THE GOLDEN AGE OF AMERICAN GARDENS

Mac Griswold • Eleanor Weller

THE GOLDEN AGE OF AMERICAN GARDENS

Proud Owners • Private Estates • 1890–1940

With research assistance by Helen E. Rollins

HARRY N. ABRAMS, INC. • PUBLISHERS • NEW YORK

in association with
THE GARDEN CLUB OF AMERICA

Editor: Ruth A. Peltason
Designer: Judith Michael

The publisher gratefully acknowledges Ernie Dieringer
for realizing the beauty of the lantern slides.

ENDPAPERS:
Panoramic view of "Longview Farm," Kansas City, Mo.

PAGE ONE:
Katharine Lane and her King Charles Spaniel dream by the lily pool at
"The Chimneys" in the fashionable Massachusetts resort Manchester-by-the-
Sea. Truncated cones of arborvitae, cascades of Clematis paniculata *in*
flower, and an elegant fence with the pierced top often seen in colonial
New England relieve the flatness of this beautiful water garden designed
by Frederick Law Olmsted, Jr., between 1902 and 1913.

FRONTISPIECE:
Airy and informal is this loggia at the Andrew Varick Stouts' long-
vanished garden in Rumson, New Jersey.

PAGE FIVE:
The George Brandeis family garden in Omaha, in September, 1917.

PAGE SIX:
A fancy gate of verdigris antique trelliswork leads tantalizingly out of the
R. W. Meades' garden near Bedford, New York.

PAGE 408:
A family of gardeners since 1652, the Sylvester descendents even had a
special bookplate by the end of the nineteenth century.

Material from the article "Carolina Grown" courtesy HG. Copyright © 1988
by the Condé Nast Publications Inc.

Selection is reprinted from I've Seen the Best of It *by Joseph W. Alsop with*
Adam Platt, by permission of the authors and W. W. Norton & Company,
Inc. Copyright © 1992 by Joseph W. Alsop and Adam Platt.

Library of Congress Cataloging-in-Publication Data

Griswold, Mac K.
The golden age of American gardens : private estates, 1890–1940 / by Mac
Griswold and Eleanor Weller with research assistance by Helen E. Rollins;
in association with the Garden Club of America.
p.   cm.
Includes bibliographical references and index.
ISBN 0–8109–3358–6
1. Gardens—United States—History.   2. Gardens—United States—
Pictorial works.   I. Weller, Eleanor.   II. Rollins, Helen E.   III. Garden
Club of America.
IV. Title.
SB466.U6G75   1991
712'.6'0973—dc20   91–8283
                              CIP

Illustrations copyright © 1991 Harry N. Abrams, Inc., except illustrations
from The Garden Club of America, copyright © 1991 The Garden Club of
America
Text copyright © 1991 Mac Griswold and Eleanor Weller
Appendix copyright © 1991 The Garden Club of America

Published in 1991 by Harry N. Abrams, Incorporated, New York
A Times Mirror Company
All rights reserved. No part of the contents of this book may be reproduced
without the written permission of the publisher

Printed and bound in Japan

*For our mothers, who showed us how to love gardens,
for our children, and for Frank and Fred*

CONTENTS

PREFACE

This book began years ago when one of us first saw a printed illustration of a glass lantern slide that had originally been part of a nationwide set commissioned by The Garden Club of America to record their members' gardens. It was this slide and countless others like it that moved us, as fragile, even more fragile, than American gardens: little three-by-four-inch glass sandwiches protecting a thin film of emulsion, glossed with the portraits of the grandest gardens, often shining with flowers so impossibly bright they reflected only the painter's vision of heliotrope or delphinium. (Each slide was painted by a specialist who worked on a black-and-white original, sometimes without ever having seen the location.) But what we knew *had* once been real, and what still exists in Riverdale, River Oaks, Woodside, and along the shores of the Great Lakes and other chosen beauty spots of fifty years ago, were the groves and hills, the solid temples and terraces that formed the backdrops and foundations seen in so many of these garden photographs.

The next step was identification, for the thread that connected the image with the real place had often snapped. If we were lucky, the glass slides, which were numbered but seldom labeled, came equipped with a similarly numbered garden club slide script that told us, for example, that the lawns were very green in Newport at Mrs. James's, or that Mrs. Schmidlapp's garden overlooked the river. Which Mrs. James and what river? Sometimes the commentary had been lost or the old black-and-white photograph of the same garden found in an institutional file had not even a scribble on the back. But we began to know certain temples by heart, and to listen to the stories of ninety-year-olds who remembered the gardens as they had been. Handwritten reminiscences and private correspondence, hand-drawn garden plans, old newspaper accounts, family photograph albums, watercolors hanging in the back halls of houses—and of course the collections of historical societies, libraries, and museums, and the books and periodicals of the period—were all part of the road map that led to a vanished life.

We were lucky in another way, for it was the dawn of garden history. The story of the glass slides, which were scattered across the United States, fell on the ears of a group of women at The Garden Club of America who recognized its importance. Their imagination, power, and resourcefulness pushed the idea of amassing a national collection of glass slides to reality. Today, 1,410 lantern slides portraying 626 gardens are safely in the Archives of American Gardens at the Office of Horticulture of the Smithsonian Institution. The collection also includes thousands of thirty-five millimeter slides of nearly 2,000 other American gardens, old and new, and the accompanying documentation. The archives, which will be open to the public by 1993, comprise a still-growing history, not just of design, art, or horticulture, but of the people who made the gardens. For women's history, and for the history of landscape architecture, the archive will prove an invaluable resource.

Our own obsessive concerns with the history of American gardens arose in childhood: from the age of four, one of us had a wisteria "throne" in her grandmother's garden pergola; the other was forced to take a daily constitutional through the slowly sliding ruins of one of the most beautiful country places in America. We grew up believing gardens were fantasy's home. If there is no other way in, we still scale walls to see a secret garden, believing that whoever loves a garden is meant to see it.

As for the actual remains, these palaces now become convents, condominiums, and asylums, surrounded by copies of Western European and Far Eastern landscapes grown up in briar and poison ivy, what is their ultimate value? They were built on the crassest piles of American loot, and the cultural history they reveal is one of frantic borrowing and adaptation of every available garden model. Yet running through their owners' lives, and implied by every casino, pagoda, and tumbling rambler rose, is a more wistful sense of appropriation: a desire to re-enter the old garden of delight. Their elaborate and often touching or hilarious masques and balls, the trees hung with apples of real gold, are expressions of what these garden makers hoped life in the garden could mean. What also emerges in the social pages of newspapers and magazines, and in freely circulated ephemera like postcards, is how *public* the rich were. Over fifty years, estate garden design history reflects a general shift from conspicuous display to a desire for privacy. Gardens were transformed from showplaces to retreats. Fifty years also saw the growth of regional, truly American garden styles, and the general disappearance of stone architecture in favor of an architectonic use of plants.

Alongside the list of near-legendary garden extravagances—in retrospect, like some American "Arabian Nights"—there is another list:

"The Lady Sapphira: A stately lady was seen advancing. A gown of rich blue trailed behind her; jewels flashed in a high headdress and she carried a wand on which blue flowers were entwined. There were excited queries and whispers and then a debutante exclaimed, 'Why, it's Mrs. James!'"
(M.H. Elliott, This Was My Newport)

gardens made for the love of gardening, and partly out of a sense of obligation to class or country to share in some way what their owners enjoyed. Some were created by thoughtful and farsighted gardeners, who saw the passing of America's flowering wilderness and wished to preserve or replicate it. Some were made by those who believed about gardening, along with nineteenth-century writer Charles Dudley Warner, that "... it is not simply beets and potatoes and corn and stringbeans that one raises ... it is the average of human life." Still others were conceived as works of art, the deeply original expressions of their makers' and designers' lives. Today, we can even rejoice that these men and women appropri-

ated the most beautiful sites in America for their "country places." Such gardens and landscapes as "Winterthur," "Ladew Topiary Gardens," "Fair Lane," "Stan Hywet," and "Lotusland" are an important part of our public legacy of cultivated beauty and preserved wilderness. In researching this book, we found surprising numbers of "country places" in almost every state of the union that are now open to the public as arboreta, wilderness areas, and as lovingly salvaged historic homes and gardens. Gardens are the slowest of the performing arts, and their lives can long exceed ours, whether they exist in reality, in memory—or only in the pages of this book.

ACKNOWLEDGMENTS

Over the five years encompassed by the book project and the twelve since The Garden Club of America slide project began, many dedicated people have given us invaluable assistance—too many for us to mention in the space allotted here. We wish to thank as a group all those not already mentioned in the picture credits or acknowledged in the footnotes who helped us find rare pictures or contributed vital information about the gardens, and we must mention some who in many ways *are* the book: Alfred Branam, aficionado of American formal gardens, whose black-and-white photograph collection contributed greatly to the book, Sadie Gwinn Blackburn, President of The Garden Club of America during the last stages of the book project, who also guided the Archive of American Gardens through the shoals from the beginning, and Harriet Jackson Phelps, who unearthed and saved the glass slides twenty years ago. We would especially like to thank Helen Rollins for her research and the appendix of glass slides. Throughout the five years there were those friends who listened, encouraged, made suggestions and interpretations, loaned books, and sometimes even provided a tranquil place to work for weeks at a stretch. They include Jane Brown, Betty and George Constable,

Evie Frost, Susan and Jonathan Galassi, Victoria and Robert Hughes, Anne Isaak and Joe Fox, T. A. Lovejoy, Ngaere Macrae, Barbara Paca, Richard Poirier, Melanie Simo, David Streatfield, the late Elisabeth Woodburn, and the astoundingly generous Susanna Zevi. Those who read large parts of the manuscript and commented wisely include Rudy Favretti, Davyd Foard-Hood, Kenneth Helphand, Robin Karson, Diane Kostial McGuire, DeCourcy McIntosh, Catha Rambusch, Suzanne Turner, and Noel Vernon.

The basis of the book, the Archives of American Gardens, would not exist in its present form without Gina Bissell, Maud Brown, Polly Ellis, Gloria Jones, Sally Meyer, and Millicent West, Co-chairmen or Advisors of the archives and the twelve Garden Club of America Zone Coordinators

ABOVE:
Miss Mildred McCormick's village house (c. 1800) in the center of Bar Harbor, Maine, had a garden by Beatrix Farrand (1923–1928) with borders of dahlias, delphiniums, baby's breath, lilies, and masses of colorful annuals. This garden was as close as Farrand got to the Colonial Revival style.

and their committees, especially Anne Wardwell, Corliss Engel, Dorrit Gutterson, Linda Jackson, Peggy Shaefer, Fran Devlin, Mary Lou Kellogg, Betty Corning, Diane Clarke, Blanche Tompkins, Molly Adams, Julie Leisenring, Laura Fisher, Margaret Bemiss, Bessy Carter, Jane Head, Harriet Ellis, Diana Norris, Libby Bishop, Virgie Lawhon, Genevieve Trimble, Jeanette Stokely, Connie White, Sally Foote, Carolyn McGregor, Becky Fouke, Ginny MacMillan, Betty Robinson, Nancy Schlosser, Tine Birkholm, Louise Hooker, Ann Jones, Joanne Titus, Barbara Carman, and Publications Procedures Advisor, Nancy Chute.

Those who helped us with documentation or introduced us to significant materials were many. In libraries, museums, universities, and other institutions the most important were Betty Bagert, Longue Vue House and Gardens; Richard Champlin, Redwood Library; Stephen Christy, Lake Forest Open Lands Association; Leslie Close, formerly director, American Garden and Landscape History Program, Wave Hill; Joyce Connolly, Frederick Law Olmsted National Historic Site; Allison Cywin, Newport Art Museum; Carol Doty, Morton Arboretum; Jennifer Eickmann, Robert Allerton Park; Franklin Garrett and Henry Wadworth, Atlanta Historical Society; David Gebhard, University of California; Robert Grese, School of Natural Resources, University of Michigan; William Grundmann, College of Design, Iowa State University; Jacqueline Haring, Research Center, Nantucket Historical Society; Tom Hayes, Edith Wharton Restoration; John Herzan, Connecticut Historic Commission; James Hodgson and Katherine Poole, Frances Loeb Library, Harvard University; Betsy Iglehart, Maine State Commission for Historic Preservation; the Junior Leagues of Greenwich, Conn., and Houston; Daniel Krall, Landscape Architecture Program, Cornell University; Lothian Linas, New York Botanical Garden Library; Doris Littlefield, Vizcaya Museum and Gardens; Elisabeth MacDougall and Laura Byers, both formerly at Dumbarton Oaks; Kit McMahon, Montecito Historical Association; Susan Ann Maney, George Eastman House; Kathryn Meechan, Office of Horticulture, Smithsonian Institution, and James Buckler, formerly at the Office of Horticulture; John Miller, Stan Hywet Hall; Paul Miller, Newport Preservation Society; Shereen Minville and Pat Kahle, Shadows-on-the-Teche, National Trust for Historic Preservation; Kevin Murphy, Essex Institute Historical Collections; Flora Nyland, SUNY, College of Environmental Science and Forestry; Janet Parks, Drawings and Archives Collection, Avery Architectural and Fine Arts Library, Columbia University; Mark Peale, New York Society Library; Ford Peatross, Library of Congress, Prints and Photographs; Holmes Perkins, formerly of University of Pennsylvania; Ellie Reichlin and Lorna Condon, Society for the Preservation of New England Antiquities; Jack Robertson, Fiske Kimball Fine Arts Library, University of Virginia; Mary Jo Sage, Cincinnati Nature Center; Dorothy Shields, Art and Architecture Library, University of Michigan; Kate Steinway, Connecticut Historical Society Museum; George Stritikus, County Agent, Montgomery, Alabama; Richard B. Trask, Danvers Historical Society Collection, Danvers Archival Center; Dory Twitchell, Montpelier, National Trust for Historic Preservation; Claire Vanderbilt, Greenwich Historical Society; Suzanne Walker, Saint-Gaudens National Historic Site; Katharine Warwick, formerly at the Hill-Stead Museum; Richard Webel, Innocenti and Webel; Dale Wheary and Richard Cheatham, Maymont; Richard Winsche, Nassau County Museum of Art Reference Library; Joanne Wurms, Bridgehampton Library; Jack Ziemer, Historic Richmond Foundation.

Help was offered all over the United States as we visited gardens or made enquiries about them, principally by Sydney Baumgartner, Polly Bryan, Meg Buck, Francis Cabot, Patrick Chassé, Susan Child, Betsy Collier, Louisa Conrad, Evan Cowles, Kitty Draper, Driwood Moulding Co., Andrew and Alice Fiske, Barry Ferguson, Maggie Gage, Louise Gillies (Mrs. George H.), Joan Gandy and Dr. Thomas H. Gandy, Mick Hales, Nan Hemingway, Susan Hayward, Peter Hornbeck, James Ireland, Libby and Brereton Jones, James S. Jones, Roger Kennedy, Robert King, Rachel Lilly, Elizabeth McLean, Elizabeth Mills-Brown, Alfred Moore, Anna C. Noll, Janis Notz, Carole Owens, Mary Beth Pastorius, William Peters, Zika Peterson, Reuben Rainey, Clara Rankin, Joy and Rudy Rasin, Mrs. Gordon Reed, Nin Ryan, Mrs. W. M. Schock, Lyman and Doris Smith, *Southern Accents* magazine, Oakleigh Thorne, Douglass Wallace, Peter and Jeanne White, Lillian Willis, and Renata Winsor.

Geoffrey James, J. Brough Schamp, and Jerry Wilson provided advice on photography or material assistance, and our agent, Robert Cornfield, gave us canny advice and held our hands. Rosie Porter, Sandy Yellott, and Fran Donahue worked with the collection day and night. Kathy Kilroy and Bea Postian at GCA headquarters, and Joan Wilhelm and Jill Palkovitz in Monkton, Maryland, typed thousands of letters and lists; Karim Tiro proofread tirelessly.

At Harry N. Abrams, Inc., we owe much to Paul Gottieb, our publisher, who bore with good-humored equanimity all the startling changes in the book, Barbara Lyons, Bob Morton, who loved the slides and helped us through the technical difficulties of getting them onto a printed page, Judith Michael, the book designer who put the crazy quilt together so beautifully, and most of all, our friend and editor, Ruth Peltason, who was there for us in the long, long haul, and in the tight squeeze at the end, never losing her vision of what the book could be.

There have been many other friends of these two projects, the AAG and the book, whose names have vanished in the years of collecting and writing or in the fifteen file drawers of correspondence and documentation the two of us have piled up; with deep apologies we know we'll remember them too late for printing here.

M.K.G. and E.C.W.

A GARDEN FOREGROUND
FOR THE AMERICAN LANDSCAPE

"The American landscape has no foreground and the American mind no background," wrote American novelist Edith Wharton to her Boston friend Sally Norton in 1905, as she was completing the garden of "The Mount," her new house in Lenox, Massachusetts.[1] Like other cultivated Americans of her day, Wharton was eager to import European garden elements to compensate for the artifice she found lacking in her native landscape. For her, the rapture of a limitless view of the Berkshire Hills could be complete only when natural scenery was contrasted with the controlled geometry of a formal garden at the foot of a terrace, such as that at "The Mount." And if the Berkshires recalled, however distantly, the hills of Tuscany, then "The Mount," though modeled after a Lincolnshire house, must incorporate the virtues of a Tuscan villa. In 1904, Wharton had assembled into book form *Italian Villas and Their Gardens,* the series of articles, strikingly illustrated by Maxfield Parrish, that she had serialized in *Scribner's* the year before. Tinged though they may have been with cultural snobbery, her observations on the greatest gardens of Italy were informed, perceptive, and deeply felt. Not surprisingly, then, the garden she created at "The Mount" was Italianate, complete with rectangular terraces, a dolphin fountain, and a *giardino segreto,* a walled rectangle made "secret" by a drop in grade below the rest of the garden. In design, "The Mount" typified American estate gardens of the period between 1890 and the beginning of World War II, when eclecticism and historicism dominated landscape as well as architectural design. Because estate gardens were an intrinsically conservative art form, their range of possibilities changed little during these fifty years. Even the appearance of Modernism in art and architecture in the 1920s had little immediate effect on these diverse and luxurious landscapes, which could easily accommodate features from every century of Western garden history, and from the Far East as well. Often a careful mixture could succeed beautifully, as at "The Mount."

American High Society and the Struggle to Get In

While Edith Wharton's garden typified its era, Wharton herself was an anomaly among American estate owners. An intellectual, independent woman who sprang almost inexplicably from old, conservative New York society, she built "The Mount" with earnings from her best-selling novel, *The House of Mirth,* not with inherited money. High society in New York, and, to a lesser degree, in Boston and Philadelphia, was constantly changing and expanding as new fortunes were made. Garden making, in 1890 as before, was a popular arena for the display of new prosperity; a great estate was intended to resemble a "family seat" with its aura of old

OPPOSITE:
Mrs. E. Ward Olney's "Square Acres" once covered most of Convent, New Jersey.

Edith Wharton wrote in bed in the mornings; her room at "The Mount" (1905) in Lenox overlooked the Red Garden seen here, which she called "her Oriental carpet, floating in the sun." Lilac and crimson stocks, and annual pinks in every shade of rose, salmon, cherry, and crimson made the garden red.

The Mount — Residence of Mr. E. R. Wharton, Lenox, Mass.

money. The struggle to become one of the elite took place at "the country place" as much as in the ballroom or boardroom, and thus a beautiful garden had the same social utility as good horses, a box at the opera, or magnificent dinner parties. Although the new rich in general had little of Wharton's concern for the American mind, they were smitten with the idea of "background." For their gardens, as for their houses and entertainments, they invented "backgrounds" with the carte blanche lent them by the stylistic eclecticism of the day.

"Money is the best manure" is an old garden saying. Despite periodic panics and busts, the American economy everywhere but in the South grew so rapidly after the Civil War that thousands of families became rich enough to afford country estates with extensive gardens. The old rich became richer, too, with the result that even the gardens of some genuine family seats were expanded and elaborated.

Gardens: A Mirror of Society

The new pattern of country and resort life began as early as the 1870s. In the Northeast, by the mid-1880s, certain preferred city outskirts had changed dramatically. Suburbs like Brookline, Massachusetts, and Morristown, New Jersey, were developing rapidly. Similar expansion occurred in the Midwest some twenty years later; the first mansions appeared in Lake Forest, Illinois, just after the turn of the century. Stone castles and commodious shingled houses, some designed by the greatest American talent of the period, H. H. Richardson, were surrounded by grounds laid out in the Victorian version of the landscape garden style known as gardenesque.[2]

By 1890, the beginning of the greatest period of estate building, tastemakers and their clientele had begun to turn away from the Shingle Style and the gardenesque. Houses grew larger and were built of more expensive, permanent materials, such as stone or brick. Architects drew liberally and indiscriminately on the Western European Renaissance tradition in order to delight a culture-hungry clientele. Then, by the middle of the decade, a new sense of restraint began to take hold, sponsored by the increasing numbers of architects trained at the Ecole des Beaux-Arts in Paris. Not only were European styles and periods deployed with greater respect for accuracy, but a more modestly conceived domestic style, the Colonial Revival, grew in popularity. The slow-ripening fruit of the 1876 Centennial Exposition in Philadelphia, the Colonial Revival survived for decades and by the Great Depression had become the sole surviving revival style of any importance. Garden design in the 1890–1940 period did not follow step-by-step every change in architectural fashion. But it's safe to say that between 1890 and 1914 gardens became more firmly structured to complement the new taste for more academic domestic architecture. Terraces, axes, and cross axes were designed to echo the symmetrical shapes and plans of the houses

they adjoined. Later, in the twenties and thirties, garden design, which is just as sensitive to changes in philosophy or behavior as any other field, moved in the direction of simplicity as garden makers looked back nostalgically to romanticized "old American ways." In this way, estate gardens remained faithful to their owners' changing sensibilities.

"Summer places" appeared. In simple eighteenth-century coastal towns, the wooden hotels built in the 1840s and 1850s began to give way to large private summer "cottages." Because the financial, social, artistic, and intellectual centers of American life were largely concentrated in the Northeast at this time, the more intrepid Midwestern or Western millionaire and his family came east, especially in the summer, to see what all the fuss was about. When they became regulars and built "cottages," their pastimes included gardening no less than polo or croquet. Most of these gardens belonged to people who owned more than one house; some had as many as three or four. As garden writer Helena Rutherfurd Ely said in 1903, "'Home' may be both town and country house, with villa by the sea and mountain camp."[3] The gardens were seasonal, designed for times when the owners were in residence. Bar Harbor, Lenox, and Newport were the resort lodestars; around them twinkled a host of other, smaller places. Regional resorts developed outside the Northeast as well. Many Midwesterners stayed close to home, making splendid lakeshore gardens in places like Lake Geneva, Wisconsin, and Grosse Pointe, Michigan. In the winter, every millionaire sought the warmth of Palm Beach or California, or a refurbished antebellum plantation in the Carolinas or Georgia.

Other congregations of estates began as weekend retreats rather than resorts. Because of their proximity to New York City, the lower Hudson River Valley and the shoreline of Connecticut rapidly became suburban, but in a grand manner inconceivable today. Weekend country places for spring and fall, rather than summer places, predominated. Moreover, the daily commute began as early as the 1870s, though at the time it was usually only a summer phenomenon. Sneden's Landing on the west bank of the Hudson, for example, was situated only one-and-a-half hours from Wall Street by horse-drawn carriage, ferry, and train. At Tuxedo Park, thirty of the 100 cottages were operating year-round by 1905. (Tuxedo Park, the first exclusive residential development in the U.S., had been established as a summer colony in 1886.) By the teens, all these places were becoming a mixture of vacation retreat, weekend country seat, and bedroom suburb.

Outside such cities as Cleveland, Indianapolis, and St. Louis, beautiful estates very much like those on the East Coast were laid out for spring and fall occupancy, on the assumption that winter and summer would be spent away from the punishing extremes of the Midwestern climate. By the teens, exclusive residential subdivisions managed by real estate speculators (who often had the largest house and garden in the development) had become an accepted pattern. As urban development accelerated in these more recently established cities of the Midwest, the prolonged exodus that had taken Boston, Philadelphia, and Baltimore three generations to accomplish took place within as little as one generation. By the teens, even the South had gathered momentum, and an estate boom, though nowhere matching in scale that on Long Island, was underway from Richmond to San Antonio.

PUBLIC DUTY AND HORTICULTURAL BEAUTY

But gardening, even estate gardening, during these years was certainly not all social climbing or urban flight. Throughout America during the nineteenth century, not just in the Northeast, there had grown up the conviction, expressed on the largest scale by the creation of Central Park in New York City (1857), that contact with nature was beneficial for everyone, and that making a garden, even a private garden to be enjoyed only by one's friends, was a socially valuable act if not actually a public duty. In those pre-Darwinian days nature's lessons were assumed to be good ones that would, in the words of John T. C. Clark, the author of *The Amateurs' Guide and Flower-Garden Directory* (1856), "inculcate a tone of refinement, afford pleasant and healthy employment, and give us exalted views of her Creator." He exhorted his readers to "make the acquaintance of Flora, whose flowery paths abound with innocent pleasures."

All through the nineteenth century, forces both cultural and horticultural conspired to raise an interest in nature and gardening. The paintings of the Hudson River School captured the sweeping majesty of the American wild — now that the wilderness frontier was safely far away. A new romanticized domesticity, complete with a garden, became the Victorian ideal, pushed by women's magazines like *Godey's Lady's Book*. During the first quarter of the century, when the Shakers began to package seeds, they became the first to conduct widespread seed merchandising. (The first American seed house, Landreth's, had been established in Philadelphia in 1784.) Shaker packets were plain brown paper, but by the time the mail-order catalogue business began to boom after the Civil War, fancy chromolithographs of dreamlike fruits, vegetables, and flowers were part of the package design. Still later, artists as well known as N. C. Wyeth and Maxfield Parrish provided the art.

American nurseries proliferated. A good nursery had a great impact on gardens in the surrounding area, since early nurseries were the botanical gardens of their day and furnished inspiration for design as well as the plants for ornamental gardens. For example, it is no exaggeration to say that Rochester, New York, would never have been known as "The Flower City" were it not for the Mount Hope Botanic and Pomological Gardens, begun in 1840 by George Ellwanger and Patrick Barry. The partners furnished what landscape architect Fletcher Steele, in a de-

Civic duty: wearing special uniforms, the ladies of the Piscataqua Garden Club in York Harbor, Maine, clear roadside trash in 1933.

scription of Rochester gardens, called "venerable rare plants that would bejewel arboretums," and they also donated 20 acres for a public park. Horticultural eminence attracts: Frederick Law Olmsted took on the landscaping there, and ravishing Chinese plants were donated in great numbers by Charles Sprague Sargent, the imperious director of the great Arnold Arboretum in Boston, who took Rochester under his horticultural wing. In 1867, Ellwanger, whose nursery had grown from 7 acres to 500, built himself a garden that inspired many others; in the twenties, Steele was asked to revise and add to the design. His stroke of genius was a formalized orchard, viewed from above, of flowering cherries, peaches, crab apples, and hawthornes, which recalled the region's hillsides quilted with fruit trees, many of them Ellwanger's own introductions.[4]

THE PRINTED WORD

Periodicals

Periodicals featuring articles on gardening and landscape design flourished: *The Magazine of Horticulture, Gardener's Monthly,* and A. J. Downing's *The Horticulturist* were all mid-nineteenth-century publications. Downing's audience was the general cultured reader, interested in what Downing called "the rural arts" and beautifying the "home grounds." Later *Country Life in America, The House Beautiful,* and *House & Garden* appeared, whose subjects were the ideal country life and how to live it. *House & Garden* published an issue entirely devoted to gardens every year.[5] *The Garden Magazine, The National Horticultural*

Magazine (precursor of *American Horticulture)*, and *Garden and Forest*, published for the Arnold Arboretum, dealt with horticulture, gardening, and landscape design. *The Gardener's Chronicle of America: A Horticultural Digest* was what could be called the professional estate gardener's magazine. All were modeled after English publications; many American library tables featured English *Country Life, The Studio,* and *The Garden* as well as the American versions.

Books

Around the turn of the century and through the 1920s, a spate of big beautiful picture books appeared on country places old and new— though mostly new. The primary focus of all these books was the gardens of the East Coast, and especially the Northeast. *American Gardens,* Guy Lowell (1901), *American Estates and Gardens,* Barr Ferree (1904), *American Country Homes and Their Gardens,* John Cordis Baker (1906), *Beautiful Gardens in America,* Louise Shelton (1915), *American Homes of Today,* Augusta Patterson (1924), and *American Landscape Architecture,* P. H. Elwood, Jr. (1924), are among the best.

Comparisons drawn between the gardens of Europe and America were widespread: Wilhelm Miller's *What England Can Teach Us About Gardening* (1911) appeared both in *Country Life in America* and in *The Garden Magazine.* English books on gardening were consulted as often as American ones, especially the works of William Robinson and Gertrude Jekyll. There were many regional books also, by climate or by state: Alice Lounsberry's *Gardens by the Sea* and *Beautiful Homes of Northern New Jersey* (1910) are typical. Many monographs on architectural firms also covered landscape design.

While the ideal of country-house life in a garden landscape had certainly been around since Mount Vernon and Monticello, its nineteenth-century fervors began with the *Treatise on the Theory and Practice of Landscape Gardening Adapted to North America; with a View to the Improvement of Country Residences* (1841), by Andrew Jackson Downing, the first American to write professionally on landscape architecture—and the first American-born landscape architect. He espoused the idea he had gathered from English garden designer, writer, and editor John Claudius Loudon that human behavior is greatly affected by environment. By the end of the century, Downing's book had gone through eight editions. The making of gardens was recognized as a civilized and civilizing activity. It was also considered healthful and a suitable activity for ladies (with the heavy work done by the gardener, who was always a man).

The Ladies

Ladies, those women who didn't have to work or actually do the household chores, had found their lives increasingly limited during the last half of the century. For their benefit, Downing had published Jane Loudon's *Gardening for Ladies* in its first American edition in 1843. But it was really after the Civil War that women fell on gardening with a whoop and in increasing numbers. Much of the pent-up frustration and energy, for which these women could find no other acceptable outlets, went into making gardens. In many places, groups of ladies met informally for tea and to look at each other's gardens, as they did on Mrs. Hamilton Fish Webster's porch in Newport in 1911 when the Newport Garden Club was founded.

The ladies soon founded their own national gardening organization, The Garden Club of America, in 1913 in Germantown, Pennsylvania, when twelve garden clubs from neighboring Main Line towns met at "Stenton," the erstwhile estate of the Logan family. By 1938 there were more than 2,000 garden clubs with various national affiliations across the country. Members not only exerted themselves in their own gardens and at flower shows, but also undertook many civic, educational, and horticultural projects. Members of garden clubs usually had old family trees as well as beautiful gardens. They lobbied successfully against billboards and for conservation; they worked hard, their families had money and political clout, and so they were often successful in their efforts. They also were, and are, serious and energetic gardeners: in the early days of some clubs, meetings were held as often as weekly. According to the bylaws of one club, members were asked "to bring to the meetings, twice during the season, interesting specimens of plants, blights, or insects, giving their personal experience with them." They visited each other's gardens, and listened to lecturers such as Charles Platt, Rose Standish Nichols, and Marian Cruger Coffin. They also went on trips together, and the numbers could be staggering. In 1924, The Garden Club of America's annual meeting junket to Virginia consisted of 740 women visiting the tidewater plantations of the James River on a steamer. Elaborate entertainments were planned for every trip: in 1930, three weeks in the Northwest included a Martha Graham performance at a ladies' club in Seattle, and a trip across Lake Washington on a barge disguised as a formal garden with flower beds, gravel paths, and park benches. Special trains with private observation cars and dining cars were put on—the sign on the board in New York's Grand Central Station read "Garden Club Special." Little booklets, green of course and printed up by the railroad, gave the schedule, and listed the ladies and their stateroom numbers. The camaraderie was intense. For many of these women, such trips were rare times—away from their husbands and families, and away from their decorous, self-disciplined daily life.[6]

Public-spirited women interested in horticulture and beautification projects were not new to the American scene: in 1853, the Laurel Hill Association had been established in Stockbridge, Massachusetts, through the efforts of Mary Hopkins Goodrich, a sort of female Paul

Revere, as she is described in Garden Club of America history, who rode around in a black riding habit on a white horse, and assembled all the townspeople to plant trees, clean up the streets, and beautify the village.

BOOKS BY THE LADIES: As amateurs, women of the period were gardeners and writers; as professionals, they were garden designers and makers of planting plans. As amateur gardeners, ladies wrote about their gardens. By the turn of the century they were responsible for most of the books that had to do with gardening per se—and there were many. Anna Gilman Hill points out in her memorable *Forty Years of Gardening* (1938), "it is the women who have worked in and loved their own gardens, who have given us the greater number of the charming and practical garden books which are now on every library table." Perennial flower gardening in all its variety, with a special interest in color harmony and massed effect in the border, is the focus of most of these works. Every single book written after the turn of the century pays homage to English garden designer and writer Gertrude Jekyll, whose influential books began to appear in 1899.

Most of these ladies gardened and wrote in the Northeast, with the notable exception of Mrs. Francis King from Michigan, author of *The Well-Considered Garden* (1915), among many other books, which has a foreword by Gertrude Jekyll. In 1938, Anna Gilman Hill called her "the best-beloved and best-known American woman gardener."

One of the first of such practical American gardening books was the wonderfully titled *Gardening by Myself* by Anna B. Warner, which appeared in 1872. Without the vote, without property rights, practically speaking, and with careers limited to teaching or nursing for those few who ventured outside the domestic sphere, how little did any woman do by herself in those days! Warner, who lived on an island in the Hudson in the shadow of West Point, went on to write another nineteen books.[7] The Colonial Revival spurred an interest in regional character, and books of local history were favorites: Sarah Orne Jewett's book about the Maine coast, *The Country of the Pointed Firs*, is one of the best examples. Garden books, such as Celia Thaxter's *An Island Garden*, occasionally verged on this genre. Daughter of a lighthouse keeper, Thaxter wrote about her cottage garden, which she made and maintained entirely herself on stony, windy Appledore, one of the Isles of Shoals off the coast of Maine. Judging from a series of watercolors by Childe Hassam, which illustrated the first edition of her book, Thaxter's garden must have been one of the most beautiful of the period, with drifts of color, annuals and perennials all melting into each other. Far from Thaxter's cottage garden, or from the practical garden books, was Alice G. B. Lockwood's immense historical work, *Gardens of Colony and State*, organized geographically and published in 1931–34 for The Garden Club of America. With great accuracy, especially given the romantic state of

garden archeology and restoration at the time, she detailed in plan, map, and photograph the extant notable gardens in the United States whose beginnings could be traced to the eighteenth century. Many gardens disappeared about a decade after Lockwood recorded them, done in by postwar suburbanization and the absence of gardeners who had left their posts in wartime and never returned.

While literary style was often of the dear-little-garden sentimental kind, the information in these books by women invariably indicated hands-on experience. Louise Beebe Wilder grew from seed all the rare and difficult plants she described in *My Garden* (1916) and *Adventures in My Garden and Rock Garden* (1923). A useful reference was Mabel Cabot Sedgewick's *The Garden Month by Month* (1907), with over four hundred pages of illustrated lists of hardy plants by color, height, bloom

Childe Hassam's oil painting, In the Garden *(1892), catches gardener and writer Celia Thaxter dreaming in her island garden on Appledore, off the New Hampshire coast. Thaxter wrote ecstatically about her flowers: "In the Iceland poppy bed the ardent light has wooed a graceful company of drooping buds to blow, and their cups of delicate fire . . . sway lightly on stems as slender as grass."*

time, and cultivation preferences. Mrs. Sedgewick, first wife of Ellery Sedgewick, editor of *The Atlantic Monthly,* for twenty-nine years was also an inspired domestic scavenger. Not only did she transplant ordinary pasture cedars, *Juniperus virginiana,* to use as effective vertical accents in her garden, but she also rescued the interior of the 1802 Isaac Ball House in Charleston and had it shipped by schooner to Boston, where the Sedgewick house, "Long Hill," was built around it by architect Philip Richardson in 1918.[8]

The ladies also discussed garden style. Critic Mariana Griswold van Rensselaer's influential *Art Out-of-Doors: Hints on Good Taste in Gardening,* which appeared in 1893, was a book of garden design for the "house beautiful."[9] She looked at the raging battle taking place among contemporary English garden writers about formal and naturalistic garden styles, and wrote that there was a place for each where "it satisfies the broad artistic sense of fitness." Her broad critical overview takes account of such design features as piazzas, formal flower beds, paths and roads, the placement of garages and stables, and the architectural components of gardens. Neltje Blanchan Doubleday, wife of the publisher and author of *The American Flower Garden* (1909), among many other books, divided gardens of the period into three theoretical categories: formal, naturalistic, and wild. In practice, American landscape architects and gardeners alike almost always had something of each, just as in England, where even William Robinson, author of *The Wild Garden,* had an enclosed flower garden with regular rectangular beds — though to be sure it was heaped with wild-looking perennials and not laid out in neat Victorian patterns of annuals.

THE GARDENS
Country estates throughout the entire fifty-year period (1890–1940), even given regional, climatic, and topographical variation, followed a regular pattern. A long drive was lined with trees, through which parkland, fields, and handsome farm buildings could be glimpsed. The drive ended in a formal court on the entrance front of the house. On the most sheltered side of the house lay a terrace or loggia, which was both a visual foundation for the building and a platform from which to look down at the rest of the garden. From this stage, hedged or walled enclosures ran down to a naturalistic lawn and trees that connected the house-surrounding to the wild landscape and the view. Somewhere in the woods or laid out as a separate garden was a place for ferns and wild flowers, or a rock garden, or a Japanese teahouse and pond, or a water garden — or all of the above.

It was also very fashionable to have still other separate gardens organized by color — the Blue Garden, the White Garden — or by species — the Iris Bowl, the Rhododendron Dell. Three other places completed the gardening arrangements on any self-sufficient country estate:

a kitchen garden for fresh vegetables, a cutting garden for flower arrangements, and a greenhouse for propagating annuals for the flower borders, for wintering over tender tubbed shrubs, and to provide cut flowers in winter for the house.

In the new estate gardens of the 1890s, flower beds, which had studded the gardenesque landscapes of the earlier part of the century, were put back into a formal framework. Patterns were outlined in tiny English boxwood; at first, in the gardens made before the turn of the century or just after, the surface of the bed was often slightly raised and filled in with plants, usually annuals, all of the same low height: dwarf marigolds, calceolaria, ageratum, and other small bright flowers. Plants with variegated foliage, such as red-and-yellow caladium and silvery santolina, added still more color. These formal parterres were magnificent and appropriate ornaments for the huge "palaces" they surrounded. By the late teens, contemporary periodicals and garden books began to inveigh against such French gardens. Gertrude Jekyll's books had appeared, and English flower gardens, rather than French parterres or Italian green gardens, took the lead in popularity. The design was formal, with a central axis and cross axes, but the plantings within the geometry of the whole were often informal. The emphasis fell on the flowers rather than on the pattern. Gardens were divided by low walls, balustrades, and steps into simple, often rectangular, sections, and were planted with luxuriant (and labor-intensive) combinations of perennials and annuals that spilled out into the walks. In still later gardens of the thirties, the garden architecture itself was often made of plants — hedges for walls, trees for statues, turf steps for stones. No layout was complete without water — a lily pool, a fountain, or a long formal rill with Japanese iris growing in it. The flower garden was punctuated with urns, sometimes cascading with vines and flowers, sometimes bristling with yucca; topiary trees in *caisses de Versailles* (big square wooden boxes, with elegant finials on the corners, first devised for Louis XIV), and statues, statues, were everywhere. Italianate gardens incorporated big old oil jars, and sculptural and architectural fragments. Special landscape features of the period included sunken gardens, pergolas covered with vines, and wide grass or herringbone brick walks that unrolled between pairs of perennial borders often as deep as twelve feet on each side.

Many such gardens were made in the days of horsepower and shovel, and a ready supply of immigrant labor was vital. The art and science of gardening reached a pitch not equaled since, thanks to a hardworking corps of highly trained English and Scots gardeners, who all seem to have known each other and who formed what can only be called a horticultural mafia. In 1931, English garden writer Marion Cran noted, "There is a new swank! Greater and more crushing at a dinner party than wearing a new rope of pearls is it to say: 'My Kew gardener has just arrived.'"

WOMEN GARDEN DESIGNERS
AND LANDSCAPE ARCHITECTS

For a woman in 1890, becoming a professional of any kind was almost as difficult as getting the vote. But at least the very newness of landscape architecture as a profession offered some hope.[10] Although courses were given in a few universities, there were no separate schools, and the American Society of Landscape Architects was only founded in 1899. When places like Harvard, MIT, and the University of Pennsylvania established separate schools of landscape design at the turn of the century, they were not open to women. Nonetheless, estate garden design, as a branch of landscape architecture, was where women won a substantial though largely unrecognized place for themselves by the end of the 1920s. They were helped on their way to a career by three design schools started by inventive and dauntless women. Mrs. Edward G. Low established the Lowthorpe School of Landscape Architecture and Horticulture for Women in Groton, Massachusetts, in 1901; the Pennsylvania School of Horticulture was founded by Jane B. Haines in 1910; and the most influential of all, the Cambridge School of Architectural and Landscape Design for Women, began with one student studying the architectural orders of Vignola on a mahogany bridge table in her living room in 1915. Her instructor was Henry Frost, who taught at the Harvard Graduate School of Architecture. He also had an infant design firm in Brattle Square with another young man, Bremer Pond, a landscape architect who had worked for several years as an assistant to Frederick Law Olmsted. Frost was a rather unwilling teaching recruit. James Sturgis Pray, chairman of the Harvard Graduate School of Landscape Architecture, called Frost into his office to explain that a Radcliffe graduate had applied for permission to study architectural drafting—"and of course," said Pray, "to permit such a thing was quite impossible." Frost continued, "I saw the blow coming as the tale unfolded . . . there was nothing for it but to accept with the best grace possible."[11]

Within very few years, "the best grace possible" included solid training in architecture as well as landscape studies. Frost and Pond, who joined his business partner in his new academic venture, overcame their early hesitations and plunged wholeheartedly into finding space, getting the best instructors—and they *were* the best—and building a library collection for their rapidly expanding school. The Pennsylvania School of Horticulture was very plant-oriented and the Lowthorpe School's curriculum only slightly less so. But at the Cambridge School, the stronger emphasis on architectural design and construction as part of the whole ensemble of landscape design gave graduates a better chance to create gardens entirely on their own—without a male architect to build the steps and balustrades while the women waited to fill the spaces with plants, so to speak. Certainly up through the Great Depression there was plenty of estate work for both men and women. The Depression and the beginning of World War II took their toll, however; in 1942 the Cambridge School was forced to close by Smith College, which for some years had been the school's home. That same year women were cautiously admitted to the Graduate School of Design at Harvard.

Public projects, which usually have been considered an architect's most important works, were out of reach until the mid-thirties for most women, with two or three exceptions, because, as one periodical article on women and landscape gardening succinctly pointed out in 1908, "In other arts there is nothing to restrain a woman from making a deliberate display of her powers. . . . But in landscape architecture success waits on invitation." Women certainly went as far as they could, given the general view of women's place in landscape architecture, which was well summarized in 1908 by Boston architect Guy Lowell when he said, "A woman will *fuss* with a garden in a way that no man will ever have the patience to do. If necessary, she will sit on a camp-stool and see every individual plant put into the ground. I have no hesitation in saying that where the relatively small garden is concerned, the average woman will do better than the average man."[12]

To get off the campstool at all, then, it was vital to have money and connections. Beatrix Farrand, then still Miss Jones, said in 1908, "I do not know of any of the women who are considered to be successful landscape gardeners who have not some means of their own assured to start with. At present I do not think there is an opportunity for many or few women who depend upon it entirely for their support."[13] Besides having some sort of independent income and family or social connections responsible for their early commissions, most successful women practitioners, such as Farrand, Marian Cruger Coffin, and Ellen Biddle Shipman, had as their mentors male professionals well known in landscape design and horticulture. Farrand (1872–1959) was trained informally by Charles Sprague Sargent and worked at the Arnold Arboretum; Ellen Shipman (1869–1950) was encouraged by architect Charles Platt and worked with him on many commissions; Marian Coffin (1876–1957) grimly studied mathematics independently in order to get into the MIT landscape architecture program in 1901 as a special student. Coffin's mentor, or rather, angel, appeared when she began to look for work: the biggest single landscape commission of her career was "Winterthur," for her friend Louise du Pont Crowninshield's brother, Harry F. du Pont. After such a start, she went on to design fifty of the finest estates on the East Coast. When the Depression came and new estate work dried up, she was able to make the transition from private to public work partly because du Pont continued to be helpful by recommending her for institutional commissions such as the rose garden at the New York Botanical Garden. Because they took up the profession before the schools existed, Farrand, Coffin, and Shipman trained themselves and used their connections instead of having a school "name" to go on (not that the name of the Cambridge School meant anything in its earliest years). All three women, and many others like them, gained their experience and worked throughout their careers by themselves or in small firms with other women, not in the big landscape architecture offices run by men. Coffin explained the difficulty: "It is hard to get a start, as there is a prejudice in many offices against employing women .... A woman has to solve many problems and learn the ropes entirely by herself, while a man has the advantage of long office training and experience."

GARDEN PHOTOGRAPHERS: Women also found careers in garden photography: Frances Benjamin Johnston, Mattie Edwards Hewitt, Jessie Tarbox Beale, Antoinette Sipprell, and Marvin Breckinridge Patterson are best known. The reason for their comparative ease of entry was the same as for landscape architecture: garden photography per se was a new field. Periodicals and lavish illustrated books created the biggest market. There was also a steady demand among estate garden owners who wanted a permanent record of their (usually new) gardens; landscape architects who needed pictures for professional reasons; and garden clubs, who commissioned hundreds of lantern slides for their afternoon meeting programs. The same photographs were circulated in many forms, so it is possible to find the same image as a black-and-white print in a periodical, in a family album, and as a hand-colored lantern slide. These photographers' styles (including men such as John Wallace Gillies and Samuel Gottscho) did not vary greatly in terms of pictorial organization, in the main because the point was to show as much of the garden as possible. Many images were organized around an architectural feature—a bench, a gazebo, a reflecting pool, or a feature, such as a path, steps, or an arch, that suggested movement through the garden. Often the photograph looked soft and romantic. However, within this narrow range, some remarkable art was produced. "The difficulty with Americans," said architectural historian Richard Guy Wilson, "is that they are always forcing themselves to make everything come true."[14] The best pictures, particularly Johnston and Hewitt's, give these American gardens a mythic quality they often lacked in real life.

In March of 1895 American artist John Singer Sargent painted Frederick Law Olmsted among the last dogwood blossoms and the mountain laurel of North Carolina at George Vanderbilt's "Biltmore." Olmsted was an old man (and already suffering the loss of memory that would force his retirement). Sargent records this, but also captures that bright unswerving optimism that had carried Olmsted through his long, prodigious life.

DESIGN AND HORTICULTURE:
FREDERICK LAW OLMSTED
AND CHARLES SPRAGUE SARGENT

Training and jobs are what Frederick Law Olmsted's (1822–1903) firm provided for many male landscape architects. As early as 1859 the Swiss emigrant Jacob Weidenmann was supervising an Olmsted project in Hartford, Connecticut, and designing estates there.[15] Charles Eliot, largely responsible for Boston's "Emerald Necklace" of parks, and Henry Codman, designer of the Chicago World's Fair, joined the Olmsted firm in the nineties. Warren Manning, Bryant Fleming, Fletcher Steele, Charles Gillette, and A. D. Taylor, all makers of notable estates nationwide, were trained by the firm or by those who themselves had trained there. In the days before public environmental action, the Olmsteds' private arboreta, from Bayard Cutting's "Westbrook" on Long Island (1887) to A. F. Sanford's "Boxwood" in Knoxville, Tennessee, made others aware of the need for conservation.[16] Harvard's Graduate School of Landscape Architecture was in some sense an Olmsted institution; its chairman was James Sturgis Pray who had worked for the Olmsted firm, and the course of studies was devised by F. L. Olmsted, Jr., working with Arthur Shurcliff. City planners who went to Harvard, like Herbert Hare of Hare and Hare in Kansas City, Missouri, made the framework for a later generation of estates when they laid out exclusive subdivisions such as River Oaks in Houston, where Ima Hogg's great garden, "Bayou Bend," is located. The Olmsted firm's influence spans nearly a century, from Olmsted's first work in Central Park in 1857 to the retirement of his son, F. L. Olmsted, Jr., in 1950.

As much as job opportunities or training, Olmsted provided inspiration. Most famous of all American landscape architects and the first to be widely recognized in the nation, he is responsible for the very notion of "park" in this country. Born in Hartford, Connecticut, and self-trained, since there was then no other way to become a landscape architect, he traveled abroad in England and in France before finding his profession. He looked not only at newly developing public parks but at the eighteenth-century English estates which served in many cases as park models. Olmsted started with Central Park, his best-known work, in 1857, from which he retired briefly in 1863 during the Civil War to serve as sanitary commissioner. He left the job permanently in 1883 in despair over government corruption, moving to Brookline, Massachusetts. He was also deeply interested in the suburban movement of post–Civil War America, of which the great estates were the most spectacular manifestation.

Olmsted was a superb and articulate observer of landscape and land use, and had a phenomenal grasp of what was local and particular. Perhaps this sensitivity to what lay before his eyes at the outset of a project, combined with his vast organizational ability, is what most distinguishes his own ability. Olmsted himself did not design many estates, proportionate to the body of his work, but those he did were important models in fundamental ways for the subsequent work of Olmsted Bros., and for the profession in general. In Massachusetts alone there are nearly 500 Olmsted gardens.

Olmsted's stroke of enduring genius in Central Park had been to divide circulation into pedestrian, horse, and wheeled traffic, and to sink the roads crossing the park. The same clarity of parts distinguishes his estates. They are divided into three: farm or forest, ornamental parkland, and the immediate house surroundings. Olmsted was really the first American to define those divisions, and to give such emphatic and attractive form to the character of each part. As for gardens—the immediate house surroundings—Olmsted was almost Californian in his belief that his gardens should allow people "to carry on daily life in the outdoors." He supplied "outdoor apartments" by means of terraces, lawns, hedged enclosures, and walled gardens. A particularly significant example of his work is "Moraine Farm," the John C. Phillips place in Beverly, Massachusetts, which is presently being restored to its original state.[17]

The house itself was designed by the Boston firm of Peabody and Stearns. Olmsted got to work on the landscaping in 1882, just before he moved to Brookline. A combination of country seat, functioning farm, and experimental forestry preserve, it is a forerunner of his later estate work at "Shelburne Farms," Vermont; "Florham Farms," New Jersey; and "Biltmore," North Carolina. Typically, the long landscaped approach alternates open and closed spaces, light, and shade. The wide view of Wenham Lake is only revealed after one passes through the house and onto the terrace. The comfortable terrace shelf, buttressed by boulders and fieldstones, has space at one end for a lawn and a sunken garden, both set apart so as not to compete with the view. A pavilion which seems to grow right out of the wall takes advantage of the elevation to overlook a wild garden below. Despite its boulders and conifers and general picturesque qualities, "Moraine Farm" is a significant early remove from the gardenesque, where lawn, woods, views, rose garden, and flower bed were supposed to run seamlessly from one to another. Olmsted, in trying to shape and order different spaces into wild and cultivated, rough and smooth, light and dark, once even said, "If the gardener shows himself outside the walls—off with his head!"

Between these first suggestions of formality at "Moraine Farm" (1882)

The great Frederick Law Olmsted's clients did not always agree with him. He had envisioned the garden below the teahouse at "Moraine Farm" in Beverly, Massachusetts, 1892, planted with "ferns and perennials seen amid groups of low trees which like the sumachs and dogwoods and Pinus Mugho *appear to advantage when looked down on." But Mrs. John C. Phillips dearly wanted a garden of fashionably bright tropical annuals, which is what she got.*

Boston's horticultural high and mighty: Horatio Hollis Hunnewell (left) and Charles Sprague Sargent sit among the orchids outside a flower show in 1901.

and the Chicago World's Fair (1893), the tone and temper of Olmsted's firm altered. Formal treatment of landscape became more extensive. The 1871 plan for Jackson Park in Chicago, the future site of the world's fair, shows a small formal basin and a big natural lake. In 1890, on the same site, a long formal pool was the axis of the world's fair plan while the natural lake had become a divertissement. The picturesque, or naturalistic, look survived at the Chicago Fair in just the same way it would survive in gardens of the period: off the central axis—importantly there—but as a contrast, not as the main theme.

If Olmsted created landscape architecture as a profession, Charles Sprague Sargent (1841–1927) was "the grand old steam-roller of horticulture."[18] At the Arnold Arboretum, Sargent combined the science of botany with what amounted to a display garden just when people were crying aloud for more decorative plants and cultural information.[19] In his fifty years at the Arboretum, Sargent put in 120,000 trees and shrubs, many of which he himself would never see come to maturity, and introduced 1,932 taxa into cultivation in the United States.[20] Sargent knew all about money, energy, and influence as well as plants. He probably spent as much of his own money every year on the Arboretum as he earned. He worked seven days a week, hired a staff that could make a dead stick grow, and cajoled Olmsted into creating an Arboretum plan. In 1881, the two strong-armed the Boston City Council into a public funding scheme with a blue-blood-studded petition that, as *The Boston Herald* said, "was the most influential ever received by that body."

What is most interesting about Sargent is neither his Arboretum and the new plants it provided, nor his own great estate garden, "Holm Lea," in Brookline. Rather, it is the close-knit complexity, both social and scientific, of his vanished world, a Boston Brahmin world that believed in, and faithfully exercised, the responsibility of privilege. The ties of family, long-term friendships, civic duty, and mutual interests that were passed from generation to generation were as strong in the fields of science and horticulture as they were in finance or the law. What's more, it was a small world. For better or worse, professionally as well as socially, everyone really *did* "know" everyone else—by reputation, if not by sight, in the upper social and financial strata of the Northeast. Not for nothing was New York society called "the 400" by social arbiter Ward McAllister in the 1880s (it soon outgrew the number but not the idea of exclusivity). There was meaning to the famous description of Boston as a place "Where the Lowells talk to the Cabots, and the Cabots talk only to God."[21]

The field of botany was smaller than most—first John Torrey in New York and then Asa Gray at Harvard *were* American botany. Gray was virtually alone at Harvard until 1872, when President Eliot of Harvard appointed four men to help Gray do what he had been doing alone since 1842. Gray created the botany department, the botanical library, and the great herbarium, which was named after him. Throughout the second half of the nineteenth century, whenever a new plant turned up in America (and many still did at that time), it was stuck in an envelope and sent to Asa Gray at Harvard; generally he wrote back.

Charles Sprague Sargent, who was the son of a successful Brahmin banker and railroad investor, grew up in Brookline. About the time of Sargent's birth Downing had written, "The whole of this neighborhood of Brookline is a kind of landscape garden, [with] an Arcadian air of rural freedom and enjoyment." Charles would inherit his father's place, "Pine Bank." Adding to it two parcels of adjoining land, he created the much-admired "Holm Lea," a masterpiece of picturesque landscape. Charles, darkly handsome and with beautiful manners, was a man emotionally restrained enough to drive his friends mad. Later in life he and his good friend, the naturalist John Muir, stood on a beautiful mountain top together. As Muir described it in his journal, he turned to Sargent, who was "standing there as cool as a rock, with a half-amused look on his face at me, but never saying a word. 'Why don't you let yourself out at a sight like that?' I asked. 'I don't wear my heart upon my sleeve,' he retorted. 'Who cares where you wear your little heart, mon?' I cried. 'There you

stand in the face of all Heaven come down to earth, like a critic of the universe, as if to say 'Come, Nature, bring on the best you have. I'm from Boston!' "[22]

Sargent, a so-so student at Harvard and one of the very few not to take the natural history course given by Asa Gray, found his first real teachers in his second cousin, Henry Winthrop Sargent, and another family connection, Horatio Hollis Hunnewell. Both were rich and gifted amateurs, whose consuming hobby was horticulture; both were plant collectors; both had magnificent gardens which held the country's two most notable conifer collections. Henry Winthrop Sargent's "Wodenethe," on the east bank of the Hudson above Fishkill Landing, New York, was directly across the river from A. J. Downing's estate. When Sargent bought his 22 acres in 1840, it was heavily wooded. Downing advised Sargent on the "expressive, harmonious, and refined imitation of the agreeable forms of nature,"[23] cutting out the views and giving good specimens room to grow. Henry Sargent always said that most of the landscaping of "Wodenethe" was done with an axe. After Downing's early death on a Hudson River steamboat, Sargent wrote a sorrowful preface to the sixth edition of Downing's *Landscape Gardening*. "Wodenethe" was an extremely influential garden: nearly 100 years later, in 1938, periodicals were still publishing articles like "The Landscape Tradition at Wodenethe: An English Inheritance Becomes an American Influence."

A. E. Anderson's engraving for The Century Magazine *depicts the house terrace of Charles Sprague Sargent's "Holm Lea" in Brookline, where 150 acres of horticultural rarities were laid out as a landscape garden. Sargent kept to a grand style indoors as well as out, with a succession of hundreds of homegrown hothouse plants to mark the seasons, and a footman behind every chair at dinner.*

H. H. Hunnewell's "Italian" topiary terraces, at "Wellesley," in Massachusetts, were actually inspired by the "Italian" gardens at Elvaston Castle in England. Hunnewell loved trees: according to Mary Jane Eastman, when a house on the property was burning, he shouted to the firemen, "Save that tree! We can build a new house!"

The rose garden of Mrs. Walter Belknap James, Mrs. Hugh D. Auchincloss, Sr.'s sister, at "Rockhurst" in Newport, had tea roses massed by color and backed with ramblers on swags and pillars—an extravagance of flowers typical of early twentieth-century gardens in Newport. The designer was society's favorite rose maven, Mrs. Harriet Foote, who also made the rose garden for the third sister, Miss Annie Burr Jennings of Fairfield, Connecticut, and the hideous rose garden for Mrs. Henry Ford at "Fair Lane" in Michigan.

From his cousin, Charles Sargent doubtless learned to love trees and the picturesque landscape.

The same age as Henry Winthrop Sargent, Hunnewell was married to Sargent's first cousin Isabella Welles, after whom first the estate, then the town of West Needham, and finally the college were named "Wellesley." Hunnewell, like many other American millionaires, made *two* fortunes: he lost the first in the panic of 1837, and started again with railroads and real estate in 1839. He bought "Wellesley" in 1854. "It will be my aim," he confided to his diary in 1867, "to plant every conifer, native or foreign, that will be found sufficiently hardy to thrive in our cold New England climate."[24] Charles Sargent, a proponent of "natural" gardening, perhaps didn't like the topiary much, but it was surely from Hunnewell that he learned early on that many trees of many species can be grouped together successfully in an outdoor museum of plants.

In 1872, President Eliot appointed Sargent professor of horticulture in charge of the Botanic Garden (then in great disarray), and curator of the fledgling Arnold Arboretum; in 1873 he became director. Sargent, who had no experience and no scientific credits to his name, was then acting as estate superintendent for his father at "Holm Lea," so it seems a singular choice. How did he get the job? One can only speculate, but since Hunnewell was a big benefactor of Harvard, a friendly acquaintance of Gray's (they played whist together and Gray advised him on his trees), and a close friend of Eliot's, Hunnewell doubtless had something to do with it, as he must have noticed Sargent's growing obsession with trees and landscape. Add to this the fact that Sargent, in the fall of 1872, after he was appointed professor of horticulture and before taking full charge of the Arboretum, spent weeks at the Botanic Garden with Asa Gray, learning as much as he could. Noticing that Gray's professional load was keeping him from completing his life's work, *A Flora of North America,*

Sargent silently, without Gray's knowledge, arranged for his father and Hunnewell each to provide $500 per annum for Gray on the condition that Gray would resign his professorship and devote himself to his researches full time. Gray did so, retaining his title and his house at the Garden, and his position as America's greatest botanist. Sargent got the directorship, in hindsight one of the landmark appointments of the century.

Always moving at top speed, Sargent was a good field botanist, one of the earliest environmentalists—and a superb fundraiser. (Eighteen separate major bequests from personal friends of Sargent's came to the Arboretum during his tenure.) He did not, however, move too fast to overlook any possible friend of the Arboretum, and he gave advice to Arboretum patrons on planting and design. (His biographer points out that there was usually an observable ratio between the patron's generosity and the time Sargent expended.) Gardens all over the Northeast were the proud recipients of Sargent's specimen lilacs, Far Eastern exotics, and splendid bay trees, but he also went as far afield with plants and advice as "Wychwood," the wild garden and nature preserve of Charles and Frances Hutchinson in Lake Geneva, Wisconsin.

Sargent's weekly *Garden and Forest* (1888–97), although never widely circulated, was read by every professional and is a chronicle of the struggle between picturesque and classical styles which took place just as landscape architects were defining their new profession. Like the elder Olmsted, his close contemporary, Sargent leaned toward the picturesque, or natural style. However, *Garden and Forest* was kindly about the formal landscaping at the Chicago World's Fair in 1893[25] and earlier that same year Sargent himself had gingerly blessed the reemergence of formal garden planning in two articles, "Formal gardening, does it conflict with the natural style?" (Conclusion: not necessarily) and "Formal gardening, where it can be used to advantage."[26]

An oak tree in relief ornaments the facade of the underground ballroom at the Joseph Desloges' "Vouziers" outside St. Louis.

The
NORTHEAST
The Powerhouse

RHODE ISLAND

"Newport by the sea, more famous than any other American summer resort, naturally possesses the greatest number of gardens on an elaborate scale. The coast at this point is somewhat sheltered, the air is mild, and there is sea moisture so beneficial to flowers. Windbreaks of hedges or walls are used where the winds blow strong off the water."[1]

"Our Social Capital," as Mrs. John King Van Rensselaer, society chronicler, called Newport in its Gilded Age heyday at the turn of the century, only came alive in summer.[2] During the winter in New York, Newport's palace owners were dancing, dining, yawning at the Opera, and heading to Palm Beach for the season. In the greenhouses of Newport, however, the gardeners, English, Scots, Italian, were planning the floral fireworks for the eight weeks of summer, July and August, when "their"

As good as a Newport party was a Portsmouth, Rhode Island, visit with Miss Alice Brayton, keeper of a green zoo— "a sheared family of Mesozoic creatures," as Mary McCarthy once called them. A camel, an ostrich, an elephant—and a policeman—plus seventeen others in yew and California privet were cut by gardener Jose Carreiro beginning in 1880; others followed. Late in her life, the wily Miss Brayton became a social climber easily up to Newport's standards. As Newport's celebrities began to pall, Newport's grandes dames discovered the pungent Miss Brayton and her special brand of "social lions."

The Northeast:
The Powerhouse

gardens had to be perfect. Bedding plants by the thousands were being sown in seed flats. The bedding plants—ageratum, dusty miller, dwarf marigold—would make the bright, flat parterre patterns at houses like Cornelius Vanderbilt's "The Breakers" or Alexander Hamilton Rice's "Miramar."[3] Annuals practically forgotten today—lavatera, godetia, mignonette—would fill in the bare spots of lavish "English borders" at Hugh D. Auchincloss's "Hammersmith Farm" or John Nicholas Brown's "Harbour Court." Thousands of the tall trained plants, known as standards, that from year to year lent height, color, and scent to marble terraces were taking their seasonal rest. Top-knotted bay trees overwintered in outdoor sunken "bay pits"; fuchsia and heliotrope were pruned to maintain their elegant shapes; orange blossom perfumed the air of the cool greenhouses.

But where were the gardens that would hold all these flowers? "The white elephants, as one may best call them, all cry and no wool, all house and no garden," were herded tightly together along Bellevue and Narragansett Avenues and on Ocean Drive under the disapproving eyes of Henry James, back in America after twenty years, visiting the resort of his childhood.[4] All these "cottages" were big enough to stand quite appropriately on huge estates; here, in the new dispensation, many had as little as half an acre.

"The chief industry of Newport, Rhode Island, is the examination and appraisal of qualifications for society."[5] In Newport, Old New York struggled to maintain what it called its standards through the eighties, but by the nineties "qualifications for society" really meant money and the ability to spend it with panache. Acres were not the point in Newport; visibility and a certain glittering, brisk, and showy style were. "Even the delivery carts are freshly-painted and new looking," writes Mrs. Van Rensselaer.[6] The flowers in the carefully planned beds were changed two or three times during the brief eight-week summer. Nothing was more appropriate to Newport's own special style than these nearly artificial displays. Thanks to the sea fogs and morning dew that can stay on the ground as late as one o'clock on a hot summer day, even the very carefully tended turf was, and is, so darkly green and deeply velvet as to appear somehow unreal as well. The last generation of Newport's famous palaces were almost all huge bricks of houses, white or brightly cream, or crystalline gray. Nothing suited them better than the firmly stylized wreaths and squares of tightly packed flowers that echoed the delicate stony garlands of their architectural decoration.

The millionaires who made these houses and gardens were, according to Tuxedoite Price Collier, "New York Society's best dish, garnished with a little cold Boston celery, and a fringe of Philadelphia and Baltimore parsley."[7] But Paul Bourget, French fin-de-siècle critic and novelist, rightly noted that in America, unlike France, each city had its own society, and from each of these the most determined (and richest) found their way to Newport. It took at least four seasons of camping out, socially speaking, in Newport to become accepted by its social arbiters.[8] So the Pembroke Joneses from North Carolina, the E. J. Berwinds from Pennsylvania, and many others hired the right architects and landscape gardeners, paraded up and down Bellevue Avenue every afternoon in the right carriage, and waited for Mrs. August Belmont, or Mrs. William Backhouse Astor, or Mrs. Stuyvesant Fish, or Mrs. O.H.P. Belmont, depending on who the reigning hostess was, to give them the ineffable nod. Ward McAllister and his successor, Harry Lehr, were the masters of ceremonies.

Newport had not always been so ferociously social. In 1852 it was still just an eighteenth-century port town on the western side of the island; Bellevue Avenue was pastureland, and little boys made money opening the gates between fields when the few summer visitors took a carriage ride every afternoon. According to town records, there were twelve cottagers: four each from New York, Boston, and Charleston.[9] Everybody else stayed in hotels, of which the biggest was Ocean House, opened in 1845. Until the Civil War made the atmosphere uncongenial up north forever, many of the Newport resorters were Southerners, "sojourning," as the Southern phrase goes, out of the heat. The only resort gardens were the cannas and geraniums at the hotels.

Cleveland Amory, in *The Last Resorts,* formulates a "Gresham's law of social resorts." First come the artists and writers looking for scenery, solitude, and low rents. Then come the professors and clergy looking for the simple life. Then they are driven out by the "nice millionaires" in search of a place for their children to lead the simple life, and last, before everyone expires of virtue, come the "naughty millionaires" who want to associate with the nice millionaires, but who build million-dollar "cottages" and clubs, dress up for dinner, give balls, and ruin the simple life altogether.[10]

Up through the sixties, Newport life was pretty quiet: flying a kite or riding on the "joggle board" were the wildest amusements, and bed at ten was the rule.[11] So the Savannah-born McAllister, who had summered in Newport as a child, didn't have to go to any great lengths to wake up the scene—just a perfectly orchestrated picnic at his farm outside Newport would do to unlimber the stiffish resorters of the early seventies. His "stepping-stones to our best New York society," as he himself grandly called his *fêtes champêtres,* took full advantage of Rhode Island's rural atmosphere. McAllister, a perfectionist party-giver, never overlooked a

single detail; he even rented sheep and cattle "to give the place an animated look." When he moved on from picnics to "cotillion dinners," they took place on the night of a full moon, "on closely-cut turf, and with the little garden filled with beautiful standing plants, the eastern side of the farm-house covered with vines, laden with pumpkins, melons, and cucumbers." They drank "Yacht Club Rum Punch" (McAllister's secret mixture was just rum over a cake of ice, with the odd bottle of champagne thrown in), danced in the barn (newly equipped with a chandelier), and drove home by moonlight.[12]

By the turn of the century, Newport had left McAllister's pumpkins far behind in a diamond-studded rout of costume balls and Chinese tea parties and Broadway shows imported for the evening. To Bourget's European eyes, Americans often seemed to substitute sport and pageantry for the "complications of amatory experience" that he would have seen in Deauville or Brighton or Biarritz or Cannes. He suggested this was because Newport's society was ruled by women—the men were too intensely preoccupied with making money.[13] Mrs. Philip Lydig, despite her Spanish birth, would have seemed typically American to him. She met an ex-beau at the ferry in her electric automobile, who confessed to her on the return drive home that unless she would have an affair with him life was not worth living. "Very well, we'll die together," said she shortly, driving her car at full speed into a telegraph pole. He went to the hospital; she walked home unscathed.[14]

By the turn of the century, Newporters were losing their almost sanitary innocence in the midst of pleasure, so that rather more standard was the behavior of Edwin Julius Berwind, builder of "The Elms," one of Newport's most beautiful cottages. A Philadelphian and a coal baron who was described in business as "dour, closemouthed, and acquisitive," he blossomed in Newport into benign bonhomie. He was also known as quite a ladies' man. Next to "The Elms," a pink villa eventually went up for his lady friend, and there were rumors about a tunnel, which disappointingly turned out to be for coal.[15]

"Devised primarily as stage settings for lavish entertainment, the most successful of these houses are those which are most consciously theatrical and exploit their artificiality most frankly."[16] The same is true of the gardens. At Ogden Goelet's "Ochre Point" (1891), and at Cornelius Vanderbilt's "The Breakers" (1893), the largest cottage in Newport built by the richest family in America, only the Atlantic Ocean could have matched the scale of the houses when the gardens were first laid out. The small aprons of formal gardens at each place are like sketches of what such houses would have had for gardens, given the space of Fontainebleau or the Palazzo Doria in Genoa, though now the rare trees fringing the lawns have grown enough to stand up to the architecture. However, at "The Breakers" in Henry James's day, the thirty-one different varieties planted by Ernest Bowditch[17] must have looked like sticks and

At Mr. and Mrs. John Nicholas Browns' "Harbour Court," landscape architect Harold Hill Blossom's flowery "old-time" enclosure, cozier than most Newport gardens, lies in the middle of an Olmsted Bros. landscape. Beyond the dense stands of phlox, lilies, and delphiniums are a pair of conically trimmed apple trees in front of a grape arbor.

Edward Van Altena, New York photographer, painted this lantern slide of the sunken parterre at the E. J. Berwinds' "The Elms" (1899) in Newport. A lantern slide specialist, Van Altena worked on this black-and-white negative sent to him with a few color notes, although more often he took the photographs he painted. A lantern slide is essentially a glass "sandwich" with a layer of film emulsion in the middle, intended for projection. "The coloring material for the slides were dyes, the same as are used in fabrics," said Van Altena, explaining his process years later to Harriet Jackson Phelps.

LEFT:

At Cornelius Vanderbilt's "The Breakers," a vine-covered pergola casts a filigree shade. Bosses of boxwood, standard topiaries, and scrolls of begonias rimmed with close-clipped English ivy made up the small parterre, a modest garden by comparison with the house.

lollipops next to the muscular, deeply shadowed facades of Richard Morris Hunt's dream palace, based on the palazzo of a Genoese merchant prince.

Back toward town, on Bellevue Avenue, past a stretch of the older, Victorian Newport of hydrangeas, shingles, and leaded panes, stands the Berwinds' "The Elms." Today, without a single elm remaining, it is still the best period garden left in Newport, miraculously preserved and grown to maturity.[18] Berwind, the son of a German immigrant who became a piano manufacturer, controlled two-thirds of the nation's supply of coal. He was one of the "boat men"; he worked five days a week till he was eighty-five and died at eighty-eight. Not among Newport's more

Jackie Onassis spent many a teen-age summer at "Hammersmith Farm" in the garden created by her stepfather's mother, Mrs. Hugh D. Auchincloss, Sr. Olmsted Bros. first laid it out in 1897, on land settled in 1639. Protected from wind and spray by walls, trees, and twin pergolas, guests lunched beneath the wisteria in this big garden bowl. The lotus- and lily-filled pool is banked with grasses and iris, both Siberian and Japanese, with clipped arborvitae and yuccas in stone planters as vertical accents. A staff of fourteen kept this, and the many other separate garden compartments, blooming all summer.

RIGHT:
Tall cryptomeria and a lattice covered with white climbing roses and blue-flowered clematis formed the background for "The Masque of the Blue Garden" at the Arthur Curtiss Jameses' "Beacon Hill House" in 1913. Tritons and mermaids swam in the blue-tiled pool, or rather danced in it, as it was only a few inches deep. Nymphs offered pink seashells full of fruit to the guests; the "spirit of water" arose dripping from the lily pond in the background, with strings of lily pads hanging from her shoulders; at the climax "Venus" was carried in on an eight-foot-wide frilly half shell.

Jacques Gréber, French parterre designer extraordinary, laid out this design at "Miramar" to harmonize with Horace Trumbauer's large, severe rendering of the Petit Trianon. The green edgings are dwarf boxwood, and the body of the pattern is filled in with foliage plants like caladium, coleus, and santolina. Blue ageratum and yellow dwarf marigolds complete the scheme.

outrageous entertainers, he and his wife, Sarah Vesta Herminie Berwind, nonetheless regularly gave dinners and balls, when the Baccarat chandeliers with crystal drops as big as small cantaloupes gleamed, and music filled the white ballroom.

Racy Miss Julia Berwind, who moved into "The Elms" almost as soon as it was built and became her brother's hostess when Herminie died in 1922, summered in Newport till she was ninety-one. "E. J. and his sister loved splendor. They knew how to create it and how to enjoy it," remembered Newport grande dame Mrs. John Nicholas Brown. She added that Julia, in winter, was "a steady patron of the chic-er nightclubs and speakeasies of Prohibition New York, flanked by buckets of champagne and a brace of handsome cavaliers."[19]

The pale biscuit-colored limestone house, a near replica of the Château d'Asnières designed by Hardouin-Mansart in 1750, is the early work (1899) of Horace Trumbauer, a little-known Philadelphia architect. His masterpiece was "Whitemarsh Hall" (1916), outside Philadelphia, for another new-money millionaire, Edward Stotesbury. The 11-acre Berwind garden, also laid out by Ernest Bowditch, is large for Newport. It faces west and once had a view of the harbor, but big walls always stood on the other three sides. Two things distinguish it: the mammoth trees and the sunken garden. Every Newport cottage worth its salt was planted with European beeches in all their late Victorian abundance. But nowhere are the broad, silvery silhouettes of weeping beeches caught with such beauty against the dark-foliaged copper variety as they are at "The Elms," set in pairing after pairing from every angle of the lawn. They frame the coolly elegant house, becalmed on its terraces freighted with sculpture, huge urns, and topiary evergreens. (The height of the terraces also conceals such tiresome necessities as the kitchen and laundry in darkness below.) Half-hidden in the beeches at the end of the lawn are a big fountain and two tiny marble temples—an inevitable invitation to walk. Arriving at the fountain, one finds a long transverse allée, with the nice surprise of a vista terminating in an arcaded facade to the north. (The beautiful mansard-roofed stable/garage complex was also designed by Trumbauer and added in 1911.) The big surprise is a sunken parterre beyond and below the temples, which are linked by a bridgelike terrace. The architectural ensemble makes a viewing platform just the right height to look down on the simple, scrolling boxwood patterns, filled with different-colored annuals in spring, summer, and fall. The gardens are among the finest collaborations between architect and landscape architect that the American Beaux-Arts movement produced, though neither Trumbauer nor Bowditch ever set foot in the Ecole des Beaux-Arts.[20]

Real French *parterres de broderie*, with the fine-lined nervosity of the best sixteenth-century marquetry, were laid out by Jacques Gréber at "Miramar," another Trumbauer creation which was begun for Philadelphian George Widener in 1912.[21] Trumbauer, ardent French neoclassical revivalist, found his landscape soulmate in Gréber, the French garden maker and city planner who so often worked with him on great estate projects. Gréber's de Gaulle nose, his quizzically cocked head, the precise set of his lips, would have let you know he was French even before he opened his mouth. "Intelligent, shrewd, cultivated, brilliant in conversation, always witty, often caustic, but otherwise courteous, and a good friend,"[22] Gréber continued to work in both America and France most of his life, taking up city planning as the vogue for formal palace gardens dimmed in the twenties and vanished in the Depression. His early, nearly royal extravagance at "Miramar" perfectly epitomized the first two decades of the century in Newport.

"Rosecliff," the beautiful white terra-cotta playhouse designed by Stanford White in 1898 for Herman and Tessie Fair Oelrichs, has all the splash of the Comstock Lode heiress herself. She was the daughter of a "Silver King," James Graham Fair, one of the four Irishmen who struck such a rich vein of silver in Nevada in the 1850s that they mined more than $500 million before it gave out in 1898.[23] Handsome, black-haired, tough, clever, and noisy, Tessie Fair grew up in San Francisco, married jolly, round Herman Oelrichs, New York member of a North German steamship family, and conquered New York and Newport.[24] Profane and eccentric enough to keep even Newport amused, Tessie Oelrichs reluctantly shared the honors with Mrs. Stuyvesant Fish, famous for her parties and her caustic wit, and Mrs. O.H.P. Belmont, formerly Mrs. William K. Vanderbilt. Alva Belmont, the Mobile, Alabama, belle who was the first in society to cycle in bloomers, the first to cut her hair, and first woman elected to the American Institute of Architects,[25] was also the first to get a divorce and not be ostracized for it. Mmes. Oelrichs, Fish, and Belmont were in constant competition, and competition meant parties, and parties meant flowers. Parties, after all, were the real meaning of flowers and gardens in Newport.

At "Rosecliff," located on the site of historian George Bancroft's former cottage, architect Stanford White's brilliant adaptation of the Grand Trianon was surrounded by rings of roses on three sides, with a lawn and fountains on the sea exposure. Sculptor Augustus Saint-Gaudens laid out the charming *cour d'amour*, as the small front garden was called. But Blanche Oelrichs, Tessie's niece, remembers that "no one glanced, save the gardener" at the hundreds of tea roses, the yards of dwarf boxwood edging, the clipped arborvitae punctuating White's exuberant facades.[26] They were merely a part of the scene, like the fleet of white cardboard silhouettes of boats moored off "Rosecliff" for the famous *bal blanc* in 1904, or the fourteen-carat gold fruits William Fahnestock of Harrisburg, Pennsylvania, hung from his trees at his cottage "Bois Doré," or the thousands of American Beauty roses that were a favorite at many balls.[27] The familiar rose, which became almost synonymous with the resort, is said to have first appeared as a sport in the Newport rose beds of George Bancroft, rose fancier par excellence. Paul Bourget writes, "It has so long a stem, it is so intensely red, so wide open, and so strongly perfumed, that it does not seem like a natural flower. It requires the greenhouse, the exposition, a public display."[28] One wonders what Bourget would have said about William K. Vanderbilt's 1899 ball, where, as an opening entertainment, six beautiful, well-brought-up young girls were tied to six American Beauty rose trees, and gentlemen drew lots for the privilege of untieing them to have a dance.[29]

Mrs. Arthur Curtiss James was the principal ornament of her own memorable garden party, *the* event of 1913, the year the income tax law was enacted that spelt eventual doom for Newport's palmiest days. But on a warm evening in mid-August, the height of the season, all that mattered was the moonlit length of the Blue Garden, the latest addition to the Italianate splendors of "Beacon Hill House's" "Italian" gardens, which stretched the distance of ten New York City blocks.[30] Down it came Mrs. James, trailing the dark-blue, Italian silk brocade train of her Renaissance costume. Prominent Newporters, including all the "power" hostesses, sat on a blue-draped stand and listened to her announce "The Masque of the Blue Garden" under the moonlight. According to reports in *The Washington Mirror*, Tessie Oelrichs's and Maymie Fish's hearts sank as they recognized that Mrs. James had the triumph of the season on her hands.

Rigged out as Cosimo di Medici, New York financier and railroad baron James, who had greeted his guests and escorted each of the older grandes dames to her seat, waved genially at the crowd as he stepped inadvertently into a spotlight.[31] Then the misty blue and gray lights went up on the new blue garden.[32] At the conclusion of the entertainment, the whole garden was lit by a blast of red and blue lights that twinkled high in the trees, and trumpeters dressed in more-or-less fifteenth-century dress

A wild flower meadow runs down to the waters of Some Sound at the Gerrish H. Millikins' "The Haven" in Northeast Harbor, Maine. Beatrix Farrand worked on this garden for twenty years (1925–1945).

showed the wondering guests the way to a banquet that included boars' heads on gilded platters. Perhaps because everyone had dined not two hours before, most preferred the strains of "In My Harem," and the smooth dance floor. Such was life in a Newport garden in 1913.

MAINE

The vagaries of Maine's climate and location have always made for a different style of resort life. Overcoming each difficulty becomes the occasion for ritual and ceremony. The numbing water means every longtime summer visitor not only has to believe that cold water is good medicine, but also is convinced that he or she knows the spot where the water is warmer than any other—just at the turn of the tide, just where the sun warms the rocks. Beaches are not sand; they are more or less pointy collections of boulders, so certain smooth flat rocks by the shore are hallowed—certainly worth a picnic and perhaps even an all-day trip. The one real beach on Mt. Desert is actually named "Sand Beach." Fog settling in for days brings long naps, books, and fires, as well as brisk wet walks and views of melting Japanese beauty.

Maine gardens endure the same privations, but Maine gardeners turn them to advantage. The three-month flowering period crams spring, summer, and fall flowers all together. Summer in the garden, like the resort season itself, seems somehow more precious because of its brevity. The deep snow cover, abundant moisture, and cool nights make for suffused color, rampant growth, and the kind of blazing displays of grenadier-guard delphiniums, trusses of roses, and stands of mildew-free phlox usually seen only in English watercolors of Edwardian gardens.

The trip to Maine, then and now, is so long that destination drops away momentarily, and the trip becomes an end in itself. By coastal steamer, and later by train and boat, the "summer people" of Maine made annual migrations in June or early July to open their Shingle-Style cottages, revamped farmhouses, and later, a certain number of palaces of the Newport type. During the twenties, one yearly trip to York Harbor went like this:

All my aunts and uncles and cousins lived in four houses surrounding "Windy Gates," our grandmother's house. When summer came all four were closed except "Windy Gates" and there was a general exodus on the Bar Harbor Express to Boston. As polio was rampant then, "Ma" (our grandmother) was very suspicious of Boston as a possible hotbed of germs. Therefore as we had to get off the sleeper and change from South to North Station we were all given gloves to wear so as to avoid Boston's contamination. Likewise if we had to spend the night, we were whisked by taxi, gloved, to the Copley Plaza, and sent immediately to our rooms where meals were sent up and where we remained until the train left next morning. My knowledge of Boston is consequently very slight.

Mother and Daddy and Ma did not always accompany us and it was left to the very competent housekeeper, Minnie, to get us there somehow. The linen came in straw trunks and the silver also travelled with us. Minnie had to settle five children, a canary, and a parrot, as well as a German nurse, an Irish nurse, a cross old butler and a wonderful fat cook into the sleeping car. Of course we would let the parrot loose to roam the upper berths and even though Minnie would get us all up when we went through Providence, we were never really ready and the Nana nurse always lost her hairpins getting off the train. One year we had to collect our dog from the baggage car and still she would get us there in one piece. After a week of frantic work we were ready for our grandmother's arrival. Summer vacation lasted three months then so it was all worthwhile.

I don't know whether it was for health reasons or just that Ma didn't care for Northern produce or dairy products but somehow a system evolved whereby all nonperishable vegetables, even corn and fresh peas, were sent from the home garden in Baltimore by refrigerator train to Boston, then Portsmouth, and picked up by Lewis the chauffeur and delivered to us in very fresh condition. Also our eggs and butter came in cylindrical wooden boxes. As Ma couldn't manage to move the cow, we drank Walker Gorden milk (unpasteurized). Also huge green glass bottles of Poland Water.

While we lived it up at York Harbor in three rented cottages, our father, uncles and older working cousins together ran a bachelors' club with a skeleton staff at Windy Gates. It must have been very lively.[33]

Bar Harbor

Of the Maine resorts, Bar Harbor was the queen, the second stop on the summer social tour, after Newport and before Saratoga or the Berkshires. Mt. Desert has a long summer resort history, beginning with the Abnaki Indians who came to eat mussels and clams on the shores of Some Sound, the only natural fjord on the East Coast. Samuel de Champlain sailed by in 1604 and christened it L'Isle des Monts Déserts because of its bare rocky peaks, the highest on the Atlantic seaboard. French and English owners gave way finally to a Senator William Bingham of Philadelphia to whom most of the owners on the east side of the island trace title. In 1844, the first resorters appeared, with the Hudson River School founder, Thomas Cole, in the van. Other artists, such as Frederic Church, and writers followed, attracted by the brilliant atmosphere, the picturesque—and cheap—life of the Maine fishermen, and the unparalleled scenery of forests, fields, and mountains rising straight from the rocky indented coast. In the 1860s and early 70s the "rusticators" followed: Boston and Philadelphia educators, professors, and clergy. They stayed in gingerbread-trimmed hotels—or at least ate their meals in them (hence the hideous description of them as "mealers") if they rented cottages newly built by the Maine natives. With their traditional pursuits becoming unprofitable, fishermen and farmers quickly latched on to the resort windfall coming their way.

Life changed quickly, even though the rusticators were determined to hang on to what they had come for—rugged New England life. In the seventies, Edith Wharton, then young Edith Jones, traveled up from Newport to flirt, converse, and walk the mountains in the strenuous fashion for which Bar Harbor had become famous. Throughout the

decade of the eighties the rusticators built their own comparatively modest summer "cottages." Gardens were either simple enclosures for flowers, fenced with pickets or hedged with hemlock, with lawns from which to see the fabulous views. Bar Harbor was famous too for a certain mystique of simplicity, a sort of "cottage modesty," as Cleveland Amory called it. When President Charles Eliot of Harvard said to his houseguest Frederick Law Olmsted, "Olmsted, you've been here a week now and you haven't told me what to do with my place," Olmsted replied, "Do with it? For heaven's sake, Charles, leave it alone."[34]

Then came the New Yorkers and Midwesterners, full of money and whoopee. By the 1890s, Mt. Desert had many colossal cottages. Two of the best formal gardens were made by New York banker Gardiner Sherman at "Keewaydin" (1898) and De Witt Clinton Blair at "Blair Eyrie" (1888). New York railroad man J. S. Kennedy's "Kenarden Lodge" (1892) had its own electric plant, as well as a magnificent Italian garden filled with pink, white, and blue flowers, a stone pergola overlooking the mountains, and extensive greenhouses. ("Kenarden Lodge" was later owned by Dr. J. T. Dorrance, inventor of condensed soup and president of the Campbell soup company.) Powdered footmen, giant yachts, and evening musicales supplemented the previous Spartan regime of popovers for lunch at rustic Jordan Pond, rides in Maine fishing boats, and lobster, lobster, lobster for every dinner. The reactionaries tended to sniff and retreat to slightly less ostentatious Seal Harbor and Northeast Harbor.

Bar Harbor Gardens

Besides "Kenarden," "Keewaydin," and "Blair Eyrie," the most noteworthy Mt. Desert gardens were "Reef Point," "The Eyrie," and "Baymeath." "Reef Point" was built for Mrs. Cadwalader Jones, Beatrix Farrand's mother, in 1883 by the architectural firm of Rotch and Tilden. By that time Mrs. Jones had divorced Frederick R. Jones, Edith Wharton's brother, but the two women remained close for the rest of their lives. After Beatrix inherited the house she and her husband, Max Farrand, professor of history at Yale and later director of the Huntington Library in California, spent their summers there.

"Reef Point" had a central axis lined up with the house. It led down the length of the point to the shore and was densely and informally planted with great sweeps of heathers and junipers. The axis terminated in a stand of huge spruce silhouetted against the Maine sky and sea. This combination of firm axial planning and bold natural planting, along with the use of tree silhouettes as focal points, can be seen in Farrand's work at "Dumbarton Oaks" in Washington, D.C., and other private gardens, and on the campuses of Princeton and Yale universities. In 1939 "Reef Point" became a botanical garden and reference library, and after Max Farrand's death in 1945, Beatrix Farrand spent more and more time at "Reef Point," becoming autocratic and peppery in her old age (she lived to a hale eighty-seven, dying in 1959). When she didn't get what she wanted—a tax abatement from the town for her horticultural institution—she tore out the gardens and gave her reference library, which included such treasures as Gertrude Jekyll's plans, drawings, and correspondence, to the University of California at Berkeley.

But her influence and her best Maine work live on in Mr. and Mrs. John D. Rockefeller, Jr.'s garden, "The Eyrie," in nearby Seal Harbor, designed and carried out in 1926–1930. The garden's original purpose was twofold: to provide a setting for the Rockefellers' collection of Chan Buddhist stelae and figures, and to ensure a never-ending supply of cut flowers for the house. The Rockefellers had fallen in love with the Far East, for these were the days when oriental gardens were the latest thing. Many such gardens were faithful Japanese renderings, occasionally even built by an imported Japanese crew, and often staffed by Japanese gardeners and tea masters. Here, instead, Beatrix Farrand designed a brilliant adaptation of a Chinese garden. A long walk known as the Spirit Walk is guarded by two lines of solemn eleventh- to fourteenth-century Korean tomb figures who stand in a sea of native ground covers. The walk leads to the principal garden, originally conceived as an English-style cutting garden—one of the loveliest and liveliest cutting gardens ever made. The surrounding dark Maine woods dramatize the pink stucco walls (one pierced with a circular Chinese moon gate), which are topped with ten thousand yellow tiles brought from the walls of Peking's Imperial City. In the first nine or ten years of its existence, annuals filled the unevenly divided quadrant beds in the central sunken panel. Later, the central panel was planted in grass, which provides an effective foil for the masses of surrounding flowers. Perennials, arranged in the drifts and washes of hot and cool colors so beloved of Gertrude Jekyll, fill the wall beds, while the walls themselves are covered with clematis and other creepers. Although "The Eyrie," with its gathering of inspirations from many sources, is by no means a Chinese garden, it has a spiritual quality of repose and mystery more often felt in Eastern than in Western gardens.

Another beautiful, entirely different early Farrand garden was that of J. P. Morgan's daughter, Mrs. Herbert Satterlee, "Great Head," which overlooked the famous Sand Beach. Curving borders, with hot colors on one side and cool on the other, framed an informal grassy path that led to the marsh and beach below. A stone folly tower looked out to sea. The Satterlees entertained no notions about the simplicity of nature belonging to all, however. When the beach became too crowded for their taste, they promptly put up a rope cordon with stout stanchions to mark "their" half.

The Edsel Fords' "Skylands" in Seal Harbor was also laid out naturalistically by Jens Jensen about 1923. There was little formal connection between the house and its surroundings, which included an exquisite rocky pool and woodland garden right next to the dining room, typical of Jensen's work. Jensen, the Danish immigrant who, beginning in the 1880s in the Midwest, was the first landscape architect to see and use the beauty of American prairies and horizons, had already made a huge natural paradise for the Fords at "Gankler Pointe" in Michigan.

But the principal style for about twenty years, from 1895 through the first years of World War I, was "Italian." From Maine to Florida to Colorado Springs, startlingly beautiful and often wild views were framed by symmetrical axes, cross axes, arbors, and pergolas. "Italian" was a loose term, however, and owners and designers continued to add random cultural dots and dashes, part of a vague Morse code of garden civilization. "Blair Eyrie's" "Japanese" garden, for instance, was an Italian garden with a Japanese bronze dragon coiled up on the fountain in the middle. What is more amazing than the combinations themselves is that they very often worked harmoniously—the gardens were beautiful. The same confident eclecticism that made the decoration of houses so often successful was almost better outdoors. All these gardens, formal and informal, were designed for parties, and for the immense clouds of houseguests that hovered over Bar Harbor every summer.

Louise deKoven Bowen's lively book of Bar Harbor memoirs, *Baymeath*, depicts life as one long, happy—and surprisingly relaxed—garden party. The sprightly Louise had come to Bar Harbor in the summers as an eighteen-year-old Midwestern girl, and when she married she persuaded her husband, Chicagoan Joseph Bowen, to build their own cottage in 1895. Money, effort, and time were poured into the place which eventually grew to 1,000 acres and took thirty-six gardeners to maintain.

Unusually for the times, the Bowens invited the public, including guests from all the hotels and boardinghouses, to their gardens "on pleasant Sunday afternoons in July and August from three to six o'clock," as their widely circulated printed invitation read. On the porch, the staff served open-faced thin white-bread raspberry sandwiches to the one to two hundred people who usually showed up to spend the afternoon. Often visitors came when the afternoon wasn't at all pleasant, but tea was served anyhow. Mrs. Bowen held court in the garden under a birch tree, while the charming Mr. Bowen enjoyed helping out by answering questions about the flowers. "Not really knowing any of the names," he said, "I just memorized the Latin for two or three and used them indiscriminately—few people seemed to know the difference." There were other garden parties at "Baymeath" too. An annual event was the party for the head gardeners of Mt. Desert. That 150 gardeners came with their wives to look at the gardens with an appraising professional eye, to have lunch, and to spend the afternoon gives some idea of the thriving estate life on Mt. Desert.

Louise Bowen's 1905 photograph shows a commanding middle-aged matriarch with kinky hair, long pearls, and a determined mouth, a

A colorful circular "Italian" garden, surrounding a Romanesque quatrefoil fountain, is the startling foreground for the woods and waters of Maine and the islands off Bar Harbor at "Keewaydin," home of New York banker Gardiner Sherman. "Keewaydin" burned in the great fire of 1947, when so many of the old cottages were consumed, somewhat to the relief of their residents, many of whom no longer had the money and staff to deal with such places.

A superb gray and green rocky corner of the John T. Dorrances' "Kenarden Lodge," a Bar Harbor garden begun by the John S. Kennedys in 1892.

LEFT, BELOW:
"Reef Point," Beatrix Farrand's Bar Harbor garden overlooking Frenchman's Bay, was her laboratory and trial ground. There she tried out Maine native shrubs and groundcovers, such as partridgeberry, bunchberry, low and high bush blueberry, and many junipers, both upright and prostrate. With them she used American plants from farther south, and introductions from China and Japan, determining their hardiness for the Maine coastal climate. What she learned she used in her neighbors' gardens, designing or revamping forty places on Mount Desert over the years.

woman entirely capable of running the huge dog-and-pony show that was "Baymeath." Only her eyes, with their sideways glance and glint of humor, betray the charm and sense of freedom her book conveys. Bowen was active in women's suffrage and for seven years was president of the Jane Addams Hull House. (Addams was her friend and neighbor both in Maine and Chicago.)

"Baymeath," one of the many flights of architectural fancy along the Bar Harbor coast, was described by Mrs. Bowen as a French Colonial house, meant to resemble the French settlers' houses of the region. Designed by Herbert Jacques of the Boston firm of Andrews, Jacques and Rantoul, on the entrance side it had a double portico of white columns topped by a Chinese Chippendale railing. There was a tight gravel circle where Louise Bowen practiced driving her huge, high four-in-hand

The walled flower garden of "The Eyrie," the Abby Aldrich and John D. Rockefeller, Jr., summer place in Seal Harbor, is reached by the Spirit Walk through the woods, one of Beatrix Farrand's most deeply felt sequences of space and light.

At the highest point on Mount Desert overlooking the sea, Farrand framed a water view for the Herbert Satterlees in native pines and curving beds.

The Joseph Bowens' head gardener, Arthur Chilman, kept the borders at "Baymeath" beautiful with his English expertise. Tall delphinium and feathery pink astilbe, too highly colored here, contribute to the bursting effect.

Publisher Joseph Pulitzer, whose New York World regularly assailed "the vulgar wealthy," shuttled between "Chatwold" in Bar Harbor (seen here), Europe, and very exclusive Jekyll Island, Georgia, where he spent the winters. In the days before security consciousness, publicly sold postcards showed the houses of the rich and famous at their various resorts.

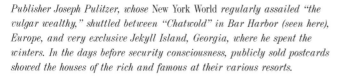

carriage, known as a tally-ho, up to the front door until she no longer ran over the grass. She had a choice of three perfectly matched teams of four—bay, chestnut, and strawberry roan, each with a spare. All were trained to run up the hills of Bar Harbor with a groom up behind, blowing madly to announce their coming. Not all her driving experiences were successful, however—one time her horse, stung by a bee, crashed her into an apple tree. Thrown out of her carriage into the road with a broken pelvis, she was found by two ladies from Philadelphia who, before they would help her, quizzed her on her name and connections, and introduced themselves, giving some idea of Philadelphia's famous "manners."

The architectural framework of "Baymeath's" gardens, a series of flowery terraces leading down to Hulls Cove with a view to the distant Goldsboro Hills, was originally laid out by Herbert Jacques, but over the years Louise Bowen and her English head gardener, Arthur Chilman, changed it all. The greenhouse became an "indoor" swimming pool; the old sunken tennis court became the formal garden, and so on. The formal garden was the most beautiful. High retaining walls on two sides were covered with actinidia vine, as were the trellises on the other sides. A balustraded grass terrace ornamented with urns looked over the simple patterns of grass, flowers, water, and shrubs below. Beyond the house was another lattice-enclosed garden where beds of roses and old-fashioned perennials were half-hidden by a profusion of climbing roses on all the fences. Another rose arbor led into the woods where lupines, daylilies, and wild roses grew. The paths of the vegetable garden were edged with flowers. One year, as a surprise for Mrs. Bowen, Chilman laid out a small garden planted entirely in yellow and orange.[35]

Other Maine Resorts

There were other summer places in Maine besides Mt. Desert, of course, such as York Harbor, mentioned above, or Prout's Neck, where Winslow Homer painted, or Kittery Point, the summer home of William Dean Howells, the American novelist and critic whose works are lively and nuanced portrayals of nineteenth-century Americans losing their innocence at home and abroad. Howells, like Mark Twain and many other artists and writers of the 1880s and 90s, found it hard to be optimistic about an America which, as he saw it, was chasing faster and faster after the almighty dollar. Agriculture failed in the East during the second half of the nineteenth century, and farmers left the land, abandoning or selling their fine old farmhouses cheap. The literary establishment's nostalgic look backward at an idealized preindustrial America spurred the development of a style of architecture and the decorative arts, and of gardening, known as the Colonial Revival, which had received its first impetus at the Philadelphia Centennial Exposition in 1876. In gardens, the Colonial Revival style meant a return to straight lines, box borders, old perennials and roses, and a final abandonment of exotic bedding-out plants in island beds, squiggly paths and any other Victorian flourishes. This return to a simpler earlier national period was the American equivalent of England's Arts and Crafts movement, which sought inspiration in the Middle Ages and the English Renaissance.

The White Garden at "Howells Place" in Kittery Point marks the spot where Mark Twain sat when he visited his dear friend, the novelist William Dean Howells. Together the two most popular American writers of their day lamented the ruinous state of the nation and looked back to more innocent, pre-industrial times. Howells had retreated to rural Maine in 1902 to find a little of that old agrarian virtue. The headless statue is Fortuna, *brought back from a European trip by Howells's son, the architect John Mead Howells, and his wife, Abby, who designed the new White Garden in the thirties.*

Maine was Howells' rural retreat. He bought an old farm on the ocean in 1902, which he called "Howells Place," christening the old barn "Barnbury." It became his study where he wrote many of his later novels. Beginning in 1910 his son, the Beaux-Arts-trained architect John Mead Howells, "restored" both his father's house and his own, right next door. Little Colonial Revival gardens, including a fashionable White Garden, connected the buildings to each other and to the ocean views.

In South Berwick, Maine, "Hamilton House" is one of the best examples of a fine old Federal house surrounded by a freely imagined version of America's colonial garden past (Colonial Revival enthusiasts often didn't take advantage of the ample historical evidence at hand and invariably made the garden grander than it had been). The Maine writer Sarah Orne Jewett, who lived in South Berwick, had always loved this distinguished eighteenth-century house. To save it from possible ruin, she persuaded her Boston friend Mrs. Tyson, widow of the president of the B&O Railroad, to buy it. Boston architect Herbert Browne renovated it to suit Mrs. Tyson's needs. Browne loved baroque palaces; his "restored" Federal houses were usually magnificent high-flown reworkings of spare New England elegance, and at "Hamilton House," completed in 1788, much remained of its past grandeur for him to work with. Colonel Jonathan Hamilton (1745–1802) had made his money in West Indian rum, sugar, and slaves. "Hamilton House," which faced the river, was surrounded by sheds, a spinning house, and slave quarters as well as wharves and warehouses along the water's edge. Hamilton, like other local gentry, owned a pleasure barge known as a "river coach," in which he would visit his neighbors up and down the Piscataqua. It was this colorful past, and such simple outdoor pleasures, that Emily Tyson wanted to revive when she began her formal sunken garden. The central axis of the garden ran from the east front of the house and framed an orchard view. A pergola acted as a tearoom and outdoor parlor, and a cottage was reconstructed from the beams and paneling of an old saltbox. Trellises and statues were scattered among the abundant flower beds that mixed annuals and perennials in cottagy profusion.

The garden's greatest days of splendor came when Mrs. Henry Vaughan, a skillful gardener and Mrs. Tyson's stepdaughter, inherited the place in 1922. She ebulliently added to the scheme flowers that no colonial dame could ever have seen. Mrs. Vaughan was unabashedly after effect and used every means to achieve it. One neighbor recalled how on the day of a garden club meeting the gardeners often would hastily stuff full-blown plants into the borders.[36]

Mrs. Vaughan left "Hamilton House" and its gardens to the Society for the Preservation of New England Antiquities. Minus the pergola, arbors, and vines, and with a sweeping new view of the river, the gardens exist today in simplified form. The progression of "Hamilton House's" gardens, from simplicity to elaboration and back to simplicity, is the story of

Emily Tyson's Colonial Revival garden at "Hamilton House" in South Berwick was built inside the foundation walls of an old barn. Arbors, arches, and a pergola were covered with hardy vines such as wisteria, akebia, honeysuckle, and ivy. Constant clipping kept "windows" open for the view of the Piscataqua River. The white wooden love seat is a typical Colonial Revival feature.

the Maine resorts and their gardens. So the Maine summer pilgrimages continue, though shorter and less complicated, as do the short brilliant Maine summers, studded with blue sky days, and enormous delphinium, larkspur, and lupine.

THE FESTIVE SUMMERS OF NEW HAMPSHIRE
New Hampshire's resort gardens in Cornish, Peterborough, and Dublin were simple—simpler, that is, than the showplaces of Newport and Bar Harbor. Their beginnings, thirty years later than the big resorts, were much the same however. The first New Hampshire resort arrivals in the

late eighties were artists, writers, and musicians who converted New England farmhouses or created fairly modest "Italian villas" on the hilltops with their spectacular views. As had happened in the grand seaside resorts, the creative types were followed eventually by lawyers, diplomats, and political figures, all looking for the simple summer life. But no New Hampshire resort succumbed to what Cleveland Amory called "the naughty millionaires," the ones who gilded the lily and had their own kind of good time doing so. Things stayed simple in New Hampshire, even though sculptor Augustus Saint-Gaudens was eventually to admit about his own house and garden that "The place has spread to be such an establishment that it requires a general, aides de camp, commissariat, wagon-trains, and what-not to run the affair."[37]

Cornish

Saint-Gaudens was the first to arrive in Cornish in 1885, renting an abandoned brick turnpike tavern, which he later bought, remodeled, and named "Aspet" after his father's birthplace in the Pyrenees. (Today "Aspet" is a National Historic Site.) "Make it smile," said Saint-Gaudens to his architect George Fletcher Babb, and indeed at first the simple red brick building with its new porches and columns reminded one friend of "an upright New England farmer with a new set of false teeth," until a coat of white paint unified the whole.[38] Saint-Gaudens himself designed the Italianate terraced garden with its long perennial borders that linked house and barn studio. A marble pool was surrounded by annuals—bachelor's-buttons, scabiosa, snapdragons, stocks, hound's-tongue, and gladiolus. Casts of classical statues (but none of Saint-Gaudens's works) stood everywhere.

Other colonists arrived in a flood after Saint-Gaudens, buying up land that was rapidly being abandoned as unprofitable for farming.[39] The Dewings, Thomas and Maria Oakey, both painters, rented a cottage and raved about the beauty of the landscape to their friends. Mrs. Dewing, a flower painter, was the first to try flower gardening in Cornish to provide herself with subject matter. Landscape architect Ellen Shipman, another early Cornishite, was one of the most indefatigable horticultural experimenters.[40] In short order followed Stephen Parrish, the etcher, and his son, Maxfield Parrish, one of the most popular artists of the early

The American version of the English "cottage garden" was the "old-fashioned garden." At "Northcote," photographed in 1902, etcher Stephen Parrish filled the beds of his eighty-foot-long rectangle with old favorites like hollyhocks, sweet william, peonies, and larkspur. Mounds of bridal wreath, prickly barberry, and the toughest roses—sweetbrier and rugosa—added mass and height, softened by washes of baby's breath and pale blue Salvia patens. In summer coreopsis, rudbeckias, and sunflowers were a blaze of gold, and wild grape and actinidia climbed to the porch eaves.

twentieth century. Stephen Parrish's house, "Northcote," designed by Philadelphia architect Wilson Eyre, was closely integrated with its garden, which spilled over with old-fashioned flowers. Saint-Gaudens's niece, Rose Standish Nichols, the successful Boston-based garden designer and writer, with her peppery temper and her "hats like velvet puddings," designed a simple but artful garden for her father's plain farmhouse. It was surrounded by low fieldstone walls, and lay separated from the house by a broad grass terrace. Regular paths were offset by soft informal plantings, and in the middle an old apple tree crouched over a shallow pool.[41] Herbert Croly, editor of *Architectural Record* and later founder of *The New Republic;* Kenyon Cox, muralist, art teacher, and critic; the musician Arthur Whiting; Everett Shinn, the painter; Learned Hand, the great justice; sculptors Herbert Adams and Paul Manship—all were Cornishites at some time. Woodrow Wilson made it his "summer White House" from 1913 to 1915. It was a tight-knit community. After the day's creative work was done, all these august personages entertained each other with the kinds of high jinks described in English novels of manners. Favorites were charades and amateur theatricals—with sets designed by Maxfield Parrish, however, and Ethel Barrymore to lend professional opinion.

The biggest spectacular took place on June 22, 1905, at "Aspet," to celebrate the twentieth anniversary of the founding of the Cornish colony. It happened in the garden: proscenium curtains were hung between pine trees and held in place by two great gilded masks made by Maxfield Parrish. More than seventy people took part in a drama written by playwright Louis Shipman, Ellen Shipman's then husband, entitled *A Masque of "Ours."* Music was provided by members of the Boston Symphony Orchestra hiding in the pines. Everyone wore classical costumes and Maxfield Parrish, playing the wise centaur, Chiron, complete with a rib cage of barrel staves with wooden hind legs. The Saint-Gaudenses themselves were drawn on stage in a golden chariot.[42]

But if Cornish is remembered for its gardens, it is chiefly because of architect and garden designer Charles Platt (1861–1933). At his own house and garden and at four other places in Cornish, he first worked out the Italian villa theme that would transform the American country house movement.[43] The houses and gardens of the preceding generation, the creations of Richard Morris Hunt working with Bowditch, or Carrère and Hastings with James Greenleaf (see "Hyde Park" and "Blairsden"), are on the whole grander and less approachable. Platt's designs had a new intimacy and sense of human scale. He came to architecture "by way of the garden gate"—he designed many gardens before he ever designed a building. He is best known for his work between 1893 and 1913, and for popularizing the idea in America that a country place, like an Italian villa, is a single design that includes house and garden. After Platt's career blossomed, he was loathe to take a commission that did not include

Sculptor Augustus Saint-Gaudens sits in the pergola of the "Little Studio" at his Cornish house, "Aspet," in 1906.

both. Planning was not the same as planting, however, and often on larger projects, such as William Mather's "Gwinn" outside Cleveland, Platt worked with landscape architects and nurserymen just as most other architects did.[44]

Gifted, witty, considerate, intelligent, Platt was a New Yorker by birth from the comfortable and cultured sort of background that his clients shared, or wished to join. He trained as an etcher and then as a painter, in New York and Paris, and won two bronze medals for his art at the Chicago World's Fair. He began his own house and garden in 1890. Over Cornish towers the purple silhouette of Mt. Ascutney (which actually stands on the opposite side of the Connecticut River in Vermont). The peak formed the principal view of almost every garden there—except Charles Platt's,[45] where he veiled his view of the mountain with a carefully thinned stand of white pines. Just like Olmsted at "Moraine Farm," Platt liked to tease, intimate, and then surprise. In many of his plans, he also used the house as a curtain for the view just as Olmsted did.

In 1892 Platt as good as kidnapped his younger brother, William, from his training at Olmsted & Co. to travel in Italy, and measure and record the architecture of Italian gardens. F. L. Olmsted expressed his misgivings in a letter to William: "I am afraid that I do not think much of the fine and costly gardening of Italy, and yet I am enthusiastic in my enjoyment of much roadside foreground scenery there in which nature contends with and is gaining upon the art of man."[46] William went anyway, and the brothers spent the spring and early summer gathering material which would be published by Charles Platt as *Italian Gardens,* in 1894, the first illustrated study of Italian gardens in English. William died tragically in a swimming accident on his return; Charles went back to Cornish and completed his own garden (which still exists today in modified form), using much he had seen in Italy.

Peterborough and Dublin

Cornish was not the only artists' colony in New Hampshire. In 1920, Boston financier Guy Currier asked his wife, an actress, if she had had any luck at an auction. "Oh yes," she said. "That's nice, did you bring it home?" "Well not exactly. It's a farm in Peterborough."[47]

The farm, "Mariearden," within two years became a summer performing arts school funded by Currier. Ted Shawn, Martha Graham, and Ruth St. Denis taught there; and Walter Pidgeon and Bette Davis were among the recruits. In the summer of 1923, Ted Shawn danced naked in the outdoor theater by moonlight, wearing only a few carefully arranged but ill-chosen leaves—poison ivy leaves. The Peterborough artists' colony, better known today as MacDowell, was founded in 1908 in memory of composer Edward MacDowell.[48]

Nearby Dublin began in 1846 as a summer colony in the usual way with a farm boardinghouse. By 1893 there were fifty-six summer houses, and ninety in 1916. Cornish was almost all New York, but Dublin reveled in Bostonians such as poet Amy Lowell and Colonel Thomas Wentworth Higginson, the Unitarian minister who had commanded the first black army unit in the Civil War and was instrumental in publishing Emily Dickinson.[49] Bostonians Mr. and Mrs. Joseph Lindon Smith carried on the amateur theatrical tradition in Dublin at "Loon Point." They had not one garden theater but two—the smaller one known as the "Teatro Bambino." The larger had Greek columns with an entablature for a proscenium arch. Paul Robeson performed there, and Mark Twain was a frequent visitor and advisor. Six generations of Smiths have also trod the boards from the time they could first walk until they no longer could. Dublin's magic mountain, Mt. Monadnock, was visible from one of New England's larger gardens, "Morelands," laid out in 1926 for the Frederick Brewsters of New Haven, Connecticut, by Boston landscape architect Arthur Shurcliff, most famous for his Colonial Revival work in Williamsburg, Virginia. First came a walled garden and a terrace facing Dublin Lake, and in 1930 a series of little enclosures, strung along a sloping grass mall and hedged in tough Canadian hemlock to withstand

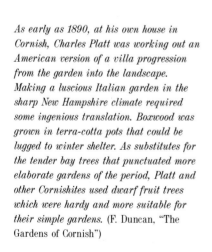

As early as 1890, at his own house in Cornish, Charles Platt was working out an American version of a villa progression from the garden into the landscape. Making a luscious Italian garden in the sharp New Hampshire climate required some ingenious translation. Boxwood was grown in terra-cotta pots that could be lugged to winter shelter. As substitutes for the tender bay trees that punctuated more elaborate gardens of the period, Platt and other Cornishites used dwarf fruit trees which were hardy and more suitable for their simple gardens. (F. Duncan, "The Gardens of Cornish")

the sustained sub-zero winter temperatures. A brilliantly formal garden by a determined gardener who knew how to work with the climate, "Morelands" was in continuous bloom from spring to frost. Greenhouses and slat houses were used effectively to grow masses of annuals and tubbed plants to take the place of more tender perennials. There was a rock garden, a sunken "English" garden ornamented with standard heliotrope and statues very white against the sheared arborvitae hedge, a "French" garden with raised beds, double hedges, and a *jet d'eau*, a "pleasaunce" or shady pleasure ground, a white garden with a waterfall, and, for an informal contrast, a "sanctuary garden" where pine-needle paths wound among plantings of ferns, bleeding-heart, and wild strawberries.[50]

The gardens of New Hampshire were among the most elegant gardens of the Gilded Age. They took every advantage of their surroundings; they were living extensions of the house, and by sight line and path, axis and terrace, they tied house and surrounding together in a classical manner. The architectural vocabulary of the garden—the statues and benches, the urns and pools—were also typical of the period. But in one important way, the owners of the gardens of New Hampshire were closer to the gardeners of today than to other Gilded Age proprietors. Though they had gardeners—mostly New Hampshire farmers-turned-hired-men left high and dry by the state's dwindling agriculture—the owners themselves *worked* in their gardens right alongside their helpers. One Dublin resorter remembers her parents-in-law:

> *She* planned, horticulted, weeded, moved, watered, stroked, and encouraged, treating each plant according to its need and merit. *He* started from seed delphinium, phlox, English pansy, Sweet William, bachelor's-button, zinnia, nicotiana, carnation, hollyhock, aster, and about forty more. He also transplanted, moved, removed, weeded, fertilized, watered (mostly with perspiration), and gave himself to the black flies—ceaselessly from April to November. Theirs was an easy, low maintenance affair, requiring no more than sixteen man hours a day.[51]

VERMONT

Only a handful of estate gardens ever flourished in Vermont. There were no resort colonies to speak of, perhaps because the state was comparatively inaccessible, but also perhaps because of Vermonters' well-known flintily democratic ways. Two showplaces were "Hildene" in Manchester (1903), the summer home of Robert Todd Lincoln, son of President Lincoln, and "The Orchards," in Bennington, where in 1910 bottle manufacturer Edward Everett made a formal garden with a thirteen-step stone cascade and many statues (100 is the number usually given). Arthur Shurcliff made formal gardens and a model farm for Willard Martin, at "Greatwood" in Plainfield in the twenties. But *the* great Vermont place was "Shelburne Farms."[52]

There were no simple Cornish apple trees for Lila Webb in her gardens at "Shelburne Farms"; she preferred tubbed bay trees lining the balustraded overlook on Lake Champlain in Vermont. Housing them in the wintertime was no problem since there were 3 acres of greenhouses. There were also 4,000 acres of Vermont farmland and a 100-room "farmhouse." To make the pastoral landscape with its winding drives and carefully tailored woodlands, Gifford Pinchot, forestry expert, had consulted with Frederick Law Olmsted. The Webbs were going in for model farming, the pastime about which Augusta Patterson, editor of *Town and Country*, once wrote, "A real number one yacht is considered about the most expensive hobby in which a rich man can indulge. That is a great popular mistake. One could support comfortably several yachts out of what it costs to be a gentleman farmer in the grand manner."[53] But "Shelburne Farms," which naturally *did* include a 117-foot-long steam yacht for lake cruising, was near-simplicity for a Vanderbilt.

Lila was the daughter of William Henry Vanderbilt, son of the Commodore and head of the New York Central Railroad, a man who had doubled the giant fortune left him by his father in the nine short years it was his. At his death in 1885 he was worth $200 million. His eight children, who were comparatively young when they received their inheritance, all immediately went on a palace-building spree.[54] Six of the children stayed in society's accustomed haunts in Newport, Bar Harbor, the Berkshires, Morristown, New Jersey, and Long Island, but Lila and her younger brother George went "back to nature" on the grandest scale, staking out new territory in distant, beautiful American landscapes. For the Webbs, model farming was also a model for life, a luxurious version of Anglo-Saxon Victorian idealized domesticity in a rural manse. Life at "Shelburne Farms" was of necessity family oriented since there weren't any other society folks willing to come to the shores of Lake Champlain unless they came as houseguests of the Webbs. Having no other Joneses to keep up with except themselves, some of the ritual and much of the display of Newport or Bar Harbor were dispensed with. What remained was the very fanciest English sporting life, with private packs of hounds and one of the earliest private golf courses in the country; driven shoots for pheasant and woodcock in the autumn; duck and geese on the lake; and a huge wooden toboggan slide that was built every winter down to the frozen lake. A niece of Lila Webb's remembers one Fourth of July weekend when twenty young people filled the house, and each couple was given a buggy, a horse, a caddy, and a canoe to keep them entertained. Sunday lunch always took place on the terrace overlooking the gardens and the lake.

The gardens at "Shelburne Farms" illustrate how taste changed from the free-form picturesqueness of the 1880s to the formal, symmetrical, architectural gardening of the early twentieth century. Almost as soon as it was made (1899), the rectangular "French" parterre patterned with

A 1916 family photograph in the gardens of "Shelburne Farms" shows three generations. Lila Vanderbilt Webb, bottom left, was especially proud of her delphiniums, ranked behind Dr. William Seward Webb, at right. Second and third from the left in the back are Frederica Webb Pulitzer and her husband, Ralph, son of the newspaper publisher.

RIGHT:

Lila Webb was inspired by English garden books and a trip to Italy to link her house to its site with perennial borders set against low walls. Her volumes of Gertrude Jekyll's writings are heavily marked, a guide for the present-day garden restoration.

The Resorts

geraniums, salvia, and alyssum next to the big Restoration Queen Anne house was slightly behind the times. Inset in the flowing lawn that encircled the house, it seemed like an afterthought, a mere accent, not an integral part of the landscape scheme. The lake, the lawn, the view, and the trees were the principal attractions.

By 1911 Lila had been exposed to ten years of *House & Garden* and *Country Life in America*, which both featured English-style borders and "Italian" gardens, and her library included many of the beautiful gardening books of the period.[55] After a trip abroad, she designed a new garden herself, with the help of photographs, memories of Europe, and the expert horticultural assistance of Englishman Alec Graham, her head gardener. Eventually there were 2,000 feet of low brick walls laid out in "rooms," a pergola, and a lily pond. Twelve-foot-deep perennial beds bordered a grass allée; a rose garden held four hundred pink, yellow, and white bushes. Other beds contained nothing but yuccas, with

their white-flowered candles ablaze in July. There was another pergola covered with climbing roses, a thyme lawn, and an 80-foot-long peony garden. Three-foot-tall potted boxwood pyramids added a little height to the garden, but not too much, so as not to obscure the magnificent lake view. Venetian stone figures, purchased abroad, stood in the formal gardens. Having an Italian garden in Vermont that made no concessions to climate was only possible as long as there were plenty of gardeners. One such, Henry Noonan, still working at the age of eighty-five in 1988, remembers "lugging those little men to the laundry building every fall and fetchin' 'em back again every spring." Another, Ernest St. George, remembers "drawing straw" each fall to mulch the perennial beds a foot-and-a-half deep.[56] "Shelburne Farms" barely lasted a generation in its full glory. Although it still belongs to the Webbs, today it is a country-house hotel and the gardens are being restored in a modified way.

MASSACHUSETTS

BROOKLINE, THE DOWAGER SUBURB

The showy world of summer resorts is left far behind on entering Brookline, dowager suburb of the United States. Brookline, which began life as Muddy River Hamlet in the seventeenth century, was the place where a large slice of Boston's upper crust lived year-round by 1890.[1] However, it was hard to tell that this was the richest suburb in America since its displays were well hidden by the winding, picturesque lanes so admired by A. J. Downing.[2] And not many people wanted showplaces: the proper Bostonian's Puritan inclination to keep things comfortable but not conspicuous inhibited garden-making on the grandest scale. (Boston's most conspicuous consumers moved to the North Shore, but even there it is hard to find many estates comparable in glitter to those on Long Island of the same period.) Then, too, hilly, wooded topography and the comparatively built-up aspect of the area by the 1890s left little room for enormous new houses and gardens.[3] To make a big garden, as Charles Sargent did at the 150-acre "Holm Lea," it was necessary to throw existing places together.

Near "Holm Lea," and near the Country Club, the earliest established in the nation (1882), Charles Platt undertook two commissions, his first outside of New Hampshire. These gardens ranked with Sargent's in

extent and display. In 1896, at Charles Sprague's "Faulkner Farm," Platt stepped into a situation that was a landscape architect's nightmare. The house was in the wrong place; the drive was laid out badly, and the rich, enthusiastic, and opinionated client was furious with everyone including the preceding landscape architect, Charles Eliot, of Olmsted, Olmsted and Eliot, writing letters from Europe to countermand orders he had just given, and so forth. Platt became famous for the kind of soothing he administered Sprague, and famous also for the garden he designed. Pictures of "Faulkner Farm" appeared in one magazine and picture book after another.[4] Critics of the period praised it almost universally, calling it a new model for American gardens and for a new American life, that of the country villa.

Charles Sprague, lawyer and politician, had married Mary Pratt, granddaughter of the owner of the largest fleet of sailing ships in America before the Civil War. On the high hill she inherited, Charles Platt created an American villa garden, using the farmland below as *campagna*, and the hill above for *boschetto*, in the Italian fashion he had just been practicing on a much smaller scale in Cornish. He tied the house to the hill with a strongly axial view down the new drive (he persuaded Sprague the old one had to go), and below the house built a

For more than forty years after Charles Platt had made his national reputation as a garden designer with "Faulkner Farm" in Brookline (1896–1901), Mary Pratt Sprague Brandegee cultivated her magnificent "Italian" gardens. Amazing floral displays such as this in the conservatory kept visitors agape and forty gardeners hard at work.

series of walled terraces and flights of stairs. Typically, the garden lies below and apart from the grand view so as not to compete with it. Platt used water in many ways, dripping from wall fountains, in basins, and in a still pool lying in front of the dominant feature of the flower garden, the graceful casino, modeled very closely after the one at Villa Lante which he had admired enough to sketch. Charles Sprague died in 1901, but the strong-willed and high-spirited Mrs. Sprague, later Mrs. Brandegee, and the garden, well cared for by up to forty gardeners, continued on right through the 1930s. The garden was regularly open to the public.

Close by at "Weld," Platt in 1901 created another version of his

Massachusetts

The beauty of the Larz Andersons' "Weld" (1901) depended on level changes, massed flowers, and garden ornaments Platt found in Europe. "My evenings I find are pretty well occupied in making lists of purchases and dividing them up among owners-to-be," he wrote to his wife.

"Italian" garden for Mrs. Sprague's cousin and her diplomat husband, Larz Anderson. Here there are fewer specific Italian architectural "quotes." As Platt's own American garden vernacular began to develop out of its Italian beginnings, the gardens themselves became simpler in plan. "Weld's" garden was just a long rectangle on flat ground extending from one side of the house. One of the finest gardens Platt ever made, it was divided in three parts: a bowling green, a little wood, and a formal flower enclosure. It's hard to remember that such garden perfection was only a tiny part of Gilded Age life. Mrs. Anderson, for instance, inherited a fortune of $17 million and was presented at the Court of St. James wearing a jeweled dress worth $500,000. She and her husband divided their time between "Weld," an equally elaborate house in Washington,

and Anderson's various posts. She also served behind the lines as a Red Cross nurse in World War I, was decorated with the Croix de Guerre, and wrote more than twenty books, including a successful travel series.[5]

THE NORTH SHORE:
RESORT AND COUNTRY PLACE

The old rockbound North Shore, east of Boston from Marblehead to Gloucester, was a land of whaling, fishing, and farming. Its thin-soiled fields had been hewn from virgin timber, and its graveyards were filled with slate slabs inscribed with skulls to remind the idle visitor of what lay ahead. Sometime in the middle of the nineteenth century all that changed forever. The precise moment could be said to be when Mr. and

Mrs. James T. Field (of the Boston publishing firm of Ticknor and Fields) decided to upgrade the fishing village of Manchester, calling it "Manchester-by-the-Sea" as if it were some English seaside resort. And resort it became, following the by-now-familiar pattern of settlement by artists and writers, followed by discreet old Boston money, followed by new money from everywhere.

In 1915, Agnes Edwards Rothery wrote, "On entering the Garden City of Beverly one enters the precincts of the fashionable North Shore: the North Shore of shaven lawns and deep bright gardens: of wide driveways curving up through the woods to the great estates hidden beyond: of high stepping horses and smartly painted traps: of limousines with chauffeurs in livery: of elegant victorias with old ladies and pug dogs."[6] In the fields of Wenham and Hamilton one heard the cry of the Myopia hounds in pursuit of their anise "fox," and the crack of mallet and ball on the polo field.[7] Boston's elite, the well-brought-up children of tight-fisted, highly successful nineteenth-century merchants, were learning how to play.[8] By 1900, one thing they had was more playtime. Though they were richer than generations of Bostonians before them, they had lost their own political arena—Boston was in the hands of the Irish machine. As New Englanders they also found themselves a minority in national politics, where the power of the West and Midwest had finally asserted itself. The North Shore became their retreat; sport, culture, philanthropy, and looking after their money their occupations. "My occupation remains the same—trustee," writes one old Bostonian, Harvard '03, for his class report.[9] Coached by the likes of the Olmsteds and Charles Sprague Sargent, uninfected by the passion for instant effect and conspicuous consumption that others of their class and period displayed, they made some of the finest gardens in America.

Old money, old proper Bostonian money, made no more beautiful garden than that at "The Chimneys," the Gardiner Lane house in Manchester-by-the-Sea. Gardiner Martin Lane had the means, the taste, the temperament, and the connections to make a beautiful garden. His father was a Harvard classics professor; his mother a Gardiner, a member of the long-established American family who owned some of the largest and prettiest chunks of Long Island. *Summa cum laude* at Harvard, Lane went into business in Boston's most important banking firm, Lee, Higginson, where his mentor was Charles Francis Adams, brother of historian Henry Adams. He was financially astute enough to have Jay Gould want to hire him (Lane refused), and at his death he was not only rich, but a director of twelve companies. Lane's cultural mentor was Charles Eliot Norton—editor, teacher, art historian, the guiding light of Boston's late nineteenth century, friend of Ruskin and Carlyle, of Isabella Stewart Gardner and Edith Wharton, of Henry Adams and Henry James. Norton aided Olmsted in his efforts to preserve Niagara Falls. It was doubtless Norton who persuaded Lane to take on the job of president of

By 1912, the harbor of Marblehead, once busy with whalers, was edged with fashionable shingle cottages like this, the summer home of Frank Gair Macomber, who spent his winters in Palm Beach. Vine-covered arches and steps lead from the garden to the veranda. Conifers, dahlias, roses, and even a fountain surrounded by a hedge fill the narrow space behind the tall breakwater.

the Museum of Fine Arts, where Lane, in his typically agreeable, low-key, high-energy way, managed to get the new building (the present building) funded and built. Lane's entire "education," in Henry Adams's sense of the word, taught him that art, culture, and nature were inextricably a part of his everyday life.

His house was designed in 1902 by his gifted brother-in-law, architect Raleigh Gildersleeve; the garden by Frederick Law Olmsted, Jr.[10] Until his death in 1914, Lane himself kept meticulous records of all the garden plantings.[11] The main walled enclosure, which held a water garden, lay off to the side of the big Georgian house, on a little plateau that Olmsted smoothed out on the bumpy cliff top. Pot plants stood everywhere, and in the wintertime were stored in a big root cellar underneath one of the two garden terraces that adjoined the enclosure on the land side. In order to enjoy a fabulous view of Massachusetts Bay and of far-off Boston, many North Shore gardens were set in constricted spaces cut into the cliff.[12] At "The Chimneys," the simplicity of the design, its flatness, and the broadness of the grass paths enlarge the small area. The softness of the flowers—lilies, roses, and water lilies and phlox in shades of pink, cream, and white—make it feel like a sanctuary, a luxurious Edwardian version of the *hortus conclusus.*

Danvers, the manufacturing town only minutes away from "The Garden City of Beverly," was definitely not part of the fashionable North Shore. But "Glen Magna," country seat first of the Peabodys and then of the Endicotts, was one of the grandest estates in Massachusetts. Open to the public today, it is a treasure house of Massachusetts decorative history; the garden is an encyclopedia of American garden styles. By 1815, what had begun as a late seventeenth-century farmhouse was already the "summer cottage" of Captain Joseph Peabody, Salem's richest merchant. Peabody hired an Alsatian landscapist who also lived in Salem to lay out a garden, and so began the slow 150-year transformation from "the farm" into "Glen Magna Farms."[13] Joseph Peabody's granddaughter, Ellen, married her double first cousin William Crowninshield Endicott, a Massachusetts Supreme Court Justice and Secretary of War under Grover Cleveland. In 1892 she inherited the farm and at once, with

At "Castle Hill" in Ipswich, steps lead down to a maze laid out by Olmsted Bros. in the twenties. Though the maze no longer exists, the view still sweeps over the salt marshes.

In 1901 Henry Clay Frick collected his loot from the Carnegie/Morgan steel merger in Pittsburgh and began to look for a grander lifestyle in the East. In 1906 in Pride's Crossing, on Boston's North Shore, he commissioned architect Arthur D. Little to design a summer cottage, "Eagle Rock." The Olmsted firm made him a garden with enough specimen trees on the grounds to constitute a mini-arboretum. This rendering shows the unbuilt garden envisioned for the seaside elevation.

Earlier than the Gilded Age fortunes in silver or railroads was New England whale oil money, and in the first half of the nineteenth century Nantucket was queen of the industry. In the large rear yard of the house her husband, Henry Swift, bought for her in 1823 on Main Street, the former Mary Coffin made the first recorded ornamental garden on Nantucket, with a typical Nantucket fence. In 1830 her brother, Captain Henry Coffin, brought her ivy and boxwood for edgings aboard his whaler.

In Dedham in the thirties no garden was more beautiful than H. Wendell Endicott's "Rockweld," with a house by Charles Platt and site planning by the Olmsted Bros. The circular formal garden laid out by previous owner General Stephen Weld came as a complete surprise to the visitor strolling on the lawn, as it was hidden below a steep drop. In May it bloomed with tulips and flowering trees.

Massachusetts

H. H. Hunnewell's topiary terraces at "Wellesley" in Massachusetts, about 1895.

Boston architect Herbert Browne, the Endicotts set about turning it into a stylish country estate. Browne was the friend and contemporary of the Endicotts' son, also William, who eventually inherited the house. Together the two kept at it for forty years, embellishing the house with salvaged marble mantels and old mahogany doors. "Glen Magna" became a cheerfully Marie-Antoinette-ish version of an old New England farm, with Mrs. William Endicott, Jr., saying things like, "This is just a farm— we only have plated silver here."[14]

The gardens were embellished as much as the house. In 1894, the Olmsted firm made new avenues and moved the farm buildings away from the house, across the meadow. They also redesigned the old flower borders. Over 1,000 plants were used for a total cost of only $93.95! Drifts of dwarf iris, candytuft, pinks, varieties of veronica and phlox, lychnis, snow-in-summer, baby's breath, scabiosa, baptisia, astilbe, sneezeweed, and Japanese anemones, among many others, assured flowers from May till frost. Plantings also include American natives like New York ironweed, *Vernonia noveboracensis,* which grows to a height of eight or nine feet, its purple discs flowering through the fall. Both generations of Endicotts were among Charles Sprague Sargent's pets, and over the years he gave many cuttings, much advice, and hours of his time to beautify "Glen Magna."

William, Jr.'s sister, Mary, had married English statesman Joseph Chamberlin, and they visited "Glen Magna" every summer. In 1897 Chamberlin designed and put in an "Italian garden" (a formal rectangle with flower beds, a central fountain, and a wisteria arbor). An observer writes that Chamberlin himself "worked like a day laborer in order to perfect it." South of it the next year he laid out a shrubbery with a Japanese air. But the capstone of the garden was still to come, the McIntyre teahouse, which the Endicotts rescued in 1901 from derelict gardens nearby. Herbert Browne designed a rose garden for it next to Chamberlin's shrubbery.[15]

"Glen Magna" is the best example of the cozy multiplicity of an add-on garden, old New England revamped as a lordly manor with old New England money. "Castle Hill" in Ipswich was the most magnificent, entirely new North Shore estate, built with Chicago plumbing magnate Richard Teller Crane, Jr.'s new money. It was not built without a hitch. The

first house on the 800-acre site was an Italianate pile that crowned the very top of Castle Hill.[16] Twelve years later Mrs. Crane decided the site was too windy, so the first building was razed and replaced in 1927 with Chicago architect David Adler's masterpiece, a very large house made of very small pink bricks, with a cupola after Sir Christopher Wren's Belton in Lincolnshire, and with architectural borrowings from half a dozen other seventeenth-century English houses. To build the "Great House," as it was called, the innards of William Hogarth's London house, Grinling Gibbons's ornamental carvings from Cassiobury Park, in Hertfordshire, and handsome scraps from other English sources were used. A plumbing millionaire like Crane, whose mission was to "make America want a better bathroom," had elaborate conveniences himself— ten of them fitted out with Italian marble and sterling silver fixtures.

The site is one of the most dramatically beautiful in America—a view in all directions of the New England coast from the top of a drumlin, a high knob of solid ground set in the middle of miles of salt marshes streaked with silver tidal rivers and fringed with beaches. The gardens, laid out by Olmsted Bros. and Arthur Shurcliff, are equally dramatic. A dark green turf allée, boldly edged with still darker spruces, runs north from the house to the Cranes' private bathing beach. Allées were more

In 1794, in the halcyon days of the Republic, Salem architect Samuel McIntire himself carved the crisp swags and other detailing that decorate merchant Elias Hasket Derby's "teahouse." A milkmaid and a reaper, American garden gods, top the roof. The little two-story building (only 20 by 20 feet) is one of the first structures built solely for pleasure in Puritan-haunted New England. In 1901 it was moved to "Glen Magna Farms" by Mrs. William Crowninshield Endicott, a descendent of Derby's wife.

common than dandelions on American estates in 1927, but this one is special: 160 feet wide and half a mile long, it rollercoasts up and down hills to an invisible conclusion. As one stands on the terrace, the long vista appears to end on an "up," a sort of ski jump in midair right into the Atlantic Ocean. Hidden beneath the first rollercoaster "bump" is an immense casino, or "playhouse" of the kind seen more often on Long Island's North Shore than Boston's. Bachelors' quarters looked onto the marble-edged saltwater pool from one side, a ballroom from the other. Twelve thousand plants of 600 varieties once flourished in the rose garden. In the sunken rectangular Italian garden, the pink, blue, and white color scheme supervised by Mrs. Crane herself was kept looking beautiful by some of the 100 gardeners and caretakers employed at "Castle Hill" in its heyday. Olmsted Bros. bills show that $13,000 worth of flowers were planted *every year* in the gardens during the twenties. Like the gardens of Newport and Bar Harbor, it was seen by its owners for only six weeks of the year; the Cranes lived in New York and wintered on Jekyll Island, Georgia, where Adler built them an Italian villa to take advantage of the mild southern winter.[17]

THE BERKSHIRE RESORTS

Lenox and Stockbridge

The old idea of country life as synonymous with the farm no longer exists. The farmhouse type of country home is by no means extinct; but in every part of the country the magnificent new mansions of the rich are putting entirely new ideas into the current conceptions of country life. The great country house is the outward visible sign of this new movement. —Barr Ferree, *American Estates and Gardens,* 1904

By 1904 Lenox, Massachusetts, had already reached its apogee: going full steam were the biggest and best known of the "cottages" such as W. D. Sloane's "Elm Court" (built with Vanderbilt money by Lila Webb's sister, Emily), Giraud Foster's "Bellefontaine," and Anson Phelps Stokes's "Shadowbrook," the largest house in America before George W. Vanderbilt's "Biltmore" in North Carolina had topped the list in 1895.[18] In 1908 the Lenox Library voted to stop renting its Assembly Room for balls, because, the minutes state, "every palace now created has its own ballroom." Cottagers and their guests included Vanderbilts and Astors, Marshall Field, Mark Hopkins, Andrew Carnegie, George Westinghouse, J. P. Morgan, Harry Payne Whitney, and Mark Hanna's son, Dan.

Lenox life was in full swing too: Mrs. Charles Lanier of "Allen Winden" was riding her pet bull to the post office every morning; Frank Crowninshield, editor of *Vanity Fair,* was complimenting beautiful women on their wit and the ugly on their beauty; at highly organized "Elm Court," weekend house guests perused the posted "Stable Order,"

which listed a choice of twenty-eight broughams, surreys, buckboards, and pony carts for their driving pleasure, not to mention saddle horses. One weekender remembered "the choice of horses and carriages was larger than at the average commercial stable in New York City; on the other hand, if Mrs. Sloane's schedule said you rode at one, you rode at one."[19]

Soon Edith Wharton, with Henry James and Walter Berry, would chug over the Berkshires in her motor car, among the first. One summer they were all busily reading the new biography of George Sand. The latest, large showy car which, Wharton said, "always started off brilliantly and then broke down at the first hill, we christened 'Alfred de Musset,' while the small but indefatigable motor which subsequently replaced 'Alfred' was naturally named 'George.' "[20]

The Berkshires' first summer visitors had been literary: Hawthorne, Melville, Longfellow, Thoreau, Oliver Wendell Holmes, the English actress Fanny Kemble, James Russell Lowell, editor of *The Atlantic Monthly*—all visited or settled in the 1840s and 50s. Catherine Sedgwick (America's best-selling woman author until Harriet Beecher Stowe wrote *Uncle Tom's Cabin)* was born and lived in Stockbridge, and William Cullen Bryant was born in Cummington and grew up in the Berkshire Hills. All saw the beautiful, still-pastoral landscape as a retreat from a vanishing New England in a rapidly industrializing America. Parts of the earlier wild forest still remained, unfarmable and unfarmed. The massive blue Berkshire Hills, cut by deep boggy hollows, had been described by one eighteenth-century traveler as a "hideous and howling wilderness."

By 1880 Lenox had thirty-five so-called cottages; by 1900 there were seventy-five. Cleveland Amory explains the use of the word "cottage." In early resort days, as the hotels overflowed, guests were put in simple cottages on the grounds which soon, because of the extra space and privacy they provided, were at a premium. The socially eminent pulled rank to get them. When these "cottagers" built their own houses, Amory says, they were loath to give up such hard-won distinction, and they kept the word to describe their marble châteaux and ninety-room half-timbered Tudors.[21]

The season to be in Lenox was early fall, after high summer in Newport, Bar Harbor, and Saratoga, and before going to New York City for the winter. For even though Lenox is in Massachusetts, it was colonized mostly by New Yorkers, the most powerful financiers, bankers, lawyers, and railroad men of America—with a sprinkling of literati and diplomats—and their enormous contingents of houseguests, coming up by rail to Stockbridge. The calm beauty of the Berkshire Hills and the excitement of the fall foliage were big draws for Lenox's devotees. Late summer and early fall were wonderful—sparkling air, deep distances, long sunny days. Perhaps Edith Wharton's grassy terrace, with its tranquil view, was part of Henry James's memory when he said to her that the two most beautiful words in the English language were "summer afternoon."[22]

But it had to be admitted that the climate was not ideal for gardens. Or at least not as good for gardens heaped with flowers as at Newport or Bar Harbor, where the nearby ocean keeps temperatures more equable. Frost before the end of September makes a short growing season, and winter temperatures of twenty degrees below zero limit the choice of plants, even with heavy winter coverings on perennials and shrubs *and* a heavy snow cover for extra insulation. Edith Wharton wrote to Sally Norton in the earliest years at "The Mount," saying that the garden is advancing in a "reluctant New England way."[23]

Four Great Gardens of the Berkshires
One of the four great gardens in the Berkshires ("The Mount," "Brookside," and the incomparable "Naumkeag" are the others), the Giraud Fosters' "Bellefontaine" had plenty of flowers but could have survived without them. Hundreds of Italian and French statues were the true flowers; the strong geometry of gardens made mostly of water and stone, with a background of American forest, was striking and beautiful. The gardens were originally laid out by Carrère and Hastings when they built the house in 1897.[24] Allegedly a copy of Louis XV's Petit Trianon, "Bellefontaine" was about four times as big and had an extra story.

Very different in size, scale, and atmosphere from this huge palace is "Chesterwood," summer home of the American sculptor Daniel Chester French, in Glendale, near Stockbridge, which now belongs to the National Trust for Historic Preservation. Like "Bellefontaine," however, it does not depend on flowers alone, though French, who designed his own garden, kept a detailed Garden Notebook, which includes his thoughts on flowers from bergamot to zinnias. He often tended the long borders within the garden walls himself. But where summers are short, he felt a garden should have other strengths. His daughter, Margaret French Cresson, wrote that "he felt pretty much about gardens as he did about statues— that if you got your essentials right . . . then the chances were that you'd have a statue—or a garden—that would stand up and look well through the years."[25]

The essentials at "Chesterwood" include a central panel of lawn to provide a resting place for the eyes, and a "frame" of woods and walls to set off its low-key formality. A grass path bordered by peonies and standard hydrangeas leads to woodland walks that eventually circle back to the formal garden. Terra-cotta urns, which French brought back from Italy, mark the small changes in level that make walking around the garden a pleasure. French loved vines, and used *Akebia quinata,* actinidia, passionflower, *Hydrangea petiolaris,* and different varieties of clematis and climbing roses on the studio and garden walls. The great view of Monument Mountain is around the corner.

At "Bellefontaine" in Lenox, the piéce de rèsistance of Carrère and Hastings' garden (1897) for the Giraud Fosters was a long pool with pale pink water lilies and a ruff of lilac pink water hyacinths. A pergola supported by white marble torsaded columns framed a magnificent fountain, the "belle fontaine." The estate's second owner, "Boy" Foster, seen here in his baby dress at two years old, was an only child, born at the Waldorf-Astoria in New York in 1904 to parents completely unused to children. When he was ten, a friend of his mother's asked, "Where will you send Boy to school?" The answer was "Groton, of course." "But," the friend continued, "can Boy read or write?" Tutors were hastily hired. (C. Owens, The Berkshire Cottages)

Sculptor Daniel Chester French sits in front of his studio, 1925, at "Chesterwood" in Stockbridge. The heart of the garden, which French designed himself, is the fountain by architect Henry Bacon, with a frieze of dancing putti by French.

Against the warm brick walls of "Brookside's" Italianate garden stood bushy perennials: boltonia, helenium, asters, and hydrangeas. The stroke of genius was underplanting all with heliotrope, whose fragrance must have been overpowering.

"Chesterwood" was designed as a place for French to work, and the garden is laid out around the studio. When the Frenches bought an old 120-acre farm for $3,000 in 1896 as a summer place, the studio was built first, designed by Henry Bacon, later the architect of the Lincoln Memorial and French's great friend. French completed his greatest work, *Seated Lincoln,* at "Chesterwood" in 1909. The first garden plan was made in 1898, and a new Colonial Revival–style house replaced the old farm in 1900. On the south side of the studio is a great covered porch, fifty feet long, its columns wreathed in wisteria and wild grape.

French designed seven other gardens in Stockbridge. Photographs of some of them are published in Frank Waugh's *Formal Design in Landscape Architecture* (1927) along with the works of well-known contemporary professionals such as Ferruccio Vitale, Paul Thiene, Jens Jensen, Arthur Shurcliff, and architect Myron Hunt. French's simple geometric compositions stand the comparison well. Like his own, they are intimate gardens, with an easy flow of levels and spaces, the mark of an artist as gifted at sculpting earth and air as bronze and stone.

At every American resort, estate-making followed the amazingly speedy rise and fall of American fortunes. William Stanley, brilliant inventor and first owner of "Brookside" in Great Barrington, had, by 1886, invented the alternating generator, transformers, and alternating-current motors. By 1908 he was broke, driven out of the power supply business by patent-infringement suits instigated by the big companies, Westinghouse (for whom he had once worked) and General Electric. He sold "Brookside," with its fireproof Tudor "cottage" by Carrère and Hastings and a circular sunken garden, to his friend, retired railroad magnate William Hall Walker. The house still exists today, as do traces of the gardens.

About ten years after Walker bought "Brookside," he commissioned landscape architect Ferruccio Vitale to make a new "Italian" rose garden as a birthday present for Mrs. Walker. Vitale was the son of a Florentine architect and had studied engineering and architecture at the Classical School in Florence. He came to the United States as military attaché to the Italian embassy in 1898, and set up a landscape architecture practice based in New York in 1904. He was deeply involved in the establishment in 1915 of the first fellowship in landscape architecture at the American Academy in Rome. Specializing in estate work, he was especially good at what might be called the "heavy artillery" of classical gardens—the steps, walls, pools, and other architectural elements.[26]

The Walker rose garden has no connection with the house, which was probably not a bad idea since their styles were so different. A screen of natural woods thickened with pine, spruce, cypress, and mountain laurel sheltered it from sight and from the north wind. It even had a separate road entrance. Vitale must have recalled his youth when he made the design: the elegant square vegetable garden was separated only by a loggia from the fountains and roses of the parterre in a way reminiscent of some small Tuscan farm/villa.

The sixty-seven marble pillars of the loggia were waxed and wrapped each year to withstand the Berkshire winters. There were elaborate electric lighting systems in the loggia, and the garden's sprinkling system, worthy of present-day Texas, had wall-to-wall sprays located every fifteen feet. An Italian marble faun formed the central focus, and the surrounding beds were planted in roses and edged in alyssum.

By Berkshire cottage standards, there is something small, civilized, and appealing about "Naumkeag," but after all what could one expect from a man like the immensely successful lawyer and diplomat Joseph Choate who, when asked what he'd like to be if he were given a second life, answered, "I'd like to be Mrs. Choate's second husband."[27] Choate saved many a situation with his wit, and he also saved the American upper classes from a graduated income tax in 1895, arguing that the right of property was the foundation of all civilized government, and that therefore any Act of Congress instituting an income tax would require a Constitutional Amendment. The Supreme Court agreed, and the 18th Amendment did not pass until 1913. Although Choate generally gets the credit, it was his notoriously skinflint partner, Charles F. Southmayd, who prepared the arguments. Of Southmayd Choate said, "Most men are endowed with only five senses. Mr. Southmayd has a sixth—the sense of property."[28]

From its beginnings in 1885 there has been a celebratory, spirited quality to "Naumkeag." Stanford White, then a young architect, designed the house with dash and warmth. It is one of the last shingle "cottages" he built before turning to the neoclassic. To catch the great view White set the house on a narrow shelf cut into a steep hill. The situation allowed almost no room for a garden, and tradition has it that F. L. Olmsted, who was first called in to look the site over, said a garden would really be impossible.

But the Choates were determined to have a garden, and hired success-ful landscape architect Nathan Barrett to design one in 1886. Barrett, sweet-natured, slow-talking, pipe-smoking, was one of the earliest designers of formal gardens (in the 1870s), and his list of other famous clients included H. O. Havemeyer, P.A.B. Widener, Stanley Mortimer, H. D. Auchincloss, and Edward Dean Adams.[29] At "Naumkeag," besides the steep fall and the need for a wider "shelf," the curving silhouette of Bear Mountain in the distance has been the other dominant factor. A note in the Olmsted records said it first: "To trim the hedges follow the contours of the mountains on the horizon."

Overlooking the big view to the west, Barrett created two broad grass terraces which united the house to the lower lawn via a precipitous ten-foot slope. On the same shelf, Barrett laid out a rose garden to the north, ending in a flower garden and a summer house. The garden evolved

somewhat as the Choates contributed their own ideas: a linden allée was planted to the south and the rose garden became a collection of topiary figures surrounded by a battlemented wall of yew, Barrett's witty allusion to the castlelike height of the garden.

"Naumkeag" remained essentially unchanged on its perch until 1925 when the Choates' daughter, Mabel, came into her inheritance. Fresh from a Garden Club of America trip to California, she had "outdoor rooms" on her mind when she met the forty-year-old Boston landscape architect, Fletcher Steele, after his lecture to the Lenox Garden Club. Over the next thirty years she and Steele worked closely together to create a whole series of enclosure gardens of great originality and style. (He could really be called the landscape architect-in-residence as he had his own room at "Naumkeag.") The whole was a virtuoso attempt to extend the amount of horizontal garden space, and to link the gardens vertically by paths and easy flights of stairs that would make conquering the grade a pleasure. It was Mabel Choate's lifework and among the very best of Steele's gardens.

Articulate, attractive, opinionated, Steele (1885–1971) passed his childhood in Upstate New York, living mainly through his eyes, as he explained it, and acutely aware of his surroundings. He attended the School of Landscape Architecture at Harvard in 1907–9 and then went abroad to look at European gardens. He saw the obligatory gardens, Italian, French, and English, yet he returned with an impression different from Charles Platt's only seventeen years earlier. Though Steele wrote his Harvard thesis in 1913 on what he had seen abroad, he would later cast his memories of the Renaissance in Art Deco and modernist molds.[30]

At the turn of the century in Europe, modernism was beginning to flourish. In Paris the leading group of architects included Le Corbusier, the most famous, Auguste Perret, and Robert Mallet-Stevens. They were

LEFT, ABOVE:
The beds of the old Moseley garden in Newburyport, Massachusetts, are as crowded with flowers as the Victorian bouquets known as "tussie-mussies." Ebenezer Moseley first gardened here in the 1820s—good family credentials for the nostalgic "old-fashioned garden" created by his descendents.

LEFT, BELOW:
"The garden room needed a giddy carpet," wrote landscape architect Fletcher Steele about Mabel Choate's Afternoon Garden at "Naumkeag." "To please both eye and ear, four little fountains, memories of Moorish gardens like the Generalife in Granada, were set to start a pattern. Between them was laid an oval of black glass covered by half an inch of water from the fountains. This makes a brilliant Claude Lorrain glass for reflection. The pool looks deep and visitors are startled when they see little dogs walking on the water." ("Naumkeag, Miss Mabel Choate's Place")

anti-Beaux-Arts, and took their inspiration from the Wiener Werkstätte and from Viollet-le-Duc, one of the precursors of functionalism. Mallet-Stevens, whose work was lighter, more playful, and more decorative than Le Corbusier's, worked with French garden designers André Vera, and Gabriel Guevrekian on private villas and exhibition buildings. In 1919 Vera published *Les Jardins,* a reworking of Le Nôtre's classical French garden tradition on an intimate scale. In 1923 Guevrekian designed the seminal modern garden for the Viscount de Noailles at Hyère while Mallet-Stevens designed the villa. The high walls that surround the garden are pierced by big openings that display the amazing view in a frankly theatrical way. In 1925 the Paris Exposition Internationale des Arts Décoratifs opened, featuring cubist gardens laid out with blocks of flowers and concrete trees. Fletcher Steele was open to these influences, and the first garden he created at "Naumkeag," the Afternoon Garden with its illusionist use of mirror and colored stone, shares the artificial and fantastic aspect of the French gardens of the 1920s which he admired. The big problem in the Afternoon Garden was how to create an enclosed feeling without destroying the great view. Steele had some tall old oak pilings carved, painted, and gilded like Venetian gondola poles, which were set up around the perimeter of the garden. Linked by swags of clematis, they hint at the idea of a colonnade. In between them lies the view, framed as theatrically as the view at the Viscount de Noailles's villa. But then the view wasn't quite right. The curved and bumpy silhouette of Bear Mountain, which Steele felt was the essence of Berkshire Hills beauty, was obscured by distant trees. He and Miss Choate called in an army of tree men and set up phone communications between garden and woods. With field glasses glued and martinis in hand, they directed the lopping operation—sometimes as much as twenty feet came off—until the curve of Bear Mountain was repeated by that of the woodland below.

There are many other extravaganzas, but perhaps the most interesting is the blue steps—a variation on the *catena d'acqua* that is almost surrealist in its trompe l'oeil tricks of perspective. Steele also carved a tour de force of a swooping south lawn, and transformed the old grass terraces into a rock garden. Many dwarf pines were added to break up the formal design of the old topiary garden. The rose garden is an essay in Art Moderne. Four winding paths of pink marble gravel are laid out like ribbons on the grass, and each curve is punctuated by a witty "knot" of floribunda roses. Above the driveway, on the highest elevation, a Chinese garden was added after Miss Choate's visit to China. In a 1950 letter, Fletcher Steele sets down his design philosophy as it relates to the entire garden:

The vital importance of curving form which was begun on the south lawn here at Naumkeag generated by the curve of Bear Mountain beyond and made clear in the curve cut in the woodland was a satisfactory experiment. So far as I know it was the first attempt that has ever been made to incorporate the form of background topography into foreground details in a unified design. Due to the limitations of the site, these particular convolutions could not go farther than the drive on one side and the Perugino View on the other. All I could do was to echo them in the curved wall of the Chinese Garden. And when the south side of that wall is completed the secret of the whole valley and surrounding hills as seen from this place will be clarified and reduced to one continuous curve.[31]

"Naumkeag," bequeathed by Mabel Choate to the Massachusetts Trustees of Reservations, is one of the comparatively few great gardens in America that are more than fifty years old. Despite its eclecticism, its many parts, and its many makers, it has unity of design without being symmetrical, and it carries the formal garden into the middle of the twentieth century.

An autochrome shows the Honorable Joseph Choate and Mrs. Choate in their garden at "Naumkeag" in Stockbridge, first designed by landscape architect Nathan Barrett in 1886.

Connecticut is the only rich suburb of New York that is also part of New England. Within the state's tiny dimensions (ninety-five by sixty miles at the outside), especially along the coast, were packed some of the really walloping European-inspired estate gardens created in this country, such as the E. C. Benedicts' "Indian Harbor." In the beautiful hill country towns, such as Litchfield and Farmington, were some of the earliest and best "old-time" and Colonial Revival gardens. Another category of Connecticut gardens comprises the work of American landscape architects as varied as the Olmsted Bros. and Bryant Fleming, working out in the twenties and thirties their versions of American garden style. There is no comprehensive definition of horticultural conditions except to say that the soil is mostly stony, but the cool summer nights upcountry and the mitigating effects of the ocean along the coast make up for such deficiencies.

Connecticut's long coastline, cut into thousands of tiny coves and harbors, with a view of nearby islands and Long Island's distant shore, was the attraction for the first summer visitors in the 1840s. This coast was flavored by the salty colonial heritage of New England, a waterborne, two-centuries-old culture shared from Maine all the way to Sag Harbor and East Hampton on Long Island's South Fork. By the turn of the century, southern Connecticut's character had changed; Greenwich, for example, was becoming what the WPA guidebook would describe in 1938 as "essentially an urban community of the New York metropolitan area with a sophisticated suburban atmosphere, quite unlike the typical Connecticut town. The home of many prominent figures in New York's social and financial life, Greenwich is distinguished by its palatial landscaped estates...."[1] Many of these houses and gardens were designed with the water view in mind.

GREENWICH AND ITS NEIGHBORS

Practically *in* the water was the estate of New York financier E. C. Benedict, "Indian Harbor," designed in 1895 by his son-in-law-to-be, Thomas Hastings of Carrère and Hastings, on a narrow peninsula just east of Greenwich Harbor. Hastings and Helen Benedict were married in the Italian Renaissance palazzo in 1900, with lots of caviar and champagne, and guests like the Andrew Carnegies and Charles Dana Gibson. Both Charles McKim and Stanford White of the firm of McKim, Mead and White beamed on their protégé and former employee. By then the gardens were in full swing. "Indian Harbor" was a rare chance for an architect who also fancied himself a landscape architect, as did Hastings.[2] He surrounded the house with formal gardens, extending the interior spaces into outdoor rooms. Thomas Hastings's work, indoors and out, tended to be predictably, if beautifully, formal and symmetrical. Nothing could have been better for him than this irregular site, which forced him to adapt the old Italian garden formulas to new conditions. Since there was little but rock underfoot, and nothing but saltwater on three sides, he created terraces to hold earth, and pergolas and balustrades for protection from the wind and spray. Box-edged flower beds filled an angle of the house to the southwest; down the 150-foot terrace marched a parade of boxwood oblongs filled with small topiary. A multi-level white pergola wreathed in vines ran along the rocky edge of the Sound, heading for the guest house.

Benedict's great passion was boats, and the view of the house and gardens from the Sound, complete with stone water stairs and a boat landing, was impressive.[3] In summertime, when one of his narrow-beamed beauties was moored offshore, against a background of columns and tubbed bay trees and awnings, there was no prettier picture of how to enjoy life at the turn of the century than "Indian Harbor."[4]

Benedict was not the first New Yorker with power and money to enjoy "Indian Harbor"; in the 1860s, the point had been the site of "Boss" Tweed's unsavory "Americus Club" of New York. After Tweed's demise a huge hotel was erected, which Benedict had had torn down to make room for his dwelling. Today "Indian Harbor" still stands, minus one story and a lot of bay trees, but otherwise an enduring landmark for sailors on the Sound.

Another Greenwich sailor with waterfront property was John Jacob Langeloth. German-born Langeloth made a fortune in metals, and with his wife, Valeria, bought the run-down Bullinger farm with its two miles of shoreline. They demolished the old house and in 1912 commissioned architect John Duncan, designer of Grant's Tomb in New York City, to build them a palace of Indiana limestone: "Walhall," one of the most beautiful estates of Greenwich. Before it was finished Langeloth died. Valeria Langeloth finally married Frederick Bonham in 1933, a *New York Times* executive. The gardens, laid out originally by landscape architects Alderson and Dell, were perfect for the tireless Mrs. Bonham's charitable parties. A long line of formal enclosures, which included a lily pool, and a walled peony and rose garden, ran east from the house. In a green enclave of sheared retinosporas stood *The Vine*, one of sculptor Harriet Frishmuth's best-known statues, tossing her hair back and ecstatically throwing her grapes in the air—an apt symbol of the highly mannered, exuberant playtimes at "Walhall."[5]

To the south where the wide lawns ran to the Sound, landscape

Miss Annie Burr Jennings' "Sunnie-Holme" was probably the most famous garden in Connecticut, since it was open regularly to the public from 1915 till the eve of World War II. The gigantic Colonial Revival house was made of two older houses joined together.

architect Noel Chamberlin designed a sunken outdoor theater which held 1,500 guests. A woodland backdrop was carpeted with more than 250,000 daffodils. "Walhall's" theater was used for everything from ballets to Gilbert and Sullivan operas to symphony concerts. One night a yacht steered too close and ran severely aground. No matter: small boats were dispatched for her passengers, who were invited to join the entertainment until the tide floated her off.[6]

The gardens on the inland hilltops had even broader views of the coast and the Sound. Landholdings were bigger on these hilltop estates, and the flavor was more farmlike, with an emphasis on self-sufficiency. Edmund C. Converse, a Boston-born inventor and a founder of U.S. Steel, had the biggest estate, "Conyers Manor"—about 1,300 acres that actually made money in apples, milk, and greenhouse crops. The real moneymaker was estate superintendent George Drew, who had taught at Massachusetts Agricultural College at Amherst. Henry Wild worked for eight years at "Conyers Manor" laying out formal gardens and a Japanese woodland garden around the eclectic European-style stone manor designed by Donn Barber in 1904.

Connecticut

William Rockefeller, John D.'s brother, was the first Rockefeller in Greenwich; he was followed by his sons, William G. and Percy, who married a pair of sisters and set up next to each other on the hilltops. Both families thought of Greenwich as home, not as a summer place. The Percy Rockefeller place, "Owenoke Farm," had formal gardens by Ferruccio Vitale, and a tree collection of thirty-nine different varieties that Percy Rockefeller had had planted in a fit of botanical enthusiasm in 1911.[7] The William G. Rockefellers were among the first American royalty to try the ostensibly low-key life that would supersede such displays as Newport's. In 1905, William took the old Federal farmhouse his father had lived in, cut it in two, and added a few dozen rooms and a cupola in the middle. The *Greenwich Graphic* said the place had "all the appearance of an extremely well-managed and prosperous farm."[8] However, who garden makers think they are will usually come out, and at the Rockefellers the truth came out in the Deer Park, a latter-day *pairidaeza*, or Paradise Garden, like those first made by Persian kings. Its artificial lakes, planted groves, trout-stocked brooks, and exotic animals were surrounded by a high wooden paling, just the sort of fence seen so often in old prints and paintings of aristocratic deer parks in Europe. Throughout history only nobles were entitled to have a deer park.[9]

Many well-known landscape architects laid out gardens in Greenwich. The Elon Hooker estate, "Chelmsford," was an early effort by Charles Gillette, the landscape architect from Wisconsin who subsequently laid out the best gardens of Richmond, Virginia. Gillette was working for Warren Manning at the time. Another Manning protégé, Bryant Fleming, later settled the Hookers' McKim, Mead and White house more comfortably on its hilltop by creating a series of grassy terraces. Manning, one of Frederick Law Olmsted's most brilliant disciples, ran a large firm in Massachusetts which was involved in public and residential work all over the country. It became a nursery for many of the good second- and third-generation landscape architects, including Fletcher Steele and Dan Kiley. The Hookers were both intensely interested in garden and landscape. He was a genuine Connecticut Yankee: an engineer, an inventor, *and* a descendent of one of the founders of Connecticut Colony, the Reverend Thomas Hooker. His wife, Blanche Ferry Hooker, was the bright, capable, Vassar-educated daughter of Dexter Ferry, owner of Ferry Seeds in Detroit, one of the biggest seed companies in America.

The gardens overflowed with flowers, doubtless from Ferry Seeds, and every day fifteen to twenty gardeners walked the two miles to and from work through the back fields from Port Chester.[10]

Close to the Westchester County border were the well-groomed towns of New Canaan and Ridgefield. Like Greenwich, New Canaan had little New England flavor; it was a country-house fantasia described in the WPA guidebook as "a community of carefully tended country estates and polo fields. This town is exclusively a residential community, situated on

Henry W. Croft and his wife put together five old farms to make "Grahampton's" 300 acres in 1915. James L. Greenleaf was the original landscape architect, but when Augusta Graham Croft wanted more room for her flowers in 1922, she called on Ellen Shipman, then at the height of her fame. American sculptor Edward McCartan's Diana *is the focal point of the garden's main vista.*

high ridges, which in many places command a view of the Sound."[11] New Canaan got its start as a summer place in the 1870s; after World War I, summer residents began to settle down year-round.[12] There were many beautiful gardens in New Canaan created in the first twenty years of the twentieth century, but the showplace, and today a public park in New Canaan, was the Lewis H. Laphams' "Waveny."[13]

On nearly 500 acres of old farmland purchased in 1904 the Laphams built a brick Jacobean house designed by Greenwich architect William B. Tubby in 1912. Mr. Lapham, then in the leather business, was lucky enough to have an oil strike on a tannery site; he became a founder of the Texas Oil Company, later Texaco. He was also a linguist, a competent organist, a skilled billiards player, and an enthusiastic golfer who could be seen suited up in knickers, stiff collar, and tie, playing three or four balls simultaneously on the holes laid out at "Waveny." "Waveny" was a busy place. One of the four Lapham children, Jack, had a summer house there; in the twenties he introduced both polo and the new daring sport of flying. Biplanes buzzed continually up and down over the tiny, tree-hung landing strip, everyone, including children, taking a turn. Once a wing was lopped off by a tree, once a plane tipped onto its nose, but there was never a severe injury. Mrs. Lapham stuck to her glass-enclosed

RIGHT:

In his Colonial Revival–Charleston–Italian-style garden in Ridgefield, architect Cass Gilbert's disposition of decorative objects was beguiling. Mrs. Gilbert (and three full-time gardeners) stuck to familiar garden perennials—roses, iris, hosta, and the like, with annual balsam to fill in the bare spots. Only a woman with a green thumb and an architect well aware of the dangers as well as the delights of eclecticism could have kept this juggling act so beautifully balanced.

BELOW:

Although it is May and the iris and pinks are blooming in the rock garden at "Rippowam," it is the contrasts of foliage color and texture, and the sinuous line of the well-laid steps that make this Ellen Shipman design so beautiful.

electric brougham, top speed fifteen mph. One of the founding members of the Garden Club of New Canaan, she was the best and the grandest of garden grande dames. Her granddaughter Caroline Valentine's description, remembered from childhood, bears repeating.

My grandmother walked through the garden every morning, accompanied by McLaughlin, the head gardener, and by me when I was visiting. We emerged from the house to the loggia, and looked south out over the terrace balustrade to a sea of lawn sloping away to a field of tall grass and wild flowers. Beyond them were oak and maple trees, and still farther, the blue of Long Island Sound.... My grandmother, walking with a firm, deliberate step, raised her parasol over her beautiful wavy white hair, took my hand, and we stepped on to the terrace ... McLaughlin met us, and we started down the steps to the main path of the garden. On either side were lilacs, mock orange, weigela, snowballs, and blossoming trees. I picked pansies while Grandmother and McLaughlin discussed the state of the lilacs. They needed pruning, and not just ordinary pruning, severe pruning: "Be brutal, McLaughlin, be brutal," Grandmother said. Her pince-nez flashed in the sun, and the pleats in her lavender silk dress quivered as she shook her head emphatically.[14]

Copyright 1905 by the Rotograph Co.
G 3218 Residence of E C Benedict on the Sound, Greenwich, Conn.
Hello Archie!   *Grace Moran*

The Italianate gardens at E. C. Benedict's "Indian Harbor" in Greenwich on Long Island Sound were designed in 1895 by two architects who loved gardens, Thomas Hastings of Carrère and Hastings, and Bostonian classicist Guy Lowell.

BELOW:

The Lewis H. Lapham garden, "Waveny," in New Canaan (1904) was one of the most beautiful in Connecticut. Hollyhocks, water lilies, and vines soften the Olmsted Bros. brick and stone garden architecture.

The Northeast:
The Powerhouse

In Caroline's childhood memories, they then covered every step of the garden, checking on the cutting garden, following a woodland path, and finishing at "a great oak tree which was circled by a bench. We stopped there to enjoy the dappled sunlight before returning slowly to the house.... If the mornings were not always warm and sunny, if all those flowers were not in bloom at the same time ... do not tell me. As far as I am concerned, this is the way it was."[15]

Ridgefield had both classical/baronial and Colonial Revival gardens. When The Garden Club of America came to visit Ridgefield in 1927, they saw classical, formal gardens such as the John H. Lynches', with a terraced green garden designed by Marian Coffin and a "Greek collonade [sic]" leading to the swimming pool. They did not see "Casagmo," the George M. Olcotts' garden, which looms large in their own great two-

Boston architect and landscape architect Guy Lowell laid out this tour de force of a sunken water garden for Morton Plant at "Branford House" in 1916 at Avery Point, near Groton. His horticultural partner, Andrew Sargent, did the plantings, which included battalions of planters filled with aloes, araucarias, standard heliotropes, the essential bay and citrus trees, and other hothouse exotics.

Morton F. Plant paid $8 million outright for the second Mrs. Plant, pictured in her summer whites and pointy shoes.

The Arnold V. Schlaet gardens in Saugatuck were designed by the Olmsted firm over eight years, 1906–1914, not an uncommon length of time to complete a garden.

volume compendium, *Gardens of Colony and State.* Laid out in 1912 when the road was widened, it replaced the remains of a very old garden in front of the original 1721 house, which the Olcotts had torn down to make room for a new house in 1897. The new garden was Colonial Revival in style, with single flowers, old-fashioned flowers, many perennials, and fewer annuals. Three shallow terraces were separated by informal deciduous hedges and low dry-stone walls.[16]

Artists came early to Connecticut, as they had to Bar Harbor and Cornish, where the living was cheap. J. Alden Weir settled between Wilton and Ridgefield in 1882, and John Twachtman in Greenwich in 1890. Charles Platt carried out some alterations on his friend Weir's house at the turn of the century, and presumably also laid out the small garden, of which only a fountain remains.[17] Other friends, including Childe Hassam, John Singer Sargent, Edmund Tarbell, and Theodore Robinson, visited as well. Weir and Twachtman, along with Hassam, are considered to be the founders of the American Impressionist group, The Ten. The shaping of these Connecticut painters' homesteads and gardens, however modest, had an impact on garden taste, as what they recorded over and over again, in works eagerly bought and prominently displayed, was the vanishing landscape of New England. This farm landscape, and its romanticized preservation, can be considered the leitmotif of inland Connecticut estate gardens after World War I.

Architect Cass Gilbert, whose fame rests on the Gothic Woolworth Building (1913) and the neoclassical U.S. Supreme Court building, came to Ridgefield with his wife in 1907.[18] Instead of building himself a big neoclassical "cottage," he bought the Keeler Tavern, the little old house that is the most historic building in Ridgefield.[19] He added an ell and many interior architectural embellishments. He and Mrs. Gilbert, a very good gardener, also made a garden. The main feature was a walled rectangle, with a fine summerhouse designed by Gilbert at one end. The wall at the far end was pierced with round-headed arches, which opened onto the croquet lawn. A "Charleston Garden" is what Gilbert called it; he had copied a gate seen there, as well as the high, blind-arched brick walls so typical of that Southern city. He must also have noticed how small Charleston gardens can seem big and mysterious because they are compartmented; the device suited his own property, which was also a long narrow town lot, one of the original twenty-four in Ridgefield.

COASTAL BARONIAL—ON UP THE COAST
From Byram Point to Stonington, the shore was lined with "places," the most prized locations being the rocky long Connecticut "necks" sloping down into the Sound. The two grandest gardens were Morton Plant's "Branford House" and the Edward Harknesses' "Eolia." The Plant house, a turreted and crenelated Late Gothic Revival pile of warm gray granite quarried on the site, was designed by English-born architect Robert William Gibson in 1902. The house, which still exists today, and the rectangular sunken garden sat next to each other, separated by the driveway and quite unconnected in style. Altogether, "Branford House" illustrates the taste of a slightly earlier day, the first flush of American money, when merely to *have* everything was enough—dollars would glue it all together.[20] Morton Plant was the son of a big Florida railroad developer, Henry B. Plant, who wanted his son nowhere near the business, so Morton chiefly learned to be a playboy and a big spender.[21] Creating "Branford House" was something of a celebration: his father had died and he had inherited the money; he was at last coming into his own.[22] By then Groton was a popular but not fashionable summer place, the brain-child of Albert Avery, who had developed his waterfront land into a resort. In 1917 the first Mrs. Plant died and Morton fell in love with the respectable Mrs. Philip Manwaring from nearby Niantic. Unfortunately there was a Mr. Manwaring, but for Morton this was no obstacle; he simply bought Mrs. Manwaring from her husband for $8 million, along with her son, Philip, and some Manwaring real estate. Plant's storybook life ended with the influenza epidemic of 1918.[23]

When Plant's house was built, the garden was laid out with a circular fountain centered within four squares of lawn embroidered with carpet bedding and mounded beds centered with palms, rather in the style of the earliest "Italian" revival gardens of the 1840s. "This stately garden suggests some of the foreign gardens familiar to us through travel and books," is Louise Shelton's only comment in 1915.[24] In 1916 a new garden was put in by Guy Lowell, Boston architect and staunch champion of the new architecturally correct "Italian" style, working with his partner, Andrew Sargent, Charles Sprague Sargent's son. This second garden, which was bulldozed into the water by the Coast Guard in the 1940s, was an ebulliency of arches, grand staircases, checkered marble paving, reflecting pools, water stairs, fountains, statues, pediments, and pink marble columns.

Lowell's monumental garden architecture was out of date almost as soon as "Branford House" garden was finished, replaced by the newer, softer style that Charles Platt introduced. Around 1902 Platt laid out a large rectangular garden and casino complex for Mrs. Randolph M. Clark at "Glen Elsinore" in Pomfret Center, Connecticut, that appeared in at least five publications.[25] The beds overflowed with loose masses of bushy perennials and shrubs.[26] In 1901–1904, at the Francis T. Maxwells' "Maxwell Court" in Rockville, mass plantings, backed with shrubs, filled out and softened Platt's severely rectangular but simple design.[27]

Edward and Mary Harkness, just minutes away in Waterford, might have been on another planet from maverick Morton—or from the garden at "Branford House." The Harknesses had eight different houses, but "Eolia" on the breezy Connecticut shore was their favorite.[28] They arrived in late June and left at the end of September; this limited stay eased the job of the landscape architect and the gardener who were expected to provide an unending sequence of bloom in the acre of formal gardens during the term of their visit. Son of Stephen Harkness, one of John D. Rockefeller's original Cleveland partners in Standard Oil, Edward S. Harkness was also second-generation money, a man whose real interest was philanthropy. He gave away over $200 million in his lifetime. Mrs. Harkness provided every U.S. lightship and tender with a new radio set during the thirties. At her death in 1950 she turned over the entire 250-acre estate (the Harknesses were childless) to the state of Connecticut, with the proviso that it somehow be used for public health. (Half is now a public park, half a facility for handicapped children.)[29]

The rectangular Italian garden was laid out immediately west of the U-shaped villa, which faces the Sound over a lawn that once was the Harknesses' eleven-hole golf course. The site overlooked nearly a mile of beach and salt marsh. The blocky house, designed in 1902 by Lord, Hull, and Hewlett, is redeemed by graceful twin loggias extending seaward. Its walls are clothed in actinidia vine up to the eaves of the low-pitched green-tiled roof. New York architect James Gamble Rogers designed the raised pergola at the north end of the Italian garden as an inspired, miniaturized echo of the house shape, matching the U of the arched and colonnaded loggias with his pergola's wings. Balancing the Italian garden was a grass tennis court disguised with flowering shrubs that later became a Chinese garden designed by Beatrix Farrand.[30] Unlike rambunctious "Branford House," "Eolia's" classic plan exemplifies the Beaux-Arts ideal of a balanced unity of house and garden.[31]

A detailed look at various planting plans during the fifty years of Harkness ownership reveals how garden taste changed from 1909, when the Italian garden was first designed, to Farrand's inspired color combinations for the same beds starting in 1919.[32] The original planting plan by landscape architects Brett & Hall of Boston, Rogers' associates, called for blocks and stripes of gladiolus, dahlias, marigolds, bright red cardinal flowers, *Lobelia cardinalis,* and double pink hollyhocks among much else.

By contrast, how very Edwardianly English some of her plantings were! Cypresses were threaded with vines, including *Tropaeolum canariense,* the canary-bird flower, a dark green-and-bright yellow combination seen in English garden paintings of the period by Helen Allingham and G. S. Elgood. Around the cypresses, which were the focal points of the three main beds, swirled drifts of blues in expanding, loosely circular patterns: grayish-blue catnip, *Nepeta Mussinii,* soft blue *Salvia patens,* nigellas, including the one named 'Miss Jekyll', veronicas, campanulas, and many others. The scarlet *Lobelia cardinalis* of Brett & Hall's scheme gave way to the downy leaved bright-blue *L. tenuior,* grown from cuttings or seed in the greenhouse. It was planted with the tiny flowered, incandescently white northern bedstraw, *Galium boreale.* However, the garden was no fluffy pastel vision. Farrand, a more daring designer than many others, including Ellen Shipman, did not omit the dark, warm colors that spiked English borders with drama. Here, used sparingly, were orange *Lilium elegans,* French marigolds named 'Mahogany', dahlia 'Black Knight', and maroon nasturtiums. For all its Jekyllesque plantings, "Eolia" was not an English garden. The outlines that remain reveal it is too open for that; the walls are too low, and Farrand planted American natives in a way perhaps only possible for a sophisticated American who had seen many European gardens. In a formal boxwood enclosure (1924–1925) she used wild sumac: its burly candles and early autumn red leaves are a striking contrast to the neatly

barbered, evergreen *Buxus sempervirens* 'Suffruticosa.'[33] In other important Farrand private gardens, such as John D. Rockefeller, Jr.'s "The Eyrie" in Maine, or the Robert Woods Blisses' "Dumbarton Oaks" in Washington, D.C., the masterful site planning, the elegance of ornament, the massing of forms, and the carving of space overshadow Farrand's virtuosity as a flower garden designer. Here at "Eolia," in spaces planned by somebody else, what stands out is her striking ability to shape a design and impart a sense of movement using little but the color and texture of perennials and annuals.[34]

"Eolia" was a garden of the very rich, who, while they were extremely civic-minded, nonetheless wished to lead a secluded, if not anonymous, life quite separate from their public. Not so Miss Annie Burr Jennings at "Sunnie-Holme," in Fairfield. Heiress to another huge chunk of Standard Oil money (her father was one of Rockefeller's partners), she was an inveterate public character. In a day when being a single woman was like having one leg, Miss Jennings made up for it by becoming a civic benefactor, pouring money and effort into every aspect of Fairfield life for nearly forty years (she died in 1939). Church, hospital, conservation, preservation—all were her causes. Openhanded but autocratic, Miss Annie, as she was called, sat way down front in almost every town meeting, dog-collared, straight-mouthed, and wielding a fan. Even though she was a Republican and a ferocious foe of the New Deal, she was close friends with the Democratic governor in the thirties, Wilbur Cross.

Miss Jennings opened her garden to the public as early as 1915. After her mother's death in 1909, she tore the old house down and erected a giant log of a Colonial Revival house, whose windows were decked with striped awnings. Gardens stretched to the Sound in compartmented profusion: evergreen, herb, iris, white, cactus, rose, wild, and many more. But within a few years, like many others, she too followed Gertrude Jekyll—to the letter, if not the spirit—grouping flowers strictly by color in some of her gardens, planting not just a white one, but strictly pink, blue, or lavender versions too (an exclusivity that Jekyll would never have practiced).[35] The rose garden was the work of Herbert Kellaway, an English-born landscape engineer, and the rose specialist Mrs. Harriet Foote, from Manchester, Massachusetts. (Kellaway and Foote also worked together on Clara Ford's infamous rose garden at "Fair Lane.") Foote is also given credit for the rose garden of Miss Annie's sister, Mrs. Walter James, and for Mrs. Arthur Curtiss James's rose garden, both in Newport.[36] Of the many Foote rose gardens the Jennings garden was easily the best; its large pool and the surrounding pergolas gave it a structure and cohesion the others lacked. It is easy to dismiss "Sunnie-Holme" as vulgar with its violent display plantings, where rows of white hydrangeas backed heaps of pink and purple petunias, along with Miss Annie's oddly thorough "effects," such as the white pebble paths in the White Garden, or the many, too many, bronze rabbits in the rock garden.

Connecticut

The gourd walk—a Colonial Revival obstacle course at Miss Annie Burr Jennings' "Sunnie-Holme" in Fairfield.

But in fact "Sunnie-Holme" exuded the robust gaiety of a circus, and Miss Annie's gardens showed off the uninhibited cartoon side of the American imagination, an imagination so literal that it insists on figures of Indians and totem poles in the wild garden.[37]

HILL COUNTRY CONNECTICUT: THE COLONIAL REVIVAL

Away from the coast and its rapidly industrializing old seaports, the new Gilded Age colonizers found the small-boned Connecticut landscape, pricked with steeples, furred with woods, patched with stone-walled pasture and worn-out field that had not yet reverted to second growth timber—village, farm, hill, stream, and wood in perfect proportion. No wonder New York City dwellers grew misty-eyed about the colonial American past, still so close at hand in Connecticut. Nowhere did the pitch of longing for an old simplicity rise higher. The Colonial Revival movement was rooted in a deep insecurity about the nation's direction after the Civil War, and in a looming recognition that the values on which the United States had been founded had been somehow dangerously lost during the

nineteenth century's rapid industrialization. For the first time in the history of the nation, progress looked threatening, and distant colonial days looked safe and attractive by comparison. The impulse to revive earlier ideals of patriotism and community was often worthy and genuine, but only precariously idealistic: there was another reason. Between 1880 and 1930 the immigrant stream doubled from 6.7 to 14.2 million, and the biggest port of entry was New York City.[38] Just as proper Boston fled to the North Shore, so did droves of upper-class New Yorkers flee their city, first for the summer, then year-round.[39] Connecticut, close at hand, with its well-documented Revolutionary past, and its handsome and available houses, was a tempting place to settle. Aesthetically speaking, this was the first time that Americans had used themselves as their own models. The effort to reimagine a particular past can be condemned, as it has been, with the same adjectives as any other revival movement: reactionary, stale, unoriginal. And yet, in photographs of the period, these gardens, with their squares and triangles of species flowers, their white picket fences and rose arbors, seem beautiful and appropriate for the distinguished Federal and Greek Revival houses they so often surrounded.[40]

West of Hartford was the Farmington River Valley. Its special upper-class limits stretched, sociologically if not geographically speaking, northwest in pockets to the New York and Massachusetts state lines near Norfolk, Lakeville, and Sharon, and southward toward the Housatonic River and such tranquil towns as Woodbury and Southbury.[41] Northwestern Connecticut is worth looking at in Henry James's *The American Scene.* Rattled by New York and by America's new wealth and greed, James headed for New England, observing, complaining, demurring all the way. Then, soothed by a few weeks in the White Mountains and on the Cape, but vaguely discomfited by what he perceived as the uncultivated, unpeopled blankness of the American landscape, he continued into the Berkshires and down to Connecticut. Both places he found to be the land "of the social idyll, of the workable, the expensively workable, American form of country life."[42] James fell for Farmington, "the New England village in its most exemplary state: the state of being both sunned and shaded; of exhibiting more fresh white paint than can be found elsewhere in equal areas. . . ." Several paragraphs are devoted to praising village streets, not just Farmington's, but the multiple Main Streets of New England: "the great elm gallery . . . the great verdurous vista, the high canopy of meeting branches." Then, the Jamesian bull's-eye: "The charming thing—if that be the way to take it—is that the scene is

OPPOSITE:
Short pants and hollyhocks in the American cottage garden of Miss Emily Wheeler in Litchfield, sometime soon after 1906. Boards have been used to edge flower beds as far back as medieval times.

everywhere the same; whereby tribute is always ready and easy, and you are spared all shocks of surprise and saved any extravagance of discrimination."[43]

This "scene . . . everywhere the same" is what makes looking for the blockbuster Gilded Age garden in Litchfield, Salisbury, Sharon, Bethlehem, Washington, or Farmington a futile experiment. Here, unlike Newport, the ensemble is what counts, and always has. The magnificent village house with its small garden on a historic narrow lot, and the Colonial Revival farmhouse with its more expansive "farm" garden, were happy companions within the same moderate, unchanging landscape. Where the exceptional was found—and there *were* a few big stone bruisers built in the twenties, with gardens to match—it seemed out of place.[44] To the new colonists, and to James, the beauty of Litchfield and Farmington was that the nineteenth-century American itch to be relentlessly personal, relentlessly original, was for once tamed by what they imagined was the spare taste of their forefathers. The gardens were often no more than charming accommodation for two thick rows of lilies or hollyhocks, two handkerchief points of flower beds, bursting with sweet william and pansies, two arbors of 'Dorothy Perkins' roses (for everywhere in these designs there was the sense of doubling for old-fashioned symmetry's sake).

Topiary of the simplest kind—blocks of hardy evergreens—was important as well. At the Ferriday garden in Bethlehem, made by Mrs. Henry Ferriday and her daughter, Caroline, a formal rose garden just behind the house still exists today. A coven of four 15-foot-tall cones of arborvitae and some cubes of Japanese yew comprised a miniature American "Sermon on the Mount," like the one at Packwood House in England.[45]

These garden makers were a group within a group, which the late Joseph Alsop, whose family "farmed" in Farmington, called the "Wasp Ascendency."[46] What that describes, he writes, is the small world of families who "got to the United States first and staked out all the best land," led and won the Revolutionary War, wrote the Constitution, set up the system of government, and then spent the next 150 years, until the Depression, running the finances of this country to their own great profit. (They were also smart enough to absorb practically anyone else who made money.) While many of them didn't shy from display (Newport, Bar Harbor, and Long Island's North Shore were by no means all new rich), the ones who gravitated to northwestern Connecticut, like Old Philadelphians in Chestnut Hill, wanted to live less conspicuously. The area already had its own conservative substratum of cultivated, well-to-do natives. They had made their money in shipping, in the professions, in real estate, and in manufacturing in Connecticut before the Civil War, and they were perfectly happy to stay where they were. Litchfield in particular had got an early start as an incubator for the Wasp Ascendency

when Tapping Reeves opened the first law school there in America in 1784. Before it closed in the 1830s, Reeves's graduates included a vice president, five cabinet members, seventeen senators, fifty-three members of Congress, and so on.

Farmington hit its peak of power beginning in 1895 when Teddy Roosevelt's forty-year-old sister, Anna, married aging naval attaché William Sheffield Cowles from Farmington. ("Bearo" Cowles later became a rear admiral.) Anna Cowles's N Street residence in Washington, known as "the Little White House," was a Wasp nexus of brains, money, and power, beginning with Henry Adams, and continuing on through Alsops, Cabots, Cuttings, Fahnestocks, Griscoms, Hays, Jays, Longworths, Reids, Stillmans, Thayers, and the other Roosevelts, including cousin Franklin and niece Eleanor. The Cowles's family house, "Oldgate," became Anna Cowles's summer base of operations. Teddy Roosevelt often visited, as did a large U.S. State Department contingent, and most of the British diplomatic corps, who found at "Oldgate" a successful American version of the ideal English country-house life, that artful mix of sport, money, sex, and politics.[47] "Oldgate" was a very large house on a very small property after Anna Cowles added an ell for servants and guests in 1905. The landscape architect who surveyed the strip of land that headed steeply downhill to the Pequabuck River must have scratched his, or her, head as to how to include everything needed for full-blown outdoor country life on only 7 acres. Family tradition says Frederick Law Olmsted, Jr., laid it out, though as yet no records have turned up. But a master hand surely was responsible for the plan, which made a virtue out of the awkward facts of the location. The plan, which has been simplified today by the incumbent Cowleses, originally included a rose garden, a cutting garden, greenhouses, a tennis court, a naturalistically planted side lawn—*and* light, air, and a long beautiful view out over the flat Farmington meadows so admired by Henry James. The continuity of the meadow vista from the house was achieved by grading so that the road that bisects the property could not be seen. A careful look confirms the fact that the axis of the garden and the line of vision are not the same, but cross each other at a narrow angle. The slight tension this creates is not jarring, but tends rather to widen the view.

Wasp Ascendency women perfected the American lady's particular brand of self-confidence and eccentricity. Joseph Alsop wrote,

We advanced across an acre or so of sward to the flower garden in search of Mrs. Barney; and there among the flowers we found a very ample lady of about sixty, in what was considered to be a ladylike nightgown of that period, made of material that I think was called lawn. At any rate it was rather thin handkerchief linen and a single waterspot made it almost completely transparent. Mrs. Barney had been working hard in strong sun for some time and large areas of her nightgown clung to her damply, transparently, and (to us children) most surprisingly. Besides the nightgown she wore a large, beflowered garden hat and large, sturdy gumboots.

This costume was completed by a trowel, already dirt-infested from heavy use, which she waved at us in a friendly way, greeting my mother with the remark, "Oh, Corinne, I do hope you won't mind how I look! I can't bear taking two baths in the morning, so I get my weeding done first and then I wash off all the dirt in one go.[48]

For her day, Mrs. Barney's garden was far more eccentric than her behavior. When the Danford Newton Barneys bought the John Treadwell Norton house in 1890, the 140-foot-wide circular hedged garden next to the house was still laid out in the same paisleyed patterns that Norton had put in, perhaps around mid-century. Greenhouses were an absolute necessity for this kind of display, and one of the paths that quartered the garden led to a small rabbitlike hole in the high green hemlock hedge.[49] Beyond it was the business end, where hundreds of plants were propagated every year. What is unusual about the Barney garden, which still survives today in simplified form, is that it lasted for at least a century exactly as it had been first laid out.[50] Mrs. Barney was above any urge to tear up the out-of-date curvy beds. Up to the mid-forties, when her daughter-in-law cut out some of the more labor-intensive plantings, not much changed within the hemlock circle, which continued on as a perfect Victorian relic, untouched by the Beaux-Arts or the Colonial Revival.[51]

By 1897 the idea of the country place was firmly established in America. But when Warren Manning (1860–1938), newly independent after eight years' employment with the Olmsted firm, received a commission from a Miss Theodate Pope in Farmington that year, he was about to make an entirely new kind of estate landscape: an American farmstead rather than an English park. Manning was the perfect choice of landscape architect. One imagines that the New England farmscape must have been among his earliest memories, since he was raised in rural Billerica, Massachusetts, as the son of a nurseryman. Previous country places he had worked on were the 1890 Hamilton McKeon Twombly place, "Florham," in Madison, New Jersey, and George Vanderbilt's French château-cum-forestry-experiment, "Biltmore," begun in 1895. Both included English-style parks and large model farms. By contrast, "Hill-Stead," which is open to the public today as a museum, is modest (250 acres), consciously American, and rural. It is also beautiful. Manning's mature vision of the purely American country place can be seen at the Frank Seiberlings' "Stan Hywet" (1915), in Akron, Ohio. "Hill-Stead" is understated, light on the ground, a sketch of what would follow.

Plump, practical-minded, authoritarian, Theodate Pope was the only child of a thoroughly likable Cleveland businessman, Alfred Atmore Pope, and the rather nebulous and social Ada Brooks Pope. At nineteen, Theodate had first come east to Farmington in 1886 to attend Miss Porter's finishing school. At this time she changed her name from Effie to Theodate, "gift of God," after her New England grandmother, beginning her own metamorphosis into a New England "character." After disastrous attempts to make Theodate fit into ordinary society (debutante party, Grand Tour), her parents were persuaded to let her live life as she wished. Her father gave her his full support. She bought a Farmington village house, and studied art and architectural history in Princeton, eventually becoming Connecticut's first licensed woman architect.[52] In 1897 she talked her parents into building a house for themselves in Farmington, which would become "Hill-Stead." Given her character, and her embrace of everything New England, there's no doubt that Theodate Pope would have had definite ideas on the landscape. One wonders what went on between her and Manning during the months before the old farms that comprised the property were bought, or the architect chosen (1898). Certainly Alfred Pope's initial ideas coincided with the eventual result. In a letter to Theodate of 1898, he writes, ". . . I would figure to improve the 'house lot' as we talked of, not to 'park' the place."[53]

McKim, Mead and White were hired as architects, but both Mr. Pope and Theodate quite openly considered her to be in charge.[54] The house was an essay in early nineteenth-century Connecticut vernacular architecture, something Theodate Pope perhaps knew more about than did her architects, after ten years spent obsessively studying the genre in Farmington. Theodate's letters to the firm show her to be defensive and disagreeable, but there's no doubt that her concept of the Colonial Revival was well founded.[55] Completion of the rambling white house was celebrated with a gaslit dinner party in May 1901. On the walls glowed the superb collection of Degas and Manet and other Impressionists collected by Alfred Pope with the guidance of his friend Mary Cassatt, for which "Hill-Stead" is famous today. After the death of her father, and her marriage to diplomat John Wallace Riddle in 1916, Theodate herself moved into "Hill-Stead" and lived there the rest of her life, until 1946.

The octagonal garden seems like an afterthought, sunk in an irregularly shaped dip separated from the house by the driveway. Perhaps Theodate had little interest in a flower garden; that was at first her mother's domain. Or perhaps the intellectual difficulty of trying to imagine a grandly ornamental, and therefore anachronistic, garden in this otherwise faithful "farmscape" was too much for her. Theodate and her husband, J. W. Riddle, moved into "Hill-Stead" in 1916, and shortly thereafter Beatrix Farrand produced a clever new plan, also an extended octagon, for the flower beds which has been carried out today.[56]

The real beauty of "Hill-Stead" is the landscape, not the garden, and its particular charm is its deliberately archaic spareness. The uncontrived shapes of barn, field, and wood stand against one another; the curve of the drive only reveals the house at the last, and at an angle. "Hill-Stead" has none of the fussiness of many other Colonial Revival gardens and landscapes. It makes the same New England statement as Henry James's "great elm gallery," which he imagined murmuring, "See with how little we do it; count over the elements and judge how few they are."[57]

NEW YORK STATE

New York includes within its borders the climates of all the New England states. Between the Adirondacks and the sea level of Long Island's South Fork, there is a month's difference in the start of spring. In 1915 Louise Shelton, writing about country places in *Beautiful Gardens in America,* pointed out that there were more fine gardens in New York, including Long Island, than in any other state. As in Massachusetts, the runner-up state according to Shelton, the uses of New York State's gardens were as varied as the climate and terrain. Some were summer gardens at seaside resorts like Southampton and East Hampton; some were parts of year-round country seats, in areas like the Hudson River Valley, Long Island's Gold Coast (the North Shore), Dutchess County, and Westchester County,

where estate life, especially weekend life, went on during spring and fall, and even winter. There was that unclassifiable and unique enclave, Tuxedo Park, founded in 1886, and—far outside Manhattan's orbit—in smaller northern cities like Buffalo, Canandaigua, and Rochester, were a few fabulous and beautiful gardens, just as fashionable and elaborate as gardens closer to New York, created by each town's leading citizens.

ABOVE:
The "Great Terrace" at the Samuel Sloans' "Lisburne Grange" (1929) in Garrison, in the Hudson River Valley, is centered with four arching sugar maples and a mirror pool designed by Kitty Sloan, Garden Club of America president and expert gardener.

HUDSON RIVER GRANDEUR

But no matter how varied New York's gardens were for reasons of climate or use, what they shared was grandeur. New York's commercial growth and ascendency over Boston and Philadelphia became noticeable after the Civil War. Control of railroads and communications meant New York was the nation's financial capital. In order to share in the high stakes, the very rich had to spend time in New York, and that meant having a house somewhere nearby as well. Fast comfortable trains, not to mention private railroad cars, went everywhere within a comfortable commuting radius of New York City. The movement away from Manhattan to the suburbs had begun even before the Civil War, however. In 1855 English traveler W. E. Baxter observed that villas on the Hudson were "starting up like mushrooms on spots which five years ago were part of the dense and tangled forest; and the value of property everywhere, but especially along the various lines of railroad, has increased in a ratio almost incredible. Small fortunes have been made by owners of real estate at Yonkers, and other places on the Hudson River."[1]

By the 1890s the concentration of wealth around New York was unprecedented, and it was well displayed in the boldness and sumptuousness of great estate architecture and garden design. The Hudson River Valley, like Newport, was no longer a collection of large handsome Dutch farmhouses on huge tracts of land, with a light sprinkling of Greek Revival temples, Gothic Revival castles, and Italianate villas, all set in picturesque grounds. It had become a riverside lineup of mansions, many with formal gardens.

In picturesque landscape architecture, the house took its place in the landscape as an incidental ornament. In formal landscaping, the house is the center and the landscape is planned around it. This was not easy when the breathtaking Hudson River was always there to steal the show, but Hudson River millionaires like John D. Rockefeller and Samuel Untermeyer gave the river a run for its money with imposing palaces and massively architectural gardens on a huge scale that almost matched that of the river.

"Hyde Park"

The idea of manorial estates was not new to the Hudson River Valley. New York State had an aristocracy as early as Virginia; it was the most northern of the manorial systems in the United States. As early as the late seventeenth century there were vast estates, huge landholdings both Dutch and English up and down the Hudson. Flowers were grown, but there were no "fine gardens," in Louise Shelton's sense of elaborate, purely ornamental gardens, until the eighteenth century. The city expanded so explosively in the nineteenth century that fewer of these old gardens or houses survive around New York than in the immediate surroundings of Boston or Philadelphia.

"Hyde Park," one of the best-known and most long-lived of these estates, was designed in 1828 for New York physician and botanist David Hosack by a Belgian emigrant, André Parmentier, a nurseryman and the first man in America to call himself a "landscape gardener."[2] Parmentier, who was much admired by A. J. Downing, the most influential American garden writer of the nineteenth century, laid out lawns and curving walks and drives planted with a legion of specimen trees including gingkos, sugar maples, white pines, and Kentucky coffee trees.[3]

The estate's inhabitant after Hosack was Walter Langdon, John Jacob Astor's son-in-law, who laid out formal "Italian" gardens, two long terraces filled with roses, reflecting pools, and fancy beds of annuals. In 1898 Frederick Vanderbilt, grandson of Commodore Cornelius, tore down the old house and had McKim, Mead and White, best-known architects of the age, build him the fifty-four-room Italian Renaissance pile of Indiana limestone that still stands on the site and is open to the public. All in all, Vanderbilt spent approximately $3 million on house and gardens — just about what he always kept in cash in his bank account, "in case," he said, "I want to buy something." Vanderbilt also commissioned James Leal Greenleaf, a New York–based civil engineer and landscape architect, to make considerable changes in Langdon's formal gardens, screening the terraces from each other with trellises and vines. (However, throughout the many changes in the garden, the sweep of the original Parmentier plan was not altered.) Greenleaf, who trained at Columbia University and began his landscape practice in the 1890s, worked with Henry Bacon on the Lincoln Memorial landscape, and created many great estate gardens, notably the Pratt gardens on Long Island and C. Ledyard Blair's splendid Italian hillside in Peapack, New Jersey. His best works featured magnificently sited reflecting pools and luxuriant and heavily textured background plantings, with many varieties of conifers. His gardens were more than a match for the richly baroque 1890s architecture of McKim, Mead and White, or Carrère and Hastings, two firms with whom he habitually worked.[4]

The Frederick Vanderbilts thought of themselves as America's royalty and enjoyed formality to the hilt — Mrs. Vanderbilt even had a rail around her bed as if preparing for a Louis XIV–style *grand lever*, complete with courtiers. The Vanderbilts' next-door neighbor, Eleanor Roosevelt, grew curious about Mrs. Vanderbilt's solitary afternoon drives with only her coachman for company. "When I go driving," replied Mrs. Vanderbilt, "I do my mental exercises." Mrs. Roosevelt grew more curious and politely inquired further. "Well," said Mrs. Vanderbilt, "first I do the kings and queens of England, forward and backward, with their dates, then I do the presidents of this country, forward and backward, with their dates, and sometimes," she added, "if I take a long drive, I get as far as the kings and queens of France."[5]

Financier Jay Gould bought "Lyndhurst," finest of the Hudson River Gothic castles, in 1880. The house was the masterwork of Alexander Jackson Davis, the landscape a rolling Downingesque triumph, but the greenhouse was what Gould loved. It became world-famous for its orchids. An annual event was the flowering of the night-blooming cereus: to witness it, every member of the household was waked and led to the greenhouse, a quarter of a mile away.

Though the "Italian" gardens are in sorry state, "Hyde Park" at least preserves an unbroken legacy of nineteenth-century garden styles, whose fragile layers must be teased apart by painstaking historians and garden archeologists.

"Springwood"

At Franklin Delano and Eleanor Roosevelt's "Springwood," the lawn above the river and modest hemlock-hedged flower garden first laid out in

the 1850s were the setting for a different kind of garden history, equally grand and far simpler. Frances Perkins, author of *The Roosevelt I Knew,* recalls the perfect scene of what today is also part of "Hyde Park":

Many times in summer, when I would be told that "the family is on the lawn," I approached through the library and saw through the open door an unforgettable picture: Mrs. Sara Roosevelt, in a soft, light summery dress with ruffles, her hair charmingly curled, sitting in a wicker chair and reading; Mrs. Roosevelt, in a white dress and white tennis shoes with a velvet band around her head to keep the hair from blowing, sitting with her longlegged, graceful posture in a low chair and knitting, always knitting; Roosevelt looking off down the river at the view he admired, with a book, often unopened, in one hand, and a walking stick in the other; dogs playing near by, and children romping a little farther down the lawn.[6]

"Lyndhurst"

Another Hudson River estate with a long garden history pedigree was "Lyndhurst," in Tarrytown, built in 1836 and purchased by financier Jay Gould in 1880. Today it belongs to the National Trust for Historic Preservation and is open to the public. Gould, the only son and youngest child of a Roxbury, New York, farmer, was a short, whiskered little man with sharp eyes and a soft voice, who loved books, flowers, and children. He was also totally unscrupulous in business—in fact his business was bribery, stock manipulation, Wall Street monopolies, and the manufacture of rumor. With Boss Tweed of New York City's Tammany Hall he effectively bribed both legislators and judges. Other robber barons did the same, but without Gould's cheerful devil-may-care air. He was the robber baron his fellow robbers loved to hate.

What Gould bought was the first and finest Hudson River Gothic villa built for New York City mayor and congressman William Paulding by Alexander Jackson Davis, inventor of the style. Downing, who was a friend of Davis's, may have advised on the grounds; the picturesque 20-acre lawn, clumped with arrangements of specimen trees, is very much in his style. There was no ornamental garden as such. But the 376-foot-long greenhouse, built by the Lord and Burnham Company, then just a local firm in Irvington, more than made up for it. Its builder, George Merritt, the second owner of "Lyndhurst," spent approximately $100,000 on his horticultural improvements—almost as much as he spent on improving the house. A bulbous Saracen cupola that served as an aviary topped the 100-foot-tall central tower. At the time it was built (c. 1865) it was the largest greenhouse in America, and would be equaled only by Horticultural Hall, built in Philadelphia for the 1876 Centennial. Gould modernized it and furnished new plant collections in 1880; then watched it burn completely in half an hour within six months of its reopening in 1881. Undeterred, he called in Lord and Burnham again to rebuild it to exactly the same dimensions on the ground, though without the big dome. He also hired John William Walter, of the renowned New York ecclesiastical architectural firm of Pugin and Walter, to design sets of Gothic doors, each with different tracery, and many other architectural details in keeping with the Gothic house.[7]

THE BEAUX-ARTS IN NEW YORK

The Frank Vanderlip garden, "Beechwood," in Scarborough, designed in 1916 and now newly restored, is a garden pared to its Beaux-Arts essentials: a reliance on garden architecture, a symmetrical plan, a fanatic attention to detail and proportion, and most of all, a fluent mastery of three-dimensional space. Screened by trees and never connected to the house, which has now vanished, it looks down over an earlier Olmsted picturesque landscape. A classical Italianate three-arched casino stands at one end of the long rectangle, a circular moated temple of the familiar kind known in periodicals as a "temple of love" at the other.[8] Between casino and temple is a long pergola that breaks up the space. All three buildings are white. It's a lot of architecture for a small garden, but the plan, with its clearly defined major and minor axes and cross axes, imparts a sense of movement. A circular reflecting pool is the same diameter as the hedge surrounding the temple's moat—a nice touch typical of the Beaux-Arts concern for detail and balance. What is

Many Beaux-Arts gardens finished with a view from the casino framed by pillars, like this one in Westchester County, the estate of Mrs. Whitney Blake, member of the Bedford Garden Club.

subtle, complex, and a perfect illustration of Beaux-Arts mastery of spatial design and dynamics is the constant and almost unnoticeable change in level. The relationship between the three buildings is determined by a slight slow grade from the casino up to the temple, which permits the domed temple roof to be framed by the arch of the pergola. Just a few steps lead down to the pool from the casino—just a few go back up to the pergola platform. In those few steps, the beautiful vaulted ceiling of the central pergola pavilion flashes into view and then vanishes. Here at its simplest is the best of the Beaux-Arts. The balance of axial planning and the tension of a controlled flow of space make a fascinating garden that is restrained in its architectural detail and its plantings.

"Beaux-Arts" implied a program even more than a style (styles ranged from Greek to Tudor) that was taught at the Ecole des Beaux-Arts in Paris, the school where, beginning in the 1880s, most young American architects and many landscape architects received their training.[9] Overall planning, from the doorknobs to the distant vista, was part of the Ecole method. An architect's master plan generally included gardens, landscape, and outbuildings as well as the house itself. He was responsible for siting; he often laid out the drive, the important entrance court, and the grades that surrounded the house—those fundamental things that really define the garden.[10] Just as with any sixteenth-century Italian villa or seventeenth-century French château, the master plan extended the axes of the house plan out into the landscape, often reaching far past the gardens *qua* gardens to distant farmland or pasture or woods or ocean. "Horizon gardening" is what one garden writer, the late Ann Leighton, called it. Beaux-Arts students were also trained to collaborate as part of an atelier. Once the master plan was roughed out, often with the help of the landscape architect, specialists worked on different aspects of the job—interior decorators, garden designers, and sometimes even other architects who specialized in outbuildings. Beaux-Arts planning and collaboration helped America's palaces rise at dizzying speeds.

The Rockefellers and "Kykuit"

"Kykuit"—Dutch for "Lookout Hill"—John D. Rockefeller's 4,180-acre estate in Pocantico Hills, is the grandest neoclassical estate designed according to the Beaux-Arts system. Rockefeller, along with Henry Flagler and other founders of Standard Oil, had gained control of 95

LEFT, ABOVE AND BELOW:
Landscape architect Welles Bosworth, classically trained at the Ecole des Beaux-Arts in Paris, made a monumental garden at the John D. Rockefellers' "Kykuit" that was a match for the four-story granite manor house. Huge trees, like these framing the Oceanus Fountain, were often moved in full grown. Hicks Nurseries, in Westbury, Long Island, seen here, were among the big tree specialists.

percent of American oil production during the last half of the nineteenth century. In 1893 he left Ohio for New York, and began to look for a summer place near New York City. In 1902, after the first "Kykuit" burned, he commissioned New York architects Delano and Aldrich to build a Georgian manor house of granite quarried on the property, and Bosworth to do the formal gardens and landscape.[11] All three had studied at the Ecole des Beaux-Arts. They had met while working briefly together in the offices of yet another Beaux-Arts team famous for their country estates, Carrère and Hastings.[12]

"Kykuit," which remains comparatively unchanged today, is much grander in scale than "Beechwood," but the same principles apply. The same changes in level, though bigger now, the same alternation of open and closed spaces, and the same exquisite and exacting attention to detail are what control the vast flow of gardens that almost entirely surround the house. Here, garden and house are closely related, the vistas and axes of the garden lining up with the doors and window bays of each elevation. The amount of marble in urns, statues (including a fine Hellenistic statue, the *Altoviti Venus*, housed in a temple of love), steps, and balustrades may seem excessive today, but in fact all is in proportion. For if you *must* have a modern facsimile of Giambologna's famous fountain in the Boboli Gardens of the Pitti Palace in Florence, with a huge white copy of *Oceanus* towering up against the eastern skyline of your entrance front, then the surrounding pools and urns and gates should be on the same giant scale, and so they are. To the west, things calm down architecturally, allowing natural scenery to take over. Steps from the piazza lead the eye out across simple terraces to the phenomenal view of the river. Below is the Japanese garden, laid out in 1908 by Japanese masters with the enthusiastic supervision of John D. Rockefeller, Jr. This garden must be where he got his first taste of the pleasures of Oriental garden-making he later enjoyed to the full in Maine with his wife, Abby Aldrich, and Beatrix Farrand.

Samuel Untermeyer's "Greystone"

On a positively pneumatic scale are the 24 acres of Greco-Roman gardens that Welles Bosworth designed at "Greystone" shortly after finishing "Kykuit." Here the familiar temple has lost its dome and been blown up into an enormous circular colonnade that projects over a pool where sea animals play on the mosaic floor. There are over 9,000 square feet of mosaics in all, and a major water network with integral lighting for more than forty fountains.[13]

In 1899 Samuel Untermeyer, a successful multimillionaire lawyer in New York and something of an amateur botanist and horticulturist, bought New York governor Samuel Tilden's place in Yonkers and set about improving the 113 acres of grounds. Untermeyer understood perfectly that one of the greatest pleasures of making gardens is the pleasure of

winging it, if you have enough money, to the furthest realms of fantasy. To assist Bosworth, he called on the landscape engineer Charles Welford Leavitt, who would later design steel magnate Charles Schwab's riotous Italian villa sculpture garden in Loretto, Pennsylvania.

In this garden, Bosworth and Leavitt explored two more Beaux-Arts interests: the connections between architecture and water, and the use of columns. The brick-walled rectangle is open along its western side to the Hudson view. The main entrance to the garden is on the south side, through an "Assyrian" portico. Instead of paths, the central axis and cross axis are long narrow reflecting pools, like those in Islamic gardens. Footpaths also run down each side of the waterways. But the eye moves faster, traveling across this long water "path" northward to the Greek amphitheater at the end of the garden on a slightly higher level. On the cross axis the water "path" fantasy leads to the temple that stands against the sky.

Down toward the river for hundreds of feet runs the vista, which terminates in a circular grass-floored landing enclosed by a Byzantine Greek balustrade. The imposing river view is effectively tamed by a simple device: a frame made of two huge antique cipollino columns. As at

At Samuel Untermeyer's "Greystone" in Yonkers, linked pairs of tall columns are topped with American sculptor Paul Manship's sphinxes, which flank a view down the main axis of the "Greek" gardens. This marble fantasy was Welles Bosworth's next project after "Kykuit."

In a watercolor by society artist Rosina Emmett Sherwood, Mrs. Robert Brewster sits on the steps of a garden temple in the woods at "Avalon" in Mt. Kisco, designed by Charles Delano of Delano and Aldrich in 1912. The temple is the terminus of the main garden vista, which continues the house axis.

"Kykuit," the bravura use of large-scale ornament succeeds, surmounting the significant risk of looking ridiculous. (The cipollino columns were imported by Stanford White, who, like Charles Platt, did quite a business finding European decorative arts treasures for his clients.) "Greystone" takes the neoclassical style to the nth degree—there is nothing like it, except for a few vast porticoes on antebellum Southern mansions that so perfectly exhibits the razzmatazz of newly rich America trying out old ideas for the fun of it.[14]

"Avalon" in Mt. Kisco

Inland from the river and north of Yonkers were such places as Mt. Kisco, Bedford, and Katonah. Mt. Kisco was the most fashionable, and the estate

residents there were known as "hilltoppers" because, beginning in the teens, they built their houses right on the tops of Westchester County's wooded hills to catch the views in all directions. By Hudson River "castle" standards, most of the houses were not ostentatious, although stylistically they partook of the same trends—Gothic, Renaissance, Tudor, Georgian, and so forth. They were not showstoppers but rather pleasant, luxurious, summer homes, well arranged inside and out for a tranquil life. Such was "Avalon," a Delano and Aldrich house designed by William Delano in 1912 for his old Yale friend, Robert S. Brewster, in Mt. Kisco.

Delano had been only twenty-nine years old when he and his partner went to work on "Kykuit" in 1902. Their partnership was formed the same year. The surge of expensive residential building created such a demand for architects that young men had breathtaking chances to execute enormous commissions. Most of them, like Delano, came from upper-class backgrounds, architecture being a suitable profession for a gentleman. This background helped them get commissions, of course, but it also meant they knew the life and manners they were designing for, and what was really wanted in a country estate. Sometimes they knew more than their clients did.

The Brewster house is a wonderful example of Beaux-Arts principles and methods in action. "Avalon" was designed as a French Renaissance château from the tip of its gleaming slate roof to the last detail of its hardware. It was stylistically all of a piece. The circulation was perfect: every reception room opened into two other rooms and to the outdoors. The visitor who came from the front door into the long central gallery was greeted by a vista that plunged through the oval stairhall and the living room, on out across the terrace, and up the steep wooded hill with its many steps to the small white temple of love, also designed by Delano.

At "Avalon" it was easy to see how interior space extended outdoors. The outward curve of the living room terrace echoed the shape of the house front, and the library and dining room each had a loggia. All three rooms had their own views: allées cut into the woods, each marked by a fountain that connected the terrace to the woods beyond.

The site planning was masterly, and yet not *too* masterly; as Samuel Howe wrote in 1915, the house is "ingeniously introduced into the woodland without a heartless cutting away of things, a too free changing of levels, or the adoption of some big engineering scheme, reducing the grounds to an artificial platform. The garden and courts have been laid out and the house located with reference to the view." Delano was not totally governed by his graph paper or by Beaux-Arts axes—the path to the elliptical sunken garden tilted eastward as site conditions required. It was a surprise to the visitor who walked down the path and then saw the whole garden at a glance from a round pergola at the top of an easy flight of curved steps.

In the twenties, landscape architect Ellen Shipman, who created a number of gardens in Mt. Kisco, was called in to enrich the plantings, but she did not alter the plan. Mrs. Brewster, while she did not work a lot in the garden herself, was quite knowledgeable horticulturally and had the happy knack of finding and keeping good gardeners. She died in 1941, and life at "Avalon" changed during World War II when labor shortages caused the downfall of many estate gardens. The Brewster children kept it up as best they could with one man, or, as one of them recalls, "he kept it up and we looked down." After the war the place was sold and became an institution, as did so many others.[15]

THE PALISADES

The west bank of the Hudson didn't develop the way the east bank did for two reasons: the Palisades made river landings difficult if not impossible, and railroad development was far more rapid on the east bank since trains could run right into the city. Anna Gilman Hill (Mrs. Robert C. Hill), the author of *Forty Years of Gardening* (1938) mentioned above, made a famous garden at "Niederhurst" in Sneden's Landing. In 1860 her grandfather, Winthrop Gilman, decided his "rural seat" in Bloemendal (now Riverside Drive and 70th Street in Manhattan) was threatened with development. At that time Nyack, on the Hudson River, was a summer place and the commute by train, ferry, and carriage was only an hour and a half. Another big draw for Mrs. Hill's grandfather was the presence of his old friend John Torrey. Torrey, who lived in a little house he had built himself on top of the Palisades cliff, was one of the two great figures of American nineteenth-century botany, along with Asa Gray.

Mrs. Winthrop Gilman, who gardened first at "Niederhurst" in 1872, belonged to the old bedding-out school of thought: "Spring was a nightmare of little plants all screaming to be set out at once."[16] Around the turn of the century when Anna Hill and her husband moved into "Niederhurst" after her mother's death, she got rid of the patterned beds and annuals and made a brilliant garden with the help of her gardener Dennis O'Brien. Landscape architect Marian Coffin designed a hidden garden below the cliff, where, on axis with the terrace and main door a long low-walled *tapis vert* led to a vista. Known as the "Claude Lorrain view," it cut through virgin timber and was floored with billowing shrubs. The terminus was a white statue of Hebe, and Mrs. Hill herself designed the garden that surrounded the statue. She also designed and put in a superb rock garden. By the twenties "Niederhurst" was a year-round place, and the Hills were summering in East Hampton, where they had yet another great garden.

Another turn-of-the-century Hudson River Valley gardener's garden was "Meadowburn Farm," in Warwick, New York, inland and north from Tuxedo Park. Helena Rutherfurd Ely was the author of the *Hardy Garden Books,* small practical volumes packed with information about

For Washington Post *owner Eugene Meyer, and Agnes Meyer, the Oriental collector, in Mt. Kisco, New York, Charles Platt designed one of his most beautiful gardens, "Seven Springs Farm" (1915–1919) in his later, more monumental style. The massive pergola at one end of the house terrace is embroidered with filigree wrought iron panels and wisteria.*

vegetables, fruits, evergreens, Bordeaux mixture, wood ashes, and barnyard manure—and exhortations to grow perennials instead of bedding-out plants. In 1914, the perennial borders in just one of her own eight gardens were divided by color—pink, blue, white, red—and they bloomed from the end of May till the first frost. However she was not a perennial purist—any bare spot that dared to show was promptly filled with homegrown annuals. Each border was four feet wide and seventy-five feet long and contained hundreds of plants. Mrs. Ely was by no means alone in her expertise, or in having such a garden. There were hundreds like her—indeed a golden age of gardening.[17]

Tuxedo Park

Just a few miles away from Mrs. Ely's garden was Tuxedo Park, the first and most influential restricted residential development, and the birth-

*Mrs. Gustavus Kirby's concrete shell fountain and blue pool are nestled
among the irises in Westchester County.*

*A garden like Mrs. Alfred Maclay's in Millbrook would have featured willowy Edwardian beauties recommended by Mrs. Ely—*Macleaya cordata, *six to eight feet tall with eighteen-inch ivory feathers and big blue-green leaves; six-foot-tall stems of* Campanula pyramidalis, *with long-lasting blue or white bells;* Aruncus sylvester, *creamy plumes on four-foot stalks; and* Boltonia asteroides *and* B. latisquama, *sheaves of tiny white or lilac autumn-flowering daisies.*

place of the dinner jacket (1886), or "tuxedo," and the Social Register (1899).[18] Pierre Lorillard IV, heir to a snuff and tobacco empire, was the founder of Tuxedo Park. The Lorillards were not members of New York's famous "Four Hundred," and Pierre IV was determined to create his own exclusive and luxurious club. The first members of the Tuxedo Club, all Lorillard's friends, included William Waldorf Astor, Lloyd S. Bryce, Robert Goelet, John G. Heckscher, C. Oliver Iselin, Grenville Kane, Lawrence Kip, Ogden Mills, Richard Mortimer, Herbert C. Pell, Augustus Schermerhorn, and William R. Travers. They were soon followed by Carharts, Colliers, Delafields, Juilliards, Wanamakers, and the like. No nonmember could own a cottage.

Lorillard owned 600,000 acres in the Ramapo Mountains, some of which he won at poker from his own relatives. In 1885 he set aside some 5,000 acres of land, including a lake, and hired architect Bruce Price who had designed hotels and cottages in Bar Harbor, Maine, Long Beach, New Jersey (a forerunner resort of the 1870s), and Oyster Bay, Long Island. The early Tuxedo Park cottages are big balloon-frame houses around which the shingles wrap and flow in dormers, porches, and verandas. Price soon left the Shingle Style behind for a range of neoclassical styles. He seems to have been able to handle any situation, architectural or social. He certainly knew how to handle Pierre Lorillard, of whom Price said, "He talked rapidly and thought twice as fast as he talked and wished his orders carried out at a speed that equaled the sum of both."[19] Together and at top speed they directed their imported work force of 1,800 Italian laborers throughout the long cold winter of 1885. Boston landscape architect Ernest Bowditch designed the grounds in a picturesque style well suited to the rough, wooded terrain. Eight months and $1.5 million later, they had a Romantic English village, complete with a pair of rustic boulder gatehouses which Price described as being like "the frontispiece of an English novel." Twenty-two cottages and the clubhouse were complete and all amenities were in, including a model sewer system, a 100-foot swimming pool, and an 8-foot barbed wire fence around the whole property. For many Tuxedoites the fence needed no explanation either to themselves or anyone else—after all, it merely stated in a balder way what every other society enclave implied: this place is only for us.

There were opportunities for every kind of sport. The lake was stocked with bass, the woods with pheasant, quail, and wild turkey, and by 1889 there was a six-hole golf course, one of the earliest in the country. There was also a race track, which was used mostly for horse and dog shows. Besides golf, court tennis, racquets, and bridge were sports pioneered at Tuxedo. The official seasons were spring and fall, but Tuxedoites loved winter too—they tobogganed on their mile-long electrically lit slide, curled on the black ice of the lake, and skated by lantern light. However romantic, life at Tuxedo was not exactly informal: Emily Post, Bruce

Price's daughter, recalled that only five men called her by her first name—and then only in private.

On Memorial Day in 1886 the grand opening was held and three special trains carried seven hundred of New York's elite to the Tuxedo Park station, where they were met by carriages painted green and gold, the Tuxedo Park colors. As they were driven around, green and gold were everywhere—even the drives were lined with gamekeepers in Tyrolean livery of green and gold. They stood out against the rustic cottages, whose shingles had been stained rust or gray. To create just the right atmosphere of age, the buildings had all been antiqued with fresh moss and lichens. But Tuxedo Park did not keep its rustic architectural airs for long. The 1890s were the heyday of transatlantic travel and Americans abroad, seeing the refinements of centuries of European aristocratic life, wanted to bring them home. In Tuxedo Park they built Tudor houses, and Spanish Mission, Georgian, Jacobean, Gothic Revival, Queen Anne, and Dutch Colonial Revival houses, all within a fifteen-year span, and getting bigger year by year. Garden staff could run to seventy people, and one household had ten greenhouses.

In 1899, Henry W. Poor commissioned New York architect T. Henry Randall to design the first really monumental house, "Woodland," situating it on top of Tower Hill, the highest point in Tuxedo. The garden was "Jacobean" too, and Stanford White, who was a close friend of Poor's, had a hand in designing it. Stone-traceried doorways gave onto balustraded terraces overlooking formal beds of roses and bedding-out plants. Two old stone fountains played, and the balustrades were ornamented with a variety of urns, both with yuccas and without.

Tuxedo Park gardens were as varied as the architecture. There were many excellent woodland gardens where lady's-slipper orchids of all kinds and rare ferns flourished along with the native laurel, *Kalmia latifolia* and pinxter-bloom, *Rhododendron nudiflorum*. There were also other formal designs besides the Poors', many of them terraced to fit the hills, just as they were in Italy.

Two Classical Gardens in Millbrook

Farther upstate, beyond any possibility of daily commuting, lay Millbrook and two extraordinary gardens. In the twenties and thirties Millbrook became a haven for those escaping increasing suburbanization farther south. The landscape was farmland, mixed and stock, and the views over the big bare hills were sweeping and fine. Fox hunting and other field sports, and coaching were the biggest entertainments. Wind was the greatest danger to gardens, and all good gardeners in Millbrook promptly planted windbreaks if they were in exposed positions.

"Thornedale," Millbrook home of the Thornes since the eighteenth century and still their home today, is situated south of a range of hills. These hills, and the big trees, some of which are as old as the house, have

Mr. and Mrs. Harry Harkness Flagler made a specialty of laurel and other spring-flowering shrubs at "Edgewood," in Millbrook, in the twenties. Landscape architect Marian Coffin made a walled shrub garden for them where rhododendron bloomed by the dark wooden entrance gate.

"Villa Blanca," Residence of Mr. Amory S. Carhart   Tuxedo Park, N. Y.

Oct. 15-25.

Postcards of New York's exclusive Tuxedo Park gardens had special allure since the club was firmly closed to all but its members. The Amory Carharts' formal garden stretched from the house (1907–1908), seen here, to a separate ballroom building.

provided ample protection for the gardens that surround the residence. The big white clapboard, vaguely Federal, house (built 1849) with its huge columned portico has endured all kinds of remodelings. Like "Glen Magna" in Massachusetts, it is an imaginative rendering of what the turn-of-the-century thought an old American country seat must have looked like. The gardens are the creation of one woman, Mrs. Oakleigh B. Thorne, grandmother of the present owner. He tells the story that in 1908, after one of the periodic panics that afflicted the American economy before any regulations were imposed, Mrs. Thorne was close to a nervous breakdown. The doctor told her, "Either go garden or go to a hospital." Mrs. Thorne promptly learned to use a compass and level, began to lay out her magnificent gardens, and stayed sane.[20] She did have professional help. Helen Page Wodell, of the little-known garden design firm of Wodell and Cottrell, advised her on the main allée; Jerome Allen, a local architect, designed a two-story water pavilion that was its terminus; Nellie B. Allen, his wife, laid out the topiary patterns in the yew garden, which was filled with white flowers all summer; and Marian Coffin helped design the stream garden.[21] But the basic plan and the plantings were essentially Mrs. Thorne's.

She was fortunate in having a volume of water; almost every garden uses its sight and sound. East of the house a terrace overlooks a large formal canal which was connected to a lower informal pond by a stream. Since Mrs. Thorne did everything on a grand scale—when she wanted to plant the stream with forget-me-nots, she scattered two pounds of seed on the waters . . . or about a million forget-me-nots. Another of Helen Thorne's strengths was her unusual choice of plants: the main route to the lower garden was a stroke of genius: a clipped allée of native sugar maples (since vanished) instead of lindens or other more traditional choices. When the leaves turned and fell, they were left on the ground to form pools of only-in-America red and yellow.

The English theme is sounded at "Wethersfield" in the Wilderness Plantings with a typical eighteenth-century device, an "eye-catcher," here a Palladian triple arch, that looks over Amenia's farm country. Chauncy Stillman began the garden in 1937.

OPPOSITE, ABOVE:
"What a view! Noble mountains thickly wooded—and Evergreens predominate—rise many hundred feet above the placid lake. Mansions, red brick, tan brick, sandstone, granite, dark wood, white clapboard, stud the surrounding land." Architect Stanford White reportedly laid out this garden for his friend Henry Poor in Tuxedo Park, a perfect viewing platform for the panorama described by the Gardener's Chronicle *reporter.*

OPPOSITE, BELOW:
One of the best garden features at "Thornedale," Millbrook home of the Thornes, is the formal pool with its "water landing," which is large and architectural enough to balance the huge white house facade behind.

RIGHT, BELOW:
Fletcher Steele's grand swimming pool for the Samuel Sloans at "Lisburne Grange," was borrowed from the Dragon Fountain at the Villa d'Este—but with a few additions, such as the iron rings "for the comfort of bathers."

One of the last gardens in this book to be created, "Wethersfield" is a masterful excursion into the preceding centuries of formal garden design. Ten acres of gardens are divided into three parts: the Inner and Outer gardens, and the Wilderness Plantings. When "Wethersfield's" owner, Chauncy Stillman, first bought the worn-out dairy farm on a hill some 1,100 feet above sea level, there was only a patchwork of eroded cow pastures.

The house, a brick and brownstone Georgian affair, was designed by architect Bancel LaFarge in 1939. Landscape architect J. Bryan Lynch completed the sheltered Inner Garden at the same time. A shallow rill with planting pockets to each side is set in a paved terrace, a reminder of such Lutyens/Jekyll gardens as The Deanery and Hestercombe, with their strong architecture and wonderfully patterned stone that set off the plantings. Terra-rosa pots overflowing with hydrangeas separate the

Cutting gardens, where flowers are grown for the house, were often beautiful, but seldom as decorative as that of George Eastman's in Rochester, seen in this pastel rendering (1921) by American artist John C. Wenrich.

Inner Garden terrace from the lawn beyond where the long east-west vista that forms the backbone of garden begins.

The important Outer Garden, whose creation was delayed by World War II, begins on the lawn where an oval pool marks the design's center. Landscape architect Evelyn N. Poehler, who had trained at the Lowthorpe School of Landscape Architecture in the 1920s, worked closely with the owner from 1947 through the mid-sixties. All different kinds of evergreens—arborvitae, yews standard and dwarf, hollies, rhododendrons—make a variety of textured walls. Color is provided by viburnums, lilacs, and dogwoods, and variegated foliage and potted plants are used throughout: gardenias gleam against dark beech leaves. The urns in the Inner Garden are designs of Stanford White's; a naiad fountain is the work of Carl Milles; a multitude of mythological figures by the Pittsburgh sculptor Josef Stachura are copies of seventeenth-century originals.

Much is made of the hill to the north. A path ascends 190 feet between 23-foot-high walls of arborvitae to a swooping view over the oval pool and miles of farmland beyond the garden. At the far end of the main vista, a left turn up a last climb crowns the garden. A small classical temple designed by W. Dean Brown stands against the sky at the top of a flight of fieldstone steps. Pairs of obelisks, urns, and cherubs mark the landings on the way up. Rough against smooth, light against dark, the play of foliage against stone: here the carefully created balance of a classical garden reaches great heights of intensity. Like "Avalon," the Brewster garden, "Wethersfield," finished in 1962, is no mere classical grid applied indiscriminately to the landscape. It takes every advantage of the rolling terrain, and the spectacularly airy views that terminate the vistas give the garden its distinctive baroque character.[22]

THE FINGER LAKES AND THE GREAT LAKES

A move to the Finger Lakes and the Great Lakes regions is a change of more than geography or climate. In these places high society was local, only peripherally part of the Boston/New York/Philadelphia seasonal resort round. Though they had summer places on the coast of Maine, shooting plantations in Georgia, and spent the winter in Palm Beach, real life was lived "at home" in Rochester and Buffalo, not on the East Coast. Garden fashions came and went a little slower there.

The Genesee River runs north to Lake Ontario through Rochester. The soil of the river valley is deep loam, the air is moist, and the temperature equalized by the adjacent lake. The summer climate both here and in Buffalo, on Lake Erie, is more like Maine than Lenox or New Hampshire. After the Revolution, pioneers came from Connecticut and up the river from Maryland. The mixture of New England moral fervor and Southern ebullience produced such phenomena as the Golden Books of Mormon, the Fox Sisters and Spiritualism, Susan B. Anthony and Women's Rights, and George Eastman, the "Kodak King."

In 1899, New York businessman Spencer Trask designed a rose garden for his wife, Katrina, at "Yaddo" in Saratoga Springs. The sundial overlooks four rose beds filled only with mass plantings of white 'Frau Karl Druschki' and pink and red 'Radiance'. A huge pine marks "Poet's Corner." True nineteenth-century idealists and philanthropists, the Trasks envisioned an artists' community as early as 1900. "Yaddo" officially opened in 1922.

In the 1870s and 1880s Eastman experimented doggedly with photography, and by the early 1890s he had come up with the first transparent and flexible film. Worth $1 million in 1890, by 1898, despite the panic of 1893, he was worth $8 million. A ruthless and energetic businessman, time transformed him into a great philanthropist. At first he was shy about it—MIT, beginning in 1912, kept receiving millions from an anonymous "Mr. Smith." Speculation over the gifts eventually

tired Eastman, and he permitted MIT to make his name public: from then on he gave openly both to Boston institutions and to his home town, Rochester. By 1924 he had given away half of his entire personal fortune. He had started the schools of music, medicine, and dentistry in Rochester, and founded almost all the local philanthropic institutions. He had the feeling there was not much left to do. Rather in the spirit that he had lived, he left a note, "My work is done. Why wait?" and took his own life at the age of seventy-eight. At his death his philanthropic total stood at $75 million in gifts.

His estate in Rochester, a city famous for its horticulture, demonstrates how architectural and garden design ideas were widely disseminated in print. Rochesterian Claude Bragdon, the architect who laid out the West Garden, had a large collection of design books and periodicals from which clients could pick their styles in that age of eclecticism. Bragdon wrote to his wife, Eugenie, in 1916, "George was in this morn-

*Like most large and elaborate American (and English) gardens of the day,
"Sonnenberg Gardens" in Canandaigua had a Japanese garden. Here a
party of visitors enjoys an August afternoon in 1908.*

ing. He's found something he liked in Lutyens book [Lawrence Weaver's] and we had quite a visit.... I'm going out to his house tomorrow morning." What "George" liked about Sir Edwin Lutyens's work seems to have been his arched facade on the orangery at Hestercombe,[23] and the detail of inset grass squares in the corners of the beds where the paths cross the rectangle of the garden. Lutyens's designs were published in Lawrence Weaver's fine monograph in 1913, and by 1916 they had been implemented in Upstate New York.[24] Eastman's 8-acre estate, whose general plan was laid out by landscape architect Alling de Forest, was an urban mini-farm with room for extensive greenhouses, vegetables, chickens, and a cow. All over the United States, during the first two decades of the century, there were compact semi-urban gardens of great charm and even grandeur.

"Sonnenberg Gardens"

Twenty-five miles south of Rochester are the "Sonnenberg Gardens" (sunny hill in German), 50 acres of Victorian-to-Beaux-Arts gardens made by a sixty-seven-year-old widow, Mary Clark Thompson, as a living memorial to her husband.[25] Even that widow of all widows, Queen Victoria, would have been impressed. One hundred eighty workmen made the gardens and ninety gardeners maintained them; such figures tell a lot about "Sonnenberg," and about the scope of Mary Clark Thompson's energy, means, ambition, and garden obsession. The daughter of a New York State governor in the 1850s, Mary Thompson was Canandaigua-born. She and her husband, Frederick Ferris Thompson, bought 200 acres in her hometown to make a summer place in 1863. (They did have another one on L'Isle au Haut, Maine, as well as a place in New York City, but Canandaigua was home.) Their second house on the site, completed in 1887, included a garden and greenhouses, but Mrs. Thompson's memorial gardens were begun in 1900.

She asked Ernest W. Bowditch, whom she knew from summers at L'Isle au Haut, to make a design and send her his three best men. Among the three was John Handrahan, who had worked at Tuxedo Park. Handrahan soon became her landscape architect-in-residence for twenty years and helped her translate all her garden ideas, for they seem mostly to have been hers, into reality.

There are both formal and informal gardens, which are open to the public today. A picturesque lawn studded with specimen trees (many planted by important visiting friends, such as Thomas Edison) sweeps up to the house from the entrance to the south. Most of the gardens lie to the west and north. First constructed was the Italian Garden of four sunken parterres embroidered in a fleur-de-lis pattern with bedding-out plants. An effective colored-foliage planting scheme used there today combines pale pink coleus with purple basil. Seventy-two conical yews outline the scheme, and the garden requires two summer plantings each

of 25,000 annuals. To the north stand an Italianate belvedere and pergola, raised a few steps in order to provide the classic overview such complex floral embroidery needs to be appreciated properly. In 1870 such beds might have stood alone on a lawn, but by 1900, no longer—they were part of an architectural complex.

On the other side of the belvedere is a huge five-lobed formal pink, white, and red rose garden of some five thousand plants. The other large formal garden is the Colonial Garden, where a central arbor is flanked by box-bordered beds of old-fashioned annuals and perennials arranged in quincunx patterns.[26] Four smaller gardens were laid out nearby: a tiny 40-by-60-foot blue-and-white garden, a pansy garden, the Sub Rosa garden (a secret garden, hence its name), and the Moonlight Garden, which had only white flowers, most of them with strong dreamy scents such as tuberoses, verbenas, and nicotiana.[27] Two big informal gardens are the rock garden and the Japanese garden. The rock garden is 3.5 acres of pudding stone (a conglomerate rock good for growing alpines that was imported from England as ballast) and a bog.[28] For the Japanese garden, Mrs. Thompson brought over Japanese garden master, K. Wadamori, and seven workmen who constructed the garden and a replica of a revered Kyoto teahouse. A deer park, aviaries, a swimming pool built like a Roman bath, and hothouses completed the tally. No wonder 7,000 people a day came when the gardens were first opened to the public.

Grandma Kellogg

In Derby, a few miles west of Buffalo on Lake Erie, was a constellation of summer houses and gardens that belonged to the high and mighty of the city. Though little known, the gardens were remarkable for their beauty and restraint. Perhaps the best was the Spencer Kellogg garden, "Lochevan." Landscape architect Ellen Shipman was asked by Mrs. Kellogg to visit and give advice when she visited Derby in the early thirties. The garden was well established by then and she told Mrs. Kellogg, "Don't touch your garden—it's the finest formal English garden I've seen in America."

A yew-hedged rectangle approximately 400 by 200 feet, the garden lay behind the house sheltered from the winds off the lake. A central axis divided the space and a circular teahouse stood at one end, facing a statue of David at the other. David was backed by a screen of arborvitae clipped to resemble Italian cypresses. A flower garden took up about a quarter of the space, and was separated from the rest by 10-foot-tall hedges. Deep perennial beds were filled with memorable color combinations that shifted annually, given Grandma Kellogg's mood, recalls a granddaughter-in-law. The other three-quarters of the garden comprised an arrangement of clipped single yews that lined the walk backed by taller specimen trees that gave depth and focus to the vista.

Grandma Kellogg did nothing by halves, whatever her mood. She quite royally sent the architect for the Kellogg town house abroad for a study tour. She knew her own mind: when she made the Derby garden in 1904, she imported many statues from Europe, but used only a few. Though she was a good plantswoman, she was not a plant collector who insisted on one of everything. Every morning she took a tour with her German head gardener, ordering this to be put in and that to be taken out. Her pruning in every field of activity could be absolutely Draconian. She commissioned William Merritt Chase to paint Grandpa Kellogg's portrait, but didn't like the way he was portrayed—too frivolous, says the family source. So she took some scissors and cut out the face! Woe to the offender of Grandma Kellogg![29]

The best Gilded Age garden stories may be those of such grandes dames, those formidable creatures who were, as Stephen Birmingham says, "stronger than all the hosts of Error and no more scrupulous than the average ward boss." With brio and exuberance, with a new confidence born of prosperity and foreign travel—and with the newly amassed arsenal of Beaux-Arts landscape architecture at hand—they set about making American Versailles and Trianons, Alhambras and Villa d'Estes. They also made just plain elegant gardens like Grandma Kellogg's. Unhampered by the past, they were free to reinvent it for themselves.

NEW YORK CITY

The rooftop garden of Mrs. Cecil Baker on East 51st Street, c. 1930s.

The city house with its own garden quickly became a rarity since country place owners used their New York houses only in the winter, or for brief stopovers. "Two generations ago social and family life centered around the city house, where more than two-thirds of the year was passed in residence," writes *Town & Country* editor Augusta Patterson in 1924.

". . . Among the many things which are charged against the automobile, it is undeniable that it has made the country house and the country life possible. Nowadays the city residence is really a place of convenience, sometimes no more than an overnight stopping place in the passage from one country spot to another."[30]

ABOVE:

Late afternoon shadows stroke the expansive lawn at the Alexander Effingham estate, on Staten Island, in 1891, photographed by Alice Austen.

This garden flourished in 1873 at the corner of Central Park West and 92nd Street, opposite Central Park. Behind these Victorian beds lie fruit trees and vegetables, including corn—a real country garden.

Turtle Bay Gardens, the square of houses enclosing a communal garden in the East Forties between Second and Third avenues in Manhattan, is one of architect William Bottomley's most graceful urban works, having the charm of an Italianate rill and a loggia in increasingly vertical New York.

LONG ISLAND

A soft climate and hard cash made the gardens of Long Island opulent as well as beautiful. Grand English- and French-style country seats predominated on the North Shore, in an enclave running from Sands Point to St. James, bounded on the north by the Sound and on the south by the Jericho Turnpike, with much spillover toward Old Westbury. Ideally, a North Shore estate was situated on one of the little peninsulas in Oyster Bay or Cold Spring Harbor known as "necks." Framed by the huge old trees that grew so abundantly in the region was a glimpse of the Sound on one side of the house and on the other a rolling country view carefully tailored from parcels of old farmland. Long Island has a fabulous garden climate and good soil because the entire island is one great long glacial dump. Four different glaciers left deep deposits of finely pulverized soil and rock as they melted. Rimmed by Long Island Sound and the Atlantic, Long Island has the English equilibrium that lets perennials and tender shrubs thrive.

Nurseries and seedsmen had existed on Long Island since the eighteenth century (Prince, in Flushing, was the earliest in 1737); by the early twentieth century the battery of landscape architects based in the Northeast found many at hand. Most East Coast architects and landscape architects, who practiced during the fifty-year period discussed, created at least one estate on Long Island. What they did was soon copied elsewhere, thanks to illustrated magazines that featured the lives of the rich and fashionable.

Long Island's estate development was powered by New York City, the same economic engine which drove the Hudson River Valley, Westchester County, New Jersey, and Connecticut. Long Island's estate heyday seems later, caught by a literary imagination that made it glow in the light of the twenties. Where the prevailing Hudson River Valley image might be Edith Wharton's *The House of Mirth*, with its bustled dresses and carriages of the gay nineties, Long Island's is F. Scott Fitzgerald's *The Great Gatsby*, where East and West Egg are modeled after Great Neck and Sands Point. Time is compressed to a single night—Gatsby's summer-long party where, "In his blue gardens men and girls came and went like moths among the whisperings and the champagne and the stars."[1]

THE NORTH SHORE

However, the pattern of development and the progression of architectural style was the same as in New York's other estate enclaves. First came Mansard- and Queen-Anne-Revival-style houses in the 1870s. In the late 80s and early 90s the Shingle Style dominated domestic architecture and it was then that the North Shore became Long Island's Gold Coast. (Other Gold Coasts were Boston's North Shore and the shoreline of

From this East Hampton garden the F. B. Wiborgs' daughter, Sara, went off to marry Gerald Murphy. The Murphys were F. Scott Fitzgerald's models for the Divers in Tender is the Night.

Garden statues, overflowing planters, and a froth of pastel flowers made Mrs. Walter Belknap Jameses' North Shore garden a pleasant place to be in spring, early summer, and fall—when she wasn't in her Newport rose garden.

Pink roses climb over verdigris treillage in the French gardens designed by landscape architect Annette Hoyt Flanders in 1927 for Helena Woolworth McCann, daughter of the five-and-dime king.

One of the last of the Newport-style palaces on Long Island was F. W. Woolworth's "Winfield Hall" (1916–1917). The photograph comes from the files of nurserymen Lewis & Valentine, who did much of the landscape contracting on the North Shore.

Chicago's Lake Michigan.) Just as in Tuxedo Park, the Shingle Style gave way on the North Shore at the turn of the century to ever-larger palaces in a variety of period and eclectic styles. There were a few Spanish haciendas like William K. Vanderbilt, Jr.'s, "Eagle's Nest," in Centerport, and Italian villas like the Guggenheims' "Trillora Court" and Gertrude Vanderbilt Whitney's exquisite studio at Roslyn. There were Georgian houses like Adele Sloane Burden's "Woodside Acres" in Syosset, Marshall Field III's "Caumsett" in Huntington, and the justly famed John S. Phipps estate, "Old Westbury Gardens," too well known to discuss here. Most astonishing of the bouldery English Tudor concoctions was "Castlegould" at Sands Point, built in 1909 for Jay Gould's son Howard and his actress/circus performer bride, Katharine Clemmons. Beaux-Arts Petit Trianons abounded, such as the Henri Bendel/Walter Chrysler house at Kings Point and F. W. Woolworth's "Winfield Hall" in Glen Cove, built for an estimated $9 million. The beginning decade of the

century had seen the first French Renaissance châteaux: houses like Clarence Mackay's "Harbour Hill," where Jacques Gréber laid out the formal gardens. O.H.P. Belmont's "Beacon Towers," writes Augusta Patterson in 1924 in her lavish picture book *American Homes of Today*, "is one of the most successful of the consciously picturesque French château types."[2] "Beacon Towers" had a painstakingly period array of towers and turrets; its builder, the flamboyant Alva Vanderbilt Belmont, toured "Blair Atholl," the ancient fortress of the Dukes of Atholl and said, "My dear, my castle at Sands Point is far more authentic."[3] The gardens of these houses extended the axial lines of the house across the landscape, and had vistas, compartments of hedges or walls, terraces, pools, fountains, and sculpture.

That nine hundred estates were built on Long Island between 1865 and 1940 doesn't sound very impressive until one takes a look at their size and ambition. They could almost be described as principalities. Their builders were laying foundations for dynasties, and their gardens and houses were statements about power and culture, just like Versailles or the Villa d'Este or Hampton Court. In contemporary American picture books the palace gardens of Europe are shown side by side with homegrown versions of the same thing. Self-sufficiency, as well as display, was what American millionaires wanted. Often everything was provided but a post office and a militia. Some estates, like Marshall Field III's "Caumsett," were laid out on town scale. The eighteenth-century fashion for model farms fascinated these people; they raised thoroughbred horses, many kinds of prizewinning cattle and other farm animals, and a dizzying variety of fruits and vegetables. Many places had their own flags, power plants, dairies—and a few even had their own veterinarians if not their own doctors.

A look at four estates gives some idea of their size and cost. Each place had a scheme with formal and informal elements, kitchen and cutting gardens, a park and woods, and impressive approaches, drives, and courts.

Where the money for these places came from is a typical sampling of Gilded Age money-making. "Planting Fields" was built on metals with a dash of old-time whale oil. "Oheka" was based on railroads and finance. "Harbour Hill's" foundations were the gigantic silver Comstock Lode and the cable communications business. Marshall Field III's money for "Caumsett" originally came from his grandfather's Chicago store, but he kept right on making it himself in the publishing business. The founder of the Pratt family fortune, Charles Pratt, began as a Brooklyn crude oil refiner. In 1887 his company merged with Rockefeller's Standard Oil, where he became a major executive.

"Planting Fields"

In 1913, when the William Robertson Coes bought about 300 acres in Oyster Bay and a half-timbered house designed by Grosvenor Atterbury (1905), the place still bore the name given it by the Matinecock Indians: "Planting Fields." In 1883 at the age of thirteen, Coe had emigrated to America. Like many another immigrant, Coe loved being American and made good use of his enthusiasm: he helped found the American studies programs both at Yale University and at the University of Wyoming. "Planting Fields," now a great public arboretum, is perhaps Coe's greatest gift to his adopted country. Coe's wife was heiress Mary Rogers, daughter of Henry Huddleston Rogers, an oil and copper millionaire

RIGHT:
From the W. R. Coes' Tudor House at "Planting Fields" in Oyster Bay (1919), the eye travels across a sunken pool and lustrous shrub plantings typical of the Olmsted Bros.'s estate work. The distant cottage has a "thatched roof" of tile.

The appropriate costume for a garden stroller at "Planting Fields" included a parasol. The roses are ramblers, and the photograph is by Mattie Edwards Hewitt, most lyrical of the garden photographers of her day.

descended from a New Bedford whaler like those Melville describes in *Moby Dick*. The "brave houses and flowering gardens" of New Bedford, and its sister port Fairhaven, both at the mouth of the Acushnet River, link the Coes and "Planting Fields" to the Boston garden oligarchy through family, friends, and mutual interests. H. H. Rogers was interested in horticulture and spent some of his fortune landscaping his hometown of Fairhaven. His friends and neighbors included James Arnold, whose bequest founded the Arnold Arboretum, and New Bedford plantsman Andrew Robeson, Charles Sprague Sargent's father-in-law. When in 1914 the Coes set about creating a 132-acre landscape and gardens, they chose the Boston firm of Guy Lowell. Charles Sargent's daughter was married to Lowell, and his eldest son, Andrew Robeson Sargent, was Lowell's partner. Andrew Robeson Sargent was in charge of the design of "Planting Fields" until his untimely death in 1918; the Coes then engaged Olmsted Bros. who assigned one of their associates, James Dawson, son of the superintendent of the Arnold Arboretum, as job foreman. The landscape of "Planting Fields" illustrates what can be done with landscape design principles refined by three-quarters of a century of practice, as were those of the Olmsteds, father, sons, and partners, and with horticultural expertise passionately pursued for fifty years, as it was by Sargent and the men trained at the Arboretum.

Greenhouses and a range of farm buildings designed by Walker and Gillette were complete by 1915. New technologies and ideas were used: a steam tractor moved trees, electrical and telephone lines were buried, and old fields were reforested (still quite a new idea in 1915) with thousands of red cedar and white pine from the State Conservation Commission. William Coe himself took the same lively interest in shaping this new landscape that he took in all his projects. Andrew Sargent got Coe interested in hybrid camellias—a huge collection was ordered from the prestigious English firm John Waterer Sons and Crisp. This first lot was sunk by a German submarine, but another was promptly sent out and formed the nucleus of the finest collection in the northern United States. When Coe's camellias arrived, he had no idea that they needed a greenhouse, and he hurried to have one built at once. Beech and linden drives were laid out and the formal Italian sunken garden, which the Coes called the Blue Pool. The formal gardens lie to the south and a long vista pierces deep into the woods underplanted with rhododendrons and azaleas and floored with ivy. "Formal" is a difficult word to use about "Planting Fields"; the design, which on paper looks tightly organized, in fact provides an invisible skeleton for artfully natural plantings.

North of the house lies the best-known part of the garden, the huge lawn and groves of specimen trees that form one of the most perfect American evocations of an English park landscape—perhaps a tribute to Coe's English childhood. On the lawn stands a gigantic copper beech, the remaining one of a pair that sheltered Mary Coe's childhood Fairhaven home. In one of the gargantuan tree-moving operations that no longer take place, because power and telephone companies are unwilling to take lines down to allow passage of a sixty-foot tree, the pair were moved across the Sound. It took twelve days to inch the trees through the town of Oyster Bay. The only bigger trees to be moved on Long Island were a pair of little-leaf lindens that traveled from the South Shore to the North Shore via Brooklyn and The Narrows. They got stuck on a mud bank for a week, but ended up safely enough at Marshall Field's "Caumsett."

By 1917 the major landscape work was complete, and the Coes were busy buying garden seats and statuary. Old privet had been replaced with tubbed bay trees from the Arnold Arboretum. (In period descriptions, plants from the Arnold Arboretum are often noted; it is astonishing how many grand places wore Sargent's lilacs, hawthornes, and bays like horticultural rosettes of the Légion d'Honneur.) The old garden house had been transformed into a teahouse, with paintings by Ash Can School painter Everett Shinn on every surface—chairs, light fixtures, walls, and ceilings.

Mary Coe loved tropical plants and birds—she even kept parrots in her bathroom at "Planting Fields." She commissioned fashionable mural painter Robert Chanler to make a tropical landscape of the new sunporch off her bedroom, complete with leaded glass windows of parrots and plants. Instead, Chanler's acetylene torch set the house afire, and the Coes were left with a finished landscape and the shell of a house. War was raging and materials and workmen hard to find, but Coe, with typical ingenuity, located a load of Indiana limestone left over from the building of St. Bartholomew's Church in Manhattan, and within months they were building again. In 1920 they moved in. When the gardens and house were complete, the local vicar came to call, and was given an extensive tour of the grounds. Afterward he turned to Coe and said, "It is a fine piece of work that you and the Lord have wrought here." Mr. Coe rather defiantly replied, "Yes, but you should have seen it when the Lord had it to himself."[4]

"Oheka"

Banking financier and railroad baron Otto H. Kahn had big eyes whose corners turned up slightly, as if he were enjoying some private joke. He also had the second biggest house in America, "Oheka" (George Vanderbilt's "Biltmore" in North Carolina remained the largest), set on what was disputedly the highest point on Long Island, in Woodbury. (Clarence Mackay claimed *his* house, "Harbour Hill," was higher, and is said to have put up a flagpole to mark the spot.) Using tons of fill and hundreds of workmen, Kahn had spent two years building his hill which was used by Orson Welles as a model for Citizen Kane's "private mountain."

"Oheka" had a garden where full-scale Metropolitan Opera productions took place in a Greek amphitheater. But the year Kahn moved into

Otto Kahn often strolled in the gardens of "Oheka" with the likes of tenor Enrico Caruso and conductor Arturo Toscanini. Landscape gardener Beatrix Farrand worked on "Oheka" from 1919 to 1928.

his palace (1919) he also published a five-point plan for improving relations between labor and business—a plan advocating public works, public housing, and public welfare. "Some people," he correctly surmised, "may regard certain of my suggestions as closely approaching socialism." Kahn, a partner in the investment firm Kuhn, Loeb, himself gave away millions to the arts, to charity, and to the war effort for the World War I.

Besides being a one-man "United Way," he was also a perfectionist: the correspondence about "Oheka's" garden between Kahn and Olmsted Bros. was an almost daily one during the years of its construction. Because of his energy, intelligence, sense of humor, and phenomenal money-making talents, he also was able to negotiate with imperturbable brio—but with eyes wide open—the social and psychological perils of being a rich Jew in rich America. It is Kahn, quietly observing American society from his Palm Beach house, whom Cleveland Amory quotes as giving the definition of "kike" as "a Jewish gentleman who has just left the room."[5]

The English writer Beverley Nichols, who traveled by rail with Kahn to California, had this to say:

Kahn was my ideal millionaire. He used his millions with taste, kindliness and understanding.... He was a patron of the arts in a sense that has been little understood since the days of the Renaissance. He was one of the few supporters of the Metropolitan who was more interested in music than tiaras. He had a poetic vision about Hollywood, which he pathetically persisted in treating as though it were worthy of his intelligence.... He was, in short, a very considerable dear.[6]

Kahn was about fifty when he embarked on "Oheka." He commissioned William Adams Delano of Delano and Aldrich to build a stucco and limestone French manor house inspired by the Château d'Effiat and ornamented with turrets. Similar little freestanding turrets, or *tourelles*, were a feature of the garden providing vertical accents and a horizontal scheme. Olmsted Bros. made dummies of the courtyard trees to site them before the cobbles were put down. For him they made miles of bridle paths and a golf course, and for her (his wife, Addie,) a 22-acre naturalistic garden with a folly ruin for thoughtful retreat. They laid out a formal French garden south of the house, which was the pièce de résistance. Plantings worth $22,000 were moved from his old house in Morristown, New Jersey (plantings that in their youth had cost $400). The long rectangular parterre had water in the parterre "beds"—geometric

CE JARDIN A ETE CREE DANS
L'AXE LATERAL DU CHATEAU
VERS L'OCCIDENT, OU LA VUE
EST LA PLUS ETENDUE SUR LA
VALLEE DE ROSLYN ET SUR LE
DETROIT DU SOUND.
GRACE A CETTE ORIENTATION FAVORABLE,
CERTAINES PLANTES D'EUROPE, UTILES A LA
DECORATION, Y PEUVENT MIEUX CROITRE QU'EN
TOUTE AUTRE PARTIE DU DOMAINE

This 1923 rendering from the Gazette Illustrée des Amateurs de Jardins *of
Clarence Mackay's "Harbour Hill" shows the French* parterre de broderie
made in 1910, intended to harmonize with the French house.

pieces of sky captured on the ground—instead of grass or flowers.[7]

What did this garden say about Kahn? In all, it was a polished, perfect performance—as urbane, suave, and clever as the man who built it. What gave it heart was Kahn's love for people and his Renaissance zest for life. Throughout the 1920s his guests were as glittering as his garden. Journalists called him the "King of New York," and "Oheka" was a setting for artists, writers, performers, financiers, and politicians who came for the weekends. "He is in touch with the romantic, ribald anarchists of art. Perhaps they make pictures and music no one understands: at least they're alive," wrote *The New Yorker*.[8]

Kahn's garden wasn't a quiet refuge, an idea made popular by the Romantic movement. His garden reflected an earlier idea, a Renaissance

idea often seen in period prints that show gardens bustling with people, and packed tight with all the pleasures, sensations, and surprises the world has to offer. Kahn said at sixty, "I feel as young as when I was twenty-five, and I hope I am not much wiser."[9]

"Harbour Hill"

Until Otto Kahn made his bid, Clarence Mackay's "Harbour Hill" overlooking Hempstead Harbor, *was* the highest point on Long Island. Clarence Mackay's father, John, a Dublin shipyard worker, was one of James Graham Fair's three partners in the Comstock Lode in Nevada, the richest known U.S. silver deposit. It yielded Clarence Mackay $200,000 per month for his lifetime, and was the foundation capital for his successful venture, the AT&T Company. Mackay himself was interested enough in gardens and horticulture to have been one of ten honorary members of The Garden Club of America in 1931. When he engaged Stanford White of McKim, Mead and White to design his $6 million French château in 1902, White was in top Beaux-Arts gear and had left the informality of the Shingle Style behind. "Harbour Hill" was a significant work for the firm; it is one of the three Long Island estates included in their monograph of 1915.

When White sited the house, he also laid out the terraces overlooking Mackay's 600 acres. Guy Lowell did the grounds and plantings with the advice of Charles Sprague Sargent. Landscape architect Jacques Gréber, then twenty-six and a freshly minted Gold Medalist of the Ecole, was brought from Europe to spread a *parterre de broderie* on what had been a *tapis vert*. It added the final touch of appropriate decorative richness to the house surroundings, just as the ebulliently carved baroque front entrance relieved the rather severe entrance facade. There were other gardens of course, and the dimensions of the trellis in the rose garden gives a sense of the scale of the garden: it was 15 feet tall and semicircular; the arc it described was 80 feet. Fifty, some say 100, gardeners were needed to do the work. At "Harbour Hill" it is difficult to separate reality from rumor—100 seems just as likely as fifty.

Jacques Gréber's father, Henri, a respected French sculptor, had made the circular "Versailles" fountain which was illuminated at night. In September, 1924, for the long-remembered visit of the Prince of Wales to watch the international polo in Old Westbury, the fountain, it is said, spouted perfumed water. The mile-long drive of sugar maples was hung with thousands of blue lights. A "lobster tree" blossomed in the tent in the garden. Twelve hundred guests ate with a Comstock Lode tableware fashioned by Tiffany. Paul Whiteman and two orchestras played till dawn. The Prince slipped away from the spectacle to have a long, long private drink (1 to 5 A.M.) with friends at a Cold Spring Harbor boathouse.[10]

There were many other entertainments at "Harbour Hill" besides music, dancing, and jumping into the swimming pool fully dressed at dawn. A casino added in 1906 had an indoor pool, a bowling alley, a gym, a theater, Turkish baths, a squash court, and shooting galleries. On the North Shore, there were many such "playhouses," as these sports palaces were called, with Mackay's being one of the earliest. A tennis court, one of the two on Long Island, had its own pro. There were stables for polo ponies, kennels for greyhounds, and a beautiful carriage house and stable designed by Warren and Wetmore which housed horses for riding, hunting, and driving. Warren, who was a Vanderbilt cousin and a graduate of the Ecole des Beaux-Arts, and his partner designed other stable/service complexes including Marshall Field's tennis casino, the stables at the Guggenheim "Trillora Court," and William K. Vanderbilt, Jr.'s "Idle Hour." They also designed Grand Central Station.

On a more purely practical note, Mackay's kingdom also had greenhouses and bay pits, a farm with full-scale dairy and poultry operations, a smithy, an auto repair shop (considered almost a necessity in the adventurous days of "motoring"), and carpentry and plumbing workshops. To get away from it all, deep in the woods was a rustic retreat. A finishing touch was a stuffed moose, half-concealed by trees, which ran back and forth on a small railroad track at the shooting range, to provide target practice for Mackay and his friends.[11]

Marshall Field and George Gillies at "Caumsett"
At "Caumsett," Marshall Field III's estate at Lloyd Neck, instead of a moose there were two donkeys that George Gillies, Field's head gardener, half-seriously insisted were kept to eat the cigarette butts on the lawn. "Caumsett's" 2,300 acres had twenty-five miles of road, and an atmosphere, as architectural writers Liisa and David Sclare have recently put it, of "a remote country village situated in the midst of the vast wilderness."[12] Marshall Field III, grandson of the founder of the Chicago department store, was the publisher of *The Chicago Sun*, World Book Encyclopedia, Simon & Schuster, and Pocket Books. He moved to New York in 1921, and by 1923 had bought the land and engaged John Russell Pope, one of America's best-known Beaux-Arts architects, to design an enormous Georgian house and stables. Pope apprenticed in Bruce Price's New York office. Much of his estate work shares the calmly monumental, handsome quality of his public commissions such as the National Gallery and the Jefferson Memorial, and his big estates required many hands.

According to census records, the number of men employed as seedsmen, nurserymen, and gardeners increased by 275 percent between 1870 and 1930. Working as gardeners on the great estates provided a secure job by the standards of the day, extra benefits, a good life for their families, an active social life, and a community that gave them standing and respect.[13] George Gillies, Marshall Field III's superintendent, came to "Caumsett" in 1923, and remained there until 1965 when he turned over the keys to the New York State Park Commission.

Gillies, who died in 1987, was born in North Devon, England, and grew up at Stevenstone, one of those English places so common ninety years ago, where every farm for six or eight miles around belonged to the owners of "the big house," and the head gardener (in this case Gillies' father) was king. In England, he worked for the Duke of Richmond and Gordon, the Duke of Westminster, and the Astors at Cliveden, where he was Lady Astor's pet. Some pet. Mr. Gillies at ninety was still a handsome 6'2" with a soft answer, a winning smile, a Humphrey Bogart nose, and the kind of silver hair that usually adorns British statesmen. His first American employer was Mrs. Whitelaw Reid, an American grande dame who wanted to create the English garden of her dreams at "Ophir Hall,"

George Gillies, Marshall Field III's superintendent at "Caumsett," is standing third from right, with other members of Long Island's professional gardeners' mafia. Most were English or Scottish; a number had trained at Kew. Friendships were close, but competition was fierce.

Head gardeners entered flower shows out of pride in their skills, as well as on behalf of their employers. No show was more important than the annual New York Flower Show. The great skill was forcing—every flower had to appear at the same time and last for a week, such as the large azaleas and fully grown dogwoods seen in George Gillies's display here.

her new estate in Purchase, New York.[14] In 1923 Marshall Field III, who was staying nearby, came to call. The real purpose of his visit was to meet George Gillies. Field, who had spent his childhood in England, and was educated at Eton and Cambridge, had just bought "Caumsett" and wanted to create a vast English country place at breakneck American speed. Getting it started from scratch at "Caumsett," however, was

another matter. In perplexity, Field revealed his problems to his English butler, Hider. "Mr. Field, I must tell you that you won't get anywhere at all until you have a good gardener," responded Hider.

British staff in America knew all the details of the kind of life their new American employers wanted to lead, and even felt duty-bound to teach them how to live it. (Hider, who had acted as valet as well as butler to Field, took the dollar bills out of his employer's pockets every night and ironed them.) Family connections in England, passionately high standards of performance, and an incredible amount of below-stairs gossip meant that reputations traveled rapidly across the Atlantic and up and down the East Coast. "Well, do you know of anyone, Hider?" said Field. "Well, as a matter of fact . . . ." answered Hider, and so it was arranged that Mr. George H. Gillies met Mr. Marshall Field III.

They took to each other at once. Gillies said of him, "Mr. Field was a typical English country gentleman, the type I was brought up with. We understood each other no matter what language we spoke." As for Field's first wife, Gillies recalls that "the fact that I was tall and not too bad-looking hired me with Mrs. Field. She was autocratic, but I got on with her." Only the second Mrs. Field, the former Audrey Coates, reputed once to have been a girlfriend of the Prince of Wales, seems to have given Gillies any difficulty at all. Not only was she English, but he added a bit darkly, "she was a gardener."

What was the job George Gillies was asked to perform? Was it the same kind of thing he would have done in England? Gillies grew the same plants he would have grown in England after experimenting with cultivation and varieties in order to adapt to the climate. But nothing is impossible for a gifted gardener who is clever, determined, has hot and cold greenhouses, cold frames, lots of labor, and a big budget! (At "Caumsett" Gillies had ten greenhouses.) But the extensive design work that exists only on an estate-in-the-making and that Gillies carried out at "Caumsett" might have been impossible for him in England, since the majority of great estates had been laid out long ago and class restrictions were tighter. What considerations went into making a big place, and how much design thinking had gone unrecorded in plans, drawings, and the notes of the landscape architects and garden designers, emerge in Gillies's story. Olmsted Bros. made the original plans based on Field's wishes. However, according to Gillies, Field's own opinions only emerged after lengthy preliminary consultation with Gillies and others on the place.[15] As Gillies told it, in one of his early conversations with Field, his new employer said, "'Now Gillies I don't want one of those damn places where there's not a piece of gravel out of place.'" Many of Gillies's landscaping ideas show a sensitivity to the environment and a delicacy of touch that is not usually associated with estate gardening. For example, he scalloped the entire margin of a fresh water inlet with candelabra primula—and left it at that. Natural effects are the first things to disappear when a garden decays. The architectural elements of a garden have a better chance, but their existence, unbalanced without the original plantings, makes old gardens seem to have been all stone and concrete. Then there was the kitchen garden, modeled on that of Gillies's childhood at Stevenstone. Gillies described Marshall Field's reaction to his preliminary sketch of the design: "He stared at it for a minute and said, 'Where did you get the idea for this—it's just like the garden I grew up in at Cadbury.'" Its 2 acres contained every kind of fruit and vegetable. A 12-foot-deep herbaceous border for cutting ran around the central vegetable beds, which were edged in roses and centered with dwarf apple trees. Espaliered fruit trees warmed themselves against the brick wall. Most kitchen gardens probably *do* have a strong family resemblance; nonetheless Field and Gillies's harmonious working relationship must have had much to do with the shared memory of that Edwardian paradise, the English country house with its woods and park, its handsome dependencies, and its comfortable self-sufficiency.

Once the task of creation was completed, the awesome daily rounds began. The biggest task of all was a perennial border 130 feet long and 30 feet wide at its widest point. This had to be kept at its shampooed best throughout the entire garden season—an intricate task Gillies supervised, marching the annuals and biennials in and out of the greenhouse when the perennial ranks thinned. Someone from the kitchen garden went up to the chef at the big house every day to get the orders. "Keeping"—the storing of vegetables before big refrigerated lockers and freezers came in—was also Gillies' domain. In a giant root cellar he used to hang cauliflower upside down to keep it perfectly fresh and sound from late summer to the end of winter. He trained the boys who fixed the flowers for the house, making sure that blooms were cut in the late afternoon, once the heat of the day was over, and then left to stand in deep water overnight to "harden off" in the special flower room, a regular feature of most big houses. The choice of flowers and their arrangement were entirely left to Gillies,[16] who also provided vegetables and flowers for Field's New York town house. (When flowers went up to town, they arrived at 9:00 A.M. and were all arranged by 10:30.) Some blossoms needed special care. 'Unique', a spider chrysanthemum, had long petals that could break or bruise. Gillies hit on doing each flower up in a rubber band.[17]

Gillies's expertise, his sense of humor, intelligence, and energy made him many good friends both in his profession and out. Montague Free, director of the Brooklyn Botanic Garden, was one, but best known was Henry F. du Pont. In the garden world du Pont and Gillies met as equals. Gillies' bustling world of professional gardeners has since vanished entirely. Because "Caumsett" was situated at the heart of the Long Island Gold Coast, the estate gardeners' Mafia, mostly English and Scots, was particularly strong there. Some of these men, including Gillies himself, also lectured about gardening, both to professionals like them-

selves and to garden clubs and horticultural societies. Gillies often did the flowers for the garden club ladies' parties. Perhaps the most memorable he devised were for a Miss Sullivan, who held a dinner on the indoor tennis courts of the Piping Rock Club. "She wanted each table to look like a garden," said Gillies, "so we cut sod to fit, and then cut holes in the sod to hold bunches of flowers. Each table was a real miniature landscape, complete right down to a handful of earthworms. . . ."

The Pratts: a Family Chronicle

As wedding presents for his six sons, Charles Pratt of Standard Oil built city houses in Brooklyn, where he founded the Pratt Art Institute in 1887.

At George D. Pratt's "Killenworth" (c. 1914), one of the six Pratt family houses in Glen Cove, the handsomest garden feature is a large tank, which mirrors the late Tudor stone house. The gardens were designed by Greenleaf, whose finest efforts were often expansive evergreen plantings, like those flowing around the tank and the distant statue.

In Glen Cove, they were neighbors too, and shared administration offices, service, and stables in a complex designed by Babb, Cook & Willard around 1904, and known as the "Pratt Oval." The six country estates were all variations on English themes laid out by the same garden designers: Martha Brookes Brown Hutcheson, James Leal Greenleaf, and Charles Platt.

The Harold I. Pratt's "Welwyn," designed by Babb, Cook & Willard in 1906 and later altered by Delano and Aldrich, was the most elaborate and extensive. The north view from the house looked over a sweeping lawn to the South, as did so many North Shore houses. A rose garden lay below where it was more sheltered and did not compete with the view, much as at "Faulkner Farm" and "Moraine Farm" in Massachusetts. The rest of the garden was laid out to the west and south in small separate compartments. Tucking the flower gardens away from the general view created an atmosphere of wide spaces and simple outlines. Charles Pratt had planted a pinetum before 1890, and "Welwyn" today is a nature preserve which features a magnificent stand of white and black pines. The grounds were designed in part by the Olmsted Bros. James Leal Greenleaf planted the background of the largest garden, the oval terraced West Garden, for which Martha Brookes Brown Hutcheson drew the plans. Hutcheson also made a simpler terraced garden featuring spring flowers and shrubs for the Frederic B. Pratt's "Poplar Hill," which was designed by Charles Platt and his sons William and Geoffrey in 1917.[18]

For the Herbert L. Pratts' "The Braes," James Greenleaf worked on a terraced garden more formal than that at "Welwyn." It complemented the rather gaunt U-shaped brick-and-limestone Jacobean house designed in 1912 by James Brite. The three terraces that led down to the Sound were tightly linked by vistas and paired stairways to the house. As at "Welwyn," the garden terrace lay below the grassed view of the Sound. Smaller sunken gardens, little box-edged treasure chests of flowers, flanked the house and were protected by pergolas from northern exposure. Garden designer Isabella E. Pendleton later altered the terraced garden and added an iris garden.[19] All the Pratts were dedicated gardeners themselves: here, the Herbert Pratts designed the rose garden and the greenhouse surroundings. At "Welwyn," Harold Pratt did the surveying for the garden border, and Mrs. Pratt devised the plantings.

At the George D. Pratt's "Killenworth," Greenleaf used hemlock hedges to divide a sunken garden from the formal forecourt of the late Tudor style house. On a level above, perennial borders were laid out in a square. Turf steps led to a small pool overhung by elms. Statues of the four seasons stood in niches around the reflecting pool. All six gardens displayed works by American artists as well known as Paul Manship, Edward McCartan, and Janet Scudder, as well as works by lesser-known sculptors such as Gail Sherman Corbett and A. Philminster Proctor, who specialized in wild animals.

The feeling at the John T. Pratt's "The Manor House" was late Georgian rather than Tudor. Here on the site of a colonial dwelling, Charles Platt designed a huge brick mansion whose long single axis was cleverly broken up by a series of pavilions and porticoes. Platt's stroke of genius at "The Manor House" was not the pleasant, easygoing garden he laid out, but the century-old elms that were transplanted to give scale (and instant age) to the towering entrance elevation with its gigantic pediment.

Three Artists' Gardens

Artists' gardens on Long Island played many roles in their owners' lives: some were works of art, outlets for creativity usually expressed in other media; some were retreats, private sanctuaries for work or thought. One small haven that still exists today as a private home is Gertrude Vanderbilt Whitney's studio complex on the original William C. Whitney place in Old Westbury. The neoclassical studio and garden were a world apart from the rest of the 1,000-acre estate, with its multi-gabled Tudor mansion, huge stables, and emphasis on sport, heavily half-timbered gymnasium, and shingled water tower in the shape of a windmill.

In 1913, when Whitney was nearly forty and her career as a sculptor was established, Delano and Aldrich designed a Palladian-style one-story studio and an adjoining garden in the country for her. As a woman, she was creating on a grand scale the same sort of refuge—a place of her own—that many of her contemporaries found for themselves in gardens. As an artist, she was one of a group of American women sculptors that included Janet Scudder, Anna Hyatt Huntington, Harriet Whitney Frishmuth, and Malvina Hoffman. Many of them got their professional start making small statues for private gardens, and then went on to create sculpture for public spaces.

Whitney's studio garden was the perfect small garden of the period. A central rectangle was sunk about three-and-a-half feet below the studio. Easy stairs descended from the grass studio terrace to the garden itself. Parallel lines of flower beds and shrubs separated by fine turf walks ran the length of the design. At the far end they met in a curve that echoed the semicircular top of the Palladian studio doorway. Wisteria shaded the building's garden elevation and covered the pergola at the bottom of the garden. Down the middle between the borders ran a narrow central rill, bridged by stepping stones at regular intervals, and paved on each side with flagstones half-covered with thyme and mint. A swimming pool was neatly fitted in at the bottom of the stairs—as good a way to place a swimming pool unobtrusively into a flower garden as has yet been devised. The finely proportioned stone cornice was ornamented with a deeply carved garland of flowers.

The lofty studio, the subtle and balanced garden, might even have seemed too perfect for work, or for real life, as if it were a stage set of an

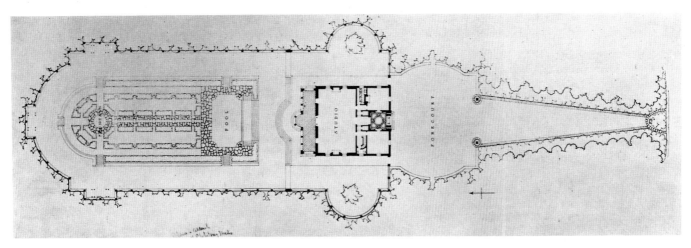

A plan of Mrs. Harry Payne Whitney's studio in Roslyn, Long Island.

artist's studio. But a look at Gertrude Vanderbilt Whitney's long list of commissions, and at the sculptures that remain in place in New York City, Washington, D.C., Spain, and France prove otherwise. Her monumental, realist work had enough merit to win a bronze medal at the Panama-Pacific International Exposition in 1915, and a major piece, *The Spirit of Flight*, appeared in the 1939 World's Fair in New York. The fountain that marks the center of the studio garden is hers, a smaller model of a piece she designed for McGill University in 1910.

Her lively and prodigal patronage of living artists made the garden a setting for memorable parties. White peacocks stalked the walks along with her artist friends and possible clients, and the encircling trees nodded with lights. The pool was inspiring, as one visitor wrote to her: "As soon as I saw the strangely dull pool [it was lined with a mosaic of small dark pebbles] I ran back to the enchanted house and stript and I dove in. Chanler [the muralist] came and waiting for him to undress I danced around your lawn like a faun a fine frenzy. . . ."[20]

A second artist's garden was Louis Comfort Tiffany's in Cold Spring Harbor. Tiffany, the son of Tiffany and Co.'s founder, was the master of Favrile glassblowing. The flower, tree, and vegetable motifs in his stained-glass windows and lampshades were based on living models grown at "Laurelton Hall." He loved wild flowers, and the two approaches to the house ran past fields, streams, and ponds planted to bloom from earliest spring days until frost. With characteristic thoroughness, Tiffany, who was his own architect and landscape architect, made a preliminary clay model of his entire 580 acres and all the buildings and landscape features on it before he began work in 1902. The gardens eventually required thirty-five men to maintain.[21]

On the terraces overlooking the water Tiffany experimented with exotic decorative elements, such as a huge rose quartz set in the middle of a pool, and a bronze Chinese dragon for a fountain head. His source for many of these ornaments was his partner, Lockwood de Forest, Sr., who founded ateliers in India where local craftsmen carved screens and panels according to the partners' designs.[22]

Tiffany also had what he called a "hanging garden," a sort of grotto supported by vine-draped poles, with an airy upper story ornamented with New Zealand cabbage trees and oleanders in beautiful containers. Slowly changing electric lights colored the fountains at night. Unlike the design and decoration, the garden flowers were not exotic—tulips, roses, peonies, iris, and many annuals were there to provide color and lots of it. Only a sophisticated designer like Tiffany could have pulled together "Laurelton Hall's" bizarre and complicated schemes into a successful Art Nouveau garden.

Architect Stanford White's "Box Hill," farther out on the North Shore at St. James, was an artist's house and garden with a very different feeling from the classical unity of the Whitney studio ensemble or Tiffany's flowery oriental fantasies. The often-remodeled and greatly enlarged summer "cottage" and its 78-acre grounds were crammed with evidences of White's inventiveness, his playful spirit, and his aesthetic theories. Born in 1854, White was a descendant of an old New England family, and had grown up in New York with the full stream of American cultural activities playing around him. His father, Richard Grant White, journalist, political activist, editor, musician, and music critic, was a friend of Howells, Lowell, Emerson, Dickens, and Browning, and White's childhood town house was almost a salon. He grew up with sure, exuberant taste, and had a wide circle of friends that included artists like Saint-Gaudens, politicians, millionaires, and playboys like James Breese of New York and Southampton.[23]

The Whites had bought the original dismal little gray Victorian house with its magnificent view of Long Island Sound because it symbolized Bessie Smith White's childhood—she was a Smithtown Smith, and the route to her favorite beach led over the hill of "Box Hill." "Box Hill" was very much a family place. White's flamboyant and well-documented Manhattan night life, which culminated in his murder by Harry K. Thaw in 1906, did not intrude here. The house, still in family hands today, is filled with testimony to their close early married life together, although they grew apart after the death of their first child and the birth of their

second son. Bessie White put on weight, and for a while White sent her a bunch of flowers every day with a note that read "Fat is Fatal."

Like most other women of her time Bessie Smith White acquiesced in White's arrangements. Perhaps even by her own choice, she led her life among her friends and neighboring family as much as with her husband who came to "Box Hill" on weekends, and took her abroad on some of his trips to Europe.

White occasionally made gardens and landscapes, a talent that is

Louis Comfort Tiffany, who used floral motifs in his art, designed a hole in his Long Island loggia roof for a pear tree and decorated the supporting colonnettes with baskets of polychrome ceramic flowers.

often overlooked in the long list of his accomplishments. At "Box Hill" he was the landscape architect making high-spirited use of architectural elements and sculpture. Behind the house and on the highest point of the property stood a cement cast of Saint-Gaudens' *Diana*, whose copper version shone at the top of White's colorful Madison Square Garden at 27th Street. Although White was not a gardener himself, he was a collector, and his horticultural specimens included huge cactus and a night-blooming cereus eighteen feet tall. All the boxwoods, like those in most other new gardens of the period, were bought from old gardens in the South, particularly Maryland and Virginia. The long lines of rhododendrons that edged the drive came from South Carolina, and the orange trees were French. "The whole exterior is embowered with plants—great boxes of hydrangeas, palms, bay trees, oleanders, and many mimic trees from Japan, most of them in their own jars or vases, some of which are rare old works of art," said Barr Ferree.[24] White seems also to have collected *impressions* of landscape. At "Box Hill" the wide view of Smithtown Bay was distantly framed by tall old chestnuts which towered over the smaller trees. White had them trimmed in the umbrella shape of Italian stone pines; they were startlingly effective, suggesting, if only for a moment, that Smithtown Bay might be Lake Como.[25]

The formal garden seemed like one more item in the collection. It was a charming little postage stamp by comparison with the nearby house, and about the same size as the large drawing room whose wide verandas overlooked it. In the central fountain pool a crouching Venus with Ingres-like haunches gazed out with doe eyes. Orange trees and cacti in pots, and a white-columned pergola at the far end provided height variations within the sunken rectangle. The four boxwood-edged flower beds, Lawrence White recalls, endured a fate that many other gardens of the period also suffered—they never escaped the relentless grasp of Joseph Gould, estate superintendent, who filled them with annual salvia, purple petunias, and pink and orange begonias.[26] Not every estate gardener was a George Gillies!

THE DOMAIN OF WOMEN

Most women who could afford to have elaborate gardens were content to be traditional wives and mothers. They were expected to create an orderly and luxurious country life, a serene counterweight to their husbands' chaotic business life in the city. They had not the slightest intention of battling this system, and often they saw what was known as "the woman's sphere" an entirely satisfactory place to be. Perhaps the making of

RIGHT:
Mrs. Edward Townsend, a member of the North Shore Garden Club, presides proudly over her garden. The freestanding arch that leads down onto the lawn is a typical period feature.

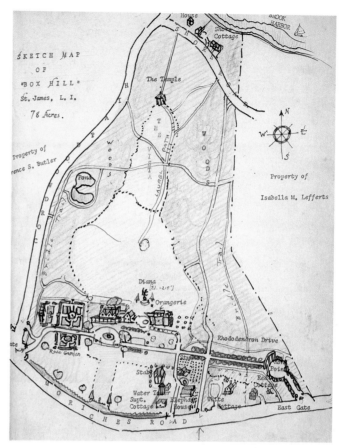

Sketch map of "Box Hill," St. James, Long Island, *from* Memoranda of the Place, and the Contents of the House, *by Lawrence Grant White for his Children.* White, himself an architect, is Stanford White's son, and had spent his childhood at "Box Hill."

gardens was the freest and most fulfilling part of this life. Since most of these sheltered upper-class women did not think of going to college, and their formal education finished at sixteen or seventeen if they were lucky, they learned from the world around them, from extensive travel, from reading, and from each other. Gardens and the making of gardens they learned from books and magazines and through their garden clubs; most of the good amateur women gardeners in this book were garden club members.

Though garden clubs, and women's organizations in general, often end up as objects of affectionate ridicule (see the cartoons of Helen Hokinson), membership gave a certain class of women a way to express their concerns about the environment and their ideas of the beautiful. At home, their gardens were places where they could make their own decisions, experiment with new information, and allow their fantasies to take tangible shape. As a group, they were able to carry out some of these ideas in the community, something they would never have dreamed of trying to do alone. They learned to take themselves seriously in a way that the world did not, and they did so without having to be revolutionaries.

Writing about his wife's grandmother, Mrs. Richard Tobin (Gertrude Vanderbilt Whitney's cousin), Louis Auchincloss describes his own Long Island fantasy of the romantic, and romanticized dichotomy of city and country life. "The two were linked only by the rattling bracelet of the commuter train, which brought the hot, tired husband home to the cool balm of his loving wife," he says, describing his visionary Long Island as "the domain of women . . . with its lush green woods and emerald lawns and gracious villas with French windows open to the velvet air. . . ."[27]

Two such private paradises were Mrs. Robert McKay's "Chelsea" in Muttontown, and Mrs. Charles E. F. McCann's estate in Oyster Bay. Alexandra Emery Moore McKay's "Chelsea" was the personal garden of an expert gardener. Her own plant lists still exist. For the pond garden, which was laid out by Ferruccio Vitale, forty pages of rough drawings by Mrs. Moore (as she was for most of her adult life) take the seasons month by month from March snowdrops through December, when red and yellow cornus twigs and Christmas roses provided color and excitement. "Chelsea," which still exists today as part of the Muttontown Reserve, was also a romantic garden. As a young bride on her wedding trip to China in 1920, she and Benjamin Moore had seen a white-and-black farmhouse framed by water. For the next sixty years Mrs. Moore lived and gardened in her version of that memory: a brilliantly white house with black shutters, a smooth black slate roof—and a moat with a bridge.

To other eyes, "Chelsea," with its *tourelles* and French windows, looks like a typical William Adams Delano exercise in French manorial architecture. Except for the moat it is not unlike the Brewsters' "Avalon" in its livability, pleasantness, lack of surface ornament, and abundant small outdoor garden spaces immediately surrounding the house.

Nonetheless, Mrs. Moore's vision of her Chinese farmhouse must have been very specific—her daughter says that Delano had to submit three sketches before her mother was satisfied. So for Mrs. Moore it was a Chinese house, and she filled it with oriental treasures from subsequent trips, as well as European finds such as the French wallpaper she picked up on a Paris street where it awaited the arrival of the garbage man. Carved wooden Chinese ornaments hung from the tree in the courtyard, Chinese lanterns shed light on many evenings spent outdoors, wind chimes filled the air, and a chinoiserie garden and a moon gate added to the oriental mood. There was hide-and-seek in the topiary, croquet on the lawn, and swimming in the moat. For children especially "Chelsea" must have been a magical place. Linda Moore Post remembers that from the tower window she and her brothers and their friends used to play Romeo and Juliet.[28]

The "domain of women" was not always such a long-term paradise. Helena Woolworth McCann, one of three daughters of five-and-dime tycoon F. W. Woolworth, had grown up on the North Shore at Glen Cove, first in a frame villa with a view of the Sound, and then in the marble château which replaced it in 1916.[29] Small wonder that when she married Charles E. F. McCann in the twenties she set about making a grand place of her own. Later, in the early thirties, she married Winston Guest, charming, good-looking, one of the best polo players in the world, heir to quite a lot of Phipps steel money, and Winston Churchill's distant cousin. The wedding took place in her own garden, among drifts of rosy Japanese cherry blossoms. A dance floor was set up on the indoor tennis court of "The Playhouse," another of the fabled Long Island indoor tennis court complexes. An entire trainload of palm trees was sent from Florida to make a tropical forest, and the walls were decorated with trellis covered with gardenias. The Guests divorced in 1944 and part of the place was purchased from Mrs. Guest in the forties by the William Woodwards.[30]

But the future must have looked bright at "The Playhouse" when landscape architect Annette Hoyt Flanders (1887–1946) began her work on the gardens there for the McCanns. Among the women landscape architects of her day, Flanders was especially well qualified. Born in Milwaukee, Wisconsin, she had majored in botany at Smith College, graduating at twenty-three in 1910, and had gone on to take a landscape architecture degree at the University of Illinois. She finished her formal schooling with civil engineering courses at Marquette University. Next she traveled abroad, studying at the Sorbonne, and on her return worked for the landscape architecture firm of Vitale, Brinckerhoff and Geiffert.

In 1922 she opened her own office in New York. Her work was varied, ranging from a three-level roof garden with a dancing floor and a huge bird cage for a children's outdoor playroom for the Walter Hochschilds in

The central reflecting pool at "Clayton" was designed by Marian Coffin for the Childs Fricks in 1925.

Umberto Innocenti's own Long Island garden was an artful mix of pattern, with the intersecting arcs of brick pavement and the long stripes of mown lawn. Both this garden and that of his partner, Richard Webel, were prototypes of the best, small liveable gardens of the forties.

New York City, to cutting and rose gardens for Mr. and Mrs. Ronald Tree at the Langhorne seat, "Mirador," in Virginia, to gardens in Canada, Texas, and Hawaii. Most of her work was on large estates.[31] Helena McCann's so-called French garden was perhaps Flanders's best work, and certainly one of her most elaborate and extensive. It was also her best known, since it won the gold medal of the Architectural League of New York in 1933. Flanders dealt firmly with changes in level, using wide, shallow turf steps to anchor the bulky brick house to its lawn. (She used exactly the same device at the very similar John Kiser house in Southampton.) A series of formal gardens was linked by allées, and informal gardens were scattered throughout the surrounding woods. She laid out bridle trails, filled woodlands with wild flowers, and made a sunken orchard carpeted with violets.

Like Farrand, she was interested in tree silhouettes. Often she directed the planting of full-grown trees and so could insist on turning the tree to display its very best profile. Sometimes, perhaps, she was too much of a perfectionist. She was working in pre-tree spade-days, and every inch meant a tremendous effort for the ten men down in the tree hole, struggling to turn the huge root ball. The foreman of the Frankenbach nurseries in Southampton recalled a technique he developed to deal with Mrs. Flanders. "Sometimes when we'd moved that tree about half way around in the hole and it looked fine to me," he says, "I'd tell the men that the next time she asked for a little more this way or that, they should just shake that tree hard, and groan a little bit. Always seemed to suit her just fine. . . ."[32] Without overwhelming the garden plantings, she very adroitly employed architectural details, such as pairs of urns, brick posts, gates, and flights of steps. Richardson Wright, editor of *House and Garden*, in a foreword to a monograph of Flanders's work,[33] says, "One is impressed with the fact that Mrs. Flanders has kept her architecture well in hand so that Nature might have a chance to complete the picture." This is a shift in emphasis from gardens of a generation before, such as Woolworth's "Winfield Hall," where plants were used more as clothing or background for architecture, not as structural elements. The overflowing ebullience and the openly derivative eclecticism of the turn of the century vanished during the twenties. Flanders's work, like that of Fletcher Steele's at "Naumkeag," was set in a lower key and looked forward to modernism.

Long Island gardens are filled with memories of all kinds. One of Martha Frick Symington's most vivid—and grisly—remembrances of "Clayton," in Roslyn Harbor where she grew up, is of the little pool under the huge oak in what she called "the woodsy garden to the north." She writes, "There was an oval lawn with a statue of a baboon whom we named 'Narcissus' as he endlessly admired himself in the water. This is where we had swimming meets between our guinea pigs, white mice, and my alligator—hilarious. The pool was also a good place for guinea pig pregnancy testing. If they were, they sank."[34] (The four ghoulish Fricks, children of paleontologist Childs Frick and grandchildren of steel magnate Henry Clay Frick, kept all kinds of pets, some clearly for a shorter time than others.)

The Fricks were the last of three private owners. The first was the poet William Cullen Bryant who built "Cedarmere," a Gothic house typical of the period in 1843. Bryant worshiped nature—*picturesque* nature—and his garden consisted mainly of an irregular lake with a rustic bridge. He loved trees, particularly native American species, and the woods are filled with his plantings. In 1895 Mr. and Mrs. Lloyd Stephens Bryce engaged Ogden Codman, Jr., to design a Georgian house on land bought

LEFT:
Landscape architects Innocenti and Webel used carved posts to "enclose" the path seen here just as Fletcher Steele had "enclosed" Mabel Choate's Afternoon Garden at "Naumkeag." Innocenti and Webel designed the gardens close to the main house at Mrs. Charles E. F. McCann's.

from the Bryant estate. Ogden Codman, Beaux-Arts-trained architect, designer of gardens, and Francophile, was also Edith Wharton's coauthor in *The Decoration of Houses.* Codman's gardens are just now being rediscovered.[35] The Bryce garden consisted of a panel of *broderie* stretched between the two handsome Palladian pavilions that flanked the north elevation. It was centered by a fountain set in a formal pool, and overlooked the rolling lawns that led down to the Sound. Separate from the house there was also a hedged garden of old-fashioned flowers.

After Bryce's death in 1917, when Henry Clay Frick bought the house and its 180 acres for his son and daughter-in-law, extensive changes were made and the place was renamed "Clayton," after Henry Clay Frick's house in Pittsburgh. The Childs Fricks made a pinetum and an extensive new garden, creating essentially what exists today.

The story of who made the Frick garden underlines some of the typical difficulties that can arise between owner and designer, even when intentions are good and the results are beautiful. The first person Mrs. Frick called on for assistance was Clarence Fowler, in 1922, but his sketch for a flower garden was turned down. By 1925 Mrs. Frick had discovered

Long Island

Marian Coffin, who by then had opened her small office in New York and was quite successful. Coffin had learned about plants from Charles Sprague Sargent's right-hand man, horticulturist John G. Jack, and about garden design at MIT where she studied as a special student under architect Guy Lowell.[36] Coffin authority Valencia Libby says that while Coffin understood the importance of flower color schemes and blooming sequences and had visited Gertrude Jekyll at Munstead Wood in later years, good spatial design was what she believed was always the backbone of a beautiful garden.[37] At "Clayton," she and Mrs. Frick transformed the site of the old Bryce greenhouse and vegetable garden into a handsome, firmly axial, rectangle divided into four "rooms" each with a different planting scheme. The main dividing "walls" were privet and the inner walls of the rooms were cedar. Boxwood, brick paths, and grass panels made interesting patterns between the perennial beds. At the central crossing she replaced a rose bed with a pool and fountain jet. The firm spatial divisions, the intricate symmetry of axis, cross axis, and parallel axes are typical of Coffin's best work.

From 1925 until the early thirties Marian Coffin worked on the garden; Mrs. Frick, a woman with a mind of her own, also worked, and watched. At some point in every successful garden that begins with a landscape architect's scheme it becomes the client's own garden. Sometimes the takeover is bloody, sometimes peaceful—sometimes coexistence is even possible. There are gardens to which the same designer returns again and again, in an advisory capacity. In others, the memory of professional assistance is deliberately extinguished. The garden becomes "the dream that Mum created"—the last hangover of the eighteenth-century tradition that the gifted amateur must be able to do everything alone. To judge from the echoes through the years, Marian Coffin and Mrs. Frick did not part friends. Mrs. Symington remembers: "Mum used Ms. Coffin for the first revamping and then they fell out. Mainly because Ms. Coffin ignored Mum's input. I do not clearly remember at what point Mum fired Ms. Coffin but I do know that the installation of the gates and the creation of the 'Tea House' lattice extravaganza at the far end (south) of the garden was done with the help of Henry Milliken, an architect—not a landscaper. In other words, Mum took over her own garden and did as she pleased."[38] The Frick garden is now the Nassau County Museum.

Marjorie Merriweather Post and her first husband, stockbroker Edward F. Hutton, also called on Marian Coffin to design their garden in Brookville. Their Tudor house was called "Hillwood." The design was more complex here than at "Clayton," but Coffin's style was the same. She used the asymmetrical but balanced mass of the house as a starting point for a formal garden that employed the same close harmonies of axis, cross axis, and parallel axis. She also managed to incorporate a putting green and tennis court in the garden scheme without distress.

She used trelliswork to screen the tennis court, and long arbors to shape space in a three-dimensional way. Coffin devoted much time to spatial definition in her book, *Trees and Shrubs for Landscape Effects*. She also designed an exquisite boxwood-edged small garden for a thatched "playhouse" for Mrs. Post's youngest daughter, actress Dina Merrill, and still another garden next to another daughter's separate but equally Tudor residence. The gardens together were notable for their circulation, which return the visitor to the main house by alternate routes.[39]

"Bayberryland"

A completely different sort of garden, and the first real beach garden described in this book was that of the Charles Sabins, set in the Shinnecock Hills overlooking Peconic Bay near Southampton. Charles Sabin was chairman of Morgan Guaranty, and Pauline Sabin the daughter of the founder of Morton Salt.[40] The house, designed in 1919 by Cross and Cross of New York, was an H-shaped ocher stucco English cottage affair with band windows and sculptural gables. The biggest difficulty was soil—how would it be possible to have any kind of garden on the dunes? The problem was solved by buying a nearby farm and removing all its topsoil to the Sabin property—certainly a lot faster than compost, though hardly an ecologically sound practice. The second difficulty was wind, and in the absence of trees Coffin built many walls which divided the seaside part of the garden in three. Farthest east, and highest, was a lawn with a tennis court; at the lowest point, a sunken garden. Between them lay the wild garden, a sea of junipers and perennials that stretched

The Tritoma Path designed by Marian Coffin at the Charles Sabins' "Bayberryland" (1919), near Southampton, is flagged and planted with tiny creepers. It curves down to the cliff overlooking Peconic Bay. On either side Coffin planted long waves of tritomas, lupines, species geraniums, and Cerastium tomentosum, *and other silvery plants that love the seaside.*

in an irregular widening triangle from the house to the edge of the bluff punctuated by the tall red cedars that grow so freely in the Shinnecock Hills. Here Marian Coffin showed how well she could design a garden whose structure depended on plantings, not symmetry.

The circulation was superb, as at "Hillwood."[41] Paths from all the sections of the garden met at the top of the bluff where a flight of stone stairs led to the beach below. The beach path wound its way down the slope amid the natural dune grasses, and just above the high tide mark stood a light pergola, last of the man-made structures in this subtly designed flowing progression from garden to wild landscape. "Bayberryland" was a perfect realization of a shore garden, of which there were many in the Hamptons during the twenties. The outlines remain today, maintained as a summer camp for the Electrical Workers Union of the Long Island Lighting Company.

THE EAST END
In the South Fork villages of Southampton and East Hampton, though the gardens were just as beautiful, the estates were much smaller and less elaborate since they were created only for a resort summer season. In 1915 Louise Shelton said that Southampton had more gardens than any other town in the state. Over all hung the sharp mid-summer incense of fourteen-foot-tall privet hedges in flower. In the 1870s, artists such as William Merritt Chase, and journalists writing in *Harper's Weekly* began to celebrate the American simplicity of the East End's quaint villages, so similar to the seacoast communities of New England. Though the first cottager didn't arrive until 1875 (New York dry goods merchant De Bost), Southampton grew as mightily during the last quarter of the nineteenth century as other earlier East Coast resorts such as Newport and Bar Harbor. The earliest cottagers were mostly New Yorkers and Pittsburghers, including Mellons, Camerons, Thaws, Dilworths, Reas, and Byerses.[42] It was a seaside summer resort but, unlike Bar Harbor or Newport, instead of rocky ledges its setting was wide white beaches, calm estuary and marsh, and flat, fertile farmland. Though a number of East End "cottage" gardens were just lawn and hydrangeas—and the incomparable ocean—many more were elaborately Colonial Revival in style. Conscious attempts at a kind of flowery cottage garden simplicity, they were suitable accompaniment to the white clapboard Colonial Revival houses like that of James Breese in Southampton, designed by Stanford White. They included those of Thomas Barber, Mrs. C. A. Bryan, Mrs. G. Warrington Curtis, Mrs. Henry E. Coe, Frederick Snow, and Mrs. Peter B. Wykoff. In a countryside where the few trees that grow naturally are all combed to the same shape by the omnipresent winds, windbreaks usually meant privet hedges or walls. Common features were "old-fashioned" box-edged perennial beds in simple patterns, vine-covered pergolas, and grass or brick walks.

"The Orchard" in Southampton
The Colonial Revival garden of James Breese's "The Orchard" celebrated the inland, farming aspect of Long Island's East End, the flat apple and pear orchards, and the potato fields. When Breese, one of Stanford White's best friends, left Tuxedo Park in 1895 and decided on a summer place in Southampton, he bought 30 acres in town, and an eighteenth-century farmhouse which he moved onto the site.[43] Breese, who had considered architecture as a career himself, chose his friend's firm to design a new dwelling, using the farmhouse as the core. At that time McKim, Mead and White were also at work on the Edwin Morgan place in Wheatley Hills, Long Island, another huge edifice, like the Breese house, in the Colonial Revival style the firm did so much to popularize. Both houses were included in the firm's 1915 monograph of their most significant works, but today the Breese house, now a twenty-nine-unit condominium, is the only Long Island house still standing that was featured in the monograph. The basic outlines of the garden have been sensitively restored, though the plantings that once gave it such style and softness have vanished.

White and Charles McKim, who drew the plans, enveloped the original structure in a very grand white clapboard building with a Mount Vernon portico on the entrance front. Symmetrical wings with complex rooflines create a U-shape on the garden side. A square formal rose garden, the first unit in the long skinny garden design, lies within the wings. On either side a columned pergola with rustic rafters extends the line of the wing down the garden's length, and continues the feeling of enclosure. The square box-edged parterres filled with fruit trees and cottage garden flowers must have brought to mind Southampton's long colonial past and the neat field shapes of the surrounding countryside.

Like many other good gardens in Southampton and East Hampton, "The Orchard" makes a virtue of the native landscape's utter flatness—the principal feature of the garden was, and still is, the alluring narrow perspective that zooms down the herringbone brick walk between the flat parterres and the two-hundred-foot-long pergolas, continues through a screen of more columns and arborvitae, and then down the central path of the vegetable garden, once lined with peach trees. It finished in infinity, more prosaically known as White's Lane, at the far end of the property, about 360 feet from the roomy curved porch that projected from the garden front. The actual distance seemed like much more since the width of the garden was only 45 feet.

Besides the usual outbuildings, Breese had wonderful sportsman's toys such as a shooting tower for clay pigeon, a garage for his newfangled motors, and a completely equipped machine shop to repair them (where one Breese son later built the engine that powered the "Spirit of St. Louis" across the Atlantic). "The Orchard" was a big boys' paradise—there was little sign of the dark and lovely, and rather noticeably sad and

The compartments of James Breese's long, skinny, beautiful rectangle of a garden at "The Orchard" in Southampton were strung along a straight brick path which leads from the house.

Beyond Cornelia Horsford's "old-fashioned" flower garden (c. 1906) are the dark shapes of centuries-old boxwood and the early eighteenth-century house, the second on the site at "Sylvester Manor."

lifeless, Mrs. Breese inside or out. Jimmy Breese was as fast and stylish as the new roadsters he constantly bought and drove. He had tremendous enthusiasms for everything from cameras (he was a serious amateur photographer with a studio in New York) to horses (he raced trotters) to antiques (traveling, often with Stanford White, he bought furnishings for "The Orchard" knowledgeably and well). He was a professional hobbyist, a playboy, a perfectionist with exquisite and original taste, and playing games seriously was what he liked best in life. There are photographs of him in fancy dress, posed in handsome heavy-lidded profile as a seventeenth-century Dutch gentleman complete with long clay pipe, or as an Italian swashbuckler in short doublet and hose that show off his long legs. In her memoirs, his daughter Frances Miller describes him as the kind of man who "when he carved a roast, was in tears if it was under or over done. He knew the exact length of time a bird should be hung, and how fruit should be ripened . . . pears in the dark, peaches in the sun. . . ."[44]

He also shared Stanford White's taste for show girls, and for years Breese's studio on West 16th Street was regularly the scene of their stag parties. Stanford White's last job before his death was James Breese's seventy-five-foot-long music room at "The Orchard." One summer afternoon in 1906, White left off advising the workmen, who were painting the coffered ceiling, to go into town for dinner with his son. He was shot that same evening by his ex-girlfriend Evelyn Nesbit's jealous and crazy husband, Harry K. Thaw.[45] Frances Miller wrote that she heard the news of White's assassination when her father rushed down the hall White had designed, shouting "Stan's been shot!"[46]

East Hampton

The shoreline of the East End is cut by river mouths, and many seaside ponds in the low, marshy landscape provide irresistible invitations for water gardeners. Naturalistic pond gardens often provided a contrast to a formal house surround. One of the most beautiful such was "The Creeks," where artists Adele and Alfred Herter's water garden ran down the estuary bank. Closer to their Grosvenor Atterbury house they laid out nearly an acre of flower beds in a formal radiating pattern, and flowers in the "room" gardens that adjoined the house matched the interior decoration—blue and lavender outside a blue-and-white room, or a red, salmon, and yellow garden outside the apricot satin-lined front hall.[47]

Another well-known water garden was that of the celebrated East Hampton gardener, Mrs. Lorenzo E. Woodhouse, on Egypt's Lane. "Considered the best piece of work in the country," according to Louise Shelton, she writes, "It is wonderfully composed, with natural pools and streams, tea-houses and rustic bridges suggestive of the Japanese art, yet lovelier than the trim Oriental type of water garden because so delightfully wild and overgrown with massive plants, vines, and shrubs, without, however, being disorderly in appearance."[48]

"Sylvester Manor": A Three-Century Garden

"Overgrown with massive plants, vines, and shrubs" certainly described E. N. Horsford's water garden on Shelter Island, laid out in 1892 by his son-in-law, Thomas Allen. Within two small ponds (one 6 by 12', the other a U-shaped basin measuring 18 by 19') grew thirty-four different aquatic species, mostly tropicals, including papyrus, *Cyperus Papyrus*, which reaches a height of eight feet, and Humboldt's Amazonian water poppy, *Limnocharis Humboldtii*. Cultural directions on Allen's plan show that he realized the problem; about the poppy he warned, it "grows ten feet or more in a season and should be trained down the pond. . . ."[49]

Horsford's garden was noted for much else besides Thomas Allen's pools. Horsford, a Harvard chemistry professor and friend of preeminent American botanist Asa Gray, had married into the family of the original patent holders of "Sylvester Manor," who still own it today. It is one of the earliest American gardens with a continuous history of cultivation since about 1655. Shelter Island is located deep within the sheltered bay between the North and South forks. What remains of the manor (700 acres) lies at the top of its own little creek. The first house was built in 1652 by the two earliest Quakers to reach America; the present-day house dates to 1732 but has been remodeled at least a little by almost every generation. "Sylvester Manor" was a safe haven for Quakers fleeing the persecutions of the 1660s in Boston, which ceased through Nathaniel Sylvester's direct intervention with Charles II, who owed money to Sylvester's father-in-law, Thomas Brinley.

The earliest mention of the garden occurs in Quaker founder George Fox's diary, where he records preaching to the Indians in "Madame Sylvester's" yard. It's possible this is the same enclosed one-and-a-half-acre rectangle that still exists today. Very old box and the remains of a seventeenth-century retaining wall attest to its age. Many trees may be record holders, and the place may well shelter rare remaining specimens of old cultivars, but no measuring has been done. As far as garden history goes, "Sylvester Manor" is an untouched spot. The oldest garden may exist in outline beneath that of today, but no garden archeology has yet been carried out.

The rectangle is divided by a box-edged path, with various compartments for ornament, cutting, vegetables, and fruit on each side. The uses and shapes of the compartments, and the plants they have contained have varied through the years. In the manor house library, plant lists, annotated garden books, garden diaries, and bills of sale dating back to the early nineteenth century form a tantalizing, though partial, record of a family with lasting horticultural interests. The last gardener to make substantial changes was Cornelia Horsford, the professor's daughter and a Garden Club of America member, who removed many Victorian traces from the oldest parts of the garden near the house to make a four-section "old-fashioned" design with a geometric parterre outlined in low box, a

The gardens of Southampton in the 1870s were as modest as this beauty.

The boathouse, at left, was part of the garden ensemble at the Albert Herters' "Près Choisis" in East Hampton. Today called "The Creeks," it is the Ossorio sculpture garden.

Anna Gilman Hill's "Grey Gardens," possibly designed with help from East Hampton garden designer Ruth Dean, were cradled in the dunes. Hill wrote the popular Forty Years of Gardening in 1938.

A thatched gazebo stands knee-deep in iris in the water garden of Mrs. Lorenzo E. Woodhouse in East Hampton, today the East Hampton Nature Reserve. A boat, the "Swamp Angel," was used to get around.

round rose garden, a box maze, and a cottage garden with a grape arbor.

The garden is a wonderfully jumbled 300-year-old record of lively, intelligent, cultivated Americans. An elm tree close to the garden, of which only the stump mark in the turf remains, was a scion of the "Quaker hanging tree" in Boston; slips of willow were brought from Elba by some nineteenth-century tourist Sylvester; a rusty metal-frame windmill, which towered over the cottage borders until the late 1980s, was the very latest model when Cornelia Horsford had it erected in 1906 to bring water to her garden. Memory and custom have had their place too—for many generations the huge box bushes were decorated with gold leaf on the day the heir brought home his bride. Today, at the garden entrance, the tiny box leaves still shine in the sun.

Long Island

115

The MIDDLE ATLANTIC

Between New York and Washington, D.C., the rich "moved countryward," fanning out from every metropolitan center, making a lacework of great estates over the agricultural countryside.[1] To some extent the estate gardens took their character from these cities; New York, Wilmington, Baltimore, Washington, and most particularly Philadelphia imposed their stamp. New York was a mecca for New Jersey—for style, society, and wealth. Philadelphia was a world apart, with its own style, its own concentrations of wealth, both old and new, and its Quaker beginnings. Pittsburgh, like Rochester or Buffalo, moved in its own orbit, and had a climate very different from seaboard America. In Wilmington, garden style meant just one family: du Pont. Getting down into Maryland, one encounters for the first time that phenomenon of the period: rich North-erners moving south for sport and for their dream of the simpler life of

antebellum days. Charles Dudley Warner went all the way to Louisiana to write about Southern[2] charm, but Maryland's Harford County or the Eastern Shore would have done as well. The great gardens of the estate period in Washington, on the other hand, did not evoke the South; they were more like European urban gardens. Most gardens were designed for spring and fall to avoid the summer heat.

ABOVE:
The "lagoon" at the George Goulds' "Georgian Court" in Lakewood, New Jersey, was designed by architect Bruce Price "to give the garden design much of the character of the famous formal gardens of Italy," which it certainly did not do. Nothing could have been more American than this garden. The bridge arching overhead which completes the composition was Price's clever solution for an unavoidable public road.

The Middle Atlantic

118

THE SOMERSET HILLS

One of the two most beautiful estate gardens in New Jersey, certainly among the most photographed, was C. Ledyard Blair's "Blairsden," in Peapack, part of the western-most expansion of the Morristown community. "Blairsden" looked south over flat New Jersey from the last big bump left by the receding glaciers. The view was magnificent. The house, designed by Carrère and Hastings (Thomas Hastings was a great friend of the Blairs), was a brick-and-stone Louis XIII château, which also was magnificent—though not remarkable by comparison with the gardens, which were among the very finest works of James Greenleaf, who often worked with Carrère and Hastings.

C. Ledyard Blair, financier and sportsman, was heir to an immense New York banking fortune. In 1897 he bought an old farm, located on top of a pointed hill covered with scrub trees, and then spent a good deal of time and money leveling part of the summit for a house site. "Blairsden's" hill was so steep that a single track railroad with a miniature woodburning engine had to be built to haul building materials.

In the gardens, Greenleaf contrasted wilderness and cultivation, formality and informality of design, contraction and expansion of space, light, and shade, and made long entrance drives which passed through a succession of landscapes. At "Blairsden" there was plenty of opportunity, as there were 2,000 acres and three major entrances. The main gate led up a mile-long allée of high-arched lindens, whose green cathedral opened out onto a sunny farm below the summit of the hill—shingle cottages with diamond panes, wide fields, creamery and cowbarns—country life picturesquely arranged.

No expense was spared. The handsome farm wall topped with flints that followed the drive on up toward the house was known as the "Norman Wall" because the workmen who made it were brought over from Normandy—naturally—and then sent back to France when they had finished. Today such attention to detail seems absurd, but, in fact, a team like Carrère and Hastings, and Greenleaf, working with a sympathetic (and rich) client like Blair, often produced landscape art as beautiful and appropriate as a *real* Italian villa or English park.

Beyond the farm the road split, the division marked by a small stone cherub fountain set among the hayfields, the first note of formality. The main drive continued up the final ascent through a high natural wood. Where the road was cut into one side of the steep hill, a natural rock "wall" had been created, a rock garden that was planted with woodland natives—wild columbine, bloodroot, arbutus, jack-in-the-pulpits, and violets of all kinds. They were followed by a variety of ferns that flourished

Maples narrow the final entrance vista of one of the most beautiful country places in America—"Blairsden," built for the C. Ledyard Blairs outside the village of Peapack, New Jersey, in 1897.

in the summer shade. The house approach was theatrical: where the woodland road began to flatten out on top of the hill a pair of 20-foot-high stone pillars formed a gate in a high brick wall. There was no view of the house beyond; nothing was visible until the carriage actually drove through the gates and turned sharply left and there you were, looking down a long formal pool toward the central limestone pediment of the house. On either side was a row of big maples. In their black shade stood tall white marble busts of the Roman emperors, housed in lattice niches painted the same verdigris as the lattice at Versailles.

There was still no sign of the great view for which Blair had purchased the Mellick farm, however. That was saved for last. Around the corner from the entrance front, two formal terraces ran the length of the house, with an orangery beneath the lower one. Down the slope below plunged steps and black-and-white mosaic ramps ornamented with tubbed bay trees, cedars, and rhododendrons. A water course with cascades, and a rill in the best Italian manner ran the length of the steps down to a fountain. On either side Greenleaf did what he did best—disposed shaggy groups of evergreens and flowering trees that merged with the new forests he planted to cover the steep old fields of the former Mellick farm. Far down at the bottom, a cut through the woods revealed more water. When Blair bought the property there was only a tiny branch of the Raritan River, which he dammed with a 100-foot stepped stone wall to form a lake before he even started building the house. It took a year to fill, and in the meantime, the Blairs' last child was born. She was promptly called "the dam baby."

The remainder of the twenty formally landscaped acres around the house included a rose garden with 1,400 kinds of rose bushes, a little walled "secret garden" behind the main house, and tennis courts with a brick-and-lattice Italian casino to cool off in. The Blairs loved sports and the outdoors—the open tennis casino had a fireplace to extend the season, and in the winter the grass courts were covered with boards and canvas so they could play then too. Like most great country estates, "Blairsden" was a sportsman's paradise, complete with miles of bridle trails, two rustic boathouses, and a trap shoot with its own shooting lodge. The Blairs summered in Bar Harbor, and also had a house in Bermuda, a sort of miniature "Blairsden." Blair was interested in racing and kept a very successful racing stable; he was a yachtsman as well—when a German boat was quarantined in Bar Harbor for the duration of World War I, it was Blair who navigated her tricky passage past Northeast Harbor and up into Some Sound.

Many of the big Morristown/Bernardsville country places built between 1880 and 1920 were set on the same Somerset Hills escarpment as "Blairsden" so that they enjoyed similar views. Though few places were as elaborate or breathtaking, they were similar to "Blairsden" in their emphasis on sport, their grandeur and conspicuous display, and their sense of leafy retreat. Other retreats belonged to John F. Dryden, Frederick P. Olcott, Charles Pfizer, James Cox Brady, James Buchanan, Percy R. Pyne (brother of Moses Taylor Pyne of Princeton), and Walter G. Ladd, who was Blair's irascible neighbor. (The road between the two places was finally closed after the two had a fight in the club car of the New York train.)[3]

Morristown

In 1897 all the Blairs' friends, according to family accounts, thought they were making a great mistake—the place to be in New Jersey was Morristown, only a few miles east of Bernardsville which during the early 1890s was transformed from a sleepy county seat with a historic past into a social hub, a spring-and-fall equivalent to the Berkshires on the social tour. By the turn of the century the old town was swamped by the new millionaires. The center of Morristown life, Madison Avenue, so-called because it ran from Madison, New Jersey, to Morristown, was known as the "Great White Way" in 1900, when the combined wealth of the estate owners along its four country-place-studded miles was approximately $500 million.[4] Proximity to New York was the lure—Morristown was a commuting town even in the nineties. The 4:15 P.M. train was known as the "millionaires' express," and carried a club car (dues only $60 per year but you had to get in) with its own porter and green-cushioned wicker chairs—a tradition that survived into the eighties on the Peapack-Gladstone train. It was filled with financiers and brokers such as Otto Kahn and Charles Henry Mellon, bankers and businessmen like Gustav E. Kissell and Marcellus Hartley Dodge, chairman of Remington Arms, and capitalists as powerful as Hamilton McKeon Twombly, a proper (and able) Bostonian who married his boss' daughter, Florence Vanderbilt.

From the time they moved to Morristown, the Twomblys were society leaders. The housewarming for their new farm buildings was a barndance for three hundred. The barn roof supports were twined with evergreens and hung with garlands of corncobs, and everywhere stood sheaves of wheat and stocks of red, white, and blue pampas grass. The hostess received in the bull barn. "Florham," named after her and him (*Flor*ence/*Ham*ilton), was another of the vast estate projects let loose on the world by the grandchildren of Commodore Cornelius Vanderbilt. (Others in this book include Frederick Vanderbilt's "Hyde Park," Lila Webb's "Shelburne Farms," where he advised but did not design, and George Washington Vanderbilt II's "Biltmore," in North Carolina.) The architects were McKim, Mead and White and the landscape architect Frederick Law Olmsted, aided by his son John Charles. Warren Manning, landscape engineer and architect, actually laid out the grounds.

The 110-room house was a replica of the West Wing of Hampton Court Palace, designed by Sir Christopher Wren. Three hundred acres were laid out as terraced formal gardens near the house and a home park, with an additional 100 acres for coachhouse, stables, orangery, kennels, and greenhouses. There were 50 gardeners, and for lawnmowers there was a flock of 100 sheep, complete with shepherds. In the usual way, flowers, vegetables, and dairy products from the 750-acre farm also supplied for the Twomblys Manhattan and Newport establishments. A playhouse, including tennis courts and swimming pool, was added in the thirties. The head gardener at Kew was lured away to run the greenhouses, and so famous were the chrysanthemums that in 1904 the Japanese Emperor's gardener came to see them. Extra flowers from the greenhouses were also sold, and in some years the profits ran as high as $25,000.[5]

Olmsted and Twombly corresponded about siting the house. Olmsted was anxious to have a building well proportioned to the location and had suggested a place. Twombly had been thinking about altering the Danforth house, which he and his wife had rented since 1887, instead of building a new one from scratch. Olmsted wrote in April, 1891, "you could spend millions [on the Danforth house] and not get anything to be distantly compared with it on the Madison Avenue site. . . . The Danforth house, however enlarged, will rank as a suburban villa. A house of half the size on the site of the Park would be a country mansion." A previous generation, inspired by A. J. Downing, had built "villas"; the Twomblys' generation, with more money and more dynastic yearnings, wanted "country mansions." In the end, Olmsted got what he wanted. In December of 1891, a tracing of the location of the proposed new house and a plan were sent from McKim, Mead and White to Olmsted so he could get an idea of how they wished to place the building on site.

Quite a few of the other great Morristown *gardens,* as opposed to estates, belonged to what Olmsted would have termed suburban villas, whose average acreage was well under 100. Their placement along both sides of Madison Avenue was similar to the still bigger houses on still smaller acreage in Newport. Mrs. Charles McAlpin's "Glen Alpine," with its deep borders, was a favorite of Louise Shelton's: she featured it both in *Beautiful Gardens in America* and in *Continuous Bloom in America* (Scribner's, 1915). In continuous bloom it was—from May 22 until frost according to Miss Shelton—in pinks, dark reds, blues, and yellows. The gardener was the brother of George Gillies, Marshall Field III's English estate superintendent. Even Miss Shelton admits how much work these wide beds took: "If there is strict adherence to their planting schemes the richness of their bloom will continue through future seasons. But, alas! how uncertain the fulfillment, when the most necessary flowers may disappoint at the eleventh hour, or the gardeners fail to abide by the plans, especially concerning the color scheme!"[6]

Another enclave of the Morristown rich, Washington Valley, had "country places" more along "Florham's" lines. "Delbarton," largest of all in Morris County (4,000 acres), a white granite manor house with dormers, loggias, and turrets, was finished in 1888 by McKim, Mead and White for banker Luther Kountze. Inside the walled Italian gardens stood two eight-foot-tall statues of the garden gods Priapus and Flora, which were carved in 1616 by the great Gian Lorenzo Bernini, working with his father when he was only eighteen. Until 1890 they stood at the gates of Cardinal Borghese's garden in Rome, where the eighteenth century English gardener, John Evelyn, saw them on his Italian tour, describing a "Dorecase adorned with divers excellent marble statues." They are now in the Metropolitan Museum of Art. Most unusual was "Giralda", the house of Mrs. William Hartley Dodge (William Rockefeller's daughter), which was separated by two miles of rolling countryside from her husband's house, but connected by sightlines along an 80-foot-wide allée lined with trees.

Llewellyn Park, Short Hills, and Rumson

The press of urbanization and industrial and corporate development has made forgotten names in the social rollcall of places closer to New York

Aerial swags of roses, conically trimmed arborvitae, dwarf boxwood edging, circular pools with flush coping, and peerless lawns were all regular features in a twenties garden. This example, the Bancroft Gherardi garden in Short Hills, is elegant because it included little else.

City such as Convent, Llewellyn Park, Rumson, and Red Bank. All once had wonderful estate gardens. Practically all of Convent was once the garden of Elam Ward Olney's "Olneyhurst/Square Acres." No members of the family who knew the garden survive, and the house burned about 1950. In the 1924 edition of *Beautiful Gardens in America*, Louise Shelton devotes five pictures to this garden. In Llewellyn Park, the first landscape-oriented planned suburb in the United States, designed by Llewellyn Huskell and architect A. J. Davis in 1854, Robert A. Franks, Andrew Carnegie's treasurer, commissioned Ellen Shipman to make an elaborate perennial garden for his place, "Bonaire." In Short Hills, the Bancroft Gherardi garden was designed by Wodell and Cottrell, two sisters who, like many others, saw garden design as one of the few career possibilities open to them. Unusually, Helen Wodell and Lois Cottrell did not begin their work until they were both in their forties. They made many gardens in New Jersey, in Upstate New York, and in Pittsburgh.[7]

In 1887 Edward Dean Adams, New York banker, took a look at the little rise he had chosen for his house site and at the red earth of Rumson, then part of Sea Bright, New Jersey, and named his new 54-acre estate "Rohallion," or "little red hill," in Gaelic. He had heard the term in Scotland on a stalking trip. The view from Adams's hill encompassed a

The turn-of-the-century childhood dream—a smart pony rig with two
ponies at "Rohallion" in Rumson.

*Seen in the distance of Edward Dean Adams's "Rohallion" is a rare
glimpse of the acres of kitchen garden that supplied every big place, and
usually the family's town house as well.*

glimpse of the Atlantic, and the curves of the Shrewsbury and Navesink rivers. Adams considered his Stanford White–designed "Rohallion" "home, while his New York pied-à-terre, one of the grand Villard Houses just behind St. Patrick's Cathedral, was merely a stopping place. At "Rohallion," the deep porches and high gables, side-by-side on a long comfortable-looking entrance front, are like those seen on the Shinnecock Club or at White's own house on Long Island. The house itself teemed with White's usual inventive details—batwing carvings inside a tiny corner cupboard, and so on. The exterior mix of stone, shingle, half-timbering, and brick was reminiscent of his house for the Choates, "Naumkeag" (1886), in the Berkshires. The gardens were similar too, since "Naumkeag's" first landscape architect, Nathan Barrett, also worked at "Rohallion" with White. Barrett worked in a gardenesque landscape style using many unusual trees and shrubs. As the Adamses were plant collectors of a sort, the gardens eventually included hundreds of specimens brought back from their trips abroad. "Rohallion's" grounds were in the charge of William H. Waite, who hybridized dahlia varieties, such as 'Jersey Delight', that were among the most popular.

Barrett's work usually incorporated certain late-Victorian "set pieces" within the informal setting—rose gardens, shrub gardens, and the like. At "Rohallion" an unusual layout was a "sand garden" of almost Islamic charm: within a hedged square on a sand ground, curving calligraphic lines of tiny boxwood (six inches high or less) were laid out with a large boxwood as a central boss. Another formal design, a lily pond, provided the setting for Frederick MacMonnies's well-known sculpture, *Pan of Rohallion*. How *Pan* was commissioned is a perfect example of the collaborative efforts that produced these big houses and gardens. When White was asked to recommend a sculptor he turned at once to his old friend Augustus Saint-Gaudens with whom he so often worked. Saint-Gaudens spoke up for his apprentice Frederick MacMonnies, then twenty-five years old and freshly returned from the Ecole des Beaux-Arts. MacMonnies's whimsical little bronze inspired a whole generation of garden statues—mischievous children and playful demigods. *Pan of Rohallion* was reproduced in many editions and even exists as a three-foot statuette in many suburban gardens today—but never again, after one single replica had been made, was he cast life-size. At "Rohallion" his lily pond ringed with roses was located at a driveway *rond-point* in front of the house. He disappeared during the garden's destruction and resurfaced in the Peacock Café in Manhattan. Today he stands, on loan from the Peacock, in the American Wing of the Metropolitan Museum of Art.[8]

Far Hills

The generations of the twenties and thirties went farther west, occupying and enlarging the white clapboard New Jersey farmhouses that had been built in the early nineteenth century. New houses and gardens were generally built in Colonial Revival style. Though Ellen Shipman designed a Spanish patio garden for the Evander B. Schleys in 1924, by that time she was making many more gardens in a simpler Colonial Revival style like the one she designed for Andrew Fowler in Peapack.

One Far Hills garden that had nothing to do either with Italian balustrades or white pickets was "Moggy Hollow," the brilliant rock garden begun in the 1930s by Leonard Buck. Buck was a mining engineer, and his first garden interest in his 50-acre property was aroused by the black basalt outcroppings scraped bare by the Wisconsin glacier on its retreat north 11,000 years ago. Buck and Zenon Schreiber, a German landscape architect and rock garden authority, sculpted twelve more rocky ledges, clearing away the thin soil and trap rock with dynamite and crowbar. Each has a name—one, Reno Rock, was so called because Helen Buck threatened divorce if Leonard did not stop blasting. Each ledge fits into the wooded landscape in a way artificial rock garden formations all too seldom do, and each provides a near-perfect habitat for those most prima-donnaish plants—alpines.

Only the most persevering and gifted gardener could create a 27-acre rock garden in a climate most alpines find inhospitable because of hot muggy summers and erratic snow cover. Buck succeeded by using alpine cultivars adapted to a lowland climate, and availing himself of the many lowland plants that are willingly planted in rocks. "Big Rock," the first tall rock face one passes on the descent into "Moggy Hollow," is a mass of rare dwarf rhododendrons, columbines, thymes, sedums, gentians, cranesbill geraniums, and pinks. All year long its shiny black surfaces are a foil for the soft gray foliage of *Arabis caucasica*.[9] He also made magnificent bog and water gardens filled with a collection of primroses, and hillsides embroidered with more rare rhododendrons and azaleas. Although Buck became an obsessive plant collector, the garden did not succumb to the one-of-this and one-of-that disease: it was a tapestry of plant colonies apparently thriving in native habitats just as they might in the wild. "Moggy Hollow" with its many plantings simplified is now open to the public as the Leonard J. Buck Gardens.

Princeton

Nothing could have been more different in atmosphere and intent from Ledyard Blair's remote mountain estate than Moses Taylor Pyne's equally beautiful and well-known "Drumthwacket." "Blairsden" was a retreat, while "Drumthwacket" was a royal court. Pyne, Princeton class of 1877, was the uncrowned king of town-and-gown, from 1890 to 1920, making and unmaking university presidents (Patton, Wilson, Hibben), running what could almost be called an extensive private university building program, and often making up annual deficits out of his own pocket. The gardens of "Drumthwacket," now the governor of New

Mrs. C. Chanler's rock garden blooms with iris—and reflections.

Mrs. Charles H. Stout's woodland path in New Jersey is planted with hosta and ferns. She was also the author of The Amateur's Book of the Dahlia *(1922).*

Pyne was instrumental in a process that was taking place all over the established Northeast and Middle Atlantic in the country place era: the challenge, and sometimes the dethronement, as here, of an older, often land-based, American social order:

an older [Princeton] resident remarked, disgruntled, there had been no "rich people" in Princeton before the Pynes came. The style of life of the well-to-do American gentry, already established in the seventeenth century and persistent really to the present, was elegant and comfortable, but it was not grandiose and extravagant on the European scale. Even the most splendid of Virginia plantations or Philadelphia country houses were modest compared with Blenheim or Petworth or most Continental palazzi, châteaux or Schlösser. During the nineteenth century, for the first time in history, there were more and more Americans rich enough to challenge the richest of Europeans. The Pynes were among these, and represented this new opportunity for conspicuous consumption as the Marquands, in Princeton at least, represented an older, traditional dispensation.[10]

Mrs. Wilson, Woodrow Wilson's wife, recognized the distinction. She wrote to a friend about her "morning at the Pynes with Mrs. Hibben. It was *all* so beautiful . . . but oh, the lotus flowers! Just think how we used to rave over *one* at the Marquand's—and then imagine hundreds, perhaps thousands in bloom at once."[11]

The lotuses and all the rest were presided over by Moses Taylor Pyne himself, with the occasional appearance of Mrs. Pyne, who was later known in her fey widowhood as "The White Queen" because of her habit of dress. In 1905 Pyne hired landscape architect Daniel Langton to make the Italian terrace garden with its marble balustrade, and an English picturesque woodland garden. There were rhododendron walks with winding paths, a marble temple of love, ponds, and a waterfall. There were also decorative livestock—peacocks, deer—an aviary with birds of

At "Constitution Hill" the Junius P. Morgans in Princeton employed Langton, who had also laid out "Drumthwacket," to make a smaller "Italian" garden, including terraces, flower parterres, and many statues.

Jersey's residence, were open to the public, like those of Versailles or any other royal residence. His grandfather, Moses Taylor, had made a fortune in Cuban sugar which he reinvested around mid-century, as so many other American moneymakers did, in banks and railroads. His father, Englishman Percy Rivington Pyne, married the boss's daughter and continued to make money. Moses Taylor Pyne himself married into an old Princeton family, the Stocktons, and settled in Princeton permanently in the nineties. At that time he was already a power in university politics. He summered in Bar Harbor and had his own *train*, not just his own car, in which to travel back and forth to New York City.

paradise, a zoo with monkeys, and Tudor farm buildings designed by Raleigh Gildersleeve, Pyne's architect.

There were other estate gardens in Princeton besides "Drumthwacket." "Edgerstoune" belonged to Pyne's sister and brother-in-law, Albertina and Archibald Douglas Russell. She was large and imposing; her husband, who was *not* a graduate of Princeton, was small and wizened. The house was definitely the biggest in Princeton, and there were not one, but two model farms on 275 acres. Russell's brother, of the New York firm of Clinton and Russell, designed the vast gray Tudor house whose piazza faced formal terraces to the west. Part of the garden was laid out like a beautiful forest. After "Drumthwacket," Russell's gardens were the most impressive in Princeton. Most distinguished of the Princeton gardens was "Guernsey Hall," the Marquand garden mentioned by Mrs. Wilson, whose grounds and house were designed by John Notman in the late 1840s. Yews, larches, cedars of Lebanon, horse chestnuts, red firs, and incense cedars were part of the gardenesque plantings, and one corner was preserved as a native woodland. Allan Marquand, who was professor of the history of art at Princeton, bought the towered sandstone house and its 40 acres in 1887, and had it enlarged in 1912 to accommodate his growing family. The architects were Cross and Cross of New York, whose partners were Mrs. Marquand's brothers.[12]

Notman also designed "Prospect," built for a Stockton connection in 1852, and home of the university president until the residence was moved to Lowrie House in 1968. When Woodrow Wilson became president, one of the first things Mrs. Wilson did was to toss out the cannas, geraniums, coleus, ageratum, and sweet alyssum that filled the long narrow plots of Notman's early Victorian bedding-out scheme, and call in Beatrix Farrand. She added a rose pergola, a central reflecting pool, and widened and joined the beds to form perennial borders, which she planted with pale-colored peonies and iris — "delicate to deepest rose, peach blossom and cream ... lavender, purple, straw-yellow, cream-yellow, rose and mauve"[13] — and many roses. Her successor, Mrs. Hibben, widened the range to make a Commencement-time display of delphinium, canterbury bells, sweet william, foxgloves, pansies, pinks, and forget-me-nots.

Princeton's "great house" for two hundred years before "Drumthwacket" had been "Morven," built by the Stocktons. The house itself was built in 1701, and the family hung on to it until 1957. The energetic Mrs. Baynard Stockton, who got to work in the gardens in 1901, seems to have been a passionate amateur garden restoration architect — the kind that makes present-day garden archeologists shudder. In the same fashionable revival spirit as Cornelia Horsford at "Sylvester Manor" — and with the same opportunity to remake an old garden — Mrs. Stockton replanted the old flower beds edged with box on the north side of the house using many "trophy plants" as was done at "Sylvester Manor": sweet williams from Walter Scott's Abbotsford, hollyhocks from Kew

The Moses Taylor Pynes' Italianate garden and an English park with a temple of love on the lake were designed by landscape architect Daniel Langton in 1905. F. Scott Fitzgerald must have been recalling "Drumthwacket" when he wrote in This Side of Paradise, *"poetry on spring afternoons in the gardens of the big estates near Princeton, while swans made effective atmosphere in the artificial pools, and low clouds sailed harmoniously above the willows."*

Gardens, and so on. Her plant list indicates what a sweet-smelling and old-fashioned garden "Morven" was: peonies, wisteria, lilac, weigela, honeysuckle, sweet shrub, meadow rue, and old roses like 'Harison's Yellow' and the damask rose.[14]

"Georgian Court" and "Shadow Lawn"

About as far as one can get from Princeton Colonial Revival good taste are "Georgian Court" and "Shadow Lawn." In these two New Jersey gardens for the first time one feels entire freedom from the straitjacket of New England conventions. They express a kind of marmoreal exuberance that eclipsed horticulture—the air smells of new millions unconfined.

In the 1880s and 90s Lakewood, New Jersey, enjoyed its brief heyday of fashion—Vanderbilts, Rockefellers, Astors, Rhinelanders, and even Oliver Wendell Holmes, William Cullen Bryant, Rudyard Kipling, and Mark Twain came to stay at the great shingle hotel in the sandy Jersey pine flats. It was advertised as a winter resort where the temperature was steadily twelve degrees warmer than New York. Twelve degrees must not have been enough: nobody stayed to build a cottage except for George Jay Gould, son of financier Jay Gould. In 1896 he hired Bruce Price to build "Georgian Court" on 200 acres in the pine forests next to a lake.

George Jay Gould was the financial manager of the Gould family's railroad millions after his father's death in 1892. (He was removed from this position for incompetence in 1919.) In 1884 he had married a beautiful young actress, Edith Kingdon. This raised few New York society eyebrows since it was felt almost anything could be expected of the

Shades of the Apollo Basin at Versailles! George Gould's birthday present to his wife, Edith, in 1902 at "Georgian Court" was sculptor John Massey Rhind's massive electrically powered version, complete with a changing light display. Gould's gardeners kept clear, for fear of electrocution.

children of the infamous Jay Gould. George and Edith had seven children. Though their professed first intention was to have a house and not a palace, "Georgian Court" soon became more than a pleasant country place in which to raise children: it became a dynastic statement and a bid for social recognition and respectability. In 1899 *Harper's Bazaar* called "Georgian Court" the finest country residence in America. In the same year, the Goulds held their first grand houseparty, to which came, among many others, Mrs. Stuyvesant Fish, the Philadelphia Drexels, and the Marquis de Talleyrand. Edith Gould played the heroine in Edith Wharton's play, "Twilight of the Gods."

Bruce Price's initial total construction budget of $70,000 was soon eclipsed by later expenditures such as the $250,000 needed to build "Bachelor's Court," one of the largest and most elaborate sporting casinos of the Gilded Age. Sport was serious for the Goulds, and they were good at it, finally winning social acceptance through their abilities: George Gould fielded international polo teams and footed the bill for America's Cup challengers. His son became the world's best tennis player.

The gardens, which exist in outline today, were also designed by Price. Formal "Italian" gardens run from an artificial inlet on the lake, known as "the lagoon," back to the casino. The low level of the lagoon is connected with the upper gardens by a branching marble staircase. Flower parterres that once held changing displays of annuals and perennials are laid out between the stables and the house. The hub that connects the two gardens is an immense fountain by John Massey Rhind, set in a white marble basin 60 feet in diameter. Besides the Rhind fountain, the garden is filled with fifteenth- and sixteenth-century marble vases, benches, and statues collected all over Europe by art dealer Sir Joseph Duveen, who advised Gould on all his art purchases. What the Goulds couldn't buy they had copied. Boni de Castellane, the Parisian exquisite and collector who married George Gould's sister, Anna, for her millions, could not get over the extraordinary mixture of works of art and cement funerary urns that dotted his brother-in-law's gardens. A lively—and hideous—birthday present for Edith from George is a giant wrought-iron eagle perched on a dragon on top of a pile of boulders. Gould arranged to buy it from the Paris Exposition Universelle of 1900. Still another gift was a one-acre Japanese garden complete with a real Japanese teahouse, laid out by Takeo Shiota, designer of the Japanese Garden at the Brooklyn Botanic Garden. "Georgian Court's" gardens are a collection of the best trophies, not a designed series of spaces.[15]

Hubert Templeton Parson, born in Canada in 1872, was F. W. Woolworth's handpicked successor in the five-and-dime business. Parsons in 1892 was "nineteen, eager, and ambitious ... a short, stocky, and somewhat swarthy young man: his large, heavy jaw suggested stubbornness and determination, and he carried his chin high with an air of hauteur. He had a rare gift for handling and ordering numbers, and a

The curving exedra of this garden at the Hubert Parsons' "Shadowlawn" in West Long Branch, designed by French landscape architect Achille Duchêne, was modeled after the famous Colonnade of Jules Hardouin-Mansart at Versailles.

photographic memory." No single kind word exists for Maysie Parson in any first-hand account. With her hair dyed copper and wearing lots of makeup, she is described as "awfully strict and changeable. And domineering, too.... And Parson would do anything for her. He would have torn the house down if she'd wanted it. *Absolutely!*"

They shared a kind of intractable social obliviousness. They just didn't need anyone else but themselves—and about $2 million a year of course. "Mrs. Parson and I don't care what people think. We're going to have what we want. And this is what we want," Parson once said. They did not want to take part in the life they so materially equipped themselves for. They went to Paris in summer, when all the Parisians were leaving town; in New York, though they had a box at the Opera, they never had parties, or schemed to be one of the "Four Hundred." Even their choice of a place to settle, Elberon, New Jersey, was an indicator of how little they cared about the social ladder. The resorts of the Jersey coast, Long Branch and Asbury Park being the best known, always limped along in a sort of sub-high-society limbo, never achieving the concentration of money, power, fashion, or exclusivity of Newport, or Bar Harbor, or the Hamptons.

The Parsons bought their 108-acre estate in 1918: a big, eccentric white house (designed in 1905 by a Chicago architect, Henri Edward Crégier) on a rolling lawn clumped with huge trees that fell gently to a lake. W. G. Eisele, a local nurseryman and gardener, had done the original landscaping. The Parsons added eight greenhouses, a two-story palm house, and had spent $1 million dollars to redecorate the house in the richest possible French gilt taste by the time it burned in 1927.

In 1928 the Parsons hired Horace Trumbauer, one of the gallery of early twentieth-century architects like F. Burral Hoffman and Addison Mizner, who built the palaces of the very rich. He had made a name for himself in Philadelphia, beginning in 1892, designing for Stotesburys, Drexels, Burdens, Belmonts, Goulds, Dukes, Wideners, Phippses, Clothiers, and Graces in places like Bar Harbor, Palm Beach, and Long Island. By 1928 his huge, correct—and often very beautiful—adaptations of classical French and English Georgian great houses had begun to seem too grand. Taste was turning to country house architects such as Delano and Aldrich whose work was less overwhelming. The Parsons' choice seemed almost reactionary, though perfectly in tune with their love of gilt and things French.

Trumbauer's chief designer and draftsman was Julian Abele, who had come to the firm in 1906. After Trumbauer had seen Abele's undergraduate architectural drawings from the University of Pennsylvania, he immediately agreed to pay all expenses for Abele's schooling at the Ecole des Beaux-Arts in Paris. Trumbauer then hired him on his return to the U.S. None of this would be remarkable except that Abele was black, and so became the first black to practice architecture professionally in the U.S.[16] Trumbauer, whose formal schooling stopped at the tenth grade, was an outsider too, the son of a poor salesman. It was a day when architecture was a "gentleman's profession," and Trumbauer and Abele were determined to succeed as well as any insider. This may well be why their work is never easy or playful—they were not able to rise above seriousness.

Achille Duchêne, the landscape architect of the second "Shadow

Lawn," was one of two remarkable Frenchmen who catered to the American palace trade. (Jacques Gréber was the other.) His father, Henri Duchêne, the scholar-artist who led the spirited late nineteenth-century reaction against the *jardin anglais*, restored a number of French gardens (Champs, Chaumont, Sully, Breteuil, among them), and was a correspondent of Frederick Law Olmsted's. The young Duchêne's broderie patterns had a lapidary sobriety. His sweeping allées, with their subtle changes of grade and level, were simultaneously intellectual and breathtaking. His garden architecture had a certain chilliness that suited Trumbauer's careful magnificence.

The Parsons must have been a heavy burden for three such classical perfectionists as Trumbauer, Abele, and Duchêne. Their clients insisted that the new house had to include many features the Parsons had loved about the first "Shadow Lawn," including a servants' wing stuck on at an odd diagonal angle to the body of the house. Parsons, financially prudent and a cool business head—his business was accounting after all—lost all control of his own expenditure on the place. The house and gardens were virtually complete, at a cost of $7.5 million in September, 1929, when Maysie announced she wanted an Aztec solarium on top of her French château. "The roof won't support it," said Trumbauer; "it's too much money" said Parson's accountant—but, "Mrs. Parson wants it," said Parson, so up it went. Work continued despite October 24, "Black Thursday," and the Parsons were ruined, marooned in their exquisitely designed French house, with its mostly marble garden attached to its side. "One must admire the expense more than the genius," said André Le Nôtre about the Colonnade designed by architect Jules Hardouin-Mansart at Versailles, the model for the Parsons' colonnade. So with Hubert and Maysie there is something to admire, but it is surely not genius.[17]

BELOW:
Mrs. Alfred Thornton Baker's garden at "Castle Howard Farm" (1863) in Princeton.

Students Photo Service

PENNSYLVANIA

NEW MONEY IN OLD PHILADELPHIA

Old Philadelphia felt the same way about Edward and Eva Stotesbury and "Whitemarsh Hall." Edward T. Stotesbury rose from office boy to become head of Drexel & Company, Philadelphia's most prestigious banking house, and a senior partner of J. P. Morgan & Co. During World War I, when J. P. Morgan was purchasing agent for the Allies, the profits of the firm were enormous. Stotesbury's share in 1915 and 1916 exceeded $7 million per year. He needed it. "Whitemarsh Hall" in Chestnut Hill, which broke ground in 1916, cost about $3 million by the most responsible estimate. Concurrently, Stotesbury had other large expenses. In 1915 he had begun the building of "Brooklands," a $1 million house in Baltimore as a wedding present for his stepdaughter, and in 1917 Addison Mizner started on "El Mirasol," the Stotesburys' Palm Beach winter palace. What had caused this frenzy of palace-building?

In 1910 at the age of sixty, Edward Stotesbury had fallen in love with and married Eva Cromwell, the beautiful forty-six-year-old widow of New York clubman and yachtsman Oliver Cromwell. Eva Cromwell made her new husband beamingly happy and changed his life entirely. Over the succeeding ten years, Stotesbury, small, dapper, keen-featured, and white-moustached, turned himself from discreet financier into the playboy of Bar Harbor and Palm Beach. To make a palace fit for his bride, Stotesbury employed Trumbauer and Jacques Gréber, landscape architect. Joseph Duveen, who was also J. P. Morgan's dealer, provided statues and vases for the garden. With taste and decisiveness Eva Stotesbury oversaw the building and furnishing of her palace from the gate lodge, which was finished first.

Jacques Gréber had already created the formal parterre gardens at "Harbour Hill" for Clarence Mackay, and had worked with Trumbauer at nearby "Lynnewood Hall" for Joseph Widener. His gardens at "Whitemarsh Hall" ran seamlessly from French parterre to English park as they extended from the house out into the wide Whitemarsh Valley farmland.[1] The garden began as terraces within the arms of the building, and continued down a five-hundred-foot-long *tapis vert* to a circular pool.

Surprise created gaiety. One passed from level to level, descending a curving staircase only to look up at a superb statue from a new angle. Everywhere water added the embroidery of sound and movement to the deliberately severe design. Lead putti spouted water in pools circled by flowers and dwarf boxwood taken from the gardens planted by Jerome Bonaparte at Woodbury, Maryland. A columned belvedere perched on the south corner of the top terrace. From the house loggia overlooking all, *The Four Seasons*, attributed to French Sculptor Pajou and purchased from a Versailles dealer in 1922, looked into the green distance.

The severity of the Henry R. Reas long lawn at Elizabethan-style "Farmhill" in Sewickley is softened by evergreen parterres which spill out onto the path as delicately as perennials.

Eva Stotesbury knew what she was getting—one of the most beautiful houses and landscapes in America. She wrote to Trumbauer, quoting a letter from a young American soldier in World War I who had returned to Paris from the trenches, and seen the Louvre again, "Heavens, there's no mistake about it being good to look at! What order, what concert, what rhythm! I am flooded in the harmony of it. I bathe myself, piously, in this silent music." She added, "I send you this because I know that, being your own creation, the house must mean even more to you than it does to me...."[2]

"Whitemarsh Hall" was opened with a party for all of Old Philadelphia in October, 1921. It was all too much for them. Although the Stotesburys were asked to join the Assembly in 1912, this was just too much money, too much open striving to be first rate. Society could not resist attending the Stotesburys' royal functions—they entertained an average of two hundred people every week for the eighteen years at "Whitemarsh Hall"—but society made fun of the Stotesburys. Even the style of the gardens was too much for Old Philadelphians. The characteristics of real Old Philadelphia gardening were understatement, the use of native stone, a lot of well-grown perennials, a cottage or Colonial Revival feeling—or even a touch, but only a discreet suggestion, of the Italian—all confined within what one Old Philadelphian refers to as a "nice scaled-down walled-type garden." "French design was for outsiders—it was not much liked," she continues.[3] ("French design" meant "palace style," because in fact a major Chestnut Hill style was Norman French, a Philadelphia suburban version of what Delano and Aldrich had done at Mrs. Benjamin Moore's in Muttontown.)

Landscape architect Jacques Gréber played optical tricks worthy of Le Nôtre at the Edward Stotesburys' "Whitemarsh Hall" outside Philadelphia: on the main drive, (upper left) the 700-foot-long gardens were hidden till the last, allowing an uninterrupted view of a perfect English country house in its home park, while from the house terrace the same view became French, as a long axial vista led up through the two circular fountains to the main gateway on the horizon.

The lower fountain in the gardens at "Whitemarsh Hall."

When the gardens of "Whitemarsh Hall" are mentioned, Jacques Gréber, "Jack Grabber," as first director of the Philadelphia Museum of Art, Fiske Kimball, said Philadelphians called him, is quickly pronounced "primarily a city planner." He *was* a great city planner who had been commissioned by Stotesbury to design the Franklin Parkway, which gave Philadelphia much needed circulation. But he was also a great landscape architect, designing magical gardens seen mainly by those who could not respond to their magic, gardens for palaces that the Depression would soon render obsolete. In 1938 Stotesbury died, two years before his money would have run out at the rate he was spending it. For another eight years, Eva Stotesbury lived on quite comfortably in Washington, D.C., on the proceeds of the sale of the estates and her jewels. In memory of her husband she gave the sculptures that had been one of the great ornaments of "Whitemarsh Hall" to Fiske Kimball at the Philadelphia Museum, where today Pajou's *Four Seasons* stand looking at each other instead of at the green horizon.

Elkins Park

Close to Chestnut Hill on the east was Elkins Park, country home of Philadelphia's new money after the Civil War. Financier Jay Cooke was among the first to arrive, building a huge mansard-roofed stone house called "Ogontz," after an Indian friend of his father's. The town was quickly also named Ogontz, which was not surprising given the fact that a common expression in America at the time was "as rich as Jay Cooke."[4]

By the turn of the century, Ogontz was an imposing suburb with houses of every description—over fifty by Horace Trumbauer alone, for example. Carrère and Hastings, Charles Platt, Ralph Adams Cram, and Frank Lloyd Wright all built houses there as well. Elkins Park, as Ogontz was again renamed after a still richer and more famous inhabitant,

P.A.B. Widener's brilliant French splendor by Trumbauer and Gréber at "Lynnewood Hall" in Elkins Park was not admired by Old Philadelphia: Too much! they said.

William Elkins, was where Trumbauer mastered his classical architectural vocabulary. His first comprehensive essay in the classical style was "Lynnewood Hall," P.A.B. Widener's 110-room house-cum-museum. Widener, a widower, and one of his two sons lived in the west wing, the other son and his family in the east, while his great collection of Old Masters, now in the National Gallery, was housed in the north wing. Built eighteen years before "Whitemarsh Hall," "Lynnewood Hall" was much more severe in style. After 1910 its severity was appropriately lapped on three sides in the most elaborate parterre embroidery Jacques Gréber could devise.

Chestnut Hill and Old Philadelphia

Sandwiched between "Whitemarsh Hall" and "Lynnewood Hall" lay Chestnut Hill, where Old Philadelphian Francis S. McIlhenny commissioned the eminent Philadelphia architectural firm of Mellor and Meigs (later Mellor, Meigs and Howe) to design a house and garden, named "Ropsley," in 1917. It was the antithesis of "Whitemarsh Hall" in every way.

"Ropsley's" site was 4 acres instead of 300. The spaces and the architectural ornament were exquisitely scaled to suit the small dimensions, so that even though there were two fountains, a gazebo, a tool shed, serpentine walls, and a swimming pool all on the same small piece of ground, the garden did not seem crowded. The site was a steep hill, and both house and garden had many changes in level, all strongly differentiated. There were "room" divisions which actually made the space seem larger: a small sunken flower garden, an entrance court, and a larger *tapis vert* rectangle. An aerial hedge of pleached linden trees running the length of the garden above the major retaining wall on the high side of the site, and the repetition of the same curve on the retaining wall, gate, niche, and porch door gave the garden unity. Various hedging materials were used: beech, hemlock, box. On one side there was a big view for breathing room.[5]

Architectural historian Holmes Perkins makes the point that until Chestnut Hill was developed (around 1915) Philadelphia's upper classes were still living in the city. They were used to asking much of small spaces, and architects like Mellor, Meigs and Howe accommodated themselves to their clients' requirements. Walled gardens on this scale can be found in other old coastal cities, such as Boston and Charleston.

Chestnut Hill was developed by the Woodward family beginning around 1915. It was essentially complete in the mid-thirties. The firm of McGoodwin, Gilchrist, Tilden, Register, and Pepper, all old Philadelphia names, were the principal architects. Two typical Chestnut Hill establishments were "Ballygarth," Mrs. B. Franklin Pepper's house and garden designed by the architectural firm of Willing and Sims in 1919, and the F. Corlies Morgan garden, redesigned in 1927 by Robert Wheel-

Pennsylvania

The intricate 4-acre garden of F. S. McIlhenney (1917) is typical of Old Philadelphia's Chestnut Hill gardens. The architectural shape of an aerial hedge of pleached lindens on the upper level is played off against the shape and void of an exedra fountain of native Pennsylvania stone. The garden, called "Ropsley," belonged to Mrs. Edgar Allan Poe at the time this lantern slide was made.

wright, who was professor of landscape architecture at the University of Pennsylvania, where he established set up the landscape program. The Pepper garden was stone dressed in green; the Morgan garden "architecture" was green with stone accents.[6]

PHILADELPHIA'S HORTICULTURAL HERITAGE

Philadelphia's list of horticultural credits is as long and old as Boston's, but much of what Philadelphia knew about plants and design stayed in Philadelphia. Philadelphians are not preachers. There is no Philadelphia triumvirate that compares to Olmsted, Platt, and Sargent in terms of national influence. But it had certainly been horticulturally sophisticated from the time of William Penn, who had five gardeners at "Pennsbury Manor"; Quaker John Bartram, America's first great naturalist; and William Hamilton, a landscape gardener and collector.

Philadelphia was the center of U.S. commercial horticulture throughout the nineteenth century, and its horticultural society is the oldest such society in continuous operation in the country (1827). The city had its equivalent to the Cambridge School for Women: The Pennsylvania School of Horticulture for Women. It was founded in 1910 by Jane Bowne Haines, and Beatrix Farrand laid out part of the campus. The

Garden Club of America was founded in Philadelphia in 1913. Until well into the nineteenth century, Philadelphia was what Penn hoped it would always be, "a green countrie towne."[7]

The Colonial Revival and Wilson Eyre

But the building of the Main Line railroad and the Philadelphia Centennial Exposition of 1876 probably have more to do with the Philadelphia estate garden story than William Penn. When the Main Line was run out to Berwyn, it opened up the towns of Haverford, Bryn Mawr, Villanova, Radnor, Devon, and others to upper-class suburban development on a larger scale than Chestnut Hill. Conceived as "farms," these estates were a nostalgic celebration of the colonial past. Philadelphia's Centennial Exposition celebrated 100 years of American independence. High Victorian gardening expertise and taste were well displayed in Horticulture Hall, a flamboyant conservatory featuring a fantastic collection of tropical exotics. But other exhibits—such as the New England kitchen, for example—were the first hints of the Colonial Revival movement, that nostalgic re-evaluation of the American past. It took time to take shape. Though McKim (who was a Philadelphian), Mead and White set right off for a New England sketching tour in 1877, it really took thirty years for an American vernacular style to become fashionable.

In Philadelphia the Colonial Revival meant something different than in New York, where the explosive growth of the city had destroyed most of the colonial past, or off the East Coast, where that past had not existed at all. Although the Colonial Revival added to the perceived worth of

George Sheaff's crenelated wall at "The Highlands" in Fort Washington was used for grapes when he built it in the 1820s. In the 1920s, owner Caroline Sinkler and architect Wilson Eyre used the wall, with its Gothic arch and terminal summer houses, as one of the focal points of the new garden.

Wallace Nutting spread the Colonial Revival gospel with such works as Pennsylvania Beautiful *(1924). His own garden, seen in his photograph, was in Framingham, Massachusetts. Morning glories cover the arbor.*

"American" gardens, Philadelphians, on the whole, already *had* their gardens. Because Philadelphians had lived continuously with the old, they tended to be less sentimental and grandiose. Wallace Nutting, ardent preacher of the Colonial Revival, manufacturer of knobby Colonial Revival furniture, photographer, and gardener, sums up the character of southeastern Pennsylvania architecture at the time, both the farmhouse models, and the new work. There is, he said in 1924, "a more careful attention to the harmonizing of dwelling with country landscape. There is a quieter tone and better taste generally manifest in this suburban district than we find in others. Furthermore, the stability and obvious attention of permanence conveyed by the Pennsylvania homesteads is most satisfying."[8] The big differences between Philadelphia and New England revival forms by such practitioners as Charles Platt and Stanford White were scale and material. Philadelphia estate buildings, for the most part, were smaller, their shapes were more

articulated, and stone was almost invariably the material. To modern eyes, these "farmhouse" designs, even though their asymmetry can seem contrived, look better than the large white frame boxes with pediments and porticos typical of the New England and the Southern Colonial Revival look.

Best of all the Philadelphia Colonial Revival architects was Wilson Eyre. Though he was born in Florence, Italy, in 1852, Wilson Eyre was himself an Old Philadelphian. He was educated in Florence, which surely affected his ideas of the importance of gardens in domestic architecture, then in Newport, Rhode Island, and then briefly at MIT. Eyre, like many other Philadelphia architects, designed and adapted old gardens as well as houses. In 1915 Miss Caroline Sinkler bought "The Highlands," located in Ambler, between Whitemarsh and Chestnut Hill. Built in 1796 by statesman Anthony Morris, "The Highlands" had a garden with 2 fanciful Gothic garden houses connected by a crenelated garden wall. By 1915 "The Highlands" was overgrown. Wilson Eyre and Caroline Sinkler laid out a new garden incorporating the old trees, the wall, and old boxwood on the site. Like "Sylvester Manor" on Long Island, begun in the 1650s and revamped by an early twentieth-century owner, "The Highlands" garden was a simple rectangular enclosure of about 2 acres. Each of the four sections had a different character—a boxwood garden in one, fruit trees in another, and different arrangements of perennial beds. Eyre's architectural additions—turreted tool and wood sheds, another wall at the end of the garden screening the greenhouse, and a curved exedra as a resolution for the cross axial view—gave Miss Sinkler's garden a grander air than Miss Horsford's home-designed rose arches and balustrades, but the two were very similar in their romantic yet sensitive approach to an old place. Today the garden is a ruin again, but heroic efforts are being made to restore it by The Highlands Historical Society. Two other Philadelphia gardens comparable to "The Highlands" are the Biddle family's "Andalusia," now open to the public,[9] and James Morris and his sister, Lydia's, "Compton," now named the Morris Arboretum.

Thomas Sears

Not many old places had been as grand as "The Highlands." The Isaac Clothiers' "Sunnybrook" was an old house in Radnor where Philadelphia landscape architect Thomas W. Sears laid out the gardens running uphill in three levels behind the house. On the second level the garden house at the end of the walk doubled as a tennis pavilion overlooking the court below. Sears was a prolific landscape architect who also worked in Maryland, and as far south as North Carolina and Palm Beach. His work ran to moderate-sized enclosure gardens—definitely not palace gardens. Often his designs were for old houses, where he comfortably worked out the problems of changing levels and living terraces, and incorporated such things as swimming pools using low stone walls and shallow, often curving, steps, and mixed shrub and perennial plantings. He was tactful, charming, and quick-witted: asked which was his favorite garden of all he had designed, he diplomatically answered, "My own!" It was not the most dramatic or extensive of his gardens (that was probably "Reynolda" in Winston-Salem), since it was simply a shallow sunken flower garden rectangular in shape, set apart by screens of trees from his house in Ardmore on the Main Line, but his answer certainly kept him out of trouble with his clients.[10]

MAKING NEW FARMSTEADS: MELLOR, MEIGS, AND HOWE

There were nowhere near enough old farmhouses to go round, and firms like Mellor, Meigs and Howe were kept busy building country pleasances like Arthur Newbold's "Laverock Farm," set on 90 acres overlooking the Whitemarsh Valley, with a goose pond, and a *potager,* set among the extensive boxwood-edged gardens surrounding the stone house. Comfort was as much a part of a gentleman's country farm as farm atmosphere. Arthur Meigs had strong ideas about the connections between house and garden. Making a complete break with a cherished American tradition, he writes in a monograph on the Newbold house in 1925, "The best kind of porch is no porch at all."[5] Instead, he advocates open terraces on all sides of the house, each shaded in turn by the house walls as the sun moves. The Newbold house had five places to sit outside, each good for a certain season or time of day. Meigs continues,

As a rule, we only have one house and one bed, and when it rains or gets cold, or when night falls, we have to go to that house and to that bed willy nilly, but if we have built ourselves a summer house with rustic posts with the bark on that collect the worms from near and far . . . have covered it with a tangled mass of honeysuckle, harboring all the flying insects that bite and sting . . . if we have to duck our heads upon entering, and beads of perspiration start forth upon our brow from the heat and smothered air contained in our darling project . . . we come out from our summer house—or rather we never go in.

Meigs goes on to say that the best summerhouse is a chair dragged out on the lawn in the shade of the trees.[11]

Outsiders Get In

Not *all* Old Philadelphian gardens were designed by Philadelphians— occasionally Charles Platt, Ellen Shipman (though she hardly counts, being a Biddle), Beatrix Farrand, Marian Coffin, and the Olmsted Bros. got a toe in the door.[12] In 1915 Charles Platt and Ellen Shipman did a wonderful brick-walled formal garden for the Isaac Tatnall Starrs in Chestnut Hill, which was a departure point for a long woodsy circuit walk that led down through a glen, past an outdoor theater, along an iris walk to a little garden house, and up again through a woodland full of ferns, trilliums, and lady's-slippers.[13] Platt and Olmsted Bros. worked together

In 1901 industrial engineer Frederick W. Taylor bought historic "Boxly" in Chestnut Hill, with its overgrown box garden dating to 1813. Taylor devised a machine to move the enormous bushes, which by 1938 were to be 10 feet high and 15 feet wide.

on the rather un-Philadelphian W. Hinckle Smith's "Timberline" in Bryn Mawr, with its wall fountain and large elaborately shaped central pool full of lotus[14] and Olmsted Bros. also laid out the splendid formal gardens and *patte d'oie* woodlands of George McFadden's "Bloomfield," designed by Trumbauer and completed in 1923. Olmsted Bros. also moved the box at "Boxly" in Chestnut Hill—one of the earliest successful instances of what was later to become almost a commonplace, as huge box bushes, mostly from down-at-heel Virginia plantations, traveled up the East Coast to new gardens. "Ancient boxwood," as it seems invariably to have been called, became a strange estate garden fetish, conferring ancestry and dignity almost as certainly as family portraits.[15]

"Allgates"

Mary Helen Wingate Lloyd was the gardener every gardener would like to be: she spent hours in her garden herself, *but* she also had a large staff. And what a toolshed she had—the handles of her garden tools were painted blue-green so no one else would use them; the potting table was mounted on hospital casters so it could be trundled outside; and her own wheelbarrow was made of wicker, for lightness in the days before aluminum.

Mrs. Lloyd painted—and she saw her garden with a painter's eye for color; she read, and she wrote regularly and well for The Garden Club of America *Bulletin.* Born in Brooklyn, as a young woman she was involved

The most famous feature of Helen Wingate Lloyd's garden at "Allgates" in Haverford was the iris bowl, three rings of plantings descending to a tiled blue pool. Iris bowls were not uncommon in the twenties, but usually only the largest gardens could afford to devote so much space to plants that performed for just a few weeks. This enormous collection was inspired by a single corm that Helen Wingate brought with her from her childhood home when she married.

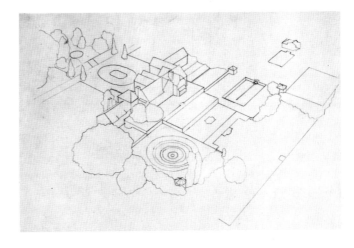

RIGHT:
A sketch of "Allgates" reveals its Beaux-Arts planning in terraces and balanced progression of enclosures. The iris bowl is at lower left.

Pennsylvania

in women's suffrage and birth control movements at the turn of the century. Intellectually curious, humorous, independent, and liberal, she was once described by a friend as *plein d'envergure*—like a ship under full sail—though she did not sail through life like a "garden lady" caricature out of a Beverley Nichols novel.

Mrs. Lloyd had three rented gardens before "Allgates," which was started in 1910. In her first, "The Yellow Box," she says, "the only thing I knew how to plant was my own foot!" The two narrow borders were filled with gifts from friends that made a screech of color—golden glow (orange-yellow), bergamot (dark red), and pink phlox—a far cry from her later subtle color combinations. In her second she began with a border 75 by 4 feet that, five years later, had stretched to 125 by 10 feet. At "Allgates," Wilson Eyre made the plans for the long creamy plaster house, sheltered by a hillcrest and facing southwest into a farm valley below. Though big, it was unpretentious and irregular; eventually, vines covered it so completely that it lay on the hillside like some great shaggy companion for the garden. Philadelphia ironworker Samuel Yellin made the gates (Julian Abele's brother, an architectural draftsman and designer, was one of his craftsmen). To the north, the house was anchored by the largest cherry tree, *Prunus avium,* in the region, and to the south by a native woodland—tulip poplar, oak, hickory, ash, sour gum, sassafras, spicebush, and all the other trees of the American forest. Mrs. Lloyd later made a primrose path through this wood that completed the circuit of the garden. Plantations of narcissus were enriched every year by the spent bulbs forced for the continuous house displays. The house was pierced by a view that signaled the presence of a great garden: it promised everything and revealed no secrets. There was nothing but grass, blue hills, and sky—and a step leading off into nowhere. The garden lay below. Mrs. Lloyd called on professional help to carry out her plans, but "Allgates" is clearly not an "H. Horace Sellers garden" (he made the general plan in 1919), or a "Vitale, Brinckerhoff and Geiffert garden" (Alfred Geiffert later laid out a rock garden in a nearby abandoned quarry). Here seems to be one of the rare true cases where Mummy *really* did do it all.[16]

PITTSBURGH

In Pittsburgh, far inland in Pennsylvania, the climate was rugged for gardening, but where the Joneses and Laughlins and Phippses and Snyders and Fricks and Byers and Hunts and Mellons and Heinzes lived, there *were* going to be gardens, somehow. Trees and shrubs, especially rhododendrons grew very well, however, and in 1829, Mrs. Trollope, who liked practically nothing about America, wrote about her tour in the Alleghenies, "the whole of this mountain region is a garden. The almost incredible variety of plants, and the lavish profusion of their growth produces an effect perfectly enchanting."[17]

Perhaps the best in-town garden (attached to the largest house yet built in Pittsburgh, in 1909) was that of R. B. Mellon, second youngest of the five sons of Thomas Mellon. (The youngest was Andrew, Harding's secretary of the Treasury and founder of the National Gallery.) R. B. Mellon's wife, Jennie King, was no stranger to grand gardens since she had grown up in Pittsburgh at "Baywood," a High Victorian house standing on a suite of terraces, now part of Highland Park. In 1909 Richard Beatty Mellon was president of the Mellon Bank, *the* merchant banking firm in a burgeoning industrial city. His sixty-room brownstone house was built by Alden and Harlow in the Tudor style, and had an octagonal Gothic crenelated tower. The 10-acre lot was surrounded by a big iron fence. Dark tapestry brick terraces, which still exist today, were topped with red terra-cotta balustrades and filled with boxwood parterres cut in emblematic shapes. There were marble pools and statues, and much garden furniture. Pittsburgh historian James van Trump, remembering the gardens from his childhood, writes "At the height of their cultivation, the Beechwood Boulevard terraces gave supremely an impression of crowded and intricate splendor unrivaled in Pittsburgh." Until the twenties, the rest of the 10 acres was a sweep of lawn with specimen trees in good nineteenth-century gardenesque fashion. There was also a tiny Japanese garden and just inside the tall polished granite gates was the oddly positioned kitchen garden. Maybe there wasn't enough sun anywhere else.[18] In the mid-twenties, Mrs. Mellon called on Ferruccio Vitale's firm to make a Renaissance garden—mostly stone, green, and water—at the end of the lawn behind the house. The work was done in concert with American sculptor Edmond Amateis, who carved the pink granite fountain and the three bronze figures in the wall niches. (Amateis's other garden sculptures include *The Four Seasons* for Mrs. R. R. McCormick in Chicago, and pieces for gardens on Long Island and in Cincinnati.[19]) A high society event that took place in the Renaissance garden was the marriage of the Mellons' only daughter, Sarah Cordelia, to Alan Magee Scaife in November, 1927. "It was certainly the most glamorous wedding ever held in Pittsburgh," says van Trump. The garden was enclosed with a $100,000 tent that held a "lake" made of mirrors and a "sky" filled with stars. The tent did triple duty: reception, wedding breakfast, dance—and was then judged so successful it was left up for that year's Hunt Ball, which always took place in November after the Rolling Rock Races. Most town houses and their gardens during the late Victorian period were built in the same district as the Mellons', the "Millionaire's Row" of the East End. The Mellons' 10 acres was not unusual.

Henry Clay Frick owned "Clayton," a house built in the 1870s and enlarged in the early 1890s. It was surrounded by 4 acres of picturesque grounds with a conservatory (1897, by Lord and Burnham) and a playhouse (1897, by Alden and Harlow). When Carnegie Steel was sold in

1901, many of the bigger players, Carnegie's partners such as Phipps and Frick, cashed in their Pittsburgh chips and left for a building spree in the East. In 1902 Frick started to summer in Pride's Crossing, Massachusetts, where he built "Eagle Rock" in 1906, and he rented an apartment in New York City. Although he hung on to "Clayton" (his daughter Miss Helen Clay Frick would eventually inherit it), his life thereafter was led mainly on the East Coast. The Morgan/Carnegie takeover had the same kind of heady effect on estate life as did the death of Commodore Vanderbilt.

Sewickley

Pittsburgh's upper-class exodus to the suburbs began as a search for sport and summer homes away from the dirt and heat of the increasingly industrial city. Some, including the Mellons, went east to Fox Chapel and to Ligonier for a sporting life with the Rolling Rock Hunt, but most went west, primarily to Sewickley. Henry Oliver, discoverer of the Mesabi iron range in northern Minnesota, and B. F. Jones, one of the founders of the Jones and Laughlin Steel Corporation, had started the fashionable retreat by buying the plateau above Allegheny City, much closer to the city than Sewickley.

Oliver and Jones "colonized" Sewickley Heights by buying two large adjacent farms as summer places. "Fair Acres," B. F. Jones, Jr.'s stone house by Hiss and Weeks, known locally as "Buckingham Palace," had a notable garden.[20] The village of Sewickley itself had been a Pittsburgh

In autumn, cascade chrysanthemums fell like lace veils in the hall of the Henry Reas' "Farmhill" in Sewickley. At right, a ceramic Pekingese sits by his bowl of fresh water.

summer colony as early as the 1870s. By the turn of the century, Sewickley Heights had the most magnificent gardens in the Pittsburgh area. "Farmhill" was created by Mrs. Henry Rea, Henry Oliver's daughter, who built a house on her father's summer place in 1898. Another was "Newington," now the garden of J. Judson Brooks, a descendent of the original Revolutionary War grant holder. The Reas' ninety-nine-room rambling Elizabethan house was covered with ivy, and stood on a 250-acre tract entirely surrounded by stone walls. The gardens stretched in all directions across the hill on which the house was located and included a water garden, rose garden, arbors, a wishing well, and curving stairs, and many statues as well as other shrub borders — all typical features of an estate garden.[21]

There was no ornamental garden as such at eighteenth-century "Newington"; in the 1870s landscape architect Samuel B. Parsons (1819–1906) created the front "park" with its undulating lawn and immense trees. Parsons, later the superintendent of Central Park, designed a number of other Pittsburgh gardens. He also made the intricate rose garden, though the English boxwood, which does not like Pittsburgh winters, was later replaced with Korean box. In 1906, Buffalo-based Bryant Fleming (1876–1946) revised the Parsons plan, and a terrace was laid across the front of the house. At "Newington," where the gardens are in perfect shape, the many paths, allées, and lawns are edged with rare cultivars and with Judson Brooks's own hybrids, as well as the big natives.

OTHER PENNSYLVANIA GARDENS

In Western Pennsylvania in 1910, at steel industrialist Charles Schwab's estate, "Immergrun," Charles Wellford Leavitt turned the plan of the Villa Farnese at Caprarola upside down and made it about four times bigger. The canephora (statues bearing vases on their heads) were at the bottom of the cascade in plain view, silhouetted against the broad Pennsylvania farm landscape. No longer mysterious and secluded in the isolation of a small space at the top of a hill as they are at Caprarola, they were instead strangely in the open, their verticality underscored by the many pillar-like American red cedars planted around them. The cascade plantings exhibited the same Italian/American pairing: a *catena d'acqua* was surrounded by bosquets of American white pine. Below, the garden flattened out into a 600-foot-long rectangle finished with a semicircular pergola at each end.[22]

Gifford and Cornelia Pinchot at "Grey Towers"

Two generations of Pinchots made their summer home at "Grey Towers," in Milford, Pennsylvania, just below Port Jervis, New York, where Pennsylvania and New Jersey meet at the Delaware River. James Pinchot made a fortune in New York City in the wallpaper business, and then, like Charles Schwab, came back to his birthplace to create his family seat.

At "Grey Towers" in Milford, former governor Gifford Pinchot lunches with friends at "The Fingerbowl," a "dining table" designed by architect William Lawrence Bottomley after examples seen in Renaissance gardens.

James Pinchot was a typical late-nineteenth-century civic-minded New Yorker. He was a founder of the Museum of Natural History and of the National Academy of Design, and one of the organizers of the first model Tenement Association in the United States. His circle included actor Edwin Booth, artists such as Sanford Robinson Gifford and Frederic Edwin Church, and poets and politicians like William Cullen Bryant, James Roosevelt, and John Jay. He was a mainstay of the American Forestry Association as early as 1875, and it was he who encouraged one of his two sons, Gifford, in the direction of conservation and forestry. Architect Richard Morris Hunt was also a friend, so it was natural that Pinchot turned to him for the design of "Grey Towers." Many years later, Hunt's son and Gifford Pinchot worked together with Frederick Law Olmsted and *his* son, John Charles, at George Vanderbilt's "Biltmore" in North Carolina.[23]

Gifford Pinchot grew up in a summer swarm of interesting visitors and country activity in the big French château made of Pennsylvania bluestone. He spent twenty years in the scientific practice of forestry, battling it out in Washington with the lumber barons at a time when the doctrine of laissez-faire was America's religion. He became Teddy Roosevelt's chief forester, and was the first to make the U.S. Forest Service a body to reckon with. He was dismissed in 1910 in a hailstorm of acrimony, broken friendships, and accusations of treachery. Gifford Pinchot was absolutist and uncompromising, a public servant who believed he always knew best—yet there *were* 193 million acres in national forests that hadn't been there when he started.

After 1910 he made "Grey Towers" his permanent residence, and became governor of Pennsylvania for two nonconsecutive terms. In 1908, he married the redoubtable red-headed Cornelia Bryce. She was the daughter of New York congressman, publisher, and politician Lloyd Bryce, second owner of "Clayton" on Long Island. A dedicated feminist in the superwoman mold, she believed that a woman "can bear children, charm her lovers, boss a business, swim the Channel, stand at Armageddon and battle for the Lord—all in the day's work!" After women got the vote, she moved on effectively to sweatshops, birth control, child labor abuse, and a whole roster of other social concerns. Cornelia Pinchot included among her many friends architects like Delano and Aldrich, journalists such as Herbert Croly, and politicians and socialites like Theodore Roosevelt and Victor Astor. Wife of a Republican governor, she openly supported the New Deal, and long after her husband's death she continued to be active in public affairs.

The Pinchots added constantly to the garden at "Grey Towers" between 1915 and 1935. When Cornelia arrived to take over her parents-in-laws' Victorian castle, she described what she saw as "a huge towered Camelot set on the side of a treeless stony hill, with the usual French dislike of shade, inherited from a Gallic ancestor." Terraces and a walled garden had been scrabbled out of the hillside beside the house, but the situation was essentially the same as "Naumkeag's"—a big house perched uncomfortably on a ledge. Cornelia Pinchot set about creating the illusion of flat land by pushing out more terraces and making compartment gardens. She took inspiration from the walled flower gardens of England, French allées and parterres, and Italian stone and green gardens. She planted well and extensively, and added several garden buildings, notably the "Letter Box," which served as Governor Pinchot's office. In 1928 Chester Aldrich built one of the most attractive features of the gardens when he pushed a big semicircular terrace out across the steep drop of the east lawn. Immediately below the necessary retaining wall was placed a semicircular "moat" filled with water lilies. The wall above was hung with vines, and topped with urns.[24]

Pinchot himself also made improvements to the landscape, practicing what he preached by planting trees. The landscape itself gradually became the focus of "Grey Towers," rather than the monumental house. The change reflects the difference between the unabashed grandeur of the late 1880s and the more sequestered style of the twenties. "Grey Towers" is now a National Historic Landscape open to the public.[25]

DELAWARE

"Longwood"

Just short of the Delaware border but still in Pennsylvania, is the first of the great du Pont gardens, "Longwood." It is not strictly true to say "first du Pont garden," since, in 1906, when Pierre du Pont bought the Pierce house and its towering late eighteenth-century private arboretum to save the rare specimen trees from a sawmill fate, du Ponts had been making gardens around Wilmington since the eighteenth century. The first du Pont garden belonged to the first du Pont in America, Eleuthère. It sat behind his 1803 house at the gunpowder mills on the Brandywine. A small square garden, it is French in feeling, but French as in *potager*, not *parterre*. Cordons of pears, a grape arbor, and squares of mixed flowers and vegetables define its rustic character.[1]

However, "Longwood," famous for its incomparable conservatory and its fountains, was the first of the great twentieth-century du Pont garden showplaces. "Nemours," begun by Alfred du Pont in 1909, is an American Beaux-Arts classical garden, full of vistas, tonsured hedges, and Carrara "sugar marble" statues. Henry Francis du Pont, a gardener's gardener, took on the management of his father's "Winterthur" in 1914. In the twenties, his sister, Louise, and her husband, Francis Crowninshield, began their garden at "Eleutherian Mills," the only garden built entirely as a ruin in America. Its classical "remains" stand on the ruins of the original du Pont gunpowder mills below Eleuthère's house. All four of these gardens are now open to the public.

Because there are so many du Ponts, there is always a du Pont to talk to about family gardens—and family gardeners. "Pierre loved beauty but he didn't know horticulture," is how one du Pont in her seventies sums up the builder of "Longwood."[2] What he was most fascinated by was water displays, and there are three at "Longwood." He cut his teeth on the Open Air Theater, constructed in 1913. Pierre du Pont's fascination with fountains might have begun in Philadelphia in 1876, where the fountains at Horticultural Hall, he said, made an indelible impression on him. Doubtless the *théâtre d'eau* at Versailles, where the water displays are the show, was also lurking somewhere in his head, since at "Longwood" seven jets, whose colors and heights are electrically controlled, stand right on stage. The Open Air Theater is unusual among American garden theaters because it has such a public character and was so clearly intended for use. American garden theaters, like English Georgian ones, were generally strictly private and peopled only by the imagination. Their use was evocative, not practical. Occasionally they were used for musical performances or for amateur theatricals by energetic house parties. However, some examples in the South and in California, such as "Vouziers" in Missouri, and "El Mirador" in Santa Barbara were as large as "Longwood" and as public.

Pierre du Pont's second waterworks came out of a European trip in 1925, when he returned, inspired by the water gardens he had seen, such as those at Vaux. He drew up the plans and computed grades, water flow, and circulation for his own new fountains in his "Italian" water garden. But du Pont dreamed of still larger fountains, fountains that would play hundreds of variations and change color almost as many times. In 1928 he began regrading the farmfields that lay in front of the main conservatory. Three years and $560,000 later, just as the Depression was deepening, the grand opening of the electric fountains was held in the great pear-shaped basin. This time du Pont drew on his recollections of the Court of Honor at the Chicago World's Fair in 1893 as well as on European memories of Versailles and the Villa d'Este, as usual "incorporating into his final plan the best features of all these" in a typically eclectic American way.[3] At full spout, 10,000 gallons per minute shoot up into the air. Unusually, the plantings were done first by the Roslyn, Long Island, firm of Lewis and Valentine, and the canals were laid out to follow the long lines of boxwood and maples instead of vice versa. Today, despite the astounding conservatory collections, it is still du Pont's fountain fantasies that catch the public's imagination.

"Nemours"

In the thirties, at "Nemours," named after the du Pont ancestral home in north-central France, "young Alfred (Alfred Victor) had the bit between his teeth," according to another du Pont who prefers a more Philadelphian style of garden to the French opulence of "Nemours." (Du Pont's taste is by no means homogenized behind the bland familial facade.) "He became an architect, or let's say, a landscape dabbler," she continues, "and Big Alfred [his father, A. I. du Pont, the builder of "Nemours" in 1909] just told him 'Make it marvelous, make it great.'"[4] Alfred Victor and his partner, Beaux-Arts-trained architect and artist Gabriel Massena, were partners in a small gentlemanly Wilmington architectural firm from 1929 to 1940. Beginning in 1929, their "Nemours" additions included a sunken garden, an oriental garden, an English rock garden, and a temple of love in which stood a *Venus* by the renowned eighteenth-century French sculptor Houdon. These were merely additions to the axial gardens that already surrounded the well-proportioned pink stucco Louis XVI house designed by Carrère and Hastings. Thomas Hastings and "Big Alfred" were responsible for the original garden design. Unusually, there was no professional landscape architect; Thomas Hastings himself acted as supervising contractor, and was responsible for all the drawings and blueprints of the garden, and for the design, or purchase, of many garden ornaments. Hastings was an ardent and well-versed Francophile, and "Nemours" certainly gave him

The "Italian" Water Garden at the Pierre du Ponts' "Longwood" was not copied from a particular European model but its flat geometric pattern certainly seems more French than Italian. Cool, green, and secluded, it is set in the distant northeast part of the garden, once a mosquito-ridden swamp. When all the fountains are playing, they use 4,500 gallons of water a minute.

The startling formal garden in front of the William du Ponts' stately portico includes, clockwise from twelve o'clock, a stirrup, a saddle, a hunting horn, a crop, a snaffle bit, and a spur, appropriate garden motifs for a place with its own private racetrack, at left.

Alfred I. du Pont's "Nemours," designed by Carrère and Hastings (1909), faces a giant colonnade, which was dedicated to the first du Ponts and added later, in the twenties, by A. I.'s son, Alfred Victor.

his chance at a French garden. The simple and elegant series of large turf steps and limestone urns that heads downhill from the house were his idea, for example. The plantings range from traditional French parterres, bedded-out with large areas of one or two varieties, to The Four Borders, about one-sixth of a mile in total of perennials supplemented with annuals for continuous color. Between the two axes, and culminating and surrounding the long vistas, are lawns with naturalized plantings of trees and shrubs. Horticulturally, "Nemours" is not very interesting; it is architecture set in greenery.

Alfred I. du Pont had built "Nemours" almost as an act of defiance when he divorced his first wife and married his cousin and lover, Alicia Bradford, who had also divorced her husband. Two divorces were just too messy for the du Ponts in 1907 and A. I. was pressed to get out of the family business. He refused, and instead built "Nemours," surrounded by 9-foot-tall walls topped with broken glass, which, A. I. reportedly said, were "to keep out intruders, mainly by the name of du Pont." After Alicia's

death in 1920, Alfred at once married a pretty school teacher, Jessie Ball, whom he had been visiting on hunting trips to her family's Virginia farm since the turn of the century. There was a vast difference in style between Alicia and Jessie. Jessie Ball relished grandeur, and much of the flashier pomp and circumstance that crept over "Nemours," both inside and out, was due to her. She was the kind of woman who, on her first day's fishing at a Maine camp, reportedly appeared in white gloves and diamonds.[5] A. I. knew how to please her: he commissioned a sculpture group for the sunken garden from Henri Crenier called *Achievement, or, What Man Can Do if He Has an Excellent Partner*. It depicts a man with an uplifted torch and a woman, both crowned with laurels. Originally, they were covered with 24-carat gold leaf; today, it's just plain gilt. The very grand colonnade—too big for the house—also dates to Jessie Ball's reign. It is just this dash of Mad King Ludwig scale and mood that distinguishes "Nemours" from the other half-dozen well-bred, finely proportioned French palaces of the period.

"Winterthur"

Nothing could have differed more from "Nemours" than "Winterthur," surely the biggest and best "natural" garden in America and the equal of Bodnant and Exbury Gardens, greatest of the English woodland gardens. Nearly 1,000 acres of meadows and woodland include 200 acres of display gardens, which are laid out with a wide variety of exotic plantings mixed with natives to look as if they had all sprouted naturally. H. F. du Pont never used large blobs of vivid color, says garden historian Valencia Libby; his harmonies were impressionistic hazes of small flowers interspersed with a lot of green. Nor was he the kind of plant collector who fell for novelty alone; he planted for form and color. Harry du Pont had decorated his room at Groton with potted plants at the age of fourteen; he then studied ornamental horticulture at Harvard's Bussey Institute. Though his formal horticultural education was cut short by the death of his mother—he came home "to housekeep for his father" as he put it—he traveled a great deal, seeing all the great gardens of Europe with an eye to the day he would inherit "Winterthur."[6] The year that he did so, 1928, he engaged his sister Louise's friend, landscape architect Marian Coffin, to make some garden improvements, and the two worked together on "Winterthur" almost until her death in 1957. Through Louise he also became part of the Arnold Arboretum network at that time, and two great specimens of Sargent's cherry flourish at "Winterthur" as testimony.

At "Winterthur" it is possible to trace American garden styles, beginning with the formal terraces that were part of the du Ponts' original 1839 landscape. At the turn of the century, H. F. began replacing the Victorian borders in his mother's enclosed garden near the house with Gertrude Jekyll's color harmonies. Over the years, he sought plants that could withstand Delaware's hot humid summers, kept exhaustive plant lists, and achieved every gardener's dream of having continuous color in the borders from May to October. As he grew as a gardener, though he never abandoned the formal garden, he turned his attention to moving those same color harmonies out into the woodlands and meadows. His first effort at naturalized gardening was the March Walk, a woodland which he planted with narcissus in 1902. H. F. was willing to wait for just the right plant for years. In 1920 he began his azalea woods, placing creamy yellow corydalis near pale Korean rhododenron, *R. mucronulatum* 'Cornell Pink'. Years later, he added hellebores that had the same tinge of pink, and in the sixties, when preeminent American rock gardener Lincoln Foster presented him with *Primula abschasica*, H. F. used its tiny bright sparks of color as underplanting to perfect his thirty-year-old pink and yellow harmonies.[7]

Thoughtful, solitary, remote, perfectionist, courteous, rigid—and a passionate lover of beauty—H. F. du Pont was more relaxed in his gardens than he was anywhere else. There, the lushness, profusion, and

H. F. du Pont and Louise, his sister, both destined to be great gardeners, stand outside "Winterthur House" long before it became a museum of decorative arts.

Marian Coffin's plan of the gardens immediately surrounding "Winterthur." The overall design, the work of both Coffin and H. F. du Pont, evolved constantly from 1928 through the 1960s.

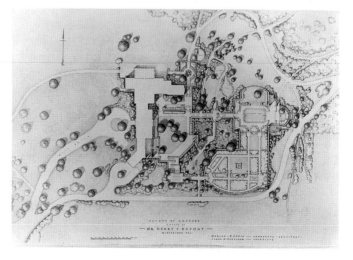

naturalness of the plantings indicated another side of his character. But inside "Winterthur" life was tightly formal. There was a liveried staff right on up through the sixties, and a strict formula for doing everything, including arranging flowers. Cut flowers were brought into the house in bunches tied with string and placed in containers; then the strings were cut and how the flowers fell was how they stayed. Harry and Louise du Pont Crowninshield had been the only children to survive of seven. For both, wanting to be outside, to be away from their father, the dictatorial Colonel Henry Algernon du Pont, encouraged an appreciation of the natural landscape. The outdoors gave them the escape hatch many other rich children found "below stairs." Jay Cantor calls their version of "Upstairs, Downstairs," "Inside, Outside."[8] Hardly coincidentally, they both became great gardeners.

"Eleutherian Mills"

In 1900, Louise married her Marblehead yachtsman, Francis Boardman Crowninshield, descendent of a great Boston mercantile family, and the typical round of foreign travel and seasonal resorts began for the young couple. In 1923, the Colonel coaxed Louise to spend more time in Delaware with the gift of "Eleutherian Mills," the old house on the Brandywine—given to her on condition that she would always pass the spring and fall in Delaware. Winters were Boca Grande, Florida, and summers, Massachusetts.

What she and Frank Crowninshield created is one of the great, original gardens of America, and all the more unusual for being a true joint effort. Not that Frank and "Dear Pussy," as he called her, weren't competitive—they were. Once she presented him with a superb copy of Luigi Dami's *The Garden*, inscribed with the following: "To the world's greatest living classical landscape architect—from the other."

Considering that in 1923 the three-story dormered stone buildings of the saltpeter refinery were still standing on the cluttered industrial site, what imagination and daring it took to knock them down and start a garden! Beginning in 1924, the foundations of the mills were transformed into five terraces, with pools created by flooding the basements of the mill houses. Huge iron saltpeter kettles, modern industrial equivalents of the ancient oil jars employed by other garden designers, were used as garden ornaments. The garden finished at the river with a bathhouse like a quarter-sized Parthenon. In 1938, when the garden was structurally complete, Nicolas de Molas, a Russian set designer who had studied with Léon Bakst, painted a conversation piece of the gardens and the Crowninshields.

What made it all possible? She was an expert and energetic gardener—despite her *very* portly shape she managed to run up and down the steps of what is virtually an eighty-foot cliff. An early and active preservationist, she had some notion of the translations that time makes.

He was obsessed with his ruins: one visitor recalls entering the garden for the first time and hearing a series of loud "whumps." On a terrace below, hidden behind the cedars, Frank Crowninshield was beating the columns of his newest temple with chains, to make them look old. The Massachusetts connection also meant they knew "Weld" and other great Italianate gardens of New England. As at "Winterthur," choice plants were sent to the gardens by Charles Sprague Sargent, who was a friend. Most important, both Frank and Louise were complete magpies; "Eleutherian Mills" is a witty condensation of all the Italian villas the two of them had visited. Their travel albums hold photos of what they liked. Some of the water effects are reminiscent of those at the Villa Gamberaia; the mosaic is a reminder of one at the Villa Giulia in Rome; pots on a high wall at the Villa Aldobrandini are echoed by agaves on the architrave of a Crowninshield wall; the gate, now demolished, that led into the garden from the river road was an exact duplicate of one at the Villa Falconieri in Frascati.[9]

Whether it was intended or not, the Crowninshields' Italian ruin is a sort of inspired nose-thumb at the du Ponts; it's so completely unlike any other du Pont form of gardening. There are no neat tricks of fountain, vista, and topiary to underline the connection between *Le Grand Monarque* and new American royalty; nor does it hark back to the good old colonial days of boxwood, homely industry, and kitchen gardens. It must have seemed outrageous, possibly decadent, and maybe even downright un-American. How ridiculous to do what Frank Crowninshield did: make brick walls deliberately out of plumb; how absurd to lay marble steps and break them up with a hammer to make them look old. THIS was hardly the way to celebrate the new American empire. . . .

Later du Ponts were not entirely comfortable with this old garden. What they wanted was a shrine to early American industry, so they knocked down some of the more flamboyant temples close to the river, including the Parthenon bathhouse. But it doesn't really matter, since this garden is a dream that could only come true after decades of actual neglect. The statue of *Antinoüs*, Hadrian's beloved, once stood in the hot white sun and not the green shade. The long vista on the top terrace is now made mysterious by red cedars that have at last achieved the height and darkness of Italian cypresses. In spring, no one misses the massed English daisies, tulips, and *Phlox subulata* in the beds below the double curving staircase—instead everywhere there are wild flourishes of old spirea, forsythia, mountain laurel, leucothoe, azaleas, and dogwood. Sprinklings of bulbs whiten the long grass. In fall, who cares that there are no chrysanthemum displays when the heavy green berries of "old age ivy" shine against their still darker foliage, and huge hickory trees light up the garden with their pale yellow fire? More a ruin now than either Frank or Louise might have envisioned, they would doubtless smile to see how time has triumphed over even their most vivid imaginings.

ABOVE AND OPPOSITE:
*Frank Crowninshield was a watercolorist, and the ruin garden he and his
wife, Louise, made at "Hagley" shares his art's allusiveness—the columns,
arches, and hints of other places are never heavy-handed.*

MARYLAND

Heading South, Baltimore is the last northern city, but Maryland, especially the Eastern Shore, is the first southern state—and Maryland is where northern and southern estate models meet. In the 1870s and 80s Barr Ferree's "movement countryward" was beginning and suburban estates were made, like the Joseph Jenkinses' family compound on Lake Avenue north of Baltimore, and John Sears Gibbs, Jr.'s, "Tyrconnell," whose Italian woodland garden was designed by Philadelphian Arthur Folsom Paul. A remnant of Maryland's land-based aristocracy had kept its acreage and eighteenth-century houses, the most notable being "Doughoregan Manor," home of Charles Carroll the Signer, built in 1720 in Ellicott City, and the Ridgelys' "Hampton," just a few miles north of Towson.

At the same time, on the Eastern Shore dozens of plantation houses on the Chesapeake Bay and the many rivers that flowed into it were still in the hands of their original builders' families. None of these plantations, though they often possessed many acres, was very imposing by the standards of turn-of-the-century northern millionaires' palaces, but they were beautiful and symbolic of an increasingly evocative past. Their owners' money and power, such as they still had in those post–Civil War and increasingly industrial days, derived from their land. Goods still moved by water. In the home landscape, the water entrance was as important as the land side, and the long allées of trees led between fields straight to the imposing garden facade. (A side track to the plantation buildings took care of the business aspect of life.) Their gardens had remained the same for over a century, give or take fifty years. They were formal, but simple eighteenth-century gardens, the Southern version of a seventeenth-century English model—few were the places where the picturesque style had intruded. Around the gardens were grouped the

A boating expedition was not uncommon at the Joseph Jenkins' "Windy Gates" outside Baltimore. The ravine beyond the stickwork bridge has been left more or less in its natural state, with some limbing-up of the trees.

handsome buildings that held the necessities of plantation domestic life: smokehouse, springhouse, and dairy; often there was a family graveyard. Sometimes the gardens were walled. Boxwood, now eight feet tall, still outlined the odd terrace parterre. Prized specimen trees in the outlying park had grown to imposing size. Many of the gardens were terraced with what are known in the South as "falls"—three, four, or five descending grassy oblongs, with grass ramps rather than steps, and with no balustrades or other stone architecture. Forty years later, in the twenties, many such plantations had new owners, mostly from the North, whose industrial fortunes spruced up—and romanticized—the old places. But in Maryland, it was as much the simple lure of wonderful sport as the mystique of the South that drew Northerners. The flocks of birds on the Eastern flyway were still almost what they had been in Audubon's days in the 1820s. Inland, fox-hunting clubs were formed around the turn of the century by homegrown Baltimore sports and Northern imports. With the pressure of the expanding city, first the big housebuilders retreated to the heights around Lutherville in the teens, and then, in the twenties and thirties, to the valleys beyond—Worthington and Green Spring, and to Harford County. They bought up the best farmhouses, just as they did in New Jersey and Pennsylvania, and they embellished them with additions and gardens.

"Windy Gates"

When Joseph W. Jenkins bought an existing house called "Idlemont" in 1880, he briefly used it as a summer house. It was situated north of Baltimore, close to Lake Roland. (Immediately south, Roland Park, that early residential suburb designed by the Olmsted firm, would be built within eleven years.) Jenkins's burgeoning family, and the growing sentiment that "country living" was better all round for health and virtue, soon led him to move out of town permanently to "Windy Gates," as he renamed his new property. Jenkins made his money in the Atlantic Coastline Railroad and in the newly powerful financial markets of the day; for him "Windy Gates" was never a farm, but a country place commensurate with his station, and a good place to raise ten children. At "Windy Gates" there was one Jersey cow and what must have been an astounding vegetable garden, but that was as far as the farm flavor went. The site was full of possibilities: by 1890 a sweeping lawn had been made, and a pond, which was spanned by a magnificent bridge of Adirondack stickwork, the work of a craftsman and former slave living at "Windy Gates." The triple-terraced "falls" surviving from the original mid-nineteenth-century landscape were laid out in busy crescent-shaped beds with a small fountain and potted agaves and other tropicals.

At the turn of the century, architect Henry Bacon remodeled "Windy Gates," taking off the Victorian gingerbread trim and adding a portico as well as big boxy dormers reminiscent of the ones he designed for Daniel

The Jenkins' stickwork playhouse (c. 1890) had a porch for each of the five children. A rope pulley with a bell connected the teahouse to the distant big house; if hunger struck, the bell was rung, and tea and cakes were shot down the rope in a basket.

Chester French's studio at "Chesterwood," in Lenox, Massachusetts. The pilasters of Bacon's new two-story sun porch were softened with vines, and a pergola and gazebo off to one side helped integrate house and garden. In 1902, Olmsted Bros. tidied the plantings of the falls, and connected the old terrace garden by a path to the woodland, planted as a garden with iris, azaleas, and wild flowers, and to a ravine. Gout slowed Mr. Jenkins up in later life, and a flying belvedere was run out over the ravine so he could enjoy the view. By the end of the first decade of the twentieth century, the Italian rage struck Baltimore, and Thomas Sears of Philadelphia made the "falls" into an elegant "Italian" garden, complete with twelve beautiful tall cedars from Lewis and Valentine, the Roslyn, Long Island, nurserymen. By the twenties, the formal gardens were full grown, with wide perennial borders on each terrace and low hedges of American box. A white wooden arbor stood against the woods at the end of the bottom terrace, providing a satisfying conclusion to the garden.

Within the five-house Jenkins compound was another Thomas Sears garden, "Edgewood," commissioned by Michael Jenkins for his unmarried sisters, Eliza and Ellen. Created at the same time as the improvements at "Windy Gates," it was a sunken rectangle reached by easy flights of stone steps from the house. Pairs of cedars stood at each step landing, a vine-covered pergola stood at one end of the garden; a lawn filled the center, and shrubs mixed with perennials lined the sides. Again it was termed "Italian," though the curving white wood benches, like the white wooden arbor at "Windy Gates," are more reminiscent of the American Colonial Revival than of the Italian Renaissance.[1]

"Tyrconnell," a "Forest Garden"

In 1923 Philadelphian landscape architect Arthur Folsom Paul wrote to Mr. and Mrs. John S. Gibbs, Jr., about their proposed garden at "Tyrconnell" in Woodbrook, still farther north from Baltimore than "Windy Gates." He said, "'a home place' should be free from ostentation and the unmistakable signs of a 'show place.'" He also stressed low maintenance and variety in plantings, and the sensible idea of "devoting particular places to a predominance of the flowers of each season of the year." Who would have guessed that all this practical and modest advice would eventually result in a stately garden with a woodland vista worthy of the Villa d'Este, climbing hundreds of stone steps, with a couple of little fountain terraces for breathers on the way? The house, which still exists today, was built in 1825. By 1919, when the Gibbses bought it, the grounds comprised 22 acres and the trees were remarkable. When Paul started work, a century-old box circle already formed the forecourt, and to the west lay a view of Lake Roland. To each of the new wings, east and west, he added "garden rooms" whose arched openings are like long windows.

But the pièce de résistance is the north garden: a long boxwood-edged allée was cut through the woodland where the big trees arched overhead.[2] Straight down the ravine march the stone steps and back up again to the summit of the next hill where a white marble swan fountain is surrounded by a circle of fourteen cedars clipped like cypresses. A horseshoe staircase like that around the Villa d'Este's Fountain of the Dragons leads from the house porch down to the formal boxwood garden from which the step walk begins.[3] In spring the long vista foams with the pale green and red of the big trees in flower and early leaf, and later with dogwood and azaleas. Along paths in the woods, thousands of wild blue phlox, spring beauties, trillium, lady-slippers, and May apples bloom before the deep summer shade overtakes them.

Arthur Folsom Paul never traveled abroad, but by the time he designed the Italian garden at "Tyrconnell" he wouldn't have had to see the Villa d'Este for inspiration. By the twenties the axial and perspective principles of European Renaissance gardens were part of American gardens too. An excellent plantsman, Paul was able to draw on a wide and sophisticated knowledge of trees and shrubs for the green architecture of a formal garden. He had graduated from Harvard in 1903, and then worked at the Arnold Arboretum under Charles Sprague Sargent, which doubtless partly accounts for his inspired treatment of this "forest" garden. Paul also landscaped part of Fairmount Park along the Schuylkill River, and designed gardens in Newport for his Philadelphia clients. In the forties he became president of the Andorra Nursery outside Philadelphia, a firm specializing in transplanting large trees.[4]

"Hampton," a "Powerhouse"

In 1859, in a supplement to A. J. Downing's *Theory and Practice of* *Landscape Gardening*, Henry Winthrop Sargent, disciple of the picturesque, wrote admiringly but uncomfortably about "Hampton" that "It belongs to the stately order of places almost unknown here at the North [at "Wodenethe" on the Hudson River], situated as it is in the midst of six thousand acres. . . . The formal terraces of exquisitely kept grass, the long rows of superb lemon and orange trees, with the adjacent orangerie and the foreign air of the house, quite disturb one's ideas of republican America."[5] "Hampton" was built in 1783–90 by the third generation of the Ridgely family to live in Maryland. Money to build one of the largest Georgian houses in America came not just from the more than 6,000 acres of farm and forest, but from the iron mines and foundry on the property about twenty miles north of Baltimore. Charles Ridgely ("the Builder") had made enormous profits during the Revolutionary War producing cannons and other armaments. "Hampton" was the only entailed estate in America; the entail was finally broken with the sale of the estate in 1949 to a preservation trust and today "Hampton" is open to the public.

"Hampton" is a living record of the revamping of a circa 1800 Southern-style formal terraced garden into a great Victorian garden in the 1840s, and its subsequent restoration in the 1940s as an interesting hybrid[6] by Alden Hopkins, successor to Arthur Shurcliff at Williamsburg. The terraces were a constant feature. Moving them in any event would have been rather difficult, since the volumes of dirt used were probably greater than for any other early American garden.[7]

The garden began during the tenure of Charles "the Builder's" nephew and successor, Charles Carnan Ridgely, who made three great terraces in 1790. By 1799 he had laid more than ten thousand feet of wooden irrigation pipes. (By 1859, hydrants had been installed in the garden.) Around 1810 the top two terraces were laid out in geometric box-edged patterns filled with ornamentals, and the bottom tier was a kitchen garden subsequently placed elsewhere. John Ridgely and his wife, Eliza, were responsible for the garden's nineteenth-century heyday. Eliza Ridgely, an heiress in her own right, was ready to spend money on her garden. She was a constant traveler as well as a gardener. She and her husband spent time in Europe and England in the late 1830s and early 40s, just as formality was returning to fashion. She planted the terraces with the new bedding-out annuals, and bought every new rose she could.

The forty marble urns Eliza also brought back from Europe are not too many for her exuberant garden, nor are the many Victorian iron benches, nor the iron wisteria "umbrellas." When she ventured into a more gardenesque style, inspired by Downing, some of her effects were not so happy. The cedar of Lebanon she reportedly brought back from the Middle East in a shoe box was plunked right in the middle of the central axis that runs through both house and garden. By the twenties, "Hampton" was cited as a "colonial" garden.[8]

A description in Appleton's Journal, *1875, of "Hampton" in Towson reads,
"in terrace after terrace strictly kept distinct in masses of color 8,000
plants are bedded out. The scarlet and orange and deep carmine of
geraniums; the blue and purple and white of the sweet-scented heliotropes;
the tawny gold and red of roses; and the ample leaves of the bronzy
crimson and yellow coleus; the borderings of vivid green." This lantern
slide was made some fifty years later.*

Harvey Ladew's "Ever-Changing Landscape"

How happy the man who was born in the 1880s in America with intelligence, a sense of humor, and plenty of money! At Harvey Ladew's garden
in Harford County, topiary fox and hounds, flat-out and belly to the
ground, streak across the approach lawn, followed by a topiary fox hunter
leaping over a white gate. Hunting and gardening were the twin passions
of Harvey's life, with painting, travel, and books a close third, fourth, and
fifth. Even more than Frank and Louise Crowninshield, Harvey Ladew
knew how to have fun in his garden and how to let his imagination roll.
Who else would have bought the box office entrance facade of the Tivoli

Theater in London and turned it into a garden teahouse — or surrounded
a window of the same teahouse with a serious gilt picture frame, complete
with a label that reads "Ever Changing Landscape by Harvey S. Ladew"?

Ladew grew up on Long Island, heir to a leather-goods fortune. After a
happy and mostly expatriate childhood in which he saw the great gardens
of Europe and avoided all formal schooling, he settled down to the
serious business of fox hunting, both in England and in America. A
member of the Prince of Wales set, Ladew was a collector of social lions
all his life, and loved houseparties and high jinks. Black-haired,
moustached, dashing, and dandyish, he knew when to wear a brown

The great bowl at "Ladew Topiary Gardens" (1929), surrounded by topiary hedges, some more than 12 feet high, was Harvey Ladew's first large-scale effort and was scooped out in horsepower days.

bowler hat and how to perk up a drooping arrangement of tulips with a little dash of gin. In the late twenties he came to hunt in Harford County, which at that time was as unspoiled as Long Island had been at the turn of the century. Intensive mixed farming, the absence of barbed wire, and the happy lay of the land made perfect fox-hunting country. For many years Harvey was Master of Foxhounds. Kennels were located just over the hill from his own establishment, and the sound of hounds was as much a part of "Pleasant Valley Farm" as the scent of flowers.

In 1929, Harvey bought 200 acres of land and a fine eighteenth-century white clapboard farmhouse, which he transformed with porticoes and pergolas and servants' quarters without making it overbearingly grand. Along the ridge, overlooking a small valley of hayfields, paddocks, and the occasional big tree, he laid out a formal garden which grew to 22 acres. He was his own head gardener; his garden attire was a smart blue denim smock, made in France, with plenty of pockets for shears and twine. "Pleasant Valley Farm," now "Ladew Topiary Gardens," seems like an American Hidcote. Indeed, given the amount of time Ladew spent in England's best fox-hunting shires, the Cotswolds, it would have been surprising if he were not familiar with the American Lawrence Johnson's great garden there, which was begun in 1919. Climate made a difference—the perennial plantings are much better at

Hidcote—and so did temperament—Harvey's garden is wittier, more impressionistic, more amusing than Hidcote. Both have long hedged vistas which form the spine of the garden, and separate secret chains of gardens that parallel the main axis. One of Ladew's best efforts is the "Garden of Eden," an apple orchard underplanted with azaleas. When they bloom at the same time, the visitor moves through shoulder-high blazing azaleas under a blush-pink cloud of apple blossom. A stone *Adam and Eve* stand in the middle. A Belgian fence of lattice-trained apple and pear trees screens the garden from the big lawn. Room enclosures hedged in hemlock and filled with gardens for different colors and different species, and whimsical yew topiary make Harvey Ladew's garden one of the best Arts and Crafts gardens in America. In 1971 when he was eighty-four years old, The Garden Club of America awarded him their Distinguished Service medal, calling his life-long work "the most outstanding topiary garden in America." But Ladew's garden is more than that—it is also a light-hearted triumph of leisure put to good use.[9]

Other New York transplants came to Harford County and one of them was James Breese from Southampton. During the teens and twenties when everyone else was amassing a fortune, Breese regularly made a little and lost a lot in his ventures on the Stock Exchange. During his periodic retrenchments he rented "The Orchard" and usually went abroad. However, one year he settled on Havre de Grace, in the most northeastern part of Harford County, as his economical retreat, where he bought the old Stumpp place, renamed it "The Blind," and did it up. The house, renamed yet again as "Oakington," later belonged to Senators Millard and then Joseph Tydings. Stanford White, who often visited, designed a wing for his friend Breese's hideout. Evelyn Nesbit came down more than once and Breese brought other New York visitors to the tranquil rural countryside, including the occasional lineup of chorus girls. One Havre de Grace neighbor, Charles Bryant, another transplanted New Yorker, remembered motoring over to "The Blind," where "the guys and dolls [were] gambolling in the buff in the garden."[10]

THE EASTERN SHORE

From Annapolis looking toward the water, on to Chestertown, St. Michaels, and Easton, and down to Cambridge and Oxford, in Kent, Queen Anne, and Talbot counties, and even as far south as Dorchester County, the old houses along the deeply indented tidewater coast were being bought up by men and women from New York, Pennsylvania, Illinois, Michigan, and other points north who could afford to enjoy life in ways celebrated in plantation novels. Such places were used mainly in the fall

for shooting, and for a spring visit or two. One frequent tidewater visitor points out that Eastern Shore owners had at least two other houses elsewhere, since summer in the Tidewater meant black flies, mosquitoes, and nettles. Summer gardens were not a great concern. Places in Talbot County were in demand, not just because the largest number of beautiful houses and gardens were there, but because the shooting was best.

New owners plunged heavily into Southern fantasy when they got to work on their old gardens. "Hope," a plantation linked to two of the oldest names on the Eastern Shore, Tilghman and Lloyd, was bought by Pittsburgher William Starr in 1908. The Starrs embellished the gardens with a brick wall topped by a marble rail, added allées and other formal gardens, and laid out a "heart garden" in quadrants with four hearts outlined in box. Revamping old gardens created a demand for landscape architects, such as Kathleen Cowgill, who practiced on the Eastern Shore.[11] Nurseries sprang up, some of which specialized in boxwood like that at "Canterbury Manor" established by Elliott Wheeler from Evanston, Illinois, who went into partnership with Ernest Hemming, previously of Kew Gardens. Occasionally new houses and gardens were built from scratch, like "Cape Centaur." In 1922 Glenn L. Stewart of New York and Pittsburgh bought most of Wye Island and built a beautiful Moorish castle of pink

Nothing more outlandish ever stood on Maryland's Eastern Shore than "Cape Centaur's" pink Moorish castle in the middle of its French formal gardens. Other Maryland enthusiasts who came for the shooting and the tranquil pace also wanted an old Maryland "place," but the Glenn Stewarts of Pittsburgh and New York were clearly not interested.

stucco which would have fitted right in at Palm Beach. To Eastern Shore eyes, its three-story tower and slit windows made it look like a fortress, an impression that three-foot-thick walls and doors of steel plate overlaid with oak did not dispel. The gardens were enormous and French and stretched each way toward the water. *Parterres de broderie* looked out over a sheltered inlet, and an immense three-way goosefoot radiated out from a lawn. "Cape Centaur" was always viewed with misgivings by its cosier brick neighbors. Henry Lockhart, Jr., a private banker in New York, came to the Eastern Shore with his family in the 1920s. They left Rye, New York, looking for that ideal sporting life *without* country clubs that Rye had offered only fifteen years or so before. They found it at "Wye Heights," an old brick house with about 1,200 acres on the Wye River, per-

fect for sailing as well as shooting. Good fox hunting wasn't far away, in Chestertown, with Wilbur Hubbard's hounds. The gardens were more than a proper appendage to a sporting household, however. Mr., Mrs., and Miss Lockhart divided the garden between them, and all gardened separately. Mrs. Lockhart's domain included the original "Wye Heights" garden and a long rose arbor which divided the rest of the garden in two. To the east of the arbor, Mr. Lockhart built his own walled garden. To the west was Miss Lockhart's azalea bowl. All three gardens were laid out without professional assistance in the mid- to late twenties. The Lockhart boys were not so interested—one of them remembers being asked one day if they would like to go down to see the gardens after lunch: "No," answered his brother, "I saw them last year."[12]

WASHINGTON, D.C.

There in the midst of Barr Ferree's 1904 lineup of fifty great American places is the White House, home of the president of the United States. It looks like a medium-sized Palladian-style country house. Though handsome, it also looks startlingly small and simple by comparison with the Newport palaces, or many other estates in the book. Many Washington houses built during the Gilded Age and the twenties were as grand as the White House for a reason—they were designed to impress, of course, but also for entertainment on a diplomatic scale. Their gardens and principal rooms were intended for the business of large formal receptions. Their occupants were often transients, and their gardens, like their interiors, underwent frequent changes. Sometimes small old Georgetown and Alexandria, Virginia, rowhouses were thrown together to make an imposing place. The present-day Gordon Gray house, for example, started off as three separate houses in 1811. In 1929 Mrs. Medill McCormick joined them and hired landscape architect Rose Greely to design a garden. A list of subsequent occupants gives an idea of how often houses can change hands in Washington: Sir John Balfour, C. V. Whitney, William M. Burden, "Scotty" Lanahan (F. Scott Fitzgerald's daughter), Arthur Krock, and Joe Alsop.

The Washington garden that best illustrates the complex relationship

LEFT:
Azaleas and dogwood light up the rhythmic portico staircase at the British Embassy and Residence in Washington, D.C., designed by Sir Edwin Lutyens. The gardens were largely the work of the American Lady Lindsay, a garden designer before her marriage, between 1930 and 1939.

between public and private spaces is that of the British Embassy, designed by Sir Edwin Lutyens in 1927. Lutyens was at the pinnacle of his fame in 1927, having already designed the Viceroy's house in New Delhi, a comparable project for which he had won his knighthood. In America, his work was known nationwide and was very influential. In 1925 he was awarded the Gold Medal by the American Institute of Architects. The plan for the new British Embassy, first presented publicly in architect William Delano's New York offices, was resoundingly endorsed by a panel of American architects including Cass Gilbert, Thomas Hastings, and Charles Platt,[1] most of whom had built great American country houses on the English model. Essentially, the British Embassy is an English country house set in the city, presenting a typical late-seventeenth-century facade to the street. A softer and more decorative early-eighteenth-century porticoed elevation gives onto the garden.[2] Like the grandest English country houses (and like their American counterparts) there was a division between public rooms and private apartments—here, between the chancery and the residence. Within the landscape scheme, the two parts are separated by the residence drive. Within the architectural design their connection is indicated by the Ambassador's study, located in the room above the porte cochere which spans the drive, connecting the two buildings. Even in Lutyens' earliest drawings the chancery and residence gardens were part of an axial, geometric vision. From Gertrude Jekyll, with whom he worked in closest partnership for more than forty years, Lutyens had learned about simplicity and directness of garden design and about the unmannered use of simple country materials such as the reddish-brown Flemish bond brick employed for the garden pavilion and walls as well as the house exterior. All kinds of exquisite Lutyens details abound. The garden gate, a narrow limestone-faced arch with steps leading up to the garden, is grandly detailed but is conceived on the most intimate human scale to hint at the quiet and seclusion within.

Lady Lindsay, wife of the first Ambassador to live in the new residence, and the person responsible for the planting plan, was unusually well qualified to realize Lutyens's inspired garden geometry. An American, she had studied architecture at Columbia University, and horticulture in Boston and in England before marrying Sir Ronald Lindsay in 1924. Lady Lindsay, who had designed gardens in Ohio and on Long Island, knew the American climate and American plants, and lavishly used the flowering trees and shrubs (dogwoods, magnolias, cherries, crepe myrtles, andromedas, and azaleas, to list just a few) that thrive in Washington. She also had the common sense to plan the Embassy garden for peak performance in spring and early summer, rather than in the height of summer when the heat of the Potomac Basin recalls the fact that Washington was once an official hardship post for diplomats during the early years of the nineteenth century.

"Dumbarton Oaks" and "The Causeway": Rus in Urbe

The grounds and gardens of the British Embassy are extensive, but they were by no means unique in the twenties, when Washington was still in many ways a country town. In 1920, "Dumbarton Oaks," the Robert Woods Bliss's new place right in Georgetown, still had farm buildings and stood on 53 acres. Robert Woods Bliss wanted a haven to retire to after a

The varied silhouettes of deodar cedar, sugar maple, and weeping cherry and willow are reflected in the swimming pool at "Dumbarton Oaks."

As originally designed by Beatrix Farrand, the swooping walk and the beautifully staggered trees of Cherry Hill were once the link between the formal gardens and the 26-acre planted woodland at "Dumbarton Oaks," which no longer exists.

Washington, D.C.

153

peripatetic life in the foreign service, and Mildred Bliss was a rich woman who wanted to use her resources to further their shared vision of the humanities. Robert Woods and Mildred Bliss were collectors who wanted to house their works of art beautifully and make them accessible to scholars. A garden to live and entertain in, and to look at in three seasons of the year was part of the grand plan.[3] Beatrix Farrand was engaged as landscape gardener, and models and maquettes of garden plantings and ornaments proliferated while letters and sketches and plans flew back and forth across the Atlantic. (Much of the garden was designed with Mrs. Bliss *in absentia*, as she accompanied her foreign service husband on his various postings, although she was nonetheless deeply involved in every decision. Farrand and Mildred Bliss became closest friends during their intense collaboration, and the correspondence between the two reveals the severe Farrand's softer side: she signed one letter "Your everloving Garden Twin."

Farrand's personal commitment to "Dumbarton Oaks" is well revealed in her *Plant Book for Dumbarton Oaks*, undertaken in 1941 when she was almost seventy. A remarkable document in the history of gardens, it is a projection of every single detail of what should be replanted, what would grow too large, what could be replaced without injuring the look of the garden. The book is a loving and imaginative feat, grounded in a lifetime of knowledge, and buoyed by the courageous assumption that gardens *can* live forever—particularly courageous given Farrand's age, and the sight of Europe crumbling in World War II.

The 10 acres of formal garden and 26 acres of planted woodland bordering on Rock Creek Park were Beatrix Farrand's magnum opus. Among private gardens, it was one of her major long-term projects, each of which occupied her for about twenty years (others included those for Rockefeller, Harkness, Satterlea, Millikin, and Straight).[4] Farrand's scheme for "Dumbarton Oaks" was a series of enclosures, fenced in every conceivable way, which unfolded in surprise after surprise down the hill on which the house stood, each enclosure growing progressively more informal and naturalistic until the garden merged with the woodland. There is no sweeping view of the entire garden. This progression has become less clear since the woodland ceased to be part of the garden. Changes that made the garden more formal were the conversion of the tennis court into a pebble-floored enclosure, the substitution of an architectural aerial hedge and a fountain for simpler boxwood, and a shallow pool in the Ellipse garden. But the separate gardens for spring and fall flowers still exist, as do many of Farrand's plant combinations. Her strong patterns of foliage and plant silhouette have flourished, and on every visit one notes another inspired and thoughtful use of trees as sculpture, or of sculpture that subtly focuses a garden or marks an entrance. "Dumbarton Oaks" does not yield all its secrets at once. It is what garden historian Eleanor McPeck has called "the chambered

At the James Parmelees' "The Causeway" in Washington, D.C., beds were filled with Ellen Shipman's usual ravishing mix of perennials, topiary shrubs, and small flowering trees. Nothing could be more effective in such a flat and regular garden than this artful informality.

nautilus of gardens, suggesting at every turn deeper levels of meaning and experience."[5]

Charles Platt and Ellen Shipman worked on a garden for the James Parmelees in Cleveland Park that had the same balance of formal and informal as "Dumbarton Oaks," though it was half the size. "The Causeways," a brick English Georgian-style country house built in 1912–14, was set on a ridge with views over an informal woodland garden with a pond to the south. The woods around the house were cut in a widening funnel; when the house was seen from the pond below, the narrowing cut through the trees created a forced perspective view of the house that made it look like a landscape painting.[6] Twenty-one acres in extent, the landscape of "The Causeways" was effectively a park in miniature, with a drive that allowed glimpses of the house as an object in the landscape on the approach. The Parmelees liked riding in the woods, so there were stables, and one year Ellen Shipman even gave them a bridle path for Christmas. The rectangular formal garden next to the house had brick paths and a simple central fountain. At the end of the brick walk vista, steps mounted to a statue framed in dark cedars—an old Italian trick. Just beyond, the high native trees made a lighter background screen. The house, renamed "Tregaron," was enlarged when Marjorie Merriweather Post married Ambassador Joseph Davies and lived there briefly in the thirties. A Russian *dacha* was built right in the middle of the formal garden.[7]

At "The Causeways," as at "Dumbarton Oaks" and the British Embassy, formal planning contrasted with flourishing broadleaf evergreens used all over the South: magnolias, camellias, azaleas, and especially English boxwood.

CITY GARDENS

Two real city gardens entirely different from such twentieth-century "country palaces" in the city are those at the grand town houses of Ambassadors Larz Anderson and Irwin Boyle Laughlin. These small elegant "rooms," both of which survive in rather institutional form, were for entertaining, not horticultural display. Places for a breath of air and a chance to enjoy the seasons and the sky, they contained only patterned pavement, statues, the sound of water, and a few flowers in pots and urns. Greenness was confined to topiary, clipped bands of ivy, and a tiny *tapis vert*. The Andersons' garden—just a terrace, really—was only a tiny pendant to their jewel of an Italian garden, "Weld," in Brookline, designed by Charles Platt for their Herbert Browne summer house. Browne, of the Boston firm of Little and Browne, was called in to do the Washington house as well, which his contemporaries considered his finest work in the Italian style. At Laughlin's impeccably French "Meridian House," designed by John Russell Pope in 1920, one has the sense of being in a small garden behind one of the *hôtels particuliers* at Versailles. No wonder since Laughlin, a passionate collector of things

French, also imported the garden's forty-one pleached linden trees from France. They now form a deep green canopy effective on the hottest day. Pope built up the level of the house's two stories on one side; the gardens are placed on top. Like a little hanging garden of Babylon, but very understated, of course, the landscaped first floor terrace is fourteen-and-a-half feet above the street below.[8]

In the Middle Atlantic states one sees the how and why of gardens in the Gilded Age, from the extravagant fantasy and immense size of places such as "Blairsden" and "Drumthwacket," "Immergrun" and "White-marsh Hall," "Longwood" and "Cape Centaur," on through the Quaker farmer fantasies of Philadelphia and the tiny triumphs of Chestnut Hill, to the *rus in urbe* of Washington. From here on, southward, time changes its shape; the Gilded Age is split in two. Before the Civil War, the South had enjoyed its own separate Gilded Age, and, after it, Northerners in search of a lost Arcady, a rural paradise, came south and created their own gilded version of Old Southern life.

BELOW:
"Grand without being grandiose; impressive without being pompous; rich without being ornate. . . ." is how architectural critic Matlack Price described "Meridian House," Irwin Laughlin's Washington, D.C., town house and garden designed by John Russell Pope in 1920. The fountain is seen here.

Washington, D.C.

155

The
SOUTH

THE OLD SOUTH

Since when has "old" been the word most often used in the South to describe gardens—and everything else—as in "Old South"? Down South, "old" seems always to mean much more than chronology. In the South, it means conservative—what has gone before.

What could have been more naturally conservative than a manorial system run by a tiny group of planters, whose agricultural organization largely comprised all effective government and social structure and whose control over their means of production, slaves, was constant oppression? "Old" had also always meant "English," which meant "good." The ties between what Southerners thought of as the Mother Country and the colonies were stronger than in the North. Beginning in pre-Revolutionary days many more upper-class Southerners than Yankees were educated in England,[1] and the South provided raw materials for England's other colonies and for its industries—rice for sugar plantations in the Caribbean, indigo for England's navy uniforms, and cotton for the cloth mills of the Midlands.

Though architecture and garden style were as conservative as the political system, gardening knowledge was up-to-the-minute. The list of great early Southern gardeners is a long one, and includes Thomas Jefferson at "Monticello," of course, but also various Middletons of "Middleton Place," South Carolina, and John Grimke Drayton of "Magnolia," also near Charleston. All three gardens exist today. The very first garden club in the world was founded in 1891 by twelve matrons of Athens, Georgia.[2] Given the wealth of the South up till the Civil War, it's no surprise that gardening reached very high levels. Southern specialties included sophisticated greenhouses for citrus and other fruits, and for other tender plants that were used in the garden in summer. Southerners could grow bulbs for all seasons, and all the tender roses, especially the Noisettes, delicate late-blooming China crosses first hybridized by an eighteenth-century Carolina rice-grower, John Champney. The best-known Noisette, and one beloved by the Victorians, was 'Marechal Niel', golden-yellow with coppery green foliage. One ninety-year-old North Carolina gardener said, "My grandmother in Mississippi had a greenhouse—a pit in the side of the hill, actually—where she kept 'Marechal Niel' roses and calla lilies. My father kept plant lists of his garden, where he grew lotus and other exotics. In fact, like most people in the South, we were not so struck when everybody discovered Thomas Jefferson's garden records—after all, we *all* had diaries like that."[3]

Nineteenth-century antebellum planters were as old-fashioned about garden design as their eighteenth-century forebears, who had built seventeenth-century-style formal gardens long after the fashion for the picturesque arrived. In the agricultural South, the symbolic import of a fine house presiding over a well-ordered landscape, productive and self-sufficient, had long-standing political and societal meanings.[4] It's no exaggeration to say that a Southern "big house" played the same part in its landscape as did Versailles in its park. All roads led to it and all vistas focused on it. In a countryside where, unlike New England or the Middle Atlantic regions, there was little county government and only a few towns, each plantation house was *the* authority. It ruled its own little kingdom, and was meant to look as if it did. The long Southern growing season and the near-jungle appearance of the native flora may also have encouraged formality. Catherine Howett, in *A Land of Our Own*, remarks on the need for Georgians to impose a civilizing order on the natural landscape. It always has seemed unnecessary to have a wilderness garden in the wilderness, since gardens generally are a contrast to the landscape that surrounds them.

As the mid-century mark was passed, old-time formality in the South also took on a new ideological vigor. Sectionalism grew, and Northern and Southern attitudes hardened, so that the planter class, those who made the great antebellum gardens of the South, became reactionary. More and more they saw themselves as Cavalier gentlemen, "the knight errants of rosewater."[5] They looked back to a time when the moral value of their society was comparatively unquestioned, when slavery was not the overriding issue, and conflict was not inevitable.[6] So "old" meant not only beautiful, but peaceful, safe, even authoritarian. A symmetrical, old-fashioned formal garden symbolized a dominance both over nature and the existing social order that was not implicit in the picturesque style, just as a big white columned "temple" spoke for power, moral purity and the sacredness of home.

But after the Civil War, "old" became a Southern badge of honor for another, bigger reason: there was no money to have anything new—not houses, not gardens, not clothes. White Southerners were destitute because the slave basis of their economy had vanished, their lands had been rifled, occupied, and sometimes burned by Northern armies, and they had ruined themselves for the Confederacy. Flower gardens grew weedy and forlorn in favor of taters and cotton. Southerners stopped making plantation gardens during Reconstruction days for another reason: the migration to the cities had begun that would alter the social order—and the gardens—of the South. In the second half of the century, while the rest of the country was experimenting with shingle houses and gardenesque layouts, the South was looking back dimly to what was becoming the Old South in fact as well as legend. In the 1880s, the faint outlines of the new order first appeared as textile manufacturers and cotton brokers began to make gardens in the cities. Generally speaking, however, poverty was what "preserved" the Old South long before there was a historic preservation movement. There was even a certain cachet to the threadbare look. At the end of the war, in 1865, only the "wrong people" (carpetbaggers) had money, and "Too poor to paint and too proud to whitewash" became the operative phrase from 1865 right on through the Gilded Age among the upper classes. And then still later, as architect

RIGHT:
"Too poor to paint, too proud to whitewash" describes the state of the South, and of the Hayes-McCance House in Richmond after the Civil War.

"Oak Island" plantation on Edisto Island in South Carolina, home of Mrs. William Seabrook, was occupied by Union soldiers during the Civil War. The garden fountain is at center, among the outline of Victorian beds.

Century-old boxwood, higgledy-piggledy borders, grass terraces, the notion that Jefferson designed something here, "quarters" and other outbuildings to convert into picturesque garden ornaments—these were the charms of old Virginia gardens bought up by Northerners who came south to revive antebellum days. Annette Hoyt Flanders worked here in the twenties on the Charles Stones' "Morven" near Charlottesville.

Henry Boykin of Camden, South Carolina, notes, "It was hard to tell when Reconstruction left off and the Depression began."[7]

Throughout the beginnings of the Gilded Age in the 1880s and 90s, the South's still-rural economy was also pinched by the North's developing industry—Southerners, like inhabitants of the Third World, had to buy all manufactured goods at Northern prices with their dwindling agricultural money. In the thirty years following the Civil War, 4,000 millionaires emerged nationwide of whom only 87 were in agriculture and the rest in industry, trade, railroads, real estate, and banking.[8] These titans congregated in the Northeast, near the nation's emerging financial and industrial centers, not in the rural South.

THE NORTHERNERS ARRIVE

But by the turn of the century, when Southerners were starting to scramble back up, these same rich Northern industrialists were heading south. Attracted by the cosmetically painted plantation life described in novels, they found in its real-life remains a tradition of Arcadian beauty and leisure lost to their own birthplaces. In Tidewater Virginia and in the Piedmont, in Camden, Aiken, and Charleston, and at the plantations on the Ashepoo, Ashley, Cape Fear, Cooper, Chee-ha, Combahee, and many other rivers in both Carolinas, in Augusta and Thomasville, Georgia, and all along the barrier reef islands, they stepped backward in time. It was easy to do, since no "modern" buildings of industry scumbled the surface.

The old plantations were rescued. Sometimes, of course, new ones were built, such as Cleveland industrialist J. H. Wade's "Mill Pond Plantation" in Thomasville, laid out in its enormous entirety by Warren Manning. W. R. Coe built "Cherokee," a Southern plantation as grand as his Long Island estate, "Planting Fields," on 10,000 acres of old rice fields on the Combahee River. The original house had burned in the Civil War, so Coe built a pillared and porticoed brick house inspired by two Virginia houses, "Sabine Hall" and "Mount Airy." The front facade and formal entrance lawn were bounded by lines of native cedars moved in from the woods. On the garden front overlooking the Combahee, a wide lawn ran down to the lake, part of the old rice plantation irrigation system. The azalea gardens, shaded by cedar, cassena, magnolia, live oak, and holly trees, flanked the lawn. A three-mile entrance drive was festooned with wisteria; pristine white-washed cabins with clay chimneys, the homes of Coe's black tenantry, stood along the way.[9]

These millionaires' gardens were similar in design and extent to those of the same period in the North, but they were richly Southern in feeling, thanks to crepe myrtles, real Italian cypresses, oleanders, the whole range of magnolias, cherry laurel, gordonia, franklinia, and a host of common flowering trees like dogwood and redbud, liriope or ribbon grass, all the tender tea roses, the rampant species climber roses like the Cherokee, *Rosa laevigata*, and the tiny Lady Banks roses, *R. Banksiae* and *R. banksiae lutescens*, and boxwood of every kind.

In 1889, in *On Horseback, A Tour in Virginia, North Carolina, and Tennessee*, Charles Dudley Warner, author with Mark Twain of *The Gilded Age*, affectionately describes Warm Springs, an old Southern watering-spot fallen on hard postbellum times. More truthfully than any conventional evocation of a Southern garden full of the lazy scent of tea olive and magnolia, it catches a certain quality that three generations of Northerners have seen and loved in the South:

The situation is very pretty, and the establishment has a picturesqueness of its own. . . . No doubt we like the place better than if it had been smart, and enjoyed the *negligé* condition, and the easy terms on which life is taken there. There was a sense of abundance in the sight of fowls tiptoeing about the verandas, and to meet a chicken in the parlor was a sort of guarantee that we should meet him later on in the dining-room. [Warner had eaten practically nothing but fatback and cornpone on his travels so far.] The long colonnade made an admirable promenade and lounging-place and point of observation. It was interesting to watch the groups under the locusts, to see the management of the ferry, the mounting and dismounting of the riding-parties, and to study the colors on the steep hill opposite, halfway up which was a neat cottage and flower garden. . . . Here came in the summer time the Southern planters in coach and four, with a great retinue of household servants, and kept up for months that unique social life, a mixture of courtly ceremony and entire freedom—the civilization which had the drawing room at one end and the negro-quarters at the other—which has passed away. It was a continuation into our own restless era of the manners and the literature of George the Third. . . .[10]

"Oatlands," "Montpelier," and "Gunston Hall"

Carter, Randolph, Byrd, and Lee. Under the schoolroom ring-and-ding of the Virginia Presidents—Washington, Jefferson, Madison, Monroe—any student of American history can also catch the resonance of this second string of names. They and others were the land-holding aristocracy of Virginia—seventeenth-century settlers who became tobacco planters, slaveholders, builders, and garden makers. Their widely known plantations and gardens, which were almost as influential as those of the Virginia presidents, set the pattern for the entire South.

In 1800 George Carter, great-grandson of Robert "King" Carter of Corotoman, in the Tidewater, built "Oatlands," about twenty miles away from the Blue Ridge Mountains. Carter's big white Federal house (complete with Corinthian columns ordered from New York) had a six-foot stone wall topped with brick to enclose his 4-acre garden. Beyond the wall was a brick orangery complete with a hypocaust (hot-water heating system); inside the garden grew as many fruits and vegetables as flowers. Garden and greenhouse provided necessities—and luxuries such as ornamental hothouse plants, figs, grapes, almonds, and apricots—for a 3,400-acre plantation. In the glory days of the 1830s, little could Carter imagine that soon the family fortunes would start a long slide down

Mrs. William Eustis's garden at "Oatlands," near Leesburg, seen here in 1903, was influenced by Gertrude Jekyll, whose writings were popular. Well-bred Americans like Mrs. Eustis steered clear of Jekyll's bolder color harmonies in favor of schemes of pastels, silver, and white. Yuccas were among Jekyll's favorites, and they grow well in Virginia clay.

The proud figure of Louis Hertle can barely be distinguished among his new boxwood patterns and perennials at historic "Gunston Hall" (1755) on the Potomac. The Hertles' effort was among the earliest Colonial Revival gardens (1913).

ending, in 1897, with the sale of "Oatlands," complete with family tomb and old oak grove. The garden fell into ruin.

By 1902, when William Corcoran Eustis and Edith Morton Eustis saw "Oatlands" on an autumn afternoon, "bricks were crumbling, weeds crowding the flowers, and yet the very moss-grown paths seemed to say 'We are still what we were,'" as Edith Eustis remembered.[11] She didn't even bother to go into the house. By spring 1903, "Oatlands" was theirs. Both of them knew just what to do with such a place, and had the money to do it. Up until World War II, life at "Oatlands" was that heady mixture of sport, politics, and perfect weekend entertainment so typical of estate life at the time. William Eustis, who trained as a lawyer, was a sportsman and a phenomenal horseman; he turned "Oatlands" into a legendary fox hunting and steeple-chasing mecca. He was also the grandson of William Corcoran, Washington banker and philanthropist. His father, George Eustis, a Louisiana congressman who married Corcoran's only daughter, came from a distinguished New Orleans family and had represented the Confederacy in France during the Civil War.[12]

Edith Eustis's mother was a Livingston from New York. Her father was Levi P. Morton, vice president under Benjamin Harrison. Her childhood was spent at "Ellerslie," one of the manor houses lining the Hudson, so her first garden sensibilities were Northern. When she began at "Oatlands," she had traveled extensively in England and had read Gertrude Jekyll just as avidly as did her counterparts in the Northeast. Edith Eustis's inclination was to create an English garden, right down to Jekyll's yuccas and her paler color harmonies of pink, blue, and white.[13] A heavily marked copy of *The Small Gardens of England* was used as a bible—and not just for planting plans: the teahouse added in the twenties is taken from one of Jekyll's designs. The head gardener, Mr. Doe, was English.

The changes made by Edith Eustis at "Oatlands"—she was a simple, direct, and gifted gardener—were typical of those carried out at most old plantations revived as second houses or summer retreats. Flower beds were enlarged, the boxwood parterre was extended, a rose garden was added (a "room garden" feature typical of the period),[14] as well as a reflecting pool. Fashionable trees like arborvitae and Japanese flowering crabs joined long lines of tree box, *B. sempervirens 'Arborescens'*, mounds of dwarf English box, *B. sempervirens 'Suffruticosa'*, old-fashioned shrubs like sweet shrub, *Calycanthus florida*, and American natives such as fringe trees, *Chionanthus virginiana*. Whatever old climbing roses had stuck it out became companions to new hybrids like pink 'Betty Prior' and white 'Dr. Van Fleet'. Standard heliotropes grown in pots on the terrace were a grace note typical of the period. Edith Eustis's own contribution was to underplant their soft lavender balls with blue cranesbill geranium—a hallucinatory, Monet-like combination. The biggest shift was to outlaw vegetables, which had been part of most eighteenth-century terraced gardens known as "falls." One entire ter-

race within the garden that had been given over to grape vines in the Carters' day was redesigned by Edith Eustis as a formal boxwood parterre. At "Oatlands," a kitchen garden proper and a cutting garden were laid out separately; additional hothouses were built, as well as cold frames dug right next to Carter's great walls.

For all her Northern birth and English taste, Edith Eustis was definitely a Southern gardener in her regard for fragrance. *Viburnum Carlesii* and mignonette were among the many smells that filled the garden. In late spring, on the sundial terrace to the east where tea was served, there were beds full of madonna lilies, probably forced in the greenhouse and sunk in their pots. Edith Eustis made a habit of visiting the garden at about 7 o'clock in the evening when fragrance was at its height.[15] The place was essentially finished in the thirties, though Mrs. Eustis continued to live there till 1964 (Mr. Eustis had died in 1921). "Oatlands" is now a National Trust property and is open to the public.

Two other notable Virginia gardens that underwent changes similar to those at "Oatlands" are "Montpelier" and "Gunston Hall." At both places, however, there were fewer traces of previous gardens than remained at "Oatlands." At 2,700-acre "Montpelier," in Orange, President James Madison's columned country seat which is now also a National Trust property, Mrs. William du Pont, Sr., jotted a brief description of the gardens in 1901, the year she and Mr. du Pont acquired the place:

When estate was bought, the garden had been destroyed, the terrace ploughed down, box bushes bare at the bottom and no paths except a mud incline from top of garden to foot, paling and Virginia worm fence in bad condition and weeds.

Terraces were remade, tiled paths made and steps put in, and marble urns added.

Replanted with grass, flowers and shrubbery, designed by Mrs. du Pont, and brick wall built, nothing of which Madison ever saw.[16]

"Nothing of which Madison ever saw" is a fine catchphrase to use in connection with almost all the early twentieth-century revival gardens. They reached heights of opulence not only unseen but unimagined by their original makers.[17] Charles Gillette, noted landscape architect of formal gardens in nearby Richmond, worked on the garden in the 1920s, but the plan, with its horseshoe-shaped terraces, fountains, elaborate topiary, and reflecting pools, was essentially Mrs. du Pont's. In 1930 the beds in the 2.5-acre formal garden were filled with "tree-roses standing about in prim precision in gay beds of larkspur and lady slippers and brilliant phlox and the white marguerite."[17] Today, huge cedars of Lebanon and boxwood over 12 feet tall provide a dramatically dark frame for Madison's house, which the du Ponts' daughter, the great steeplechase patroness Marion du Pont Scott, painted a pale and becoming pink.[18]

At "Gunston Hall" overlooking the Potomac River, Louis and Eleanor Hertle also made an "oldtime"[19] garden. When the Hertles bought "Gunston Hall" in 1912, the finely proportioned brick building was encrusted with additions. The garden was a skeleton—but what a skeleton! From a few feet beyond the delicate semioctagonal portico on the garden front, an English boxwood allée stretched south for 220 feet, seemingly ending in the sky. At the end, "falls," or terraces, softened a steep drop to meadows sloping down to the river, with the Maryland hills on the opposite bank.

Temptingly, to either side of the boxwood stretched the blank grassy spaces where once was "an extensive garden touching the house on one side and reduced from the natural irregularity of the hill top to a perfect level platform. . . ."[20] George Mason's son, General John Mason, did not elaborate his description further, so it was all fair game for Mr. Hertle and his architect, Glenn Brown, of the Washington, D.C., firm of Glenn and Bedford Brown. They created elaborate parterre patterns, and below the first fall they made a rose garden whose design still exists today, although plants that were grown in colonial times have been substituted for the roses. "Gunston Hall's" garden is now a Garden Club of Virginia restoration, and both house and garden are open to the public.

Those were the baby days of garden reconstruction, pre-Williamsburg days, without even the rudiments of archeology. In addition to the trees and shrubs that remained on any site,[21] plant lists, letters, and hearsay were the primary sources. Garden makers who wanted to make an old-fashioned garden to go with a Georgian house also relied on modern historical surveys such as Inigo Triggs's *The Formal Gardens of England and Scotland*[22] in the belief that such gardens had close American counterparts. Arguments can be made as to how much valuable garden history was destroyed by the early garden "restorers." However, if one discards the idea that authenticity is the only trump card, one sees the beauty of such gardens. Italian garden makers during the Renaissance were quite sure they were reinterpreting Pliny's gardens faithfully; instead they made the finest new gardens the world had seen in a thousand years. "Gunston Hall" in its rather busy Hertle incarnation was not a new Villa Lante, but it was beautiful with boxwood, peonies, iris, heliotrope, phlox, delphinium, foxgloves, and roses. Lilacs and flowering cherries, along with thousands of bulbs, made spring displays. The bowling green was edged with pleached fruit trees. There were lemon verbena and rose geranium to pinch for their pungent aromas, and in the fall, brilliant chrysanthemums were massed in the beds.

John D. Rockefeller, Jr., and Colonial Williamsburg
In the twenties and thirties, John D. Rockefeller, Jr., created a vision of pre-Revolutionary Virginia—a past that included gardens, of course. Because Williamsburg was well publicized and much visited, it exerted a tremendous influence on private garden design. Because it enshrined a design period that had been familiar to Americans since the Philadelphia Centennial, Williamsburg's thirties brand of Colonial Revival garden was also easily accessible as a concept—it was not a new idea to grapple with.

But the scope of Williamsburg's garden influence went well beyond the details of style. Williamsburg changed the scale of American gardens at a time when such a change was imperative due to diminishing acreage, income, and available labor. Small gardens became a distinctly fashionable possibility. It's not going too far to say that garden designers of the second quarter of the twentieth century, such as Loutrel Briggs in the South and Innocenti and Webel in the Northeast, drew inspiration from Williamsburg and improved on it. A tidy simplicity, as opposed to the overflowing look of the "old-fashioned" garden, the use of wrought iron and patterned brick, and the revival of the ornamental kitchen garden, all owe something to Williamsburg.

"Rockefeller's interest in Williamsburg was based on his conviction that the eighteenth century was far more beautiful than the twentieth";[23] after World War I, the Crash of 1929, and the Depression, that must have been easy to believe. Rockefeller and his architects, Perry, Shaw and Hepburn, and Arthur Shurcliff, his landscape architect, saw the gardens as frames for the buildings, which were the main focus of the restoration. Though the conviction had strengthened that restored gardens should also be authentic since the Hertles' joyful "restoration" of "Gunston Hall" in 1913, there was still great difficulty agreeing on what "authentic" meant. Certainly to Arthur Shurcliff it did not mean the bare, and probably untidy, look we now think existed at Williamsburg in the eighteenth century.

Arthur A. Shurcliff was fascinating and persuasive—a sort of landscape prestidigitator who was able to impress his vision on people *who actually knew* his ideas were too elaborate and often entirely undocumented. Shurcliff's enthusiasm and artistic vision simply blew away the finer points of garden archeology[24] as it was then emerging. For accuracy he substituted a sort of garden hagiography, which put a halo around the ancestral portrait of industry and neatness that Rockefeller wanted. Shurcliff was a city planner as well as a landscape architect. He had been the first "junior member" admitted by the founders to the ASLA in 1899. Bostonian but no Brahmin, he changed his name from Shurtleff to the more anglicized Shurcliff. In 1928, in a recommendation letter from Perry, Shaw and Hepburn to the Colonial Williamsburg staff, he is described as "clear, simple, direct, energetic and personally, very charming," and as having "a personality which is most adaptable to collaboration with others."[25] Not everyone was so sure at first. In an interview, Mrs. George P. Coleman, the hapless resident of a Georgetown house whose garden was about to be restored, recalled her first impressions of Shurcliff: "This is such a terribly enthusiastic man! He startled me the first time I met him, when he addressed the Garden Club on the subject of old gardens, and hoped that the modern species of flowers would be banned from gardens here, and urged us all to grow red geraniums in profusion! I have grave doubts as to the presence of red geraniums in Virginia in Colonial Days, and have no partiality for them at any time!"[26] Later in the year she continued, "Mr. Shurcliff came down like a wolf on the fold again today. He rushed in and out several times with charts and plans for all sorts of alarming 'landscapes' in our yard. He has boxwood on the brain." But in fact Mrs. Coleman herself was eventually won over and loved the garden Shurcliff designed, as have so many thousands of visitors to Williamsburg since her day. Shurcliff's theory, which can be roughly stated as: "Look for the evidence, but if you can't find any, no holds barred," should not take away from the undeniable charm of his gardens.[27]

"Biltmore," the Ultimate Estate Garden

Long before Rockefeller had gone to Virginia to raise Williamsburg from the dead, another great Northern fortune had gone farther south with a

vision. "Biltmore" in Asheville, North Carolina, was both the most traditional and the most innovative of all the Vanderbilt estates built by the grandchildren of Commodore Cornelius. The French Renaissance style that George Vanderbilt and Richard Morris Hunt, favorite architect of the first generation of great estate builders, chose for the house was already almost old-fashioned in 1888, the year building commenced. The kind of royal architecture that Hunt built in Newport—or for James Pinchot at "Grey Towers" in Pennsylvania—would soon seem ostentatious and heavy-handed. Sitting on the dramatic forested bluff above the confluence of the French Broad and the Swannanoa rivers, however, "Biltmore" looks right. The 35 acres of formal gardens that stretch to south and east are just what's needed to provide a platform for such an immense building. "Most innovative" because Vanderbilt, under Frederick Law Olmsted's tutelage, was way ahead of his time in his environmental concerns. Thousands of acres (Biltmore comprised 125,000) were reforested; thousands more, farmed-out and eroded, were scientifically

At George Vanderbilt's "Biltmore" in Asheville, North Carolina, in 1888, F. L. Olmsted began the job that his sons and Warren Manning would finish in 1893. Though it was an anomaly in the South at the time it was created, "Biltmore" was the blueprint for the country places of the next forty years, especially in the North. Architectural and planting styles would change, but formal gardens near the house (upper left), a grand approach (upper right), and a separate complex for cutting flowers and greenhouse would be retained.

restored to use and profit. At "Biltmore" the first School of Forestry in the United States was founded and the first comprehensive forest plan put into effect. For advice on reforestation, Olmsted recruited Gifford Pinchot,[28] who became head of the newly founded American Division of Forestry in 1898. "Biltmore's" forestry program was a national model and an important experimental station. So it was not just size alone that distinguished "Biltmore"; it was the scope of its endeavor. Olmsted, who was near retirement when he began the project, always foresaw its public character and importance. When he gave up all other private commissions, he kept "Biltmore" on until 1895, the year he finally was unable to work.

As for size, "Biltmore" is like something out of the Arabian Nights. One thousand men labored for five years to complete the house, outbuildings, and gardens; there are 265 miles of trails in the forest, 70 miles of wagon roads, and 38 of macadam drives. As for style, in France today there is a sumptuous but cozy, brocaded and bibelot-filled decorating style known as "le style Rothschild"; "Biltmore" and the other Vanderbilt estates provided its American equivalent, inside and out.

We are also back with that American innocence—the feeling we could do it all, that it was *proper* to have it all, and since "Biltmore" is so well preserved, there it all still is to see. There are 250 rooms, and a bathroom for every bedroom (not including the servants of course), as well as central heat, mechanical refrigeration, and electric lights—each among the earliest installations in the nation. There is a real working deer park, grandest symbol of European aristocracy, and an immense model dairy farm. There are over 2,500 roses in the rose garden, an Italian garden with pools, hedges, statues, and a magnificent walled garden and conservatory. Farther off from the house, as the formal landscape begins to give way to Olmsted's beautiful "wild" landscaping, there is also the most complete collection of wild azaleas in the United States.

These azaleas bring up the question of what kind of life could be led on such a place by someone who was not the owner, but an employee. In the case of Chauncey Beadle, the answer was "Wonderful." Estate superintendent jobs on big estates like "Biltmore" were really quite high-level management positions, which required intelligence and judgment as well as various technical skills; they were also positions that could be shaped to fit the job-holder's own interests. A Cornell-educated young Canadian, Beadle was originally persuaded by Olmsted to take on "Biltmore," which required someone equally good at forestry and gardening. The initial five years of work began, unusual even for a big estate, with a topographic survey of the entire 125,000 acres as they were acquired, and with a program called "openwood," which involved clearing undergrowth and young saplings selectively to promote a high cover. Beadle then stayed on for fifty-five years. In the thirties, believing that the native deciduous azalea was the finest American shrub, he began

collecting in earnest. He and three companions, two doctors and a chauffeur, who called themselves the "azalea hunters," scoured the eastern United States for native species, climbing mountains and forests, finding such beauties as the pink-shell, the flame, and the pinxter-bloom azaleas. When Beadle gave his collection to Biltmore in 1940 it included more than 3,000 plants. He had gathered fourteen species and many forms and hybrids. They were planted in a garden which is actually Beadle's own contribution to "Biltmore's" landscape. Though it had been laid out originally by Olmsted Bros., it was Beadle who enriched and enlarged the plan by adding conifers, magnolias, hollies, and rare plants such as franklinia and elliottia to make a rich green background for his azaleas. Collecting, selecting, propagating, designing, and just plain gardening—surely Beadle was able to exercise his talents at "Biltmore" as fully and variously as he would have anywhere else.[29]

GREAT SOUTHERN PLANTATION GARDENS

But when the North came South, they did not look to "Biltmore" for a model—they wanted something much more authentically plantation Southern. For inspiration, every casual visitor—or prospective Gilded Age plantation buyer—would have looked at the two most famous Carolina Low Country gardens, both located on the Ashley River, "Middleton Place" and "Magnolia Plantation." After 1909 when Benjamin Kittredge bought "Dean Hall," he would also have visited "Cypress Gardens," as he named his extraordinary water garden. The first two were created and restored by the same Charleston families that maintain them today; the

When Northerners came south, they all visited "Middleton Place," the supreme example of the eighteenth-century formal garden, as hung with legend and tradition as a live oak with Spanish moss. Seen here is the Middleton Oak, which marked a Native American trail for centuries before the English came to Charleston in 1673.

third was the dream come true of a transplanted New Yorker. All are open to the public today. Together the three include every possible feature of ornamental landscape on a southern plantation.

At "Middleton Place," turn-of-the-century visitors would have seen the renowned butterfly lakes and the green terraces of eighteenth-century Henry Middleton's day, the camellias, and all the other plants from the Orient reputedly brought to the garden in 1785 by French botanist André Michaux. Such imports, including the Chinese azalea and the candleberry tree, became synonymous with the South. They would also have seen the later picturesque landscaping of nineteenth-century Middletons, the romantic rice mill, the views across the Ashley River and its magnificent marshes, the remains of the great house, burnt to the ground in the Civil War except for one wing, and the immense live oaks hung with moss. By the twenties they would also have remarked on the garden restoration efforts of J. J. Pringle Smith, a Middleton descendent, and his wife, which culminated in the planting of 35,000 azaleas on the hill above the Rice Mill Pond. "Middleton" would have seemed a great place in the grand manner, redolent of history and of plantation life, with its business, its satisfying complexity.[30]

"Magnolia," on the other hand, was the creation of just one man, the Reverend John Grimke Drayton. Advised to garden for his health, he traveled abroad, saw most of the great gardens early in the nineteenth century, and returned to the Low Country to sweep away the old formal garden of the plantation he had inherited, replacing it with a picturesque landscape. Beginning about 1840, he planted hundreds of varieties of *Rhododendrom indicum* and *Camellia japonica,* which by 1900 had grown to tremendous size. Visitors came to "Magnolia" with high expec-tations, because, as E.T.H. Shaffer wrote in 1937, "Mr. Baedecker double stars only three places in the whole United States—the Grand Canyon and Niagara Falls because they are big—Magnolia Gardens because it is beautiful."[31] Drayton's creation is timeless, not historical; the focus is on the garden, not on the parade of plantation life, or the house, which was Drayton's simple replacement for the big house burned in the Civil War. At "Magnolia" Northern visitors would have been struck by the variety of unfamiliar plants, by the beauty of Drayton's phantasmagoric combina-tions, and by the jungly vigor of ornamental vines that love the long Carolina growing season: Lady Banks roses, jessamines, both yellow and white, and wisteria that climbs to the top of the tallest pines.[32]

"Cypress Gardens" is at once the strangest and the most beautiful of

LEFT:
As early as 1874, only nine years after the Civil War, when Harry Fenn's wood engraving of "Magnolia Garden" appeared in William Cullen Bryant's Picturesque America, *the image of the South as a wilderness paradise was set: swamp, water lilies, oleander (at right), and Spanish moss in the* Magnolia grandiflora, *above left.*

the three gardens. It is a sort of Miltonic hymn to wilderness, and has nothing to do with houses or gardens in the usual sense. In fact Kittredge created it about a mile from the old plantation house of "Dean Hall" in the abandoned backwater swamp among the old rice fields. Huge gray-trunked cypress trees grow in the ponds, raising their knobby Peer Gyntish knees and staining the water as black as good coffee and as clear. The gardens are well-known today: floating islands of pale or fiery azaleas, dizzying sweetness of *Daphne odora* in the air, thick fringes of daffodils, and extraordinary birds—white owlets peering soberly down from nests in the cypress crowns, etc. Above all there is the play of reflections in the water, and the pleasure of wandering silently by boat on the surface of black streams lit by those bright mirrored flowers. But when the first plantation-minded visitors came down, these effects must have been stunningly unfamiliar. "Cypress Gardens" would have impressed them with the idea of a wilder paradise to be regained than just the straight plantation model. Few but the foolish would have tried to duplicate these peerless gardens, but there were lessons to be learned about plants, plantings, the use of water in a Southern garden, how best to reuse a rice plantation, and how to create a romantic atmosphere.

The best variations on the Southern themes of history, horticulture, and wilderness include "Medway," "Mulberry Castle," and "Harrietta" in South Carolina, "Orton," and "Airlie" in North Carolina, and "Greenwood," "Goshen Plantation," and "Wormsloe" in Georgia. Some, like "Orton," "Airlie," and "Wormsloe" were owned and restored by Southerners, but most were revived by the Northern migration—or smartened up, at least, for not all plantations were ruins after the war.

Four lines of the darkest live oaks, and five sober green terraces make a perfect, restrained setting for "Medway," the pre-1690, medieval-looking house made of brown and lavender plantation brick that is set on a branch of the Cooper River near Charleston. Sixty years of luxurious sporting life, passionately and idiosyncratically pursued by New Yorkers Sidney and Gertrude Legendre and a ringful of international guests, hover in the air.

"Mulberry Castle's" name commemorates both the short-lived silk culture of the Carolinas and the unique detached ornamental pavilions, with hipped roofs and bell-shaped turrets that are positioned like defensive flankers in front of the house, built in 1714. Charleston landscape architect Loutrel Briggs took advantage of the location on the bluffs above the Cooper River to make a garden on three levels: a long river-level garden that finishes with a wall fountain under a live oak; an informal camellia garden under the oaks on the slope closer to the house; and nearest the house, a traditional formal garden, outlined in dwarf box and filled with daisies, phlox, roses, tulips, and violets. Briggs took every chance available to celebrate local color, and at "Mulberry Castle" a typical Low Country feature—the boat landing at the edge of the barge

canal that once led from the river through the home rice fields to the house—is made much of with a round court planted with azaleas and steps that lead to the house lawn above.[33]

Eighteenth-century "Harrietta," farther north on the Santee River in South Carolina, also has a wonderful garden that runs from a formal boxwood-and-brick design close to the house through lawns edged with camellias to live oaks and the river view. Most notable at "Harrietta" is H. S. Shonnard's early twentieth-century restoration of the barge canal and the rice fields themselves. The quilted marsh, the regular rise and fall of the waters, and the profusion of migrating birds, especially wild duck, fill in the background of the garden picture as it once existed at all these river rice plantations.

At "Orton," on the Cape Fear River, near Wilmington, North Carolina, the gardens that surround the white-columned house (begun 1760) were only really started in 1910 by Dr. James Sprunt and his wife, Luola. Third-generation Sprunts now own "Orton," which is open to the public. The house and gardens are set on a ridge, with the rice fields in front and a fresh water marsh behind that is full of egrets. Banana shrub, *Michelia Figo*, perfumes the air with its heavy scent. A grove of pale-green camphor trees, *Cinnamomum camphora*, stands witness to the tendency of gardeners everywhere, but especially in the South, to grow what they *almost* cannot grow—to try to be just that little bit more tropical and exotic than experience should permit. One hard winter, in other words, and good-bye camphor tree. "Orton's" great features include a Scroll garden where the kind of cookie-cutter beds so beloved by the Victorians shine to advantage. A pair of gazebos on stilts permits the proper view down onto the parterre, where slightly humpy crescents and kidneys, outlined in podocarpus and filled with bright annuals, look like so many garnet-studded brooches and necklets on the grass. All over the garden stand little folly buildings and bridges, including a memorial chapel to Luola built after her death in 1916.[34]

Mr. and Mrs. Pembroke Jones's "Airlie" on Wrightsville Sound, since destroyed, was not properly a plantation, but a large hunting and garden preserve—an estate in short. Jones was one of the few Southerners who worked on Wall Street; he made money, had houses in Newport and New York as well as in Wilmington, and invited his New York friends, who included Vanderbilts and Harrimans, down to "Airlie."

At first just a two-room bungalow, the house soon grew to thirty-eight rooms, including a ballroom and a dining room big enough for eighty. Set right in the forest, but within view of the Inland Waterway, was a beautifully Italianate classical folly known as the Lodge, designed by John Russell Pope. Near the Lodge, which was miles away from the main house, Pope also designed a pillared temple of love—appropriately enough, as he soon married Pembroke Jones's daughter, Jane. Pembroke Jones died in 1919, and in 1922 Mrs. Jones married his old friend Henry

At "Goshen Plantation" outside Augusta, Georgia, one of the garden terraces is embroidered with huge Cherokee roses in pansies and dwarf box. Silly, literal, and charming, this was a successful early twentieth-century version of the parterre de broderie.

The entrance gate at "Wormsloe" (1735), oldest of the Georgia plantations.

Walters, founder of the Atlantic Coast Line Railroad and of the Walters Art Gallery in Baltimore. She continued to work on her 150-acre natural garden in the woods, planting primarily magnolias, azaleas, camellias, and wisteria. Her gardener, Topel, once an undergardener to the Kaiser, estimated the azaleas planted at 150,000 and camellias at over 5,000.[35]

At "Greenwood" near Thomasville, Georgia, Stanford White was called in by the Payne Whitneys of Long Island to make alterations on the house and to create new gardens. "Greenwood," a Greek Revival house built in 1835, was the work of master-carver and English-trained architect John Wind. It was a particularly splendid example of the houses built by cotton-planting Georgians as they expanded westward into lands that were newly opened up and free from the threat of Indians. (The Indians had just been deported en masse to Oklahoma.)

It had belonged to New Yorkers since 1889. Writer William Robert Mitchell points out in an article on another Thomasville plantation, "Pebble Hill," that by now shooting plantation life in pinewood Georgia has lasted longer than the cotton culture it replaced.[36] Thomasville was known as "Yankee Paradise" as early as the 1870s when private Pullman cars brought visitors to stay in the elaborate resort hotels and breathe the warm piny air. They then moved on to dove and quail and hunting dogs. As Cleveland Amory points out in *The Last Resorts*, hotels came before cottages from Maine to Florida. Hotel-keeper Karl Abbott, who began in the White Mountains of New Hampshire and finished with some of the biggest resorts of the twenties in Florida, writes that for Northerners the next step after a hotel visit was to "buy an old plantation house from a local real estate man who gave them a beating only to be

compared with that given the Union Army at the first battle of Bull Run." The house was always in a terrible state of disrepair so that the local contractors had a field day.[37]

Much to White's credit, he said he wouldn't touch the house at "Greenwood"; it was perfect as it stood, surrounded by a grove of palmettos and magnolias. Before the Civil War it had been encircled by formal gardens, the typical mosaic of little beds so beloved by eighteenth- and early-nineteenth-century Georgians. White made one of his typical Italianate gardens, importing statues, balustrades, and fountains from Pompeii. It looked odd but good, as did a palm garden filled with every species that would grow as far north as Thomasville. The woodlands were thick with azaleas, and the driveway was banked with Cherokee rose.[38]

The Cherokee rose, *Rosa laevigata*, is one of the glories of the South— again it is not an American native, but a plant from the Orient introduced to this continent at an unknown date. A delicate large white single flower with heavy sculptured tassels of gold stamens and dark polished leaves, it's an accomplished climber that will run up trees or over banks for twenty feet or more. The Cherokee rose has an especially honored place at "Goshen Plantation" outside Augusta looking toward the low hills of South Carolina. A formal garden on three levels had the usual accents of the period—a sundial copied from Hampton Court, and the usual divisions—a top terrace at house level, a box garden on the next, and a water garden planted with iris, azaleas, and flowering trees below. Four acres of daffodils extended from one side of the garden, and up the hill on the other was a rock garden full of Atamasco lilies and gentians. But the glory of the garden was the pair of Cherokee roses, stems, and leaves that made the box garden design.[39]

"Wormsloe," the oldest estate in Georgia, was begun in 1735 by another Jones, Noble Jones, one of the founders of Savannah. The garden has been changed and added to since then, and has always been in the possession of the same family. Many garden features on long-lived plantations commemorate family events (and almost always there is a family burying ground); the late-eighteenth-century mile-long oak allée at "Wormsloe" celebrated the birth of a son. In the 1920s, Augusta Floyd De Renne, wife of then incumbent Jones, added a formal garden. It was enclosed by warm old brick walls and iron grilles, and divided into three sections. Busy and cheerful, it featured modern plantings of blue larkspur, pale pink arctotis, and valerian, in combination with native yuccas and palmettos. Augusta Floyd De Renne also included many statues, both old and new, in her plan, and even extended a warm welcome to those Victorian outcasts—garden gnomes! An entire third of the layout was actually called "The Gnome Garden."[40]

Chauncey Beadle collected azaleas; the Reverend Drayton collected camellias; Augusta Floyd De Renne collected gnomes; Anna Hyatt Hunt-

Actaeon, *in gilt bronze by Paul Manship, flees the hounds of Diana against a background of rice fields at "Brookgreen Gardens" in Murrell's Inlet, South Carolina. Manship sketched this group and its companion,* Diana, *in 1915 when he was living in the artists' colony of Cornish, New Hampshire.*

ington collected sculpture. A sculptor herself, she and her husband, Archer Milton Huntington of the railroad and shipping family, bought an old plantation, "Brook Green," birthplace of nineteenth-century painter Washington Allston, on the Waccamaw River at Murrell's Inlet, South Carolina, in the twenties. "Brookgreen Gardens" was intended to be a quiet, salubrious place for Anna Hyatt Huntington to recover from a bout of tuberculosis. The Huntingtons also wanted to create a preserve for the flora and fauna of the Southeast, and a garden surrounding for her sculpture. Anna Huntington's sculpture required a lot of surrounding, one might say, as many of her works were monumental equestrian groups, or very large animals, such as *Fighting Stallions,* an aluminum group of two horses that stands fifteen feet high. Her first sculpture to receive official acclaim was an equestrian *Joan of Arc,* which received honorable mention at the Paris Salon of 1910.[41] At first, since the statue was so big (it had required more than a ton of clay to model), the judges had refused to believe it had been made by a woman.

When she recovered from her tuberculosis, the idea of "Brookgreen" gathered steam—three adjoining plantations were purchased, and the sculpture collection was expanded. It is an outline collection representative of the history of American sculpture[42] in the realist tradition, beginning in the nineteenth century (when American sculpture really began) and continuing through the first half of the twentieth century. The Huntingtons' collection is important because it has preserved an aspect of garden art and sculpture that fell from fashion for fifty years and is only being rediscovered today. "Brookgreen" is also that rare thing, a successful sculpture garden. Big works are given enough room, and in the smaller courts and enclosures smaller works are sympathetically related to one another. Statues that need particular placement in a garden get the treatment they deserve: Harriet Frishmuth's *Call of the Sea* sits in an iris-fringed lily pool; Anna Huntington's *Reaching Jaguar* is appropriately planted with cactus. Immense live oaks and a network of white-washed "Charleston" walls provide flickering shade, background, and Southern atmosphere.[43]

Horse Heaven

There were other horses in the Southern landscape besides Anna Huntington's stupendous steeds. From the 1880s on through the twenties, the big Southern attractions for Northern fox hunters, polo players, and steeplechasers were the soft going underfoot, the mild winters, and a countryside free from the kind of development that was just beginning to inhibit field sports around Northern cities. There was also golf in the pinelands and superb upland bird shooting. Southern comfort abounded in the form of good servants and old houses. The people who flocked to Aiken and Camden, to Augusta and Thomasville, were the same people who made gardens around Boston and New York, and cities farther west such as Cleveland, Detroit, and Chicago. Many of them were second-generation rich, freed from the cares of having to make money on a daily basis; their yearly round included three winter months in the Southern pines. A garden and a house full of flowers were as much a part of their lives as a good hunter or polo pony. Often they employed the same architects and garden designers for their winter houses as for the houses up north. In Carolina and Georgia resorts one finds gardens by Rose Standish Nichols; Herbert, Pray and White; Warren Manning; Peabody, Wilson and Brown,[44] and many more. It was a wonderful opportunity for owner and designer alike to experiment with a new unfamiliar flora, and with plants too tender to grow up north.

Nurseries such as Berckmans' Fruitlands in Augusta, Georgia, which was one of the earliest in that state (1857–1858), provided exotic materials; native plants used in these resort gardens were often wild specimens. Prosper Jules Alphonse Berckmans, a Belgian, was responsible for many important introductions from Europe and the Far East that became Southern garden staples, such as Amur privet. He also introduced into commerce a wide variety of oriental thujas, or arborvitae, less hardy but lusher than the American species. These dense, cylindrical conifers stood in for cypresses in many a Southern "Italian" garden of the early twentieth century. Fruitlands is now the Augusta National Golf Course.[45]

Aiken, in southern South Carolina, just seventeen miles from Augusta, Georgia, became known around the turn of the century as Aiken, Long Island. It had had a history as an antebellum Charleston summer resort, as did Camden and Augusta. Beginning in the 1880s, Aikenites cut a bigger social—though perhaps not horticultural—dash than the others since it was to Aiken that the tastemakers and the money of New York came in greater numbers. Paradoxically, Aiken was "colonized" as a Northern resort by a New Orleans family, the same Eustises who had revived "Oatlands." The Eustis children, William, George, and Louise, were taken to Aiken by their aunt, Celestine Eustis, after their parents' death of tuberculosis in France in 1872. Little Louise, known as Lulie, was frail. (How many good gardens in this country owe their existence to the nineteenth-century search for "good air," then supposed to be the only prevention and cure for TB?[46])

When the boys went away to boarding school, Lulie and Celestine settled into a house that had once been the summer retreat of an old Charleston family, the Legares. Celestine, known as Tantine to one and all, christened the place "Mon Repos" and made the garden that would be the model for many others in Aiken. The tall longleaf pines made a lofty and ubiquitous background, and Tantine added camellias, honeysuckle, bamboo, and tea olives. Against the white clapboard house walls wisteria, jessamine, and Lady Banks roses clambered up to the second story. A green picket fence separated the garden from the road.

Tantine came from New Orleans, had spent much time in Europe, and every summer she took Lulie to one Northern watering spot or another—Newport, Bar Harbor, Saratoga, or Boston's North Shore.[47] She had probably seen most of the beautiful gardens of her day, and thanks to the Corcoran fortune she certainly did not lack for money to spend on a garden. But she also must have understood the real meaning of the phrase "genius of the place." At "Mon Repos," there were to be no exotic fantasies for her—no New Orleans courtyards, no Newport or Riviera grandeur. Instead, she simply chose to emphasize the natural beauty of the area, and the Southern romance of fragrance and drooping vines. She also fixed up a number of other cottages to rent to interested Northern friends. Lulie married Tommy Hitchcock, Sr., and Aiken was off and running.

Hitchcock Senior, who had inherited a comfortable fortune from his father, the best financial columnist of his day—and a very successful stock market operator—was one of the best polo players of his generation, and a superb all-around horseman. Simple and courteous, but severe-seeming and almost ascetic, Tommy Hitchcock, Sr., also had the magic gift of leading the rich to join him in new (but only healthy!) pleasures and new places. When he married Lulie Corcoran Eustis and came down to her sleepy haven of Aiken, his "set" happily followed right along. By 1898 Aiken regulars included Traverses (as in Saratoga's Travers Stakes, one of the great American stakes races), Hunnewells, Sanfords, Vanderbilts, Elkinses from Philadelphia's Elkin Park, and Rutherfurds and Schleys from New Jersey. By 1929 sportsmen from every fashionable rich suburb in America were enjoying Aiken's winters—they came from Grosse Pointe, Lake Forest, Indian Hill, and Sewickley.

By then, Aiken had become the polo mecca of America, thanks to the admirable Lulie, the patron saint of the sport. A pied piper for the sporting young in Aiken, her protégés included almost all the 10-goal players in the United States at that time. Her horsemanship was legendary: though she could not see more than about ten feet in front of her, until her last days she was always up front in the draghunts, jumping the five-foot-tall timber fences banked with brush that were typical Aiken obstacles of their day.[48] Those who could stay with her as she rode beside her husband would hear him calmly say, "Now, Lulie, we are coming to a fence."[49]

William C. Whitney was one of the Long Islanders who joined Hitchcock in Aiken and helped buy up the fifteen to twenty square miles of land that comprised the Hitchcock Woods, where the famous Aiken drags were held. The woods were a natural garden, and the Hitchcocks planted them every year with new wild flowers to add to the display, which began with the first few mild blue-and-gold days of December and ran through April. There were also stands of bamboo, descended from Tantine's first introductions. Ivy covered the ground and climbed the trees.

Equestrian life influenced the landscape of pineland resorts in countless ways. Horses themselves, and their paraphernalia, were thought of as ornamental, not utilitarian. In Aiken the roads were kept unpaved to provide soft going, and the pale sand made a vivid contrast to the surrounding green. Paddocks, polo fields, stables, and training sheds were part of the look of these estates.[50] At Alexander House in Thomasville, designed by K. B. Schley, a vista of green paddocks and horses grazing behind the crisp verticals and horizontals of fences was an integral part of the camellia garden laid out by landscape architect Earl Draper.[51] In Aiken in 1929, architect Thomas Hastings actually built a house combined with stable for himself and called it "Horse Haven."[52]

In Aiken, and even more in Augusta,[53] there were also gardens that were less deliberately Arcadian than the Hitchcock Woods, or the many plantation wild gardens, with their hundreds of camellia and azalea varieties flourishing under the pines. With fewer acres than plantations, the town gardens were necessarily more pulled-together and designed-looking. Two typical formal gardens were the C. Oliver Iselins' "Hopelands" in Aiken, and the H. P. Crowells' "Green Court" in the Sand Hills of Augusta.

In Brookville, Long Island, Mrs. Iselin, who was the gardener and horse lover of the family (he was a well-known yachtsman), had a wild garden full of azaleas. At "Hopelands" on Whisky Road, the most desirable address in Aiken, formal garden compartments of flowers or lawn were surrounded by a serpentine brick wall like the one Thomas Jefferson designed for the University of Virginia. An old Southern favorite, cherry laurel, was used as hedging and for the clipped mounds and pillars that were such a prominent feature of the garden.

At "Green Court," the garden was as secluded from its close neighbors and from the road as any Chestnut Hill, Philadelphia, garden. A straight path ran the length of the garden, with flower borders on the left and a thick screen planting on the right. A pergola canopied with climbing roses finished the straight line of the path. Behind the house was a square sunken garden hedged in privet, which was reached via other square, grassed compartments set on slightly varying levels. A succession of low, fat, and handsome privet arches flanked by somber Italian cedars formed the dominant motif of the garden; statues, benches, fountains, and a square reflecting pool were bordered with iris and box. The one informal part of the design was a walk that wound its way around the perimeter of the estate within feet of the encircling iron fence, a fence so thickly planted out that no one could have guessed it lay behind the spring blaze of hundreds of azaleas and tall shrubs.[54] The April show over, the Northerners departed to do it all over again up North in June. The pinelands were left for another year for the Southerners who lived there all year round to enjoy, and especially for their small children who

wiggled through the estate fences to pick the remaining flowers and run wild in the empty gardens.[55]

CAMDEN AND COLUMBIA, SOUTH CAROLINA

Camden: "Plane Hill," "Holly Hedge," and "Kamschatka"

Camden was more of a Southerners' town. An eighteenth-century history, a tightly knit plantation oligarchy, and close connections with Charleston via the Wateree River, whose navigable course ended in rapids at Camden, made for a town proud of its own history and of its own culture, which included a number of notable gardens. Throughout the nineteenth century, plants came upriver from the nurseries around Charleston, packed in Spanish moss to keep them cool, or planted in barrels.[56] The grandest gardens were terraced in the same fashion as the falls of Maryland and Virginia houses.

"Plane Hill," a plantation built before 1817 and later known as "The Terraces," was the childhood home of Mary Boykin Chesnut, that redoubtable diarist of the Civil War. The terrace garden was laid out around 1840 by Hamilton Boykin with the help of John McRae, a Scotsman, who had already terraced his own garden at nearby "Horsebranch Hall." "Plane Hill's" garden had four levels, each reached by three flights of steps. The bottom level was planted with cedars and looked out over the fields; there was also an ornamental grotto with a spring. On the top three terraces specimen shrubs were planted in the same nineteenth-century gardenesque fashion[57] as on the bottom "wilderness" level of Sarah Coleman Ferrell's very well-known garden, also called "The Terraces," in La Grange, Georgia, which was first laid out in 1841. Among the shrubs were the earliest Indian azaleas in the area, imported by Mrs. Boykin.[58] In spring, the sides of the falls were bright with yellow jessamine, South Carolina's state flower.

Both in Kirkwood, the tiny village north of Camden that became the resort neighborhood, and on the Wateree River south of the town, there were other places, such as "Holly Hedge," "Mulberry," and "Mt. Pleasant," with important gardens or landscape surroundings. So in the 1870s when Northerners began to come for the winter season by railroad they found a proud, down-at-heel, but handsome town with public buildings by Robert Mills, South Carolina–born architect of the Washington Monument, and an assemblage of overgrown terraced gardens. Some of the old in-town plantations, as they were called, took paying guests. Following the traditional pattern of resort colonization, Yankees also bought places and "fixed them up," though Camden was never very ostentatious as far as gardens went—more splash was spent on the horses, and perhaps on transportation (the usual private railroad sidings were built for the usual private cars, for example).

"Holly Hedge," the largest and most elaborate early garden in

Camden, is located in Kirkwood (today a Camden neighborhood) on the sand hills. The handsome raised-cottage house was built around 1842, but the gardens had been laid out some fifteen years before.[59] Its 32 acres of landscape included terraces that cascaded down from the house to a series of ornamental ponds. These mixed-garden terraces of fruit, flowers, and vegetables were still in place at "Holly Hedge" when it was bought by Ernest Woodward, fondly known as "the Jello King." Charles Garnett, the Virginian who came to "Holly Hedge" in Marian du Pont Scott's employ when she bought it in 1942, and who has been there ever since, remembers how the asparagus kept coming up through the grass year after year. Both at "Holly Hedge" and at "Kamschatka," which the William Buckleys bought in 1938, the new owners made the improvements themselves without professional help—or rather with the professionals who were part of their house staff. Charles Garnett remembers Mrs. Scott (also the owner of "Montpelier" in Virginia) laid out the curves of the seven-foot-tall Jeffersonian serpentine brick wall that now surrounds the flower garden near the house. A Virginia-born mason, whom she had also brought south with her, laid the wall, and her own house carpenter made the low wooden entrance gates.[60]

The garden made by the William Buckleys at "Kamschatka" followed the familiar axial terraced garden model. Any reader of Mary Chesnut's memorable diary will recognize her playful wit, with its faintly complaining undertone, in the story of the naming of "Kamschatka."[61] A great Southern belle, imperious and sharply intelligent, Mary Boykin Miller married fellow Camdenite James Chesnut, who became first a U.S. Senator and then a Confederate general. The childless couple lived at the Chesnut family plantation for eight years with her parents-in-law. As difficult as this situation was for her, nonetheless, when she and her husband finally built their own dream house in 1854, the very name she chose was a complaint. Because, she said, the new house was so far from town—two miles—she called it "Kamschatka" after the remote Russian peninsula. Mary Chesnut always liked to make it clear she knew what perfect was, *and* what it wasn't.[62]

When the Buckleys bought "Kamschatka" it had suffered neglect, the effect of the Civil War, Reconstruction, and the Great Depression. Nevertheless, as Priscilla Buckley remembers, everyone in Camden still knew how to have a good time. "All of Camden of my Father's generation (80s and up)," she writes in 1987, "remembered a fancy dress ball that was given in the shell by the Watsons and the Pomeroys (who then owned it) during the Depression. They danced by candlelight in the ghostly structure on top of a sand dune, disturbing the rest of a mule that was stabled on the ground floor in what would be our breakfast dining room."[63]

Around the slightly Gothicized Greek Revival white frame house, the Buckleys added four outlying cottages, a swimming pool, stables, a laundry, and an office building. "The garden had fallen into disarray," continues Priscilla Buckley, "and had reverted to jungle tangles, but it still had magnificent trees." Buckley may have worked from original plans made by James Chesnut when he laid out his ten terraces on the entrance side of the house, but even without plans, all Buckley would have had to do was look around at other terraced Camden gardens for inspiration.[64] In true twentieth-century enclosure garden fashion, the terraces were hedged with clipped osmanthus to form outdoor "rooms," and statues and fountains were brought back from London. The brick walks were laid in fancy patterns, and everywhere were the signature plants of this particular version of the South—Lady Banks roses, dogwood, azaleas, magnolias, and towering pines.

Columbia

Forty miles southwest of Camden is Columbia, the state capital, where a vivid and wonderfully raucous social life, the happiest mixture of North and South, unfolded in an extraordinary Gilded Age garden. Not all Yankees who came south for the winter lived on remote plantations or were maniacs for hunting, shooting, fishing, and polo.

Sarah Porter Smith Boylston was more interested in gossip and conversation, parties, bridge, the jokes life plays, afternoon cocktails, and her garden.[65] Miss Sarah, as she was known, was the sort of woman who wore a green eyeshade to play what she called cheating bridge, where the rules allowed you to peep in other people's hands if possible. At the end of the season, just before she shut up the house to go north for the summer, Miss Sarah, the best of hostesses, would have her most splen-

The gardens of "Hampton-Preston House" as they appeared in the pages of Harper's Weekly *in April 1865, the year the Civil War ended.*

diferous garden party, and would serve "doubtful punch" — the leavings of all the old bottles she could round up, mixed with fruit juice and soda and poured over ice. According to one participant, "One time the punch would have little power but next time it might knock your head off. The beautiful setting and the air of *adventure*, caused by the drinks, made for a grand evening." Columbia loved Miss Sarah, and never for a moment thought of her as a Yankee.

Born in the Palmer House Hotel in Chicago, Sarah Boylston came to Columbia for the first time when she was eight years old, in 1889, part of that great aimless railroad drift of successful Northerners seeking warmer climates. Her Wilkes-Barre, Pennsylvania, businessman father made Columbia their winter home, and in 1909 Sarah married Samuel Shoemaker Boylston, a good ole boy from a fine South Carolina family. They settled in across the street from her father's Victorian house.

With her considerable inheritance, Miss Sarah also settled down to making a two-and-a-half-acre garden using what remained of the old garden on site. This was quite a lot, as original owner John Caldwell, the wealthy merchant who built his splendid Greek Revival house around 1830, had laid out three terraces with a central walkway, transverse walks, and many specimen trees. The new garden, which is being restored today, is divided into compartments, which Miss Sarah called her "parlors." Walls were made not only of boxwood, but of cherry laurel, *Prunus caroliniana*, pruned high to make lacy screens so the sun would reach the box below. There were arbors and fountains and summer-houses, a flower parterre, and a memorial garden dedicated to the dead of World War II, and to her deceased husband and son. Miss Sarah had her gardeners root every piece of box they pruned in a capacious rooting garden. There was also an old-fashioned glass-covered "pit" for propagation. From a notable collection of South Carolina wild flowers and ferns at her country plantation near Winnsboro she often brought specimens for the town garden. It was a real Southern garden, filled with high flickering shade, vines, old-fashioned roses, bulbs in their season, and perfumes that ran from the old-fashioned sweet shrub to the spicy breath of incense cedar in the sun. It was also filled endlessly with people — Ethel Barrymore, Tallulah Bankhead, Edgar Lee Masters, Jane Addams, Winston Churchill, and Lord Mountbatten were all visitors, basking in Miss Sarah's convivial glow.

High Victorian gardens had not been unknown before the Civil War. The memory, and the remains, of other old gardens must have influenced a gardener like Miss Sarah who was doubtless familiar with the outstanding nearby local examples, "Hampton-Preston House," designed by Robert Mills in 1818[66] and as well known for its 4-acre gardens and plant collections as for its famous second owner, General Wade Hampton, hero of the Revolution and of the War of 1812. Naturalists and botanists as noteworthy as Audubon, Le Conte, and Agassiz all had commented admiringly on the parterres, the trees, and the fountains.

In 1861, Northern landscape gardener and rural architect W. R. Bergholz described the collection of intricate and highly colored conifers so beloved by the Victorians:[67] "large old trees . . . over eighty feet high, whose huge trunks and wide spread branches are, in many cases, densely wreathed and draped with masses of English ivy, forming the most picturesque sylvan objects so rarely met with." He continues, "The grounds . . . are layed out [sic] strictly in the geometrical style. All the symetry [sic], uniformity of the old school, introduced in Europe several centuries ago, are displayed here, in formal walks and small figures, mixed plantations, trellises, grottoes, artificial water, etc."[68]

At the end of the Civil War, pictures of the "Hampton-Preston" garden summed up the vanquished South in the pages of *Harper's Weekly*. The garden is depicted with its long evergreen allées, and the house, the Union Headquarters, has the Union Jack flying from the porch.

Though she had a huge garden library, Sarah Boylston might not have read Bergholz or an 1865 *Harper's Weekly*, but she surely would have seen *Country Life in America*, where Helen Ashe Hays described the garden in 1910 as "A Colonial [sic!] Garden Down South." Hays's description of the garden in winter conveys its newly desirable romantic desolation: "the vines take possession of the upper air, make it their playground, romping from tree to tree and flinging themselves across paths and over walls. . . . Most audacious is the wisteria which unites the whole garden in its embrace, casting ropes and nets between the branches. . . . Where it springs out of the ground under the wall, its trunk is like great cables, thicker than a man's thigh. . . . The dainty Carolina jasmine [jessamine] . . . entwines itself delicately over shrubs and pillars. . . . The fountain stands encircled by high walls of clipped box. . . . Its setting of high green walls and arching trees is in harmony with its classic grace. Fountain and surroundings call to mind the somber simplicity of Roman gardens."[69]

Fragonard and Hubert Robert's sketches and paintings of overgrown Italian gardens influenced French garden taste in the last quarter of the eighteenth century. Similarly, at the turn of the nineteenth century, the green look of Southern ruin and age was admired. Overgrown boxwood and tall trees bound together with vines cast a Fragonard shade over gardens that, had they been kept up as their original Victorian owners intended, would have promptly been swept away. As it was, these shaggy gardens became romantic, nostalgic models, the American gardens of Tivoli for gardeners like Miss Sarah. Today "Hampton-Preston" gardens, which were bulldozed in the forties, are being re-created with a full range of old-fashioned Southern planting, things like the great spring snowdrop, the cinnamon and musk roses, and all the lilies with funny names, most of which aren't lilies at all: milk and wine, ginger, magic, red spider, and trout.[70]

Coming down the coast, the southernmost barrier reef islands of Georgia tell you that Florida is near, and that the mythological weathervane is shifting from "Southern" to "Mediterranean," but with a distinct turn toward the tropical. Thomas Wentworth Higginson of Massachusetts, who published his Civil War memoirs in 1870, wrote about St. Simon's Island,

when we afterwards landed, the air had that peculiar Mediterranean translucency which southern islands wear, and the plantation we visited had the loveliest tropical garden, though tangled and desolate, which I have ever seen in the South. . . . The deserted house was embowered in the great blossoming shrubs and filled with hyacinthine odors, among which predominated that of the little Chickasaw roses which everywhere bloomed and trailed around. There were fig trees, date palms, crepe-myrtles, and wax-myrtles, Mexican agaves and English ivy, japonicas, bananas, oranges, lemons, oleanders, jonquils, great cactuses and Florida lilies [*Zephyranthes atamasco*].[1]

Higginson is writing about "Retreat Plantation," which was later bought by Howard E. Coffin, of Detroit, Michigan, founder of the Hudson Motorcar Company and Georgia's first big-time resort promoter.[2] Coffin had first visited Georgia in 1911 and bought Sapelo Island, where he built "South-End House," a Spanish house and gardens, on the ruins of an Italianate plantation house and its original huge gardens. Beginning in 1926, he transformed "Retreat" into a golf course, part of the Spanish-style resort "The Cloisters" on adjoining Sea Island. Addison Mizner, the virtual creator of the Palm Beach Spanish style, was the hotel architect.

"Vizcaya"

Before Mizner, there was only one well-known Florida estate garden: "Vizcaya."[3] There is almost too much to say about "Vizcaya," and most of it has been said. In 1924, *Town & Country* art editor, Augusta Patterson, wrote about the days when the house was being built, c. 1912–19: ". . . it was a sensation. Everywhere everyone seemed to know someone who was doing something for the Deering house."[4] "Vizcaya," which is open to the public today, is a sort of Venetian palace set on what was originally 180 acres of the black marshy shoreland — known as "Florida hammock" — of Biscayne Bay. Fanning out to the west and south is a fabulous Italian Renaissance formal garden carried out in tropical plantings. Instead of strictly shaped plane trees, there are live oaks, and traditional parterre patterns are traced in clipped Florida jasmine and colored sand. The dramatic black shade and dazzling Florida light inspired John Singer Sargent to paint the best watercolors of his life when he visited Deering's brother and "Vizcaya" in 1917.[5]

The house, whose original inspiration was the Villa Rezzonico, a Venetian summer escape on the "Brenta Riviera," is the best-known work of Beaux-Arts-trained architect F. Burrall Hoffman, Jr.[6] Its structure and interiors incorporate thousands of decorative works of art spanning four centuries of European history, mainly Italian. The gardens were designed by Diego Suarez, who was born in Bogotá, and trained in Florence under the discriminating eye of Arthur Acton, who owned and restored Villa La Pietra.[7] The entire operation was overseen by Paul Chalfin, an American art expert and would-be painter who studied in Paris first with Gérôme and then with Whistler.[8] He was also an associate of New York decorator and stylish girl-about-town Elsie de Wolfe, who in 1910 introduced Chalfin to her friend James Deering, of the Chicago harvesting machinery fortune. Chalfin and Deering traveled in Europe for six years, collecting furniture, decorative elements — and impressions — for their tour de force. "Their" is the word to use, because, while the idea and the money were Deering's, the driving artistic force behind the coruscating vision of "Vizcaya" was certainly Chalfin's. Deering had been put out to pasture by his family company and found himself at the age of forty-nine with a lot of money and nothing to do. His real life's work turned out to be building "Vizcaya," and perhaps his interest and excitement in the grand design helped keep him alive for many more years than might have been expected — he suffered from pernicious anemia.[9] He died in 1925, only two years after the great baroque gardens were finally completed.

So much for "Vizcaya's" genealogy. Where does it stand in the list of American gardens? "Vizcaya" is more than an encyclopedic collection of garden compartments and European architectural features. It is a garden whose brilliance gives the word "pastiche" a new meaning. Although it is often compared to William Randolph Hearst's "castle" at San Simeon because of its crazy opulence and many statues, it is actually closer to Platt's greatest Italianate gardens, with their carefully reasoned spaces, or even to Beatrix Farrand's masterpiece, "Dumbarton Oaks," in its mastery of levels and horizons — though Suarez was never a match for Farrand in plantsmanship. All of the treasures from abroad and all of Hoffman or Chalfin or Suarez's flights of fancy — for each contributed to the garden — are strongly knit into the design. The great stone barge modeled after that at the Villa Borromeo on Lake Maggiore breaks up the flat sea view and creates a harbor, as well as providing the final top note of fantasy in the garden. The mount crowned with a casino at the western end of the garden not only provides something to look at from the house

Painter John Singer Sargent said of Vizcaya in 1917, as the Americans were joining World War I, that "it combines Venice, Frascati, and Aranjuez and all that one is likely never to see again." (At Frascati are some of the most famous villas of Italy; Aranjuez is a rococo royal palace in Spain whose garden exhibits the same mix of Spanish, Italian, and French influences as Vizcaya.)

terrace, and a welcome change in elevation, but also eliminates the glare from the lake beyond.

The sensibility expressed at "Vizcaya" is also very different from Mizner's. The palace and its gardens are elevated beyond the admittedly marvelous estates of Palm Beach by the quality of Deering and Chalfin's collection of decorative arts, and by the exquisite unity achieved by Chalfin, Hoffman, and Suarez. Mizner's taste was more robust,

and expressed a much heartier hedonism. "Vizcaya" is set apart by a melancholy that permeates the place, a contrast to Mizner's cheerful stage business. In Europe, the melancholy one sometimes feels in great gardens gone public comes from a sense of vanished pleasures. But at "Vizcaya," as at so many other American palaces, it comes from a sense of life never lived. Rich Americans *wanted* to enjoy themselves as Europeans did; that was how they pictured themselves as living, but often they couldn't quite do it. Unbridled indulgence was all right in fantasy—but maybe that was as far as they really wanted to go. Certainly Chalfin was able to express what he *fantasized* about life in the gardens:

What was a casino for? For one to dream in or perhaps to weep; for two to steal to; for three to sing and for eight to dance in. Or perhaps the footmen—just liveried boys from the farm—had fetched and displayed hampers of cold fowls and sherry and sorbets made from the strawberries that ripened—even in winter.[10]

And certainly he and James Deering had a good time, but the heart of it is this: the life led was a life of luncheons for twelve with two butlers in tailcoats, when it should have been orgies. It was hard to live up to a place like "Vizcaya." What animated Deering's life was something that Americans enjoy possibly more than anything else to this day—planning, collecting, building, blissfully unaware that they are creating realities in which they won't *quite* be able to carry out their fantasies.

Palm Beach and Flagler

"Vizcaya" gave developers a promotional rallying point to describe Florida as *the* new, fashionable resort paradise: "See," they were able to say in effect, "the rich and famous are here to keep you company." In 1913, the originator of Palm Beach, Henry Morrison Flagler, broke the news

The Palm Beach house and garden of Mr. and Mrs. Alfred G. Kay, designed by Addison Mizner in 1921, had purple bougainvillea, pale blue plumbago, and the salmon-colored shrimp plant, Justicia Brandegeana, *covering the loggia and wall.*

The Palm Beach gardens of promoter Henry Flagler's day were at the resort hotels. In The American Scene, *Henry James, visiting the Flagler Royal Poinciana in 1904, describes the "gardens and groves, the vistas and avenues between the alignments of palms, the fostered insolence of flame-colored flower and golden fruit."*

about "Vizcaya" in a publication distributed by his land company to his hotel guests.[11] By 1913 Flagler, a Standard Oil partner and one of the great entrepreneurs of the nineteenth century, was well on his way to realizing the "American Riviera" he had always dreamed Florida could be. Like everyone else, he first began to visit Florida for his health. In 1888 he opened the Ponce de Leon Hotel in St. Augustine, designed by Carrère and Hastings in a Hispano-Moresque style. Flagler started Palm Beach as an upper-crust resort in 1896 when he brought down a trainload of New York's fashionable and curious, including four Vanderbilts. Colonel Edward R. Bradley's "Beach Club," a demure, white clapboard casino with stakes as high as Monte Carlo and famously delicious food, opened in 1898. In Palm Beach Flagler himself lived on the shores of Lake Worth, then a tranquil tropical lagoon with clear water and wooded shores. In 1901 Carrère and Hastings had been called in again to design "Whitehall" as a wedding present for Flagler's third wife, Mary Lily Kenan. The immense house was a handsome but odd mixture of Spanish Colonial and Southern plantation motifs: it had red tile roofs and a central courtyard with tropical plantings, but the huge Doric portico definitely said "Southern." It was built on only 6 acres. A promenade led from each bedroom to the central garden, where a copy of the *Bathing Venus* from the Boboli Garden in Florence presided.

As yet, nothing else in Palm Beach was remotely "Spanish." Up until 1919 there were a few Beaux-Arts mansions, a small colony of shingle houses, and, on the ocean front, Michael Grace and Henry C. Phipps.

Flagler's two big hotels, the "Royal Poinciana" and the "Palm Beach Inn," later named "The Breakers," were verandahed frame buildings painted "Flagler yellow" that could have fitted right into any resort palace on the East Coast.

Addison Mizner

It would be up to Addison Mizner to blend and refine a style that would typify the Palm Beach style, as Richardson's Shingle Style had somehow typified the idea of a northern resort cottage. Mizner's eclectic training, his natural attributes, and his ideas of what domestic architecture could be, were peculiarly suited to the job. Born in San Francisco in 1872 to a prominent California pioneer family, Mizner spent a year in Central America when he was sixteen. He absorbed Spanish culture, and learned to speak Spanish fluently. After trips to Spain and the Far East, he apprenticed himself to Willis Polk, a young California architect who was also a master builder. Mizner learned how to lay bricks and plaster walls expertly, and quite a lot about plumbing, electricity, and carpentry. He was a big spender, a man-about-town, and his tastes in the early days outran his pocketbook. Getting out of town was sometimes imperative because of his debts. A stint mining gold in the Klondike, some miniature painting in Hawaii, a little lantern-slide painting in Samoa, and a lot of European travel and sketching, broadened his architectural vocabulary. On another trip to Guatemala he almost bought out the Roman Catholic Church, which had fallen on hard times. From cathedral and monastery he purchased silver, carvings, textiles, and furniture. Information, impressions, techniques—Mizner absorbed them too, just as quickly as he picked up antiques. Everywhere he went his best friends invariably were the women who ran society. In Hawaii, it was Queen Liliuokalani, and when he moved to New York City to start an architectural practice in 1904, who did he know but Birdie and Tessie Fair, the San Francisco daughters of James G. Fair, the "Silver Bonanza King," who had respectively become Mrs. William K. Vanderbilt, Jr., and Mrs. Herman Oelrichs. They all loved him because he was razor-witted, entertaining, curious, and full of the unexpected. Weighing in at over 300 pounds, Mizner was never a beauty, though very much a dandy.

After fourteen years as a minor society architect in New York, in 1918 he found himself in Florida, recuperating from an old injury in the company of Paris Singer, the gorgeous blond sewing-machine heir, and Singer's latest love, the English nurse Joan Bates. (Singer's previous long, flamboyant, and stormy love affair with Isadora Duncan had ended in 1917.) Mizner's first Palm Beach commission was to revamp Singer's white bungalow, which she had grown bored with. The result was the "Chinese Villa," multicolored, with a sweeping pagoda roof. Mizner also designed a Chinese gate and garden, and a woven bamboo fence. Paris Singer put a five-foot-long stuffed alligator on the roof "to defy good taste," a totally appropriate way to start the Mizner Palm Beach era.[12]

But despite this, and all the highly colored stories about sketching plans in the sand, or hornswoggling clients into thinking the plans were unnecessary altogether, or forgetting the staircases on houses—most of which were promulgated by Mizner himself—his most important attributes were his organization, his inventiveness, his American "can-do" character. The workshops he set up to make tile, ironwork, Woodite panels, and "antiques" according to his own specifications, meant he could readily achieve his "look"—as could the many other South Florida architects who bought from Mizner Industries. His construction methods—stucco over hollow tile with molded cement ornament—meant his designs could be built by ordinary workmen, not by artisans, which meant much smaller price tags.

It wasn't just architecture or interior decorating, either. He developed his own methods of root pruning and transplanting; before Mizner, Florida natives believed tropical plants would not stand transplanting at all. He also invented some desperate shortcuts: the day before the opening of the Everglades Club he had the "lawn" planted with grass seed that had been soaked in warm water for two days—it sprouted as the workmen raked! (He even hung oranges on the trees with hairpins.) But he also was the first developer to save wild Florida plants: when the golf course was put in and he was responsible for tearing up 60 acres of jungle "hammock," Mizner saved all the wildlings and replanted them with remarkably little loss. He figured out when to prune shrubs for maximum bloom during the short Palm Beach season. His eye for scale led him to manufacture terra-cotta planters for terraces that were big enough to hold the root ball of a full-grown orange tree. He always insisted on being involved in the landscape planning of his projects.[13]

Like Frank Lloyd Wright, like Stanford White, who befriended him in New York with minor commissions on several occasions, Mizner was an overall designer. His houses were created for a kind of relaxed fun his clients couldn't have in any place in the world but Palm Beach: a sort of sun-on-the-skin easiness, a lazy take-it-or-leave-it sporting life not nearly as religiously outdoorsy as, say, Northeast Harbor. Many of Mizner's clients were the new American rich, proud to be playing the social game at Palm Beach, perhaps the best resort of all in which to start moving up the social ladder because it seemed to matter less there how or where you had made your money than how you spent it. Mizner's incorporations and adaptations of old material were a reassuring substitute for family history. His clients could point with pride to the furniture, sculpture fragments, or old tiles which he brought back annually from Europe, or to Woodite panels modeled after the paneling from the room where Ferdinand and Isabella met with Columbus.

Sometimes to lighten up the Spanish look, he used a touch of Venice, especially in houses right on Lake Worth,[14] and always there was the indefinable gaiety of the Riviera. This was not all Mizner's magic — real Riviera-ites did indeed come to Palm Beach, bringing, besides their titles, espadrilles, and striped jerseys for daytime wear, the idea that sport and wicked glamor could go together. The staid Garden Club of Palm Beach history states, "World War I brought here a number of visitors who normally spent their winters on the Riviera or in Mediterranean resorts." The Prince of Monaco, Prince Rainier's father, eventually came to have a look, to find out why so many of his American regulars were deserting Monte Carlo.

Singer and Mizner's brainchild, the Everglades Club, opened on January 25, 1919, in Palm Beach, and with it dawned the era of Palm Beach private gardens. That same winter, Mizner received his commission for "El Mirasol" from Mrs. Edward T. Stotesbury, who was so entranced by the Spanish splendors of the Everglades Club that she got rid of Horace Trumbauer and his already completed plans for a classical mansion. No one could miss "El Mirasol" or the fact that it helped Mrs. Stotesbury attain the social ascendency in Palm Beach she had failed to achieve at "Whitemarsh Hall" in Philadelphia. Besides the marvelous house, to which Mizner added something every year, there was a private zoo, an aviary, an orange grove, housing for fifty servants, an underground garage for forty cars, a reception lounge for visitors' chauffeurs and, more practically, a vegetable garden and a chicken house. Though in general Mizner's clients adored him, that didn't always make it easy for him to mastermind everything. After his "El Mirasol" experience with Mrs. Stotesbury, he said, "If an architect could chloroform a client, the house would be more attractive and coherent."[15]

The "cottage" idea spread more slowly in Palm Beach than at other resorts because the season was so short: at first just from the beginning of January until George Washington's Birthday, February 22. Not that there wasn't plenty of opportunity to make wonderful gardens, beginning with the climate itself. Starting at a point fifty miles north of Palm Beach, the Gulf Stream runs closer to the shore than at any other point in its course, making the water about 80 degrees F. all year round, and creating a microclimate that, unlike the rest of South Florida, really *is* tropical. The soil is surprisingly good for such a sandy looking place. Palm Beach's garden liabilities are strong winds and the salt spray they carry, which can be borne inland for half a mile.

SOUTH FLORIDA FLORA — A SURPRISE FOR THE NORTH

The Noah's Ark of plants listed in 1870 by Thomas Wentworth Higginson would also be typical of the wild mixture found in Florida gardens fifty years later. Lady gardeners who came south and their gardeners had to start all over again in a decidedly new climate. One Palm Beach lady in the thirties wrote,

. . . gardening in South Florida has been an exciting new adventure — a new type of pioneering. We have all had to start from "scratch" as it is only in the last decade that any gardening has been attempted in this part of the world. Imagine a place where trees often grow ten or twelve feet a year (and what that can do to the contour of your garden); and where hollyhocks, delphinium, and such, are grown as annuals, if at all. Most of us even grow our roses as annuals, digging up the beds each spring and replanting them with new bushes in October. Needless to say we use only inexpensive ones. . . .[16]

It was hard to keep to "well-bred" pale colors, given the tempting red-hot exotics that throve and bloomed in winter, though for pale colors there were quite a few: the soft blue plumbago, *P. capensis,* hibiscus *H. Rosa-sinensis* in white and pink, (as well as all shades of scarlet and red), and pink and white poinsettias. Gerberas from South Africa came in pale colors too, and for white flowers there were small trees like the fragrant white-flowered frangipani, *Plumeria alba,* from the West Indies, or the datura, *Brugmansia candida,* from Peru, with its huge crisply faceted flowers, dramatically called "angels' trumpets." More familiar from greenhouse culture in the North were gardenias and different jasmines. There were vines like allamanda, *A. cathartica,* a South American vine with clear yellow flowers all year long; Mexican golden chalice, *Solandra nitida,* with creamy red-veined flowers; passionflower, *Passiflora violacea,* and many other cultivars from Brazil; tropical varieties of morning glory, *Ipomoea,* in blue, yellow, lilac, white, and pink as well as magenta, red, and deep rose; and clock vine, *Thunbergia grandiflora,* with its blue-purple, yellow-throated trumpets. Northern gardeners slowly learned about the effects of strong sunshine on pale colors — they glare or look bleached-out unless there is some shade — and they began to see what happened to red-hot colors in Florida.

Against the dense, tropically green background, or the bright blue sky, or the bold Spanish facades with their deep-shadowed loggias, lots of strange new plants looked fine. Among the strangest were bird of paradise, *Strelitzia reginae,* from South America, with winged flowers colored orange and blue like match flames, and cathedral bells, or air plants, *Kalanchoe pinnata,* from the Far East, with candelabras of pendant pale green pods.[17] Some people grew orchids. Crotons, *Codiaeum variegatum var. pictum,* with their thick leaves streaked and spotted with red, yellow, and cream, and bronzy-leaved cannas, usually red, had been staples since late-Victorian hotel days. Caladiums, elephant's-ear, *Colocasia antiquorum,* beefsteak begonia, *B. × erythrophylla,* and Moses-in-the-bulrushes, *Rhoeo spathacea,* with its stiff green and magenta swords, were good for foliage interest. Brightly flowered vines, like bougainvillea, of course, and orange-flowered cape honeysuckle, *Tecomaria capensis,* were perfect with tile roofs. Shrimp plant, *Justicia Brandegeana,* from Mexico — salmon-red and with a vague resemblance to boiled shrimp — was found to be a good ground cover, as was *Catharanthus roseus*, the Madagascar periwinkle whose many patterns are figured in deep rose and white. South American shrubs like Brazilian pepper, *Schinus terebinthifolius*, also known as Florida holly, and golden-dewdrop, *Duranta repens*, decorated the garden with big clusters of berries, respectively scarlet and bright yellow.

There was a great variety of hedging material: turk's-cap, *Malvaviscus arboreus* var. *mexicanus*, from Mexico, crown-of-thorns, *Euphorbia milii*, from Madagascar, South African natal plum, *Carissa grandiflora*, the common oleander, *Nerium Oleander*, also called rose bay, originally from the Middle East, and the kinds of privet that like hot weather, like *Ligustrum Walkeri*, from Ceylon. Prized courtyard trees included banyans, *Ficus benghalensis*, whose elephantine chalk-white trunks and strange epiphytic growing habit were especially prized; feathery acacias with their sprays of yellow puff balls, bananas, figs, oranges, guavas, and lemons; and different palms—some used most often included arecas, *Chrysalidocarpus lutescens*, the pygmy date palm, *Phoenix Roebelenii*, and the sago, *Cycas revoluta*. Palms particularly favored for lawns and avenues were the graceful Queen Palm, *Arecastrum Romanzoffianum*, from Brazil, about 50–60 feet tall, and the Royal Palm, *Roystonea elata*, a South Florida native, which until it matures to 100 feet looks very like the Queen. Additionally, it has the advantage of having no "skirt" of dead leaves to be cut away. Cabbage palms, *Livistona australis*, were a common feature of the native South Florida landscape, and in Palm Beach a particular local feature was the great clusterings of coconut palms, the result of the fortuitous 1878 shipwreck of the Spanish brigantine, *Providencia*, with its cargo of 175 tons of coconuts.

This long list only begins to touch the range of plants that were grown. There was a tremendous amount of plant carnage until the new Floridians and their gardeners got the hang of it—new watering and fertilizer requirements, new growing season, a blasting sun. Often the most beautiful Palm Beach gardens were created by those, like Mrs. Henry Rea, who had the finest gardens up north, people who knew that heartbreaking experimentation is always part of the art of gardening. The Garden Club of Palm Beach was founded in 1928, and shortly thereafter professional gardeners got together as the Palm Beach Gardeners' Association. Together the ladies and their gardeners discovered there *were* ways to grow roses, thereby disproving part of the old Palm Beach complaint, "Roses are unthinkable; lawns impossible; summers unthinkable; milk undrinkable."[18]

Because of the salt, few ornamentals were grown on the ocean front except the sea grape, *Cocoloba uvifera*, which *would* survive salt, drought, and wind. Its round metallic leaves and heavy clusters of fruit decorated the laboriously maintained oceanfront lawns along with palms (often Washingtonias since they are so salt resistant), and the tall cream-colored candles of Spanish bayonet, *Yucca aloifolia*.[19]

PALM BEACH GARDENS

Mizner-style houses and gardens were perfect for the South Florida landscape. It was flat; they were not. It was low-key; they were dramatic. Gardens always exist in apposition to what's outside them, and nothing could have been more enlivening after the monotony of land and sea than to be in a garden surrounded by Mizner's towers and varied rooflines and chimney caps and leaping arches and flying staircases. He set the mold for gardens at houses designed by other Palm Beach architects: Marion Sims Wyeth,[20] Maurice Fatio,[21] and Joseph Urban.[22] The entrance facade was usually rather severe, and the plantings formal. Inside the house were fabulous displays of pots and cut flowers, which were changed regularly. On the other side of the house one found the "front lawn" on the ocean, and on another exposure the sheltered courtyard, or patio, that was the heart of the house. Almost always there was a fountain or a pool in the middle to center the design, and Mizner also used a variety of low retaining walls and steps. Galleries, balconies, and decks looked down into the patio from above.

Palm Beach "patios" often were not entirely surrounded by house walls. South Florida architects like Hoffman and Mizner had wisely opened up traditional Spanish architecture to adapt to the heat and to admit as much breeze as possible. At "Vizcaya," the roofed central cortile of the Villa Rezzonico became an open courtyard with an airy double-story loggia that looks both ways—into the courtyard and out to the sea;[23] in Palm Beach Mizner rang a hundred changes on the patio theme. "What I really did," said Mizner, "was to turn the Spanish inside out like a glove."[31] The courtyard *was* the garden: the sounds of the wind and the ocean were hushed, the walls were covered with vines, there was swaying shade, the music of a fountain, and in the evening the fragrance captured inside the walls was incredible. Moonlight was a must—at "Mar-a-Lago" Marjorie Merriweather Post had a blue electric "moon" mounted in the seventy-five-foot tower of the house. The view of the garden from inside the house was often framed by the arches of the loggia, that delicious vaulted and arched Mediterranean porch, where the people of Palm Beach lived.

Two places exhibit the diversity of Palm Beach gardens and gardeners. The first, "Audita," on South Ocean Boulevard, was designed for Mr. and Mrs. Alfred G. Kay by Mizner in 1921, one of six houses built by his firm that year. By Mizner standards the house was small; the restrained exterior had only a few trefoil-surrounded windows for ornament, making it a good example of Mizner's dictum: "If [the clients] have money, let them keep it inside."[24] The patio garden was framed by house walls, and faced west toward the ocean. Growing up the tower staircase and across the loggia was the main feature of the garden, a very old bougainvillea vine flowering freely with plumbago, which grows rampantly on the island. Here, its delicate clusters of pale blue phloxlike flowers cooled

The E. T. Stotesburys (perhaps under Mizner's giddy influence) took the idea of the Palm Beach patio as an outdoor living room literally: an Oriental rug covers their tiles.

Mrs. Henry R. Rea gardened in Florida as lavishly as she did in Sewickley, Pennsylvania. She later befriended Addison Mizner, who designed her Palm Beach house and garden during his later, leaner years. The garden was inspired by the rill at the Generalife in Granada, and the Gothic arches at the far end were one of Mizner's architectural finds.

down the hot purple bougainvillea bracts. The wall below was covered with shrimp plant, its deep salmon-red flowers all that was needed to complete the tropical color harmony.

The Kays gardened every inch of the property, beautifully and fancifully.[25] Unusually, they had preserved a part of the original jungle, or "hammock"—it was one of their most treasured possessions. From the main garden, with its peaceful Spanish convent atmosphere, a small path led through the jungle to the cutting garden at the back of the property. On the south side of the house was a small cloister garden, full of flowers throughout the entire season.

The Kays also had a house in Chester, New Jersey, and a camp in the Berkshires; both were deeply interested in botany as well as being good gardeners, and both belonged to the Garden Club of Palm Beach. Alfred Kay was a small, slight man, gentle, intelligent, sweet, and soft-spoken; his wife, Elizabeth, was tall, magnificently ramrod straight, brilliantly white-haired in her old age, given to wearing the softest and most flowery Liberty lawn dresses, and to making pronouncements in her sonorous and commanding voice that began "Alfred thinks. . . ." Elizabeth Kay was not above the "Mummy-did-it-all" temptation that afflicted so many

RIGHT:
Most of Marjorie Merriweather Post's entertaining at "Mar-a-Lago" took place in this crescent-shaped patio, which echoes the shape of the Bargello Palace in Florence. The round paving pebbles, found by Mrs. Post on a beach at Great South Bay, were shipped by the carload to Palm Beach and set in designs she had copied from the Alhambra.

The tiled cloister garden at the Alfred G. Kays in Palm Beach.

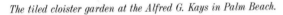

people of her generation—it was considered somehow less than perfection to call in a professional to decorate your house or to design your garden. Her description of the Palm Beach place states firmly that she was responsible for the design of both house and garden. She and Alfred had no children and did most everything together. Among other things, together they prepared *The Plant World of Florida,* a useful guide based on the notes of a German botanist and horticulturist, Henry Nehrling, who spent many years in Florida. Their decorous and well-ordered Palm Beach life was one never chronicled in memoirs or newspapers, and was typical of many Palm Beachers.

Nothing could have been more different from the Kays than the very public life and many marriages of Marjorie Merriweather Post and "Mar-a-Lago," both too well-known to describe again here. During the 1920–21 season, villas began to be built along the newly completed golf course, where in 1923 "Mar-a-Lago" would rise to challenge "El Mirasol." Mrs. Post, then Mrs. E. F. Hutton, competed with Mrs. Stotesbury for the crown of Palm Beach, and eventually won. The Hispano-Moresque house, designed by Joseph Urban in association with Marion Wyeth, consisted of

This covered pool in the south loggia of the John S. Phipps' "Casa Bendita" in Palm Beach was designed by Addison Mizner. There was also an outdoor pool.

115 rooms built in a crescent shape on South Ocean Boulevard, 17 acres of lawns and gardens, and a 9-hole par-3 golf course. Although the first sight of "Mar-a-Lago" tends to produce a laugh of amazement, in fact the terraces, exterior arches, swooping garden walls, and flights of stairs are beautifully, if stagily, planned, and tie the huge building into the landscape very well. The plantings are immense, and equal to the house in weight and flamboyance, and best of all, the staggeringly beautiful palms all around are big enough to keep the four-story tower from looking like a lighthouse.

Palm Beach patios, loggias, and terraces had to be big enough for entertainment and Palm Beach believed in the grand scale, but only "Mar-a-Lago"—and Marjorie Merriweather Post—were up to having the Ringling Brothers Circus perform on the lawn. The property stretches from Lake Worth to the sea, and had a private tunnel beneath the roadway for access. Construction was finished in 1927. Joseph Urban is most famous for working with Florenz Ziegfeld and his Follies, and that zany, sexy opulence shows up at "Mar-a-Lago" as well. Wyeth, who had originally been asked to design "Mar-a-Lago" and at first stayed on when Urban got the commission, eventually disclaimed all responsibility for the house, saying, "I don't want anyone to think *I* was the architect in charge." Mizner's biographer Donald Curl conjectures that the very extravagance of Urban's Palm Beach "Spanish" style, which we now so admire, is what contributed to its demise in the thirties.[26]

OTHER RESORTS

Mountain Lake

Just at the time Palm Beach was getting started, another less well-known Florida resort was also getting under way, powered by that wacky utopianism Americans had in abundance at the time. In 1907, Fred Ruth, soon to be a Florida real estate developer, was driving across the greenish, flattish, cattle-and-citrus country of central Florida near Lake Wales. He noticed a perfect conical hill. It was not very high, but it didn't need to be—it was, and still is, the biggest thing around. In fact, no bigger hill exists within sixty miles of the Atlantic coast between northern New Jersey and the very tip of Florida. "Iron Mountain" is the rather grand name of this 300-foot-high bump. "It seemed a sort of Floridian joke upon the prevailing flatness of the rest of the state," wrote Frederick Law Olmsted, Jr., in December, 1914, in a memo to Ruth[27] about the proposed private golf resort community to be nestled into the flank of Iron Mountain, on 2,500 acres of land Ruth had just bought. (It was the time of the Florida land boom, and many speculators were gulping chunks of land as big as a million acres, so Ruth's purchase was comparatively modest.) The bump itself was bought by Edward Bok, founder of the *Ladies' Home Journal,* the first successful mass circulation magazine in

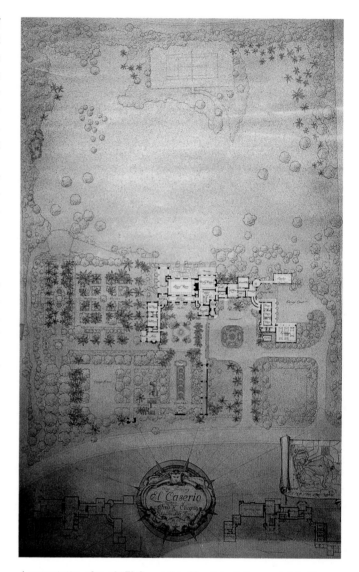

A presentation plan of "El Caserio" in Mountain Lake, created by the Olmsted firm, hangs in the house today.

the world. A Dutch emigrant, Bok was intelligent, serious, energetic, moral. He was saved from being the very embodiment of American middle-class virtue by his amiable visionary eccentricity. He had seen the carillon tower that John D. Rockefeller, Jr., had just raised above the Park Avenue Baptist Church in New York City. How much farther the bells would resound over the Florida flats![28]

By 1929, the 500-acre resort was surrounded by 2,000 acres of commercial citrus groves, and the bump was completely covered with luxuriantly deep green live oaks, a contrast to the prevailing scraggy cabbage palms, longleaf pine, and turkey oak of the surrounding countryside. For the mountain top, Olmsted imported miles of irrigation pipe—and nightingales and flamingoes—not to mention rare American trees like gordonia and thousands of lilies and azaleas. A pink marble carillon tower rises above the trees. "Bok Tower Gardens," Edward Bok's gift to the nation, is now open to the public. On any warm late winter day the golden notes of "My Old Kentucky Home" shower down onto the roof tiles of the big pastel Spanish Revival houses in the golf resort below. The lake golf course and the Mountain Lake Club, which Olmsted designed before Bok's gardens, stretch out in all directions. In landscaping Mountain Lake, a private residential community, Olmsted used native plant materials and an abundance of callitris, *C. Preissii,* an Australian conifer with a dark, billowing, columnar shape that gives the landscape a vaguely Mediterranean look. In the gardens of "El Caserio," the long pink house built for Massachusetts businessman Alfred H. Chapin in 1923–1930, brilliant painted glazers shine in the fountain basins. Silvery fountain spray cuts a silhouette against the callitris trees. A bell tower dominates the red tile roofs that cover seven master bedroom suites, room for six in staff, and reception rooms with painted beams and velvet sofas. The view to the south looks over a lawn down to the lake.

The delicate business of translating a formal garden into semitropical terms has been treated by the usually sober Olmsted, Jr., with a sense of fun and fantasy not often seen elsewhere in his work.[29] The square beds of a formal parterre, known as the "Portuguese" garden, are filled with roses, outlined with dwarf mondo grass, *Ophiopogon japonicus,* and centered with Chinese fan palms, *Livistona chinensis.* Live oak trees are pruned to wineglass elm shape. At night, a "glorietta" garden, a circle of stone benches punctuated by carved stone lanterns, is a reminder of medieval Moorish-flavored "gloriets," or pavilions, when the lanterns' pale light makes a ghostly tent of the surrounding tall trees. The living room loggia opens onto a central patio at the bottom of a *catena d'acqua* that drops from the hill facing the house as it would in the garden of an Italian villa. At the top there is a grotto of rusticated stone. The tiny sound of dripping water echoes off a cloistered walk that runs along one side, a high stucco wall on the other. Instead of the cypresses of Italy, there are camphor trees, *Cinnamomum Camphora,* that arch overhead, underplanted with rustling sago palms, *Cycas revoluta.* Tiny pygmy date palms, *Phoenix Roebelenii,* stand in a row, and ornamental guavas, *Feijoa Sellowiana,* press up against the house. Next door to the cascade garden is a quick change of pace from formality: a large two-story pink playhouse with a door for a mouth and windows for eyes. Its "expression" is a happy howl. Who could have been responsible for this Disney Bomarzo? Surely it was Gaudí or some other wild Catalan. Not at all—it was created by the perfectly reputable Boston architectural firm of Parsons, Wait, and Goodell,[30] and the staid Frederick Law Olmsted, Jr. What had caused them to lose their heads in such a charming way? During the high-rolling twenties, resort architecture everywhere in Florida announced the state as *the* place where successful

Mizner's Venetian-style landing in Palm Beach for the Barclay Warburtons.

In Palm Beach, a loggia designed by architect Maurice Fatio for Philadelphian Joseph P. Widener looks out at Lake Worth.

America could cast off its cares. Even Northern architects and landscape architects felt free to invent there. Olmsted, Ruth, and Bok were American dreamers, members of a generation that believed anything was possible.

Olmsted, Jr., son of America's greatest landscape architect, was the leading partner of the McMillan Commission in Washington, D.C., that planned the Mall. As much a conservationist as landscape architect, Olmsted, Jr., saw an opportunity at Iron Mountain to create a haven for wildlife and a plant repository for native Florida species. City planning projects and planned suburban communities were another deep interest (one of the best and most enduring he created was Roland Park, in Baltimore). Fred Ruth loved Olmsted's work because he had grown up in Roland Park. His zany all-American dream was to create a self-supporting resort—a paradise for American captains of industry where all maintenance would be paid for by citrus profits. Some of his early directors and stockholders (Bok came a bit later) included Frank Washburn, president of American Cyanamid; James Mitchell, president of Alabama Traction, Power, and Light; E. W. Rice, Jr., president of General Electric; Elmer A. Sperry, president of Sperry Gyroscope; E. T. Bedford, who was responsible for much of Standard Oil's development abroad; and August Heckscher, who began in coal mining, saying, "all I knew about coal at the time was that it was black," and who finished as one of the most powerful men in mining and metals in the United States and as a great philanthropist. These were not East Coast society and the people who wanted to be part of it, but the heart of American business, the people who, in the Coolidge years, were the engine of the prosperity that was the twenties.

Ruth figured that 2,000 acres of citrus groves could support his 500-acre winter playland, and Olmsted fitted the groves to the landscape instead of planting them in rows, interspersing them with stands of longleaf pine and scrub oak. At Iron Mountain one sees the American capacity for reinvention at its wildest and best: a barren mountaintop transformed, a stately carillon playing Stephen Foster, a big pink head masquerading as a garden gazebo,[31] and a golfing paradise maintained by orange juice profits.

Rodney Sharp and Boca Grande

The late-nineteenth-century discovery of phosphate deposits in the South had rescued a few plantation owners like the Reverend John Grimke Drayton from a moribund economy. The expansion and maintenance of the garden at "Magnolia" was the result of strip-mining phosphate-rich land. In Florida the railroad lines built to carry the phosphate away were put to another use during the first decade of the twentieth century, bringing the tourists in at the time of the great Florida land boom. The Gulf Coast of Florida had wonderful beaches, not that anyone cared much in those days, superb fishing, and strings of little offshore islands. The C. H. & N. Railroad southern terminal on Gasparilla Island, named after the pirate José Gasparilla, was a phosphate loading station for transatlantic freighters. Years later, long-time Gasparilla Inn operator Karl Abbott remembered his first trip across to the island to start building the hotel:

As the train crawled across the four-mile trestle from the Florida mainland to Gasparilla Island I knew it was the beginning of a great adventure. . . . the water seemed painted with a gigantic brush—splashes of pink, green, indigo, and saffron delicately blended, dotted with tiny white sandspits and islands. Pelicans sailed above the shimmering waters and dived for fish, and as we approached the draw and the engineer gave long blasts on the whistle, great flocks of sea birds rose screaming into the cloudless sky and circled our train. . . . The landscape was covered with a scattered growth of cabbage palms, sea grapes, and cactus. Here and there were shacks, a fishhouse with longs racks of fish nets drying in the sun.[32]

In December, 1913 a white frame hotel opened in the tiny railroad junction of Boca Grande, and a golf course soon followed. Success was assured from the start by the early arrival of a socially impressive group from Boston, Philadelphia, and Wilmington: Ames, Cabots, Saltonstalls, and Frothinghams; Drexels, Biddles, and Pauls; du Ponts and Sharps. Others came from points west like Rochester, Evanston, Illinois, and Grosse Pointe. Some of the great American gardens of the epoch were theirs at home, but in Boca Grande life was simpler. Those redoubtable garden makers, Frank and Louise du Pont Crowninshield of Wilmington and Marblehead, Massachusetts, had a small enclosed garden at their Gulf Coast Spanish-style house.[33] Mrs. Russell Alger, whose impressive Ellen Shipman garden in Grosse Pointe is now the Grosse Pointe War Memorial, did not garden in Boca Grande, she fished. Soon the Gulf Coast sprouted invisible villas, hidden behind walls and gates, entrance arches and oleanders. In Boca Grande, a fetish of simplicity, even of secrecy, unusual in the high-calorie conspicuous consumption twenties, meant there was little outward show. Long accessible only by train or boat (and usually only to people in the social register), it has always remained proudly and stuffily low-key, with the emphasis on sport, not on entertainment for hundreds, or dressing for dinner. Spanish gardens—not the Addison Mizner variety, "turned inside-out like a glove," but the kind that keep their secrets to themselves, that are like Moorish gardens—were perfect for Boca Grande. Climate was one compelling reason to build completely enclosed gardens. In Boca Grande the wind off the Gulf blows steadily all year long, and the salt flies through the air. Without walls there would be no gardens. Almost as wonderful as the sights and scents that open up through an arched wooden door is the sudden hush, the absence of surf and wind; the reemergence of smaller sounds, like bees, or the delicate rustle of leaves, or a trickle of water.

ABOVE:
One of the most beautiful gardens in Florida was designed in the twenties by Marian Coffin for Rodney Sharp of Wilmington, Delaware, in Boca Grande. The tank garden echoes in well-proportioned miniature the Patio de los Arrayanes in the Alhambra. The blue-and-yellow zigzag tile design is a Moorish pattern for "waves." Wide, low flower beds are reminiscent of those in Persian miniature paintings; the "burladores," or jets, and the small raised fountain break up the flatness.

The biggest, grandest Moorish garden on Boca Grande was H. Rodney Sharp's "The Hacienda," affectionately known to all as "the winter palace." It was designed by Marian Coffin, as was "Gibralta," Sharp's other garden in Wilmington. Sharp himself was very involved in the design and execution of both gardens. While the house and garden are hidden from the public, the entrance gives a good hint about what will be found inside. Along the main road runs a long, high, white-stuccoed wall. Over the top peer cabbage and royal palms, and many other varieties, as well as jacaranda, live oaks, and immense oleanders. Through the entrance gate a line of palms runs down a pink sandy road to finish in an arch that frames—nothing. Nothing, that is, except the blue Gulf and the blue sky. The reverberations of that vast expanding space linger as one turns down a narrow, darkly shaded entrance road to the forecourt of the house. Again a full stop. In the circular forecourt there is only a windowless house front—a wall space just big enough to hold the tall arch of the door, framed in the pink coquina rock used everywhere on the island for trim.[34] One classical pink stone urn and an immense ligustrum stand on each side. The only extravagance is the top of the enclosing wall, which leaps around the driveway circle in a series of swooping Saracenic curves.

The garden is an unfolding progression of many steps, a set of contrasts between open and constricted, up and down, soft and hard, black and white, ornamented and plain. Marian Coffin designed many

Florida—Making It All Up From Scratch

187

beautiful gardens, but the same Florida freedom and fantasy that Olmsted felt at "El Caserio" likewise inspired her at "The Hacienda" to an increased boldness and elegance. The house was designed by Albert Ely Ives, who had worked with Mizner before setting up his own practice in Wilmington, Delaware.[35] The house was finished in 1925, but Rodney Sharp always continued to work on the garden. Right up to the year before his death (1968) he was always buying a thousand tiles here or there and then finding a place to put them.[36]

The 4-acre garden comprises a series of white-walled enclosures. There was a tennis court, today a rose garden, but happily no one would ever have known unless they wanted to play, it was so well concealed by walls and vines. Paths are brick, and many planters are terra-cotta. Coffin went abroad with Rodney Sharp to collect the sculpture for the garden, both freestanding pieces and architectural elements. Jasmine, bougainvillea, plumbago, ficus, and other vines clothe the walls. Annuals, perennials grown as annuals, and tropical and Riviera plants fill strictly defined beds. Atop a triple-arched Moorish pavilion a pierced balustrade runs round a viewing platform, one of two in the garden. Since the entire property is totally flat, this upper level is the brilliant stroke that creates the third dimension the garden needs. From the platforms, one can pretend to be a muezzin—or just look at the colorful garden patterns spread out like an Isfahan carpet.

"Ca d'Zan": The Waters of Youth

Mable Ringling, wife of John Ringling of "The Greatest Show on Earth," wanted her house on Sarasota Bay, "Ca d'Zan," to look like the Doge's Palace in Venice—but with a tower rising above it like the one Stanford White had created for Madison Square Garden.[37] She *almost* got what she wanted—the tower is shorter, only a section of the Doge's Palace was reproduced—but the effect is there.[38] Today the Ringling residence and the John and Mable Ringling Museum of Art are both open to the public. They produce in the average visitor exactly the same sequence of effects as the circus—at first, amazement, just plain jaw-dislocating surprise at the sights; then gaiety and curiosity—how *do* they do it? and finally, overdose. But just like cotton candy, how good it is going down. Unlike most of the other gardens in this book, "Ca d'Zan" has no sequence. You can start anywhere. Like the circus there are three rings: the house itself and its setting on the bay, the museum with its cortile garden chock-a-block with modern bronze castings of famous Greek and Roman statues, and the gardens in between the two buildings. There is a Rose Garden, a Secret Garden, a Dwarf Garden, and a Jungle Garden.

Mable Ringling laid all these gardens out herself. Since what she was gardening was actually a mangrove swamp full of rattlesnakes, copperheads, and alligators, she often wore high boots and a hip pistol.[39] On her head was a solar topee to shield her from the sun. Later on, when the gardens were tamer, on her strolls round the gardens she herself would break the neck of any snake that crossed her path because, the story goes, she was braver than the gardeners.[40] Whatever the truth of it all, it makes her typical early twentieth-century rose garden a more interesting place to be. Located about halfway between house and museum, it is a wheel of hybrid tea roses circling around a wire-topped gazebo covered with confederate jasmine, *Trachelospermum jasminoides*. Everywhere, and that word cannot convey how many there are, not only in the rose garden but *everywhere*, are knee-high limestone statues of putti, dwarfs, and lions. There is a satyr positioned in front of the banyan grove; a Hermes parked nearby; a pair of lead sphinxes smiling at the entrance to the house walk; a pint-sized replica of Cellini's *Perseus with the Head of Medusa* in the house patio; and a double-sized Michelangelo *David* at the end of the museum garden. Then too—wasn't there a copy of the Pompeiian *Victory* on a column among the oak trees? If so, why is it at hedge level in the shrubbery, watching traffic on the Tamiami Trail (now U.S. Route 41)? It seems that when John Ringling liked a statue, he

OPPOSITE:
The gardens of John and Mable Ringling's museum of art at "Ca d'Zan" on Sarasota Bay are water, stone, and green; the buildings are pink and white. A mammoth copy of Michelangelo's David *presides over all.*

bought more than one copy—two *Victories*, three *Discoboluses*, and so on.

John and Mable Ringling had a good time at "Ca d'Zan;" they led the kind of life everyone likes to read about. John Ringling, floridly good-looking, six-foot-four, and 240 pounds, rose at two in the afternoon and stayed up all night. He hired bands to play on the marble terraces; the yacht *Zalopus* swung just offshore; he kept eight refrigerators full to take care of his friends in show biz, politics, and business like James J. Walker, the dapper mayor of New York, Will Rogers, Florenz Ziegfeld and his wife, Billie Burke, Irvin Cobb, the humorist, and Frank Phillips, founder of Phillips Petroleum.[41] Piquant and demure-looking as an early pinup, the dark-haired Mable collected fans, lace, and cockatoos when she wasn't killing snakes. Best of all, they loved each other. (Nothing lasts forever—she died a few months before the Crash in 1929, and John Ringling died a few years later, bankrupt, and crippled by stroke and heart attacks.) It is very easy to make fun of the Ringlings in their funny, fantastic prime, but in fact what Henry Ringling North, John's nephew, wrote is true:

Ca d'Zan ... was neither ugly nor vulgar. It was so riotously, exuberantly, gorgeously fantastic, so far out of the world of normality, that it surpassed the ordinary criteria for such things and emerged a thing of style and beauty by its magnificent indifference to all the so-called canons of good taste. It was, in fact, the epitome of its owner.[42]

The garden of the pink stucco museum, which has a notable and early collection of Italian baroque art, contains a collection that is meant to be instructive as well as impressive: thirty-two modern casts of ancient and Renaissance statues fill the 350-foot-long garden. Right below *David*, a stage apron and two doors indicate a garden theater with dressing rooms.[43] All around the garden runs a cloister whose eighty-four columns of varying height, style, thickness, and age were cleverly put together by the museum's architect, John H. Phillips. How can this be charming? Again, the circus flavor saves it. On the building's balustraded top cornice, silhouetted against the brilliant blue overhead, are huge white statues of gods, goddesses, warriors, and athletes, which break up and lighten the long lines of the building very effectively. Hauled up into place by John Ringling's circus employees, they themselves are like so many heavenly roustabouts waiting for the show to begin. The real show is Florida—the Florida sun, the Florida sky. Following the dizzy skyline of the statues one's eye finds an immense allée of eighty-foot-tall Italian cypresses, *Cupressus sempervirens*. (Like nothing else at "Ca d'Zan," they have grown up!) Their two dark shaggy lines tower westward to Sarasota Bay from the end of the museum garden. At their terminus they mark what the Ringlings came for, what everyone has come to Florida for since Ponce de León—the warm blue waters of youth and happiness.

SOUTHERNERS AT HOME

A great migration cityward took place in the South during the second half of the nineteenth century, and many gardeners left the home place to tenants and eventual neglect. There was little to remind those genuine Southerners who stayed on the plantation of circuses or sunshine. Keeping a roof on the house was more like it, and most often the furthest thing from anybody's mind—or pocketbook—was making a new garden. But plantation-owning Southerners, never a puritanical lot, always seized a good time when they could—they stylishly turned their threadbare circumstances to good advantage, given the slightest opportunity. Often it was the charming, handsome and high-spirited women who managed to keep the home place going, sometimes even to improve it. Two such Virginians were Amelie Rives Chanler Troubetzkoy of "Castle Hill" and Nancy Perkins Field Tree Lancaster of "Mirador." Both places are in the Piedmont, not far from Charlottesville.

BELOW:
"Belmont," in Nashville, Tennessee, epitomized the high Victorian have-it-all-ness of the last decade before the Civil War, the South's own brief Gilded Age. A romantic 1860 oil painting of "Belmont" by an anonymous American painter shows the 105-foot-tall water tower and the greenhouses at left, and the gardens beyond in all their incredible variety.

Romance at "Castle Hill"

"The beautiful Amelie did not appear for some time, when she finally did the effect was dazzling, especially to the young men. . . . She was full of life and had a slight Southern drawl that was attractive. A siren, a goddess, perhaps a genius—at all events we were well repaid for our expedition," is a description of the young Amelie in 1888, at the age of twenty-five.[1] What a stock romantic heroine, straight out of one of her own novels! No genius, despite the description, she *was* talented and industrious enough to live by her pen. From 1888 to 1930 she churned out a stream of slightly steamy novels, poems, and plays, and even screenplays for the "silents." The theme of "Castle Hill" as the most beautiful place in the world, and as the ultimate refuge *from* the world, runs through her work.[2]

In Amelie Rives's family history, names like Thomas Jefferson (her great-great-grandfather was Jefferson's guardian), the Marquis de Lafayette (her father's godfather), and Robert E. Lee (her own godfather) are commonplace. Her own visitors included H. L. Mencken, William Faulkner, Adlai Stevenson, and Katharine Hepburn. In the twenties it was said to be "the only house in Virginia where you could be entertained in five languages in one evening."[3] Add to the mix an elegantly shabby, sun-warmed pink brick house with columns, ghosts in crinolines, phantom birds that appear to warn of death, fifty-foot-tall—*fifty-foot-tall*—American box that shields the old terraced garden from the north wind—and a forty-year happy marriage to an impecunious Russian prince, Pierre Troubetzkoy, to whom she was introduced by Oscar Wilde—and the profile of "Castle Hill" and its owner begins to emerge.[4] Louis Auchincloss, who visited her in her old age when he was a law student at the University of Virginia, described her as "small and straight, with white hair, carefully waved, and with delicately penciled dark eyebrows. . . . One felt that she had been a great beauty in a day when great beauties had been made much of. There was no nonsense about asking why a law student should want to spend a Saturday afternoon with a woman of seventy-five."[5]

Despite, or perhaps because of her sophistication, the Princess Troubetzkoy liked "Castle Hill's" old gardens the way they were, the way they had always been. Besides, there was no money to change anything. The days were long gone when "Castle Hill's" land, shrunk to a mere 1,200 acres at the turn of the century from its original 18,000, could provide a living in the style to which its owners were accustomed. The house grounds were, and are, divided into three parts. A block of existing house was built in 1765 by Dr. Thomas Walker, Amelie's great-great-grandfather. Next to it a bowling green faces north for a dramatic view of the Blue Ridge mountains. On either side stands a row of dependencies, nearly concealed by very old lilacs and rose-of-Sharon bushes. To the south, on the approach side, stretching from the pink brick front to the

"I could hardly believe the boxwood that lined the narrow drive," wrote Louis Auchincloss in A Writer's Capital *about his first visit to "Castle Hill," near Charlottesville, Virginia, "It towered over my Pontiac, and scratched against the doors on both sides as I drove slowly through it. I learned later that a tree surgeon had warned the Princess that it would die unless treated for a price beyond her means, and she retorted 'It was planted by a gardener who worked for George II. I think it will last my time—and yours.' It has."*

road, is a lawn laid out by Amelie's grandmother, Judith, in 1832 in the fashionable picturesque style. Its hour-glass shape, rather like that at Mt. Vernon, is outlined by two driveways.[6] Thirty-foot-high walls of boxwood edge each side of the entrance, making a narrow tunnel that shields "Castle Hill" from the road and from the world. To the southwest side of the lawn among the huge American specimen trees stands the King's Tree, a gigantic horse chestnut grown from a nut Judith also brought back from Paris.[7] West of this lawn the terraces of the oldest garden slope away below the biggest line of boxwood. This garden is not axially related to the house at all—perhaps an older pattern of house and garden asserts

itself here, as at "Sylvester Manor." (There had been a house on the "Castle Hill" site since 1725.) About this garden where everything was grown together in the old higgledy-piggledy style, Amelie's sister Gertrude writes,

The highest terrace, where one enters the garden through an arch in the hedge, and down a flight of old brick steps sunk deep in the bank, is devoted entirely to flowers. There are the old garden shrubs and flowers, some so old that their names are now almost forgotten . . . a broad turf walk leads down to the second and down more steps to the third level, and so to the lowest terrace of all. The great square beds on each side of the walk are bordered by fruit trees, and grass paths lead everywhere around the terraces. Beginning on the second level, a grape arbor stretches over the broad turf walk, and as one passes down from terrace to terrace, one sees the orderly rows of vegetables stretching away on either side, for the Castle Hill garden is not only beautiful and full of old world charm, but it is noted throughout the countryside as the best vegetable garden.[8]

When "Castle Hill" was sold in 1947 after Amelie's death, the new owners employed Alden Hopkins to redesign the terraces. Hopkins was responsible for the post-Hertle restoration garden at "Gunston Hall" and carried on at Williamsburg after Arthur Shurcliff. His work at "Castle Hill" was historically sympathetic to the terraced design and the mixed quality of the plantings. He made a formal boxwood parterre on the upper level, but kept grapes and fruit trees on the lower two, adding wisteria, crepe myrtle, and dogwoods. The vegetables disappeared, but a sense of farmscape was kept by adding horse paddocks.

"Mirador"

Like most Virginia places, "Mirador" evolved over the generations. But even more than at "Castle Hill," the character of one woman is what has shaped the garden that exists today. At "Castle Hill," Amelie Rives heightened the threadbare charms of Ole Virginny—what Charles Dudley Warner called the "*negligé* condition"—the chicken-in-the-parlor quality so attractive in the South. At "Mirador" in the twenties and thirties, Nancy Perkins Field Tree Lancaster smartened and enlarged the gardens, but without entirely losing that Southern air.

White brick piers linked with roses define the back of a long border at "Chatham," part of a 1924 revamping of an old Virginia country place by Ellen Shipman for Colonel and Mrs. Daniel Devore.

OPPOSITE:
It took great skill to suggest a sense of moving through a garden, as Frances Benjamin Johnston does here at "Belvoir" in Fairfax County. She photographed a garden entrance, the distant archway, centrally but not insistently, and included the details of garden architecture and plantings, as well as the relationship of the garden to the house.

Back in the
Real Old South

Nancy Perkins was the daughter of one of the famously beautiful Langhorne girls of the 1890s. Two of them became symbols of their times. Her Aunt Irene married the dazzled Charles Dana Gibson, the illustrator, who proposed to her on the front steps of "Mirador," and soon her pompadour, her shirtwaist, and her pert but demure profile were famous from coast to coast. Nancy Perkins's Aunt Nancy, the Viscountess Astor, was the first woman to become a member of Parliament. Nancy Perkins's own mother, Elisabeth, the eldest, died young, and little Nancy spent many summers in England with Lady Astor. Just as for impoverished British peers, the imperatives for Virginia girls were to make "good marriages"—ones that brought home the bacon. The Langhornes did it better than anybody, and when it came time for Nancy Perkins to make her choice, she did well. She married Marshall Field's grandson, Henry Field, and then, when he died, in 1919, his first cousin, Ronald Tree. The Trees returned to "Mirador" in the early twenties to set up an American country life for the spring and fall seasons.

"Mirador," elegantly square, brick, and Federal (1825), was equipped with the Virginia usuals: lawns, great trees, boxwood, and a small mixed garden, enclosed in a typical picket fence. There were also a number of old pink brick dependencies—office, schoolhouse, separate kitchen building, and smokehouse—the little buildings that any good garden maker instantly seizes on to focus the design. At the turn of the century, a flower garden had been made between the rear of the house and the nearest pair of little buildings.

When Nancy Tree arrived, she hired Delano and Aldrich and set to work, perfecting the actuality of that welcoming Southern life which had always existed at "Mirador"—but existed always partly as illusion. For perfection, a great deal of money is always needed to jump from illusion to reality: the revamped "Mirador" garden, designed by Annette Hoyt Flanders after Delano had made a site plan, was maintained by thirteen men.[9] By the late twenties a network of gardens stretched northward behind the house, webbing the little dependencies in symmetrical patterns of brick paths, hedges, shrub plantings to cut the wind, and enclosure gardens. The pattern was English—the Arts and Crafts enclosure garden, the Renaissance revival garden popularized by Lutyens and Jekyll which Nancy Tree must have seen hundreds of times in England—but the flavor was Southern. Perhaps due to a joint classical and Italian inspiration, the style of the garden seems naturally compatible with the Federal house, whose architectural style is so much later.

Of all American gardens, those of the antebellum Upper and Coastal South are closest in feeling and form to country-house gardens of the late English Renaissance with their terraces, topiary, and axial symmetry—and to the gardens of the English Arts and Crafts Revival. What Arts and Crafts garden enthusiasts revived, often calling them "medieval," were Italian Renaissance architectual forms, simplified and

transposed into living greenery. In Virginia and elsewhere in the Coastal South for about a century (1725 to 1825), house builders had drawn on the same architectural vocabulary, sometimes working directly from the books of Vitruvius and Palladio. With such a shared formal heritage, no wonder that simple classical "Mirador," with its brick fabric, arched openings, and plain white marble keystones, was perfectly suited by Nancy Tree's series of relaxed rectangular gardens.

Directly behind the house a sunken square of green was placed, a visual jumping-off point for a central axis that continued up a small Bramante-ish horseshoe staircase between huge box hedges, and finished with a view down an arched wisteria walk. Nancy Tree, W. A. Delano, and Annette Hoyt Flanders all knew the value of interruption—of things that half-conceal or frame a view. One of their great strokes was to break the length of the lawn by linking the two dependencies closest to the house with a white wooden pergola in a very Thomas Jefferson, University of Virginia, style. Its wide round-headed arches defined the inner garden and created a series of vignettes from either side. A tennis court lurked in the boxwood—Nancy was determined to conceal its vulgar shape from the rest of the garden. A big flower garden, with brilliantly planted serpentine borders of shrubs, annuals, and perennials, lay beyond the farthest dependencies to the northwest. To the east was the rectangular rose garden, once the old picket-fenced enclosure. Beyond the roses were the orchard, the beautiful cutting and kitchen garden framed in grape arbors, and a tiny garden known as "the sandbox." Still farther east was a wild walk that led past a serpentine brick wall—shades of Jefferson again—and on down through woods filled with dogwood to a pond.

Flower Gardens Old and New

Other gardens in Virginia, both old and new, followed the patterns seen at "Castle Hill" and "Mirador." "Chatham," on the Rappahannock River overlooking Fredericksburg, passed through many hands from the time it was built in 1750 for William Fitzhugh. The most romantic story about "Chatham" is that of General Robert E. Lee's refusal to turn his cannons on the place during the battle of Fredericksburg, even though it was occupied by Union troops. Chatham's then owner, Major Lacy, stood by Lee's side on the other side of the river, urging Lee not to spare his house. But Lee had become engaged to his wife, Mary Randolph Custis, in the gardens of "Chatham" and he held his fire. In 1924 Ellen Shipman laid out a garden for "Chatham's" new owners, Colonel and Mrs. Daniel B. Devore. Although it is described as a "restored" garden,[10] like "Mirador" it was really a twentieth-century garden designed by a landscape architect sensitive to the historic atmosphere. From the wide living terrace that ran the length of the house (210 feet), a central grass axis bisected the garden. At the end of the allée, a terra-cotta statue of *Diana* set against a screen of red cedars finished the view. To one side was an iris garden and to the other a rose garden. Close to the house were low boxedged parterres, which Shipman planted solidly with single colors of different flowers—pink English daisies in one, forget-me-nots in another, yellow wallflowers in a third. Characteristic Shipman touches were the interesting flowering standardized shrubs she used to center the parterres and give them height—forsythia and weigela as well as wisteria.[11]

The bird garden was unique—a set of eight pheasant runs where vividly colored pairs of rare pheasants strutted among old boxwood and cedar. Each enclosure had a birdhouse, and the wire net fences were concealed by dogwood.

Entirely new, very extensive, and much admired and published was "Rose Hill" in Greenwood, Albemarle County, not far from Charlottesville. Mrs. William R. Massie of Richmond bought "Rose Cottage" in 1903, and built a summer house on a nearby hill. The site was quite unprepossessing, but it had a beautiful view. Soon the first version of the garden was laid out in traditional old style "falls." Unfortunately, instead of traditional low geometric parterres, Mrs. Massie put in borders of informally massed perennials on each terrace. Period photographs show the two-to-three-foot-tall plants looking like a stubbly beard blurring the smooth edge of the fall.[12] In 1930 the original house burned. Within

the year New York architect William Lawrence Bottomley, who had a thriving Richmond practice, had created a new Georgian dwelling. Bottomley, like W. A. Delano and Thomas Hastings, often involved himself deeply in site planning. Perhaps he had something to do with the changes in the garden. By the thirties, a new and sophisticated garden had emerged that combined old and new very successfully. The perennials disappeared from the horizontal surfaces of the "falls," and a truly innovative rock garden was planted on the vertical faces instead, which traditionally had always been left as plain grassy banks. A single row of formal clipped evergreens ran along the middle level of the garden, a foil for the flowery richness of the banks.

Suzanne Williams Massie herself was familiar with every nuance of traditional Virginia garden style. With Frances Archer Christian, she edited one of the two "bibles" of Virginia garden history, *Homes and Gardens in Old Virginia*. Such books, with separate entries for each house and garden written by family members, often descend to mere hagiography.[13] However, the lists of gardens, and the description of their plantings in the first few decades of the twentieth century are invaluable for the history of gardens and that of taste. Though often inaccurate and romanticized, these accounts are the first systematic look backward at the plantation gardens of Virginia which, to a great extent, had been the starting point for all the other regions of the South.

OVER THE ALLEGHENIES

THE SOUTH'S OWN GILDED AGE
—AND RECOVERY FIFTY YEARS LATER

In the last decade before the Civil War, Southerners had briefly enjoyed what can be called their own Gilded Age. Houses and gardens exhibited the same joyous and flamboyant ornateness as did those at the turn of the century in the Northeast. This building spree was bankrolled by a booming slave economy producing tobacco, rice, cane, and indigo, as well as the staple crop, cotton. Few of these gorgeous new establishments sprang up in the long-settled and exhausted soil of the coast, however. By the 1850s, prosperity in the South had migrated westward over the mountains, where the cotton gin made short staple cotton (the only kind that would flourish on upland plantations) a profitable crop on land made safe by the deportation of Native Americans. Conservative planter taste meant most of the houses were still in the Greek Revival style, but a few ultra-fashionable Italianate "villas" such as "Belmont" gave a hint of

what might have happened had there been no war. For their gardens, planters brought boxwood cuttings in their wagons on their trip over the Alleghenies. In their heads they carried the old Virginia Tidewater dream garden, with its box-edged beds brimming with what Gertrude Jekyll and Alice Morse Earle would later bring back into cultivation as "cottage flowers" and "old-time gardens." So, in addition to the sweeping lawns, curving drives, and clumps of exotic trees demanded by early Victorian taste, these domestic landscapes almost always retained areas, especially near the house, that were nearly as formal and axial as any eighteenth-century garden. Southern garden makers simply incorporated into a formal grid the brilliant stars and crescents full of bedding-out plants that irregularly dotted lawns in other regions of America during Victorian times.

The war ended all this. Sixty years passed, the gardenesque style came in and went out elsewhere in the country; the public park took

An unidentified twentieth-century Southern garden, probably in North or South Carolina, was captured in watercolor by Harold C. Beckett on October 19, 1932.

shape as did the profession of landscape architecture and the demand for it in the private sector. Then Charles Platt's and Edith Wharton's Italian revolution began in the nineties up north. In the South, the original "old-time gardens" just got a little older. Not until the second decade of the twentieth century, in the suburbs of Louisville and Nashville, Richmond and Atlanta, were houses and gardens again built by Southerners in numbers that indicated prosperity. Like the much earlier gardens in Brookline, Massachusetts, and Morristown, New Jersey, these twentieth-century suburban gardens were not land-based. They were refuges from the urban world of banking, finance, railroads, engineering, textile, and tobacco manufacturing, real estate, newspapers and other communications—all the occupations that began to make money as the South arose again. These twentieth-century Southerners, as a general rule, were building principal residences in the suburbs—they were not restoring old plantations as sporting second homes. Turning Barr Ferree upside down, one could say that in the South the estate movement, which came forty years later than up north, was a "movement cityward" of Southerners finding another ideal life model besides the plantation. A few resort gardens existed in traditional Southern watering spots, such as Camden, South Carolina, Flat Rock, Roaring Gap, and Blowing Rock, North Carolina, or on Lookout Mountain, on the Georgia/Tennessee border. Landscape architects like Charles Gillette in Richmond or William C. Pauley in Atlanta, architects who designed gardens and interiors as well as residences like Neel Reid and Philip Trammell Schutze, created large formal gardens that complemented finely detailed Revival-style houses, mostly Georgian or Federal.

Eastern-based landscape architects as well known as the Olmsted Bros., Warren Manning, Marian Coffin, and Ellen Shipman, worked in Kentucky and Tennessee, but perhaps the most interesting gardens were made by Jens Jensen and Bryant Fleming, two landscape artists who worked mostly in this world beyond the East Coast. Jensen had a new vision of the "prairie garden," a landscape garden that made the most of regional topography and planting; Fleming worked out formal Italian and Georgian models in a vocabulary suited to the climate. His gardens were closely, and axially, related to the houses they surrounded.

Creating lavish great estates based on European models was difficult in the Upper South as the climate is untempered by any nearby large body of water, and temperatures can fluctuate by as much as 110 degrees between summer and winter. All the sudden weather disasters occur with some regularity—hailstorms, tornadoes, black frosts, sudden withering heat waves, and blistering droughts. Anne Bruce Haldeman, graduate of the Cambridge School and Ellen Shipman's long-time associate, has practiced landscape architecture in Kentucky and Piedmont North Carolina since 1937. She says that the most difficult things about gardening in the region are "the heat, the drought, and the changing winter climate." Her extensive list of most commonly planted perennials includes almost no summer-blooming flowers.[1] Native trees are among the greatest beauties of the Upper South—elm, ash, tulip poplar, maples, various oaks, and locust, often despised as a "trash" tree because of its irregular form, splintery yellow wood, and the litter it deposits on the lawn or driveway. But the honey smell of the locust in bloom is one of the most evocative scents of the South. Roses do extremely well, including all the more tender varieties, both climbers, such as the Lady Banks rose and the Bourbons, and the delicate tea roses. Almost every garden mentioned in these pages had a collection of boxwood: dwarf, *Buxus sempervirens 'Suffruticosa', B. sempervirens* and *B. sempervirens 'Arborescens',* known in the South as "tree box."

"Oxmoor," the Plantation Model

First, a look at the original model, the plantation, as it survived the trip over the mountains, the Civil War, and the entry into the twentieth century. "Oxmoor," named after Oxmoor in *Tristram Shandy,* is the family seat of the Bullitts. The 1,000-acre holding, nine miles east of Louisville and close to the Ohio River, is still farmed today, although the law and financial investments have long since taken the place of agriculture as the base of the family's wealth.

"It has never been owned by anyone except the Bullitt family," writes Thomas W. Bullitt, the present occupant.[2] His great-great-great-grandfather, Colonel William Christian, who was married to Patrick Henry's sister, came from Virginia to Kentucky in 1785. The family continued at "Oxmoor" until in 1863, the middle of the Civil War, the house was closed for forty-six years. In 1909 William Marshall Bullitt and his wife, Nora, returned to a typical modest plantation house of the antebellum Upper South: an old white frame house with a brick front and a small central portico. A straight half-mile avenue of locust trees led to the portico; the plantation included a family graveyard, slave quarters, separate kitchen, icehouse, smokehouse, springhouse, and all the other familiar plantation dependencies and features. At the time of the Civil War, the Bullitts had been the third largest slaveholders in the state with 120 slaves. "Oxmoor's" greatest attractions are its proportion and the orderliness of a functional landscape. The small scale of the house, even today in its enlarged state, is very pleasing in relation to the large trees, and to the big, flattish pasturelands and fields. Firmly axial, just like so many other plantations, the garden on the south side of the house was on line with the mile-long locust entrance avenue on the north. The Bullitts turned "Oxmoor" into a grand estate house with two waves of building, 1915 and 1925 to 1927, finishing with a magnificent 60-foot-long library to the east. The Bullitts had long-standing Philadelphia connections, sent their children to Eastern schools like St. Mark's and Harvard, and were well traveled. William M. Bullitt eventually became Solicitor General of the U.S. His wife, Nora Yassigi Bullitt, whose well-heeled Boston Brahmin mother had married a Turkish diplomat, had been the sort of girl Frank Crowninshield squired around New York. The Bullitts were in no way a backwoods Kentucky family.[3] Before they added the library they had called on Marian Coffin to redesign the plantation home landscape. She laid out a simple formal flower garden southeast of the old house, whose three circular plantings were echoed by a gazebo at each end. Coffin also firmed up the axial plan, emphasizing cross axial paths with arbors, and defining the beds of the old back-door garden more elegantly. Even though the big brick addition later dwarfed and cramped the flower garden somewhat, Coffin's design as a whole is still strong and in tune with the grand simplicity that is "Oxmoor."[4]

"Belmont," Showplace of Nashville

Entirely different from "Oxmoor" is "Belmont," outside Nashville, built in 1852 by Adelicia Acklen and her second husband, Joseph. "Belmont's" gardens have the showboat glitter and fantasy of the Deep South rather than the Upper South, and indeed it was built on Mississippi cotton money. Today, the remains stand as a monument to the South's first Gilded Age. (As Belmont College, some of the grounds have been built over, though the house and the main outlines of the garden still exist.) The place was built as a summer villa on a 65-acre tract, with an adjoining 104-acre farm to provide the amenities—truly an estate or country seat, not a plantation. The architect, Adolphus Heiman, who seems to have been the landscape architect as well, had a Nashville practice. He was the son of the superintendent of Sans Souci, the extravagant summer palace of Frederick the Great in Potsdam. In its crowded complexity, its many garden buildings and conservatories, statues, fountains, and its gaiety, it is somehow a robust Victorian "Sans

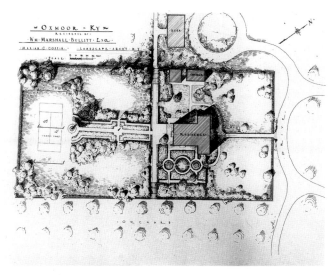

Landscape architect Marian Coffin's circle-in-a-square at "Oxmoor," the Bullitt family's old plantation house near Louisville, Kentucky, is planted mainly for spring. She used the same simple flat geometry beloved all over the South.

Souci." Called "South Park" by Nashvilleans, and open to everyone much of the time, "Belmont" indeed seemed like a public park—or a circus. The rectangular grounds, bounded by streets on four sides, were laid out as a picturesque park on the outskirts, and as a formal rectangular garden near the cupola-ed Italianate house with its richly Corinthian pillared front. The main greenhouse, which was backed by a 105-foot-tall brick water tower, and seven others grew everything from tropical fruits and flowers to cacti, jasmine, lilies, and camellias. The steam-engine-powered water tower supplied what must be one of the earliest underground lawn sprinkling systems. Three large circles contained a variety of stylish Victorian parterres. There were also five summer houses wreathed in roses, a two-story octagonal bearhouse, a Greek Revival style art gallery, a bowling alley, and six fountains, including one in the front hall of the house. In the zoological garden were animals from all over—monkeys, parrots, a panther, a deer park, and an artificial lake with alligators from Louisiana.

Adelicia Acklen was a grand opportunist. She broke all the rules and survived, thanks to her adroit mixture of prudence and brazenness. She appears tiny (ninety-five pounds), dark-haired, with intense black eyes and dramatic eyebrows, but a second look reveals her extremely tight mouth. A strong constitution must have had as much to do with her success as her determination. She bore ten children to her first two husbands in thirteen years. Only five children survived; the others died in infancy or as young victims of croup, bronchitis, or diphtheria.

Adelicia's first husband, Isaac Franklin, twenty-eight years her senior and one of the richest men in Tennessee, was an ex–slave trader—even then considered unsavory. On his death in 1846 she broke the will that left the bulk of his fortune to charity. Next was a handsome lawyer and veteran of the Mexican Wars, Joseph Acklen. Adelicia made sure this time that the marital agreement spelled out that what was hers was hers. Acklen increased their fortunes greatly. By 1860, "Belmont" was complete, and the Acklens were worth $3 million. War broke out, Acklen died of a fever, and Adelicia went on to carry out the greatest coup of her life.

The Confederacy decreed that cotton on the plantations was to be burned so that the Federal Army could not benefit from its sale. Somehow Adelicia wheedled her way into getting Confederate permission to pick her cotton, and a Confederate guard squad to protect it—and then talked the U.S. Army into providing wagons and teams to get the crop to New Orleans. Letters, statements, and official records indicate confusion among both Confederates and Yankees. The eventual 2,000 bales brought Adelicia $960,000 on the English market, probably paid in gold. She took off from Louisiana for New York by boat and returned to Nashville for the end of the war. "Belmont" was actually on the battle lines at one point, but survived almost intact, just like Adelicia. She became Nashville's social queen after the war, but there is a certain bleakness to her later years. Rumbles of family disagreements pursued her.[5] Without slaves to man the plantations, in 1880 she wisely decided to sell (one buyer held the lease for convict labor in Louisiana). Finally, in 1885, she sold "Belmont," separated from her third husband, William Cheatham, and moved to Washington to join her daughter Pauline. She died in New York on a furniture-buying trip for her new Washington house—too mundane an ending for a real-life Scarlett O'Hara. "Belmont" became a school for young ladies.

JENS JENSEN AND THE PRAIRIE LANDSCAPE
Few grand gardens were made in Tennessee and Kentucky between 1865 and 1900. When the demand rose again in the first two decades of the twentieth century, most people wanted formal, symmetrical gardens with axes and cross axes, clipped hedges, pergolas, fountains, and statues, gardens that hinted at an easy familiarity with European culture, or at least the fashionable East Coast's estate garden version of it. At the same time a new school of architecture and landscape was evolving in Chicago: the Prairie Style. In landscape, this meant the Danish immigrant Jens Jensen's work: massing native species in a newly flexible kind of landscape garden with a minimum of garden ornament. Jensen was the first great landscape architect in America to practice outside the influence of the East Coast establishment. Born in Jutland the son of a Danish squire, Jensen (1860–1951) arrived in Chicago in 1886 where he worked as gardener for the city Parks Department for fourteen years, and then as

a park designer. His most productive years of private estate practice (1906–1934) ended when he retired to his summer home, "The Clearing," in Wisconsin in 1935. There he lectured and wrote, and started a school for artists and craftsmen interested in landscape and nature. Little of his work remains, and most of his records were destroyed in a disastrous office fire in 1937. The best Jensen landscapes open to the public are the newly restored Humboldt Park Prairie River in Chicago, and the Lincoln Memorial Garden in Springfield, Illinois.[6] In architecture, the Prairie School was chiefly the work of Louis Sullivan and Frank Lloyd Wright. Briefly, their residential architecture had horizontal lines, uncompartmentalized spaces, and detailing that was not derived from the then-fashionable Beaux-Arts models. In the light of contemporary architecture and landscape, the Prairie School has great importance now as a forerunner. Then, it was never a dominant style but always an alternative to the Beaux-Arts among the generally conservative ranks of estate makers.

The Prairie School was a political statement as well as a design movement. Wright, Sullivan, Jensen, and their followers were rejecting the domination of the Beaux-Arts establishment, just as the Republicans of the Midwest were challenging the East Coast financial oligarchy. Many Midwestern magnates with names like Ford, Armour, McCormick, and Ryerson took Jensen up. Across the region and extending down into the South, leading citizens of small towns like Bloomington, Indiana, or Frankfort, Kentucky, followed suit. The Prairie Style marked the coming-of-age of the Midwest. At the time, the loudest Prairie proselytizer was Wilhelm Miller, who wrote the Prairie garden's manifesto, *The Prairie Spirit in Landscape Gardening*, in 1915.[7] Miller defines the Prairie Style as "an American mode of design based upon the practical needs of the middle-western people and characterized by preservation of typical western scenery, by restoration of local color, and by repetition of the horizontal line of land or sky which is the strongest feature of prairie scenery."[8]

A marked identification with the Midwest unfortunately prevented national recognition of the fact that preservation, restoration, and repetition of native plantings constituted a valid and attractive way to make a landscape in any region. (The idea was not entirely new: for example, Frederick Law Olmsted, Sr., throughout his career, and O. C. Simonds, in Chicago in the 1880s, had stressed the beauty and usefulness of native plants. Simonds' masterpiece is Graceland cemetery in Chicago, which was much praised by that English proponent of the wild garden William Robinson.)

"Airdrie," a Complete Surviving Jensen Landscape
Leonard K. Eaton, Jens Jensen's biographer, points out that Prairie Style gardens were almost never built on the prairies, but rather on the rolling

and often wooded land of the newly suburban North Shore of Chicago, or along the shores of the Great Lakes near other industrial cities.[9] Similarly, some of Wright's best early houses are scattered from Wisconsin to California. And although Jensen's story rightly belongs to the Midwest, what may be the best-preserved example of a Jens Jensen private estate garden, "Airdrie," is located far from the Great Plains, in the bluegrass country of Lexington, Kentucky.

At "Airdrie" one is instantly aware of a great work of art on the ground, shaped by growth and thoughtful maintenance for over seventy-five years. Jensen started work there for Mr. and Mrs. W. E. Simms in 1916, on 4,000 acres of idyllic Kentucky landscape, a natural limestone grassland dotted with huge specimen oak, ash, and hickory.

In 1906 William Simms from eastern Kentucky married Lucy Alexander, whose family had owned the land since the eighteenth century. They built a portly brick house in restrained Southern Classic Revival style on a gentle hill.[10] Then a tornado ripped up most of the huge trees that dotted the green meadows. When Jensen arrived in 1915, he discovered that instead of making a garden he was about to restore a landscape. Somehow he and Simms decided "restoration" meant replanting a forest primeval, a symbol of the great wilderness that had once been America.[11] To plant a big untidy forest was a bold stroke for the bluegrass country, where the beautiful shaven fields are squared by tall black fences, but

then both Jensen and Simms were bold men. The older Jensen became (he was forty when he finally left the Chicago Parks Department to embark on a career as a landscape architect) the more he cultivated his bold Viking image—head thrown back, neck scarves with a silver wolf clasp, flowing white hair, and moustache. Jensen's biographer quotes a nameless client who said, "I always agreed with everything he did—I'm sure that it would have been most unpleasant if I hadn't."[12] Simms was brave enough in the first place to seek out Jensen at a time when most Kentucky gardens were either geometric layouts of boxwood and herringbone brick, or Italian balustraded terraces. At "Airdrie," Jensen used the few large trees that remained after the tornado as pivot points for his design and as symbols of the region and the past. A single giant blue ash, *Fraxinus quadrangulata*, at least 200 years old and native only to a small area of the Midwest running south of the Great Lakes, could be seen from the house a half mile away. Its craggy growth habit and platelike bark of pale, red-tinted gray made it look like a ghost of another time, a dinosaur of a tree. Just as any palace garden maker would have framed a distant statue, Jensen used the ash as the focal point of the garden. Promontories of hemlock are highlighted by the sinuous limbs of native wild cherry. Stage wings of sugar maples, their lower branches sweeping the ground, funnel down to the slice of pasture view where the blue ash stands.

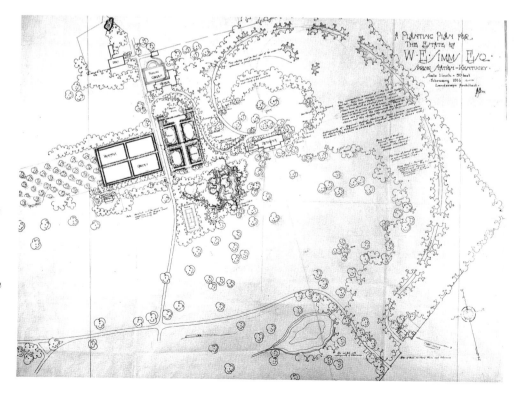

Jens Jensen created two great gardens in Springs Station in the bluegrass country of Kentucky, "Lanark" and "Airdrie." At "Airdrie" for the W. E. Simms in 1916 he planted an entire forest and made what is essentially an American "palace garden." The long entrance drive, seen on the plan as a slow curve beginning at lower right, defines the central experience of "Airdrie" as moving through wilderness space.

As a European, he'd perhaps preferred to see only what was strikingly American, whereas American-born Charles Platt, for example, might see how similar a garden in Massachusetts could be to an Italian garden. However, Jensen also employed the conventions of formal landscape, subverting them to suit his own view of nature and democracy in America.[13] Here at "Airdrie," essentially an American palace garden, Jensen created axis and cross axis, an ornamental water garden, a formal flower garden, a garden theater, and a grand approach drive, but all in a Kentucky vernacular.

On the vista path, close to the house and near one of the big sugar maples, he characteristically preserved a unique Kentucky feature, a "sink hole," by making it part of the lawn. A "sink hole" is a wide circular depression created when the limestone crust beneath the topsoil gives way and sinks sometimes three or four feet taking the soil with it like icing on a cake. This sink hole now looks like a big dimple in the lawn since the short grass has softened its jagged shape. Light haloes the rim and soft shadows form within its shallow bowl. Jensen has romanticized what many other landscape architects would have eliminated.

"I am a northern man, and to me the light is very precious," said Jensen.[14] How he used light to model his design can be seen in his "sun openings" throughout the woods, in glades often centered on the few remaining large burr oaks. Jensen originally planted these "sun openings" and "sun lanes" (sometimes they are marked as such on plans), in shapes that took advantage of the arc of the sun to cast long slanting rays. At "Airdrie" a cross axis traverses the woods that frame the main vista. Sun lanes create chiaroscuro effects as startling as those in any Italian garden along this straight path. Carefully chosen tree foliage and flowers enhance the light/dark contrast. On the north side of the main vista, the cross axis is defined by a row of the largest koelreuteria trees in the United States,[15] which bloom chrome-yellow in June. On the south the path becomes a black tunnel of yews and sixty-foot-tall hemlocks that leads to the flower garden and the vegetable garden. On the way are glimpses of one of Jensen's famous rock pools and a sunken rock garden, both within another, larger "sink hole" whose limestone ledges were cleared of soil. The exposed rock was planted with a variety of ferns and wildlings, but no exotic alpines.[16]

Farther down the cross-axial allée, the darkness gives way on the right to the flower garden, a sunken rectangle measuring a generous 125 by 85 feet. At the west end a regular semicircular apse of hemlocks outlines a "Players Green"—the garden theater. A handsome rectangular vegetable garden and quincunx-style orchard are aligned with the flower garden cross axis. The main body of the garden is divided into four equal rectangular parterres, lined with American box. But Jensen has made a quirkily wonderful decision here—the rectangles are back to back; that is to say, they do not open into each other. The only entrances are on the *outside* edges, making each rectangle a secret garden. The two inside paths that cut the garden into its four quarters are lined with smoothly bulging box walls that today have reached a height of ten feet, making a view of the whole garden impossible. It has become a labyrinth. Jensen has turned the classical parterre inside out, bringing a humdrum design alive with mystery and an unexpected sense of humor. Wherever he used a formal element, like this flower garden on an estate,[17] he situated it far from the house, allowing the lawns and trees to roll right up to the building in English landscape style. Formality is always a walk away—something to visit, not something to be surrounded by. In a sense, Jensen turned Beaux-Arts landscape convention, where formal terraces and gardens gradually give way to lawns and then to the natural landscape of field and wood, inside out.[18] Up the hill beyond the vegetable garden is a "council ring," another favorite Jensen feature. Council rings, constructions of low stone sitting walls, or rings of loose stones, or just rings of trees, were Jensen's tribute to Native American heritage and to his ideas of democracy. The council ring at "Airdrie," just a circle of osage orange trees now forty-feet-tall and half lost in the woods, illustrates the simplicity and beauty of Jensen's idea.

Jensen's best works, those that assure him of a high place in the canon of American landscape, are sometimes too large in scale and too subtle to comprehend easily. One simply exists in them, aware that the large easy volumes of space and flowing lines of plantings are different from other designs. Eventually, it seems to be his perception of space, even more than his generous and ecologically sound planting practices, that sets him apart and distinguishes him as the first modern American landscape architect. His handling of space has more to do with fluid movement through it than with the creation of "landscape pictures." Thus it is a break with previous landscape tradition which had utilized pictorial devices like framing, and divisions into foreground, middle ground, and background.[19] Photographs, which necessarily are taken from a fixed point, usually fragment and distort Jensen landscapes. His plans are much better illustrations of his work.

The long nautilus-shell curve of the driveway at "Airdrie" reveals Jensen's new spatial resonance. All sense of time or direction is lost in the smooth, continuous blind curve and the rush of trees on either side. It is a landscape of abstraction. There is no definition of foreground or background, no landmark to indicate the distance traveled through space, and no sense of historical time—the wilderness past has become the present experience. The branches of understory flowering trees flourish in the sun of the road cut: wild red cherry, yellowwood, and mountain silver-bell. Behind them the high walls of oak and white ash, and other American forest natives, looped with wild grape and honeysuckle, open and close in constant motion. The openings reveal more trees, but never a horizon until, just as the ground levels off, the drive bursts out of the woods. The approach to the front door is at an oblique angle, emphasizing the large free space in front of house, not the building itself. Huge elms and ginkgos (natives of China) arch over the roadbed and the house.

Though Jensen is known as the master of regional planting, in practice he interpreted the word "regional" more loosely than his writings or Miller's indicate. "Fitting," a word which occurs again and again in his instructions and letters, better describes the very wide range of plants he worked with. It doesn't always mean strictly indigenous. For example, Simms's home landscape in the mountains of Bourbon County was forested with hemlocks and white pines as well as with the deciduous trees found in the bluegrass. Perhaps to remind him of home, both conifers were planted extensively at "Airdrie." Although the white pines have all died out, the mountain hemlocks survive and are the backbone of the vista plantings.[20]

Jensen's correspondence and his planting notes and directives on plans make better reading than the high-blown philosophizing on nature in his book, *Siftings,* published in 1956. A single directive note from the "Airdrie" plan illuminates his fluid control of large plantations, his command of landscape architecture as an art form in three dimensions, and his reliance on natural growth as part of design. Explaining how the forest trees are to be planted, he says, "These trees should be planted from 6 to 20 feet apart, sometimes in groves of 10 to 40 trees; sometimes in pairs or threes; and sometimes single. Where the trees are far apart, the undergrowth has a better chance and this changes the skyline of the forest floor."[21]

Jensen's ability to redefine landscape in an entirely new way surely stems in part from his immigrant keenness of vision. However, his art transcends mere observation. He was a mystic, and an artist whose medium happened to be landscape. He believed in the beauty and redeeming power of pure nature much as Wordsworth or Thoreau or Emerson, and his works expressively communicate his faith. His longtime associate Alfred Caldwell wrote, "To Jensen, as to the ancient Greeks, there was an essence, or being, proper to a spring, a hill, a meadow, a ledge of rocks. The art is not to impress, but to make this being clear, to make the landscape speak. Each place was planned to reveal the inner meaning of the landscape. When the landscape became itself, it became more than the landscape because it then revealed what had once been obscure."[22]

Italian Variations

Bryant Fleming in Kentucky and Tennessee
Bryant Fleming (1876–1946), almost completely unknown today, was one of the busiest regional landscape architects of his day.[23] During the thirty years of his practice, which was divided by World War I and essentially finished by the Depression, Fleming worked in a wide Midwestern tier from Toronto on down through Michigan and Illinois to Kentucky and Tennessee. Although he designed parks and campuses and exposition grounds, perhaps his best works were the large estates for which he designed or chose everything from the gatehouse and its surrounding shrubbery to the quilts on the beds in the main house. Fleming was born in Buffalo, the son of a lumberman, and grew up on his grandparents' farm near the Canadian border. Like Charles Platt, he came to architecture by way of the garden gate—that is, he took a degree in agriculture at Cornell in 1901 (there was as yet no school of landscape architecture) and practiced as a landscape architect before registering as an architect in New York State. Intending to be a landscape architect, he devised his own curriculum with the help of Professor Liberty Hyde Bailey, who around the turn of the century began to publish the series of horticultural encyclopedias that would culminate in his great standard manual of cultivated plants, *Hortus,* first published in 1930. However, Fleming's interests were certainly not exclusively horticultural. At college he took courses in architecture—both history and practice—the history of art and ornament, and in free-hand drawing. His self-set curriculum became the basis for the course in landscape design at Cornell, which served as a model for many other institutions. (Fleming taught at Cornell from 1904 to 1915, and was the landscape architecture consultant to the School of Architecture for many years thereafter.) Following Cornell, he joined Warren Manning's Boston firm for three years, and traveled in Europe to visit houses and gardens, returning in 1904 to Buffalo. Like Manning, he was an inspirational teacher and employer: four of the men he trained went on to win the Prix de Rome in landscape architecture. Like Manning, who for many years was the big push behind the American Society of Landscape Architects, he was a joiner, serving on multiple committees in both his disciplines. During the teens and twenties, practitioners like Fleming were the ones who carried the country house ethos to almost every small prosperous city in the country.

Fleming was as interested in architecture and lifestyle as in horticulture and design. His periodic obsession with the Colonial Revival reminds one of Wallace Nutting; his trips abroad with clients to see gardens and to choose an architectural style for the house of their dreams are like Stanford White's trips. Again like White or Platt, he was always in search of the perfect European eighteenth-century garden urns or gazelle statues, or a grand staircase or lapis lazuli mantelpiece, though he bought without quite the same free-wheeling splendor as White. His work was consistently more theatrical and robust than Platt's; once the fever of historical imagination gripped him, discretion was thrown to the winds. Norman T. Newton, whose *Design on the Land: The*

TO·HOLD·AS·'TWERE·THE·MIRROR·UP·TO·NATURE

Development of Landscape Architecture chronicles the history of the profession, describes Fleming's work as "extremely individual and unorthodox, at times challenging all rationality, often guilty of the most

ABOVE:
The Bingham newspaper family estate at Louisville, Kentucky, has a Carrère and Hastings classical theater where events like the Kentucky Home School for Girls' annual play, seen here, took place. The grand marble reality of this Doric colonnade—surely intended to link the Binghams to history—also suggests that Louisville would be another Athens and every Bingham another Pericles. Shakespeare's words across the lintel frame the idealized "nature" of the man-made landscape.

whimsical exaggeration, yet somehow invariably delightful."[24] A letter describing one of his early commissions gives a good idea of Fleming in full cry: "He designed everything; the stables, the enlarged house, and the grounds to be nice early-North-American-Colonial. He insisted that the focus of the court around which the house forms a U should be a large honest-to-goodness maple sap boil-down kettle with water in it. (no European fountains!)"[25] Like Platt, Fleming arrived quickly at the conclusion that houses and gardens work best if designed together. His early series of renovated New York State farmhouses in the village of Wyoming, New York, are the equivalents of Platt's first house and garden essays in Dublin, New Hampshire. There, Fleming worked out some of the formulas and variations he would use in the groups of houses and gardens in Tennessee and Kentucky in the twenties. Like any eclectic architect/garden designer worth his salt, he ended up by working in a wide variety of styles, from Colonial Revival to Italianate to Georgian to "Jacobean" to "Country French" to Neo-Grec, a handsome kind of brick Regency revival.

His garden designs exhibit the typical Beaux-Arts progression from formal courtyard to outer woodland, with the accompanying compartments—iris, rock, rose, water, wild flower—so fashionable when there was plenty of labor to keep them up. Fleming used many, sometimes too many, lead and stone ornaments, though generally the strong lines of his gardens and of his architecture kept things under control. The wide variety of stone and brick paving patterns he used is reminiscent of Edwin Lutyens, though Fleming's paving designs ultimately lack Lutyens's delicacy and spatial resonance. Massive walls were a favorite Fleming feature, and he often lightened them with stone balustrades, wrought-iron railings and gates, scalloped tops, and accents such as finials or statuettes. For his Southern clients, he located enough specimen box to satisfy their desire for instant ancestral dignity—old boxwood was almost as good as family portraits. His deep perennial borders often included vertical notes like boxwood, flowering shrubs, and dwarf evergreens; he used vines lavishly. He created picture-book plantings of flowering trees along driveways, and made dramatic use of water and views.

Fleming's Wyoming patroness, Lydia Avery Coonley Ward, came from Louisville, and was undoubtedly his original Southern contact. He played the same part in her life as did Fletcher Steele in Mabel Choate's. Lydia Ward was a perfect Helen Hokinson cartoon right out of the pages of *The New Yorker*, a woman who could seriously write a poem for Fleming that begins, "The fairies brought you cradle gifts, dear architect and friend." She was also the sort of woman who couldn't be happy unless something was being torn apart and put together. Fleming was her live-in architect and garden designer (actually he had his own house close by, where Steele had to be content with a mere bedroom at "Naumkeag"). Like Mabel and Fletcher, Lydia and Bryant undoubtedly did not have a sexual relationship; but in each case one can hazard that they were closer to each other than to any other person of the opposite sex. For both women, the relationship and the garden-making was a means of expression; for both men, it was their opportunity to carry out over a long period their most cherished, experimental—and often most expensive—ideas. For Lydia Ward and for her Gilbert and Sullivan *Pinafore*-esque collection of "her sisters and her cousins and her aunts," Fleming realized an entire rural world of houses, barns, cottages, and gardens at the enormous place called "Hillside" between 1908 and 1917.

The twenties were Bryant Fleming's heyday. Of the dozens of places he worked on in Kentucky and Tennessee during that decade the best-known today is "Cheekwood," begun for Mr. and Mrs. Leslie Cheek in 1929. Leslie Cheek, who had made his money as a wholesale grocer before moving to Nashville, where he made millions in the coffee business, came home one day to find that Mrs. Cheek had bought a mirror too big for the house. "We will either have to sell the mirror or build a house to fit it," he said. "She called his bluff," recounted their daughter Mrs. Walter Sharp, who later inherited "Cheekwood." Today it is the Tennessee Botanical Gardens and Fine Art Center.[26]

The Cheeks bought 100 acres and hired Fleming to do both house and gardens. The three settled on the Georgian style and then took off for a long European trip. They visited Crowther's, England's famous rag-and-bones shop to which all the decorative fragments of England's destroyed great houses and gardens eventually find their way. They returned with doors from the Duke of Westminster's Grosvenor House (the hardware bears the ducal crest), and Queen Charlotte's staircase from her palace at Kew—not to mention a magnificent Georgian urn, statues representing *Alchemy and The Arts*, wrought-iron gates, and stone pineapples. We

Around the grotto, situated below the terrace on the garden elevation of the Leslie Cheeks' "Cheekwood," in Nashville, Bryant Fleming placed a fantastical but effective assortment of plants. Besides the papyrus and water lilies in the water, there is boxwood, mahonia, juniper, red cedar, and white pine to soften the huge retaining wall and to link it with the towering wisteria arbor above.

A walk along Richland Creek at "Watersmeet," designed by Bryant Fleming for the C. Runcie Clements of Nashville.

The W. C. Rosses of "Rostrevor" (1928) in Knoxville, mastered the art of keeping their "Italian" garden in full bloom right through the long hot Tennessee summer.

may find Fleming's work too busy and crowded with "features," but for his clients, the fields of architecture, landscape design, and horticulture were cultural warehouses from which they were entitled to pull out any number of emblems—that is, emblems of success. By the twenties, the permissable limits of eclecticism had contracted since the 1880s. An architect or landscape designer was supposed to keep his client on the straight-and-narrow of some style or other. However, within the broad confines of the style chosen, the clients' pleasure was to find as many period objects as possible, and the designer's job was to fit them all together. Extra dollars often meant extra features. Hence "Cheekwood," where Fleming designed a tall, rough-surfaced limestone mansion, impressive but severe. The gardens are elaborate, and started off with a real bang, you could say: the Cheeks assembled one of the finest boxwood collections in the country, but when it came time to plant them, holes had to be dynamited in the limestone crust of "Cheekwood's" hill to give them the depth of soil they needed. On the south front, Fleming tied the lofty, unornamented elevation to its hillside with a complex series of garden features. On the house terrace is an arched wrought-iron wisteria arbor that overlooks a naturalistic pool-and-grotto garden immediately below the balustraded terrace wall. Below that, stone terraces descend the hill to a rectangular pool which reflects the house facade. Two sets of divided staircases with wrought-iron railings curve down to the terraces, and at the bottom of the garden a central lawn vista has been cut through the woods. Off to the left is a series of three irregular ponds linked by waterfalls.

The Olmsteds in the Upper South: "Boxwood" and "Gardencourt"
"Boxwood," the Alfred F. Sanford arboretum and gardens begun in 1924 near Knoxville, Tennessee, was the work of the Olmsted firm. Its particular mix of formal axial gardens, picturesque lawns, and richly underplanted woodlands, all firmly linked by paths, are a good example of how the firm could carry out their model estate-cum-arboretum plan in any climate. Perhaps because Sanford was a shrub enthusiast like William Coe, the pictures of his garden in *History of Homes and Gardens of Tennessee* recall "Planting Fields" arboretum on Long Island, where the Olmsteds took on the job in 1918 following the death of Roland Sargent, Charles Sprague Sargent's son. The similarity derives from more than planting choices; even the compact, curvy, vine-covered profile of the teahouse in the water garden is very similar to that of the cottage, "thatched" with tiles at the end of the sunken pool garden at "Coe Hall." At "Boxwood" we first encounter John Staub, *the* Houston architect during the twenties and thirties. Early in his career Staub chose to go to Texas and build houses in Houston for Harrie T. Lindeberg, the New York country house architect, rather than to become a partner of Barber & McMurry in his native Knoxville. Staub's gently

eclectic, impressive but comfortable houses were perfect partners for the relaxed formal gardens that usually surrounded them. He renovated "Boxwood" for the Sanfords in 1925.[27]

The Olmsted firm did a lot of work in Louisville both public and private. How their Louisville projects developed typifies their pattern in other cities. Nationwide, beginning in the 1870s, their municipal park systems acted as magnets for upper-class suburban development. Ironically, the civic urge to beautify fueled the first urban exodus, since the city fathers who hired the firm often bought up the property adjacent to the new parks, which were frequently located on the then-outskirts of the city. There they built houses and gardens for themselves, and sold off the rest of the real estate in large parcels to the equally rich and powerful. Often they hired Olmsted Bros. to do their private landscaping. In Louisville, Olmsted Senior began the park system in 1875; the last of the parks was completed around 1900 after his retirement. All the parks were named after tribes of the Iroquois nation, with Cherokee, east and south of the city center, as the first. Alta Vista Road, on a hill overlooking Cherokee Park, was one of the most exclusive addresses.

In 1906, three sisters, the Misses Lucie and Mattie Norton, and Mrs. Minnie Norton Caldwell, all daughters of Louisville financier George Washington Norton, called on Olmsted Bros. to make a garden around their new imposing L-shaped brick Georgian house, "Gardencourt," on its 14-acre site. Carriages swept up a drive that curved along the ridgeline and ended at the house in a formal enclosed forecourt. On the final approach, a visitor would notice the top of a long garden pergola above the top of a high wall to the left. But the garden itself, and the wide grassy tree-dotted slopes beyond it, were kept a secret until one walked through the house, and stepped out onto one of the two white stone piazzas. The surprise garden, the surprise view, with its release from the tension of the enclosed arrival court and the enclosed volumes of the house, are part of an old garden formula of spatial constriction and expansion that dates back at least to the Renaissance.

By no means one of the Olmsteds' larger efforts, "Gardencourt," which still exists today and was purchased at auction in 1986 for $2.2 million, could even be called cozy. From the piazza level a short flight of steps leads down into the rectangular garden nestled between the pergola and a low wall on the view side. At the far end, a pair of brick pavilions connected by a wall frame a circular pool with a cherub fountain. A wide flower border lay next to the pergola, and the central space was crisscrossed with four brick paths and filled with more flowers—a design that was simplified to lawn after the death of the last sister, Miss Mattie, in 1946. The Kentucky landscape architect Anne Bruce Haldeman recalls that there was a strict territorial division between the two sisters who survived longest. "Miss Lucie did the house," she recalled, "and Miss Mattie got the garden."[28]

RICHMOND RISES AGAIN

Richmond, Virginia, capital of the Confederacy, enjoyed a special status during the estate era as the place that bounced back the fastest after the Civil War. A mercantile city of almost Tuscan sturdiness and sobriety, Richmond was one of the most urban and urbane cities of the South, with a flavor as distinct as that of Charleston, New Orleans, and San Antonio. Although it has a legacy of eighteenth-century houses, punctuated by the magnificently restrained Greek Revival buildings of Robert Mills, first native-born American architect, it had been largely rebuilt as a Victorian city after the devastation of the Civil War.[1] However, Richmond exists at the center of a dense network of the great plantations of Tidewater Virginia. Given this heritage, and the length of Richmond's English tradition, the affection for English styles in domestic architecture and gardens is hardly surprising.

During the teens and the twenties, a number of Tudor houses were built. Inspiration for the Georgian is self-evident in Virginia, but where did houses in this earlier style come from? The eclectic building habits of the nineteenth century had spread an architectural smorgasbord, widening the choice beyond Georgian and Federal. For Southerners used to making the romantic connection between Southern and English aristocracies, and especially for the newly rich seeking "ancestors," perhaps it seemed appropriate and satisfying to choose the Tudor style, the style of the earliest period of Virginia's settlement, in order to celebrate their past. The most fashionable new area lay south of Monument Avenue, which when it opened in 1890, became the new axis of the city and was one of the first Beaux-Arts city planning efforts in the nation.[2] At the James River fall line, the Kanawha Canal had been built to bypass the rapids. "Maymont," "Agecroft Hall," and "Virginia House," three examples of the new Virginia gardens, lie near the beautiful Kanawha Canal elbow.

"Maymont," "Agecroft Hall," and "Virginia House"

"Maymont," the first of the three, was built in 1893. The gardens on the 100-acre estate were created over the following twenty years. Both house and garden, largely restored, are open to the public today. Major James Henry Dooley and his wife, Sallie May, built a turreted stone castle with a pink-granite-pillared porch, surrounded by an intricate late-Victorian picturesque landscape that featured 185 different kinds of trees collected by the Dooleys all over the world.

In 1909 the local architectural and engineering firm of Noland and

Baskervill transformed the steep forty-foot drop from the house site to the Kanawha Canal into an up-to-the-minute formal terraced "Italian" garden with a *catena d'acqua* at one end and a natural cascade at the other.[3] On the level below was a grotto with stalactites and stalagmites chipped from a cave in western Virginia and a Japanese stroll garden. Indoors, a potpourri of Old Master copies, tapestries, and bibelots collected abroad exhibits an engaging but undifferentiating innocence typical of late Victorian eclectic taste in America. Such exuberant conglomerations would eventually vanish in favor of more stylistically unified designs. "Agecroft Hall" and "Virginia House" are the best such examples. Next-door neighbors, the pair were built by the same architect, Homer Grant Morse of Essex Fells, New Jersey, and their gardens were laid out by the same landscape architect, Charles Gillette of Richmond.[4] When Americans embraced a single historical style, collecting things of just the right period became an obsession. At "Agecroft Hall" and "Virginia House," both dwellings were constructed largely of materials brought from old houses in England. "Virginia House," begun in the early twenties, incorporates the golden sandstone remains of the Priory of the Holy Sepulchre at Warwick, originally built in 1125. Queen Elizabeth I slept at the Priory, and it was later the home of Henry Wise, Royal Gardener to William and Mary, and to Queen Anne. Ambassador Alexander Wilbourne Weddell and his wife, Virginia Chase Steedman, bought it as a ruin, sight unseen, over the telephone in 1925.[5] Most of fifteenth-century half-timbered "Agecroft Hall" once stood in Lancashire and was brought to this country over British protest, although by the time the Richmond owners, Mr. and Mrs. Thomas C. Williams, Jr., acquired the place, it was no longer inhabited and stood desolately in the new British industrial landscape of Midlands cotton mills. Both houses are now house museums open to the public.

Windsor Farms, where the houses are located, is part of a 600-acre tract once farmed by Martha Washington's nephew. It was, and is, the most desirable residential neighborhood in Richmond. Its developer, the builder of "Agecroft Hall," Thomas Williams, Jr., envisioned Windsor Farms as an English village. "Agecroft Hall" was to be the manor house. The engineer who laid out Windsor Farms was John P. Noland, the Richmond-born engineer who had designed the gardens of "Maymont" with his former partner, Henry E. Baskervill.

Besides a south-facing view of the James River, the gardens of "Agecroft Hall" and "Virginia House" have many traits in common. Both

A Tudor house with a garden by local landscape architect Charles Gillette was a Richmond way of life in the 1920s. At "Meadowbrook Manor," the Jeffresses played cards in shingled gazebos shaded from the sun and swam in the pool guarded by tubbed oleanders and gardenias.

are intimately associated with the houses they surround and have many outdoor rooms for privacy or entertaining. They share an Italian-flavored English Renaissance style very reminiscent of Edwin Lutyens's gardens, though the plantings, due to climate, are very different from Gertrude Jekyll's. (Gillette did subscribe to Jekyll's "drift" theory for flowers, though he put it rather differently, saying that one should mass them boldly "like a farmer plants corn.")[6] But since there can be no long-term summertime displays of perennials like delphiniums, due to the heat and humidity, spring-flowering bulbs, shrubs, and trees, and later, annual displays, and a burst of color in the fall, are the floral mainstays. However, these are heightened by Charles Gillette's exquisite and strongly structured mixed plantings of broadleaf evergreens, which were one of his specialties.

Charles Gillette, who has been called the Innocenti of the South, was

also a master of garden architecture. Like Bryant Fleming, Gillette was often called on to incorporate into his designs dozens of imported European garden decorations. His ability to do so gracefully was tested at "Virginia House," where, though many of the statues and urns are very fine, thirty years of State Department posts and a keen longing to be back in Virginia meant the Weddells were always returning with a memento, whether it was an entire garden loggia or a copy of the *Birth of Venus.*

Along with Fletcher Steele and Bryant Fleming, Charles Gillette (1886–1968) received his training as a landscape architect under Warren Manning. Gillette was born in Wisconsin, and attended the state university. In 1903, with no background in landscape except rides through the Wisconsin countryside, he moved to Boston to work for Manning for ten years. In 1911 he came to Richmond to supervise the Manning firm's extensive College of Richmond job, which was part of the Richmond park system. He was taken abroad by one of Manning's clients in 1912 and was very impressed by the lush landscape parks of Ireland, the cottage gardens of Stratford-upon-Avon, and the formalities of palace gardens such as Hampton Court and Versailles. In 1913 he moved to Richmond permanently and started his own practice there, working until his death in 1968.[7] Like Steele and Fleming, Gillette has been forgotten until just recently, when the reevaluation of America's twentieth-century classical heritage began to extend to landscape as well as architecture. The Manning training all three landscape architects received gave them a common horticultural vocabulary that emphasized a free use of shrubs and bold combinations of native species with trees from all over the world (seldom did any of them plant a woodland that didn't include at least a dozen species). In their estate work, all three men designed in a Beaux-Arts mode, stressing axial clarity, separation of parts according to function, the use of sightlines to tie the house and garden together, and a gradual shading from formal to informal as the garden plan extended outward from the house. Each worked in a variety of styles according to what his clients wanted. Each designed the architecture for his gardens, though Fleming was the only one to design houses as well. Each had his own distinctive character, inspiration, and stylistic affinity. If just one phrase had to describe the flavor of each man's work, "French" would sum up Fletcher Steele, "Italian Baroque" Fleming, and "English" Gillette. Steele's precisionist tricks, his forced perspectives, and his wit in garden design seem akin to Le Nôtre's optics, and spring from the cubist gardens he saw in Paris in the twenties. Fleming's most memorable gardens are not his Colonial Revival adventures in New York State, but the massy stonework and opulent plantings of gardens like "Cheekwood."

Gillette's gardens at "Agecroft" and "Virginia House," just like those of his contemporaries, Inigo Triggs and Harold Peto in Great Britain, were inspired by the Renaissance and filtered through the English Arts and

Richmond's mild climate allowed Charles Gillette to use tender evergreens like the beautiful Photinea serrulata, *seen here in the background at the rill garden at "Virginia House," in Richmond. Its soft shape, red juvenile foliage, sweetly perfumed white flowers, and flat corymbs of brilliant coral berries enhance every season.*

Crafts movement. As we have seen, such enclosure gardens formed sympathetic surroundings for English, or English-style, Renaissance houses, and were particularly suited to the suburbs, where walls and hedges were really necessary for privacy.[8] For country residences, such as "Lochiel" near Gordonsville, Virginia,[9] Gillette developed a broader eighteenth-century English landscape style, tying the house into the forests and fields with the long formal sightlines already familiar to Southerners from their old plantations. He also adapted this simpler style to in-town or suburban Georgian houses old and new like "York Hall," in Yorktown, or "Milburne," in Richmond, designed for the Walter Robertsons by William Lawrence Bottomley.

"Milburne" and Its Four Designers

William Lawrence Bottomley, architect, was a virtuoso interpreter of the classical tradition whose work was primarily directed toward the needs of "that peculiarly American, twentieth-century, New World suburban gentry who had become the backbone of our emerging country club/corporate culture."[10] His thirty-seven Richmond projects comprise a body of work that, as Jaquelin T. Robertson points out in his foreword to *William Lawrence Bottomley in Richmond,* "gave architectural distinction to the notion of 'Banker's Georgian.' "[11] A McKim Fellow at the American Academy in Rome in 1907, and a Beaux-Arts graduate in 1908, Bottomley's achievements in the twenties included River House in New York, as well as the inspired urban ensemble of Turtle Bay.[12] In the nineteen-thirties he edited the definitive two-volume work, *Great Georgian Houses of America,* still in print today. "Milburne," the last and the finest of the houses Bottomley designed between the World Wars, was highly praised by architect Louis Kahn. One can guess at the attraction of Bottomley's work by noting that the boy who grew up at "Milburne," Jaquelin T. Robertson, became the dean of the School of Architecture at the University of Virginia. Bottomley's buildings did not exist in isolation. Masters of modern landscape classicism such as Dan Kiley and Laurie Olin have paid tribute to his masterful site handling.[13] Bottomley's secret was to recognize that, although his clients' lives and work were inextricably entwined with the city, their "hearts were in an idealized and domesticated countryside."[14] His greatest achievement, in terms of gardens, was to scale down the Virginian plantation with all its widespread parts to a harmonious suburban villa with a forecourt, service area, garden, woodland, and view (usually screened to eliminate the neighbors). In this, his closest collaborator was Charles Gillette, who shaped and executed Bottomley's rough site and garden ideas.[15]

Like "Maymont," "Agecroft Hall," and "Virginia House," "Milburne" stands on the bluff overlooking the James River and the Kanawha Canal in Windsor Farms. But all resemblance ends there. Although Bottomley uses the vernacular of the eighteenth century, "Milburne" does not transport the visitor to another century—nor does that seem to be the intent. "Milburne" is solidly here and now, an early twentieth-century house and garden happily reaffirming the strength of the classical tradition today. A pebbled forecourt fronts the symmetrical pale pink brick house built in 1934; from the modeled brick urns on the carefully wrought entrance posts to the delicate plantings of andromeda, yaupon, azalea, columbine, and tiarella on a side path, to the terraces and trees that frame the magnificent canal view, everything breathes restraint, balance, an air of perfect choices carefully made. Though Walter Robertson was the director and architectural aficionado of the Robertson pair (his correspondence with Bottomley during the project amounted to nearly 200 letters), Mrs. Robertson can stand for all the American domestic generals from Lady Jean Skipwith[16] onward, who marshaled their skills, intuitions, wits, opinions, and prejudices to create such serene house-and-garden ensembles. And it is through the shorthand of Mrs. Robertson's anecdotes about her landscape architects that the story of "Milburne" comes alive.[17] First, of course, there was Gillette, who, says Mrs. R., "did the boxwood in front and on the upper terrace. But every time he came to the house he'd say 'You've got to take those two limbs off that tree.' We felt that big tree was one of the best things on the place, and we could see he just couldn't get his mind off it. So finally we got rid of one limb—and Gillette!" Next in line was Arthur Shurcliff, who had been working nearby at Colonial Williamsburg. "He ate raw eggs, wore boots, and drank tea like water—a very nice man but very eccentric," reminisces Mrs. R., adding, "he made the terrace and went back to New England." Shurcliff's replacement at Williamsburg, D. Alden Hopkins, then also replaced him at "Milburne." Last in line and fondest in her memories is Umberto Innocenti who, during the forties, was at the height of his fame and powers as a designer of sympathetic garden surroundings for old houses. Mrs. Robertson admired him not for what he added but for what he took away. "There are entirely too many trees," she remembers him saying on his first visit. "All he did was to take out four trees on the lower terrace, and one in the courtyard," she marvels, "but it made all the difference."

Just as classical Georgian architecture was a living and honored tradition in and around Richmond, so were gardens of a certain formality like "Milburne's." Places like "Bremo" and "Sabine Hall," "Westover," "Shirley," and "Berkeley" existed to teach lessons about the grandeur and sweetness of simplicity in a garden. Put together right, all one needed were well-articulated spaces, a few bricks and box bushes, wonderful trees, a good view, hot sun, and some shade. Bulbs, old roses, and the ubiquitous azaleas and camellias were the flowers. Why should a gardener experiment with the newfangled or the grandiose? The weight of social aspirations as well as of successful experience were all on the side of tradition. Richmond's society was small but strong, and insular enough to keep its power and test newcomers for admission, rather than being overwhelmed by them. Edith Wharton would have had a hard time setting *The House of Mirth* in Richmond. Add to this the mystique of the "Old South" and the importance of the restoration movement—most upper-class women, or those who had social ambitions, did a stint for the Garden Club of Virginia garden restorations—and the reasons for the reactionary nature of twentieth-century garden design all over the South become apparent.

TWENTIETH-CENTURY GARDENS FARTHER SOUTH

Ellen Shipman, Mrs. Ralph Hanes, and Winston-Salem, North Carolina
If anyone ever gave the lie to the notion that perennials are impossible outside of Maine, Long Island, California, and the uppermost tier of the Midwest, it was Ellen Shipman. From Cornish, New Hampshire, to New Orleans, to Cleveland, to Winston-Salem, she designed gardens filled with the most demanding perennials for the most demanding clients who had usually seen the best England had to offer. They included Fords,

Algers, Seiberlings, Knoxes, Goulds, Huttons, and Haneses. How did she do it? First, Ellen Shipman never said it was easy. Her planting plans bristle with the most daunting—and sometimes bizarre—cultural instructions. Try this mysterious recipe for the best way to grow delphinium in the South: "Early in the spring make a trench around each delphinium not too close to the plant and deep enough to touch the roots, put enough salt to go on a ten cent piece in a trowel full of lime, cover and water."[1] No one today seems to know what this will do for delphinium.

The fountain at the Ralph Haneses in Winston-Salem is wreathed with creeping saxifrage, ivy, and hydrangeas, and with a few fine grassy leaves of spent spring bulbs.

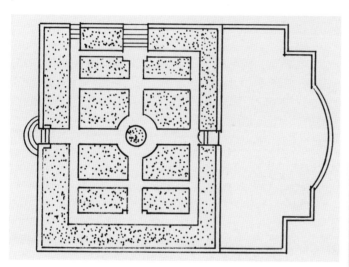

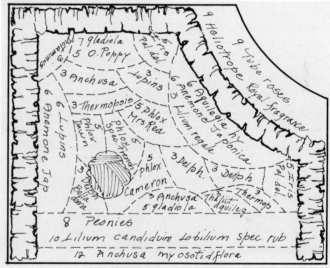

ABOVE AND RIGHT:
Redrawn from Ellen Shipman's original 1929 blueprint are the overall design, the planting detail of one of the central beds, and some of the cultural notes Ellen Shipman always added to her plans.

NOTES

STAKING— After the preparation of the soil and the planting, the next most important thing for the success of the garden is proper staking. This should be attended to most diligently, as most plants, if not staked from the beginning, form roots on their stems and spread out, leaving little or no room for less hardy and less vigorous plants.

DELPHINIUM CULTURE — Follow- Hybrid with dahlias; delphinium belladonna with salvia farinacea, peonies with pots set in of such plants as fairy lilies (pink and white); Hemerocallis, crinum kirki, Crinum fimbriatulum, hyacinthus candicans, from H. H. Berger Co., New York.

Remove biennials promptly and replace with annuals.

Plant lilies among peonies, as indicated on plan in groups of three and five staggered ×× ××× ×
                                                    ×× ××

Cut back nepeta mussini To induce second bloom. Nepeta should be divided every spring.

Seed annual poppies among Iris for September bloom.

Second, she never said it didn't take time, or that some things weren't purely experimental, or would last; she knew herself, and taught her clients, that gardening is a continuous balancing act. Third, from her early days gardening in the inhospitable Cornish climate, she knew the special efforts that must be made to help each plant thrive and look well. For instance, on the same southern garden plan she said, "Plant anemone japonica and aquilegia in staggered rows. Cut back aquilegia leaving only the lower leaves [which are pretty and feathery] as a mulch to keep the roots of the anemone cool during hot summer days." Fourth, Ellen Shipman kept her standards up and never ignored the limitations of the possible. Offered an important job in Atlanta where the clients were in too big a hurry to do the three-foot-deep double digging she felt was imperative for a good garden, she turned it down.

Born a comparatively poor Biddle in West Virginia in 1869 and raised by her grandparents, Shipman went to Southern schools, attended Radcliffe College, married the playwright Louis Shipman (they were later divorced), and in the nineties, met Charles Platt in the artists' colony of Cornish, where both had summer houses. He encouraged her to become a landscape architect; the first planting plans she made were for his Cornish houses. She continued to work with him throughout their careers. But for more than forty years she also had her own nationwide independent practice with its main office in New York City. She never let go of what she had learned in Cornish about garden geometry and "simpler, not nurserymanic" flowers.[2] She shared the fashionable taste of her contemporaries for single flowers and for pale color harmonies—no bright red. Shipman also had strict rules about appropriate planting inside and outside the garden proper: "Don't you ever plant one thing outside the wall that isn't native," she told Mrs. Ralph Hanes of Winston-Salem, in 1929, "but you can plant anything you want inside."[3] Her enclosed gardens were the heart of her landscapes, and were designed to show off the packed abundance and fabulous beauty of her plantings. Even in her largest gardens, such as "Halfred Farms," Cleveland, Ohio, and "Longue Vue," New Orleans, she stuck to her simple design formula, "A path, a coping around a bed, a tree, a place to sit—that is a garden." Color, seasonal sequence, and pattern were her strong points, rather than manipulation of space. When Shipman was in her seventies, she told an interviewer that "Until women took up landscaping, gardening was at its lowest ebb. The renaissance of the art was due largely to the fact that women instead of working over their boards, used plants as if they were painting pictures, and as an artist would."[4] However, she was proud of her ability to design her own garden architecture, and once said, "I like stones as well as I like flowers."[5] In the garden next to the Haneses' brick Georgian house, designed by the Boston firm of Peabody and Stearns, a tall cylindrical stone dovecote[6] and a finely detailed white Chippendale gate anchor the garden at opposite corners. The surrounding brick walls

swing up and down in their changing heights elevating the garden's small level changes. Shipman also loved designing the refinements of life indoors. She once told Mrs. Hanes, "No dining table is any good unless knees touch," and instantly designed four interchangeable different-sized table tops. Nor did her ideas about color end in the perennial border; at her Beekman Place apartment she served raspberry ice on powder blue plates. Most of Shipman's clients became passionate gardeners under her tutelage. Her practice was to make twice-yearly visits, if budget permitted, to revise the planting plans as the garden developed. Shipman was sixty when she first came to Winston-Salem for the Haneses. "She had a sweet face like a dried apple," remembers Mrs. Hanes, "and she and I became darling friends." The guest book records twenty years of her visits.[7]

DeWitt Chatham (as in blankets) Hanes (as in stockings) is tiny but very upright, and wears a sturdy blue smock with ruffles at neck and wrists. Her white hair stands out magnificently with an electric-shock effect. No one could miss the fact that she is a grande dame—the grandest, the oldest, and perhaps the most sophisticated of them all. Although DeWitt Hanes styles herself a "mountain woman," and pioneered the current revival of Appalachian arts and crafts, she and her family also founded the very contemporary Southeastern Center for the Visual Arts and the School for the Arts. Visitors to this lively house have included Henry Mencken, Amelia Earhart, Serge Lifar, Carlos Segovia, Walt Kuhn, Sister Parrish, George Balanchine, Cornelia Otis Skinner, Helen Hayes, and the entire American Ballet Theater, among many others. Aldous Huxley almost stayed longer than he wished: one morning after breakfast he fell through the cellar trap door in the dining room floor which had accidentally been left open. Another guest then told Ralph Hanes he knew his host's secret method for fine boxwood: "you invite the brains of the world," he said, "then you open the trap door, and later you just sweep up the bones to feed your box." (Boxwood loves bonemeal fertilizer.) Indeed Ralph Hanes, who worked long hours in the garden himself, loved boxwood. Shipman taught him how to prune. "Ralph," she said, "there are only two things that man can really control; one is a tree and one is a vine. Always cut out anything that goes up, and make sure you don't leave any nubbins."[8]

Although the Haneses' house can be called a "power house," their garden is not a showplace garden like those of Bar Harbor or Newport. It is significant for its sense of family continuity and vivid social, artistic, and family concerns. Shaggy today, but brimming with boxwood, roses, wild phlox, Virginia bluebells, and volunteer Johnny-jump-ups, it is very much DeWitt Hanes's garden, full of the madcap and impromptu spirit of its owner. It is also precious as a private Ellen Shipman garden, kept faithfully for fifty years by someone who remembers everything Ellen Shipman told her.[9]

At "Reynolda," begun in 1916 in Winston-Salem, a boulder bridge spans the spillway into Lake Katharine, named after Katharine Reynolds.

"Reynolda"

Bellwether estates—places built by leading citizens that inspired surprising numbers of copies in the same region—are an interesting phenomenon in the small cities of the South during the estate-building boom of approximately 1910–1929. Although the same regional preference for certain architects, landscape architects, and styles existed up North, in the South it seems more noticeable, perhaps because there was a smaller range of designers to choose from. When the Weddells or the Jeffresses or the Williamses built English Renaissance houses and gardens in Richmond, those places became symbols of success, actualizations of ideal domestic life for others who arrived later. Often when a new millionaire said, "Make me a place like the Joneses," the easiest way to do it was with the Joneses' architect and landscape architect—hence the thirty-seven houses in Richmond, where Bottomley, often working with Charles Gillette, played out so many graceful variations on the Georgian theme.

The bellwether estate in Winston-Salem was the 1,065-acre "Reynolda," completed in 1917 for R. J. Reynolds, the tobacco magnate. Reynolds had opened his first tobacco plant in 1875, and though Winston-

Salem's economy was thriving and diversified, it was really tobacco that made Winston-Salem rich. As in Richmond, where there is one most desirable place to live—in Windsor Park on the James River—so in Winston-Salem the best address was Reynolda Park, which grew up adjacent to "Reynolda House" when lots were sold off after Reynolds's death in 1918, only a year after he moved in.[10] R. J. Reynolds's tobacco business had the same effect on Winston-Salem's domestic architecture and landscape design as did Carnegie's steel company in Pittsburgh—it provided its top executives with enough money to build what they wanted in the latest style. "Reynolda House," designed by Philadelphia architect Charles Barton Keen, was really the brainchild of Katharine Smith Reynolds, R. J.'s private secretary, whom he married in 1905. Their daughter, Mary Reynolds Babcock, bought out the estate after her mother's death in 1924 and changed the house and garden to suit herself. "Reynolda House" now belongs to Wake Forest University, and the gardens are open to the public.

Many 1920s and 30s houses in Winston-Salem repeat its bulky and comfortable Dutch Colonial style, with white-stuccoed brick walls and green tile roof. But no one else in town had an entire village, complete with a church, power plant, central heating system for all houses, early phone system, a model farm, a polo field, and a private post office named after the estate. Like Marshall Field, Jr.'s "Caumsett," or George Vanderbilt's "Biltmore," "Reynolda" is properly called an estate rather than a plantation since it was not crop-supported.[11] Thomas W. Sears, also of Philadelphia, who often worked with Keen, designed the landscape and gardens in two major stages. Sears loved Repton and Olmsted. Here in 1916, the rolling North Carolina countryside and the abundant Piedmont flora seem at first to have inspired him to make a picturesque landscape. He framed long views with native trees and shrubs, and allowed the lawns to roll up to the house. The only formal garden feature near the house was a small oval sunken garden centered with an oval reflecting pool. A winding drive finished with a circle on the west front, where a Tuscan-columned porte cochere extended from the long verandah on the south front.[12] Like "Belmont" in Nashville, "Reynolda" was not just a private showplace, open only to the Reynolds's friends and business associates. It was also open to the "villagers" of Reynolda, and to the Winston-Salem public. So at a time (1916) when a mansion and its garden were often conceived as a unit, Sears laid out Reynolda's 4-acre formal garden proper far away from the house, partly to allow public access to the gardens without disturbing the family.[13]

The east-west oriented layout is entered from the west through a magnificent conservatory, part of the Lord and Burnham greenhouse complex which, along with the village church, was built even before the house (in 1912). On the other side, an avenue of huge chamaecyparis frames the conservatory's beautiful facade and leads to box quadrants and two Arts and Crafts pergolas. A row of espaliered grapes separates a lily pool from the kitchen garden still farther beyond to the east. Saucer magnolias and Japanese weeping cherries form the background on either side. In the thirties Sears eliminated the old picturesque-style circular drive and formalized the landscape of the house, adding a sunken garden on the south front, on axis with the fine circular steps that lead down toward the great views on the north. To the conservatory complex he added a formal rose garden beyond the vegetable plot, separated from it by a rose arbor. At the western end, two dark rustic pergolas frame a rill and reflecting pool, whose curved gable-like details echo the Dutch Colonial style of the house.

ATLANTA ESTATES
Believe it or not, Georgia is the largest state east of the Mississippi River, even larger than New York. There are 400 different types of soil, and a two-months' difference in the start of spring. The climate ranges from the subtropical to the boreal; there are winter resorts and summer resorts scarcely 300 miles apart. In the southern part of the state, palms flourish, as well as banana shrub, *Michelia Figo*, tea plant, *Camellia*

sinensis, and camphor tree, *Cinnamomum Camphora*. But even in the Piedmont where Atlanta is located, where the climate is not as mild as the semitropical coast, shrubs like Cape jasmine, *Gardenia jasminoides*, the most commonly planted gardenia, and vines like coral vine, *Antigonon leptopus*, and Confederate jasmine, *Trachelospermum jasminoides*, lend a luxuriant tropical air. They are joined by smoke tree and snowball, spikenard and pomegranate, and by the narcotic moonflower, *Ipomoea alba*, tuberose, *Polianthes tuberosa*, and 'sweet syringa', as the mock orange, *Philadelphus coronarius*, was called in the South. In the red clay soil of the hills around Atlanta, roses thrive and every estate garden had a collection of old-fashioned tea roses like 'Maman Cochet'. Walls were covered not only with tender old climbing noisettes such as 'Cloth-of-Gold', but with the creamy white of 'Silver Moon', the soft pink of 'Dr. W. van Fleet', and the music hall gaiety of 'American Pillar', cerise with a white center, all introduced after the turn of the century. Boxwood flourished on the clay soil, as well as other broadleaf evergreens that were used to make the green garden walls and patterning that were so much a part of every Atlanta estate garden. Many of them are intensely fragrant, such as the tea olive, *Osmanthus fragrans*, euonymus, *E. japonica*, and pittosporum, *P. Tobira*.[14]

Atlanta was founded in 1837 as a rail terminus for the upland cotton economy which dominated the state for thirty years before the Civil War. After the war, Atlanta rebuilt itself following Sherman's massive depredations, and cotton farming pulled itself together as a tenant farmer business. Life in Atlanta was very different from that on the old romantic coastal plantations, which the North had come to imagine were the South. The region's resourceful merchants and entrepreneurs struggled to diversify away from cotton—and succeeded. By the end of the first decade of the twentieth century, thanks largely to textile manufacturing, and to Coca-Cola, the Candlers, and the Olmsted firm, lavish modern estate gardening was coming into bloom. In 1892 Frederick Law Olmsted arrived to make suggestions for the 1895 Cotton States Exposition. He also advised Joel Hurt, a foresighted developer, on Druid Hills, his 1,500-acre residential development tract northeast of Atlanta. In 1908, the Coca-Cola Candlers bought Druid Hills, and called in Olmsted Bros. to complete their new purchase, which is still one of Atlanta's most exclusive neighborhoods. The Candlers sold Coca-Cola in 1919, and built houses for themselves in Druid Hills, as well as a campus for Emory University.[15]

Atlanta's estate-making history is close to that of Richmond, and Druid Hills was the counterpart of Windsor Farms. Both developments were begun in the early twenties; at both, the bellwether houses—"Agecroft Hall" and "Callanwolde"—were the homes of the developers themselves. Both were Tudor or English Renaissance in style, and inspired a host of imitations. Year-round houses for elite commuters are what they were—not weekend houses or seasonal resorts. In Atlanta,

"A man and a mule" were all the professional help the Robert F. Maddoxes used to terrace a ravine at "Woodhaven" in Atlanta. What began as a rose and perennial garden, as seen here c. 1908, eventually became a garden theater seating 600 by the twenties.

At "Trygvesson" (1919), in Atlanta, a youthful work of neoclassical architect Philip Trammell Schutze, the formal garden was a boxwood and ivy parterre with teardrop beds centered on an imitation tufa-bordered pool. A robust horseshoe staircase curves down from the house terrace to a tiny grotto-esque fountain on the landing above the garden.

banker Robert Maddox's half-timbered "Woodhaven" — "the first formal garden of any pretensions in Atlanta" — with its 75-acre landscape and immense terraced garden, was begun around 1906.[16] The estate lies about four miles north and west of Druid Hills, on Pace's Ferry Road. In the same area, known as Buckhead, two of the most beautiful formal gardens of Atlanta were located.

Just as in Windsor Farms, in Druid Hills there were a few Tudor houses, but classical forms were its stylistic bedrock. In architecture and garden design, the classical is the language Southerners are most comfortable speaking, and which has had the most meaning and resonance for them. As country-house architecture nationwide turned to variations on the Italian Renaissance, and to the English and American Palladian, Georgians followed suit, producing some of the most beautiful Classical Revival houses and gardens of the period.

At "Trygvesson" and "Swan House," Philip Trammell Schutze, first notable Georgia-born architect, indulged his clients with learned graceful Italian villa garden essays to go with houses that are acknowledged classical masterpieces in the Georgian Revival style. Why Georgian Revival? The answer is self-evident here in a countryside where white wooden porticoes with columns adorn the majority of country houses. The Andrew Calhouns and the Edward Inmans were among those "who had known a more rural south, where ladies and gentlemen were reared to respect the classical house as a symbol of a family's social position and cultural status."[17] Mary Trigg Calhoun told her architects, the Atlanta firm of Hentz and Reid,[18] that she didn't care what they designed for her and her husband, Andrew, who had made his money in real estate — they just wanted a house big enough for their five children. What they got was one of the most poetic baroque villas in America, with formal gardens in a 100-acre setting of pine woods and orchards. From the front gates there was a tantalizing view of the garden front up a long lawn (more precious than an Isfahan carpet in Georgia), lined with double rows of *Magnolia grandiflora* and sheared arborvitae. Then the road dived into the pines. The woods hid a wild garden, a cutting garden with a loggia, a tennis court, and an elaborate playhouse, which "was as big as a real house," remembers the Calhouns' daughter, Mrs. Charles Motz, "and in fact later on it was turned into a servants' house." It stood not far from the stables and the vegetable gardens. "Father did a lot of gentleman farming on his fifty acres, which were behind the house," adds Mrs. Motz, "and Mother had the front fifty."[19]

The "front fifty" contains the earliest important work of Schutze when he returned to Atlanta to apprentice with Neel Reid in 1919. Reid, whose classical masterwork is "Hills and Dales," was by that time already weakened by the cancer that would kill him in 1926. "Trygvesson's" house, garden, and interiors are all the work of Schutze, who was the same sort of master-of-all-trades as Charles Platt. The Piedmontese villa feeling

"Swan House" in Atlanta, "the villa ideal, long courted in Georgia, ideally realized," was created in 1926 by Schutze for the Edward Inmans. The cascade is taken directly from that of the Palazzo Corsini which Schutze had sketched. (Martin & Mitchell, Landmark Homes of Georgia)

LEFT:

The boxwood maze at "Bankshaven," a billowing wealth of box as it flourishes in the South, came from an old Georgia plantation. Numbered and lifted, it was replanted by Atlanta landscape architect William Pauley for the William Banks, Sr., in Newnan in 1929. Pattern—whether a boxwood maze, a doily of flower beds, or the sand or clay of a traditional vernacular "swept garden"—has always entranced Georgians.

began in the entrance court lined with terra-cotta pots of pomegranate, oleander, and orange trees. Below the house terrace is a parterre garden from which stairs descend to the long lawn below. The tall, slightly-too-decorative, slightly-too-flat three-story facade rises behind, topped with flaming urns. But when "Trygvesson" was going full steam in the twenties and thirties, and the garden was ornamented with large Italian statues, when immense, five-foot-tall *ollas* held aloes and azaleas, when 'Paul's Scarlet' roses twined in the balustrades, it looked right. The garden's elaboration was the perfect match for the curvy complexity of the soft buff stucco building.[20] "Trygvesson" has the slightly gawky grace of a first effort. It was, and is, the joyful work of a talented young man trying out all his new Italian ideas—a little Villa Cuzzano here, a little Villa Gori there, a touch of Villa Spada.[21]

Perfect fusion came with "Swan House," which is, as Martin and Mitchell point out, "the villa ideal, long courted in Georgia, ideally realized." "Swan House,"[22] built in 1926 for the Edward Inmans, and now open to the public as a house museum, belongs to the Atlanta Historical Society; the gardens and grounds are maintained by thirty-two different local garden clubs. Here on 45 acres of woodland Schutze used many of the architectural and landscape ideas he had tried out at "Trygvesson." There is the same long shot of the garden front from the entrance gates before the house disappears from view, screened by woods, and a similar terrace-and-divided stair configuration in the garden.

But "Swan House" has a gravitas, a majesty, unfelt at lighter, more fairy-tale "Trygvesson." Perhaps it is because many of the house's architectural features are baroque English rather than Italian.[23] However, the five-basin garden cascade flanked by steps is taken directly from the Italian. Line for line, it is that of the Palazzo Corsini, in Rome, which Schutze had seen and sketched.[24] The cascade is flanked on either side by two massive stone-walled terraces: the top is a simple green shelf for the house to stand on, trimmed with boxwood, the lower once featured gardenias.[25] Schutze's favored tufa stone encrusts the urns that still stand on the high terrace wall. (The same tufa-festooned urns punctuate a little *giardino segreto* off to the west side of the house.) Jasmine and roses wreathe the walls around the cascade, and the strong lines of the

basins and stairs are softened by many pots. Below the cascade a beautifully maintained lawn spreads out in three more terraces. The lowest is shored up by a retaining wall with seven niches, which inevitably recalls William Kent's Portico Praeneste in the Venus Vale at Rousham, in Oxfordshire, one of the earliest and best-known English landscape gardens.[26] Emily McDougald Inman was a recondite English house and garden fan, and she particularly loved the first half of the eighteenth century.[27]

Edward Inman, a prominent Atlanta cotton broker, died only three years after they moved in, but Emily Inman lived on—for forty years in, and with, her house and garden. Hers was a life liberated and given meaning by the creation of its own setting, a setting where the garden equaled the interior and the architecture in importance. In fact one might argue that it is the garden that makes the whole thing possible, aesthetically speaking. Schutze's deep understanding of Italian garden design is what makes this bird-of-paradise Palladian house fit into the Atlanta suburb of Buckhead appropriately and easily, as if it belonged there, as indeed it does.

Piedmont Georgia: "Dunaway Gardens" and "Hills and Dales"

In Newnan, about thirty-five miles south of Atlanta, is "Dunaway Gardens," a wonderful example of the sweet unself-conscious gaudiness that can overtake the South in its sillier moments. Hettie Jane Dunaway, an Arkansas-born actress who became the highest paid performer on the Chautauqua circuit in the early years of the century, married Wayne P. Sewall, who is always described as "a dashing booking agent from Atlanta." Together the two set up "Dunaway Gardens" on the Sewall family's worn-out cotton plantation on a tributary of the Chattahoochee River. During the Depression, the making of "Dunaway Gardens" provided jobs for hundreds of laborers. A sort of artists' colony, "Dunaway Gardens," which billed itself as a "theatrical training center and floral rock garden," was, in the thirties and forties and into the fifties, filled with the likes of Minnie Pearl, the Grand Ole Opry star. "Dunaway Gardens" was nothing if not eclectic. In the cotton-barn-turned-theater, dancers rehearsed, ranging from Broadway show choreographer Edwin Strawbridge's hoofers to the Ballets Russes de Monte Carlo. On "Dunaway Gardens" 22-acre hillside there were miles of drystone retaining walls and steps, pagoda-topped gazebos, rustic cottages with names like "Little Windy," where the performers-in-residence lived, not to mention one called "Shangrila," where honeymooners could put up. There was an iris garden, endless pools and springs, and a sunken garden with a wishing well. A tearoom called "The Blue Bonnett," once the Sewall family home, regaled tourists with fried chicken and a chance to rub elbows with the performers, who also ate there. But the most prominent garden feature of all was the 1,000-seat grass-terraced outdoor theater, a

In its heyday (the thirties and forties) "Dunaway Gardens" in Newnan was a show biz artists' colony. Broadway choreographer Edwin Strawbridge's show girls perform on the grass steps of the 1,000-seat garden theater.

Around 1914 at "Hills and Dales" in La Grange, the Fuller Callaways added two boxwood inscriptions taken from his family's coat-of-arms, "Ora Pro Mi" and "St. Callaway," to Sarah Ferrell's "God Is Love" and "Fiat Justicia," planted as part of the original garden laid out beginning in 1841. The plan shows Ferrell's original terraces and her intricate gardenesque plantings, as well as the new central axis and circular pool, at bottom. Neil Reid designed the Callaways' big new house, and sympathetically reordered the garden.

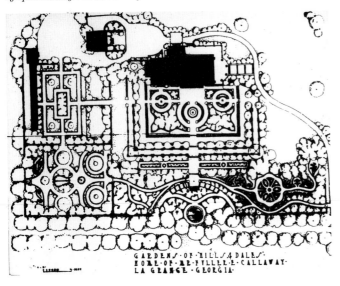

GARDENS · OF · HILLS · & · DALES ·
HOME · OF · MR · FULLER · E · CALLAWAY ·
LA · GRANGE · GEORGIA ·

wonderful populist version of the garden theater, which is being restored today, as is "The Blue Bonnett." Pines, red cedars, and magnolias formed the backdrop, and a forty-foot totem pole crowned the highest slope.[28] This is inspired American show-biz hokiness of a kind that rarely, if ever, has been expressed in garden form.

The most important modern estate garden near Atlanta is actually a garden started in 1841 by a tiny little woman with big green thumbs, Sarah Coleman Ferrell.[29] Sarah Ferrell was that rarity, a plant collector with a sound, if idiosyncratic, sense of design. (Prosper Berckmans' great nursery, Fruitlands, established in 1857 in nearby Augusta, meant she could find many unusual and newly introduced plants.) She also believed in the morality of garden-making espoused by every nineteenth-century garden book and periodical of the nineteenth century. Toward the end of her fifty-two years of gardening, she even admitted that plants and flowers were more for her than an agreeable pastime or a wholesome domestic duty. They were not just "a part of my life," she wrote to a friend, in what seems to be self-reproach, "they were life itself."[30] There are few gardens in the world where one feels more the personality of its creator, or the pleasure she took in making and tending her quirky masterpiece — five terraces of differing widths and lengths whose framework is clipped boxwood, magnolia, and cherry laurel. Her boxwood topiary is the fullest expression of her feelings. On the top level of "The Terraces," as she called her garden, Sarah Ferrell embroidered her own motto, "God is Love," and that of her husband, Judge Blount Ferrell, "Fiat Justitia," both in dwarf box. At the garden's east entrance is the word "God," very large in more boxwood. At the western end of the garden Sarah's imagination soared in what has been called the Sanctuary, where one finds a boxwood harp with strings of gold-leaved alternanthera, a low, easily sheared annual, and a pulpit and pews in boxwood, filled in with flowers.[31] There is also a lumpy, figure-eightish pattern, which turns out to be a waterless *catena d'acqua* worked in boxwood, a strangely touching provincial translation of the glittering water chains at Villa Torlonia, or Villa Lante.

Sarah Ferrell died in 1906, but before she did, she entreated Fuller E. Callaway, a member of the Atlanta textile manufacturing family, to save her garden. In 1912, he and his wife bought the 5-acre garden and the rest of the place,[32] which they renamed "Hills and Dales," and an additional 3,000 acres of surrounding farmland.[33] The Callaways knew they were saving something important, but it is interesting to speculate on what they, and their architect, Neel Reid, thought they were getting, and, given that, what they did with it. Sarah Ferrell had gardened for so long that one might say she had gardened straight through two styles. The first was the early Victorian gardenesque, the second, the early Victorian form of the "Italian" style. On her garden terraces, there are many of the meandering paths and irregular plantings of mixed shrubs and newly introduced trees so characteristic of the picturesque. The "Italian" gardens of the 1840s were the latest revision of the formal garden, which had taken shape in Italy in the Renaissance. But the "Italian" gardens of the nineteenth century that would have influenced Sarah Ferrell were English variations on the theme designed by Charles

Barry, with symmetrical *parterres de broderie* of bedding-out plants laid out in conjunction with the house, clipped hedges and topiary figures, trellises, and statues. H. H. Hunnewell's topiary garden, "Wellesley," in Massachusetts (1854), is a good American example of the style.

However, the fundamental design of Sarah Ferrell's garden long antedates the Victorian gardenesque or the newly revived "Italian." That is to say, for all her interest in new plants, she was a conservative Southern lady whose most basic design ideas were typically those of her part of the South. She made terraces,[34] she edged her beds with box, and made her garden paths of hard, swept, whitish clay. Though the Ferrells built a fashionable "cocked-hat Yankee cottage," as Alexander Jackson Downing's favorite gable-and-gingerbread wooden houses were occasionally labeled in the South,[35] they did not reorder their traditional home landscape. The Fuller Callaways were native Georgians, philanthropists, and millionaires. Besides saving Sarah Ferrell's garden, they wanted a classical house to match their position as important Southerners. Neel Reid had come to Atlanta in 1909 where he made his specialty residential architecture, and classical architecture at that. His Beaux-Arts training, his year of work in New York during 1908 to 1909, and his interest in landscape architecture meant he would have known Platt's *Italian Gardens,* and Wharton's *Italian Villas.* So what struck him and the Callaways was the garden's Italian-ness. Doubtless, if they had been Yankees making an Arcadian plantation retreat, they would have emphasized the traditional Southern aspects of the garden. But both aspects were there to choose from, an incomparably rich and complicated mixture.

Reid proceeded to build the masterpiece of his short life,[36] a graceful, spacious house he described to Mrs. Callaway as "Georgian Italian," meaning English Palladian of the Georgian period.[37] To the main garden, Reid and the Callaways added a rock garden, a sunken garden,[38] and a cutting garden—all the usual features of any self-respecting estate. (They also improved Sarah Ferrell's greenhouses.) The changes made in the main garden did not alter Mrs. Ferrell's designs, but transformed the whole garden, subtly and sympathetically shifting the balance of the garden to the classical. They added very fine statues and urns throughout the gardens. (Sarah Ferrell had used some urns but no statues.) The top parterre pattern was doubled to match the larger mass of the new house, so that the new garden pediment now looks down on two circular sets of mottos. Although "Hills and Dales" is primarily a topiary garden, it is by no means a green garden. There is the full range of flowering shrubs, trees, and vines, from the commonly used azalea, oleander, gardenia, magnolia, dogwood, crepe myrtle, and wisteria, to more old-fashioned smokebush, flowering quince, and golden-bells, and fruit trees like peach, pear, and pomegranate. In 1932 landscape architect Earl Draper made a partial list of the wonderful period combinations grown in the sunny top parterre beds in Ida Cason Callaway's time:

amaryllis, madonna lilies, coreopsis, gaillardia, clove pink, physostegia, gladiolus, peonies, spider lilies, and many other perennials and annuals.[39]

To the broad bottom terrace Reid added a circular reflecting pool reached by a pair of widely curved steps. There had been no water in Sarah Ferrell's garden except for covered wells. Reid placed a large, beautiful stone fountain with a jet on the top terrace on line with the central door and with the lower reflecting pool. His additions gave a new axial quality to the old garden, stringing the terraces and the house together with a beautiful visual shot. The high flashing jet on the top terrace gave the parterre the movement and verticality it needed to be a match for the very grand new garden facade, with its two-story engaged Ionic columns.[40]

Sensitive, intelligent, and gifted, Reid was as good a gardener as he was architect and landscape architect. Descriptions of his own garden at "Mimosa Hall" in Roswell, north of Atlanta, show how simply and evocatively he used plants familiar in the South. The most conspicuous ornament at his pedimented and columned front door[41] was a chaste tree, *Vitex Agnus-castus,* a tall shrub beloved by old Southern gardeners for its cool blue flowers, so rare in August. Over it Reid threw a veil of Lady Banks roses, the climbing rose of the South that runs wild everywhere along with the Cherokee rose, and begins to bloom early in April.[42]

"Hills and Dales" has been called "the apotheosis of all Georgia box gardens."[43] In a sense, it can be seen as much more—it embodies the conservative spirit, the design elements, and the plantings characteristic of Southern gardens along the coast and back into the Piedmont, from Maryland to Georgia. Although it was never a plantation, and by Southern standards is not very old, "Hills and Dales" is grounded in the formal planting patterns and the terraces of the Tidewater region. Any visitor senses the wonderful speed and savagery of Southern growth, and the softness of climate, in a garden where a yellow multiflora rose festoons the very top of a 60-foot tall silver-leaved poplar,[44] where Cherokee roses, wisteria, and Confederate jasmine form a roof above giant tender cunninghamias, where violets bloom everywhere in December, and camellias in January.[45] Sarah Ferrell's runic inscriptions and naive pictorial devices in boxwood have something of the idiosyncratic, unself-conscious charm seen in gardens like "Belmont," remnants of the South's own antebellum Gilded Age. Most important of all, "Hills and Dales" continued to grow in the twentieth century. Sarah Ferrell's energy and obsession were met at just the right time by the sympathetic eye and classical abilities of Reid, the means, and the gardening fervor of not just one, but two, generations of Callaways. With its Classical Revival house, it is a genuine Southern estate garden in the modern sense, as well as the unique example of perfect garden continuity in the South,—the bridge between the two opulent Southern garden-making eras: the 1850s and the teens and twenties of the new century.

The
DEEP SOUTH
Alabama · Mississippi
Louisiana · Texas

Moving west and south into Alabama, Mississippi, Louisiana, and Arkansas, one moves back forty years into the heart of the South's own Gilded Age: cotton culture in the last decade before the Civil War. (Though cotton culture architecture and gardens were the models for east Texas, and continued to be right on down through the suburban style known as Southern Colonial, the enabling money for the estate-scale gardens of Texas actually came from oil and its leveraging effect on the Texan economy, after Spindletop blew in Beaumont in 1901.) What do forty years mean in terms of garden literature and horticulture? Large plantation owners in the South, the "big bugs" as they were sometimes called, had libraries full of practical horticulture books.[1] It was a matter of pride to have a fine flower garden and to be able to provide every kind of fruit and vegetable for the table. There were no landscape architects as such, though a "European gardener," sometimes actual and sometimes merely apocryphal, hovers around the making of many Southern gardens. Without widespread photographic reproduction, there was as yet no great explosion of garden picture books; periodicals like *Godey's Lady's Book* and horticultural magazines[2] were the important disseminators of

garden style. Diaries and letters are the best sources for information about specific gardens of this period in the Deep South.[3]

While many plants that are the staples of Southern gardens as we know them today (crepe myrtle, camellias, mimosa, tea olive) had already been introduced from the Far East, many tender and tropical plants from South America and South Africa,[4] and species from Korea and Australia,[5] were just making their entry into Southern horticulture. Greenhouses were often magnificent,[6] and many who did not have a greenhouse or conservatory proper had a "pit," a sort of walk-in cold-frame, half

ABOVE:

An 1860 John Sartain engraving (later hand-colored) shows "Gaineswood" in Demopolis, Alabama, the "Home Place" for a 1,500-acre cotton plantation in the rich soil of the Black Belt. General Nathan Whitfield, owner, architect, builder, and garden designer, and his family are enjoying the springtime. Lombardy poplars, fashionable when Whitfield began his garden in 1843, are a feature of the landscape. The temple was used as a bandstand for parties. In front of the house the balustrade and retaining wall of the formal south parterre can be discerned.

below ground and roofed in glass. Nurseries were in short supply outside the big cities[7]—fruit trees, for example, were often imported from northern nurseries such as Prince on Long Island. (However, due to the change in climate, northern trees often did not flourish in the South.) There was plenty of opportunity for an enterprising horticulturist like Thomas Affleck to start a local nursery business.[8] A Scot, Affleck came to the Natchez area in 1841, married a widow—a plantation owner—and set up Southern Nurseries, getting a sound start with fruit trees of all kinds. For hedging, he provided a choice of evergreens (photinia, pittosporum, aucuba, viburnum) besides the eternal native cherry laurel. He also sold lots of annuals (verbenas were his favorites), dahlias, and 175 kinds of roses. In 1851 he published *Affleck's Southern Rural Almanac and Plantation and Garden Calendar,* which was influential throughout the South. A brilliant salesman, Affleck opened offices in New Orleans (where there *was* plenty of competition), and in Brenham, Texas, where he is buried. He also found a captive audience aboard the Mississippi riverboat *Princess,* where he sold potted plants and cut flowers weekly from the hurricane deck. Always enterprising, he took advantage of his European connections, experimenting with firs from England (without much success), and getting an early start on the importation of Ghent azaleas, the first hardy varieties.[9] In 1861 he moved to Houston, where he became known as the Father of Texas Horticulture.

There was no shortage of labor or money for gardens in the Deep South. Planters whose well-to-do tobacco-growing grandfathers in the Coastal South had owned at the most fifty to a hundred slaves now could own as many as several hundred. The cotton and cane trades were at their height, throwing off money for those lucky few whose lifestyle and gardens make the parallel to the Gilded Age an apt one. Money spent in quantity was what made the 1850s the Deep South's Gilded Age. Although there were nowhere near as many millionaires in the antebellum South as there were later to be in the Northeast, they spent money in the same unashamed style as New Yorkers would do in the nineties.

Handy parallels can be drawn between Newport, Rhode Island, in the 1890s and Natchez in the 1850s. Natchez, just like Newport, was a collection of massive and elaborate mansions in a port town, built quite close together by people who shared the same life and interests—and made their money by the same speculative capitalism that caused similar huge swings of fortune. In Newport it was high finance—banks and railroads and land speculation; in Natchez it was high cotton prices. The result was the same exaggeration of style and obsession with detail, the same boisterous but wonderful show. Houses were elephantine, doorknobs were made of silver, and spoons and forks of gold,[10] and platoons of plants came and went in the gardens. In Natchez or New Orleans, just as in Newport forty years later, the same eager interest existed in European culture and the Grand Tour. Garden ornaments were shipped back to the Deep South surprisingly often from the Continent. But thanks to the French influence of New Orleans and to the English cotton trade, antebellum Southern planter families were often more sophisticated in their tastes, and had closer ties with Europe, than did Northern Gilded Age millionaires two generations later.

ALABAMA

It is always surprising to discover how young the Deep South really is. The garden history of Alabama begins when the region was settled by white planters in numbers after the Creek Nation was finally defeated in 1814 by Andrew Jackson.[1] That defeat, the end of the 1812 war, and the increasingly worn-out state of the land on the East Coast, brought a tide of settlers south and west to the Black Belt.[2] At first life moved on the rivers, but by the 1850s railroads began to compete seriously with water traffic for the cotton trade. Alabama was known as "the heart of Dixie"; it is where the Confederacy was formed on February 4, 1861, and where the first Confederate flag was sewn.[3] The state was also a center for the kind of Southern expansionist thinking that led to the annexation of Texas and the war with Mexico. Nowhere did the current of Southern national-ism run stronger than in Alabama.[4] Spontaneous, childlike, fantastic, romantic, and intensely conservative, cotton planters, who explained themselves and their lives in terms of cavalier mythology, made gardens that reflected many of these same characteristics. As conservatives, they kept the straight avenues and geometric parterres that were their East Coast Tidewater seventeenth-century legacy; as romantics, they added the curving paths, lawns, and groves inspired by the picturesque.

In Demopolis,[5] about 100 miles west of Montgomery on a bluff overlooking the Tombigbee River, stands "Gaineswood," the most opulent surviving antebellum mansion in Alabama, surrounded by the preeminent landscape of the period in the state. The gleaming white Doric-pillared house was designed and built by General Nathan B.

Whitfield, starting in 1843, the year he purchased his 480 acres with its log house. Inside, the classical orders continue—Ionic pillars and pilasters throughout, except for the drawing room, which is finished in the Corinthian style. All around the house lay a picturesque park of 15 acres, landscaped by Whitfield and surrounded by a cypress board fence, the last addition before the Civil War. On the north and south fronts of the house are double-story porticoes 51-feet long which opened out onto flower parterres. Each garden was surrounded by a classical balustrade, whose corner piers were topped with huge Greek urns. In the middle of each parterre stood an Italian marble statue, one a Greek goddess, the other a dancing girl. Beyond the south garden lay the working part of the estate—a kitchen garden of several acres, barns, stables, workshop, slave quarters, the traditional separate kitchen, and even a still house with cypress tanks where brandies were distilled from peaches and apples grown on the place. On the north side of the house was the ornamental landscape. The parterre itself was laid out in intricate patterns of tea olive, hyacinth, buttercups, kiss-me-at-the-gate, *Viola tricolor*, flowering quince, bridal wreath, and many tea roses.[6] The rose that General Whitfield's grandson, Jesse, remembered best was the fragrant, soft sulphur-yellow noisette, 'Cloth-of-Gold'.[7] 'Cloth-of-Gold', or 'Chromatella', was hybridized in France in 1843, the year that Nathan Whitfield began to build his mansion. Beyond the north parterre a lawn ran down to an artificial lake, with two islands and a classical pavilion. Improving the views was very important to the general: in 1859 he was "busily engaged grading the ground in front of the house, sloping it down to the lake so as to let us see the water better." He laid out the north and south drives so that the approaching visitor would always see the house in a picturesque perspective. Besides the parterres, the other formal garden elements were a "lovers' lane" of two straight lines of crepe myrtles, which led from house to the boathouse, and a curving cedar-lined drive, which led from the main north entrance up to the house and back down again to the south gate. After the war, fortunes declined: a mulberry tree grew up through the dining room floor, and goats roamed the halls. "Gaineswood" was restored in 1896 by Whitfield's sister, Mrs. Charles Duncan. It was restored again in 1946 and now belongs to the state.

"Bellingrath Gardens"

A twentieth-century garden, "Bellingrath," near Mobile, is a freewheeling Southern variation on the American worship of European culture. It shares the eclecticism of much earlier estate gardens in the Northeast or a place like "Ca d'Zan" in Florida. But where Northern millionaires generally went to the same small group of architects and landscape architects to buy their taste, the Bellingraths unself-consciously went their own way. They engaged professional help to carry out their schemes, but without censoring their rambunctious ideas.

The Bellingraths were childless; their vast garden became a very important part of their life. A comforting sense of immortality must have been gained by knowing their creation would live after them. Like a museum, the garden offered opportunities to collect (the Bellingraths collected camellias and azaleas), a chance to exercise their philanthropy and express their civic pride. Designed to be open to the public almost from inception, "Bellingrath Gardens" seems institutional. It is difficult to like the almost military displays of massed daffodils or chrysanthemums, the wide hard-surfaced paths that allow so many people to visit, or the sense of zealous moral or fundamentalist uplift. Yet "Bellingrath Gardens" has its moments of Spanish moss-covered magic.

In 1903 Walter Duncan Bellingrath acquired the franchise rights for Coca-Cola for most of Alabama, and made millions by advertising Coca-Cola year-round instead of as a "summer drink." Bellingrath was also the first to sell a six-pack. He and his wife, Bessie Mae, made their European Grand Tour in 1927, and when they returned they set about transforming their fishing camp twenty miles south of Mobile into a 65-acre garden, with a plantation surrounding of 750 acres. The Bellingraths wanted to combine typical Southern plantings—azaleas, camellias, moss-hung live oaks—with European garden features. In 1935 Walter and Bessie Mae began to build a big house in the center of the gardens and they asked George B. Rogers, *the* Mobile architect of the day, to use all the features they liked: Roman arches, Italian fountains, New Orleans ironwork, English stone dolphins, and Chicago roof tile. Rogers also supervised the creation of the gardens, employing as many as 100 workers at a time to build the rock gardens, grottos, ravines, cascades, and fountains.[8] Continuous succession of bloom was the aim. Twenty-five hundred camellias start to bloom in October, and are followed by a mad rush of 250,000 azaleas in February. There are over 140 azalea varieties, and about 900 kinds of camellias. Like Easterners with their boxwood, the Bellingraths collected specimen camellia plants up to 100 years old from neighboring places and "yards." Some were huge. Just ten camellia bushes, more like trees, completely filled an entire railroad boxcar which arrived on the Bellingraths' private siding sometime in the thirties when the garden was nearly finished.[9] Late spring azaleas are followed by mountain laurel, then hydrangeas and gardenias, with color through the

OPPOSITE:
A 1931 visitor admires just a few of the original 20,000 azaleas planted by Coca-Cola millionaire Walter Bellingrath and his wife, Bessie Mae, at "Bellingrath Gardens" south of Mobile. Local designer George Rogers employed the same architectural forms estate garden makers all over the United States had been using for a quarter of a century: the rill, the divided stair, and the grotto and semicircular pool popularized by Sir Edwin Lutyens.

summer from crepe myrtle, oleander, hibiscus, and the yellow-flowered allamanda vine. The formal rose garden, surrounded by rose-wreathed chains, was laid out to resemble the Rotary Club's emblem, the pilot's wheel.[10] Nearby are extensive conservatories. There are more than seventy different kinds of trees.

The place opened to the public with a traffic jam in 1932. "Bellingrath Gardens" are flamboyant, not subtle; they have a populist appeal which the public-spirited Bellingraths must have fostered from the first. Gardens as "Southern" as these are almost a caricature of themselves.

They are just as fabulous as Walter Bellingrath, or "Mr. Bell," himself, who was the archetypal American self-made man. An enthusiastic philanthropist, a colorful money-maker who believed in the Protestant virtues of self-help *and* of helping his neighbor,[11] he kept his ole' country boy charms as he grew richer and richer, so that even in his eighties, he was still drinking whisky out of the bottle (in private; Coca-Cola in public), doing a little buck-and-wing dance step to his own whistled tune, and playing hillbilly tunes on his mouth organ almost till the day he died.[12]

MISSISSIPPI

In 1835, in *The Southwest by a Yankee*, Joseph Holt Ingraham wrote about Natchez as a town "whose suburbs are peculiarly rich in tasteful country seats."[1] Not only is the word "suburbs" startling at such an early date, but so is the phrase "tasteful country seats," with its Reptonian ring, in a part of the country where the working cotton plantation would have seemed to be the prevailing reality. In fact, Mississippi and Louisiana cotton planters often escaped their isolated, breathlessly hot, yellow-fever-ridden lowlands for the high breezy bluffs of Natchez—the first really high land on the Mississippi north of New Orleans—and the comfort of their own society. In this sense, Natchez was a resort town, with all the gaiety, luxury, and beauty that implied. By the 1850s, Natchez was very old in Deep Southern terms: it had been an established white settler's town for nearly 150 years. The Natchez Indians and a succession of French, Spanish, and Americans beginning in 1716 made Natchez an important travel depot. The town marked the end of the Natchez Trace, the long Native American trail that was the main route from Virginia through Tennessee to the banks of the Mississippi. Historian Roger Kennedy, in *Architecture: Men, Women and Money*, describes what a cultural oasis, architecturally speaking, Natchez was in the Deep South before the Civil War. He writes,

Any unsentimental survey of the region between the Fall Line in the seaboard South and the Mississippi River—that is, the inland region settled by emigrants from the oldest South—will yield the conclusion that in the nineteenth century, in that vast domain, there were no great clients for architecture.... There was a profusion of wealth, suddenly acquired and concentrated in the hands of people avid for display.... The frontier magnates of the Middle South showed their ambitions in houses that were large but that were not architecturally very bold.... Natchez was always the great exception among southern interior cities. In Natchez arose a class of literate, cosmopolitan clients—many of them doctors of medicine as well as planters—whose architecture represents a unique accomplishment in the new South.[2]

The architectural styles of Natchez's well-preserved town houses and "tasteful country seats," range from late eighteenth-century Federal[3] to a huge spread of Greek Revival,[4] to a light sprinkling of eclectic and Italianate houses built in the fifties.[5] Every last one has columns somewhere, and all have magnolias, cherry laurel, and the other plants that belong to what the great Southern gardener and garden writer Elizabeth Lawrence disparages as the "cast-iron Southern" garden—that is to say, whatever will endure the summer blaze. On the whole, these gardens, unlike the houses, are beautiful but not interesting. Some have retained the vestiges of old terraced or formal gardens,[6] more are purely pictur-

esque, others are combinations of both styles. The two most interesting estate gardens created in Natchez during the 1850s are "Brown's Gardens," still surviving and known as "Magnolia Vale," and the lost gardens of the incomparable "Longwood." Though the houses were notable as well, both gardens were much more than mere settings. Both indicate the old high state of Southern horticulture—combined with eccentricity—during the last decade before the Civil War.

"Brown's Gardens"
"Brown's Gardens" sit on a ledge below the high loess bluffs of Natchez. Loess, the calcareous dust heaped up by thousands of years of prairie winds is fertile soil. It is easily eroded by the Mississippi River's changing course, however. Consequently, "Brown's Gardens" are a lot closer to the river now than they once were. The sawmill that made Andrew Brown, and later, his son-in-law, Rufus Learned, their first fortunes, was once located hundreds of yards closer to the river. A new one was rebuilt in 1917 on what was the magnolia avenue and the lower, picturesquely laid-out part of the gardens. (The replacement mill was torn down in 1962. Though the original house, built in 1834, burned in 1946 and was subsequently rebuilt, the wonderfully eccentric geometry of Andrew Brown's parterre remains. "Magnolia Vale" is open to the public.)

Andrew Brown, tall, Scottish, and narrow in Presbyterian black, came to Mississippi in 1820 from Edinburgh, that city still lit by the excitement of the eighteenth-century Enlightenment and its afterglow of interest in the sciences, including botany. Edinburgh has a botanical garden renowned for its beauty and its science; many notable nineteenth-century plant hunters were Scots.[7] Brown was a graduate of the University of Edinburgh, and in later life became a member of the American Society for the Advancement of Science. His 15-acre garden, where a Scots professional gardener propagated all kinds of rare plants and Brown's "museum," a wing of the house devoted to mastodon bones and Indian stones, attest to the strength of his Scottish-born fascination with the natural world.

"Brown's Gardens" had a sort of municipal status, like "Belmont" in Nashville or "Gaineswood" in Demopolis: they were often used for civic events and enjoyed by the citizens of Natchez. There were also many out-of-town visitors, for the gardens were a Mississippi river boat tourist spot from the 1840s onward. Steamers tied up at Brown's Landing and, in those early days of tourism, visitors to the gardens were very well treated: there was no entrance fee, they were allowed to cut bunches of flowers, and in the afternoon ices and cakes were often served.[8] Peacocks stalked

A domed "living teahouse" where children drank lemonade in the afternoon and the dense perfume of banana shrub and tea olive were a few of the attractions at "Magnolia Vale," also known as "Brown's Gardens" in Natchez. Hedges of the red noisette rose 'Agrippina' were much admired. A half-mile avenue of Magnolia grandiflora *with its plate-sized creamy flowers led from the Mississippi River landing to the garden entrance, seen below on an 1872 map. "Brown's Gardens," with its whimsical paisley-like beds and zany topiary and standardized shrubs, is similar to Sarah Ferrell's "The Terraces" in La Grange, Georgia; both were laid out primarily in the 1840s.*

among the many varieties of camellias. The garden entrance was flanked by a pair of mounts topped with oaks, equipped with benches to view the river. An abundance of arbors and bowers, covered with white and yellow Lady Banks roses, provided shade. Andrew Brown's garden, like Hunnewell's "Wellesley" or the Braytons' "Green Animals" is another of those lovable and unsophisticated re-creations of English topiary forms that became important local landmarks. For many visitors, such gardens must have been not just a pleasure to walk through, but the closest thing to Europe they would ever see.

"Longwood," an "Oriental Villa"

As eye-popping as it is, there is nothing unsophisticated about Haller and Julia Nutt's unfinished "Longwood," long known as "Nutt's Folly," the largest and most elaborate octagonal house ever created in the United States.[9] Dr. Haller Nutt was heir to a great planter's fortune and, almost more important, to a tradition of learning, science, invention, and medicine rooted in the great days of the Philadelphia Enlightenment at the turn of the eighteenth century.[10] Rushford Nutt, Haller Nutt's father who settled in Natchez about 1805, hybridized Petit Gulf, or Nutt, cotton, a disease-resistant strain still planted often in the South; he and Haller together adapted the cotton gin to steam power in 1830, and were among

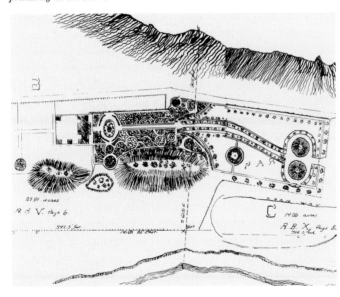

RIGHT:
In 1861, Godey's Lady's Book *illustrated Philadelphia architect Samuel Sloan's sketch for an octagonal "Oriental Villa." By then, the actual octagon for Haller and Julia Nutt, "Longwood," was nearing completion. One of the most ambitious and extravagant houses of the South's Gilded Age, it was left unfinished when the Civil War came to Mississippi.*

Mississippi

227

the first to plow under cover crops of field peas to maintain the fertility of the cotton soil, and to practice contour plowing.[11] By 1860 Haller Nutt owned or controlled plantations comprising 43,000 acres, which annually produced 3,000 to 4,000 bales of cotton so fine it brought at least a dollar a bale more than other cotton on the New Orleans market.[12] His sugar plantations brought him equally large returns.[13] The Nutts traveled, had Kentucky-bred horses, thirty-two house servants, a fine library—Haller was a proficient scholar of Hebrew, Greek, and Latin—sent their children away to good schools,[14] and spent thousands of dollars on clothes and jewels. They were to spend much more on the furnishings for their new house—marble statues from Italy, gold-leaf mirrors, and furniture from New York, New Orleans, and Philadelphia.

Given his passion for order and productivity, it's no wonder the new-fangled charm and elegant but useful geometry of an octagon house appealed to Haller Nutt. The architect of "Longwood" was the well-known Philadelphian Samuel Sloan, whose works were widely popularized by *Godey's Lady's Book*.[15] Nutt and his wife, Julia, who had much to do with the creation of the house,[16] planned the up-to-date features of "Longwood" with Sloan. A central rotunda had carefully placed mirrors that cast sunlight into each room. A furnace system was planned, along with twenty-six fireplaces. Laundry chutes led to the bottom floor; there were closets, a new idea at the time, and even a bathroom with running water for washing, though the toilets were still in the outdoor privy. Romantic "oriental" gingerbread trim was to hang from the double galleries on the exterior. The Nutts lived in the old plantation house on the place during construction, which began in 1859.[17] Seventy skilled workmen from Philadelphia labored to finish the building after the brick foundations had been laid by slaves. By 1861, Haller Nutt estimated that another six to eight months would be required to complete and furnish the octagon. That same year the Northern workmen laid down their tools, which still lie on the floor, and never returned. The upper floors are only a shell. The ground floor was hastily finished as a dwelling by the Nutts' slaves. Generations of the family continued to live there till 1939, but the elaborate gardens only lasted till the 1870s; no visible trace remains. "Longwood," now open to the public, is encircled today by a jungle of live oaks and magnolias hung with Spanish moss. The Pilgrimage Garden Club of Natchez plans to bring back at least part of the gardens.

The scale of the "Longwood" landscape and gardens was impressive, and not at all typical of a Southern plantation. The comparatively small 90-acre estate was laid out entirely as parkland and ornamental garden, looking south over the broad panorama of the Mississippi about two miles outside Natchez. (A couple of miles away was what, on a Northern estate, would be called "the farm": the plantation "Cloverdale," which daily provided by wagon all the meat and poultry, fruit and vegetables, milk and eggs for the Nutt family.) The bulbous Byzantine-Mauresque house

dome looked down from five stories on a picturesque landscape where groves of native magnolia and live oak were mixed with the exotic oriental varnish tree, *Rhus verniciflua*. Mimosas, crepe myrtle, wisteria, dogwood, and redbud provided color. For almost a year, a Philadelphia nurseryman or landscape gardener, Mark Kyle, worked on the park and gardens.[18] The formal flower garden, a terraced series of diaper-patterned beds some 15 acres in extent, was tucked away to the southeast of the house, near the entrance gates.[19] There, until 1863, in the midst of war and destruction, 500 varieties of roses flourished.[20] But much else was left unfinished when the war came: an ornamental mound, a shady children's playground with a fancy playhouse, an artificial lake ringed by a system of paths and bridle paths, and a marble teahouse designed to sit at the water's edge.

Haller Nutt's portrait, now hanging at "Longwood," shows a thin-faced, gentle-looking man whose dark, bright eyes are shadowed by quizzical eyebrows. There is about him none of the empty-headed, pompous look that mars so many masculine portraits of the period. Ingenious, intelligent, energetic, perfectionist—and sentimental and affectionate—his energy and vision must sometimes have made him hard to keep up with on a daily basis. However, it appears that jokes on the subject were possible. Once, when Julia was absent from "Longwood," Haller bought hundreds of rose bushes, her favorites, and made a surprise for her—a 10-acre garden.[21] On her return, she reportedly remarked that she did indeed love roses, but it seemed she was going to have to have the horse and buggy hitched up each morning in order to pick a few flowers for the house.[22] Nutt's life seems sustained by an Enlightenment belief in the perfectibility of man and nature, a belief which must have been somewhat tested by his own frequent illnesses, the loss of three children out of the eleven Julia bore, and the very contradictions of his own life as a strong Union sympathizer and a slaveholder. He was a "southern Yankee," a Unionist, and as the nation headed toward war and both sides became more extreme in their views, there was no middle ground left for Haller Nutt. It is easy to condemn Nutt as an opportunist, a man who was willing to take advantage of a system (slavery) that he was not willing to defend. Yet, as a man who liked solving problems, he must have believed that reason, along with a little care and practical application, could nudge almost any compromise into shape. As the conditions of war and embargo worsened, Nutt fought fiercely to finish his dream house. His struggle seems disproportionate, as though a completed "Longwood" were to be a sign for him that reason could prevail, fortunes be reversed, the war halted, the Union restored. In 1863 the Emancipation Proclamation freed his slaves, and the Union armies destroyed his plantations (an estimated loss on the Louisiana plantations alone of over $1 million in 1864 dollars.)[23] In 1864 Nutt died at "Longwood" of pneumonia—and grief, despair, and rage, according to Julia.

She lived on in the basement till 1897, raising the children and extracting approximately $200,000 in damages from the U.S. government. "Longwood" is unfinished still, and the whole idea of the octagon house now seems like a bizarre joke—truly a "folly." Nonetheless, there is something satisfying about it and its owners. In the get-rich-quick story of the Deep South, with its ignorance and smothering gentility, the Nutts were a beacon of lively intellectual curiosity, erudition, charm, and humanity. For once, one can sympathize with the predicament of slave owners who, as Thomas Jefferson once said, knew "we have the wolf by the ears, and we can neither hold him, nor safely let him go."[24]

LOUISIANA

"Rosedown": "My Gardens Are in Perfect Order"

Some twenty miles south of Natchez where the Mississippi crosses the Louisiana state line, are the Feliciana parishes of Louisiana, settled for the most part by Anglo-Saxon planters who came westward with the cotton gin. In this delta bottom between Natchez and New Orleans were the richest plantations in America in the 1850s. In the high years of cotton prices, three successive good crops could make a millionaire.[1] Whatever the hideous moral dilemma posed by slavery, whatever the ecological damage done by one-crop agriculture, with its built-in expectation of exhausted soil, there is no doubt that the Deep South plantation was one of the most beautiful and functional landscapes in America. The satisfying, symmetrical layout imposed a rhythmic, predictable order on the recently tamed wilderness, and reinforced the hierarchy of buildings: plantation house, plantation office, slave cabin, and cotton gin or sugar mill.

The plantation landscape reached its apogee in such exquisite creations as "Rosedown," home of Daniel and Martha Turnbull, and her cousin, Daniel Barrow's, "Afton Villa." Both gardens, which are in St. Francisville, have been restored to nearly their original state and are open to the public. Daniel Turnbull was one of the "extra heavy men" of Louisiana—that is,[2] he was one of the largest cotton planters in the industry, with approximately 450 slaves by the 1850s. (In the 1850s, only 3,000 cotton planters nationwide owned more than 100 slaves; thirty-eight lived in West Feliciana Parish. Only two of these owned more than 500 slaves.)[3] In 1828, Turnbull, the son of a Scots immigrant trader-turned-planter, had married Martha Barrow, one of a numerous and powerful planter family. The Barrows had followed the familiar trail from Virginia to the Carolinas, to Tennessee, and finally, in 1800, to Louisiana. They were famous for their beautiful houses and gardens and their grand style. Who but the Barrows had a pleasure boat, a seventy-five-foot-long steamer called the *Nimrod*, that could carry twelve horses and six packs of hounds? Sporting equipment aboard included fishing tackle, shotguns and rifles, as well as a bar. The black crew wore

A Carrara marble statue brought back from Europe in the 1830s by Martha Turnbull of "Rosedown" looks pensively down from her plinth among the hydrangeas and the live oaks.

tailcoats.[4] Rich, fashionable Southerners, the Turnbulls spent their summers in Saratoga,[5] visited Philadelphia frequently, and made a number of trips to Europe. For her garden, Martha Turnbull brought back Carrara marble statues of the seasons and the continents, not to mention urns and vases. The garden ideas she brought back were as important as the marbles. Versailles and other famous French gardens — the Jardin du Luxembourg, for example — were at the height of their Third Empire style, their superb formal seventeenth-century designs had been thickened by the growth of trees, and embroidered with brilliant bedding-out schemes that included many newly introduced exotics. Martha came home to try her own hand at it in the American vernacular, creating 28 acres of formal gardens.

The plantation house, a straightforward double-galleried white frame Greek Revival house similar to the hill plantations the Barrow family had left behind on their way to Louisiana, was named after a play the Turnbulls had seen during their European travels. The typical moss-hung live oak plantation entrance avenue — a straight black tunnel of coolness leading to distant white columns — is one of the most magnificent and stately in the South today; the white statues and urns still punctuate its length. Martha flanked the avenue with picturesque lawns dotted with summer houses and clumps of shrubs and trees (now thickly grown, so that a sort of bosquet effect has been created). She also had a "moss house," which was freshly covered every year — an up-to-date Victorian variation on the English landscape park hermitage theme.

South of the house is the flower garden, roughly square, and divided into beds. Martha Turnbull grew all the old-fashioned flowers, such as mignonette, sweet william, violet, verbena, snapdragon, and annual pinks and phlox in her flower garden. From her journal we know she also grew the most extravagant exotics to put out in blooming sequence, such as *Eupatorium elegans*, a pale-pink-flowered Mexican introduction that grows eight feet tall. In beds, and as shrubs and hedges, she grew all the great roses of her day, including many white moss roses, and Tuscany, a black-purple rose with heavy gold stamens, known as the 'Old Velvet Rose'. Sometimes the roses bloomed on till December. Martha Turnbull made great use of hotbeds, cold frames, glass forcing bells, and a conservatory. By the 1850s, the production of delicacies for the planter's table, of bedding-out plants for the flower garden, and of ornamentals for the house had reached great heights.[6] Greenhouse construction had become specialized. At nearby "Oakley,"[7] James Bowman, who had married Sarah Turnbull, in 1860 built a winter-forcing greenhouse, the duplicate of one found in a book in the Turnbull library at "Rosedown."[8] In Martha Turnbull's garden diary there are pages devoted to greenhouse management.[9] At "Rosedown," the original hotbed was later joined by a large, handsome conservatory where thousands of cuttings were raised to keep the flower garden bright almost every day of the year. Of course, because the Turnbulls "sojourned," meaning went away for the summer, the hot months were not as important, but everything had to look wonderful on their return in September.

Martha Turnbull's garden journal, which spans sixty years beginning in 1835, when "Rosedown" was built, is even more remarkable than the garden itself. It vividly presents all the details of plantation domesticity and horticulture: for example, on November 11, 1852, she writes, "Quite warm and now raining. Put down vines around ladies' privy." Her entries, the notes of an accomplished and knowledgeable gardener, establish the rhythm of a Southern garden, where annual seedlings can be planted out in November, and dahlias, put in the beds in January, are blooming in May. In September she regularly sowed pinks and sweet william to set out in her flowerbeds in November. She recorded her very early introduction of azaleas — 1836 — and her extensive camellia cultivation: the Turnbulls were among the first to bring camellias to Louisiana, in the 1830s. In April, 1857, she counted 196 new *Camellia japonica* seedlings. There are recipes for fertilizer and engrafting mixtures, lists of what flowered in winter, and of what never "did" for her at all. She tried everything, and what didn't work the first time, she tried again before giving up. There are still other lists of what was propagated from cuttings or layers, or grown from seed. In pre–Civil War days, the quantities were staggering and by today's standards seem on an almost commercial scale. Annual entries in the fifties often record fifty successful cuttings of tea olive, *Osmanthus fragrans*, for example. Even in 1864, at the height of the war, she noted she had 1,617 pots for the greenhouse. Before the war, large orders had been placed with nurseries on Long Island[10] and in Philadelphia,[11] as well as New Orleans. In the catalogues she jotted down her orders, and what her gardeners so successfully propagated from what she bought. "My gardens are in perfect order," she wrote again and again at the end of entries in her journal during her first twenty-five gardening years.

In 1852 the family's portraits were painted by Thomas Sully. By then, Martha Turnbull, forty-two years old, had borne her three children and lost her youngest son to fever in 1843. Her husband and surviving two grown children look out of their frames into a romantic middle distance, but not Martha, who glances at us directly — confidently but coolly, with a little half-smile — from under her lifted eyebrows. Everything else is in its proper place: flat wings of shiny black hair emphasize her pale, clear complexion and her oval face; a tiny round white collar and a gauzy black bertha do not *really* hide a swanlike neck. She looks like a compact little person, made smaller by her black dress, which outlines a fashionably sloping shoulder against a sober fawn background. By 1852, the year of the portrait, her garden was essentially complete, except for the new greenhouse, finished in 1856, and a rockery added in 1858. For the next forty years she would need all the confidence and coolness she could muster to keep it going, and to deal with the tragedies of her life.

In 1856 William, her remaining son, drowned in a Mississippi River accident; in 1861 Daniel Turnbull died; in 1862 the war began in earnest, and in 1863 "Rosedown" was overrun and sacked by the Union Army. What she had left was her daughter, Sarah Bowman, now married and living nearby.[12] Martha still had her garden, though, as she wrote in her diary in January, 1864, "Up to this time, since the Federals landed in May, neither field or garden has been worked. The garden is a wilderness, sedgegrass. It looks melancholly [sic]." However, Martha Turnbull had not lost her courage or her taste for gardening, so her entry continues, "I have commenced work, but slowly."[13]

What the years show from 1864 onward to her death in 1896 is her dogged determination to keep going. She grew cotton under the sharecropping system, and handled the contracts, taxes, and war repatation requests. (Nothing was ever paid to her, though she eventually received a pension of $8.00 per month as a widow of a veteran of the War of 1812.) She rented land out in exchange for work around the place. She bargained with her former slaves to save her garden, and paid them in coffee, sugar, and molasses for the chores they performed. Some of her entries are filled with complaint and despair. On January 4, 1869, she writes: ". . . Hay all over the truck patch & no manure yet hawled . . . no hands yet in garden but John Prenter and he is worse than nothing." But what is so likeable about Martha Turnbull, despite her bitterness, what makes her leap off the pages of her journal, is her spontaneous delight in whatever she had left. Deep into Reconstruction days, and sixty-six years old, on May 15, 1876, she writes, "Everything now is spring like. Box looking green." She died in September, 1896, leaving her invaluable journal and enough of her gardens behind to bring them back to life.

"Afton Villa Gardens"

About five miles north of St. Francisville are the remains of "Afton Villa"[14] — the four-foot-high brick foundation walls of what, until 1963 when it burned, was a forty-room Gothic Revival house with two tall towers. Though "Afton Villa" would have been quite unremarkable along the Hudson in 1849, it was a rarity in the antebellum South, where "plantation" often meant "Greek Revival." The home of David Barrow, Martha Turnbull's first cousin, "Afton Villa" was built over an existing small house on the site. He was the third generation of his family to own the property, and in the 1840s his ballooning cotton prosperity on this 3,000-acre plantation was what allowed him to build such a high-style dwelling in 1849. According to the 1860 Louisiana State Census, he was the richest planter in West Feliciana Parish. He died in 1874. After the war and various vicissitudes including a stint as a young ladies' academy, the place was bought in 1915 by a couple from Illinois, the Dr. Robert Lewises — surely among the earliest plantation buffs in the Deep South. They restored the gardens and added a few new touches such as a ruff of azaleas around the artificial lake. Lewis also propagated a red *Rhododendron indicum* unique to the property, calling it 'Pride of Afton' or

'Afton Villa Red', and planting it by the hundreds. Today a simple inventory of the gardens' features would allow one to imagine "Afton Villa" to be a typical Deep South plantation: an oak avenue or "alley" four-trees wide underplanted with azaleas; seven massive terraces that fall away from the house down to what once were pineapple beds and hothouses, a boxwood maze, and a box-bordered parterre. But what makes this garden so different is the influence of the picturesque aesthetic on the symmetrical and rectilenear plantation plan—*and* the reluctance of its makers to dispense with the traditional garden features. The mile-and-a-half avenue is serpentine, not straight—but it still exists. The seven terraces with their elaborate system of underground brick drains are curved, not rectangular, but they are still certainly terraces. Once they were ornately planted with flowers, now they are in grass. Serpentine avenues and curving terraces were a more common feature in grand Deep Southern gardens than might be supposed: four other such avenues remain in West Feliciana today, and one set of terraces has survived. The Feliciana planters' vast wealth, their travels, their education and sophistication, gave them more than a book acquaintance with garden fashions like the picturesque, and an opportunity to incorporate them into their new country seats. The "Tara" image—white-box-with-columns-and-straight-driveway—has tended to obscure such variant forms. In Louisiana alone before the Civil War there were at least 100 gardens comparable to "Afton Villa"; five survive today. That anything survives of "Afton Villa" is fortuitous; even though the house is gone, the remaining landscape greatly extends our understanding of how garden style was changing the look of the plantation in the last decades before the Civil War. Today the three acres of terraces, the "ruin garden" built among the foundations of the burned house, and the 65-acre park of "Afton Villa Gardens" are open to the public.

FRENCH PLANTATION LOUISIANA

Moving south down the river toward New Orleans we move from English to French, from cotton to sugar, and into the distinct orbit of New Orleans. New Orleans culture, intricate and sophisticated, always remained distinctly French. English would not be heard frequently in the region until after the Civil War, even though a number of the very richest men in the region were American from the 1830s onward, including Natchez planters such as Haller Nutt and slave traders such as Isaac Franklin. Between 1803 and 1860 there was a quantum leap in wealth, thanks to the widespread use of the cotton gin, the successful granulation of sugar (1793), and the increase in world consumption of both. In 1833 Louisiana produced only one-fifteenth of the world's exported supply of sugar; by the 1850s that percentage had risen to more than one-quarter. By the 1850s cotton represented more than one-half the United States' total exports,[15] and the bulk of it left the country via New Orleans.

The invention of the steamboat (1811) was what gave the planters access to their market. Both the new American planters, and the Creoles who had been there for 150 years, enjoyed this prosperity. Small wonder that there was plenty of money for gardens.

In Southern Louisiana the grand plantation landscape with its raised-

Traveling artist Adrian Persac painted the bayou side of "Albania" in 1861. Behind the white fence is the garden.

During the 1920s at beautiful "Shadows on the Teche" in New Iberia, Louisiana, Weeks Hall, grand romantic and great gardener, planted the dark shade of his live oaks with English ivy, sown with thousands of pink Zephyranthes graudiflora.

cottage house, *garçonnières* (separate bachelor's quarters), and elaborate *pigeonniers* (in France, pigeonhouses, by law, could only be erected by the nobility), owed little to the Old South over the mountains; instead, as Roger Kennedy points out, it comes direct from the West Indies. The climate is mild: the mean temperature in Southern Louisiana is 68 degrees, with summer averages in the low 80s (though often it seems much hotter because of the humidity) and winter averages seldom below 52 degrees. Besides the famous and productive plantations on the banks of the Mississippi itself, there were additional hundreds on the smaller rivers of the delta, such as Bayou Teche to the west of the city. A series of superb watercolors rendered in 1861 by the French architect, civil engineer, and artist Adrian Persac[16] show the gardens on the eve of the Civil War.

Architecturally, "Albania" was a typical Bayou Teche plantation. Charles Grevemberg, a French emigrant and the original plantation owner, completed construction in 1842. He and his wife were both killed in the storm that leveled the grand resort hotel on Last Island in the Gulf of Mexico in August, 1856, but their son was raised at "Albania" by his grandmother. Persac's 1861 painting shows the bayou side of the house with its columned portico. The tops of bushes that may indicate a parterre pattern are visible over a white picket fence that defines the garden. The highly decorative pair of *garçonnières* are part of the scheme. Included in the painting is a *pigeonnier* outside the fence, and slave quarters. Many of Persac's paintings display similar fences, gardens, and paired outbuildings.

The best-known house in the region, beautiful salmon-pink brick "Shadows on the Teche," in New Iberia, built by David Weeks in 1834, was

painted twice by Persac. The view of the north side shows the bayou, only 100 feet away from the house, and the profusion of trees and shrubs gives some idea of the picturesque plantings on this side. The road view sports another handsome white fence which enclosed grounds of nearly 3 acres, but Persac does not give any hints of Mrs. Weeks's famous garden, with its cuttings from as far away as Philadelphia and Charleston.

Beginning in 1922, great-great-grandson William Weeks Hall restored the house and made purely ornamental gardens, front and back, that were typical of his own time. A bamboo hedge gave privacy from the street; symmetrical boxwood hedges and stands of bamboo created enclosure gardens. A formal rectangular flower garden was hedged in bamboo, ornamented with marble statues of the four seasons, and planted with an eye to the salmon brick of the house in subtle colors such as silver, gray, bronze, pale pink, lemon, white, and a salmon salvia that almost matched the house brick. A lily pool filled the hole where the greenhouse once stood. Hall added azaleas, which had never existed on the property, and rare specimens of hard-to-find old camellia varieties to those originally planted by Mrs. David Weeks. Hall's garden was visited by filmmakers and writers such as Cecil B. DeMille, Walt Disney, D. W. Griffith, H. L. Mencken, and Henry Miller, and doubtless helped form their idea of the antebellum South. Most of this important twentieth-century garden has been destroyed;[17] restoration efforts were begun in 1991.

Valcour Aime and "Le Petit Versailles"

On the west bank of the Mississippi just above the town of Vacherie, a small jungle of trees and vines represents all that once was known as "Le Petit Versailles," perhaps the most fantastic plantation garden in the entire South, the creation of the legendary Valcour Aime. In 1847, young Eliza Ripley came south to visit her Creole relations in New Orleans, paid a brief visit to the plantation by steamboat, and described Valcour Aime, then fifty-one, as ". . . tall and graceful . . . my ideal of a French Marquis."[18] Aime owned over 9,000 acres and was in the vanguard of the sugar industry. At one time, his sugar refinery was the largest in the business.[19] He and his wife, the daughter of another powerful Creole family, the Romans, had four daughters and a son, Gabriel. Reputedly the richest man in the South, Aime enjoyed every luxury, including his own steamboat, which was named the *Gabriel Aime*, after his son.[20] Like so many later millionaires of the 1890s, he also had his own railroad car—though it was only a flatcar that ran back and forth on a spur from the boat landing on the Mississippi to the house. By 1838 the house itself, built by his father in 1799, seemed inconsequential, given his immense wealth. Columns were thickened, marble floors, marble mantels, and marble stairs were added, and the two ends of the house extended to form a galleried U-shaped patio.

But the gardens, not the house, were what earned the nickname "Le Petit Versailles." Beginning in 1842, the marshy ground between the house and the river was drained and filled, and a *jardin anglais* put in. Like the gardens at "Afton Villa," Aime's garden was influenced by the picturesque. Doubtless Aime was not inspired by Downing but by an earlier and less earnest version of the landscape garden, the gaily busy *jardin anglais* in France of the preceding generation. Bagatelle, Ermenonville, the Désert de Retz, the Parc Monceau, and the Hubert Robert garden at the Petit Trianon would have been among the best known at this time. All were recorded by Georges Le Rouge in 1787, in *Détails de nouveaux jardins à la mode*. Aime's gardener, Joseph Muller, is said to have trained at the Jardin des Plantes in Paris; if so, he might easily have seen these gardens. Even in their post-Revolutionary state, they would have been impressive. Aime's winding layout covered 12 acres (about half the size of Martha Turnbull's garden at "Rosedown") and included many typical late-eighteenth-century follies. There was an icehouse whose ten-foot-tall mound was topped by a Chinese pagoda trimmed with silver bells, a miniature fort (La Roche de Ste. Hélène, in memory of Napoleon) with a real cannon that boomed a salute for distinguished guests, cascade fountains, and a fenced section known as the Petite Forêt, where a log cabin housed rabbits, deer, and kangaroos. Black-and-white swans swam and peacocks strutted. There were groves of palms and camphor trees, supposedly the first imported from Korea, specimen ginkgos, also recently introduced, and many orange trees standing in tubs. (The oranges were used in battles between all the family children.) Full-grown live oaks were transplanted to create an impression of age.[21] The central element of the garden was an artificial lake and a little wiggly river, both fed by a pump from the Mississippi. The rivulet was crossed and recrossed by little high-arched bridges. A carriage drive divided at the entrance to encircle the main part of the garden, and provided a view of its hectic delights.

The English traveler Alexander Garden visited the Aimes in 1847. Though the garden was still young, he was able to say that "its extent, the vast and varied collection of plants, trees and shrubs, its hothouses and ornamental buildings [are] unsurpassed, if equalled by any in the union." In those hothouses and in various kitchen garden plots, Aime carried the planter's dream of self-sufficiency to magnificent excess. There is an often-told story about a $10,000 bet between Aime and a visiting French epicure: could he provide a dinner up to Parisian standards? Indeed he could, and what's more, everything was grown on the place. (Aime, so the story goes, did not accept the $10,000 he won.) Up to thirty gardeners tended many kinds of tropical fruits, including mangoes, besides the pineapples that every self-respecting grand Louisiana planter grew. Coffee was grown, a vineyard provided wine, and the local Perique tobacco cigars. Terrapin were kept in a holding pond, and of course fish and game were readily available.

In fact, perhaps all this is not so extraordinary—one has read quite similar accounts before. Even the amazing garden looks a bit pale and provincial in the cold light of garden history. What animates it is the operatic story of Valcour Aime, the man who had everything—and lost it all. In 1854 his son died of yellow fever; two days later Valcour Aime wrote his last diary entry, "Let him who wishes continue. My time is finished. He died on September 18. I kissed him at five o'clock, also on the following day." Valcour Aime became a recluse and spent many hours praying. The garden was tended, but he ceased to make improvements, nor did he carry on with his sugar experiments. Within a few years his wife died, followed by two of his daughters. Mourning, Aime lived on comparatively undisturbed through the Civil War, and died of pneumonia on New Year's Day in 1867. The garden grew up, the gates fell down, other gardeners came and took the big camellias. In 1920 the house, never inhabited by anyone but the Aimes, burned to the ground.

New Orleans and "Longue Vue"

By 1860, New Orleans was the only real city south of the Mason-Dixon Line, since Charleston, economically speaking at least, had become a backwater. After New York City, New Orleans was the biggest seaport in the nation. For the plantation aristocracy who had their town houses in New Orleans, or who came to town for culture and cotton trading, it was the center of fashion and culture, where every kind of entertainment and sport went on: horse- and steamboat-racing, opera and theater, cock and dog fighting, dueling and gambling, dancing and intriguing and making love. It was also a city of fire, flood, and yellow fever, voodoo, openly acknowledged mistresses, a hierarchy of color—quadroon, octoroon— and all the other exotica that, from the 1870s onward, so attracted Northern writers such as Charles Dudley Warner.

By 1850, New Orleans's famous cultural mixture, an Indian/French/ black/Acadian/Spanish/American melting pot, had produced two distinctly different types of city gardens. Both sorts were attached to grand town houses of planters, merchants, slave traders, or cotton brokers who generally also had country properties. In the *Vieux Carré,* the old French Quarter, the interior courtyards of L-shaped houses were laid out in formal mixed gardens of flowers and many fruit trees, in a style that dated back to the early days of the city. The utilitarian rectangular beds were softened by the tropical luxuriance of Louisiana growth. Beginning in the 1820s, the gardens of the Garden District, south and east of the French Quarter, were created by Americans who brought with them their own particular classical style, the colossal Greek Revival. Many of the most imposing houses and gardens date from the South's Gilded Age, the 1850s. The courtyard garden had been private, an extension of the house

and a room to live in, but a typical garden in the Garden District was a surround, a suitably beautiful backdrop for a twenty-to-thirty-room house set back from the front property line. Where elaborate suburban gardens of the same period up north would have invariably been laid out with star or crescent beds and winding paths, these Garden District designs often did not abandon a certain French formal simplicity until as late as the 1880s. Many gardens, especially in the Lower Garden District, kept the old rectangular or diamond-shaped beds in regular geometric patterns, divided by paths. If size allowed, there might be a bower, an arbor, or a gazebo.[22] The specimen trees and cast iron fences of the Garden District are particularly fine.

Just within the city limits to the west is "Longue Vue," the only place in or near New Orleans that is unequivocally a twentieth-century estate. The property, which is now open to the public, is grandly Beaux-Arts in scale and feeling though it comprises only 8 acres. The central garden vista is on the long axis of the Neo-Palladian house; there are walled and hedged room enclosures closely related to the building, garden sculptures, water features, intricately planned borders (now considerably simplified), and an artful balance between formal and wild areas. Pines, magnolias, and crepe myrtles screen out any view of nearby houses. Although the plantings are deeply regional in the most informed way,[23] the design has little to do either with plantations or New Orleans city gardens. Despite the Southern oak avenue, the boxwood parterre, the tall south portico, the *pigeonnier* that is a copy of one at the lost Louisiana plantation "Uncle Sam," and the Mississippi sandstone that lines the basin in the wild garden, all one would have to do is change the flora, and "Longue Vue" could be one of those lavish but understated, tastefully eclectic gardens made in the Northeast in the 1920s. And no wonder, since its original designer was Ellen Biddle Shipman.

Shipman was sixty-six when she began the "Longue Vue" project, which turned out to be one of her largest. In Edith and Edgar Stern she found the same kind of lively and sympathetic clients and friends she had in DeWitt and Ralph Hanes in Winston-Salem—and the same large budget, since Edith Rosenwald Stern was the Sears, Roebuck heiress. Intelligent and curious, the Sterns, especially Edith, were perfectionists, determined to get the details right.[24] Civic-minded, philanthropic, and serious, they also enjoyed life and took themselves lightly—for instance, they referred to their splendid oak avenue, with its elegant forecourt, as the "estately entrance." The Sterns had a wonderful time with Ellen Shipman; they called her "Lady Ellen," and she took them in hand, just as she had the Haneses, to teach them the grand and pleasant sequences of life in a country-house garden that, by 1935, was a life that almost *had* to be taught, so quickly was it becoming obsolete. For the Sterns, Shipman's tutelage extended further than the garden. Since she had often designed her own garden architecture, at "Longue Vue" Shipman gave designing

Huge camellias were hauled into place to make a long vista, the spine of the Edgar Sterns' "Longue Vue" in New Orleans, designed by Ellen Shipman beginning in 1935.

"A portion of our party was quartered in the former residence of the rebel General Albert Pike," wrote a Union soldier in Little Rock, Arkansas, in 1864. "The house was of brick . . . with wide piazzas supported by huge columns of Mongrel Doric . . . heavily wreathed with ivy." Three acres of gardens were laid out picturesquely, though Pike did not dispense with the conventional straight entrance walk. From 1874 to 1889 the residence was the Arkansas Female College, seen here. (See Brown & Douglas, A Garden Heritage)

the house a try, until, it is said, the fireplace kept coming up in the middle of the drawing room in her plans.[25] At that point, William and Geoffrey Platt, sons of her old friend and mentor, Charles Platt, and architects by profession, were called in. It was a happy collaboration.

Coming, as it does, so far along in Shipman's long life of design, it is not surprising that "Longue Vue" is a sort of estate garden summation within its mere 8 acres. Besides the ornamental gardens there is also a large, efficient cutting garden/coldframe/bath house/greenhouse complex. The beautiful kitchen garden was a loving tribute to the idea of growing every single vegetable one might need. In the fan-shaped beds of its walled octagon were all the usuals—broccoli, cabbage, carrots, lettuce, leeks, onions—planted in double rows. For fruit there were espaliered plum and pear trees, strawberries, rhubarb, raspberries, and even grapefruit. The beds were edged with parsley, rue, basil, sage, thyme, lavender, and chives, and the corners were marked by tufts of lemon verbena and clumps of geraniums.

Even for the very rich, like the Sterns, the American entry into World War II effectively marked the end of easily available labor. (In the early days at "Longue Vue" there were up to sixteen gardeners for the 8-acre estate.) In 1940 the kitchen garden was merged with the cutting garden, and renamed the Walled Garden. It was planted with a three-season floral display that was somewhat less work than the vegetables: early spring tulips were taken up every year and replaced with delphiniums for late spring, which were in turn also replaced every year with chrysanthemums for fall. Today it is a permanent rose garden planted in orange, red, and yellow. The plantings of the Portico Garden, the boxwood parterre near the house, were also simplified. Hundreds of daffodils, narcissus, hyacinths, tulips, and poppies, all in groups of 25 to 100, gave way to floribunda and standard roses, with an elegant row of large pleached gardenias along the portico. Despite the changes, it is still a small, sweet-smelling, sunny, quiet flower garden, whose low broad steps invite the visitor to proceed out into the long garden view.

The south lawn was at its best seen from the upstairs drawing room. Until the mid-sixties, it included only a circular temple and reflecting pool reached via a wide grass allée bordered by camellia "trees"—large specimen camellias transplanted with great labor and expense—and many replacements—from the plantation country around Lafayette. These had been conveniently pruned to "tree" shape by several generations of cows nibbling as high as they could reach.[26] To judge from photographs made at the time, the south lawn in its quiet entirety looked like a silvery Woollett engraving of a mid-eighteenth-century landscape. In the sixties, Edith Stern, by now widowed, made a trip to Spain with William Platt. Inspired by the Generalife Gardens at the Alhambra, in Granada, they transformed the south lawn into a Spanish water garden, adding high fountain jets, pots of flowers, and a painted tile surround to

Louisiana

the reflecting pool. Fountains and clipped boxwood parterres took the place of the camellias, azaleas, and roses along the sides. Shrubs of beautifully contrasting textures and colors filled the planters next to the brick walls. The temple became a semicircular loggia. To the left of the loggia was another water garden, a Portuguese canal. Effectively, the formality of the Portico Garden was carried the full length of the lawn. The pattern and color of the Spanish court at the far end of the garden has been substituted for the former horticultural richness of the Portico Garden near the house. The sustained high key is perfect for a public garden, which is what "Longue Vue" has become. Were it still a private garden, however, one would have to say the balance had been slightly upset by William Platt's alterations. Shipman's design had shaded gradually from formality to informality as the distance from the house increased—a happy transition she had perhaps learned to make long ago from Charles Platt, who did the same thing so well. His son's changes made an unrelievedly rich palace garden procession out of what had been an American country house circuit walk of contrasting enclosures and vistas.[27]

TEXAS

A very young Texan gardener, C. J. Sweeney of Galveston, stands on the lawn of "Ashton Villa" next to an enormous century plant in 1915.

Texas is a place apart from the rest of the Deep South. While the state is as deeply Southern as pecan pie, cotton was never the staple crop, labor was never entirely slave labor, and its opulence and prosperity in the last decade before the war was no match for that of Natchez, St. Francisville, or New Orleans. Then too, Texas is Western as well as Southern: its long Spanish and Mexican history, its sense of its own separate destiny (Texas was an independent republic for a heady ten years, 1836–1846), the cattle ranching that is such a feature of the western half of the state, and the very geography of its vast plains and deserts make it Texas, and no place

else. The late-nineteenth-century role of finance and industry in creating millionaires in the Northeast and Midwest was in Texas played most noticeably by the explosion of oil at Spindletop in 1901, but also by a booming lumber industry, and rice and cane plantations in the southeastern part of the state. Texas's estate garden period roughly coincides with that of the rest of the United States.

Southern gentility, the sense that everyone was determined to be ladies and gentlemen, could be awfully thick in Texas during estate garden days, but mercifully it often broke down, leaving big holes for all the hyperbole, all the genuine warmth and hospitality, and the ornery eccentricity Texans are famous for to pop through. Just as they prize the notion that they are a match for any other cultured or refined society, Texans treasure their own eccentrics, their own richly high-handed way of doing things. This was true for their estate gardens as for everything else: Lutcher Brown, in San Antonio, imported every single thing, right down to the actual dirt, to make a Southern garden, Miss Ima Hogg of Houston, on record in a taped interview, fought gaily with her architect, John Staub, about who had done what in the garden at "Bayou Bend," forty-eight years earlier. (Who but Miss Ima could make a statement to a professional architect like Staub, "All the Greek architecture, you know, was pale pink. Did you know that?" Staub, exhibiting what must have been his unvarying firm courtesy with his talented and obstreperous client and friend, simply answered, "No, I didn't.")[1]

As for climate, it is as varied as the people and as often remarked on. Texas "northers," when the temperature can drop 50 degrees in ten hours or so, can strike anywhere in the state. The one other safe generalization to make is that it's very hot in summer and, in the days before air conditioning, gardens were soft green oases of comfort and delight. Water was often used in gardens for its refreshing sound and cool appearance. In most regions, watering throughout the summer had to be frequent and heavy. Rainfall ranges from only 9 inches a year in the semidesert of El Paso on the Mexican border to 55 inches on the eastern edge of the state.

GARDENS OF THE COASTAL PRAIRIE: BEAUMONT, GALVESTON, AND HOUSTON

Rainfall alone would make the coastal prairie the easiest place to make gardens in Texas—add easier transportation than in the rest of the state, a lot of money from lumber, rice, railroads, banking, and above all oil, plus a tradition in neighboring Louisiana of ornamental gardens as a mark of the elite—and it's no wonder that many of the best gardens in the state were there, with San Antonio the only notable exception. In the Gulf region, it's interesting to trace the progression from Victorian gardens in the 90s to Beaux-Arts-style axial gardens in the 30s. In these later gardens, whether they were antebellum plantation style, or Spanish mission, the point was a romantic shaping of regional history, a return to some previous historical era in the Southwest. What is most remarkable about Texan estate gardens, given the amounts of money available, is how few there were that approached Eastern, or even Midwestern, standards of grandeur.

In Beaumont, a picture of what an early estate garden in Texas was, and how it developed, can be seen at the McFaddin-Ward house, built in 1906 on what was then the prairie. Today, the house and gardens are open to the public. Third-generation Texan W.P.H. (Perry) McFaddin was "the wealthiest man in Southeast Texas" at the time he bought his new house outside town in 1907, according to the *Beaumont Enterprise*. In 1907 that meant a lot, since Spindletop had famously "come in" in 1901, and Southeast Texas was full of people like J. S. Cullinan, founder of the Texas Company and James Stephen Hogg, ex-governor of Texas and the first man smart enough to buy oil instead of wells. But then Spindletop was located on McFaddin land, property on the southern outskirts of the town. Architect Henry Conrad Mauer, who came from La Grange, Texas, an old cotton plantation town west of Houston on the Colorado River, had trained at the Pratt Institute in New York. The large white squarish three-story frame house has an irregularly gabled roofline and is encircled by a deep porch supported by Ionic columns. The bold double portico is topped with a deep swagged cornice with a railing above. The style has been termed Beaux-Arts Colonial, and it *is* reminiscent both of the American turn-of-the-century classical style, and the Colonial Revival. However, more than anything else the McFaddin-Ward house recalls the white columns of all the plantations that marched with cotton across the South, symbols of stability and gentility. In the feverish early oil days, Mauer built fifteen of these houses in Beaumont, but this is the

only large one still standing. The extant original interiors are ornate: the entry hall is paneled with marquetry and floored with Persian rugs; the deeply carved newel posts of the central staircase act as *torchères*—they are topped with gilded electrified candelabra hung with heavy crystal drops.

The garden was far less elaborate than the house—it was merely a suitable setting. The immediate house surround was about 300 feet square, and had a paved path running around the building, a lawn, spindling plantations of trees, and a large carriagehouse and stable, topped with a tiny widow's walk standing to the rear of the house. Soon the trees would grow, especially the pair of live oaks called "Rachel" and "William," planted to the west to screen the hot afternoon sun. Privet and camellias would shield the corner lot from the street. There would be azaleas, magnolias, and date palms, and, with a formal rose garden just behind the house, the roster of Deep South signature plants would be complete. The rectangular beds of the rose garden held over two hundred China and tea rose bushes; old shrub roses were scattered throughout the grounds, and the only time roses were not in bloom somewhere on the places was from mid-December to March.[2]

GALVESTON

There were no fabulously rich pioneer oilmen in Galveston in 1907 to experiment with estate gardens: Galveston's glory days were over. In the 1880s and 90s, Galveston had been the premier port of Texas—the only deep-water port—and, with San Antonio, the richest and most cosmopolitan city in the state. The metropolis became a backwater thanks to the tightly monopolistic Galveston Wharf Company, which controlled the waterfront; the discovery of oil in Beaumont; and the effects of the 1900 hurricane. Shut out of Galveston by exorbitant port fees, the state's big businessmen began to look elsewhere for a deep-water port as early as the 1870s. By 1917, both Houston and Beaumont were dredged deep-water ports, due to the power of oil money. By that time, Galveston had just finished the grade raising that had absorbed most of the city's energy since the hurricane, when the full force of the blow had struck the city. Winds reached 110 miles an hour, and at the height of the storm, a four-foot wave washed over the island. Six thousand people were killed. Their bodies were placed on a barge and buried at sea; the next day's tide brought most of them back to shore, so they were gathered up again and burned in immense funeral pyres on the beaches.[3] Galveston, on a long skinny island only eight feet above sea level, was determined to prevent such disaster again, so the city built a massive seawall, and undertook to raise the level of the entire site. Thousands of acres were raised by at least eight feet. Galveston's houses had always been built on raised basements or stilts for fear of flooding—even these spaces were filled in. Seventy years of gardening and tree growth were either removed or smothered in salty clay and sand. No tree, no garden in Galveston antedates 1903. What remained were the houses, and the lots they were built on, small by comparison with the turreted and crocketed edifices themselves. Broadway, a downtown main street, was where the leading citizens lived, and "Ashton Villa," the J. M. Brown residence built in 1859, was a typical house and garden. A three-story bracketed Italianate villa, brick with white stony eyebrows and door sills, was encircled with fruit trees, palms, oaks, and palmettos, and protected by a decorative iron fence. Nothing remains of the garden, which was well known before the grade raising. Local legend has it that Brown cared enough about his garden to import several hundred English sparrows to eat the bugs in his yard, an ecological disaster whose consequences were not then foreseen.[4]

Also on Broadway was "Open Gates," the Sealy home, where the remains of the garden and gardening efforts were more substantial. John Sealy had been one of the founders of the Galveston Wharf Company in 1854, and by 1889, Galveston's zenith, the family was rich enough, and sophisticated enough, to look to New York for an architect. They chose McKim, Mead and White to design a house which local architect Nicholas Clayton built; Stanford White made the ballroom with furnishings from his own decorative supplies. After some years, the French Renaissance brick château, with stacked chimneys, balconied turrets at every corner, and a red tile roof, had to peer out over Mrs. George Sealy, Sr.'s collection of oleanders, the Sealy family's considerable contribution to the beauty of Galveston, which is known as the "Oleander City."

Mrs. Sealy was the kind of serious gardener who returned from every trip abroad with cuttings stashed in her pockets. When she got interested in oleanders, she got even more serious and financed a project of her son, George, Jr., who was as interested in civic beautification as she was, to hybridize oleanders. George and horticulturist Edward Barr came up with thirty-four new colors and forms, making a total of sixty known varieties, which were planted along the sidewalks and boulevards, and in the gardens of Galveston, forming a riot of color from early spring right through November. They were named for the friends who took them in and raised them in their gardens. The Sealy garden was the official "garden party garden" of Galveston just as "Brown's Gardens" were in Natchez. Important visitors to town went to the Sealys and enjoyed the fish pond, which was filled with lotus, the many kinds of palms rustling in the breeze, and the perfume of jasmine and tea olive on the air. Mrs. Sealy was also famous for indoor plants: giant maidenhair, staghorn, Boston, hare's-foot, and Davallia ferns; many kinds of orchids, and exotic ivies. Between parties, they rested up in a special greenhouse, where they were cared for by a special gardener, Mr. Millage. "Open Gates" and all its oleanders, which have now reached the second story, was given to the University of Texas Medical College of Galveston as a memorial to George Sealy and his mother, Magnolia.[5]

HOUSTON

"Inglenook"

In Houston, the most elaborate early estate garden was at "Inglenook," the John Henry Kirby home, which was written up in a twelve-page article in the *Southern Industrial and Lumber Review* of December, 1906, covering Miss Bessie May Kirby's marriage to Mr. James Schuyler Stewart of New York. An idea of Kirby's wealth and prominence can be gathered from the 1940 WPA Guide which still acknowledged the East Texas lumber baron as one of the three "Houston business leaders [who] have gained national repute"—despite the fact that Kirby had gone virtually broke in the Depression.

Like George Eastman's house and garden in Rochester, the Kirby home and its garden covered an entire city block, about 3 acres. The ornamental garden and pleasure buildings covered most of the land. Servants and horses were housed on the adjacent block. A low granite wall topped with an iron fence ran around the house property and was punctuated by two wrought iron gates. Sago palms and yuccas were planted next to the gateposts, but it's clear that all sides of the house and much of the garden were visible from the street—privacy was not a high priority for the Kirbys, or for any important family of the period. Visible exclusivity was the goal.

The house, in its first guise, was built in 1893 by J. Sterling Price, and purchased by the Kirbys in 1896. A large Victorian frame building, it had a three-story tower topped with a bulbous dome, while the rest of the entrance facade was broken out with bays and porches, and the roofline was exuberantly crowded with dormers and gables of all different shapes. The Kirbys' makeover of Price's rather strict and spiky Victorian garden began in 1901, when the house was remodeled and enlarged, and a loggia was tacked on the garden side. From the loggia a curving white wood pergola covered with roses sprang out to connect the house with the new ballroom building. Serpentine paths wove among endless palms, bananas, and live oaks. Newspaper photos show an attached conservatory, a separate and ornamental greenhouse, an Italianate garden, a lily pond, a circular seat wreathed with allamanda vine, and a rustic bridge over what was called Mirror Lake, which was ringed with weeping willows. All told, "Inglenook" contained the entire arsenal of a pleasure garden of the Gilded Age. Most newfangled of all was the natatorium, or "Roman bath," an indoor pool with gothic-paned windows, which occupied the ground floor beneath the ballroom. The *Lumber Review* described it ecstatically as "A Wilderness of Exotic Beauty and Elaborate Electrical Design." Like any casino or playhouse on the East Coast, the natatorium building was in the latest architectural style: in Texas, in 1906—Beaux-Arts Colonial, of course! A gigantic Ionic-columned-and-pedimented double gallery encircled the building.[6]

By 1926, along with the rest of the country's millionaires, the Kirbys were learning to be more circumspect: in post-income-tax days, conspicuous architectural display was giving way to a more sober taste. Architect James Ruskin Bailey transformed the frame house into a brick Tudor house with tall ornamental chimneys and a few modest crenelations. The natatorium was demolished. Finally, a hedge was planted as a barrier instead of the see-through iron fence. The natural growth of shrubs and trees also increased privacy, and the wild and sinuous curves of the Kirbys' turn-of-the-century layout gave way to the more restrained straight lines of an Italianate terrace, complete with balustraded stone rail, low, square stone urns, and a straight flagstone path leading to a simple white arbor.

Henry T. Staiti

Who knows if there was a professional hand at work in the garden extravaganza at "Inglenook" in 1901 or at the McFaddin-Ward house in 1907? Certainly by 1917, Henry T. Staiti was employing Edward Dewson, the earliest known professional landscape architect in Houston, to make a garden for him at his newly renovated house in the Westmoreland addition. When the house was designed in 1905 by architect Olle J. Lorehn, Westmoreland, along with Courtland Place, was one of the most fashionable new neighborhoods.

Texas-born Henry Thomas Staiti was a Spindletop oilman, a colorful character whose idea of garden entertainment, recalls his niece, Jeanette King, was to set off a lot of firecrackers on the Fourth of July. "I think he set fire to several houses around there," she adds.[7] Staiti and his wife, Odelia, had moved to Houston in 1904. To repair hurricane damage in 1915, they employed young Alfred C. Finn, the flamboyant Houston architect who later designed the Gulf Building and other early downtown skyscrapers.[8] Stylistically, the house ended up somewhere between the Prairie Style and Restoration Queen Anne.

In an area only 160 by 80 feet at the side of the house, Dewson laid out a fan-shaped flower garden, a rectangular rose garden, a flower-bordered lawn with a big flagpole, and a white lattice teahouse connected to the house by a lattice pergola. The latticework, which also covered the side of the house, was an inspired idea. Its neat, airy pattern lightened the formidably clunky house.[9] The rose garden was backed with a greenhouse; the flower garden was neatly separated from the service yard by flowering shrubs, and the clever partitioning of space actually contrived to make the garden seem bigger. (In the twenties and thirties, architect John Staub, and the landscape architects who created the gardens around his houses, would manage the same trick on comparatively limited lots of 2 to 5 acres.) In 1986 the garden was moved to Sam Houston Park.[10] Reunited with the pergola and teahouse, and with a

In pre-air-conditioning days in Houston, Staiti, a Spindletop oilman, and his family spent much time in the vine-covered teahouse, enjoying what breeze there was.

In winter at Ima Hogg's "Bayou Bend" in Houston, the "Diana Garden" is seen against a dark, glistening background of holly, podocarpus, and yew.

replica of Dewson's garden, the Staiti "estate" will soon be open to the public—a monument to the first generation of houses and gardens built by pioneer Texas oilmen.

Residential enclaves, or "coterie neighborhoods," as architectural historian Howard Barnstone termed them,[11] were where the most notable gardens in Texas cities were located. The suburban pattern begun in Brookline, Massachusetts, in the middle of the nineteenth century, had become a national pattern; from 1900 on, most new upper-class neighborhoods on the outskirts of cities were speculative ventures governed by restrictive covenants. Houston's new millionaires wanted to make sure they had millionaire neighbors. Westmoreland, where Henry Staiti lived, was among the earliest; it was followed by Shadyside, Shadowlawn, West Eleventh Place, Broadacres, and eventually by River Oaks, begun in 1924, the brainchild of oilmen Will and Michael Hogg. River Oaks was situated on the other side of town from the other great developments, at the great distance of three miles west of Houston, on the upper reaches of Buffalo Bayou. The model was Kansas City's Country Club District, and the Houston subdivision was designed largely by the Kansas City landscape architects, Hare and Hare.[12] In the 30s, Herbert Hare, who also designed the gardens of "Villa Philbrook" in Tulsa, Oklahoma, would create large weekend playground estates (40 to 100 acres) for what Barnstone calls Houston's Best Oil Money (BOM) in the development of Post Oaks, west of River Oaks. While the flamboyant Wildcatters, men like Glenn McCarthy, who appeared thinly disguised in Edna Ferber's *Giant*, were making

headlines, men like the Farishes were quietly intermarrying with the old Houston lumber, cotton, real estate, and banking interests like the Rice, Carter, and Neuhaus families. Still today, they form a large, tight, oligarchy, who are likely to send their children east to school, and are absolutely fanatic about no publicity.[13] The center of Post Oaks is the Bayou Club (designed by John Staub), for polo, riding, and tennis: this is where the BOM feel most at home, although they also belong to the River Oaks Club and the Houston Country Club, the oldest golf club in town.

As always, the biggest house and garden belonged to the developer, and at River Oaks "Bayou Bend" was to be the star attraction. "Bayou Bend's" architect, thirty-four-year-old John F. Staub, was already well known in Houston when he was offered the job by the three Hogg children, who wanted a house they could share. Born in Knoxville, Tennessee, in 1892, Staub took his master's degree in architecture at MIT, studying at the same time with architect Ralph Adams Cram (who had just completed Rice University in Houston). Staub then worked for Harrie T. Lindeberg, the New York–based country-house architect, on estates from Stockbridge to Greenwich to Morristown to Lake Forest.[14] World War I gave him a brief look at Europe before he headed back to Lindeberg's employ. In 1921, new commissions for the firm in Houston led to the River Oaks job; Staub moved permanently to Houston, and became *the* residential architect of the South in the late twenties and thirties, just as Bottomley was in Richmond. As restrained, gentle, handsome, and quietly witty as the eclectic houses he designed, he formed many close, lifelong friendships with his clients, and even designed a number of second-generation houses. Staub's work, again like Bottomley's in Richmond, is highly valued in Houston today.[15] Staub's interest in siting his houses went well beyond the aesthetic; on the hot and humid Gulf Coast location was paramount. (The very design of a garden—the location of trees for shade and avenues to admit breeze—was part of the art of Southern living.) But beyond the location and sight lines, Staub actually designed very few gardens. In addition to Hare and Hare, the landscape architects and garden designers he worked with in Houston most often included C. C. "Pat" Fleming of Fleming & Shepard, and Ruth London. In Dallas and Fort Worth, his best-known collaborator was Joe Lambert.

"Bayou Bend"

One reason the Hoggs built "Bayou Bend" was to encourage others to join them, since, in 1926, River Oaks' lots, even in the premier section of Homewoods, were hardly being snapped up more than two years after the development opened. "Bayou Bend" was going to be the biggest and the best, if only to demonstrate the Hogg family's intention to back River Oaks.[16] But "bigger"—even in Texas—meant something different in the twenties than it had at the turn of the century in Newport or Morristown. Architectural critic C. Matlack Price defines the new discretion in an article on Lindeberg's work saying, "I have always thought that the very term 'show place,' which was applied to large country places when the demand for them was at their height, foretold their ultimate decline and fall. Who wants to live in a 'show place'? Very few people today."[17] "Bayou Bend," for all its elegant pale pink formality, is small by comparison with such places, as are the gardens, whose statues, fountains, and thousands of plants comprise 14 acres, with a native woodland surrounding that is now a bird sanctuary belonging to the city of Houston. Like Harvey Ladew's garden in Monkton, Maryland, which is exactly the same size and more or less the same period, "Bayou Bend" is extraordinary because of its exceptionally strong design, charm, taste, and a certain pervasive whimsy. Neither garden feels institutional; each is a place that, even after years of public ownership, feels like *somebody's.*

The three Hoggs, Will, Mike, and Ima, were the children of James Stephen Hogg, governor of Texas from 1891 to 1895, one of the biggest original players in the Spindletop boom. Will Hogg was an important oilman in his own right. The family was well known in Houston when they left their old cane plantation in West Columbia, Texas, and moved to the city to play in the big leagues. Just fighting for her joke name might have been enough for others, but Ima Hogg did more. Imperious, intelligent, and forever unmarried, her big-nosed, small-eyed face was made charming by her quickness, canniness, and sense of humor. More than just a "hostess with the mostest," she was truly public-spirited; her principal contribution was in the decorative arts, where, along with a scant

handful of other rich collectors (including John D. Rockefeller at Williamsburg), she early on felt the history and saw the beauty of American regionalism in architecture, objects, furniture, and paintings. "Bayou Bend," now a nationally known museum of American decorative arts, was Ima Hogg's gift to the Houston Museum of Fine Arts.

The style of the gardens was determined by John Staub and Miss Ima's choice of house site and by the architectural vocabulary they worked out together, which became known as "Latin Colonial"—a variation "that is Georgian in form and Latin in flavor," meaning Creole French or Spanish.[18] Staub and Miss Ima were seduced by Creole architecture, its soft, exotic colors, its ironwork, its adaptations to damp heat and fierce sun. "Bayou Bend," a long, narrow, three-part house based on "Homewood," an eighteenth-century Georgian house in Maryland, has many details taken from New Orleans town houses and Louisiana plantations. Similarly, "Bayou Bend's" garden is an eclectic version of an antebellum Southern garden.

The work of no single landscape architect, "Bayou Bend" is really the imaginative creation of its owner. Hare and Hare's design was turned down; Ellen Shipman, who was doing other gardens in Houston at the time,[19] submitted a sketch to Miss Ima, and visited for a few years after the house was built, then disappeared from view.[20] The east garden, located right next to the house, is usually credited to Ruth London, a 1928 Lowthorpe graduate who apprenticed with Ellen Shipman among others, and practiced in Houston for forty years. A formal enclosed space, the east garden has low boxwood embroidery parterres, tiered azaleas in soft pinks and corals, and a shady terrace at the end farthest from the house. It is hedged with ligustrum and with *Camellia japonica* 'Duchesse de Caze Pink', an old variety of camellia now difficult to find commercially, that is also known as the 'Opelousas Peony'. Ima Hogg's meticulous garden records show she purchased both the azaleas and the camellias from I. H. McIlhenney of Avery Island in Louisiana; they were among the very earliest such flowers in Houston.[21] What seems unbelievable is that no other ornamental gardens existed—or were planned—until 1936. (The driveway was planted as an informal woodland; there was a peach orchard and a kitchen garden, and a formally laid-out annual garden attached to the gardener's cottage, but there was no other landscape feature commensurate with the scale and grandeur of the house.) "Bayou Bend's" fine north portico and terrace stared right into a thicket of brambles and briars, loblolly pine, yaupon holly, *Ilex vomitoria*, cherry laurel, and bay, and Miss Ima loved it just that way.[22] So did the mosquitoes, and in 1936 she was persuaded by a particularly airless and hot luncheon party to cut some "airways" through the woods. She hired Dallas landscape architect Joseph O. Lambert and left for the summer. In a typical Ima Hogg maneuver, she then fired him by letter before her return, fearing that he might be cutting out the wrong things. When she came back, Pat Fleming managed to get her to resume the job. Eventually Fleming and Miss Ima and some mule trains and dump scoops carved out the major feature, the sweeping 250-foot lawn, divided into three shallow grass terraces connected with turf flights of steps. A long reflecting pool pointed toward the bayou view. Big cypresses formed a terminus, but they seemed inadequate.

A vista garden with not enough to look at was what they had on their hands by July 1937, when Miss Ima found a copy of the *Diana* of Versailles in white Carrara marble at the Frilli carving studio in Florence. Her dogged correspondence with Frilli finally beat the price down by $1,000, Fleming drily recalls.[23] *Diana*'s arrival in April, 1938 was followed by a November order for copies of the muses of history and music, *Clio* and *Euterpe*, from statues in the Vatican collections. Miss Ima and Pat had at last had the idea of a cross axis finished at each end with a statue. The garden was complete—conceptually, that is. But The Garden Club of America was arriving in March, 1939—could the statues be there in

time? Anyone who has opened a garden to the public knows the agony of wanting to have everything perfect, only discovering afterward that it doesn't matter. The Garden Club of America ladies had a wonderful time at "Bayou Bend" in March and the statues arrived in mid-April. Since 1966 more than 540,000 visitors have walked through these gardens, through six months of frothing azaleas and the longest stretch possible of camellia blossoms, past the goddesses in their little clipped temples of eternally green podocarpus and yew, under the giant pines and the pale sycamores that brighten the leafless woods in winter.

Was "Bayou Bend" a model for Texan gardeners? A bellwether estate like "Reynolda" or "Belmont," it exerted a tremendous influence as a horticultural model. Just as the earlier foursquare buildings like the Kirby or Staiti houses gave way in the 20s to Staub's graceful tributes to Southern cross ventilation, so did the Victorians' favorite tropical exotics largely vanish from fashionable gardens, to be replaced by backbone plantings of azaleas, camellias, and a wealth of indigenous trees: oaks of many kinds, pine, magnolia, hickory, sweet gum, tupelo, winged elm, buckeye, redbud, dogwood, and many others. Today, broadleaf evergreen gardens in a woodland setting seem uninventive, but in the twenties and thirties they were something new in Texas. Just like white columns, camellias and azaleas stood for Southern conservatism, for the antebellum Southern tradition revived and revised to fit the large suburban estate lot. Although "Bayou Bend" was certainly not the first of its kind, it consecrated and popularized the formula for hundreds of later gardens.

THE SPANISH COLONIAL ALTERNATIVE

The runner-up in popularity to a Southern antebellum house with columns and azaleas was a Spanish Colonial house with a red tile roof and patio garden. The Spanish Colonial Revival movement in the Southwest was not a fond look back at family roots like the Colonial Revival or antebellum styles, but a search for a legitimizing regional historical past—and the first American attempt to come to grips with the actuality of the climate and the soil of the semi-arid region. Spanish garden style was disseminated through books like Bynes's *Spanish Gardens and Patios,* published in 1924 which, incidentally, was one of only three books on gardens in John Staub's extensive architecture library. Other important works were Rose Standish Nichols's *Spanish and Portuguese Gardens* (1924) and Rexford Newcomb's *The Spanish House for America: Its Design, Furnishing, and Garden* (1927). Earliest had been the English volume, C. M. Villiers-Stuart's *Gardens of the Great Mughals* (1913). Staub designed one of the handsomest Spanish Revival domestic essays in Houston for the William Crabbs in 1935; in Dallas the outstanding work was the Everett DeGolyer place (1939) where the Spanish-style terrace extended smoothly out into a typical Beaux-Arts landscape. The patio, completely enclosed by the house walls, was a dense tapestry of

Landscape architect Joe Lambert of Dallas designed a succession of garden compartments that surrounded the patio of the William Crabbs' Spanish Colonial house (1935) in Houston, designed by John Staub. Pat Fleming put in the pool garden. Bright annuals were a fitting match for the white walls and red tiles.

*Spanish Colonial was the style chosen in 1915 by cattle baron Captain
Richard King, for his new house at the King Ranch, less than one hundred
miles from the Mexican border. A lawn—the symbolic Anglo landscape
garden—triumphs over the dust, and is planted with clumps of exotics like
date palms and bananas, as well as native willow, huisache, and
mesquite. A flower-filled patio lies within the U of the house. Outbuildings
include ranch-hand bunkhouses and a commissary, all part of the huge
working operation of nearly a million acres that still exists today.*

pebble mosaic flooring, wrought iron, many different ground covers, and favored common tropicals, such as bananas and bird of paradise.[24]

Spanish Colonial also seemed appropriate style for the biggest cattle ranch in Texas, located as it was less than 100 miles from the Mexican border, south and west of Corpus Christi. In 1915, in the dry, dusty cattle country on the site of cattle baron Captain Richard King's original 1853 cow camp next to the Santa Gertrudis Creek, a young architect from San Antonio, Carleton Adams, began his first major project. He designed a huge white house for Captain King's widow to replace the old frame house, which had burned down. Built to resemble a Spanish Colonial *casco de casa,* it has crenelations, corbels, arches, and a large tower, and looks today almost exactly as it did in 1915. It is a house that followed both Mrs. King's own instruction to make a place where "Men could walk in in boots," and that of her son-in-law, Robert Kleberg, Jr., to create "A monument to Mrs. King's hospitality." The dining room, floored with native Texas slate, seats fifty. Everywhere in Texas, entertainment is almost a religious duty, and most gardens were made with entertainment in mind, for both large groups and small, rather than for solitude or purely horticultural pleasure. The ranch landholdings by 1915 comprised nearly 1 million acres, so the Santa Gertrudis headquarters was more than an entertainment center; it was the heart of a working ranch in wild, near-desert country. In addition to the main house, there were stables, homes for the ranch employees, a huge water tank, and a commissary, or general store, for people living on the ranch. All of these were grouped quite closely together; they comprised a feudal village, but how different from Marshall Field's "Caumsett," for instance, where the working estate operations were all out of sight of the big house.

Around the Santa Gertrudis mansion a lawn was encouraged to grow—a thick, smooth mat of carpet grass. More in tune with the house architecture was the enclosed patio where nothing but the lushest greenery surrounded the central Spanish-tiled pool. Yellow Lady Banks roses provided the only flower color. Behind the house was a cutting garden with rows of zinnias, carnations, larkspur, periwinkle, marigolds, anemones, and other flowers. Captain King himself had planned the original landscape around the old frame house, and had planted the ebony trees that alternated with palms along the imposing entrance drive.[25]

RIGHT:

The dauntless Joanna Steves, wife of San Antonio German settler Edward Steves, sits in her rocker in her wintry garden under the pecan trees she so carefully watered. Behind the house, seen here c. 1890–1900, was an indoor swimming pool, the first in the city, called "River Haus." Neighborhood children were welcome, but everybody had to clear out at two o'clock, time for Mrs. Steve's daily afternoon swim.

SAN ANTONIO

"Among the Nation's sizable cities San Antonio is one of the eight or ten which, in the same sense as Boston, Charleston, New Orleans, and San Francisco, are wholly distinctive in their individual atmosphere," says the 1940 WPA guide for Texas. San Antonio's cultural mix took many centuries to achieve its flavor. Founded by the Payaya Indians as Yanaguana, the town was renamed by the Spaniards in 1691, and remained Spanish and Indian in feeling until the 1830s when Americans started to appear in the Republic of Texas. German immigrants poured into Texas in the 1840s, escaping the revolutions of Europe. Southwestern cowboy culture added its particular tang when the big cattle drives began after the Civil War. By the 1890s San Antonio was truly urban, prosperous, and confident of its own cultural traditions. It had history—it had the Alamo. Downtown on King William Street, there were rows of grand Victorian houses with gardens full of trees and roses and

vines. Later, when ranchers and cattlemen struck oil in the twentieth century, they often moved into town and built big houses.

San Antonio has enjoyed certain advantages when it comes to making gardens. First, the climate is mild enough to grow tropical plants in sheltered places, and the city is far north enough to grow temperate zone plants as well. Second, there has historically been plenty of underground water. Third, San Antonio has always been a city interested in its own looks: its beautiful river, its architecture, and its public squares and places have been important throughout its history. Fourth, both Mexican and German traditions have fostered celebrations, fiestas, fests, parties of all kinds, and in a mild, dry climate, outdoors is the place to have them. Perhaps more important than anything else has been the influence of the surrounding countryside: though the Edwards plateau is very beautiful, it is thorny, hot, dry, and inhospitable enough to make people long for the exact opposite. Nature presents formidable challenges to human control. San Antonio landscape architect Sarah Westkaemper writes that San Antonians of the estate garden period wanted to "create garden schemes which are not an extension or enhancement of the landscape," but which are, she continues, "a replacement for the appearance of the landscape of Bexar county. . . . The physical environment of the area is one not easily tamed. . . . Perhaps the popularity of geometric forms in gardens of San Antonio lies in part in the symbolism of control that straight lines and symmetry embody, important in an area where the land is not receptive or forgiving."[26] Two gardens in San Antonio, dating from 1876 and 1936, reveal much of the city's garden history. The story of the Steves Homestead spans sixty years of family occupancy. And in 1936, the year that Joanna Steves died, Lutcher Brown's garden was planted on Ivy Lane.

Edward and Joanna Steves

Edward Steves made a one-generation leap from frontier farmer in 1848 to respected city burgher, with enough money and sophistication in 1876 to go to the Philadelphia Centennial and treat himself to a cast-iron garden fountain to take back to San Antonio. Steves, who emigrated from Germany at the age of nineteen, came straight to Texas and bought a threshing machine. He threshed his way to prosperity, hauling his precious equipment as far as 120 miles for a job, leaving his wife, Johanna, and three young sons to the vicissitudes of lonely frontier farm life. He took his pay in grain, hauling it by oxcart to Dallas to grind into flour, and then traveling to Mexico to sell it for silver. After ten hard years, the family moved to San Antonio in 1866, set up a lumber business, and bought 5 acres of what had been a Spanish mission farm field, close to the Alamo and to the San Antonio River.[27] At the time of their purchase, the land all around them was being bought up by other prosperous Germans—so many that the district became known as "sauerkraut bend." The solid limestone houses were set on lots of 10 acres or less running back to the river. When F. L. Olmsted traveled through Texas in 1854, again and again he remarked that the only well-cared-for yards he saw belonged to the Germans. Edward and Johanna Steves built a fashionable mansard-roofed house on King William Street, but even before they built it, they put up an elaborate picket fence to keep out the neighbors' cows. How the fence got to San Antonio gives an idea of the difficulties house-proud owners went through to create their dream estates in Texas even as late as 1871: the fence was prefabricated in Florida and shipped to the Texas port of Indianola; from there it came overland by oxcart to San Antonio. The lumber business prospered, the boys went to college in Virginia, and the whole family traveled back East and to Europe. In addition to the fountain from the Philadelphia Centennial, the garden grew to include boxwood-edged cookie-cutout beds of old-fashioned annuals on either side of the front walk—the cherished memory of the parterre gardens they saw abroad. Palms and all the exotics so dear to Victorian hearts were planted. In old photographs, everything is rigidly clipped, pruned, trimmed, and staked—but then, the Steveses had surely not journeyed from their frontier farm to have an untidy, wild-looking garden in San Antonio. Later, a certain luxuriance crept in: the boxwood in the front garden grew thick and high, and a shaggy copse of *Sophora secundiflora,* the fragrant blue violet-flowered native shrub Texans call "mountain laurel," flourished. But long after the frontier days, this garden must have signified hard-won safety and cultivation for the family that made it.

"Oak Court"

After World War I, King William Street lost its luster and elite neighborhoods developed on the hills north and east of the city. Lutcher and Emily Brown came to San Antonio from Houston in the thirties, she originally from Sherman, he a member of a lumber baron family from Orange, an old cotton plantation town right on the Louisiana border at the Sabine River, where camellias, live oaks, Spanish moss, and azaleas grow. At "Oak Court," Lutcher Brown would have camellias and azaleas too, far from the humid lazy heat and peaty soil of the Gulf coast. "Oak Court's" 24 acres in Terrell Hills comprised one of the biggest estate gardens in San Antonio, and Brown was the first person to grow acid-loving shrubs and trees on the alien, alkaline, semiarid soil of the Edwards Plateau. At the start, Brown didn't feel strongly about what style he wanted—when he went to the architectural firm of Ayres & Ayres in 1934, the first proposal they discussed was a Mediterranean house. The preeminent local architects of the period, the Ayres were best known for their residences in Spanish Colonial style. Ayres & Ayres's chief draftsman for five years, J. Fred Buenz, recalls that after Brown chose the Georgian style, Atlee Ayres lost interest so his son, Robert, took on supervising the job. But it seems that Brown and Buenz together did most of the work: Brown would come up with a detail for an entrance or paneling, and Buenz would draw it. The project became Brown's chief obsession. "Morning, noon, and almost night, he would hang over the drafting table," remembers Buenz, "that house was his bedfellow, so to speak."[28]

Brown's absorption in the garden was just as profound. In Houston, the Browns were friends with Ima Hogg, who was hacking out her woods to make the great north vista at "Bayou Bend" the same year, 1936, that Brown was making what he thought of as an English Georgian garden, in reality a full-blown American neoclassical fantasy. This friendship

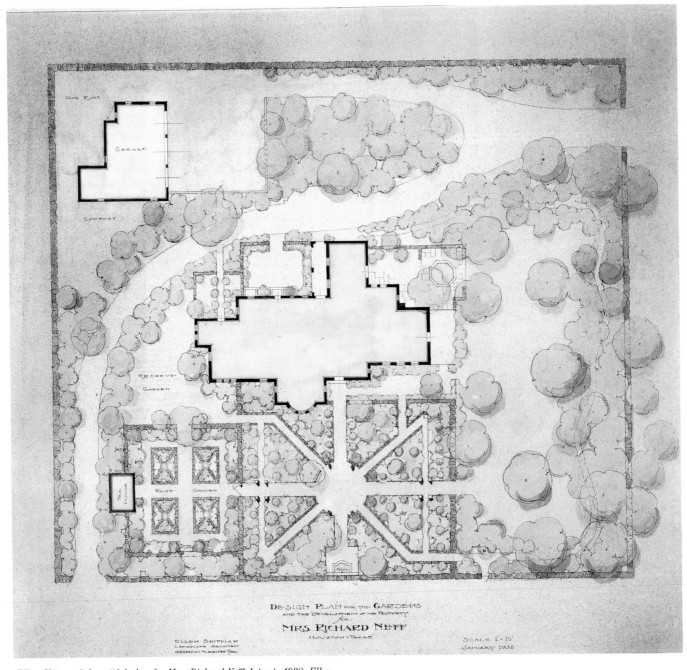

*Ellen Shipman's beautiful plan for Mrs. Richard Neff dates to 1938. Ellen
Shipman designed a number of gardens in Texas.*

might have occasioned the brief appearance of Ellen Shipman, who made a fairly complete set of garden sketch plans. According to Mrs. Joan Winter, one of the Brown daughters, it was the presentation of a bill for $4,000 for these sketches that made her father decide to execute the design himself.[29] Regular, majestic, and unsurprising, the garden has an axial oak-avenue, a lawn vista garden with a columned bath house and a swimming pool doubling as a reflecting pool to terminate the view. To the west is a walled azalea garden, to the east a formal rose garden with a gazebo. A little circular domed temple stands above the old spring; statues and urns are everywhere. The house is located on a knoll; the land slopes off softly to the east to a beautiful view, and there were extensive planted woods circling the outermost edges of the estate. In the early days the corridor between the woods and the house was a natural draw for doves, who flew through by the thousands over the formal gardens. This is Texas, after all, and in dove season the men of the family, all great hunters, could practically sit on the back porch—a columned loggia—and bag their daily limit.

Despite the well-grown plantings and the perfection of the arrangements, "Oak Court" only becomes interesting when one knows the exhausting facts of its creation. Buenz and Brown spent hours over the gate design, for example, and it was only after sleepless nights that Brown came triumphantly to Buenz's office with a design of his initials for the gate that could be read from both directions. Nothing seems special about the avenue underplanted with the deep pink of Formosa azaleas except perhaps its very large scale—till one considers that every live oak was trucked in nearly full grown from a ranch miles away. Each tree, in those long-ago pre–automatic sprinkler days, had a faucet to provide enough water year-round. Brown invented his own version of the tree spade and a conveyance that, according to Emily Brown, could move three trees at once. In all, Brown transplanted more than 700 large trees, elms, and magnolias, as well as live oaks. He made a wide and thorough sweep of the area in his search for good specimens. After moving two big oaks to a spot behind the house near the swimming pool, he said, "I hope neither of them die, because if they do, they could never be replaced because there isn't another tree left in Bexar County that tall."[30] He also made a wide sweep for garden ornaments and ideas. Much came from England. The stone temple was shipped just before the Battle of Britain in World War II, Mrs. Winter remembers. Expected to crumble before it reached London from the country, it survived its long dangerous trip by nearly fifty years. A small-waisted lead shepherdess did not fare as well. The hot Texas summer was too much for her—she melted and bent over double. She was given some extra backbone, and has stood straight up in her corner of the pool garden ever since.[31] Brown also took many ideas from his books. The bathhouse facade was faithfully copied from a photograph and elevation drawings of a springhouse at "Oaklands" in

Maryland, which has been preserved on the grounds of the Baltimore Museum of Art.[32] The gazebo was said to be inspired by the octagonal entrance on the garden front of "Gunston Hall" in Virginia.[33]

Every azalea and camellia on the place grew in a capacious planting hole filled with acid soil, some of it brought from East Texas. The water in San Antonio wasn't right either, so Lutcher Brown weekly mixed up acid water in his workshop in a decorative dovecote. Plants responded magnificently to all the special care: one camellia nicknamed Pinky bore 1,500 blossoms one year. (All the big camellia lovers knew each other; Brown and Mr. McIlhenney used to hunt camellias on rundown Louisiana plantations and shoot birds together. McIlhenny even named one of his camellia hybrids 'Emily Brown' because, he said, its pointed petals made him think of the Lone Star State.)[34]

Of all the gardens in this book, "Oak Court" most nakedly represents that triumph of will and control over nature which is part of the making of any garden. Perhaps part of the intensity of Brown's garden-making came from not having enough to do. He ran a family papermill in Monroe, Louisiana, but it practically took care of itself, and he was, as were most rich Texans, "a little bit in the oil business." Like so many others of his generation, he had money and energy to spare. Shooting and boats—he was a champion skeet shot and a racing sailor—did not absorb all his energies. Sports aside, leisure time is not something Texans have felt easy with, however, and Brown was no exception to the rule. Rapid, competitive, quickly proficient at whatever he turned to, he must have been an engaging though problematic man. Only in his forties when he began "Oak Court," he threw himself into the venture as if it were his salvation, which, for a while it was. Restlessly, only a few years after the estate was finished, he began to visit South America, where he set up a bank in Uruguay, dabbled in real estate, and bought a big boat in which he spent many hours sailing on the Gulf. Not too long after that, he gave "Oak Court" away to the University of Texas system, which used it as a reception center. (Something of a white elephant, it has since been resold as a private home.) Brown began to spend more and more time in Uruguay. The reasons for the gift and the move are murky, and no doubt there is some truth to the story of unpaid income taxes, but it's probably just as much to the point to say that Lutcher Brown was bored again. The pillars of the gates at "Oak Court" are sunk thirty feet deep in the ground. The walls that closed the avenue in on each side were built so the Brown children could feel comfortable building their own houses right next door on the other side. It's the kind of dynastic thinking that went into the making of every great estate but which was almost always thwarted in America. The restless founders of these twentieth-century principalities were as responsible for the demise of their own creations as were income tax, labor shortages, war, or changing tastes. Once the place was finished, then what?

The
MIDWEST
and
BEYOND

Blazing maples light the Laurence H. Armours' drive at "Two Gables"
(1928), the work of Chicago's society architect, David Adler, in Lake
Forest, heart of the Gold Coast on Lake Michigan.

Vast estates—estates of thousands of acres, with every stylistic variation on the garden—were no oddity in the Midwest. Illinois, Ohio, and Michigan were the big three, where commodities and industry exploded into fortunes big enough to support hundreds of country houses and suburban estates. In Wisconsin and Minnesota, there was a sudden rush of summer places on the lakes. In Missouri, Indiana, and Kansas, as elsewhere in the country, an exodus from the city took place, fueled as much by the increasing distress of the city centers as by the "country house" mystique. Nothing was simultaneously more rural and more industrialized than the Midwest during the estate garden years: called the breadbasket or the heartland, it was also the center of American invention, technology, and heavy manufacturing.

In the Midwest, gardeners deal with real wintertime, as well as startlingly abrupt changes in temperature, fierce searing winds both hot and cold, and a long summer when 90-degree heat and both drought and humidity are the norm. Finding the hardy plants to duplicate Italian or English estate garden "looks" was the first hurdle. To the narrow range of dwarf barberry-for-boxwood, cedar-for-cypress worked out on Eastern estates, soon were added native trees, shrubs, and wild flowers—hawthorns, viburnums, rudbeckia, native iris, trillium, species roses—the full complement of Jensen's Prairie Style. The climate of the lake states, Michigan, Minnesota, and Wisconsin, is tempered by the surrounding water and by latitude: in the short clear summer, flowers bunch up and bloom together within three months. There were enough gardeners to cram the perennial beds to flowery fullness with annuals started in hothouse and cold frame so that an English border was a real possibility. The air is like Maine's, laden with moisture from the many lakes of the region. "In Missouri, as in Kansas and elsewhere in the Middle West, there is great variableness of climate from year to year, and never is it an ideal district for summer flower gardens," says Louise Shelton in 1914[1], and goes on to quote "an experienced amateur gardener"—

The climate of Kansas City, Missouri, is subject to every eccentricity, and at times is very trying. One of my experiences was a four or five inch snow-storm on the 3rd of May after a month of warm spring weather; when German iris and many other things were in full bloom, and Peonies in bud. Everything was mashed down and then it froze.... The greatest trouble with the summer garden is the extreme heat and dryness of the air. The earth can be kept moist around the plants, but many things wither in the dry air. With the greatest care a garden of annuals might be kept looking fairly well through July and August, but I am glad to get away from mine early in July.[2]

Only in the Midwest does it make sense to divide American estate gardens along formal/informal lines. By 1910, most rich Americans wanted both—and both they could have, thanks to the ubiquitous and flexible scheme evolved by Charles Platt and by the many Beaux-Arts

At the James Simpsons' "Roscrana," Chicago landscape architect Ralph Rodney Root designed the magnificent perennial borders. Even in a difficult climate, an "English garden" like this could be made with a little ingenuity—and a greenhouse and many gardeners to replant annually what was blasted by cold, heat, drought, and wind. Hardy stalwarts identifiable here include iris, and peony foliage in the foreground. Delphiniums raise their spears the length of both borders. Jens Jensen did the original landscaping at "Roscrana."

practitioners where formal gardens around the house melted into magnificent "wild" surroundings. But in the Midwest, the Prairie Style that rolled meadows and woods right up to the house was a home-grown alternative with its own characteristic plantings and a well-defined creed (preservation of natural scenery, restoration of local color, and repetition of the horizontal lines of land and sky). Though it flourished only for the first twenty years of the century, and was never widely popular among estate garden makers, basically a conservative lot, the Prairie Movement carried within it the genesis of modern, ecologically conscious American landscape design, and the natural four-season garden.[3]

Although tradition has it[4] that the death knell of the Prairie School sounded at the World's Columbian Exposition of 1893 in Chicago,[5] in fact the competition between neoclassicism and the Prairie Style was as fast and furious as Wimbledon tennis for more than twenty years after that date, with Jens Jensen, Ossian Cole Simonds (the first non-Eastern president of the ASLA in 1913), and the Chicago School architects on one side.[6] Wilhelm Miller preached the prairie gospel in print and at the University of Illinois. Jensen said things to his Lake Forest clients like,

"You are an American. Why do you want to be a stuffed shirt?";[7] he designed enormous gardens for the likes of Henry and Edsel Ford, and did over $6 million worth of work between 1901 and 1915, an impressive comment on the Prairie Style's popularity.[8] Playing more politely on the other side of the net were classicists Charles Platt, Howard Van Doren Shaw, and David Adler, all Beaux-Arts architects who designed beautiful, calm, easily understood gardens, usually in collaboration with landscape architects, often women such as Ellen Shipman and Rose Standish Nichols. Landscape architect Warren Manning remained magnificently in the middle, resolving the struggle in a series of brilliant, very American estates, of which the best is "Stan Hywet" in Akron, Ohio. In 1912, the Prairie School was gingerly referred to in the pages of *Architectural Record* as "insurgent architecture."[9] A client of Howard Van Doren Shaw's said that Frank Lloyd Wright's houses looked like gas stations—probably the common verdict of Chicago/Lake Forest society people who would never have dreamed of living in the idealistic, solidly middle-class suburbs of Oak Park, Glencoe, and Winnetka, where the best examples of the Prairie Style were created.[10] By the twenties, what H. L. Mencken called the "Bozart" indeed *had* won.[11] Just as the Midwest's millions became part of the national system controlled by New York's financial markets so did the Prairie School collapse into an attractive but mild national eclecticism best typified in the Midwest by Howard Van Doren Shaw's work. In 1922 architect Thomas Tallmadge wrote, "Twenty years ago, when the Middle West was mentioned, the brilliant and original ornament and philosophy of Louis Sullivan, the long, low casemented houses of Frank Wright, the enthusiastic and courageous work of the other members of the Chicago School arose before one's eyes, but no longer is this typical."[12]

FORMAL GARDENS IN THE MIDWEST

Landscape architect Ralph Rodney Root, who taught at the University of Illinois, was a formalist who favored long axial *tapis verts* lined with allées of trees, parterres, high formal cascades, and rectangular reflecting pools. In 1924, writing about Midwestern estate gardens and how they developed, he accurately sums up the prevailing style,

> . . . almost without exception the sites for the houses have been selected because of some magnificent view of lake, river, valley or open prairie. . . . What is deprecated as our "meager" selection of plant material and our "peculiar" climatic conditions which handicap fine lawns, so far from militating against good design, have been a distinct aid in forming country places with pleasing composition. . . . We plan to have a real show of flowers during the two seasons [spring and fall] and then depend upon the architectural features and the strong masses of shrub and perennial foliage to carry the garden through the few hot summer weeks that intervene. . . . The entourage of ample open and wooded areas, with the house and its terraces, gardens and courts . . . gives a certain magnificence and grandeur that one finds in the gardens of the Renaissance.[1]

"Melody Farm"
Lake Forest began as the Olmsted-designed preserve of Presbyterians who had moved out of Chicago in the 1850s to find a better place to raise their children than the Windy City. In the nineties, the first summer houses were built: flush Chicago businessmen wanted to summer outside Chicago *and* go to work every day, and the seventy-five miles to the fashionable summer resort, Lake Geneva, just seemed too far. Golf then hit Chicago—the Onwentsia Club was founded, and in 1904 the high society note was struck by J. Ogden Armour, son of the P. D. Armour who almost single-handedly founded the Chicago stockyards. Ogden Armour bought 1,200 acres of farmland well west of what was then Lake Forest, in Libertyville. Four years and $10 million later, he moved into his 419-foot-long palace with his wife, Lolita. According to Arthur Meeker, the chatty, irreverent, quick-witted son of a meat packer, and the best guide to the Gilded Age in the Midwest, Lolita was "a fidgety, discontented creature," despite "her biting wit and brilliant, commanding brunette beauty."[2] Armour himself was shy, handsome, tongue-tied, and brown-eyed—and he did all the things that a rich man's son who doesn't know what to do with himself does—piling up possessions, making unlikely friends like circus man John Ringling, or the local druggist, falling in love with Scots opera singer Mary Garden, having the Prince of Wales visit his "farm," and, in 1923, losing the Armour fortune only to recoup it, a financial somersault common among Chicago millionaires.[3] "Melody Farm" became Lake Forest Academy/Ferry Hall in 1947; the house remains but the gardens are gone. Little Lolita, the Armours' only grandchild, would carry on with the family garden tradition on a Brobdingnagian scale in California. "A certain magnificence and grandeur that one finds in the gardens of the Renaissance" well describes the 40 acres of formal compartments and elaborate park landscape surrounding the Armours' pink plaster and white marble dwelling, designed by architect Arthur Heun.[4] "It was, naturally, an Italian villa," writes Arthur Meeker; "I always felt the trouble with it was that it was too

ABOVE:
Earliest of the grand gardens in Lake Forest was the J. Ogden Armours' "Melody Farm" begun in 1904. The site planning and garden architecture were probably the work of architect Arthur Heun, but the shaggy plantings of grasses around the pool are doubtless that of Jensen, who laid out the landscape beyond the casino with O. C. Simonds.

damned Italian. Nothing could have looked more lamentably inappropriate under the high, thin prairie sky than this ponderous pleasure palace, with its fountains and rose-gardens and formal, cypress-lined terraces, in which nobody took any pleasure."[5]

But despite Meeker, how beautiful the gardens must have been—especially the 350-foot-long water garden, with the arched white marble casino and its oddly successful bronze statue of a wrestler standing on a black marble table, silhouetted against that prairie sky. Tall, billowing plantings of grasses and bamboo softened the edges of the three long pools, and beyond the casino lay a surprise view of a 20-acre artificial lake dotted with islands, and surrounded by gently undulating meadows. Walks, shaded by willow, larch, alder, and mountain ash, along with spirea and viburnums, led around the lake.[6] The strikingly original grass plantings by the pool, and the wealth of native flora around the lake are all that tell us this is an early estate work of Jens Jensen, begun in

1909, the year that he was rehired by the city to redesign the entire West Park System, which he did on prairie principles. He had been fired for exposing graft in the city park system in 1900, and had had six lean years with little work. "Melody Farm," the early showplace of rich and social Lake Forest, must have been an important commission for Jensen both financially and as an advertisement that he was ready to work in the private sector on a grand scale.[7]

As for the work itself, a description of 1920 depicts a bold, ornate garden typical of its period—and atypical of Jensen as he is thought today.[8] The rose garden, with its white gravel walks and bright green lawn edgings, was filled with roses grown as standards and on pillars and umbrella forms, and underplanted with gladiolus for later color. 'Dorothy Perkins' and 'Lady Gay', favored roses of the decade, covered the walls with pink, yellow, and white. Not that "Melody Farm" shied away from suffused color, or from those fainting shades, like mauve, so favored by the Victorians: in the center of the "Dutch" garden was a solid circle of mauve cannas. The rest of the geometric beds were planted in petunias of all shades from white to darkest purple. Edgings were dwarf clipped juniper—a common Midwestern stand-in for boxwood—and here too the walls cascaded with 'Dorothy Perkins' and 'Lady Gay' roses. As a matter of course, "Melody Farm" had vegetable and cutting gardens, greenhouses, orchards, additional truck and fruit gardens, and a couple of tennis courts. It also had a nuttery, an orangery, a deer park, and its own train station. Quite in keeping with all this, says Meeker, was Mrs. Armour herself, whose "idea of a picnic was to set up a board with a damask table-cloth on the *tapis vert* fifty yards from her front door and be served on the second-best Meissen by the butler and the footman."[9] He also recalls his mother's and Mrs. Armour's dance exercise ". . . in black bloomers, making a dashing entrance to the strains of a fandango as they banged tambourines with abandon on their knees."[10]

"Gwinn," "The Moorings," and "Villa Turicum": Platt's Italianate Lakefront Villas

Just as "Melody Farm" was completed (1907–1908), Charles Platt was designing the equally grand "Gwinn" for Cleveland iron ore magnate William Mather in what was then the Lake Erie shore village of Bratenahl, outside Cleveland.[11] Platt's restraint produced subtle, controlled effects entirely unlike "Melody Farm's" highly colored, highly wrought Chicago magnificence. In his forties, Platt was starting on the succession of country houses that would bring him national recognition. The three best known were in the Midwest; the other two besides "Gwinn" were the Russell Alger, Jr.'s "The Moorings," in Grosse Pointe, Michigan (1908–1910), and "Villa Turicum," in Lake Forest, for the Harold McCormicks, (1908–1918).[12] All were lakefront villas. At each place Platt created an architectural landscape feature that decisively tied the house to the site; each master stroke made the ridiculous idea of a sunny Italian villa perched on the banks of American Lake Erie, Lake St. Clair, or Michigan seem perfectly appropriate. At "Gwinn," the encircling curved arms of

Mrs. Russell Alger and Ellen Shipman (right) take a break from garden planning chores (they are hardly dressed for digging). Shipman became friends with many clients, and checked on their gardens biannually.

the breakwater still give an impression of harbor safety today. At "The Moorings," now the Grosse Pointe War Memorial, a long vine-covered pergola stretched the lakefront elevation out till the house seemed to relax and sun itself behind the Venetian barge moorings that were stuck so bravely in the waters of Lake St. Clair.[13] At "Villa Turicum," since destroyed, Platt made the most of the seventy-foot drop to Lake Michigan by dropping a torrent of curving steps, terraces, water stairs, and dolphins down from the imposing house perched on the bluff.[14]

In its extravagance, "Villa Turicum" seemed more Roman than Italian (it actually had a Pompeiian-red atrium with a fountain). There were 300 acres, and two huge fortunes to spend (Edith McCormick was John D. Rockefeller's daughter, Harold McCormick was one of the reaper family). Platt, aided by landscape designer Phelps Wyman, let fly a salvo of references from the great Italian villas—Mondragone, d'Este, Lante.[15] Platt's biographer, Keith Morgan, writes, "The scale was immense and the money available encouraged Platt to reproduce, more than adapt, the villas of Italy."[16] "Villa Turicum" was indeed a Villa d'Este, an American country palace, a throwback to the "showplace" great estates of the nineties, from which Platt himself had weaned his clients with his ideal "country place," based on the Italian villa. However, Edith Rockefeller McCormick *was* grand. According to Meeker, she didn't know how else to be, and Chicagoans didn't know what to make of her.[17] One McCormick in-town garden party at their Lake Shore Drive palace was a *fête champêtre*, with Chicago's *gratin* in white wigs and eighteenth-century dress wandering about among the newly landscaped lilac clumps—or *bosquets* to Edith. Unluckily, the wind turned into a gale from the lake, and the guests fled to the McCormicks' neighbors for hot toddies. The marriage did not last. Harold eventually—but briefly—married the glamorous would-be opera singer Ganna Walska, who later made a fabulous garden in California with her McCormick settlement. Edith, intelligent, eccentric, neurotic, resourceful, and humorless, learned to play the violoncello, and took up both a Swiss architect boyfriend, Edwin Krenn, and Jungian analysis with the master in Zurich, eventually practicing herself. She also quietly supported James Joyce for a number of years, as well as continuing to erase much of the deficit of the Chicago Opera, a habit she and Harold had developed during their marriage. Although she spent almost no time at "Villa Turicum," the house was kept fully staffed. The crash caught her badly, and poor Edith Rockefeller McCormick died at the Drake Hotel in Chicago in 1932, leaving assets of only $1.5 million, and debts of $3 million.[18]

By contrast with "Villa Turicum," "Gwinn" seems quietly balanced, set perfectly on a mere 5 acres, with what seems like plenty of room for a bosky woodland garden, an exquisite flower garden, a spacious central lawn set between parallel drives, a tennis court, and large greenhouses. As always with Platt, the bravura effects were reserved till last and worth

ABOVE:

The curved double portico of one of the most beautiful houses Charles Platt ever designed, the William Mathers' "Gwinn" (1919–1920), overlooks Lake Erie outside Cleveland. The landscape architect was Warren Manning; the walled garden at the right was replanted by Ellen Shipman in the twenties.

waiting for. The view across the water opens up only from inside the house, through the high, rotundalike double portico set right above the water.[19] Across Lake Shore Drive, the view from the central axis of the house continued down an allée cut through woodlands. Warren Manning

worked on all parts of the Gwinn garden with Platt; Ellen Shipman later redid the flower garden.

Classical Favorites: Rose Standish Nichols,
Howard Van Doren Shaw, and David Adler
Also in Lake Forest were many of the gently formal gardens of Rose Standish Nichols, who often teamed up with Howard Van Doren Shaw, the Midwest's homegrown version of Charles Platt. Shaw, from a well-to-do Chicago family, went to Yale and MIT, and then traveled in Europe, except for France—he didn't like French classicism, preferring cosier English

architects like Lutyens and Voysey for inspiration. He set up his Chicago practice in 1895, and in 1898 he designed his own Arts and Crafts house, "Ragdale," in Lake Forest. Though he preferred English styles, he would also oblige with Spanish houses and Italian palazzos when required—and he nearly always finished his houses within budget! For the next thirty years rich Midwesterners lined up for his handsome, comfortable, well-built, well-bred houses, made of brick or stone, with French windows opening onto terrace and garden. Shaw often designed the gardens as well, and his daughter, Sylvia Shaw Judson, became a well-known sculptor of garden statues.[20]

"Tall, gaunt, patrician, with an individual style that made no concession to changing fashion,"[21] Rose Standish Nichols, born in 1870, was the genuine New England article: she was Augustus Saint-Gaudens's niece; she lived in Cornish, New Hampshire, in the summers, along with Platt and Shipman, and spent her winters in a Bulfinch house in Boston. Definitely a garden designer, though not a very innovative one, she had nonetheless studied with architect Thomas Hastings, of Carrère and Hastings, at MIT, and at the Ecole des Beaux-Arts in Paris. Her clientele was spread across the United States from Massachusetts to Santa Barbara, with stops in Georgia, Arizona, and the Midwest. She was also a bluestocking, and always a lady. Sharp-tongued and intelligent, she espoused social and feminist causes worldwide from the thirties onward; she was famous for her salonesque Boston "Sunday teas," and she had the dash, spark, and almost-always charming pushiness of a person who has been taught from birth that she can get away with anything. She was the author of four books on European garden styles—Italian, English, Spanish, Portuguese. One might say that style was her specialty, the ability to intimate a Spanish garden rather than copy it, and make it look at home next to a dark brown brick house designed by Shaw. Such was the effect of plantings she did for Mrs. Hugh J. McBirney, at "The House of the Four Winds," in Lake Forest, where Shaw laid out the garden "after the Generalife." Like other women designers, Nichols sometimes seemed doomed to the planting-plan circuit. For instance, at the Charles H. Scheppes, also in Lake Forest, Pray, Hubbard and White of Cambridge, Massachusetts, did the terraces, forecourt, and parterre (1914), and Fletcher Steele did the theatrical swimming pool and hornbeam arcades, while she did the plantings for the long perennial border and the rose garden. However, she also did some gardens on her own, as at the William E. Clows' in Lake Forest, where she made a dramatic sunken garden. Nichols also designed formal summer and autumn gardens for the Laurence H. Armours in 1914. When the original house burned down in 1928, it was replaced with another by architect David Adler, then at the height of his fame as Shaw's successor as the North Shore's fashionable country-house architect.[22]

Adler, who was born in Milwaukee in 1882, had worked for Shaw after

A copy of Giambologna's Winged Mercury *hailed a cab in many American estate gardens. Here he stands in a long canal in the "Spanish" garden at the Hugh J. McBirneys' "House of the Four Winds" in Lake Forest.*

The pink granite pillars of a belvedere designed by David Adler (1928) at the Alfred Hamills in Lake Forest are topped with nymphs by the American sculptor John Storrs. Hamill was a renowned bibliophile; the twirling staircases recall the stairs in an English gentleman's library.

his return from the Ecole des Beaux-Arts before setting up practice with his Beaux-Arts colleague and friend, Henry Dangler, in 1912.[23] Slight, shy, nervous, and handsome, Adler was a terrible, impatient draftsman, who made up for his technical drawbacks with a cameralike eye for scale and detail, and a creative worship of the past. Like Shaw and Platt, he was interested in every aspect of decoration and lifestyle, and often designed the gardens for his houses. That is to say, though not a gardener himself, he allowed room for elegant, formal garden spaces which were filled by Ellen Shipman,[24] Ferruccio Vitale,[25] and other well-known landscape architects or by the owners themselves.

One of Adler's earliest and finest garden essays, which still survives today, was for the Charles B. Pikes, in Lake Forest in 1917. A wide green sunken lawn is flanked, on the upper level, by rows of statues and the tight-clipped geometry of yews kept low. Like a dress rehearsal for the 1927 Richard Cranes' great roller coaster down to the Atlantic in Ipswich, Massachusetts, the Pikes' lawn spills down over the bluff, making the wide water horizon part of the garden. Sinking the lawn was a stroke of genius—it provides the perfect modicum of relief from all the flatness. The low, rectangular villa, very reminiscent of Platt and executed by Adler and Henry Dangler together, is made of pink-buff bricks softened still further by a worn coat of whitewash. On the entrance side is a walled courtyard garden, the perfect counterpoint to the stately water vista.[26]

The Charles B. Pikes' garden by David Adler (1917) boldly faces Lake Michigan.

A copy of Bertel Thorvaldsen's nineteenth-century work The Three Graces *terminates the broad main vista of the formal garden laid out by Percival Gallagher of Olmsted Bros. in 1920 at pharmaceutical manufacturer J. K. Lilly's "Oldfields" in Indianapolis. "Oldfields," which was a gift to the Indianapolis Museum of Art on Lilly's death, now houses the museum's decorative arts collection.*

Vernacular Formal Gardens

Not all the Italian gardens in the Midwest were such pure exercises in the villa form. At the turn of the century, Italians from Calabria came to the Greater Cleveland area in numbers and worked as laborers, gardeners, and cemetery caretakers. Angelo Palermo dug graves, lived on macaroni and beans, and attended sculpture classes at the Cleveland School of Art (now the Cleveland Institute). By the time World War I broke out, he had established his own gardening business, and by the early 1920s he was designing gardens in the new suburbs, known as the Heights. Palermo was a mason as well as a gardener.[27] His layouts were filled with flagstone and crazy paving, and with arches, bridges, fountains, walls, and curving flights of stairs all in the same monumentally rustic, closely fitted style. He worked as far south as Canton, Ohio, where, in a garden for E. A. Langenbach (c. 1925), he created an utterly original summerhouse on a bridge—a sort of homegrown Bridge of Sighs. At that time, the gardens of Walnut Hills and the various Heights, Euclid, Cleveland, and Shaker— were filled with "Italian" bridges, flower beds, and arbors designed by establishment landscape architects. It's as though Palermo seized on them, and transformed what he saw into vivid, vernacular approximations of their already translated selves.[28]

The Missouri River flows below the overlook that finishes the 1,000-foot central allée of the Joseph Desloges' "Vouziers" outside St. Louis, Missouri.

LEFT:

The clear blue of scores of agapanthus are the only flower color in this superb Italianate garden on only half an acre, designed in 1910 by Massachusetts architect Henry Ayling Phillips for the Irwin family of Columbus, Indiana.

A Château and a Villa in Missouri
Some formal gardens were in the French style. Inspiration for Joseph Desloge's seventeenth-century-style château, "Vouziers," in Florissant, ten miles north of St. Louis, came to him while serving in France during World War I near the town of Vouziers. He also met his wife-to-be there,

ABOVE:
Angelo Palermo, first of many Italian-Americans to start a landscaping business in Cleveland, designed this flowery garden in the twenties for the Charles J. Patersons of Euclid, Ohio. A party must be going on, to judge from the many motorcars back by the house.

who was a Red Cross nurse. They began construction of their new home on its 2,000 acres in 1925, and kept building this and that for another twenty-seven years. "Vouziers" today is still a private home.

"Some magnificent view of lake, river, valley or open prairie," said Ralph Rodney Root in 1924, and what "Vouziers" overlooks is the breathtaking confluence of the Missouri and Mississippi rivers, at the plain called Portage des Sioux, where for 5,000 years travelers have camped on their trans-American voyages—the route of Indian tribes, Marquette and Joliet, La Salle, Lewis and Clark, Daniel Boone, and the westering pioneers. Stone arrowheads still turn up daily in spring plowing. Joseph Desloge was a lead baron; he made a fortune in the Missouri mines

A stereopticon slide catches "Selma Hall" in spring, with a view of the old boxwood walk along the river bluffs. This old Italianate "castle" overlooks the Mississippi River at Festus, Missouri, south of St. Louis.

place. Ann Desloge Bates, daughter of Joseph, remembers that "During July and August, every evening at eight, a crew of seven men watered the box, and in winter the bushes were wrapped in burlap. During the second war, in 1940 and 41, it became impossible to get help, the boxwood died, and they were replaced with juniper." But "Vouziers" remained staggering. When English garden designer Russell Page flew into St. Louis, he spotted "Vouziers" from the air, and drove around and around until he found it.[29]

In Festus, south of St. Louis on the western bluffs of the Mississippi River, stands "Selma Hall," built in 1850 as "a copy of a villa on Lake Como." "Villa" here means a house and gardens in its earlier Andrew Jackson Downing incarnation, with a picturesque landscape instead of a formal garden. The formal gardens, arbor, and gazebo were created in the 1920s by Richmond landscape architect Charles Gillette for Mr. and Mrs. William Schock, according to family records.[30] Long known as "Kennett's Castle," after its builder, the crenelated white limestone building at one time surveyed 4,500 acres and five miles of Mississippi river frontage. The architect was George I. Barnett, who also designed Henry Shaw's "Tower Grove" in St. Louis, now the Missouri Botanical Garden. "Selma Hall" today belongs to the Mississippi River Fuel Corporation and is open to the public. The garden, which has vanished, lay deep in the valley below the house on the land side. Its strong circular pattern, hedged with evergreens more than six feet tall, was meant to be viewed from above. It formed a complex with the tennis court and pool; behind them were the vegetable garden and the farm barns—a compact, handsome estate ensemble when seen from the castle on the hill. Redbud and dogwood, punctuated with cedars, clothed the bluff's steep slope on the garden side. On top of the bluffs, near the house and running parallel to the river, once were long double lines of boxwood, marking the approaches to the castle from land and river. Like Missouri itself, "Selma Hall" is more than half Southern. Though it was founded on salt and lead mines, not on cotton, its builders' families were from Kentucky and Tennessee, and it was constructed by slave labor. There was even a separate kitchen building, sure sign of Southern plantation tradition. Its flamboyant history is one of duels and Union occupation; there is also the boxwood, Southern garden symbol supreme. Boxwood does not like St. Louis: it's either too hot and dry, or too cold and windy, so the shrub needs a lot of coddling, is very expensive, and frequently dies. But the late Mrs. Schock, like many St. Louisans of her day, was determined to have lots of the soft green bushes. According to her daughter-in-law, there was a nurseryman who regularly traveled up from New Orleans with a load of old boxwood which he would peddle to gardeners in St. Louis. He visited "Selma Hall" regularly, but it was only on his return down the Mississippi Valley that the canny Mrs. Schock would buy. She always made a deal to take all he was unable to sell upriver—for half the price.[31]

which, until the northern Minnesota ranges opened up, were the richest in metals in the West. A fortune was what was needed to create a house and garden to match the scale of the site. Shaded by maples, American elms, and beech trees, and without foundation planting, like a proper French château, the three-story mansard-roofed stone house looks rather starkly upon the river and the huge view. More than life-sized, just like everything else, a pair of bronze Great Danes guards the front door. A 1,000-foot allée of Siberian elms that leads from the house to the ballroom terrace is the backbone of the garden. From the balustraded stone terrace, the terminus of the allée, one views the Missouri River; beneath the terrace is the underground ballroom, which still frequently holds 140 people for a dinner dance. The ballroom's long French windows look out on a grass terrace, where a large fountain lined with pink marble sends a jet thirty feet in the air. There is also an outdoor proscenium theater, whose handsome two-story stone columns come from an old hotel, and an amphitheater that seats 500, which, during the thirties and forties, was actually used regularly for civic events as well as private musicales. The boxwood hedges that ran everywhere were the pride of the

The Edsel Fords and Jensen at "Gankler Pointe"

Edsel Ford, Henry Ford's son, and his wife, Eleanor Clay, said they wanted "a modest and picturesque home—not a palace or a fortress," for themselves and their four children when they decided to build "Gankler Pointe" on a beautiful 65-acre peninsula in Grosse Pointe Shores in 1926. Albert Kahn, their architect, and the Fords went to England, returning with oak staircases, mantels, paneling, building stones, and stone shingles—and English craftsmen. The sixty-room Tudor manor house, a bit more than a "modest home," is now a house museum; the gardens are presently being restored.

Jensen, who in 1914 had created the great landscape at "Fair Lane" for Henry Ford, was called in. Like "Fair Lane," or "Airdrie," in Kentucky, "Gankler Pointe" is an American palace garden that exalts the native

ABOVE:

In 1928, at the Edsel Fords' "Gankler Pointe" in Grosse Pointe Shores, Michigan, Jens Jensen planted the long island at right as a bird sanctuary with companionate trees and berried shrubs; the island banks were a tangle of native golden currant and wild roses. Nesting houses stood in the forest areas, and sand was dumped offshore to make shallow beaches for the birds.

landscape. Many of the features are the same in all three places. However, water on three sides of the house at "Gankler Pointe" meant Jensen, unusually, had to integrate the wooded drive, a great meadow, and formal gardens together into a smoothly flowing design on the landward side of the house. These elements are separated by his characteristic woodland plantings, with skirts of his favorite American flowering trees and shrubs—dogwood, shadblow, native plum, redbud, ninebark, and red-osier dogwood, among many others. The framework of the scalloped bays is sugar maples and elms; the tapestry of ground covers includes blue *Phlox divaricata*, yellow lady's-slipper, and the purple and yellow of violets, along with *Cornus canadensis* and *Trillium grandiflorum*, signature flowers of the northern woods. In 1928, the year after the house was finished, Jensen made a plan for "Bird Island," the unique feature of "Gankler Pointe." (When Jensen arrived in Chicago in 1886, he had been struck by the prairie, that great sea of grasses blazing with acres of purple phlox and burnt-orange rudbeckia still surrounding the city. During his fourteen years as a gardener in the park system, he made regular weekend trips to the prairie and the wooded bluffs of the North Shore. His familiarity with the entire Midwestern range of plants, his sensitivity to their individual personalities, to their growth habits, and their companions in the wild, all date to this long apprenticeship.) From

ABOVE AND LEFT:
*Jensen's "Great Meadow" at
Henry Ford's "Fair Lane,"
in Dearborn, Michigan, is
skirted by "stage wings" of
trees. The rock wall of the
boathouse on the Rouge River
is an example of Jensen's
finely striated work that looks
like a naturally occurring
Midwestern limestone
outcropping. Offshore is Clara
Ford's electric motor boat, the
Callie B.*

"Bird Island" one can wander back across the meadow and enter a trail of enclosures that includes a rectangular reflecting pool garden and a formal circular rose garden in a traditional wheel pattern. Here, just as at "Airdrie," Jensen successfully solved the Prairie Style problem of gardens that look man-made by hiding them within the woods at a distance from the house. Next to the rose garden is a tennis court enclosure and one of his famous natural-looking rock swimming pools.[1]

Fighting at "Fair Lane"

The problem had not been solved so felicitously at "Fair Lane," where in 1920 Jensen broke off abruptly with his biggest and most important private clients, Henry and Clara Ford, after a battle over the formal gardens she intended to superimpose on Jensen's prairie masterpiece. Ford had hired Jensen in 1914 to make a landscape on the 1,240 acres surrounding the big battlemented stone house then going up on the Rouge River only two miles from Ford's birthplace in Dearborn, and far from the fashionable suburbs of Grosse Pointe or Bloomfield.[2] Jensen got the job after Ford asked him what he would do with a newly arrived boxcar full of Scotch pine seedlings. Send them back, said Jensen, explaining he seldom used exotic species, especially evergreens, in the Midwestern landscape. They began with nearly treeless farmland. Jensen landscaped 60 acres, leaving 17 in lawn or meadow, with most of the rest planted as another of his great reforestation projects. The main elements of the scheme were a winding drive, after which "Fair Lane" is named, developments along the river, including a cascade, laid in rugged courses of Ohio limestone that looked like a naturally occurring Midwestern waterfall, and trail gardens—glade openings in the woods, that skirted three long meadows on the way to a council ring. The biggest of these meadows, on Jensen's 1915 plan labeled "The Path of the Setting Sun," where the sun drops into a distant notch of trees, could be called the grandest "sun lane" he ever created. Now known as The Great Meadow, it has been recognized as one of the supreme works of landscape art in this country.[3] Much has been written about The Great Meadow's dog-leg design, which creates a feeling of mysterious distance. But Jensen's detailed knowledge of Midwestern plants and the unornamented quality of his designs also contribute greatly to the general effect.[4] Of the 135 species of hawthorn, Jensen chose two, *Crataegus crus-galli* and *C. mollis,* which bloom one after the other, to plant together as the pivots of the meadow's woodland wings. Their constant counterpoint of slightly differing leaf shape and color draws the eye down the meadow and subtly enriches the prospect in a way two more contrasting species could never

RIGHT:
The Edward H. Haslers' "Aldingbourne Cottage" had a rustic pergola that covered the Spring Walk, which led from the west gate to the house, set on 2 acres designed by Jensen.

At the Edward L. Ryersons' "Havenwood" (1912) in Lake Forest, Jensen was the landscape architect and Howard Van Doren Shaw, with whom he often collaborated, was the architect of the house and the designer of the fountain with its four Italian statues, just visible in the foreground. Rose Standish Nichols later planted the borders for Mrs. Ryerson. Jensen made formal gardens on many estates, but unlike this one, they were usually set far from the house and screened in woods.

do. As at "Airdrie," Jensen used a tree instead of a statue or a temple as the terminus of his vista. Here, a group of white birch was planted, whose trunks emerge in winter as a focal point. (Birches are short-lived; this group will be replanted as part of the ongoing restoration which will return "Fair Lane" to Jensen's plan as far as can be practically implemented.)[5]

There were many other gardens. Jensen also made a grotto close to the house dedicated to Ford's friend, John Burroughs, the naturalist and writer. Ford and Burroughs were filmed laying the first stone, which came from Burroughs's New York home. When Burroughs died, Ford kept a lantern lit at the grotto for ten years. Most unusually, perhaps as a concession to Clara Ford's interest in flowers, Jensen made conventional formal gardens right next to the house, which included a blue garden and a rectangular rose garden. However, by 1920, Clara Ford had made little impression on the landscape; it reflected Henry Ford's interests in conservation, birding (there were feeding stations, 500 nesting houses, and a steam-heated birdbath in Burroughs's grotto), and wild landscape. It was also a masterpiece of prairie gardening.

That year, the house decoration completed, Clara Ford began to look outdoors. Like so many women of her era, she saw the gardens as her domain. Clara Ford did not brook opposition to her views. Throughout their fifty-nine-year marriage, Henry Ford often bowed to her interests, even claiming that he signed with the unions because she threatened to leave him if he didn't. Clara Bryant was a farmer's daughter, a neighbor of Henry Ford's in his youth. She, like her husband, never lost what amounted to a sturdy, almost pioneerlike belief in her own abilities and judgment.[6] She also had a lot of garden ideas, all of them bad, or at best pedestrian. Perhaps they look as dreadful as they do because of where she put them—right in the middle of a Jensen masterwork. Jensen, who considered "Fair Lane" essentially complete after six years' work, quit in a rage, and, though he worked again for the Fords, never at "Fair Lane."[7] The only parts of the garden that kept their looks were the blue garden, which stayed mostly blue, and the small rose garden. It retained its shape, but was redesigned by Ellen Shipman in 1927 as a handsome English garden, that is to say with flower beds of perennials and annuals, a teahouse, lilac hedges, and Japanese flowering cherries. "No statues," said Clara Ford to Shipman, perhaps the only thing she ever said with which Jensen would have agreed.[8] Clara Ford went about systematically making a display garden with compartments full of showy flowers. Like many collectors, she always wanted to have the newest kinds, and every variety, of whatever she planted. First was a waving acre of peonies, 1,200 plants of 40 varieties, oddly placed beyond the service drive in 1921. In 1922 she ripped up the beautiful closely laid limestone courses of Jensen's lily pool/rock garden/cascade ensemble on the river, and replaced them with crazy paving and a European-style alpine rock

garden. Along the trail gardens, among the shadblow, gray dogwood, and wild grapevine, she planted delphinium and dahlias, and bordered the most distant glade with yellow tea roses. But all this was nothing to her rose garden, which occupied the entire flat length of the second meadow.[9] The ruins remain today. An old aerial photograph shows rings and colonies of roses dotting the turf like so many fungal growths spotting a Petri dish in a laboratory. Twelve thousand bushes, 300 standards, and 400 climbers, 350 varieties in all, covered nearly 3 acres, all visible at one horrifying glance from the entrance casino. Henry Ford would not let her touch The Great Meadow because he found it restful to walk alone there at the end of a hard day.[10]

The fate of Jensen's gardens was almost always to be remodeled. Why? First, his designs did not include the sort of permanent architectural features that make even the most extravagant remodeler think twice about removing them. He also failed to take into account the gardener's eternal itch to improve the garden—a sort of gardener's agoraphobia. His large, luminous, simple spaces often must have made their owners antsy to fill them up. There was room for more in a Jensen landscape, and more they would have. Ideally, Jensen's gardens were to be started by Jensen and finished by nature and time. Over and over on Jensen's plans one finds the notation, "This plan will suffer in composition if any changes are made in the planting." Essentially, all the gardener had to do was prevent invasive and unwanted species from taking over, or interrupting the natural succession. Fletcher Steele, that sharp observer of human nature, dealt with the same problem differently. He added to gardens over many years only partly because of the staggering costs; he also knew that his clients had to have something to fiddle with. Perhaps Jensen's spaces were too grandly theoretical and too simple to suit the social needs of some of his private clients, especially the imperious hostesses of the era.

Jensen's vision sprang from the largest natural American spaces, the prairies and woodlands. The almost narrative flow of his gardens, his perfect control of mass plantings, and of ground and horizon lines, are best shown off in his largest works, such as "Airdrie," "Gankler Pointe," and "Fair Lane." His small gardens are not so resoundingly successful. There is something cramped about a council ring stuck off at the end of just one acre, or the "trail" that goes nowhere but around the smallish lawn through the woods. The lengthy Midwestern oscillation between the Prairie Style and the formal garden is most often described as a struggle, but it is better viewed as the parallel development of different spaces and different resources. In the long run, the virtue of the formal garden is the plan: the sequence of enclosures that gives mystery and an air of additional space to any garden, no matter how small. The Prairie Style's lasting gift to the American garden was not design, but planting, the use of native trees and shrubs as the backbone of the garden, and the recognition of the beauty of plants' life cycles.

A city-by-city survey of Midwestern estates turns up other rationales for making gardens, many of them more national in application than the Prairie Style/formal garden debate. Far more illuminating than a forced march through every Midwestern state is a look at the entire region, grouping gardens loosely by types. There were bucolic gentlemen farmers' estates, where the garden was only a small part of the show. There were English manor gardens, where their owners imagined they were re-creating earlier, simpler, saner times. There were resort gardens just for the summer. Finally, in the Midwest as everywhere in the U.S., there were those few great gardens made for the sake of gardening, assemblages of plants grown for curiosity and love.

GENTLEMEN FARMERS IN THE MIDWEST

"The farm" was always an important part of any estate, and the tradition of upper-class interest in agricultural improvements inherited from England had been part of American estate life since George Washington and Thomas Jefferson's day at least, a faint but clear echo of Virgil's *Georgics*.[1] The Webbs' "Shelburne Farms" in Vermont, or Marshall Field's "Caumsett" on Long Island, or R. J. Reynolds "Reynolda" in North Carolina, and many others like them, were model farms that brought the pastoral ideal to new grandeur, and expense. In those halcyon pre–income tax days, there was no need to show a profit every five years, or to keep losing money to maintain tax benefits! The farming was serious and the competition at flower shows and county fairs and livestock shows was cutthroat. But the purpose of such farms was pleasure. Two "farms" in Missouri and Wisconsin illustrate how the garden fit in.[2]

"Long's barns were better than most people's houses," says historian, art critic, and *Kansas City Star* reporter Donald Hoffman about lumber baron Robert A. Long's "Longview Farm," begun in 1912, eighteen miles south of Kansas City, Missouri.[3] When Long's company, Long-Bell, became the largest lumber company in the world, Long bought 1,700 acres of rolling farmland, "scenery that only wanted a castle, or a gentleman's seat here and there interspersed to have equaled some of the most celebrated park scenery of England,"[4] and spent $2.5 million on his own "gentleman's seat." Long toured the dairy farms of Wisconsin and Illinois and the horse farms of Kentucky, and then commissioned Henry Ford Hoit, of the Kansas City architectural firm of Van Brunt and Howe, to design the forty buildings needed for his dream farm. There were nine horse barns, including the harness horse and show stable, which was the largest barn west of the Mississippi when it was built in 1912. Thirty miles of whitewashed Kentucky board fences enclosed the property; it took eight men, full time, to keep them white. (For Long's surprised neighbors, even barbed wire fences in good repair were a luxury.)[5] Every building on the place was white stucco with a red tile roof, a beautiful contrast with the green Missouri hills. "Longview" was always on view. A

BELOW:
A panoramic photograph shows the front garden at lumber baron Robert A. Long's "Longview Farm" (1912). A throwback—but a beautiful one—to the old Victorian days of bedding-out, this garden was as meticulously manicured as the rest of Long's 1,700 acres, a model farm on the grandest scale.

*The Farm,
the Manor,
the Resort, the
Escape from
the City,
the Gardener's
Garden*

267

bankers' convention of 6,000 came to visit one day in 1916, a real estate convention of 2,500 in 1920, and regularly scheduled livestock and horse shows (there was both a race track and horse-show grounds) to raise money for local charities, were among the many public events over the years. A special camp, with permanent buildings on the grounds and a round-the-clock staff of ten to twelve nurses, was held every summer for two weeks for unwed mothers and their babies. Eight people were kept on staff as tour guides for those who wished to visit "Longview," any day except Sundays.[6]

The formal flower garden, designed by Hare and Hare, was more like a municipal garden than a private one. The landscape was wide open: 300 acres of lawn meant there was little sense of privacy or seclusion. On the south side of "the big house," and separated from it by the drive, which had electric lights on lampposts, just like a park or city street, was a large sunken garden. It was laid out in perfectly mounded Victorian crescents and scallops and curves of bedding-out plants encircling a brick-edged pool filled with water lilies and a small fountain. Classical benches of white marble and small standard trees in Versailles tubs kept the level uniformly low. By 1916 when this garden was made, such Victorian style had passed from the private to the public domain (where it still finds a place). The 1890s are when the curvaceous bedding-out era in fashionable private gardens began definitely to give way to "old-fashioned" gardens of perennials and annuals set within the "Italian" framework of walls and balustrades popularized by Wharton and Platt, and the many shelter magazine articles on the subject. As though the passage of twenty-five years had allowed a settling process to take place, "Longview's" throwback parterre is surprisingly beautiful.[7]

"Lone Tree Farm"

A dairy farm on the grand scale (1,100 acres) with a homemade formal garden was what the Victor Lawsons of Chicago created on beautiful Green Lake, in central Wisconsin, in 1888. Jessie Lawson was eccentric, strong-minded, very religious, and a semi-invalid. With no love for Chicago society, she spent her summers at "Lone Tree Farm,"[8] while Victor, who was the founder of Associated Press, came up on weekends. "Lone Tree Farm" was Jessie's refuge as well as her occupation. She was still building and adding in 1913 when her eccentricity gave way to madness. She died in 1914, but Victor Lawson maintained the estate till his death in 1925. Today, "Lone Tree Farm" is the Greenlake Conference Center, run by the American Baptists.

Jessie Lawson collected animals the way other Gilded Age Americans collected paintings. There were doves, all kinds of chickens, turkeys, geese, black-and-white swans, many dogs, and a balky white donkey bought from a circus going out of business. A special graveyard was set aside just for the Lawson carriage horses. There were two herds of cows,

Jerseys and Guernseys, and Mrs. Lawson held white glove inspections. If a finger came up dusty, off went the cow to be washed. In a state that has many big barns, the Lawson's Guernsey barn was the biggest of all, standing magnificently at the main entrance as if to say "This is a Farm." Tall Palladian windows ornamented the gable ends, and majestic tile silos stood at either side. Hideous but enthralling, "Lone Tree Farm's" squarish, stuccoed, green-tiled architectural style was all its own, and owed little either to the Prairie School or to the Beaux-Arts. In addition to the farm buildings, there was a boathouse, what was called a "Tee House" for the nine-hole golf course, and no less than seven tile-topped water towers. The pace of building was feverish to suit its owner's obsessive demands. Harold Mitchell, today's director of operations, remembered the day-to-day construction he witnessed as a child, saying of Mrs. Lawson, "She knew how to whip a crew—I wish I could dig the old gal up!"[9] So far, no architect or landscape architect has been unearthed; credit must go to Jessie Lawson and to a Mr. Cohen, a resident engineer. The water towers (no one can really say why so many were built) and the miles of boulder walls are what make the handsome park landscape an unforgettable sight. Scattered on the grounds are other typical estate garden features such as an outdoor theater, and the remains of a lily pool with a gazebo and a rustic bridge. The formal garden, which survives in outline today, is a large grassy square inlaid with bright geometric beds of flowers, mostly annuals, tucked below a boulder retaining wall at least fifteen feet high and facing the lake. On the level above is an elaborate conservatory[10] and terraces with more flower beds and fruit trees, right alongside the chicken houses, tool sheds, farm hands' quarters, and a brick-paved horse yard. Like the gardens at "Selma Hall," in Missouri, this garden is part of a large, decorative toy, the home farm complex.[11]

ENGLISH GARDENS—WHICH GENERALLY ENDED UP ECLECTIC

In the South, estate makers relied heavily on a single regional model, the plantation. In the Midwest, there was no single model to refer to, but rather a collection of architectural and garden design daydreams. One of the most popular of these was the English manor, an idea that owed much of its early twentieth-century vitality to William Morris and the Arts and Crafts Movement, and to Edwin Lutyens and Gertrude Jekyll. Like the plantation, the English manor ideal was more than an architectural style. Half-timbering and casement windows implied a wholesome family life on the land, aristocratic culture and pleasures, and permanence. Of course there were numbers of Georgian brick manors, too. The gardens surrounding these various houses are difficult to categorize. They were as eclectic as English gardens in England themselves became at the time, with their various enclosures dedicated not only to different colored flowers and plants' different cultural requirements, but to different cultures—Japanese, for example. Seven gardens in Ohio, Illinois, and Michigan illustrate the range.

"Winding Creek Farm," Julius and Dorette Fleischmann's 1,600-acre place, was created in the mid-twenties as one of the biggest and most elaborate estates in the newly formed Camargo Club's 12,000-acre tract outside Cincinnati, now Indian Hill. This planned development and real estate venture was begun in 1924 by a group of Cincinnati investors, some of whom already owned property on the run-down farmlands east of the city. Cincinnati's elite flocked to Camargo. In the twenties, ten estates were built for between $500,000 and $1 million dollars (land ran $150 to $200 an acre), and by 1930 there were sixty houses. Trainloads of fertilizer improved the worn-out farmland, and two polo fields, a large riding stable, tennis courts, a shooting range, and a golf course were built.[12] In 1925, a pack of English foxhounds was presented to the newly founded Camargo Hunt by Fleischmann, known as "Junky," one of the principal movers of Camargo and the third generation of the Fleischmann Yeast Company.[13] The pack was kenneled at "Winding Creek Farm," where Cincinnati architect Stanley Matthews[14] designed a magnificent limestone building for it, not to mention stables and barns and a limestone manor house with tall gables and traceried windows for the Fleischmanns. The gardens and grounds, designed in 1926 by A. D. Taylor of Cleveland, who did many other well-known Cincinnati gardens,[15] were a match for the house and stables. Out front, there was a cobbled courtyard big enough to hold hounds, hunt staff, and a field of fifty or more mounted foxhunters. In the gardens, a line of formal enclosures ran parallel to this romantic flight of fantasy, a long moated wall topped with a wide grassy walk that connected the house terrace to a gazebo.[16] Though the views from this parapet were of the beautiful Ohio fields and woods, the flavor of "Winding Creek Farm" was definitely English, down to the sound of the hounds in kennels. It seemed like a Norman fortified demesne that had softened through the centuries, moving from crenelated wall and defense moat to Lutyensesque pleasure garden. (However, as was so often the case, aging had in fact happened overnight.) Nurserymen all over the United States hustled to fill the Midwestern millionaires' demands for full-grown trees. Fleischmann was one of the satisfied customers mentioned by the Long Island firm of Lewis and Valentine in a form letter entitled, "Special Letter to List of Chicago Millionaires, Send Special Delivery, Marked Personal," a list that also included Pierre du Pont, Otto Kahn, Charles Schwab, E. T. Stotesbury, and other Midwesterners such as Cyrus McCormick.[17]

Largest of all the English manor types is "The Farms," Robert Allerton's 12,000-acre estate on the Sangamon River near Monticello, in central Illinois, of which about 1,600 acres were laid out in formal gardens and a gigantic sculpture garden. Allerton was the only son of

English Ham House was the direct inspiration for Robert Allerton's "Allerton House" (1900) at "The Farms," 12,000 acres of Illinois countryside and farmland.

energetic, civic-minded Samuel Allerton, Chicago livestock baron, a go-getter Mayflower descendent, who made a fortune on hog sales to the Union Army during the Civil War. Samuel grew up poor in Amenia, New York, and became a founder of both the Chicago Union Stockyards and the First National Bank of Chicago. He also amassed huge tracts of Illinois real estate. His son, Robert, went to St. Paul's School in Massachusetts, and then took off to study in Munich and Paris to become a painter. Already a stern art critic at twenty-four, he judged he would never succeed as an artist, so, burning all his canvases and leaving bohemian life behind, he came home, and in 1897 took on his father's gift, "The Farms." His garden would become his occupation; it provided him with the outlet both for his own talents as a collector and connoisseur, and with a lifetime of friends, associates, and companions, who helped him shape his vast creation. Inspiration began in England, with Ham House, outside London on the Thames, as a model for Allerton's architect, his art-school colleague, John Borie. The Illinois house was finished in 1900. Today it is a conference center for the University of Illinois, and the gardens, home park, forest, and a 50-acre stretch of prairie are open to the public.[18]

The restrained, early Georgian-style brick house sits at the very edge of a pond, overlooking two straight brick-faced terraces which make a platform from which to enjoy the beautiful landscape park. A pergola and peach orchard screen the kitchen wing as one walks toward the processional allée leading to the formal gardens, set far away from the

The Walter Brewsters' "Covin Tree" in Lake Forest was landscaped by Mrs. Brewster around their Lutyensesque house designed by Howard Van Doren Shaw.

house. A traditional kitchen garden laid out in 1902 and known as the Brick Garden, which was later used briefly as a rose garden and is now filled with annuals, provided the starting point for other enclosures that would eventually stretch for miles. They evolved as a series of rectangles, strung along the axis of the Brick Garden. Many are filled with strict evergreen geometric patterns in privet, including one based on the Chinese character for good luck—Allerton enjoyed telling his friends he'd copied the motif off his Chinese silk pajamas. There is also a long, hedged flower garden, mostly hardy iris and peonies. The greenhouse is cleverly worked into the formal garden scheme. In 1922 Allerton met John Gregg, a young architectural student at the University of Illinois, who became his lifelong companion and eventually his adopted son.[19] The conventional English estate garden began to take on exotic dimensions with Gregg's new gardens, which focused primarily on Art Deco and Asian decorative objects. The Garden of the Fu Dogs was his first, a long allée of Colorado white firs, with two lines of bright blue ceramic nineteenth-century Chinese dogs, and a vine-covered garden house for a pair of gold-leafed Buddhas. In the same year, 1922, Gregg added a serene sunken garden, walled with pyramidal arborvitae, to the end of the long enfilade of existing topiary gardens. In 1932 he redesigned it as a Balinese garden, walled-in pines, with tall temple pillars framing the view back through the older gardens.

During the twenties Allerton had bought a great deal of contemporary sculpture. The two largest pieces, Emile Antoine Bourdelle's *Death of the Last Centaur* (1914), and Carl Milles's *The Sun Singer*, demanded that gardens be created especially for them. Bourdelle's monumental gold-flecked piece was placed in a clearing a mile from the end of the formal gardens. Its brooding presence is strongly framed by dark Canadian hemlocks and white oaks, whose leaves turn blood-red in autumn. The purchase of *The Sun Singer*, Milles's Apollo, was a magnificent mistake. Allerton and Gregg thought they had ordered a half-size casting of the piece they had seen in the harbor in Stockholm, but when the immense crate arrived, there was an exact duplicate of the harbor version, over sixteen feet tall, and weighing 1,600 pounds. Big enough to peer in the second-story windows, it was hardly a tractable garden object. Allerton and Gregg solved the problem brilliantly by extending the garden axis another mile from the *Centaur*, to a high open pasture. Gregg designed a dramatic circular base inspired by the Altar of Heaven in Peking's Forbidden City. With his huge bronze arms uplifted toward the rising sun *The Sun Singer* stands alone in the wide fields, silhouetted against the sky. Last of Gregg's designs carried out at "The Farms,"[20] it is the most striking, original, and effective.[21]

Allerton was necessarily interested in what would grow in his harsh climate and as soon as he took possession of "The Farms" he began to plant in the Prairie Style.[22] He used native species in the formal gardens:

his Rodin *Adam* was backed with elm and hackberry. The woods were planted with thousands of wild flowers and bulbs, with fritillaries and wild ginger among the native jack-in-the-pulpit and columbine. He massed sumac, honey locust, and shingle oak, all swagged with summer fox grapes, along the drives. In 1915 Wilhelm Miller wrote, "The Allerton drives are the mellowest and purest examples of roadside planting in the prairie country with which I am acquainted."[23] Not all ran smoothly: Allerton tried box in the Chinese maze, but soon had to retreat to the tough Amur privet. Beaten down by the climate, the English gardener hired in 1902 took to drink, was sacked, and retired to Phoenix (surely no more hospitable for gardening than central Illinois).[24] But Allerton and Gregg kept on, slowly transforming the English manor house and landscape park into a Shangri-la, a passionately eclectic, Art Deco-flavored, American estate garden.

Mrs. Brewster, Landscape Gardener

Charitable, social, clever, Mrs. W. J. Brewster of Lake Forest, Illinois, also had the luck to look like a Greuze nymph, according to her admirer Arthur Meeker. But behind those poetic blue eyes and fragile air he claimed there was a will of steel.[25] She needed it to wrestle a beautiful garden out of the entirely flat, treeless, cut-over 25 acres in Lake Forest where architect Howard Van Doren Shaw built a long low English house, "Covin Tree." One can see Shaw's admiration for Lutyens in the careful, agreeable use of contrasting materials (small yellow brick and smoothly

At "Stan Hywet" in Akron, Ohio, Gertrude Seiberling gazes over the "West Lookout." To Warren Manning, the landscape architect who orchestrated that tremendous view of farmland and woods, it symbolized the best of America's westering instincts and wide opportunities.

The Farm, the Manor, the Resort, the Escape from the City, the Gardener's Garden

cut stone), and the classic but nicely varied rhythm of the fenestration. Shaw, who designed many gardens around his houses, sited the building on a low terrace, with a striking balustrade to emphasize the tiny change in elevation. The single natural feature was a shapeless farm pond. Mrs. B. took the landscaping in hand herself,[26] fringing the water's edge with flags and other wild bog plants, and introducing a couple of swans for ripples. Out back, she designed an informal garden around a strong central axis. She made screens of trees and poked peepholes in them. She invented her principal view by planting out most of it, and putting as many tantalizing obstacles in the way of the rest as she could. Walls with gates to look through, and a U-shaped arbor arched with vines made the twelve-foot-wide chunk of remaining skyline-meets-Illinois exciting.[27] (In the terrace wall was a statue, *St. Brigid*, by Shaw's daughter, Silvia Shaw Judson, one of the favorite garden sculptors of her generation.) There were three separate enclosure gardens for April, May, and June; each was planted strictly for that month and never visited at all the rest of the year.[28]

Warren Bicknell

Warren Bicknell's Jacobean house, "Beacon Hill,"[29] in Cleveland, Ohio, sat on its lawn looking north, where the trees were kept well pruned to allow what is called, on the Olmsted Bros.'s plan of 1921, "A Glimpse of Lake Erie." Although comparatively small,[30] the garden was literally a prize winner, gaining the Landscape Architecture Medal in 1922 at the exhibition of the Architectural League of New York.[31] It was described as a "formal English garden,"—a term understandable only if one admits Italianate water stairs to the category.[32] The beautiful Cleveland garden ran in terraces, steps, fountains, and pools down a ravine south of the house. The leafy shade of tall woodland plantings to either side made the small water jets and falls look whiter, sound louder. Every feature of an estate garden was fitted in; a square rose garden stood at the top, a grape arbor made the transition to a terraced vegetable garden at the bottom, a swimming pool disguised as a reflecting pool was part of the garden's descent, and a tennis court lay hidden off in the trees to the south.

"Cranbrook"

Half-timbered "Cranbrook," north of Detroit in Bloomfield Hills, was to become more than a family seat, but that was how it began. Out of its Arts and Crafts beginnings, it became the great hatchery of American design, which produced artists and craftsmen such as Harry Bertoia, Florence Knoll, and Charles Eames. Cranbrook House and Gardens are only part of the 300-acre complex of schools, ateliers, and art colony. In the early twentieth century, Bloomfield Hills could be called the only socially acceptable suburb of Detroit that was not on Lake St. Clair, with Henry Ford as the solitary Dearborn pioneer. Ellen Scripps Booth, of the

Scripps-Howard newspaper chain family, and George Booth, president of the *Detroit News*, bought a run-down farm in 1904 as a summer place for their family of five. The first thing they did was to name the place "Cranbrook," after the Kentish village from which the Booth family had emigrated sixty years before. Booth, an architect *manqué*, who was later the founder of the Detroit Arts and Crafts Society, made the original house plan for Detroit architect Albert Kahn. The large and cozy looking dwelling, with bulging bays and leaded casement windows, was completed in 1908. The gardens on the nearly treeless hill were divided into different enclosures by changes in level, hedges, and walls, which were mainly constructed of the glacial limestone that cluttered the site. In 1922 Czech sculptor Mario Korbel carved many statues for the gardens, including the smoothly neoclassical *Harmony, Dawn, Eve,* and *Morning and Evening*. There are other original works, superb ornaments like the pair of eighteenth-century lead sphinxes from Osmaston Manor, in Derbyshire, and craft work done at "Cranbrook" itself. The most successful garden is the simple Pine Hill Cascade, which was constructed by seventy-year-old Henry Booth, George Booth's father, with an assistant, in 1914. The semicircular stone theater holds 400 people. The dedication ceremonies in 1916 included a masque with a cast of over 100 and a chorus of 40. The large scale of the theater gives a clue to the evolving nature of "Cranbrook." At the same time that the Booth's were making their gardens, the idea for a utopian community in the form of an American Arts and Crafts enterprise was taking shape. (The family would eventually invest over $20 million in the "Cranbrook" experiment.)[33] In 1932, the famous Academy of Art was founded, which used the American Academy in Rome as a model. Finnish architect Eliel Saarinen was chief architect and first president; Carl Milles was head of the sculpture department. But as a garden, "Cranbrook" is too full of statues and walls. One senses didacticism at work: statues and fountains—perhaps even flowers and trees—are there to enlighten, not to give pleasure. There is a self-consciousness, a sense of moral uplift here that prevents the place from being what all gardens should be: an escape, a pleasure, and a work of art.[34]

"Stan Hywet"

At "Stan Hywet," in Akron, Ohio, Frank A. Seiberling, founder of Goodyear Tire and Rubber, commissioned his manor gardens and landscape from Warren Manning, the landscape architect who passed the flame from Frederick Law Olmsted to Fletcher Steele, Charles Gillette, Bryant Fleming, A. D. Taylor, and Dan Kiley, all of whom trained in his Massachusetts-based firm. Manning and Seiberling, continually corresponding and exchanging ideas, worked with the same elements as the Booths at "Cranbrook": a Tudor house,[35] a deep affection for the Arts and Crafts movement, a determination to create an enduring family seat, a

Most of Cyrus McCormick's great lakeside estate, "Walden," in Lake Forest
was the work of Warren Manning beginning in 1894, but this charming
formal flower garden was the work of Pittsburgh landscape architect Ralph
Griswold in 1902.

The Farm,
the Manor,
the Resort, the
Escape from
the City,
the Gardener's
Garden

273

formal garden design, a severe climate—and a great deal of money. Unlike "Cranbrook," "Stan Hywet" is one of the great estate gardens of America. It is also Manning's best surviving work for a private client, displaying his sensitivity to place and his vast vocabulary of plant knowledge. The exquisite landscape is presently being restored to reflect Manning's design intentions, and the house and gardens are open to the public today.[36]

Frank Seiberling is one of the legendary American successes. In 1898 he borrowed $3,500 and made the rounds of his Akron neighbors to interest them in Dr. Benjamin Franklin Goodyear's languishing twenty-year-old scheme to use rubber commercially. Those few who went along with Seiberling saw their Goodyear Tire and Rubber stock multiply 10,000 times in the next twenty-five years—$10,000 ballooned to $1 million. By 1911 Seiberling himself was already a very rich man. He believed in America, in American business, American energy, American opportunity. Why not an American country place, and American aesthetics? In Warren Manning, Seiberling picked exactly the right landscape designer for the job. In keeping with the spirit of their times, both men believed that the best was possible in their world. "To him [Manning] the world was and would be good—exasperating and often strangely blind and temporarily stupid, but always good. . . . No trait was more endearing in Mr. Manning than his nervous exasperation when he saw evidence that an individual, a community, or a nation was refusing to do something for its own good; and he was always sure in his creative mind just what that something should be."[37]

Born in 1860, Manning was fifty-one and well-established in public and private practice by the time of the "Stan Hywet" commission. By 1911, he had created estate gardens all the way from Long Island's Gold Coast to Tennessee, Georgia, Minnesota, and Illinois.[38] (He also did small private gardens on occasion, for which he made no charge—such works were listed in the office as "love jobs.")[39] At the time of the "Stan Hywet" project, he had just finished the symmetrical, classical gardens of "Gwinn" with Charles Platt, and, in Chattanooga, Tennessee, at Lookout Mountain, he had used the huge natural rock outcroppings, and Piedmont trees, shrubs, and wild flowers to frame the views of the Tennessee River far below.[40] Although the taste of the times ran to lavish European garden ornament, and Manning's gardens certainly contained their share of imported fountains, statues, and urns, the real ornaments of his works were the plants, especially American ones. Plants were never "plant material" for Manning. Nowhere is this better displayed than at "Stan Hywet."

On a summer afternoon in 1920, driving up the winding Seiberling driveway (the estate acreage fluctuated, running as high at times as 4,000 acres), it wouldn't have been the long-drawn-out façade of the Tudor house, unfolding its 300 feet in a procession of gables, wings, and

Elizabethan brick chimneys, that first took your attention. Instead, your eye would have been caught by the squat, frosty-green old apple trees, the remains of a farm orchard, left at the entrance by Manning "to preserve the rural character of the estate." Next came the wide uninflected lawn, a real Midwestern space with barely a roll to it. No sheep-cropped English greensward this; Manning's planting plan calls for grasses of different heights on different sections of the lawn. Finally came the house itself, deep in the high shade of American chestnuts already growing on the site and of the spreading fans of American elms, transplanted full-grown by Manning to give "the long-established character" Seiberling desired.[41] South of the house runs an allée of London plane, rhododendron, and azalea, which terminates in a niche of pine trees. Northward is one of Manning's best effects, a cathedral nave of white birches ending in twin teahouses that frame a view across the lagoon pond to steep hills.[42] The so-called lagoons, drowned quarries, are what Manning felt would give "Stan Hywet" its greatest distinction, and here he did some of his most inspired naturalistic plantings on the quarry faces. (All these gardens, changed by growth and loss, will benefit from the ongoing interpretive restoration.)

Closely integrated with the house design are the myriad enclosures of the Arts and Crafts layout, the ten-foot-deep perennial borders, the rose garden, the Japanese garden, and so on.[43] In the English garden, the walls, walks, and verdigris square-topped trellis arches were designed by Manning, with plantings by Ellen Shipman, whom Manning proposed for the job, telling the Seiberlings she was "one of the best, if not the very best Flower Garden Maker in America."[44] The English garden was Mrs. Seiberling's favorite, where she retreated (the Seiberlings had six children) to think, read, and write poetry. There is also a breakfast garden, where once the yellow and blue planting scheme matched the Fiestaware indoors. A visitor can move smoothly from one garden to another; the various compartments are interwoven with the interior spaces, making a living net of sunny and shady spots, of places to have tea, or play croquet or bowls, or just to be alone. "Stan Hywet" was the hub of Akron; the Seiberlings' house guests included four U.S. presidents (Taft, Harding, Coolidge, and Hoover), and a raft of celebrities, scientists, and artists, from Will Rogers, Helen Keller, and Thomas Edison, to Rosa Ponselle and Paderewski.

Manning and the architect, Charles F. Schneider, had worked closely together, siting the house for views. On the long western elevation, the skein of garden enclosures gives way to a pair of broad terraces and a cut through the woods. The sense of space is immense: thousands and thousands of acres of Ohio farmland, orchard, and wood are visible from the top of this sandstone escarpment. Manning thinned the woods on either side, accenting the beautiful silhouettes of the original forest trees, some stagheaded, some with the long angular branches that are the sign of a tree reaching for the light. One hears Manning quoting Jefferson on the bounty of the American landscape: "we have only to cut out the superabundant plants...."[45] Manning was the least heavy handed, the most poetic, of landscape architects.[46] Although one knows from his extensive correspondence with Seiberling[47] that the west terrace view was planned to evoke the idea of "the American West's unlimited possibility for individuals of vision, energy and enterprise," there is no inscription in the floor of the overlook, no statue of a boy looking west, or a girl with a sheaf of corn. Just the immensity of woods, fields, horizon, and western sky does the job without words, a landscape metaphor.

The Mini-Manor of Standish Backus

Plants were the stars of Warren Manning's gardens, but Fletcher Steele loved space better—and the illusion of space even more. On Standish Backus's narrow 5-acre strip of land in Grosse Pointe Shores, Michigan, around the bulky forty-room English Gothic mansion designed by Ralph Cram, Steele created a garden in seven parts that sustained the illusion of many manorial acres. It was not at all an English garden, however. English garden ornament and Elizabethan garden design details were used, but the crispness and wit were Fletcher Steele's best French idiom.[48] He used trick perspectives worthy of André Le Nôtre, and worked out his most elegant variation on the cubist gardens that had inspired him in Paris in 1925. The Backus garden was one of the three Steele considered his best works when he summed up his career.

Standish Backus was Steele's ideal client: a man quite sure he could afford whatever Steele designed, a man who, as a child, had sketched the houses and castles of Europe and dreamed of being an architect before becoming a successful lawyer and businessman. For Backus, as for so many garden makers of the period, men and women alike, it was a creative outlet. Above all, for Backus, it was an absorbing playground where experiment was possible and decisions not irrevocable, where he could happily try out the beaverboard maquettes provided by Steele for architectural features, or take a trip to local nurseries, hunting for specimens with Steele's assistant, Virginia Cavendish. Backus was, for all intents and purposes, the job foreman as well as the obsessed client. "This place is a bloody, muddy mess," Backus wrote to Steele in 1934, six years into the job. "I am home with a ptomaine attack in my ptummy. There are a steam shovel and two or three motor trucks engaged in transporting the East Mound to the South Stage.... As I wrote you before, we are following the contour lines on your blueprints just as closely as little steam shovel is able, and when we get it polished off by hand, it ought to look just as you have indicated."[49] Backus was willing to listen to any wild idea Steele proposed, including one for a garden entrance: a pair of red marble posts, each topped, perhaps appropriately

enough for the organizer of the Cadillac Motor Car Company, with a car headlight shining straight up. He was also perfectly willing to turn anything down if he didn't like it (the pillars were never executed), but what both men seem to enjoy most was discussion—in person, by telegram, and by mail. Their correspondence runs to 500 letters. Toward the end of Backus's life, Steele wrote him, saying "I imagine that in some ways you feel as I do—that the building and planning is almost better than the finished job with nothing much to do with it except enjoy the fruit of the work. It is harder for me to sit down and enjoy things than it is to work at them."[50]

Out of this close, playful (and argumentative) collaboration between two boyishly restless Americans came "The Long Shot," a narrowing vista garden, whose triangular bays hid brilliant patterns of flowers which only became visible to the delighted garden stroller walking down the lawn. Turning around at the far point, one saw the full collection of gardens. The plantings, all in different colors, were linked by a front line of gray: artemisia, veronica, lamb's-ears, and santolina. This was a trick Steele had picked up from Beatrix Farrand, who herself was perhaps inspired by Gertrude Jekyll. Describing a Farrand garden in Bar Harbor, Steele writes, "... in one respect her planting was more knowing than ours. In order to keep the color keyed up, Mrs. Farrand had hidden so far as possible, the green foliage of the perennials behind the whitish grey leaves of common and uncommon grey-foliage plants.... the effect was as much gayer and brighter than the usual planting as a luminous Monet is more full of light than a Claude."[51] One forgets how much cross-pollination of ideas must have gone on all across the country. The garden owners made yearly pilgrimages from home to summer place, and visited their friends within the nationwide network of family, social, club (especially The Garden Club of America), and business interests that knit them surprisingly tightly together. The professionals also shared their clients' lifestyles and followed the same social circuit. Designers often worked with each other in the same gardens—or on top of each other, as gardens were added or replaced.

MIDWESTERN RESORTS

Grosse Pointe: A Summer Cottage Colony Becomes Detroit's Year-Round Gold Coast

Grosse Pointe was originally cut up into "ribbon farms" as early as 1701 by French settlers from Quebec, the first permanent white inhabitants of Detroit. Each farm had water frontage of a few hundred feet on Lake St. Clair and ran from one to three miles back into the wilderness. These "long lots" would later give rise to many innovative garden plans, such as the Standish Backus garden, as designers tried to maneuver around the large houses which always threatened to throttle the skinny sites.

Like Bar Harbor, Grosse Pointe's life as a resort began in a small way before the Civil War in 1846, but wasn't widely fashionable as a "summer place" till the 1870s. For 200 years Detroit had developed slowly, calling itself "the most beautiful city in America" by 1890. Its best neighborhood was a couple of lines of Victorian mansions set behind iron fences on handsome boulevards, just like every other middle-sized American city of the Midwest.[52] By 1900, its elite "formed a moderate-sized community, conservative, complacent, provincial and yet urbane, closely knit by ties of intermarriage. In 1900 the population was 280,000. Old Detroiters will tell you this was the Golden Age of the city."[53] Then came Henry Ford—and Buick, Durant, Leland, R. E. Olds, and the Fisher brothers, and the workers needed for the assembly lines. Detroit boomed like a mining town, and, like a mining town, it grew without any of the amenities of other American cities. Its old civic structure and habits gave way under the strain of thousands more people than it could absorb.[54] "Old Detroiters" fled in a body to their Grosse Pointe summer playland, turning it into a year-round restricted residential community known as Detroit's Gold Coast.

The automobile also put an end to the Detroit businessman's favorite mode of travel: the yacht. Up to the turn of the century, to and from Grosse Pointe all summer long puffed the private steam yachts of Detroit's elite. Mssrs. Newberry and McMillan, the Damian and Pythias of Detroit in the 1880s and 90s, owned the long white-hulled elegant *Truant* together.[55] In fact, they did just about everything together, and the story of their business partnership is the story of Detroit's pre-automobile transformation from a commercial port to a manufacturing city. Both men turned to politics in later life: John Newberry became a U.S. Representative (his campaign was managed by McMillan); James McMillan a Senator. McMillan was profoundly interested in landscape. When he was Detroit Park Commissioner in 1881–1883, he hired Frederick Law Olmsted, Sr., to create Detroit's only beautiful park, Belle Isle. Later, he even advanced his own money[56] to send his hand-picked team, the McMillan Commission, on a "refresher course" to Europe to prepare them to redesign the Mall in the District of Columbia.[57] The Newberrys and the McMillans together also transformed Grosse Pointe. They set the stamp of approval on it as *the* Detroit summer place when, in 1875, they built mirror-image "cottages" side-by-side on the shore of Lake St. Clair. Instead of two names, they shared one, calling the compound "Lake Terrace." Not that the families were above a bit of competition, especially about gardens: "If one put a potted palm out in front," said a latter-day McMillan, "the other family put in a fancy flower bed."[58] Both shingled houses had lacy verandahs, and the rolling greenswards they stood on had been specially landscaped for lawn bowls.[59] Down on the lakefront sat their airy white boathouse, its feet in the water, with a sort of pagoda-shaped Coleridgean fantasy for a roof—a real pleasure dome.

At the B. E. Taylors, in Grosse Pointe, landscape architect Bryant Fleming indulged himself and his clients in a typical flight of fancy by connecting the octagonal teahouse at left to the house terrace by an arched bridge, barely visible at right. The "bridge" is actually a wall to screen the swimming pool on the other side from the rest of the garden.

What happened later at "Lake Terrace" is typical of the rest of the Grosse Pointe development. In 1908 the old house was demolished, and the Newberrys' son, John, Jr., built another house on the site, while his wife, an expert gardener, had landscape architect A. B. Yeomans make a compartment garden in a big rectangle behind the new house. (In the mid-to-late twenties, Ellen Shipman redesigned and replanted some of the gardens.) It was a place for entertainment as well as gardening: the big lawn just behind the house was often dotted with tables for summer luncheons and dinners, and hidden behind the pergola covered with polygonum, actinidia, and grape vines was a perfectly equipped kitchenette, used to make teas, picnics, and alfresco suppers.[60] Mrs. Newberry was a Garden Club grande dame, serving twice as president of the Garden Club of Michigan. The high point of Mrs. Newberry's year was the trip to the New York Flower Show, when all her greenhouses were variously stoked or banked to bring every flower to pre-peak perfection, and every gardener held his breath. Mrs. Newberry and her friend, Mrs. Dexter Ferry, would take their masses of flowers, vases, and all the other equipment needed to make their arrangements—and their personal maids, gardeners, and chauffeurs—and climb aboard the crack train for New York.[61] There were so many flowers that an entire drawingroom was set aside especially for them.[62] Needless to say, Mrs. Newberry won many, many ribbons for the splendor and beauty of her arrangements.

A beautiful Grosse Pointe garden was Burt Eddy Taylor's, designed by Bryant Fleming in the twenties.[63] Burt Eddy Taylor, Jr., now in his seventies, still sees it all with a tranquil child's eye:

In the David Wintons' garden at Wayzata, a rustic seat encircles a huge white oak, the vantage point for sailboat races on Lake Minnetonka.

At "Southways" in Wayzata, Mrs. John S. Pillsbury kept her garden low and horizontal to maximize the prized view of Lake Minnetonka.

*St. Paul's favorite resort was White Bear Lake, east of the Twin Cities,
where Mrs. Lucius Ordway laid out her summer cottage garden.*

It was one of the loveliest in the state. Sixteen gardeners were employed to keep it up. Brick walks and terraces led from the house to the octagonal garden lounge which was two stories, in which tea was served . . . you could go towards the garden lounge through brick-walked gardens, great squares were filled with vinca, a fountain splashed water in an interesting way (the spout was trued upright so the water fell back on itself), then on through another flagstone pathed garden to a pair of columns with lead figures atop, then down a few steps to a grass area where you could sit and watch dancers and actors on the raised stage at the back.

There was a large orchard, a summer camp building or two for children to enjoy sleeping in cool surroundings in summer heat, and gardens behind. There was a small dairy as we kept cows in early days. There was an ice house as we cut ice from the lake, brought it back to the ice house with a horsedrawn sled, and stored it with sawdust. A barn housed cows, etc., then the head gardener's house, then a fenced-in area for my rabbits to play in, then a huge rock known to Indians in early days. Going back from the house on the other side, you first came to a tea garden, then a rose garden, then a lily garden with curved paths like a butterfly, then lilacs as a divider and then a large cutting and vegetable garden.

Mr. Fleming used walls a great deal. My mother wanted peacocks (live) to strut around, but my father would not allow it due to screeching, so Mr. Fleming solved it by placing a grille in a wall with ironwork in the shape of peacock tail feathers. Mr. F. demanded $60,000 be kept as a drawable balance by him in a local bank, and what the whole thing must have cost I would have no guess. It was beautiful. Then came the crash of 1929 [Burt Eddy, Jr., was twelve], and all was lost to us as the banks foreclosed on the place. Later, my father bought it back for a short while, and when he died it was sold by my mother to Henry Ford II. Then it was later torn down and subdivided which is how it is today. When a friend of mine asked me for plans [to copy the gardens], I declined saying I wished it to exist only as a beautiful dream.[64]

Lake Minnetonka and White Bear Lake in Minnesota

Another lake resort that slowly succumbed to everyday life was Lake Minnetonka, west of Minneapolis by about thirteen miles. Minneapo-

lis/St. Paul lay at the navigable headwaters of the Mississippi River, and in the last decade before the Civil War Southern planters with their families and household slaves came up the river on the palatial steamboats to "sojourn" in the cool summers. Just as in Bar Harbor and Newport, these first summer visitors stayed in hotels. The grandest was the Lafayette, completed in 1882 by James J. Hill, Northwest promoter, Minnesota's greatest, most ruthless, and most colorful entrepreneur, and the man who took the American railroad to the West Coast. In the 1880s, the summer people, by then mostly from Minneapolis, began to build their own cottages. By the twenties, the hotels had burned or been torn down, and the big private gardens of important lumber, mining, and flour-milling families from the Twin Cities lined the wooded shore. And what a shore: Lake Minnetonka is only twelve miles long, but the coast is so deeply indented it runs for 250 miles. Transportation was by steamboat up through the twenties. But sailing was the great sport. In the earliest resort days, after an all-day sailing party, hungry sailors would return to "Orono," the Brackett place on Starvation Point, for a picnic of baked beans and blackberry ice cream. Mr. Brackett cooked the beans for several days in a kettle sunk in a hole in the ground.[65] As the summer houses were being converted to year-round residences, the idea of a garden was reshaped from a simple display of summer flowers, good for three months of tight-packed bloom, to fit the new year-round requirements, which included temperatures ranging from a winter low of 40 degrees below to 100 degrees in summer. Two typical gardens were the John S. Pillsburys' "Southways" and the Russell M. Bennetts' "Cedarhurst," which both used the lake view as a background. "Cedarhurst," originally known as "Northome," had belonged to a St. Louis summer sojourner, Charles Gibson, who built the first "cottage" on the site in 1870. At that time, four long straight allées were cut through

the virgin forest, reportedly by "a Boston landscape architect." Then the fashionable Minneapolis landscape architects, Morell and Nichols, designed architectural gardens for the Bennetts, a successful flour-milling family, when the original cottage burned and was replaced. The new formal garden, one of the two grandest on Lake Minnetonka (the other was at the Peavey/Heffelfinger "Highcroft," designed by Warren Manning in 1895),[66] was laid out in herringbone brick paths and rect-angular beds. At the end of the central path, a few easy steps led up to a balustraded viewing platform, grass-floored and with a curved exedra at

Mrs. Russell Bennett explains the sundial at "Cedarhurst" on Lake Minnetonka in Minnesota to one of her many grandchildren. Although Lake Minnetonka, Minneapolis's beloved resort, eventually became a suburb, for many years the slow-paced life there was that unique American "summer place" existence where nothing ever changes.

one end. The intricate pattern of grass, bricks, flowers, and shrubs was kept low, and the trees along the shore were limbed up high enough for a layered view of lake, hill, and sky. Plantations of pale phlox mixed with nicotiana filled the air with fragrance at the height of the summer.[67]

East of the Twin Cities is White Bear Lake, the St. Paul answer to Lake Minnetonka. The same process of assimilation went on here, a summer resort expanding to a year-round residential area. One of the most beautiful gardens was that of Mrs. Lucius Pond Ordway, probably laid out by her, and photographed in 1905 or 1906. Below the half-timbered summer cottage it spread out in all its glory, in parterre beds that were veritable tussie-mussies of flowers, and with a cutting garden and veg-etable garden included right alongside. The Ordway garden is a rare example of family continuity in Midwestern gardens: it is in its third generation of Ordways, and has recently been redesigned as a green garden.

Lake Geneva, Newport of the West

Seventy miles north of Chicago is the city's first and favorite resort, Lake Geneva. Hunting clubs were the first to arrive, in the 1870s, coming up for the good bird shooting along the wooded shores. By the 1880s Lake Geneva was booming, and Chicagoans like Wrigley, Swift, Wacker, and the Morton Salt family were building big shingle cottages. The houses themselves were built on the lake shore, with the road that ran around the lake behind them; on the opposite side of the road everyone had bountiful vegetable and cutting gardens. One of the major social gathering places was Horticultural Hall, where flower shows and vegetable competitions were held, and where the very active estate gardeners' association met.[68]

A familiar cast of characters assembled to create Lake Geneva's gardens. In 1907, for Adolphus Clay Bartlett, the wholesale hardware

The Farm, the Manor, the Resort, the Escape from the City, the Gardener's Garden

279

RESIDENCE OF JOHN J. MITCHELL.
LAKE GENEVA, WIS.

The most exotic summer cottage in Lake Geneva was the John T. Mitchells'
"Ceylon Court," a copy of a Buddhist temple which had been one of the
pavilions at the Chicago World's Fair of 1893. Appropriately enough, all
the plants in the Mitchells' garden were exotic too.

magnate who was one of the first generation of Chicago's merchant princes, Olmsted Bros. made a formal courtyard garden cradled in the arms of one of Howard Van Doren Shaw's typical long stuccoed houses, called "House in the Woods." At the far end of the reflecting pool, with its wide paved surround and flanking deep flower beds, steps rose to a little studio with a Palladian front, arched windows, and pergolas at either end. Hothouse standards and small potted conifers provided a continuous play of small verticals. "House in the Woods'" garden was created as a contrast to the surrounding tall woods. Frankly artificial, it was a villa garden, an outdoor room, somewhere to grow the most delicate flowers and to lounge in the sun.[69]

At the other end of the range of garden possibilities was Jensen's first large-scale prairie garden, created in 1901 for the Chalmers family. Planting like nature, he used hundreds of prairie phlox, *P. paniculata*, purple flags, *Iris versicolor*, and swamp roses. In August, the banks and shallows of the river were lit by the five-inch pink flowers of the common mallow, *Hibiscus Moscheutos.* For his friend Edward A. Uihlein, the Chicago parks commissioner who helped Jensen get many private commissions after he was fired by the city, he made a ravine garden, banked with the distinctive rockwork for which he would later become renowned at Henry Ford's "Fair Lane."

The most interesting garden in Lake Geneva was "Wychwood," home of Charles and Frances Kinsley Hutchinson. "Wychwood" was the work of J. C. Olmsted in 1901, one of the private commissions the Olmsted firm carried out in the wake of their first Lake Geneva job, the Yerkes Observatory grounds for the University of Chicago, in 1895.[70] Charles Hutchinson, a trustee of the University of Chicago, doubtless had first

come to know the Olmsteds during the planning for the Chicago World's Fair, since Horticultural Hall had been his inspiration. He and his wife were founding members of the Lake Geneva Garden Club, and The Garden Club of America gave them a special award for service and conservation. She wrote two garden books, *Our Country Home* (1908) and *Our Country Life* (1912), both of which were illustrated with her own photographs of "Wychwood." She was the ultimate "lady garden writer," a real gusher, whose prose is littered with "fairy circles" and "feathered folk," "friendly tree trunks" and "gladsome spectacles." Not without wit, however—her husband became known to her readers as "The Constant Improver"; she was also a good photographer and ultimately, her books are winning because they present such a detailed chronicle of the great garden she and her husband created. Other details are a pleasure too, such as her "simple, sensible, and comfortable working costume," which consisted of a big loose sailor blouse, "a short straight skirt to match, a wide-brimmed hat, stout low-heeled shoes, and large loose-wristed gloves . . . pieced out to the elbow with heavy silesia finished by an elastic to keep them from slipping." She designed a gardener's apron with enough pockets to hold a hammer, a paper bag for mushrooms, a pad and pencil, a ball of twine, scissors, a large knife, a pair of pruning shears "designed for the gentlemen orange-growers of California," staples for vines, and hairpins to tack brambles back off the paths. She completed her arrangements with a small bird book, binoculars around her neck, and a few peanuts for the squirrels.[71] In this outfit she would work for many hours.

"Wychwood," located on 72 acres of untouched forest, was an exemplary private American conservation effort, similar to Biltmore's forests in intent, but much smaller in scale. By 1903, when the Hutchinsons began their country place, intelligent Americans were viewing the devastation of American nature with alarm. Nowhere was it more immediately apparent than in the Great Lakes states, where, since 1865, hundreds of thousands of acres of forest, both hard- and softwood, had vanished in the lumber boom, taking the native flora and fauna with them, and leaving behind poverty, unemployment, and unfarmable land. Many Midwestern estate owners, including J. Ogden Armour, Robert Allerton, and Henry and Edsel Ford, were conservation-minded, and used their properties as experimental planting stations. Professionals, like Charles Sprague Sargent,[72] and interested politicians, such as Gifford Pinchot, looked to the private sector even more than to the government for conservation aid. ". . . it seems that the only hope for real accomplishment is the establishment of sanctuaries or refuges by public spirited individuals, who are financially able to donate tracts of greater or less extent for the express purpose of providing a safe refuge for the numerous forms of wild life which are an essential part of our beloved country," writes Robert Ridgway, noted American ornithologist and author of *The Birds of North America,* in his introduction to a new edition of Frances Hutchinson's writings in 1928.

The Hutchinsons knew from the start they didn't want, as she writes, "stiff formal gardening, little box trees and hedging"; they wanted their new abode "to look like a house dropped down in the woods, rather by chance"—the hardest kind of garden to make.[73] The large, simply planned, half-timbered house, designed by Shepley, Rutan & Coolidge of Boston, was located only 100 yards from the lake shore. The Hutchinsons and Olmsted turned the conventional lakeside estate plan inside out. Instead of running lawns down to the lake, they heaped the shore with thousands of dog roses, prairie roses, sweetbriers, and many other species roses, with silvery sea buckthorn and wild olive, with "the Rocky Mountain plum, the Missouri currant, and the New Jersey tea," and hundreds of other shrubs that birds love.[74] They mixed orange jewelweed with yellow flags by the shore, and left the tangles of milkweed and wild grape at the transition line of shrubbery with forest. The lawn went behind the house, where it created a breathing space in the forest, which was cut out to admit light, and laced with paths but not "landscaped." It was what Prairie-Style writer Wilhelm Miller calls a "pleasure woods," made beautiful not only by what grew naturally, but with thousands of carefully placed wild plants, including many dug up by farm neighbors, who were only too glad to sell to the Hutchinsons things they didn't value themselves.[75]

"Wychwood" also had all the usual features of a turn-of-the-century garden: a pergola with a hardy perennial border, a formal garden, window boxes, a terrace crowded with greenhouse specimens in beautiful glazed and terra-cotta containers. Hardier than most, the Hutchinsons would often come up on weekends in winter to slog through the deep snowy woods, to hear the ice crack and boom, and to sit by a big fire. One November they stuffed their empty window boxes full of berries and seedheads. The silver stars of New England asters' empty calyces, the warm brown flat heads of *Sedum spectabile,* the dark orange sumac berries, and the pale rose and deep magenta coralberry, *Symphoricarpos vulgaris,* stood in the window boxes all winter long, attracting the birds, and shining with ice and snow.[76]

A more prolific and professional garden writer from the Great Lakes states was Louisa Yeomans King, who wrote nine books, beginning in 1915 with *The Well-Considered Garden.* She was friends with the garden mafia both here and in England; *The Well-Considered Garden* has an introduction by Gertrude Jekyll, and her *The Little Garden* (1912) is dedicated to Fletcher Steele. King wrote for *House & Garden, House Beautiful, The Garden, Country Life, Landscape Architecture,* and many other periodicals. Her own garden, "The Orchards," in Alma, in Central Michigan, became familiar to thousands of readers through her books. A large, compartment garden, it spilled over with that beautiful,

toppling abundance usually only seen in England, with plantings ". . . all balanced in predominating colors of rose, lavender, white, and palest yellow. Gray foliage and white flowers are freely used, and through the entire summer there is not one week when the whole garden is not gay with flowers from June until frost."[77] In her books she combines practical garden advice, luscious and detailed plant description, critiques of tools, catalogues, and books, with a sort of high-class travelogue and photo-

No cannas on a smooth-shaven lawn down to the water for the Charles Hutchinsons at "Wychwood" in Lake Geneva, but a tangle of native shrubs and vines for the birds—and the wilderness-loving Hutchinsons. On the other side of the rambling half-timbered house, paralleling the pergola seen here in 1905, would eventually be a garden to gladden the heart of any English gardener (and the Hutchinsons' was English). One morning in July 110 Madonna lilies were in bloom.

graphs of American and English gardens. Her readers must have loved not only her horticultural expertise, but the feeling that they too were friends with Mrs. John H. Newberry of Grosse Pointe, or familiar with the Mountain Lake Club in Florida, or a visitor to Gertrude Jekyll's Munstead Wood for afternoon tea.

THE ESCAPE FROM THE CITY

From the 1870s onward, every Midwestern city had had its highly visible "Millionaire's Row." After 1900, these were followed by more secluded—and distant—"nice neighborhoods," with at least a handful of impressive estates set among the many large suburban houses on smaller grounds. In Lake Forest and Grosse Pointe there were estates with gardens that in extent and grandeur matched those of Boston's North Shore, or Long Island's Gold Coast, but in Ohio and even in the small cities of Kansas like Topeka there were magnificent gardens as well, little known to the world at large. Unlucky Midwestern nabobs, who were never glorified by a Margaret Mitchell, nor painted by a Henry James or an Edith Wharton so brilliantly that their warts almost ceased to be defects! The Midwest's native writers, from William Dean Howells to F. Scott Fitzgerald, all left in a body to write about the East instead. In fiction, the Midwest was a place to come from, not to stay; the Midwestern millionaire is the hayseed who appears in stories of West-comes-East, or America-goes-to-Europe. Midwesterners like Theodore Dreiser, Sinclair Lewis, Sherwood Anderson, and Willa Cather (who was actually born in Virginia and moved to Nebraska as a small child), who did write about their birthplaces, certainly did not celebrate, or even chronicle, high society life in Lake Forest or on Lake Minnetonka. In real life and in fiction, Eastern nabobs seem more colorful, more magnificently excessive, than their Midwestern counterparts, who appear smug and dreary. One wonders how much difference there really was.

Nowhere were the outward leaps of estate makers more pronounced than in Cleveland. Developers responded to the surge of prosperity, to the idea of planned neighborhoods spawned by the City Beautiful, and to the possibilities of the automobile. The first outward-bound move was to Euclid Avenue, Cleveland's "Millionaire's Mile." Only slightly east of downtown, it was lined solidly in the eighties and nineties with mansions and Victorian gardens for a mile. There lived Jeptha Wade, John D. Rockefeller, Marcus Alonzo Hanna, and Samuel Mather, the first generation of millionaires who were making their fortunes in communications and real estate, the new oil industry, iron ore, and steel. Their partners and lieutenants—Harkness, Severance, Flagler, among others—also accumulated major fortunes. These industries and their spinoffs, such as paint and automobile manufacturing, made Cleveland a fabulously rich city by the 1890s. For the men who made it, nothing better expressed their feelings about their success and their new social status than a big,

stylish new house and a garden that, besides being a place that smelled and looked good, also embodied, for themselves and for everyone who strolled in it, money, culture, and a love of nature. But by the turn of the century, Cleveland had become a dirty, disquieting place for a millionaire to live in, strike-prone, and full of the thousands of European immigrants who made up much of Cleveland's work force. For the next two decades, Euclid Avenue's inhabitants simultaneously made civic improvements downtown—museums, parks, hospitals, libraries—and left for the hills, or rather Cleveland and Shaker Heights, with a brief stop on the way at University Circle, near Wade Park and Western Reserve University.[78] For instance, Mrs. Leonard Hanna in 1919 snapped up a University Circle house with an Olmsted Bros. garden that had been newly completed, but was never lived in by the Harry Payne Binghams, and the Hannas' old Greek Revival house on Euclid became the Museum of Natural History. The last grand garden made on Euclid Avenue was the F. E. Drurys' 4-acre "The Oasis," designed in 1916–1917 by Vitale, Brinckerhoff, and Geiffert.[79] Its flower garden, grotto, cascade, lawns, and graceful naturalistic plantings had vanished by 1927. Two great Cleveland Heights gardens were those of J. L. Severance, and his sister, Mrs. F. F. Prentiss. Inheritors of Standard Oil money, they spared no expense.[80] Mentor nurseryman and landscape architect M. V. Horvath designed the Severance garden, and worked on the Prentiss garden with Warren Manning. Another notable Cleveland Heights garden was that of Charles E. Briggs, where, in 1906, Bryant Fleming made formal English gardens, with a reflecting pool to double the image of the house crenelations and towers. All that remains today is the Briggs's poolside loggia, which Fleming topped with a ballroom, another of his soaring flights of whimsy. Shaker Heights, the elite restricted development less than ten miles from downtown Cleveland, was the brainchild of the Van Sweringen brothers, legendary real estate speculators, known as "the millionaires who were always broke." The key to Shaker Heights success was rapid transit: when the Van Sweringens purchased their development tract, they also bought the railroad that connected it to the city.

As each new development filled in, on went the topflight Clevelanders, searching for the country life, out to Willoughby, Gates Mills, and Chagrin Falls after World War I and in the twenties. Not that there hadn't been a few "country places" as far out as Mentor or Willoughby earlier. In addition to their University Place town house, the Leonard Hannas had "Hi-Lo Farm" in Mentor, an English manor. In 1906 the Francis Sherwins, of the Sherwin-Williams Paint Company, bought an early nineteenth-century farmhouse as a summer place, calling it "South Farm." They too summoned Bryant Fleming, who did one of his best assemblages using bricks, stones, timbers, and paneling, iron grillwork and railings collected from old houses and barns. The large gardens, also designed by Fleming, overlooked a pond; there was a rose garden

Ellen Shipman's recipe to keep a show like this going at "Halfred Farms" in Chagrin Falls, Ohio, was to stake, thoroughly and unobtrusively, every plant that even thought of sprawling. Extra volume was added by bushes of single pink floribunda roses and handsome terra-cotta pots of flowers like that at lower right.

with a fountain next to the house, and a beautifully planted courtyard.[81] Mrs. Sherwin was a keen horticulturist, a charter member of the Garden Club of Cleveland, and the donor of the Fine Arts Garden at the Cleveland Museum of Art.

Mr. and Mrs. Windsor T. White (he was the chairman of the White Motor Company) moved out to Hunting Valley, near Chagrin Falls, in 1916, where at "Halfred Farms," an 1860 farmhouse, Ellen Shipman planned a beautiful garden in 1921, and made her usual biannual follow-up visits. (Once she got back to New York quicker than usual when she met aviator Lindbergh at the Whites, and accepted a ride in his airplane at once.) The garden, a typical Shipman low-walled rectangle lined with deep borders, lay south of the main house. Old pictures show the beautiful little porticoed guesthouse, which made a sheltering L to the west, awash in flowers up to its windowsills.[82] For a garden that would continue overflowing after the great flush of June, she planted things like the great globe thistle, *Echinops sphaerocephalus,* which made a six-foot-tall steel-blue haze in the outside border, and lasted for weeks in full summer. The gorgeous tough native American joe-pye weed, *Eupatorium maculatum,* bloomed in late summer and autumn, its flat heads of pinkish-purple standing four feet in the air. In fall, three-foot-tall mounds of deeply cut leaves were covered with the flowers of Japanese anemone, first the silvery lavender and later the single and double whites.

The garden survives in simplified form today, along with many of Shipman's original plantings, including thick edgings of creamy primroses that come up every spring along the south walk.[83]

Cincinnati

Two Cincinnati gardens in East Walnut Hills, *the* in-town suburb before everyone moved out to Camargo/Indian Hill, and before "suburb" was a dirty word, illustrate the pleasures of those gardens of the twenties. Walnut Hills got its start in the last decade before the Civil War, when enterprising citizens first began to move up to the hills, prosperous from river trade with the big cotton plantations in corn, pork, and other necessities.[84] For two subsequent generations, Cincinnati's estate makers stayed in Walnut Hills, where they enjoyed "... all natural beauty, of flowers and trees, and all changes which came with the march of the seasons."[85] "Ca Sole," the Horace Schmidlapp's Walnut Hills house and garden on Grandin Street, was hunkered down on the steep slope overlooking a dramatic bend in the Ohio River, looking south. The name and the red-tiled roof were a hint that this was meant to be an Italian garden. However, it was not a villa, but an Italian farmhouse, with rough masonry and rustic wooden shutters. Every inch of the garden was intended to create a feeling of horizontal space, or to show off the view. Ferruccio Vitale, and his then-associate, the young Umberto Innocenti, later of Innocenti and Webel, cut four narrow flower garden terraces below the house Grosvenor Atterbury had designed. On the brick-topped stone walls in summer stood many pots of plumbago and figs. But the

At Jean Maxwell Schmidlapp's "Ca Sole" in Cincinnati, windows were cut in the garden wall, lower left, to give a better view of the Ohio River. This finely detailed lantern slide was painted by Gladys Pratt, who also worked on dioramas for the American Museum of Natural History in New York.

The Farm, the Manor, the Resort, the Escape from the City, the Gardener's Garden

283

master stroke of the garden was a strange hexagonal space, floored with grass, furnished with wicker and a fountain, and surrounded by high walls that curved out from below the loggia terrace, making a perfect sun trap and windbreak for such an exposed location. A room garden indeed, it even had arched windows cut all around, framing the wide view on every side. Some of the windows looked down at an oval swimming pool on the level below, surrounded with evergreens, overhung by a large magnolia, edged in spring with tulips and in summer with lilies and heliotrope for a sweet-smelling swim.

Also on Grandin Street were the H. F. Woods, who "did battle in the garden and held a truce at the dinner table." Every year he pruned her flowering shrubs just before they bloomed; every day she cut him up at the afternoon tea table. The rather sweeter-tempered Miss Beatrice Wood, Aunt Bea, who painted, printed batiks, and designed the garden, lived on the top floor of the house built in 1890. Next door lived Mrs. Wood's mother, and next to her, the Wood grandchildren. Beyond that lived Great Aunt Ema and a scattering of elderly cousins. The garden was always full of children digging dandelions at 25 cents a bucket, or painting watercolors of flowers under orders from their grandmother, or rehearsing playlets she had written for performance in the little amphitheater at the bottom of the steep riverbank. On one occasion Mrs. Wood herself performed, dancing around veiled in diaphanous shawls batiked by Aunt Bea. "On a spring evening Grandpa's garden was especially enchanting when the Island Queen, the stern-wheeler party boat, would play its calliope as it went by on the river," writes Wood granddaughter Angela Campbell. "I remember the first time I was ever in Cincinnati in the middle of the summer. [Most summers were spent in a log cabin on Lake Michigan.] I arrived late at night to stay with my grandmother. The tropical sounds and smells from the ponds of the garden below brought a sense of mystery, and then the calliope added its soft hoarse hoot. . . ."[86]

Topeka, Kansas

Topeka, Kansas's capital city, is located in the eastern part of the state, where the rolling hills that look something like the big landscapes around Ithaca, New York, have not yet flattened out and become the Great Plains. M. Roy Linscott, a Kansas city planner who had worked for J. C. Nichols, the far-sighted developer who made his name with Country Club Estates in Kansas City, Missouri, promoted a 160-acre development, Westboro, just outside Topeka in the mid-twenties. Nearby, an "Italian" garden-cum-English-landscape park was created in 1925 by Frederick Anton. His buff brick house was approached via a driveway that curved past a man-made pond and a circular garden temple that jutted out into the water. Near the house was a formal, balustraded Italian garden in three terraces, with a rectangular reflecting pool and a fountain.

Other estates sprang up nearby, in what rapidly became Topeka's "best

The classical garden temple of love continued its march across the United States, and by 1930 could be found in the Topeka, Kansas, in the gardens of Frederick Anton, a pup-tent manufacturer who had made a fortune in World War I.

address." Next door to Fred Anton's "Terrace Lake" was "Georgian Court," where Mr. and Mrs. George Moore lived in a white Southern Colonial house with columns. Georgia Moore was Southern, daughter of a doctor from Liberty, Missouri, hence the columns. George Moore, an insurance company president, raised and showed saddle horses, hence the stables and horse-show ring; he was also internationally known as a dog trainer and breeder (pointers and setters), hence the kennels. In addition, on the 50-acre estate there were lighted tennis courts, a swimming pool, a garden gazebo, and a maze garden ornamented with Georgian urns. A block-and-a-half away was a handsome Greek Revival raised cottage that Moore reportedly had built for his mistress, Iva G. Hayter.[87] Linscott's partner in the Westboro development, attorney Tinkham Veale, also had terraced gardens behind his handsome Mediterranean Revival stone house, designed by Topeka's leading architect, W. E. Glover.[88] Veale raised Tennessee Walkers and thoroughbreds; he loved riding, hunting, fishing, and golf—and roses, which he raised in a rose garden designed for him by Hare and Hare in 1938. (The roses Tinkham Veale didn't like he gave to Mrs. Veale for *her* rose garden.)

"Cedar Crest," the largest of the important Topeka estates, and the only one that could be called a real "country place" in Barr Ferree's terms, had no formal garden. *Topeka State Journal* publisher Frank MacLennan built a buff stucco Scots Baronial castle on 224 acres of farmland east of Topeka, on the other side of the city from Westboro. MacLennan and his Kansas City architect William Drewin Wight (as yet no landscape architect of record has been located) sited the house magnificently on the crest of a ridge overlooking the Kaw River to the north, and a long sweep of farmland to the south. The previous owner, a farmer, had planted a three-quarter-mile-long double line of ash trees, which MacLennan continued to use as a driveway. MacLennan's garden was his beautiful landscape: he dug ponds, planted clumps of oak, ash, and hickory across the rolling pastureland on either side of the drive, and added specimen shrubs and trees as he found them. Today "Cedar Crest" is the Kansas Governor's Mansion, and is open to the public by appointment. Though none of these houses or gardens was large or grand by East Coast standards of the period, the number, variety, and comparative stylishness of Topeka's gardens of the twenties can be considered representative of many small cities in the Midwest.

For the Love of Gardens
One man in the Midwest who was as possessed by his gardens as H. F. du Pont at "Winterthur" was Henry Shaw of St. Louis, Missouri, whose creation would eventually become the Missouri Botanical Garden. In 1851, the year of London's Crystal Palace Exhibition, fifty-one-year-old Henry Shaw, a successful St. Louis, Missouri, wholesale supplier, found

The broadly terraced garden of the John Horns, in Kansas City, Missouri, was photographed in the summer of 1929 when the borders were bursting with phlox. The garden was designed by the local firm of Hare & Hare, who did most of the big estates, parks, city planning, and residential subdivisions in the Southwest.

Victoria amazonica *was a big public attraction at Henry Shaw's Missouri Botanical Garden, which today is a major center for research on tropical plants. Linnaean House, at rear, was designed by George Barnett, who also designed "Selma Hall."*

himself walking around the gardens of Chatsworth, seat of the Duke of Devonshire. There Shaw saw a quarter-mile cascade laid out by a pupil of Le Nôtre, a vast Capability Brown landscape, and the sixth duke's and Joseph Paxton's Victorian improvements: the Emperor Fountain, with its 290-foot jet, the pinetum, the arboretum, rockeries, ruins, and lakes. Most dazzling of all was Paxton's "Great Stove," the conservatory (1836) that comprised the largest area of glass in the world. Only slightly more than a year before Shaw's visit, *Victoria regia*, the Amazon lily with six-foot-wide leaves that was the marvel of the age, had flowered there for the first time in Britain. Shaw had been born in Sheffield in 1800, twenty-five miles away from Chatsworth, and in childhood it must have been a legend, a place he had vaguely heard of, the "big house" of his small life. In 1851 Chatsworth must have summarized everything good and desirable about his own times to Henry Shaw: history, power, aristocracy, culture, science, exploration, invention, and public weal, all beautifully wrapped up in what an Englishman likes best: a garden.[89]

Inspired, Shaw came home to plan a new grand garden at his Missouri country house in St. Louis, "Tower Grove House," designed in 1849 by English-born St. Louis architect George Ingram Barnett. Its first developments included a walled 10-acre pleasure garden, a 25-acre American arboretum that would display what grew best on the prairie, and 6 acres of fruitbearing shrubs and trees—what Shaw called a fruticetum.[90] Later he would add greenhouses, an herbarium, a museum, a botanical library, and a school of botany. The Missouri Botanical Garden, as it was officially named, was opened to the public in 1859. These were the earliest days of public parks: Birkenhead, in England, designed by Paxton and first of its kind, had opened in 1847; in 1859 Central Park was just being built.[91] Shaw continued to live at "Tower Grove House" until his death in 1889, watching every development from the balustraded observation post on top of his three-story house. In 1868 he gave 276 acres to the city as a public park, which he and his new English head gardener, James Gurney, then landscaped with 20,000 trees from all over the world. Shaw designed the park's ten gazebos himself. There was a lake with a fountain and jet, and a ruin. Then came the conservatory, Linnaean House, also designed by Barnett, as were most of the buildings at "Shaw's Garden," the name commonly given to the Garden. In the water gardens in front of the brick arches flowered huge Amazonian water lilies. Shaw's Chatsworth was complete.

Shaw's mentors-by-correspondence were botanists Asa Gray in Boston and Sir William Hooker, director of Kew Garden. His resident botanist in St. Louis was Dr. George Engelmann, the German whom Asa Gray described as "by his own researches and authorship . . . unalterably associated with the buffalo grass of the plains, the noblest conifers of the Rocky Mountains, the most stately cactus in the world, and with most associated species."[92] Shaw's main interest was not botany or horticulture, however; his shelves contained many more books of travel, history, and literature than anything else. He was a Victorian enthusiast of beauty and culture, not a scientist. He filled his gardens with statues and busts of Shakespeare, of Rossini, Mozart, and other composers, along with statues of Columbus and von Humboldt, the German naturalist and explorer of the Amazon, as well as busts of botanists Linnaeus, Thomas Nuttal, and Asa Gray. Ever meticulous, Shaw also planned his own pink granite mausoleum in the tall sassafras grove that gave "Tower Grove" its name. There lies his marble effigy, resting on his tomb like a proper English nobleman. (Leaving nothing to chance, Shaw had had photographs made for the sculptor years before his death, dressed in a suit, with his eyes closed and a rose in his hand.) In May, English bluebells and wood hyacinths spring at his feet.

In their day, in the second half of the nineteenth century, the Missouri Botanical Garden was quite simply the most important and best-known garden west of the East Coast. Its importance as a major scientific establishment also made it the botanical gateway to the West.[93] The gardens were a famous pleasure ground for all, rich and poor. Some of the

Mrs. Clyde Carr's primrose path in Lake Forest was strewn with pale yellow English cowslips, Primula veris, *and splashed with the many vivid colors of the polyantha hybrids. Although these are not native plants, this garden by Warren Manning (1910) does convey the atmosphere of flower-spangled American woodlands.*

casual visitors who came for the day must have been inspired by "Shaw's Garden" to have gardens of their own, perhaps even a "country seat," just as Shaw had been inspired by Chatsworth.[94]

Carl Krippendorf: Portrait of a Gardener

One of the great garden pleasures is reading. There is no more appealing American garden character than Carl Krippendorf, gardener in Perintown, Ohio, outside Cincinnati, as he appears in the pages of Elizabeth Lawrence's *The Little Bulbs.*

Sometimes I am not so sure which is more real to me: finding an early flower in my own garden, or following Mr. Krippendorf's solitary ramblings across his wooded hills. At the top of one hill there is the house, and at the bottom there is a clear wide creek. On the far side of the creek the limestone banks are hung with ferns and wild flowers. On the near side is a little green meadow, long and narrow and embroidered with blue phlox. A broad path winds from the house to the meadow, with gray bridges across the ravines. In the steep places there are steps made of great, flat stones drawn up from the creek bottom. From the main path tributaries lead to other parts of the woods. Along these you can walk up and down hill for hours, and never come to an end of squills and daffodils. When the leaves are off the trees you can see through the branches to other hills, far away. Those hills are wooded too, and I suppose they are full of bulbs. There is nothing else in sight—only Mr. Krippendorf in his leaf-colored jacket, with a red bandanna around his neck.[95]

Carl Krippendorf began his garden, "Lobs Wood," in 1895. Henry Shaw had planted the prairie; Krippendorf was saving 175 acres of beech and maple climax forest from the ax. (It was about to be sold as a tobacco farm.) It was land he had walked over as a child, sent out of smoky Cincinnati for the summer to a country doctor's farm to recuperate from an illness. Krippendorf's father was the founder of a Cincinnati shoe company that would later become U.S. Shoe, largest in the nation. Carl Krippendorf ran the company all his working life, but his garden was his real vocation.[96] He corresponded with all the notables of the garden world for fifty years, trading bulbs and plants across America and England. Experimenting with hundreds, perhaps thousands, of exotics, he found what suited him and his woods. "There was a time when I tried to grow every plant I could get," he writes to Lawrence. "Now I want only those things suited to woodland conditions and limestone soil, and able to survive zero weather. But I want plenty of them." Mr. Krippendorf liked plenty of everything including work. "I potted up thirty-one pots of lilies for the terrace [mostly *Lilium speciosum Album* and *L. sp. Rubrum*]," he wrote to Lawrence one February, "... After potting the lilies I chopped wood, kept three brush fires going, raked paths six inches deep in leaves, and had a good time generally." In spring the terrace was covered with pans of hyacinths, 100 of them, pink, blue, rose, yellow, and white, followed by 200 pans of tulips whose staggered bloom lasted for five weeks. Each pan weighed fifteen pounds. Every year bulbs of all

kinds were planted, sometimes as many as 15,000. He planted them all himself, and always sent some of whatever might be new to Lawrence. Once he wrote to her, "I am sending you a box of bulbs. One of the bags is marked 'Old Lady'. Give these to someone with a cottage garden, who would like something in bloom next spring that none of her neighbors have."

Entries from Krippendorf's diarylike letters to Lawrence tell the story of his garden year. In January there could be winter aconites, snowdrops, and Christmas roses—or nothing. By February he could write, "When it goes down to twelve degrees the snowdrops look sad, and the aconites shut up tight; but as soon as the sun comes out, the aconites open and the snowdrops look as if nothing has happened. . . . Today it has warmed up to fifty degrees, the sun is out, the bees are flying, and all through the woods there are patches of gold. Five hundred kinds of daffodils were the big spring show; the ground was solid with them. I picked seventy-five stems without moving my feet. I think I could have picked a hundred, but I couldn't hold any more." By the end of April he writes, "I walked through wild flowers all afternoon, and I couldn't see the trees for the flowers on the ground. . . ." Primulas, camassias, blue phlox, and sweet rocket advanced the summer season. Then the deep shade of the woods meant flowers mostly to be found along roadsides, or in a cutting garden full of tuberoses (and zinnias, gladiolus, and pompom dahlias). "I suppose anyone is slightly mad who grows seven or eight hundred feet of tuberoses," he confesses to Lawrence. The turn of the year came in August, with the first katydid, and tens of thousands of the clear pink wood lily with the ugly name, *Lycoris squamigera.* "When I go beyond the path in front of the house, and look into the distance, carpets of lavender pink are repeated as far as I can see . . . It frightens me when I think that practically every clump was planted by me, and that all of them came from one bulb planted in 1895."

Lawrence writes, "Whenever I reread *Landscape Artist in America,* the life and works of Jens Jensen, the creator of the great Chicago city parks and the Lincoln Memorial Garden at Springfield, I think how he would have felt at home in Lob's Wood. He and Mr. Krippendorf had the same purity of conception; both worked with plants, rocks, water and space, and depended on changing seasons and varying lights and shadows for dramatic effect. Both dealt with large areas, and planted them in lavish measure. Both felt the kinship of great trees and small wildflowers."[97]

"Lob's Wood" is now the Cincinnati Nature Center, 800 acres of preserve. The lycoris are still blooming there. Whether or not they were labeled Prairie Style, gardens like "Lob's Wood," or "Fair Lane," or "Stan Hywet," the creations of farsighted human beings who wanted to make explicit the vital connections between horticulture and American nature, are the enduring legacy of the Gilded Age in the Midwest.

"Joslyn Castle," the home of the richest man in Nebraska, George Joslyn, and his wife, Sarah, was designed in 1902 by John McDonald. Solidly Scotch Baronial, it sat on the equivalent of four city blocks in Omaha, surrounded by 200 trees of 48 varieties and hundreds of shrubs and vines.

At "Villa Philbrook" in Tulsa (1926), the Waite Phillips and their guests could change in the garden temple, which had lockers below, and swim in the naturalistic pool while they looked up at the Italianate facade of the house, from which this view is taken. The diagonal parterre pattern with its central rill is a motif adapted from Vignola's design for the Villa Lante; the large fountain basin echoes that at the Villa Farnese.

The George Brandeis family garden in Omaha, photographed in September, 1917.

In the northern Plains States, Nebraska, Iowa, Idaho, Montana, and the Dakotas, which stretch west toward the Rocky Mountains, estate gardens were rare. Scanty rains and what is politely called the "continental climate," indicating extremes of temperature from 110 degrees in the summer to well below zero in winter, make gardening a difficult art. More importantly, these were farm states, without the urban concentrations of wealth that led to the making of estate gardens, and those who made fortunes in flour and cereals, or milling, soon left town. Most Easterners who came west were entranced with the idea of the Wild West, like Teddy Roosevelt, who ranched in Medora, North Dakota.

In these largely treeless states, planting trees came first—no wonder Arbor Day was instituted by a Nebraskan, J. Sterling Morton, Secretary of Agriculture under Grover Cleveland, and the man for whom the Morton Arboretum in Illinois is named. Morton's own homestead, "Arbor Lodge," in Nebraska City, was remodeled for his sons as a white-porticoed summer residence in 1902 by Chicago architect Jarvis Hunt, Richard Morris Hunt's nephew. The surrounding 65 acres which Sterling Morton had planted with more than 200 kinds of trees, beginning in 1855, were revamped in part by Warren Manning, and terraces and a sunken garden were added. In 1922 "Arbor Lodge" became a state park.[1]

South of the Great Plains, in Oklahoma, a state that manages to be both Midwestern and Southwestern, oil was the mainspring of the economy by the twenties. Spanish haciendas and Italian palazzos were created, with formal gardens like those at H. Vernon Foster's "La Quinta," designed by Kansas City architect Edward Buehler Delk in Bartlesville, and E. W. Marland's 80-acre ornamental garden and gold course in Ponca City. Marland employed a Scots gardener; he imported scores of magnolias from Avery Island, Louisiana; he edged his long geometric layout with three miles of Amur privet—and he asked the entire town to his housewarming in 1916.[2] In the northeast corner of Oklahoma, the part that is definitely not the Southwest, the rolling foothills of the Ozarks is Tulsa, and the grandest garden, Waite and Genevieve Phillips' "Villa Philbrook." "Villa Philbrook," today the Philbrook Museum of Art, is Italian in style and was also designed by Delk. The 23-acre gardens, the work of Herbert Hare, spill down the hill to Crow Creek, and spread out into the surrounding woodlands.[3]

DESERT AND MOUNTAIN

Mountains and desert: the resorts of the Rockies and the Southwest were built on the tubercular sanitarium business—and on silver, gold, and copper fortunes. Many cure-seekers stayed on to enjoy the slower pace and the informal atmosphere of the region, as well as the benefits of climate. When it came to making gardens in New Mexico and Arizona, both the Eastern contingent and the local millionaires wanted to have what they were familiar with; while they loved the desert and enthusiastically adopted Spanish Revival styles, they still wanted a lawn, and many a patio was planted with roses and perennials as well as cactus.

The same was true in mountain resorts. General William Jackson Palmer, a Union cavalry officer from Philadelphia who explored railroad routes west through the Rockies after the Civil War, settled in the beautiful small valley at the foot of Pikes Peak and called it Colorado Springs in 1871. Palmer's attempts to start a tourist and health resort were aided by a Dr. William Bell, who hustled tubercular patients from the East and from London to Colorado Springs. By the eighties, there were so many English people it became known as "Little London."

Despite the discovery of mammoth silver deposits in nearby Leadville in 1878, Colorado Springs languished because it was so inaccessible. Then J. J. Hagerman, a Wisconsin iron tycoon who had arrived in Colorado Springs on a stretcher, built a railroad and regained his health. Colorado Springs' good luck continued: just as the U.S. went off the silver standard in 1893, gold was found at Cripple Creek. The boom that ensued produced fifty millionaires, and estate gardens were created like the Charles Baldwins' "Claremont," modeled after the Grand Trianon, with gardens to match—a startling sight below the rugged peaks of the Rampart Range. Gold ran out and Spencer Penrose arrived, an Old Philadelphian maverick who made millions on copper in Utah. As Colorado Springs' greatest booster and public benefactor, Penrose turned to Olmsted Bros. to make gardens at his "El Pomar" in 1916, located next to his other big real estate venture, the Broadmoor Hotel. No more bravura example of eclectic American cultural imperialism exists—a Spanish Colonial Revival house with an Italianate garden, filled with English garden flowers—all set beneath the towering profile of Cheyenne Mountain.[4]

*Californians went to Lake Tahoe in Nevada for their dose of mountain air,
setting up in camps just as luxurious as those in the Adirondacks. At Mrs.
Lorne J. Knight's "Vikingsholm," the roar of Eagle Falls could be heard
everywhere. Already by the 1860s, San Franciscans were enjoying the
summer* pasear, *camping elegantly in the mountains with "a charming
blend of frontier and* belle tourneur.*"* (Starr, Americans and the California
Dream)

ABOVE AND BELOW:
*The first "estate garden" in
Colorado Springs was
already there when General
William Jackson Palmer
founded the resort in 1871:
the great eroded sandstone
formation known as the
Garden of the Gods. Palmer
built "Glen Eyrie"
adjoining the canyon and
made a garden simply by
placing a rustic pergola and
casino in front of the rocks.
The house seen here was
later replaced at the turn of
the century with a huge
Tudor pile, and new
gardens by Olmsted Bros.*

For "Claremont," built in Colorado
Springs in 1907, Charles Baldwin,
a polo-playing Harrow and
Harvard graduate who had
married Comstock Lode silver
heiress Virginia Hobart, sent his
architect, Thomas McLaren, abroad
for a year to study the Grand
Trianon.

EL POMAR - BROADMOOR, END OF GARDEN
LOOKING SOUTH TOWARDS CHEYENNE MOUNTAIN, AUGUST 1920.

The sunken garden at the Spencer
Penroses' "El Pomar" in Colorado
Springs, designed by Olmsted Bros.
1916–1925.

The
WEST COAST
and
HAWAII

In 1874 Ward McAllister was teaching stiff New York society and a few *arrivistes* how to unbend on the soft green turf of his Newport *ferme ornée*. In the new transcontinental railhead of Tacoma, Washington, south of Seattle on Puget Sound, Alice Blackwell was planting the first garden of the new city. She planted it on a dock in large wooden boxes (forty by six by one foot) filled with the centuries-old leaf mold brought to her by railroad workers of the Northern Pacific line, who had just hacked a rail bed through the virgin timber of the Pacific Northwest. She picked this peculiar spot because she and her husband, Will, a Civil War veteran, were the live-in managers of the brand-new railroad hotel, which also stood on the wharf at the end of the tracks (not yet completed) at the edge of the bay. For her floating pioneer garden, Mrs. Blackwell "had 200 boxes made and painted which held my tender plants that I took in the house during the winter."[1]

That same year, 1874, Tacoma also turned down Frederick Law Olmsted's plan for the city, a curvilinear layout that emphasized the natural outline of the bay and minimized the steep hills of the site. The disgruntled town fathers, accustomed to grids, said that the great man's plan resembled "a basket of melons, peas, and sweet potatoes."[2] Finances, rather than aesthetics, were the real determining factor, however. In 1873 Jay Cooke's railroad bubble had burst, and his major speculation, the transcontinental railroad, was desperately underfinanced. Every lot sold meant a little more money in the railroad company till, and so Tacoma turned back to the grid, since square lots were obviously going to sell better than the unfamiliar curvy ones.

But good fortune returned speedily to the Northwest. By the end of the century, the railroads were completed, and timber was running out in the Midwest so the lumber barons, the "sawdust aristocracy," came west. Outfitting the Alaska Gold Rush of 1896, and the discovery of other rich mineral deposits such as the Kennecott copper claim in 1906, gave an extra boost to the region's economy. Boom times had arrived for gardens as well. By the end of the first decade of the twentieth century, there were gardens in the Northwest to equal those of Newport and Long Island. Only a handful, it is true, but one has to take into account the reasons why there were so few. The settlers of the Northwest telescoped into less than a century the clearing of land and development of gardens that had taken almost 300 years to complete on the East Coast. Neither was there the same great concentration of wealth as in the Northeast at the end of the nineteenth century, since the Northwest was not a great financial or transportation center, but a producer of raw materials—timber, copper, gold, wheat. Many of the owners of these vast deposits lived in the East or

in California. Of course, local producers and local capitalists made their piles as well, but in modest numbers by comparison with the Northeast. Population was part of it too: in 1900 Portland had only 90,426 inhabitants for example, whereas New York City had 2,025,515 souls!

However, one great advantage distinguished estate garden development in the Northwest from that in any other region. Garden makers discovered that *everything* (except tropical plants) grew better, faster, and bigger in the mild, temperate, rainy climate. On the western, coastal fringe of the area, in Portland, Seattle, and Tacoma, the only places that concern us, winters average between 35 and 40 degrees, or just above freezing, and in summer the thermometer hovers coolly in the 70s. And the rain falls and falls, something the local inhabitants prefer not to think about. In 1914 Louise Shelton described it this way:

In this coast region of the Northwest, shrubs, trees, and vines develop rapidly and give sooner to the garden the appearance of completeness than is the case in the drier climates. . . . the whole coast is ideal for flowers. . . . The variety of vegetation is almost endless. Plants native to England will grow here that will not thrive in other parts of the United States, and the gardening tasks are simple in comparison to the toil necessary where gardens are subject to greater extremes of heat, cold, drought, and similar problems.[3]

Such weather made it especially easy to create the grand English-style garden that came into fashion at the turn of the century. One has to start with Portland, the oldest city in the Northwest, founded in 1844. Estate garden development began after the disastrous fires of 1872 and 1873. The emerging pattern was similar to that in Midwestern cities, such as Cleveland or Detroit, where the growth of heavy industry and the arrival of the automobile made it both desirable and possible for the elite to move out to the suburbs from the "downtown" neighborhood that had first served as their home.

In the 1870s, Portland's *gratin* lived next to each other in big mansard-roofed houses on the local version of "Millionaires' Row," the parts of the city known as the Park Blocks and Nob Hill. Their picturesque-style Victorian grounds and gardens were often designed by nurserymen who also provided the plants. This was a contrast to the pattern only a decade before, when exotic plants had arrived in the holds of sailing ships. Tight corsets of shrubs encircled the houses, fine wooden or iron fences protected the grounds, and specimen araucarias, ginkgos, and Camperdown elms dotted the lawns. Flowers, including tropical bedding-out plants, were massed in circles, hearts, and squiggles on the lawns as well. It was discovered that roses thrived in Portland,

The Gilded Age view of the West Coast in 1912 was this: purple mountains seen in a golden haze, under eucalyptus trees and above Italian steps, just like George Owen Knapp's appropriately named "Arcady" in Santa Barbara, one of the most visited of California gardens.

which eventually became known as the City of Roses. Drives were lined with flowering shrubs—weigela, lilac, deutzia, viburnum—and privacy was not at a premium. Such gardens made a neighborhood, and porches looked out on the street so that residents could see what was going on next door or in the street. Because Portland's blocks were small, many a fine house stood on its own block. The grandest of these early places was the W. S. Ladd place, which took up two blocks and included an arboretum and a conservatory surrounded by elaborate annual beds.

After the Philadelphia Centennial, Restoration Queen Anne houses became the rage, though since the houses were still built within the city proper, garden design continued to be confined by the block pattern. A change in garden design occurred in the 1890s when the new, robust Richardsonian Romanesque houses of the latest style were placed on firmer foundations than the lighter, wooden Queen Anne–style houses. Stone loggias and terraces, their balustrades covered with vines, replaced the ubiquitous porch as the structural link between house and garden, and began the march of architectural form back out-of-doors. Finally, the World's Columbian Exposition in Chicago in 1893, which took ten years to have an impact architecturally on the Northwest, and the reappearance in 1903 of the Olmsted firm in the Northwest to plan the 1905 Lewis and Clark Exposition, introduced the neoclassical garden style.[4]

J. C. Olmsted seemed to be everywhere in the region in 1903. He and his firm were responsible not only for the Exposition's plan, but for bringing the talented Emil T. Mische to Portland as park superintendent and designer from 1908 to 1914, the city's formative period. In 1903 J. C. Olmsted also visited Seattle to begin planning the park system there. At the same time, just as had happened in Lake Wales, Florida, and at Lake Geneva, Wisconsin, the town movers and shakers began to commission their own gardens from the firm. J. C. Olmsted complained to the Seattle park commissioners that whenever he or any member of the firm set foot in the Puget Sound area to work on a public project, they were besieged by the fashionable and rich for help on their own gardens.[5] Between 1903 and 1927 Olmsted Bros. designed about thirty private gardens in Portland, and in Seattle approximately forty between 1905 and 1939. In Spokane, which in the 1890s grew from a population of 350 to 19,992, Olmsted Bros. laid out at least nineteen gardens by 1936. (Spokane, the biggest city between Seattle and Minneapolis-St. Paul in the Northern tier, was reveling in the profits of the great Coeur d'Alene silver lode, the wheat of the eastern prairie half of the state, and the rapid timbering of the inland forests.)

"Elk Rock"

On the eve of his marriage, Peter Kerr, emigrant Scottish gentleman and successful Portland grain merchant, called on J. C. Olmsted in 1905 to transform what had been his 13-acre bachelor establishment, "Cliff Cottage," overlooking the Willamette River. The first big decision was where to locate the new Scottish baronial "castle" that would replace "Cliff Cottage." Kerr felt it should stand right on the cliff; Olmsted argued for a location set back from the edge, so that the mountains would still form the view, but the increasingly unsightly city in the river valley below would be shut out.[6] Olmsted prevailed, and a wide lawn soon stretched across the front of what had been renamed "Elk Rock." The garden rose behind the house in four narrow terraces; not long afterward their number was reduced to two, since even six gardeners could not keep up with the work. One of the terraces was filled with roses and the other with more than fifty kinds of carnations; both gardens were outlined in boxwood. There was also a conservatory filled with rare cactus, a rock garden that became famous in later years, and a wonderful tennis lawn surrounded by rock walls whose cracks sprouted rare ferns, alpines, and mosses.

Tennis was not the only garden activity at "Elk Rock": there were parties grand enough to require an orchestra in the garden, and an annual midnight celebration of the night-blooming cereus. Throughout the garden the rattle of two tiny wheelbarrows could often be heard—the Kerr girls on their way to their own small plots. That early training took. Jane Kerr Platt's own garden in Portland, "Curchie Hill," was to be the most innovative garden of the next generation. Her sister, Lady Anne

Cascading down a retaining wall at the Peter Kerrs' "Elk Rock" (1905) in Portland, Oregon, are common rock garden flowers that grow quite easily all over the United States: yellow alyssum, violet blue aubrieta, pink dianthus and androsace, and white arabis. But how they grow here is the point—such a flood is proof the West Coast is gardeners' heaven. Kerr, a noted plant collector, also grew many rarities.

Peter and Laurie Kerr with their daughters, Anne and Jane, in the south corner of the garden about 1918.

McDonald, chose as her Portland landscape architect the Salem, Oregon, firm of Lord and Schryver, which created some of the most subtle and beautifully planted gardens in the Northwest. The two daughters also supervised "Elk Rock," now the property of the Episcopal diocese, which is open to the public 365 days a year. Such watchful eyes, combined with a healthy endowment, mean Peter Kerr's garden still has the luxuriant feeling of a private garden, which most public places lack.

"Elk Rock" was, and is, the most important garden in Portland for many reasons. The "rich background of primeval trees" that Louise Shelton remarked on in 1915 was in fact more than a background.[7] The native flora—madrones, Douglas firs, cedars, western dogwood, Oregon grape, and on through an extensive list—were woven into the garden design. The Northwest was at last admitting its own "exotics" into the cultivated landscape, instead of cutting them all down and replacing

The Northwest

them with outsiders. Then too, in those halcyon days before import licenses, "Elk Rock" was the West Coast port of entry for a multitude of English and Japanese plants, including many unusual flowering cherries and the beautiful vine, *Actinidia Kolomikta*. Kerr also collected camellias, rhododendrons, and every species of magnolia that would grow for him. Most important of all, however, is the lesson his garden taught about making choices. In a region where so much was possible horticulturally, "Elk Rock" was notable for the firm design that imposed control on such a multitude of plants. Though Kerr was an impassioned collector, he and J. C. Olmsted made sure "Elk Rock" was not a Noah's Ark of plants.

Entirely different from the Kerr garden was the T. B. Wilcox garden, "Glenwood," where landscape architect L. M. Thielen carried out a completely symmetrical, entirely enclosed, highly neoclassical design. A large handsome Colonial Revival house looked down over balustraded and hedged levels to a broad rectangular lawn where a white Italianate casino curved its arms around a water lily pool. Although the small wooden building with its central arch, colonnades, and pool was similar to Charles Platt's arrangement at "Faulkner Farm," the Wilcox version lacked "Faulkner Farm's" proportions and grace. However, this garden, with its stepped brick walls and white balusters and pilasters, *was* reminiscent in one especially important way of another New England garden: Ferruccio Vitale's two-part walled enclosure for William Walker's "Brookside" in Great Barrington, Massachusetts. Both are vivid contrasts to the surrounding dark woodland. The landscape architect in each case dispensed with any idea of having the edges of the garden extend out into the natural scenery. Being *inside* is in fact the point of the Wilcox garden, and the "scenery" is exactly that—a "set" against which the garden performance is played.[8]

"Fir Acres"

Another formal design imposed on the wild Oregon forest was "Fir Acres," the mid-twenties house and garden of M. Lloyd and Edna Frank on Palatine Hill overlooking the Willamette River. House architect Herman Brookman, who also laid out the garden, made the panoramic view of the Cascade Mountains the dominant theme. Except for the garden theater (a round clearing centered with a paved circle of Belgian block) and a few side paths in the woods, the axially placed profile of Mt. Hood could be seen from every part of the garden. Vast as the view was, the five huge, carefully shaped grass terraces were a match for it. The turf itself was the pride and joy of a Kew-trained English gardener, who must have shaken his fists in the air after The Garden Club of America, several hundred strong, came to call in 1930. "Never had we seen such grass," wrote the official reporter of their visit, "Near the house it was of the serviceable variety, but down the long panels of the garden it was of the

At the Lloyd Franks' "Fir Acres" (1922) in Portland, the Beaux Arts set its huge classical footprint on the wild landscape. The terraces that fall from the house all have a view of Mt. Hood.

finest putting-green kind, and I fear the high heels of the visitors created havoc thereon."

The garden axis stretched nearly 1,100 feet from the lawn that fanned out between the wings of the asymmetrical brick house. On the first major level below the house lawn, the view was framed by a pair of teahouses, whose elegantly shaped tiled roofs were held up by stout oak pillars. Every detail Brookman designed took account of the scale of the mountain beyond. In brilliant parterres and beds to either side of the fourth and biggest terrace were an abundance of flowers and a magnificent conservatory. The virtuoso planting plans for this garden, and in fact for the entire estate, were the work of landscape architect Emil Mische, who had stayed on in the Northwest after his stint as Portland's park commissioner.

Below the flower garden terrace was the sixty-foot-long swimming pool, surrounded by a "beach" (one of Brookman's happiest design fantasies): a ten-foot-deep stretch of dazzling white sand for sunbathing.

The pool attracted many visitors—friends, relatives, neighbors. Edna Frank, while a hospitable woman, nonetheless kept a telescope in her bedroom so she could see who had dropped in. "If I liked them, I'd go down; if I didn't, I'd stay home," she remembered years later.[9] A surprise that lay out of sight below the last terrace was the elaborately patterned rose garden, also fan shaped. Rose bushes grew here, and are just one of the reasons why the 77-acre estate needed thirty-two gardeners to stay in perfect trim. One of Brookman's not-so-subtle but very effective devices was to widen the garden as it descended the slope, making it seem even larger than it really was. About 40 feet wide at the top of the steps by the house, it stretched 340 feet across on the lowest terrace. The fan shapes of the house itself, the top lawn, and the rose garden added to the expansionary effect. The lowest lawn, overlooking the rose garden, was flanked by grass tennis courts and a children's playground, and was rather municipally punctuated by an immense flagpole.

Architect Herman Brookman had received a telegram from Lloyd Frank while in England in 1922, where he was completing a leisurely study of English manor houses and gardens. It was perfect timing for his first important independent commission. Born in New York in 1891, Brookman had gone to work at eighteen, after finishing high school, as an apprentice for the New York–based firm of Allbro and Lindeberg, the same country-house architects who had trained Texas-based John Staub. Like Staub, Brookman moved away from New York and set up a successful practice translating the country-house style to another region. Brookman admired English architect Edwin Lutyens's work. At "Fir Acres" there are many echoes of Lutyens in the plan and the garden architecture. Brookman also shared Lutyens's Arts and Crafts–inspired reverence for good materials, painstaking craftsmanship and handmade detail. However, Mische's planting plans for the beds and borders were more regular than anything Gertrude Jekyll would have done, and consequently the exquisite tension between formal plan and overflowing plantings so typical of Jekyll and Lutyens's best gardens didn't exist here. "The garden, the largest and most extensive I have ever seen . . . was like some enormous showplace in England. . . . It would take one weeks to see it thoroughly and it was overwhelming in its magnificence," writes the Garden Club lady. Brilliant, ingenious, amusing, a bit heartless, and almost mechanical in its perfection, "Fir Acres" was like Lutyens's later gardens, such as those at Tyringham (1924), in Buckinghamshire, executed when Gertrude Jekyll wasn't around to take off the shine and add the glow. And yet, thanks to its incomparable wild setting, "Fir Acres," while it stretched the limits of grandeur, never toppled over into vulgarity or boredom.

A statement of power, display, and social position, "Fir Acres" indeed had an almost public character. And well it might, since it functioned as an important gathering place for Portland's Jewish society. Portland's Gentile society, like that of the rest of the United States at the time, barred Jews from their country clubs and other social organizations. Jewish families such as the Franks, or their partners in the department store business, the Meiers, insulated themselves with perfection and luxury like that found at "Fir Acres," or at Julius Meier's "Menucha" overlooking the Columbia River. (Brookman designed Meier's house and gardens as well.) In business and political circles, however, prejudice in the Northwest seems to have been less intractable than in the East. Historically, German Jews who had arrived as part of the Gold Rush as early as the 1850s had participated fully in their communities' growth. In Portland, there had already been two Jewish mayors by the time the state elected Julius Meier as state governor for a term in 1931.[10]

The Lloyd Franks' tenure at "Fir Acres" was short. The house was finished in 1925, and the gardens in 1929; they divorced in 1931, and only a year or two later the place was sold and became what it still is today, a campus of Lewis and Clark College. The rose garden has been restored; the house and the outlines of the rest of the garden remain.

WASHINGTON

Seattle

Oregon became part of the Union a year before the Civil War began in 1859; thirty years later Washington became a state. The Gold Rush that helped Portland boom was California's 1849 strike; Seattle reached top speed after the Alaskan Gold Rush of 1897. It also picked up a spectacularly bad name. The term "Skid Row" got its start in Seattle, where a "skid road" was merely the slippery mud trail down which the big logs had been "skidded" to the waterfront. "By 1901, the more lurid districts . . . fastened upon the city a violence, criminality, drunkenness, and competitive prostitution that projected a counterculture blatantly in defiance of the Victorian rectitude on Capitol Hill."[11] Victorian rectitude—the "sawdust aristocracy," and the financiers and bankers, shipping magnates, railroad men and merchants—established themselves in exclusive neighborhoods set high on the steep surrounding hills, not only on Capitol Hill, but on Queen Anne Hill and in Washington Park. Summer colonies also sprang up, first in "The Highlands" in 1907, then on the beautiful points and islands of Puget Sound, and around Lake Washington on the mainland side of Seattle. Who were the "sawdust aristocracy"? Andrew J. Pope, William C. Talbot, Asa Mead Simpson, William Renton, and other Yankee merchants, had arrived in the Pacific Northwest as early as 1849. They had been based in San Francisco, where they established lumberyards to take advantage of the Gold Rush, but found their new source of timber and serviceable ports on Puget Sound, both in Seattle and Tacoma. Generally, they sent their junior partners to endure the rigors of the Puget Sound area.[12] In the eighties, the more farsighted timber barons from the Great Lakes began to relocate in Washington.

By 1901, the Olmsted firm was by far the largest and most prestigious landscape architecture firm in the country. Senior partner J. C. Olmsted, Frederick Law's stepson and nephew, was well equipped to deal with public and private projects in the Pacific Northwest. As an inquisitive and observant eleven-year-old in 1863, he had moved to the Sierra Nevadas for two years while Frederick Law Olmsted managed a gold mine, and his summer jobs had included surveying in Nevada and Utah. Familiar with the topography and flora of the West from his early days, he integrated the shape and feel of the land, as well as indigenous plants, into his work.[13] Beginning in 1903, he created the Seattle park system, lacing together forty-five parks with a system of boulevards, weaving existing specimens into the design, using native species as a recurring motif. Two or three local nurseries sprang up after Olmsted's arrival; before that, gardeners had relied on plants shipped in by train or boat, and on specimens collected in the wild. As nurserymen discovered the fabulous advantages of climate and growing conditions, the Pacific Northwest became famous for its monster delphinium, the Mt. Hood and Puyallup hybrids, and for such sights as 200,000 regal lilies in bloom at once on Vashon Island, in Puget Sound between Seattle and Tacoma, where fifty lily growers had their fields.[14] The Olmsted team in the Northwest included not only landscape architect Emil Mische mentioned above, but also A. A. McDougall, a landscape engineer, and James Frederick Dawson, one of the unsung associates of the Olmsted firm, who worked for the firm from 1896 to his death in 1941. All contributed to "The Highlands," which was started in 1907 as a private summer colony and golf course ten miles north of the city limits on Puget Sound. Taken as a group, the four "Highlands" gardens of the Stimson family cover the design history of estate gardens in Seattle.

C. D. Stimson's Michigan father had sent him on a trip prospecting for timber in 1884, and, after a nationwide survey he settled on the Puget Sound area as potentially the richest. C. D. Stimson had worked in his family's Michigan sawmills as a boy during his summer vacations; he moved to Seattle in 1889 as a fully seasoned, second-generation lumberman. By 1890, he had started the sawmills, land companies, and logging railroads that would make the Stimson enterprise the biggest in Seattle. How hard it is not to judge C. D. Stimson by today's standards: he took full advantage of the Timber and Stone Act—that federal boondoggle engineered by the timber industry to acquire huge land claims, and his logging methods were destructive and wasteful. To him, timber was there to be taken and used. Banker Jay Cooke's adjutant, Samuel Wilkeson, accurately described the lumberman's mind in 1870 when he

called the Pacific Northwest "a vast wilderness waiting like a rich heiress to be appropriated and enjoyed."[15] But by the standards of his own day, Stimson was a good man, not only a good sport—commodore of the local yacht club—but a civic-minded citizen who served as a director of the Alaska-Yukon-Pacific Exposition in 1909. He was also a joiner: he belonged to all the clubs in town, as well as in Pasadena, California, where the Stimsons wintered. Like so many other Seattleites, the family had strong California ties; many "Highlanders" belonged to the Bohemian Club in San Francisco, for example. Stimson was patriotic and generous with his own time and effort, setting aside all his business interests during World War I to manage the local Red Cross effort full time for a dollar a year. Finally, like many another logger, he became an ardent conservationist *after* the timber was down, acting as a trustee for the Izaak Walton Conservation Foundation. From 1909 to 1919 he was also the president of "The Highlands," which was formed as a private residential corporation in 1907.[16]

The C. D. Stimson garden, one of the oldest in "The Highlands," still exists today. It was laid out in 1909 by the Olmsted firm, and by 1917 the stucco house was covered with vines, *Akebia quinata*, and roses. The flower garden next to the house, since simplified, was a forest of perennials, with towers of delphinium and huge clumps of lilies and phlox. An ivy-covered balustrade gives onto Puget Sound a view that is a feature of the most desirable sites in "The Highlands." Then one looked directly down from the terrace into a green garden with a fountain. Far off beneath the Douglas firs there is still a shingled playhouse, which was once surrounded by an inspired miniature planting of forget-me-nots and the tiny pinky-white English daisy, *Bellis perennis*. In the Stimson garden one also finds the work of the local landscape architects who sprang up to supplement Olmsted Bros. In the twenties, Edith Schryver, of the firm of Lord and Schryver, did a new planting plan, and in the thirties, Butler Sturtevant, whose work links the Beaux-Arts period with the modern era, changed and added to the gardens yet again.

The other Stimson gardens round out the design story. C. W. Stimson, C. D.'s nephew, also a lumberman, had a garden close by laid out by A. A. McDougall, after he set up his own practice. McDougall's Olmsted training is apparent in the plans, but his emphasis on architectural details is heavier. Garden steps are a little wider, walls a little higher, and so forth than would have been the case in a garden laid out by James Frederick Dawson.[17] Roberta Wightman, a retired landscape architect in Seattle, recalls that the Olmsted Bros.'s work in Seattle was characterized by a "marvellous ability to handle slopes without always building terraces and walls, walls and terraces."[18] At the C. W. Stimsons', the entire surface of the formal garden not covered with flowers was paved with bricks, whose crevices were filled with tiny flowers and with moss that flourished in the decidedly damp climate. The color schemes of the four

The C. D. Stimsons, members of Seattle's "sawdust aristocracy," had a perfect forest of perennials in the flower garden next to their house in "The Highlands."

corner beds are worth mentioning as they are so typical of the thirties. Each bed was planted differently—shades of yellow in one, lavender and pink in another, blue and white in the third, and in the fourth, pink double pyrethrum, blue lobelia, and a saffron hybrid tea rose combined the colors. The central bed was filled with roses, and everything was underplanted with lavender violas, a unifying carpet.[19]

Next door to the C. D. Stimsons lived their daughter, Dorothy, who had married A. Scott Bullitt, from Kentucky, whose family estate, "Oxmoor," near Louisville, had gardens designed by Marian Coffin.

The Bullitt garden in Seattle was formal and sunken, with a site plan possibly by the Olmsted Bros., and plantings by Edith Schryver, who at that time was establishing herself as a landscape architect in the Pacific Northwest. Here, she combined regal lilies, standard roses, delphinium, clematis, and heliotrope. The fragrance of this garden must have been one of its greatest charms. Defining the path that led to the rose garden were low brick walls, against which were planted more lilies and *Daphne odora*, while climbers sprayed the walls of the rose garden itself. Roses of all kinds were a standard garden feature in the Northwest, from hybrid teas like clear pink 'Mme. Caroline Testout', the official rose of Portland, which was used everywhere as a hedge since it could reach fourteen feet in the ideal growing conditions, to new climbers such as shell-tinted 'Dr. W. Van Fleet', and old ones, like the prized and delicate lemon-ice-colored 'Mermaid'.

The Thomas D. Stimsons, C. D.'s son and daughter-in-law, commissioned a house, garden, swimming pool, and casino from Charles Platt—the full Platt country-place complement. Platt even painted four large landscape panels for the dining room in 1929. The house was designed in 1923, and the garden in 1927, but when some 300 members of The

The bright annuals of the R. D. Merrills' town garden in Seattle were the garden's second planting plan incarnation, a new look for the thirties, though Charles Platt's classic 1923 design remained the same. The caisses de Versailles *filled with oleanders were painted white instead of gray-green, perhaps to harmonize with the new bright key of the flower beds.*

Garden Club of America came to lunch in 1930, the garden was not yet finished. Not that it mattered much, really; there was so much going on at the Thomas Stimsons on July 10th that one hardly missed the garden. For one thing, lunch was 600 brook trout![20] It was served under copper-and-blue awnings on the level side lawn next to the house which, Mrs. Stimson explained, would eventually become the garden. For a lunchtime spectacle, two tiny ponies were harnessed to miniature Roman chariots, and the little pair raced against each other while the ladies fileted their trouts. Their racecourse was the huge lawn below the house terrace, a lawn that served both as a playground for the Stimson children, and—a new use for the picturesque home landscape—as an airstrip for the family airplane.

In the handsome green program printed for the occasion, O. E. Holmdahl, a Swedish naval architect who would design many Seattle gardens in the thirties, is listed as "Landscape Gardener," while Platt appears as "Garden Architect." Holmdahl, who got his start as a designing contractor, an "installer," was creating gardens by the late thirties that integrated the native landscape closely with the designed garden. Two early naturalistic Holmdahl gardens, both set in lakeside ravines, in Medina, the summer colony across Lake Washington from Seattle, presaged his development.[21] Both gardens were visited by the garden club ladies the day before they visited "The Highlands"; they boated across Lake Washington, enjoying views of snow-covered mountains from a

huge barge laid out as a formal garden, complete with gravel paths, beds of flowers, garden benches, and a bright blue tent.

By 1923, when the Thomas Stimsons called on him, Charles Platt had already designed his best and only other work in Seattle—a town house and garden for lumber baron R. D. Merrill in the old suburban district of Capitol Hill, which by then had become "the city."[22] Seattleites found hundreds of ingenious solutions to growing plants on the forty-five-degree slopes of their city.[23] Platt's was to set the Merrill house close to the street, so there would be more room for a garden to the west. He then created the flat space so necessary for his kind of Italian garden by terracing out over a garage on the slope below the house. The pale, handsome house still sits on a low terrace facing a casino, whose three square bays repeat the divisions of the house facade. The nearly square garden is also divided in three: gravel paths separate a central lawn from box-edged rectangular beds to either side. Only the planting schemes of the beds and borders have changed during the eighty years of the garden's life—the house and garden were designed in 1909—but each of the three alterations has startlingly transformed the balance and mood of this small, dignified masterpiece.

In July, 1930, the beds were filled with pale perennials, perhaps still the original 1909 scheme. Writes a garden club correspondent, "White is the underlying color of the garden—white lilies of all varieties, pale

At Gravelly Lake near Tacoma, the first garden on the site of "Lakewold,"
the well-known Corydon Wagner place, was the H. F. Alexanders'
"Inglewood" (1909) where Mrs. Alexander posed in 1920 with her dogs.
California landscape architect Thomas Church later enlarged the garden,
but the teahouse remains.

straw-colored centaurea, pale Canterbury bells, and light-blue towering delphinium, strengthened here and there by choice pieces of box and other evergreens. Just as Whistler signed his etchings with a butterfly, so Charles Platt signs his gardens by cutting a piece out of a corner and setting a huge grey pot of flowering plants or a bay tree on that spot."[24] Sometime in the mid-thirties, the tall perennial drifts were replaced with splendid, flat patterns of annuals—lobelia, dwarf snapdragons, verbena, sweet alyssum, apricot-colored Drummond's phlox, godetia, petunia, mignonette. "The cool moist climate of the area is what makes possible this type of garden, just as a similar climate favors the Luxembourg Gardens in Paris, of which it is so reminiscent..." write garden authors Fitch and Rockwell.[25] The use of bright annuals and

defined pattern changed the garden mood radically, from the romantic "Italian" style Platt had made so fashionable to that of the most gaily sophisticated of Parisian royal parks. Why was the change made? Certainly annuals like this are easier to maintain than perfect perennials. However, a look at the 1930s photographs reveals how the shorter-growing annuals seem a better balance for the mature permanent plantings, grown tall and thick after twenty-five years of growth. The final metamorphosis occurred when the Merrill Foundation, which keeps up the garden today, substituted colored gravels and boxwood scrolls for the annuals to reduce maintenance.

For many years, Lord and Schryver had charge of the Merrill garden. Both Edith Schryver and her partner, Elizabeth Lord, trained at the

Lowthorpe School in Massachusetts; after graduating, Schryver worked for Ellen Shipman in New York for five years. Given Shipman's long association with Platt, it seems likely that Shipman recommended Schryver to the Merrills through Platt when she came to the Pacific Northwest in 1929 with Lord. The two young landscape architects settled in Salem, Oregon, at a time "when people in the Northwest scarcely knew what landscape architecture was."[26] Like Annette Hoyt Flanders, they were members of the second generation of landscape architects who used plants as increasingly sophisticated and subtle green architecture to make the smaller, more intimate garden enclosures the thirties preferred and the forties required, when the professional gardeners vanished. Although their spaces were smaller and their flower border plans less lavish than Ellen Shipman's, the firm's encyclopedic knowledge of plants and their skillful treatment of bloom sequence and foliage color and texture is surely in part her legacy.[27] As a postscript, one can guess how much the garden meant to the Merrills by looking at what their two daughters created. In the 1950s, Virginia Merrill Bloedel and her husband, timber family scion Prentice, began what has become one of the most famous gardens in America, the Bloedel Reserve on Bainbridge Island, now the property of the University of Washington and open to the public.

Virginia Merrill's sister, Eulalie, a self-described "uncontrollable plant collector," also married a lumber baron—Corydon Wagner, from Tacoma. In 1938 she set to work on an old estate, originally called "Inglewood," on Gravelly Lake about ten miles south of Tacoma. Its most recent owner had been her husband's uncle, Everett Griggs. Griggs had renamed the place "Lakewold" because of the nearby lake and the magnificent stands of native trees—Douglas fir, of course, but also Oregon oak, *Quercus Garryana*, an oak indigenous to the West Coast from British Columbia to northern California, which can reach 100 feet. Over a fifty-year period, Eulalie Wagner transformed a simple, linear turn-of-the-century layout hacked out of the forest into a complex series of modern gardens with the help, starting in the 50s, of California landscape architect Thomas Church. When she started, not much hacking had been done. "This was like a little forest, dripping with moss, when we came here," recalled Eulalie. "Since Uncle Everett was in the lumber business, he couldn't bear to cut down a single fir tree unless he knew he was going to use it." Eulalie promptly eliminated 200 trees to gain the necessary light, air, and views. She successfully grew temperamental alpines near the lowland lake, and gray plants in the kind of wet climate they dislike. If and when the tulips threatened to bloom too early to suit her, she topped off their beds with cakes of ice to fool them.

In old age Mrs. Wagner writes, "When we first came to 'Lakewold' in the spring of 1938, I was very much in awe of the place and felt I could never do it justice." But she must have felt something else as well. Perhaps growing up in that sunny square shelter filled with flowers, poised above the grand Seattle view, was what sparked her determination to make a garden, her boldness in selecting Thomas Church (a novel choice in the fifties to revamp a Beaux-Arts period piece), and even her plant collecting fevers. For her, as for so many other great gardeners, it is clear that her garden was more than an ornament or a pastime, it was her deepest expression of what life was meant to be.[28]

Tacoma

Tacoma, south of Seattle on Puget Sound by about twenty-five miles, had more than its share of estate gardens. Many of the grandest, like "Lakewold," were on Gravelly, American, and Steilacoom lakes, south of

"Piranhurst," a terraced Italianate villa in Santa Barbara designed for San Francisco industrialist Henry Bothin by Redlands architect F. Garvin Hodson in 1914, was famous for its outdoor theater, modeled after that at Villa Gori in Italy. Its Monterey cypress wings and ivied proscenium apron are seen here through the window of one of its six boxes, also clipped cypress.

the city. A terrific rivalry existed between Tacoma and Seattle; Tacoma children used to chant, "Seattle, Seattle, death rattle, death rattle," while the Seattle newspapers called Tacoma "a railroad promotion." The last decade of the nineteenth century saw the two run nearly neck and neck. Seattle's population ballooned from 3,500 to over 43,000, Tacoma's from 1,000 to 36,000. The two cities competed over the timber business, over the number of railroad terminals in each city, and the number of boats coming and going in their harbors. They also battled over the name of the biggest mountain; Seattle voted for Mt. Rainier, explorer George Vancouver's choice of name, while Tacoma understandably lobbied for Mt. Tacoma, the original Indian name for the peak. By 1899 Tacoma had lost that battle (Congress named the national park Mt. Rainier). It remained such a sore subject for years that in 1930 the Garden Club reporter, either in confusion or in excess of tact, actually discussed the mountain as if it were two separate peaks. By 1910 it was clear that Seattle was the winner after the pump-up effect of the Alaska Gold Rush on the city's economy, the arrival of the Chicago, Milwaukee, & St. Paul Railroad in 1909, and the publicity and city planning benefits resulting from the Alaska-Yukon-Pacific Exposition of the same year.

But whether or not Tacoma ruled Puget Sound, during the first decades of the twentieth century the city was riding high on the prosperity of being the headquarters of the timber industry in the U.S., if not the world. The Weyerhaeuser Timber Company had its main offices there (1914), though Frederick Weyerhaeuser himself continued to live in St. Paul, Minnesota, right next door to railroad magnate James J. Hill.[29] Tacoma high society also included the lawyers, bankers, real estate speculators, and manufacturers typical of any small rapidly developing American city—and many Tacomans actually did their business in Seattle. As an anonymous *Harper's Weekly* correspondent wrote in 1894, "Well, gentlemen, if I were a man of wealth seeking a home and investments on Puget Sound, I would live in Tacoma and invest in Seattle."[30]

People like Joseph Carman agreed. Known as "the mattress czar of the Northwest," Carman had made a fortune in the soft furniture business, and by 1904 he had companies in Seattle, Spokane, and Portland. He and his wife, Margaret, lived in Tacoma and summered on Gravelly Lake until they bought a 25-acre lakeside piece of land there in 1918 to build a permanent home. On the shore, Kirtland K. Cutter, of the Spokane firm of Cutter and Malmgren and a favorite society architect in the Pacific Northwest, designed a Mediterranean villa for them, white stuccoed and red tile-roofed. Frederick J. Cole, a talented Seattle landscape architect, and Margaret Carman, who was a fervent gardener, made a superb curving entrance avenue lined with native hemlock and cedars underplanted with big groups of the native *Rhododendron macrophyllum*,

known locally as "pink pearl rhododendrons." The drive wound beneath an imposing 400-year-old "wolf tree," one of the crooked firs scorned— and spared—by the loggers. Over 19 acres of the property were laid out as gardens, including what they called a "formal Roman garden" of long borders terminating in a pergola. Just like the Rockefellers at "Kykuit," the Huntingtons in California, and the Emorys at "Sonnenberg Gardens" in Canandaigua, New York, Margaret Carman imported not only stones, plants, and temple lanterns, but a Japanese gardener to make the Japanese garden.[31] Frederick Cole made sympathetic use of native plants and used them as the springboard for his designs; for example, the wide green lawns were fringed with all kinds of dogwoods besides the tender native *Cornus Nuttallii*.[32] His unforced use of the local flora made for harmony with the surroundings—and for a less labor-intensive garden: only three gardeners, a small number by the standards of those days, cared for the entire estate. Unlike so many other houses of the twenties, "Villa Carman" remains liveable—at least by Hollywood standards: the house and 3½ acres of gardens now belong to actress Linda Evans, though much of the original detail has vanished. The loggia of the house, overlooking the lake, was the finest "garden feature," a real outdoor room that was the heart of summer bathed in the translucent light of a big green-and-white awning bellying from the wall of the house across to four stone columns.[33] Many of the houses and gardens of Tacoma's lakes shared the dreamlike quality of "Villa Carman's" loggia. This was due in part to the surreal pace at which plants grew. The land and climate were ideal, combining the soil of the glacial meadows at the foot of Mt. Rainier, moisture-laden air from the lakes, and mild winters where "only a few weeks intervene between the last blooms in December and the early flowers of February, and the water in the lily pond is rarely frozen."[34]

"Thornewood"

Best of all these better-than-real-life-gardens was "Thornewood," the Olmsted Bros.'s estate masterpiece in the Northwest, which was given the international prize by the American Garden Association in 1930. Everyone who saw it burst into song, describing it as "one of the three most beautiful gardens in America," and "a thunderclap of astounding beauty . . . the perfect consummation of the ideal garden."[35] Louise Shelton may have been the first to write about it in the 1915 edition of her book, *Beautiful Gardens in America*.[36] The garden was then only two years old. What made this garden so admired and loved?

By 1908, the year the first plans for the 100-acre estate were made, the basic themes and variations on the great American estate and its garden were well established. Besides the obligatory practical features, such as kitchen garden, cutting garden, greenhouse, and service court, there were standard features that had become absolutely de rigueur in the

*The most breathtaking view of the Chester Thornes' "Thornewood" was
over the sunken garden where the "color gardener," a man who did
nothing but orchestrate the changing schemes from year to year, was kept
very busy.*

The teahouse in Miss Millicent Estabrook's Santa Barbara garden was designed by Lockwood de Forest. Climbing rose 'Cecile Brunner', a California hybrid, covers the roof, and the North African ground morning glory, Convolvulus sabatius, *creeps onto the walk.*

ornamental landscape. In addition to those eighteenth-century inheritances, the rolling lawn dotted with trees, and the sweeping entrance drive, these now included the rock, water, rose, and wood or wild gardens, a formal garden of some kind, and a grand view. Composition often verged on the formulaic. How the separate gardens at "Thornewood" were related to the house and to each other was an important part of the success story. Unusually, there was no integration of house and garden, no terrace overlooking the flower beds and statues below. Instead, the main garden, known by the family as the Sunken Garden, was a separate walled enclosure west of the big Gothic/Tudor house, with its cheerfully anachronistic white jigsaw bargeboards on every gable. (Over the years, everything but the windows, chimneys, and roof became smothered in ivy.) The house was entirely surrounded by lawns and groups of firs, and the reception rooms looked east, at the lake. It was a picturesque house in an old-style picturesque landscape. The view of Mt. Rainier had been saved for the garden alone—and for Mr. and Mrs. Thorne's bedside: the garden rectangle was on axis with their second-story bedroom and with a view that had been cut out of the forest and framed by two brick garden houses and a balustrade.

This tantalizing use of the most obvious view was not a design unique to "Thornewood" in the Northwest. The Olmsted firm did something similar for a Seattle client at "The Highlands," the D. E. Fredericks house, whose enclosure garden of stone, green, and water was surrounded by woods, and was one of their late, great works in the thirties. When Mr. Fredericks was asked why he didn't choose to look at the Sound and the Olympic mountains, he is said to have replied that he saw enough of those views on his daily drive home from Seattle.[37] No view at all may be a bit extreme, but, by comparison with the Lloyd Franks' "Fir Acres" in Portland, where the big view of Mt. Hood is present at all times, how much more interesting is the variety at "Thornewood."[38]

The second stroke of genius was siting the water garden. After the high note of the big white mountain peak and a stroll along the sunken garden, whose mixed beds were crammed with flowers, shrubs, vines, and bulbs of all description, one stepped up on the brick-paved cross walk connecting the two garden houses at the far corners of the enclosure. There to the left and quite far away, through the arched openings of the garden house, was another arch, and in front of it an intriguing glimpse of green water. One walked through the garden house and six feet down a pair of ramps into the intimate seclusion of pink and blue water lilies, iris, papyrus, and lotus. The distant arch structure came into full view; it was a niche for a statue, the main feature of a large wall fountain. Where the sunken garden was all straight lines, the water garden was all curves, a three-lobed garden whose separate pools were heated to keep the tropical water lilies happy. Wide-set brick pillars topped with a light wooden rail made a series of flat-topped arches that ran around the curving perimeter of the garden—enclosed, but not closed in.

Everyone admired the view, the velvet lawns, the surprising design, the stately completeness of "Thornewood," but what everyone fell in love with were the colors in the Sunken Garden. "At last we have seen Sutton's catalogue come to life," said a Garden Club lady, and indeed the list of annuals alone that were grown at "Thornewood" was as long as a catalogue test garden, running from familiar plants like blue bedding lobelia and fragrant stocks, to such obscure tongue-twisters as *Ursinia anthemoides* (small South African yellow daisies). The beds were structured around the familiar giant delphinium and regal lilies. Sometimes the garden was mostly white—to match snowy Mt. Rainier, one visitor suggested; at other times it was all misty blues and lavenders, pale pink, gray, and purple. It was the kind of luxuriance of color almost never seen in America and seldom, if truth be told, in England. "Not since I visited Mrs. Gertrude Jekyll in her Surrey garden have I seen such brilliant, soft and glowing combinations of color," is how a Garden Club lady's enthusiastic description finishes.[39] Whatever the color scheme, there were always huge perfect globes of tubbed orange and bay trees that wintered in the greenhouse, and tangles of old roses on the walls (pale yellow 'Maréchal Niel', silvery pink climbing 'La France', and white 'Mme. Alfred Carrière'). There was a fountain in the wall, and one in the reflecting pool in the middle of the central lawn panel. Box edging defined the central beds. In spring, its little dark greenness was lit from below with lines of crocus in spring, which were followed by violas that lasted all summer long. For this was a four-season garden, a "country estate" as labeled on the Olmsted Bros. plan. The intention was to make a family seat in the grandest way.

Chester Thorne, who moved to Tacoma as a young man in 1890 to become a financial tycoon, must have known what he wanted. He himself had grown up at a grand, old family seat, "Thornedale," in Millbrook, New York, the home of his elder brother, Oakleigh.[40] Although the perfection of "Thornewood's" garden has traditionally been attributed to Mrs. Thorne, one wonders what part family memory plays here. Certainly Chester Thorne wanted everything to go perfectly from the start: he had hired Kirtland Cutter, the leading local architect, for the house, and Olmsted Bros., the most famous landscaping firm in the country, for the garden, and just to make sure everything would grow forever, he enriched the already fine land of "Thornewood" with tons of still richer soil brought by horse-drawn wagons from the distant Nisqually River delta.[41] "Thornewood" represents a perfection of the expected, the English family seat come true, and in a place perhaps sunnier than England. Southward on the West Coast, in California, the expectations were different, and the prevailing dream was that of the Mediterranean South—Greece, Italy, Spain, Morocco. California's garden dreams would be less concerned with permanence than with pleasure.

When The Garden Club of America, hundreds strong, jumped aboard their private train in Grand Central Station, New York City, for a three-week trip to California in 1926, they were planning to see fifty-six gardens *just in Santa Barbara alone.* In the twenties, it's doubtful whether any other state, even double-barreled New York, with both the Hudson River estates and Long Island, offered as many beautiful, important estate gardens as California. Besides a nearly unlimited supply of money, Californians also enjoyed an unlimited range of plants and a nearly perpetual growing season—no wonder more of their gardens were truly beautiful. Californians were, and are, garden-conscious; even then they lived and entertained in them, especially in southern California, for much of the year. As early as 1906, architect Bernard Maybeck defined "hillside architecture" as "landscape gardening around a few rooms for use in case of rain. . . ."[1] California gardens are important to us because from them sprang the most significant and vital work of the next generation: the work of Thomas Church, Garrett Eckbo, and other great modernist landscape architects. During the estate garden era, the California garden was transformed from a lawn displaying a collection of tropical plants into the "Mediterranean" garden. The California gardens seen in this volume were chosen to illustrate that long development, as well as to display the imagination and flamboyant exuberance that were so typical of the California dream.

By 1890, it was dawning on a few discerning Californians that a lawn might not be the perfect garden solution, and that the English park model seemed at odds with the California climate. Intent on establishing an American order on a land that had only been formally annexed in 1848, and had become a state in 1850, those mid-nineteenth-century Californians, who were in a position to make an ornamental landscape, had tried, from the fifties onward, to re-create what they knew. What this meant for the first estate garden makers, the "bonanza kings" of the 1860s who made summer places in the San Francisco Peninsula, was following as best they could the current fashion for gardenesque villas derived from the English country place. The opportunity to grow tropical plants that would flourish only in a conservatory back East proposed lawn, shrubbery, flower bed, and driveway plantings as crowded and richly colored as a Victorian parlor.

RIGHT:
The William Proctors' elegant French flower parterre at their garden in Piedmont is centered with a pool paved with water lilies. Most patterned gardens like this had an overlook like the balustraded one in the foreground, from which to better take in the view.

In downtown Santa Barbara is this "city" garden where Mrs. Schuyler Coe's white freesias light up the foreground at left, and a bright yellow acacia blooms in front of a dark Kauri pine.

The Duncan McDuffies' pergola with its comfortable rattan chairs is a version of the great California innovation, the "outdoor living room." The 10-acre Berkeley garden was designed by Frederick Dawson of Olmsted Bros. in the twenties.

After 1890, the garden model was more likely to be Mediterranean, first meaning Mission, that newly romanticized take on Old California, then Italian, Moorish, and Spanish Colonial. In part, these architecturally based garden models were an expression of the nationwide movement toward formal planning and neoclassical architecture that occurred after the 1893 Chicago World's Fair. However, they were also part of the search for regional style, like the blossoming of the Prairie Style between 1890 and 1930 in the Midwest. California simultaneously experienced the beginnings of an original, indigenous gardening style in the assemblages of drought-resistant plants made by Kate Sessions of San Diego for architects Eric Gill and William Templeton Johnson's adobe houses, and in the informal bungalow gardens of the Craftsman firm of Greene and Greene. But in 1915 conservative taste was reinforced locally by the San Francisco and San Diego expositions, both of which presented formal layouts and neoclassical or Mexican Churrigueresque architecture as ideal garden planning solutions. As did other revival styles elsewhere in America, this formal, historicist landscape architecture dominated California through the twenties. Designers of private gardens found that formal styles offered a welcome methodology for limiting choices in a climate where anything would grow.

Leaving the English picturesque mode had not been easy at first. Even as experienced and sensitive a natural observer as Frederick Law Olmsted was taken aback by the wild California landscape. On his first voyage in 1864 (to improve his health), California must have looked especially arid and forbidding, since he arrived from green and tropical Panama. More than that, Olmsted was still wearing the spectacles of an English country gentleman of the first quarter of the nineteenth century. His ideal landscape ran to smooth green hills, not bare mountains, the curving lines of well-grown, well-watered woodland and field first experienced in his Hartford, Connecticut, childhood, not the severe geometry of the water-conserving Hispanic mission landscape, or the fragile ecology of rancho life. "The whole aspect of the country is detestable. . . ." he wrote to his wife, "The style is Cyclopean, but the vegetation is Lilliputian."[2] The different rhythms of the seasons and of California's natural succession escaped him at first, as it did practically everybody who came, except Scottish naturalist and writer John Muir.

But by 1887, when Leland Stanford commissioned the great landscape architect to make a plan for his new university at Palo Alto on the San Francisco Peninsula, Olmsted had developed an understanding of the semi-arid California landscape and its beauties. His campus was the first significant American-made design on the land that harmonized with its Californian surroundings. The layout was based on the Spanish mission plan where buildings were massed around patios. Irrigation for the campus was minimal, confined to small beds in the middle of the courts. The only lawn was a single panel in the entrance court.[3] Shepley,

Rutan and Coolidge, H. H. Richardson's successors, and the firm that would design Charles and Frances Hutchinson's environmentally sensitive house in Lake Geneva, Wisconsin, in 1901, were the architects of the mellow Romanesque/Mission-style buildings. H. S. Codman, Olmsted's young partner, went to Spain and North Africa to look for plants that would flourish with a minimum of water and maintenance. Water was paramount: no matter what the style, securing an adequate supply was the most important first step in making a great garden, especially in Southern California. Despite the example of Stanford and even though estate owners took up the Moorish and Spanish architectural forms that conveyed the *idea* of a sparing use of water—small rills, small fountains that could be used for dipping—they still watered extensively. Deep wells were sunk, and in Santa Barbara tunnels were dug through the mountains behind some of the gardens. Henry Huntington even diverted entire streams for his garden in San Marino.

Climate and topography caused the reliance on irrigation. In 1915, architect Louis Christian Mullgardt described the climate, writing in *The Architectural Record,*

The Pacific Coast States, Washington, Oregon, and California, are topographically and climatically separated from the other forty-five States of the Union. . . . Each year is climatically divided into two seasons over the greater area—rainy and rainless; the latter extends from April to November. When the north winds of the Central and Eastern States blow cold and bring their blankets of snow, then the Pacific Coast States don their new shades of spring green intermingled with flowers and trees in foliage and blossom.[4]

Coastal mountains running the entire range of the littoral mean that the cool, moist air blowing off the Pacific is turned back and falls as rain or fog, never reaching the long interior valley of the state. The valley remains dry and hot, but gardens along the coast enjoy a terrific climate. Especially in San Francisco, where the mountains are right next to the Pacific, the cold white fogs come every summer night to water the gardens. As important as climate or topography in shaping the estate gardens were the attitudes Californians took toward their new land. David Streatfield, the California garden historian, sketches the Californian themes: "a mythical sense of the past, a passionate avowal of hedonism, an experimental approach to life, a close association with nature, and a comparison of California with the Mediterranean littoral."[5]

The 1849 Gold Rush, which became myth almost as soon as it happened, came to stand for roistering American individualism in every form, an individualism seen in some of the wackier garden features of the Pacific Coast, such as Ganna Walska's Coke-bottle glass edgings for her Japanese garden at "Lotusland" in Santa Barbara, or Lolita Armour Mitchell's toothy grotto at "El Mirador." That same individualism, the same experimental attitude toward life, is what made Golden Gate Park out of acres of shifting sand dunes, saw new technology developed to irrigate desert land, and produced new growing and pruning methods effective in the unfamiliar, nearly seasonless climate. But the fundamental premise of the Gold Rush—that California was a place to be rifled, not settled or husbanded—was at odds with the other prevailing Californian myth of an Arcadian life, often a community life, outdoors under a perpetually golden sun. As elsewhere in America, there was no shortage of utopian collectives: for example, Pasadena got its start when a group of Indianapolis residents, fed up with a particularly hard Midwestern winter, decided to grow oranges cooperatively in the San Gabriel Valley in the early 1870s. However, California's community ventures did not spring primarily from the opportunities offered by a better climate or an especially strong run of Protestant utopian thinking. The American dream has always been to build a better place; certainly California's natural advantages made it not only the *best* "better place," but also the last one, since that final jumping-off spot had been reached: the Pacific Ocean. Bigger and better opportunities, but also a last chance—a good reason for the California Dream to become "an intensification of the American Dream," as historians David Streatfield and Kevin Starr have both called it.[6] California real estate interests capitalized heavily on these utopian yearnings beginning in the eighties, when the direct-line railroad arrived in Los Angeles from the East. The writers hired to promote land sales did more than sell lots with luscious descriptions: they crystallized the California dream by fictionalizing the region's Hispanic past as the reality of pre-annexation history receded. Novelists followed the same fictionalizing route, and their revisions were powerful validations almost as captivating as the myth of the Old South. Ironically, out of the Hispanic myth grew a new California reality, one created chiefly by the estate garden makers. Inspired by Gertrude Atherton's novels, and even more by Helen Hunt Jackson's wildly popular *Ramona*, California's American elite made the gardens, and set out to live the "half-barbaric, half-elegant, wholly-generous and free-handed life . . . [of] Mexican men and women of degree in the early part of this century" that their favorite novelists had invented.[7]

Long before Jackson or Atherton, however, John Charles Frémont had begun the romanticizing of Old California with his widely read *Report of the Exploring Expedition to Oregon and North California* (1845) and his *Geographical Memoir Upon Upper California* (1848). Struck by the bare and shapely landscape, the colorful atmosphere, and by what he perceived as the Mediterranean cast of the mission gardens, Frémont made an extended comparison to Italy throughout his descriptions. When he settled in the Mariposa foothills near the Yosemite Valley, he built a villa-style house, one of the first, and consulted with Olmsted on the landscaping. Besides setting up the Italian analogy for the first time, Frémont and his wife, Jessie Benton, also cast the mold for freewheeling

American romanticism in California. Born in Savannah, the son of a French émigré and a Virginia mother, West Point–trained Frémont was a soldier and an adventurer imbued with the code of Southern honor, and easily at home in the Creole cultures, both French and Spanish, of the American South. He took part in the conquest of California, and when the Spanish-speaking ranchers, the *Californios,* surrendered to the Americans, it was to Colonel Frémont they insisted on handing in their swords; in spirit he was one of them. His wife, daughter of Missouri Senator Thomas Hart Benton, grew up in St. Louis at a time when that river port city combined Yankee, Creole, and Southern influences. She spoke French and Spanish and was well educated for a woman of her day by the nuns of the Sacred Heart. Life in Mariposa was like a stylish opera performance: both Frémonts, theatrically handsome and dark haired, wore Old Californian dress; in the house, outbuildings, and gardens Indian women of the Mariposa tribe worked, dressed in bright calico. When the Frémonts rode out in their carriage in grand style, their outriders were two Delaware Indians, with classy mounts and Mexican costumes.[8] California lent itself to another analogy besides the Italian and the Spanish, however. The clear air, the white heat, the stark hills, the mystical quality of so many of its natural sites—no wonder men and women brought up to consider the Greeks and Romans as their inheritance rushed to make the comparison to a classical Mediterranean world.[9] Thinking back on his life Frémont said, "I lived its earliest part with the true Greek joy of existence—in the gladness of living."[10]

Most Americans were no Frémonts, but for many of them reaching this exotic Pacific shore meant it was time to relax. Here it was possible to be "Mediterranean" at leisure while remaining staunchly Anglo-Saxon at work. David Starr Jordan, Stanford University's first president, reveled in the Old California atmosphere, "The color of romance, which must be something between the hue of a purple grape and the red haze of Indian summer, hangs over everything Spanish."[11] Not that California didn't exert religious and psychological imperatives to live up to such natural splendor, of course, but it also might be a place where, as travel writer Charles Dudley Warner said in his book on California, *Our Italy* (1891) "engagements will not be kept with desired punctuality, under the impression that the enjoyment of life does not depend upon exact response to the second-hand of a watch; and it is not unpleasant to think that there is a corner of the Union where there will be a little more leisure, a little more of serene waiting on Providence . . . that this land might offer for thousands at least a winter of content."[12]

The Bohemian Club of San Francisco is the best example of the mild but heartfelt hedonism practiced on the West Coast. Roughly a counterpart of the Century Club in New York, it was founded in 1872 by a group of journalists as a haven for those interested in the arts. Businessmen flocked to join the free-and-easy gathering of artists, writers, and the press, just as they flocked to the Century Club. By 1882, when Oscar Wilde came to visit California in his velvet suit, sombrero, and puce cravat, he noted that never in his life had he seen "so many well-dressed, well-fed, business-like looking Bohemians."[13] Businessmen who became members were of course partly seeking the powerful network found in any city's important social clubs. But the difference between New York and San Francisco can be summed up in two words, "Midsummer Jinks," which were the theatrical revels held year after year (and still today) in the Bohemian Club's redwood grove in Sonoma County. The level of participation in these weeklong events measured how earnestly, and perhaps naively, San Franciscans believed they could combine a love for culture and for nature with the search for the almighty dollar.[14]

THE GARDENS OF THE BAY AREA

In the Bay region the large estates that appeared on the San Francisco peninsula during the 1850s and 60s were, according to David Streatfield, "the earliest appearance of such a landscape type west of the Mississippi."[15] However, unlike the equally palatial houses of Natchez, which were built at the same time, these estates possessed vast surrounding acreage. Unlike the plantations of Louisiana which had large pleasure gardens, but which were working landscapes, these were seasonal homes, summer retreats away from the San Francisco fogs. In appearance they were modeled on European country estates, with extensive gardens, large stables, enclosed deer parks, and even private racetracks. None was smaller than 500 acres. The largest, 6,500 acres, was also the very first: "El Cerrito," purchased from pre-annexation Rancho San Mateo by William Davis Merry Howard, a Boston merchant in 1850.[16] "El Cerrito" later became a Beaux-Arts showplace in 1907 when Panamanian-born hydroelectric power developer Eugene Joly de Sabla, Jr., had San Francisco architect Willis Polk design a large Tudor house, which the newspapers of the day claimed would be the "the first large country home constructed entirely of brick and stone." The estate had by this time shrunk to only 30 acres, of which 14 were Howard's original landscape gardens. They were dotted with magnificent mature specimen trees that had been set out by John McLaren, the near-legendary Scots plantsman and gardener, later the renowned park superintendent at Golden Gate Park and the dominant horticultural figure in the Bay Area during the estate garden period.[17]

Another early Peninsular estate of a different kind was "Valparaiso Park," the 1860 Menlo Park estate of Faxon Dean Atherton, like Howard also a transplanted New Englander (and the future father-in-law of Gertrude Atherton). His colonnaded T-shaped house was surrounded by elaborate formal flower beds edged with curving boxwood hedges, a familiar New England Victorian garden feature.[18] By the 1880s, the multimillionaires of San Francisco were putting up crocketed, man-sarded palaces whose towering pinnacles were incongruous vertical notes in the wide expanses of ranch landscape around San Mateo. The five-story towers of "Millbrae," the country estate of Darius Ogden Mills, who made a fortune in banking, looked down on all four sides at a writhing pattern of paths, beds, clumps of trees, and drives, and on a huge domed conservatory not unlike Jay Gould's "Lyndhurst" on the Hudson. Mills also had a house on the Hudson, designed by McKim, Mead and White, as well as residences in Paris, Newport, and New York City.

"Flood's Wedding Cake"

Also in Menlo Park was what was known locally as "Flood's Wedding Cake," topped with a pinnacled six-story tower and encircled by white-painted porches hung with gingerbread, the country house of James C. Flood, otherwise more staidly known as "Linden Towers." Flood, once a San Francisco tavernkeeper, was one of the Silver Kings, the four Irishmen whose first silver claim, in 1859, was the Comstock Lode.[19] Flood's 1880s garden at "Linden Towers" was as flamboyant as his house. First he approached William Hammond Hall, the brilliant young engineer who created Golden Gate Park. Finding Hall's proposed charges too high (Hall believed in grading and on-site visits by the landscape architect, which seemed like extravagances to Flood), Flood turned to a German landscape gardener, Rudolph Ulrich, who did many Peninsular gardens during the 80s. Ulrich's work may indeed have been cheaper, but it was also perhaps more ostentatious than anything Hall would have done. Ulrich tended to the formal, rather than to the gardenesque of the preceding decades. He used large numbers of imported tropicals, ribbon bedding, imposing cast-iron fountains, urns, and deer and other statues as focal points in his designs, and like most other gardeners of the day he relied heavily on evergreens of every kind. Besides being a staple of Victorian taste, they require less water than deciduous trees (especially important in California).[20] Interestingly, Ulrich did include what he called an "Arizona Garden" on each of the estates he designed; this was usually a small enclosure planted with cactus as if it were a desert and mounded with stones.[21] John McLaren disliked Ulrich's gardens intensely and spoke up for what he called natural gardens. In reality, as Streatfield points out, the difference between the two was more of degree rather than philosophy.[22] Ulrich made gardens where the plantings were meant to look like a cornucopia of the world's flora. Gardeners who trained at Kew in the mid-nineteenth century, or at the Royal Botanic Garden in Edinburgh, as did McLaren, were taught to make garden pictures arranged by climate, or plant groups, so that the effect was a series of garden pictures, accurate in every detail. In Golden Gate Park, one walked from the Sierras to the desert, to a rhododendron glen that might have been in Scotland, all arranged as if they might have grown in nature, but actually no more natural to San Francisco than Ulrich's efforts. Such separate groupings would evolve into the garden "rooms" of the twenties. During his lifetime McLaren introduced between 600 and 700 plants into Northern California.[23]

The only one of the old mansions to survive is "Belmont," the summer home of William C. Ralston, president of the Bank of California. Like the house, the gardens, which have vanished, were conspicuously Italianate, and the garden ran downhill in many urn-bedecked terraces.[24] "Belmont" was the largest of all the Peninsular palaces when it was built in the 1860s. It reportedly had 100 bedrooms, all with silver doorknobs, but despite the doorknobs San Francisco high society remained unsophisticated. William Sharon, Ralston's partner, inherited "Belmont" after Ralston's death, and in 1880 his daughter married a titled Englishman. In his book, *California Rich*, Stephen Birmingham quotes the *San Francisco Examiner's* breathlessly confused description of the flowers, "Every pillar of the many in the house was invisible for the smilax and camellias with which they had been covered. Boxes of evergreens, hanging baskets of shrubs and cut flowers had been again gracefully disposed in all the rooms."[25] His account of the transportation arrangements for Sharon's daughter's wedding conveys the period flavor even better: "Special trains had been engaged. . . . At the San Francisco station a woman guest, magnificently dressed in white silk from head to toe, tried to jump from the running board of her carriage to the curb and landed on her hands and knees in a pool of mud. Before the press could identify her she had climbed back into her carriage shouting unprintable words."[26]

But the days of San Francisco society's raucous childhood were numbered, and the headlong forty-ninerish lifestyle of its members was doomed to become slightly more staid. Ranch land became estate land; where once William Ralston raced the train to Belmont from San Francisco, bucketing along the roads with a pair of horses, people now hunted the fox in pink coats, and both men and women played polo.[27] The second generation, the sons and daughters of the men who made millions digging for gold and silver, speculating on railroads, land, and shiploads of goods and lumber, were coming into their own. What they wanted was respectability and culture. They believed that San Francisco could truly become the Florence, the Athens, of the Pacific.

No one believed it more ardently than James Duval Phelan, son of an Irish forty-niner who had made his millions. The Irish held a different place in San Francisco than they did in any other American city. Arriving with everyone else in 1848 and making just as much money, they were part of the establishment from the beginning, not an immigrant class clawing their way up after the fact. If ever there was an Irish ascendency in America, it was here. To be Catholic was also different in San Francisco, once part of Catholic Spain. Civilized, cultivated, urbane, and educated by the Italian Jesuits in San Francisco, Phelan was a man whose Mediterraneanism came naturally to him. Revering Italy, he also

felt at home there, and wished that "San Francisco might one day emerge as a city in the style of Rome: sun-splashed, spacious and baroque."[28] In 1897 Phelan served a term as "San Francisco's first honest mayor" and made a heroic attempt to clean up city corruption; he improved the water supply and the streets and parks.[29] He also played an important role in organizing the Panama-Pacific International Exposition of 1915. Phelan worked unceasingly, and undiscriminatingly, to foster the arts. His weakness for anything created in San Francisco, which led him to support many embarrassingly second-rate efforts, were part of his high-spirited dream that San Francisco be "a city of art and sound governance."[30]

Gertrude Atherton considered him California's most elegant, accomplished gentleman, which he probably was, says Kevin Starr.[31] He wrote poetry and essays, served as president of the Bohemian Club, and was a fluent public speaker. In his fifties, white-goateed, piercing-eyed, inveterately stiff-collared, and dignified, Phelan did two things that capped his career as a public man and his vision of himself as a new-age Florentine patron of the arts. He ran successfully for the U.S. Senate, and he bought 175 acres in Santa Clara, south of San Mateo in the Peninsula. "Villa Montalvo," named after the sixteenth century Spanish writer Garcia Ordonez de Montalvo, was finished in 1915 just as he took office.[32] The elegant Spanish Renaissance house was designed by local architect William Curlett. The house and gardens were surrounded by orchards of fruit trees, just like the rest of the Santa Clara Valley. Phelan did all the approved garden things: in the Italian garden (which lay apart from the house, screened by conifers) stood four large statues of Roman emperors, which he had brought back from his travels, and when his beloved dog, Boz, died, he was buried under a large obelisk in the garden. With Gertrude Atherton, who often presided with him at "Villa Montalvo" as girlfriend (probably Platonic) and muse, Phelan encouraged San Francisco's literati and artists to visit.

San Francisco's real sobering-up came with the earthquake and fire of 1906, when the city, rebuilt along its old ugly lines, lost the raffish, temporary charm of its first beginnings and became the suitably gray business capital of the West Coast. "It is as though a pretty, frivolous woman had passed through a great tragedy. She survives, but she is sobered and different," wrote an ex-San Franciscan journalist the night the news of the fire reached New York.[33] For the owners of the big estates in San Mateo, still more sobering was the news that many San Franciscans wanted to move out of the city after the 1906 disaster—to the exclusive green fields of San Mateo. Quickly, in 1908, the village of Burlingame was incorporated as a city to avoid being gobbled up by San Mateo; no sooner was that done than the Burlingame Country Club members, threatened with annexation by Burlingame, incorporated their own city in 1911, the noncity of Hillsborough, with no sidewalks, no street pattern, and no business or commercial enterprises. It rapidly became the

A tent pitched for a naval reception at James Duval Phelan's "Villa Montalvo" in the Santa Clara valley was a typical Californian entertainment fantasy captured by the peerless lens of San Francisco photographer Gabriel Moulin.

Not even the diving board, barely visible at the far end of the pool, can bring C. Templeton Crocker's "Uplands" (1913) to earth, one of the great gardens of the San Francisco Peninsula.

most exclusive address.[34] Within the next generation the gardens of the Peninsula, like San Francisco itself, would shift from braggadocio to gilt-edged restraint. No more grandly reticent group of houses and gardens could be found than "Uplands," "La Dolphine," and "Filoli," the country places of C. Templeton Crocker, George Newhall, and William Bourn II. Classical in their exterior architectural detailing, sumptuous in materials inside and out, symmetrical in plan, they were California's answer to the Gold Coast of Long Island—though less flamboyant.

C. Templeton Crocker's "Uplands"

C. Templeton Crocker was one of the three sons of Charles Crocker, the huge red-bearded partner of Collis Huntington, Mark Hopkins, and Leland Stanford, founders of the Central Pacific, the first railroad to cross the country in 1869. Charles Crocker had been the partner in charge of building the track, sleeping in his private railroad car by night, and riding his horse up and down the line by day, pushing his 16,000 Chinese workers hard. Along with the Silver Kings, the foursome made the biggest fortunes in San Francisco.[35] Young Crocker grew up in San Francisco, a member of the Bohemian Club and a contemporary of architect Willis Polk. Polk had apprenticed with Bernard Maybeck, the most innovative of the Bay Region–style architects, who, in 1915 for the Panama-Pacific International Exposition, would create *the* memorable public building in San Francisco, the Palace of Fine Arts — "a russet-hued evocation of time, tragedy, and romance."[36] For C. Templeton Crocker, Willis Polk built "Uplands," a 35,000-square-foot white Renaissance palace, which survives today as the Crystal Springs School for Girls. Compact and self-contained, the house would have looked at home in Newport on the day it was built; Crocker, unlike Californians of only a few years later, was clearly not interested in the exchange between indoor and outdoor space. The gardens were a different story. "Uplands" stood on the site of an older house, so the trees, planted in 1878, were magnificent, and the highly architectural terraces of the Italian garden were inviting with classical seats in shade and sun, cool pools of water, and wide views of the still unbuilt hills of Hillsborough.[37] The "Italian" garden in America was never happier than in California, and while Californians often invoked classical allusions, they turned most often to the richness of Renaissance Italy for their grandest gardens, such as "Uplands," built mostly during the first two decades of the twentieth century. The Mission gardens of the nineties and the Spanish Colonial gardens of the twenties were restrained by comparison.

Polk was one of *Les Jeunes*, a recherché group influenced by the Pre-Raphaelites, who came together in the nineties, searching for a California style that would be fresh, innovative, and yet somehow ancient in its civilized associations.[38] Many of them were interested in the decorative arts; the world of the country house offered a place where they could express themselves. Porter Garnett, for example, wrote a valuable record of the pre-World War I estates, *Stately Homes of California* (1915), and also sketched, bound books, and arranged flowers. Bruce Porter, a painter, poet, and maker of stained glass, also designed gardens, including not only the famous "Filoli," but also notably "New Place," the green, Italianate garden of Charles Templeton Crocker's brother, William, which in its "bold and simple handling of scale and detail invites comparison with the best work of C. A. Platt."[39] The Renaissance house at "New Place" was designed in 1906 by favorite Peninsular architect Lewis P. Hobart, who was also responsible for both house and garden at "La Dolphine."

"La Dolphine"

The embodiment of "tremendous grandeur and dignity and extreme simplicity" is what budding modernist landscape architect Garrett Eckbo called "La Dolphine," when he made a tour of famous Bay Area gardens as a student in the early thirties. Of all the gardens he visited, this severely axial, symmetrical beauty was his favorite.[40] Indeed, the same qualities of abstract formalism and clean geometry can be seen in Eckbo's own later work and that of Thomas Church, Dan Kiley, and other modernists. Like Fletcher Steele, whom they admired, the new generation of landscape architects preferred outright artifice such as that of Le Nôtre, to the naturalistic designs of the Humphrey Repton/William Robinson school.

In 1914, when Hobart designed what was then called "Newmar" for the George Newhalls, a French garden was a rarity in California. But the low French-windowed stone house was inspired by the Petit Trianon, and Hobart, following what by then had become a Beaux-Arts tradition of unity between house and garden, went on to make a brilliant French garden. The plan itself was hardly striking. A cypress-edged *tapis vert* extended an axial view from the entrance court; on the garden front, on the same axis, a 175-foot allée was framed with lines of pink and white hawthorns, and terminated in a temple of love. Just below the house terrace, a wide grass parterre was strictly divided into four grass rectangles, and centered with a reflecting pool. The parterre was surrounded on all four sides with nearly 100 perfectly pollarded plane trees. Outside the confines of the main view, things relaxed: a rose garden and abundant orchards lay just beyond the severe cypress hedges.[41]

There was another French-style garden in California, also in Hillsborough, that deserves mention even though it was never finished. Harriet Pullman Carolan, heir to George Pullman's huge railroad-car fortune, had married the son of an old Sacramento family, Francis J. Carolan, in 1892, and moved to San Francisco. Along with the rest of the millionaires, they moved to Burlingame in the 90s and took up polo, fox hunting, beagling, and horse breeding at "Crossways Farm." They also entertained lavishly, and a string of Harrimans, Rockefellers, Vanderbilts, and Roosevelts came through their doors. This was competition indeed for San Francisco society. In 1907 Mrs. William Crocker opened "New Place"; by 1913 "Uplands" and "La Dolphine" were being developed.

"Crossways Farm" began to seem a bit insignificant to Harriet Pullman Carolan. That same year, she gathered her sleeping car pennies and bought 500 acres on the ridge just above "Uplands." She was setting out to build a country place bigger than anything the West Coast had ever seen. She chose French architect Paul-Ernest Sanson, with Willis Polk as the California back-up on the job. By 1915 the house was finished, but the Carolans themselves were falling apart (he moved back to "Crossways," she to New York and a marriage with A. F. Schermerhorn). The immense gardens designed by Achille Duchêne, the biggest single commission he ever received, were never to be executed. The beautiful drawings published in the *Gazette illustrée des amateurs de jardins* show three vistas that between them encompass nearly the entire 500 acres. Duchêne's plan took advantage of the topography, with views from the house itself stretching to San Francisco Bay and the East Bay Hills, to the Burlingame Hills on the north, and across the Crystal Springs Lakes to the west.[42]

"Filoli"

A garden that has become one of the most beautiful in California, if not the world, is seventy-five-year-old "Filoli," in Woodside, which is now familiar to everyone as the setting of "Dynasty"; it is open to the public, a property of the National Trust. William Bowers Bourn II began his business career by managing his family's gold mine, but in addition he owned a vineyard, a major water supply company (as good an investment as gold in California), and a gas company. In 1915, he and his wife bought 645 fantastically beautiful acres in Woodside because they reminded him of the soft landscape around the Killarney Lakes in Ireland. A forty-three-room, soft-pink brick manor house was designed by Willis Polk, who had also designed Bourn's town house and his previous country "cottage." Georgian, but with many eclectic touches, "Filoli" was a triumph for the architect, who was working here with a knowledgeable, participatory client with strong, sophisticated tastes, who was also familiar with the architect's work. Paderewski played at the housewarming, and on the walls of the drawing room were portraits of the Bourns, not by just any San Francisco society painter, but by that sardonic English version of John Singer Sargent: William Orpen. (The Bourns' daughter, Maud, *was* in fact painted by Sargent.) The ballroom murals, the work of Ernest Peixotto, a book and magazine illustrator who was also a member of *Les Jeunes*, depicted the Bourns' Irish demesne, the great abbey estate of Muckross, in Killarney. (Muckross was her parents' wedding present to Maud, who married an Irishman.) In many ways, the language of "Filoli" is Irish, right down to the 300 spectacular Irish yews in the gardens, but the intonation is Anglo-Irish, not Celtic. Of course, being in California it is larger, more perfect, and saner than any real Anglo-Irish place, where the ramshackle, the fine-boned, and the totally idiosyncratic lie companionably side-by-side.

"Filoli's" 16 acres of gardens, almost too well-known to describe, consist of terraces around the house, a sunken garden, and an intricately compartmented walled garden, all set within a landscape of green fields, huge oaks, and low purple mountains. One is reminded of Anne's Grove, Mount Congreve, or Glenveagh, and other great twentieth-century gardens in the south and west of Ireland, where the climate, terrain, and design are similar. Bruce Porter, a friend of Bourn's and one of his hunting companions, was the garden architect, and Isabella Worn, a San Francisco society florist, as well as an active horticulturist, did the planting plans.[43] Unlike so many other gardens of the Peninsula, no attempt was made here to create a semitropical atmosphere. While tender plants have been used, such as plumbago, they were generally the ones

that have also adorned equivalently grand Irish houses. The exceptions are the olives and the native live oaks, which respectively provide a constantly shimmering silver presence and a dense, cool darkness as a backdrop.

"Filoli" has had the luck as well as the looks of the Irish: it sits atop the San Andreas Fault—so far so good—and, after the death of the Bourns, it was bought in 1937 by William Roth and his wife, Lurline, who was the daughter of the founder of the Matson Navigation Company. They filled the house with family, the stables with champion hackneys, and the garden with plants from around the world. Today, "Filoli's" gardens have reached what Bruce Porter hoped they would attain, "the consummation of their beauty and mystery, conferred by Nature herself wherever gardens grow old."[44]

Fleishhacker and "Green Gables"

Only a few minutes away from "Filoli" in Woodside was a garden that couldn't have been created anywhere else but California in the first quarter of the twentieth century: "Green Gables," the country place of the Mortimer Fleishhackers, still in family hands today. Fleishhacker, a banker and prominent figure in the San Francisco Jewish community, and his wife, Bella, wanted an English house with a thatched roof on their magnificent 75-acre site at the foot of the Santa Cruz Mountains. After a considerable search for an architect, they decided on Charles Greene, of the Southern Californian Craftsman firm of Greene & Greene, famous for their "ultimate bungalows" in Pasadena, built between 1906 and 1909. It was an odd choice; there was no evidence to suppose that Greene was the best man for the job. The Japanese-inspired bungalows

Charles Greene's sketches show the curved arcade at the end of Mortimer Fleishhacker's pool at "Green Gables," the masterstroke of Greene's inspired garden design.

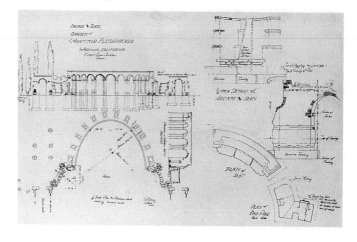

At the George Newhalls'
"Newmar" (1914), later "La
Dolphine," architect Lewis
Hobart doubled the low hedges
and staggered the pollarded plane
trees in strict quincunx pattern.
Perfect maintenance in a perfect
climate also contributes for a
uniquely hallucinatory effect.

Famous "Filoli" (1915), in
Woodside, is the California
version of an Irish Georgian
garden. The columnar Irish yews
beyond the sunken garden were
all raised from cuttings taken at
historic Muckross Abbey in
Killarney, which the William
Bourns also owned.

Northern
California

321

designed by Charles and Henry, his brothers, had little appeal for the Fleishhackers, who made a special trip to Pasadena to see them. In general, the Greenes' imaginative and progressive but unpretentious architecture was not favored by the rich, who preferred Mediterranean styles for their estates.[45] David Streatfield conjectures that Greene's artistic personality and the firm's reputation for lapidary craftsmanship may have appealed more to the Fleishhackers' fastidious, almost austere tastes than the more ornate estate work of architects like Polk and Hobart.[46]

Streatfield identifies "Green Gables" as the most challenging commission of Charles Greene's career: it was by far the largest; there was a shortage of water, and the prospect of inventing an English thatched house that would fit harmoniously into a California setting was enough all on its own to terrify any sensitive architect.[47] Greene, who had just made a long visit to England, abstracted the textures and profiles of the simple but rambling houses he had seen hidden in the combes of Devonshire—the same sort of Arts-and-Crafts inspiration Edwin Lutyens had found in the village architecture of Surrey. The walls were sprayed with Gunnite to suggest the rounded shapes of English plastered stone walls, and the mounded thick edge of a thatched roof was suggested by the curve of redwood shingles, each individually steamed and molded.

In the garden, the major problem that Greene faced was a common one in California: how to accord the colossal scale of a mountainscape with a domestic scale. At the Fleishhackers it was the Santa Cruz range; further south, in Santa Barbara, the Santa Ynez mountains loomed, and in Pasadena, the San Gabriel. To his clients' consternation, Greene sat for days on the hill he eventually chose as the house site, meditating. His first steps were conventional enough solutions used by garden makers through the centuries. He located the house behind a huge existing oak, doubtless both to shade the garden terrace and to break the immensity of the view. He ran a wide-spaced pair of paths out across a sloping lawn toward a lily pool, making the central rectangular panel into a *tapis vert*-like focusing axis. Thinking of the textural richness of the mountains, he kept the colors and planes of the garden simple: no flowers except a band just below the house windows on the terrace, and in dark brown glazed pots he designed for the steps. By 1913, the garden was handsome but not truly effective; the terrace, lawn, and lily pool that connected the house to the mountain view seemed too small. Greene must have sensed this; he experimented with large vertical plantings—poplars, Atlas cedars—at the far end corners of the lawn. Not until 1927 did he solve the problem satisfactorily, when the Fleishhackers asked him to design something for the steep slope below the lily pool. Greene added a 300-foot-long pool, which terminated in a series of huge arches. Their rough stone construction, monumental size, and the way they are tied together as an arcade

instantly but not insistently evoke a Roman ruin. Both pool and arches are invisible until the steps just above the lily pool are reached. The gardens finally became part of the landscape, thanks to the massive scale of the swirling divided stairs that lead down to the new pool, the use of local stone, and the arches, which simultaneously suggest a garden boundary and hint at more beyond. After the new garden architecture was complete, the tree planting rationale seemed to fall into place as well. For instance, a pair of Monterey pines at the edge of the stairs, which have now reached maturity, restrict the mountain view from the house and make a screen behind the lily pool from above; they also, a few steps later, dramatically frame the first view of the water garden. Greene's eclectic, allusive masterpiece was easily the most important estate garden completed in the twenties in the Bay Area.[48]

"It was typical of Charles Greene just to 'wing out' when working alone and not pressed," says his biographer, Randall Makinson.[49] Makinson speculates that the inspiration for the water garden, the rocky stairs, the masterstroke of the arcade, the intimation of ruin, may have come from Greene's long-held memory of a stone arch at Tintagel, in Cornwall. On his visit in 1909, he spent nine months in Clovelly and painted watercolors of the arch; one of these hung, framed, in his own house at Carmel for years.[50] On the other hand, there is no denying the baroque Italian curves of the masonry and the balustrade from which one looks over the long pool, the Villa Aldobrandini-esque character of the grotto, or the fact that Greene spent time in Italy as well.[51] Like Fletcher Steele's Blue Steps at "Naumkeag," like Jens Jensen's great entrance drive which is the mainspring of "Airdrie," the water garden at "Green Gables" is the deep, intricately fused response of an artist to his or her material, a response almost impossible to plumb. Even if the creator offers an explanation afterward, one can never be sure what has really happened—the only sure thing is that the grandeur of the solution often seems to equal the difficulty of the problem.[52]

"Casa Amesti" and "La Cuesta Encantada": Poles Apart

Moving down the West Coast from San Francisco, one comes first to the Monterey Peninsula, where fine gardens were made around the nineteenth-century adobes of Monterey starting in the late teens. The prized architecture of the little seacoast town, the old capital of California, was Monterey Colonial, a fusion of New England construction and California materials which yielded two-story, verandahed adobes that were among the few fruits of the short-lived Yankee-California harmony of the 1830s and 40s.[53] Monterey-style gardens were like those at the house of Thomas Larkin, first and only American consul to California: town gardens with fenced yards, often informally planted, surrounding long rectangular adobes. Pots were arranged in large groups, and the vertical verandah posts were wreathed in vines. A more formal garden

Hearst often swam in the Neptune pool, taking his pet dachshunds with him.

was that of "Casa Amesti," now a National Trust property: cool, green, and Italian, hidden behind high adobe walls. Chicago architect David Adler remodeled the house and created the garden for his sister, interior decorator Mrs. Frances Adler Elkins, after 1918.[54]

On the other side of the Peninsula, in the posh resort development of Pebble Beach, English garden writer Marion Cran walked along the coast, "rocky as Cornwall and far more vivid in color." She found one of those California garden sights that make even the most experienced gardener rave: "Accustomed to see James Carter's solemn presentment of carefully-grown hothouse cinerarias in England at the Chelsea Flower Show every year, I was much taken aback to find this, the most lovely groundsel, positively boiling out of Mrs. Dan Murphy's garden on the roadside in a bewildering confusion of size and color. . . ."[55] In the early thirties, the gardens of the new houses of Pebble Beach were very different from the gardens of the upper Peninsula made twenty years before. Beaux-Arts giants like "Uplands" were no longer fashionable; people instead preferred smaller, simpler Spanish Colonial courtyards by such Bay Area architects as Clarence Tantau, with many variations on the verandah and the exterior stair, a flow of interior/exterior space, and a livable mixture of sun and shade. These gardens, and some of the more modest ones in Santa Barbara by architects George Washington Smith or James Osborne Craig, are the ancestors of today's California gardens. However, to judge from photographs in Winifred Dobyns's book, the flower beds in these smaller gardens still "positively boiled" with labor-intensive, thirsty *Phlox paniculata*, heliotrope, ferns, and elephant's-ears plus other tropicals and native plants.[56]

Two hundred and fifty miles south of San Francisco, and south of the Big Sur, was "La Cuesta Encantada," William Randolph Hearst's palace set five vertical miles above the Pacific at San Simeon. In glitter, extravagance, and fantasy, the "Hearst Castle," as it was soon called, was the herald of "The Southland," which is how Southern Californians still refer to the land below the Tehachapi Mountains. The distance from the consciously simple garden at the Thomas Larkin house in Monterey to San Simeon was more than a geographical seventy-five miles—the two were the antipodes of California gardens. Hearst was the son of a flamboyant, foulmouthed, poker-playing, millionaire senator from California, George Hearst, and Phoebe Apperson Hearst, who became one of the grandes dames of California. Even before San Simeon, the Hearst family was given to extravagant domestic architecture (W. R.'s mother's "Hacienda Del Pozo de Verona" in Livermore was a Spanish-Moorish fantasy.[57] "Wyntoon," her shingle castle on the McCloud River near Mount Shasta, was designed by Bernard Maybeck. "Wyntoon" was rebuilt by Julia Morgan, W. R.'s San Simeon architect after a fire in 1929; Marion Davies, W. R.'s constant companion, hated the place and called it "Spittoon."). Phoebe Apperson was the cultivated daughter of a Missouri preacher, and following the custom of the day frequently took her young son to Europe. Such trips must have fueled W. R.'s first collecting instincts—only instead of stamps or dead beetles, he had higher aims. It's reported that when he saw the Louvre for the first time, he said to his mother, "Buy it for me, Mom! We can afford it."[58] After Harvard, he returned to California and was given the *San Francisco Examiner* to run by his father. Thus were set the two most important aspects of Hearst's life as an American prince, with all its pleasures, prejudices, and mercurial enthusiasms: he was a publisher for sixty-six years and a ravenous collector every day he breathed.

Like Louis XIV, Hearst had building fever, and his architect, Julia Morgan, was in constant attendance, working at San Simeon from 1919, when his mother died and left him the property and $11 million till 1947, when Hearst and Davies moved to Beverly Hills on account of ill health. Because building was constant, and money no object, it is difficult to make out any rationale for the site plan or the planting plans—they were always changing. It usually depended on what gigantic European architectural trophies Hearst had recently bought or what plants he had just seen. It is a tribute to the startling eclectic skills of Julia Morgan, and such landscape architects as Los Angeles–based Charles Gibbs Adams, that the gardens of the lavish hilltop village were a luxuriant synthesis, not merely a Tower of Babel speaking many different Mediterranean tongues. (Spanish, Italian, and French Renaissance were spoken here, as well as Art Moderne and first century A.D. Pompeian.) But appropriately enough for California, the prominent feature of the landscape besides the palm-sprinkled terraces was the neoclassical swimming pool, clad in green tile and white marble, and known as the Neptune Pool.

Apart from citing numbers—700,000 annuals were grown in five greenhouses each year, 4,000 to 5,000 trees of all species were planted *yearly* on the castle's approach slopes—the best period description of the gardens is a short one by Marion Cran. An invited guest, she arrived at the 245,000-acre ranch (one-third the size of Rhode Island) from Los Angeles as the evening mists were rising up from the Pacific. "A huge gate barred the way, bearing the legend 'Wild Animals; Unsafe For Pedestrians,'" she wrote, "and just inside the gate a gnu lay across the path. . . ." She made it to the castle itself, where, she continues, "We ascended marble stairs, passed the plash of fountains among marble limbs of naiads, trod wide terraces of marble hung with roses; I glanced up at the familiar sky to catch the sense of a common world in this staggering Arabian Nights place . . . but the mist had blotted out the stars. . . . In one spot a cluster gleamed; and to that my eyes clung . . . 'The Pleiades have changed their shape here,' I said at last, faintly. The escort smiled. 'Those are the lights on the castle towers.'"[59]

Hearst's virtually unknown architect, tiny Julia Morgan, was the first woman to take engineering at Berkeley, where she also studied architecture under such Bay Area notables as Bernard Maybeck and John Galen Howard. Then off she went to Europe, where she fell under the spell of the Gothic, with its mystique of the architect as part of a team of skilled craftsmen. In Paris, in 1898, she became the first woman to study architecture at the Ecole des Beaux-Arts, where she absorbed the widest range of historical styles. She returned to San Francisco in 1902, and five decades later, she had created a stream of houses of varying styles, from the informal redwood Colby House in Berkeley to cast concrete Italian Gothic structures, to San Simeon itself. Nearly every Friday evening—along with other Hearst guests such as Clark Gable, Charlie Chaplin, and P. G. Wodehouse—she boarded the train for San Simeon, "like a neat bantam hen among peacocks," said one guest. She spent the weekend working, often with Hearst himself in attendance. A memorable sight in a narrow-brimmed hat, tailored gray suit, and white French silk blouse, she climbed the scaffolding herself to direct the 100 workmen on every detail of what has only recently been acknowledged as her Mediterranean masterpiece as much as William Randolph Hearst's.[60]

SOUTHERN CALIFORNIA

SANTA BARBARA

"January and part of February are the spring in southern California," said Mrs. Francis King, eminent garden writer, in 1921,[1] explaining why, from Santa Barbara southward, California became winter vacationland for Easterners and Midwesterners. Though development started in the Southland after the railroads arrived in 1876 and 1886, vacation for earlier visitors often cloaked a more serious concern: the search for health. Santa Barbara, like Pasadena and other resorts farther south, had its beginnings in the escape from illness. By the 1880s Eastern consumptives, asthmatics, and those just feeling poorly had transformed the small Spanish town below the Santa Ynez mountains into a flourishing sanitarium, coming for the air and sun, the sulphur mud baths, the mineral waters, and the hot spring above Montecito. Just as in Florida, visitors first stayed in hotels, and by the eighties there were four large ones.

But the big estate makers who arrived in Santa Barbara and Montecito in the 1890s were not seeking a cure; they simply were sick of East Coast winters. These millionaires who arrived yearly in their private railroad cars became known as the "hill barons," because they settled in the foothills of the mountains that reared up just three to five miles from the coast.[2] The Santa Ynez range has always been Santa Barbara's greatest attraction and protection. Because the 4,000-foot-tall peaks prevented direct rail linkage with the East, and the coastal plain was too narrow for extensive developments, Santa Barbara was spared the kind of epidemic land boom that took place farther south in the Los Angeles Basin. The unique climate of Santa Barbara and Montecito is also created by the mountains: they run east-west instead of north-south, the only place along the entire Pacific Coast that this occurs. Called the "American Mentone" by Baedeker's *Guide* as early as 1893, Santa Barbara and Montecito actually do enjoy what is known as a "Mediterranean climate." Both weather and topography are similar to that of the Côte d'Azur and the Riviera, parts of Australia, South Africa, and Chile. The floras of all these regions flourish in Santa Barbara and Montecito, where the winters are cool and moist, with a hard frost only every ten to fifteen years, and the summers are long, warm, and dry. If anything, the climate of Montecito's woodland belt above the seashore, where the greatest of the estates were located, is marginally better than Santa Barbara's, with additional rainfall annually and extra heat, thanks to the proximity and orientation of the mountains, which act like a gigantic solar screen.

In their first Santa Barbara gardens, Easterners planted the showiest,

The crisp maze on the terrace at the Kirk B. Johnsons' "La Toscana" was finished by landscape architect A. E. Hanson just before the Crash.

largest, tenderest, plants available at the time, as if to celebrate escaping Eastern winters. Every garden had cup-of-gold, the *copa de oro* vine *Solandra maxima*, which is native to Mexico. It flowers most prolifically in winter, smells like a coconut, and blooms while you watch.[3] Other early favorites were palms of all sorts; brilliantly colored bird of paradise, *Strelitzia maxima*, from South Africa; the frangipani, *Plumeria rubra*, from Mexico and the West Indies; easily recognized banana; and the sixty-foot dragon tree, *Dracaena Draco*, with two-foot long leaves, the cousin of the dracaenas that Victorians had grown in their greenhouses.[4] Australian plants were also favored, such as the bizarre grevilleas and banksias, with their flowers like bottle brushes and huge upholstery tassels, and the ubiquitous eugenia, *Syzygium paniculatum*, a perfect hedge, with its waxy, substantial leaves and rosy new growth in the winter time. Eucalyptus was planted everywhere and then naturalized, becoming one of the most attractive features of the landscape. Blue gum and sugar gum were special favorites. Freesias, sparaxis, ixias, and other little South African bulbs also naturalized in gardens; pelargonium, known commonly as geranium, ramped like a groundcover instead of growing sedately in pots, and agapanthus, the blue lily-of-the-Nile, grew wild. The wonga-wonga vine, *Pandorea pandorana*, a purple-spotted Australian cousin of the trumpet vine, threw itself about, and gardeners gloried in strange and ever-stranger plants.

But in all this tropical splendor, something was lacking. Mary Kennedy Woodhouse, visiting Southern California from East Hampton, in 1914, put her finger on the intangible that was absent from a California garden for her.

There is something . . . in the ease and abundance with which plants, shrubs and vines run riot, that furnishes a clue to the something that one misses. . . . The quality of tenderness, of delicate care bestowed, that the gardens in more difficult climes demand, one misses in California especially on the great estates, where the tendency is constantly to increase in size. The lawns encroach upon woodland, flowers appear where they do not belong, the place gets out of hand, for one cannot administer an intimate affection over half a county.[5]

She was certainly no stranger to "the tendency to increase in size"; her own very large garden was a paradise of pergolas, arbors, statues, walled enclosures, reflecting pools and water gardens, and thousands of flowers. Her discomfort arose for other reasons: first, the feeling that gardening was all too easy in California, and second, because of that easiness, that there was no thoughtful sense of scale, appropriate planting, or place. Two of the three gardens Mrs. Woodhouse *did* admire that she felt were well designed in all respects were J. Waldron Gillespie's "El Fureidis" and George Owen Knapp's "Arcady" in Santa Barbara. (The third was Henry Huntington's estate in San Marino.) Gillespie's garden was inspired by Persia; Knapp's by Italy, both among the Mediterranean cultures to which Olmsted had resorted for the plan of Stanford University, and the Bay Area designers for the Peninsular gardens. Over the course of the estate garden period, which in Santa Barbara ran from the turn of the century to the beginning of World War II, most great gardens were in these two styles for the first twenty years; the Spanish Colonial style reigned for the succeeding twenty. In the thirties, landscape architect Lockwood de Forest was the first to free garden design from historical styles, making abstract gardens based on the formal qualities of plants themselves, gardens that also obeyed the imperatives of climate and fit harmoniously into the California landscape.

Who were the garden makers of Santa Barbara? Sophisticated, well-traveled, stylish, conservative, secure in their own taste, their wealth, and in themselves, they constituted a special group unlike other Californians. Second- or third-generation wealth made them accustomed to having what they wanted, and knowing how to get it. Often when they arrived they were expert gardeners, or at least owned large gardens back East. Just a few of the most accomplished or enthusiastic bi-coastal gardeners in Santa Barbara were Mrs. Oakleigh Thorne of "Thornedale" in Millbrook, New York, Mrs. Alfred Herter of "The Creeks" in East Hampton, the Arthur Meekers of Chicago and Lake Forest, and Lolita Armour Mitchell, whose garden heritage included her grandfather's extensive Italian villa gardens at "Melody Farm" in Lake Forest.[6]

"El Fureidis"

In 1890, J. Waldron Gillespie arrived from New York and bought 33 acres and a small house. (Gillespie, a member of an old New York family, also kept a family place in Granville, north of Albany, a house in Manhattan,

The garden that started the Mediterranean craze in Santa Barbara was the J. Waldron Gillespies' Persian rill at "El Fueridis" (1901), which ends at the bottom of a hill in what became this lush water garden.

and a villa in Havana.) For the next ten years he left the old house untouched on its magnificent site overlooking mountains and sea, and concentrated on the landscape, planting an arboretum with 125 varieties of palm and 25 different acacias. Many of Gillespie's acquisitions came from Kinton Stevens, one of the early nurserymen who experimented with introductions and propagated the regional flora.[7]

In 1901 Gillespie engaged New York architect Bertram Grosvenor Goodhue to build a new house; he himself already had ideas for the garden. In 1902, the two took a trip to Spain and Italy, and on to Persia,

where they rode 400 miles on horseback from the Caspian Sea to the Persian Gulf. They traveled to Isfahan, Shiraz, and Samarkand, and came back with two garden ideas new to Santa Barbara: a respect for water and a fascination with geometry. "El Fureidis," credited with being the first formal garden of Santa Barbara, was very influential; almost every other design after 1906 paid lip service at least to a sparing use of water and employed a formal, geometric scheme.[8] Francis T. Underhill, a gifted amateur architect and garden designer, helped with the plantings. A colorful, polo-playing New Yorker from Oyster Bay, and an ex-Congressman who became a Santa Barbara fixture, the versatile Underhill also designed other local landmarks, including the luxurious Bartlett Polo Field complex, which opened in 1916.[9]

The grounds of "El Fureidis," which means "Place of Happiness" in Arabic, were divided in two parts. The well-irrigated outer landscape, which grew up into a near jungle, was threaded with trails that led to views, and to such attractions as a reservoir ornamented with columns from which ran a tiny, shiny Islamic channel of water set in the pavement, a Javanese temple, a tile shrine to the Madonna, and a naturalistic water garden planted with the mauve canyon or broom lupine, *L. cytisoides*. The breathtaking second part of the design was the narrow enfilade of water gardens that descended the hill from the small, white concrete and stone "Roman villa," with its central atrium and red-tiled roof. Nothing was planted in the terrace tank next to the Ionic-columned garden front of the house, and nothing in the "water garden" just beneath the shallow pools reflected only the blue sky, the white house, and the surrounding dense greenness of Gillespie's palms. The long flight of white-walled masonry steps to the garden far below was equally strict—nothing but high, dark, clipped cypress on either side, with the tops of the palms and other tropical trees peering over. Some fifty feet below lay the final pool, shaded by the branches of surrounding trees and planted with purple and yellow water lilies. Beyond it stood a tea pavilion consisting of two plain white cubes connected by an Ionic portico. The exotic severity of design and plantings in this part of the garden impressed visitors—and there were plenty of them, for Gillespie opened his gardens every day of the week except Sunday, beginning in 1915. "El Fureidis," claimed one travel book, "after the mission, is probably the most distinctive attraction of Santa Barbara."[10] For Gillespie's own guests another attraction was the atrium garden, planted with oranges, bananas, and *Cocos plumosa*, where *absinthes frappés* were served around a marble pool, under the benign gaze of a full-sized statue of *Antinoüs*.[11]

"Arcady"
The other garden Mrs. Woodhouse admired in Montecito was "Arcady," which surrounded the tile-roofed, yellow stucco Italian Renaissance villa designed by Santa Barbara architect Carleton Monroe Winslow for George Owen Knapp in 1912. Winslow is also credited with the terrace and the upper garden, but another well-known Southern California landscape architect, Ralph D. Cornell, also worked at "Arcady" in 1920, as did Charles Gibbs Adams, who was responsible for some of the planting at San Simeon.[12] Francis Underhill's tour de force at "Arcady" was the lower garden, a series of formal pools that stretched 1,200 feet below a splendid swimming pool enclosed in a classical casino with an electrically powered sun roof, which he also designed. "Arcady's" broad terrace with a central fountain, and the wide, curved "Bramante steps"

guarded by a pair of cherubs, all bathed in golden afternoon light and positioned to catch some of the most romantic folds and valleys of the Santa Ynez range, embodied Charles Dudley Warner's *Our Italy* for all, including Mrs. Woodhouse, who remarked on the "very strong Italian atmosphere." But Marion Cran, who came to visit "Arcady" some fifteen years after Mrs. Woodhouse, saw another aspect of the garden: "It looks like Italy and England *mixed*," she said, looking at the vast lawn, the biggest in Montecito, "where," she added, "water is scarce and gardening a great luxury."[13] That luxurious lawn, and the way in which, as Porter Garnett said in 1915, "roads and paths seem to have been governed by the position of the trees and the configuration of the land," and "little attention has been paid to formal design," are part of the older California garden aesthetic—the English picturesque applied to the semiarid California landscape.[14] "Arcady" was also famous for the richness and variety of its plant collections, which required a 75-page booklet to catalogue. There was also a grotto, and a half-timbered construction called "The Hut," roofed with redwood bark and used for informal entertainment. Knapp's passion for *Sequoia gigantea* later led him to buy a fifty-foot-tall chunk of redwood which he "planted" in the ground so that it looked like an enormous stump. Inside this folly, stairs climbed to a sweeping view of the ocean.[15]

"Las Tejas"
In 1917, when Mrs. Oakleigh Thorne began her gardens at "Las Tejas," she adopted the aesthetics of irrigation and water conservation that Gillespie had pioneered. Though her gardens had easily as much variety as "Arcady," and she used quantities of what she called in 1921 "the evanescent, decorative planting consisting of practically the same material which supplies color in our Eastern gardens," she also intentionally used drought-resistant shrubs as the backbone of her garden and "reduced the grass to a negligible and ornamental quantity." She made the connection between straight lines and efficient watering, pointing out that "a dependence upon irrigation is, I believe, an economic factor forcing California gardening into those formal lines which lend themselves to its practice. A hedge is much more readily watered than broad irregularly planted borders."[16]

"Las Tejas" was built for William Alston Hayne II, as a Mission-style adobe in 1898 and roofed with old red tiles from the original Spanish houses of the town, hence the name "Las Tejas," "the tiles."[17] When the Thornes bought the property in 1917, Mrs. Thorne and Santa Barbara architect Francis W. Wilson transformed the house into an Italian villa.[18] With Wilson's help, Helen Thorne, who had surveying implements and knew how to use them, laid out her stunning chain of water gardens below the loggia on the garden front. Like Lila Vanderbilt Webb at "Shelburne Farms" in Vermont, though to a much greater degree, Helen

The powerful descent of the Oakleigh Thornes' "Las Tejas" (1917) in Santa Barbara was engineered by the capable Helen Thorne. The distant casino is modeled on that in the sixteenth-century gardens of the Farnese Palace in Viterbo. In the fern garden, below, one of the many separate compartments of "Las Tejas," those two precious California commodities, water and shade, are put to lavish use.

Thorne was interested in garden architecture as well as in plants. She had the freedom, the money, and the skills to garden "like a man"—that is to say with bricks and mortar, rock, dynamite, and soil—instead of "painting pictures with flowers," as did most women gardeners of her day.

Like other great gardeners, Helen Thorne also studied her own work, minutely chronicling in photographs and extensive notes the placement of trees, the effects of various shapes, and her color schemes. Sensitive and intelligent, she was acutely aware of the connections possible between landscape and garden, especially color, using garden plants of the same hues as those of the naturally occurring rocks and vegetation.

The gardens of "Las Tejas" eventually covered 26 acres, with a virtuoso Japanese garden, compartments such as a heliotrope garden, and Spanish gardens up near the front of the house. George Washington Smith, Santa Barbara architect and Helen Thorne's close friend, laid these out beginning in 1926 when he remodeled the entrance front and closed in the house patio, making it into a sumptuous Italianate room. Smith, the man most responsible for the rise of the smaller, simpler Spanish Colonial houses that would set the tone for the next generation of Santa Barbara gardens, made plain the difference between the Italian gardens and the newer Spanish style: "In the Spanish garden the long open vista of the Italian garden is transformed into a vista through many gateways, so that a feeling of intimacy and mystery is achieved rather than an effect of formality and grandeur. One is not overcome by seeing it all at once, but one has new surprises as he progresses through the gardens."[19] In the twenties on the West Coast, just as on the East, in such enclaves as Santa Barbara or Long Island's Gold Coast, taste was beginning to change among garden sophisticates. The forthright and strongly architectural statement of power and wealth seen in the work of such landscape architects as James Greenleaf, or the occasional brilliant amateur such as Helen Thorne, was giving way to a less ostentatious, though no less architectural, style like Smith's, or to the green architecture of Annette Hoyt Flanders and Lockwood de Forest.

George Washington Smith and the Small Spanish Garden

George Washington Smith was not a landscape architect, but he was probably the best designer of houses on the West Coast, and his influence on estate gardens in Santa Barbara, at least in terms of design, was as great as that of any landscape architect working at the time.[20] Smith was born in East Liberty, Pennsylvania, in 1876, and after attending Philadelphia's Academy of Fine Arts and studying architecture at Harvard, he traveled abroad for several years, especially in Italy and Spain. After several career starts, he settled on architecture. In 1915 Smith came to California to paint, and to visit the San Francisco and San Diego Expositions with his wife. They stayed on, and he built his first house in Montecito in 1916. Painting soon gave way to architecture, since, as Smith himself said, "I soon found that people were not really [as] eager to buy my paintings, which I was laboring over, as they were to have a whitewashed house like mine."[21] Until his early death in 1930 he practiced in Santa Barbara, simplifying for his conservative clients the shapes of an old regional vernacular,[22] just as architect Wilson Eyre did with the Georgian farmhouse in Pennsylvania.

One of the great pleasures of being rich in Santa Barbara during the twenties would have been working with George Washington Smith on a new house. Agreeable, accomplished, workmanlike, gentlemanly—his pose was always that of gentleman architect—,Smith was unruffled to the point of being phlegmatic.

Smith designed the gardens of his smaller houses, and the two gardens that he made for himself were brilliant essays on the straight line, the enclosed, intimate space, and the use of the strong California light and shadow. The first, "El Hogar," later the Craig Heberton house, turned its back to the street; to the rear was a formal garden with a long path, as a strong central axis, laid in brick, his usual paving material. As Elizabeth Kellam de Forest, landscape designer and widow of Lockwood de Forest wrote, "it was the inspiration for scores of other Santa Barbara gardens made in the Spanish style," with its "tall trees, the paths and beds laid out symmetrically, all straight lines emphasized by edgings of dwarf box, sunlight and shadow playing over an oblong sunken pool on the terrace."[23] "El Hogar" was built in 1916; "Casa del Greco," his second, smaller and less formal house and garden created in 1920, was what David Streatfield calls "a perfect example of the planning tradition of the teens and twenties; the entrance court was placed on the southern side of the house with small openings, while the living area on the eastern side faced across shaded terraces to the sunlit gardens beyond, providing a sequence of light ranging from the deep shade of the interiors of the house, through the partial shade of the terraces, to the full sunlight of the garden."[24] The two organizing features of the garden were a box maze and a brick pavement with an Islamic water channel. At "El Hogar" and "Casa del Greco," Smith rendered the Mediterranean theme with which Gillespie had first experimented in a way suited to an urban or suburban site and small acreage.

THREE LARGE MEDITERRANEAN GARDENS
"The formal Mediterranean gardens of southern California were designed on two scales," continues David Streatfield, "the smaller ones were usually completely formal while the larger ones were designed in one of two ways, they were either axially related to the house with groves of trees around them or they were planned as a series of separate garden 'rooms' arranged around a lawn or within a grove."[25] "El Hogar" and "Casa del Greco" fit the first category; the gardens of three other George Washington Smith houses fell into the second. On large places such as these Smith worked with every Southern California garden designer of note.

"Casa del Herrero," "house of the blacksmith," epitomizes the Spanish tradition as it developed in its own particular way in California in the twenties. The simplicity of Smith's unadorned adobe walls and the architectural detailing of the house were Spanish, though there were some additional Italian touches, such as the main south loggia. St. Louis businessman George F. Steedman, and his wife, Carrie Howard, traveled to Spain and Italy, collecting architectural fragments for use in the house and the garden, and consulted with Hispanic experts Mildred Stapley Byne and Arthur Byne, authors of *Spanish Gardens and Patios*, even traveling to Spain with them in 1923.[26]

The flavor of the garden is Spanish, the plan is typically American Beaux-Arts, and the plantings are pure California. The entrance court-yard with its black-and-white pebble paving is reminiscent of the Patio de la Reja at the Alhambra, and there are many magnificent Spanish carvings and other ornaments, tiles, and pieces of wrought iron throughout the gardens. The typical estate garden layout has a central green vista that lines up with the axis of the house, while enclosure gardens run alongside or project from the other house elevations. The sand-floored cactus garden, brilliant with scarlet kniphofia and beautifully located below the sightline of the allée, is a California specialty, the final form of Ulrich's "Arizona garden." The plantings were a mixture of temperate, semitropical and tropical plants. Ralph Stevens, son of nurseryman Kinton Stevens, made the original estate plan; the richly varied courtyard plantings are an especially good example of his work. Stevens, who opened his own Santa Barbara office in 1917, continued planting in the lavish style of the nineties, using a wide range of exotics to carry out superbly the old fantasy of California-as-tropics. Francis Underhill and Lockwood de Forest, more formal and abstract in their approaches, were called upon to make changes in the basic Stevens plan and plantings. Steedman himself, an enthusiastic perfectionist and gardener, carried out some of his own ideas in addition to all the rest he had solicited. Peter Riedel, early California naturalist Emanuele Orazio Fenzi's partner in the Southern California Acclimatizing Association, also worked at "Casa del Herrero."[27] Smith died in 1930 with the house still unfinished, though the Steedmans had moved in on June 29, 1925, the day of Santa Barbara's famous earthquake (the house was untouched).[28]

In 1923, a year after he began work for the Steedmans, Smith also began "Il Brolino," a handsome L-shaped Italian-style villa for Mrs. Mary Stewart, the daughter of a lumber baron with interests in Wisconsin, Oregon, and California. Smith endowed his Italianate houses with the same simplicity, gravity, and attention to detail that he gave his Spanish Colonial work. At "Il Brolino," the severe entrance front looks across the courtyard, up over a mighty rampart wall to an enclosed garden teeming with antic topiary figures, which give only a hint of the richness and variety of the gardens.

The 6 cultivated acres of "Il Brolino" are an early work of Florence Yoch, a California-born landscape architect whose estate garden practice stretched from such specifically Italian gardens as this, with its topiary features and dignified direct quotes from the Villa Medici and Villa Vicobello, to theatrical Hollywood gardens of an almost Roman extravagance for movieland figures such as Dorothy Arzner, David O. Selznick, George Cukor, and Jack Warner. In addition to the sets for such films as *Gone with the Wind* and Cukor's *Romeo and Juliet,* she also designed over 100 gardens in Pasadena and nearby San Marino, many of which were modest flowery places in what we now can consider the best laid-back California tradition. In 1923, when she did "Il Brolino," she had not yet met Lucille Council, the woman who would join her practice and her life in a thirty-nine-year-long partnership. Of the two women, whom Cukor described as "a couple of tough customers," Yoch was the designing partner. Council seems to have been the enabler; the one who found the perfect olive tree for a client's garden, who managed the office and the accounts, and who gave Yoch the support and understanding she needed to be a practicing landscape architect in what was essentially a man's world.[29]

In the 1880s, Yoch spent her earliest childhood in Santa Ana in an Italianate villa, and grew up at Laguna Beach, where her oddball but successful German emigrant father, who had sold his Illinois coal fields to Jay Gould at a profit, ran the Laguna Beach Hotel. Her family was close friends with Madame Helena Modjeska, the legendary Polish actress. Modjeska, and her husband, Count Karol Chlapowski, made a fabulous estate in Santa Ana, with an elaborate bungalow by Stanford White and a garden by Englishman Theodore Payne, who later became a nurseryman in Los Angeles and one of the greatest experts on California native plants.[30] Modjeska and her garden, which formed the nucleus of the Rancho Santa Ana Botanical Garden, doubtless had a formative effect on Yoch.

Even in such an early and atypical garden as "Il Brolino" (Yoch did no other topiary garden), Yoch worked according to the principles that would govern all her later work. Formal gardens were symmetrical but never arbitrarily so—she adjusted the plan on site. The symmetry was always waylaid by an odd tree or a statue set off center. Yoch fuzzed the edges of her grandeur with coziness: around the splendid wellhead in the sunken garden at "Il Brolino" is a humble, assorted collection of flowerpots. Lacking the crisp precision of most American villa garden replicas, such as Charles Platt's, the not-quite-straight lines of the enclosure gardens at "Il Brolino" suggest that they seem to have arisen organically, over time, in response to the land forms and to need, rather than as a single designed sequence. Paths lead off to a cutting garden and to a quiet shaded terrace where the classical aura of a stone balustrade and a pair of Roman chairs is softened by an off-center oak.[31]

Third of the trio of Smith houses was the Kirk B. Johnson place, "La Toscana," where the unlikeliest partnership produced one of the most beautiful villas of Santa Barbara, which still exists, comparatively intact,

in private hands today. No one could have seemed less compatible with George Washington Smith than A. E. Hanson, hard-driving son of a small-time, Southern California orange-grove developer. If Smith's temperament and art could be called Apollonian, then Hanson's was some kind of new-minted American Dionysian.

Hanson finished his formal schooling with two years of high school and then went to work for seed collector and nurseryman Theodore Payne for a year in 1915. A trip to the San Francisco and San Diego Expositions convinced him he wanted to be a landscape architect. How to do this with practically no education and no formal training? No problem for Hanson—he was the very model of the brash salesman/entrepreneur, but an engaging talented honest one. He hired other landscape architects to do the designs, a team of carpenters and gardeners to carry them out with plants from the best nurseries, and he found a Miss Johnson whose botanical Latin was impeccable—"no longer would I have to sit up at night making a plant list, trying to spell the names."[32] He eventually hired a superb Beaux-Arts-trained designer, Lee Rombotis, and Geraldine Knight, a horticulturist, to do the planting plans. Hanson made the calls, sized up the clients, and got the commissions. Hanson's robust account has the full, Fitzgerald flavor of the twenties—"There was Bill Menzies, who later became the art director for *Gone with the Wind;* there was a casting director for Fox; there was a stock broker. We'd all sit around at our house with bootleg liquor, fried chicken, and one man playing the piano while we sang, drank, and ate chicken. Time meant nothing on a Sunday night." Because of the Depression, his spellbinding career was short: by 1922 he had streamlined his Mediterranean landscaping system; by 1925 he had Harold Lloyd as a client; between February, 1928 and October, 1929 he designed some of the most flamboyant gardens of California, and "wouldn't bother with any garden that didn't cost $10,000 or more."[33] In 1932 he was doing his last estate garden, the Dan Murphy garden in Los Angeles, and had already become a land developer in the new estate garden–less world after Black Thursday, October 24, 1929.

Hanson himself considered the Johnson garden one of the five most important of his career.[34] His thrill at getting the commission, his first in the lofty old-money world of Santa Barbara, didn't diminish his ability to describe his clients in hard-headed terms. "Mrs. Johnson had inherited the money," he writes in his memoirs, "and I was told (not by Mr. Smith) that she was one of the five richest heiresses in the United States. Amongst other business ventures, her father had financed King C. Gillette, the safety razor man, and in doing so had made a lot of money. Mr. Johnson's only business that I knew of was handling Mrs. Johnson's money."[35]

Smith had heard about Hanson from his longtime lieutenant, the talented architect Lutah Maria Riggs, who had worked with Hanson in

1925 on the Henry Kern house in Holmby Hills that Smith had designed. Smith called Hanson in on the Johnson job just as the house was nearing completion, in early 1928. In November, 1927, Hanson and his wife had whirled around Europe in six weeks, and he was enthralled by the gardens he'd seen, especially in Spain. Some of the European features of his earlier gardens were unassimilated and crude, distinguished only by their lively brutality—a cascade at the Kerns that looked like a three-story escalator, for example. The Johnsons' 8 landscaped acres were different, no doubt partly due to Smith's influence, but also to the impact of the real thing on Hanson's active imagination and practical intelligence.

Serene and elegant, the gardens surround the tawny Tuscan villa with a smoothly flowing collection of enclosures and a wide lawn. It's hard to choose one feature over another; whether the parterre garden with its subtle topiary echo of the curving steps is finer than the ramped pergola garden that terminates in a tiny platform, pebble-floored in a Maltese Cross pattern, or than the shadowed network of paths that make a *bosquet* of the woods leading to the rose garden. The huge south lawn makes a

Distant, double rows of pink and white hawthornes pick up the color of petunias just below the garden terrace at the George Newhalls' precisely splendid "Newmar," later "La Dolphine," in San Mateo.

perfect stage for the long low house and immense old cypress and oaks. Perhaps the north garden, which runs off the dining room, is the best of all. Here, double lines of lemon trees in beautiful terra-cotta pots, what Hanson called "the honor guard," run up a gentle hill from a small water garden to a white fountain set in more black-and-white pebble patterns. "To me, the landscape architect, this is the epitome of what a garden should be," said Hanson, "not because of what the landscape architect did, but because of the magnificent setting, the superb, dark green live oaks on either side, and the soft grey of the coast range in the background. . . . It was like a Maxfield Parrish painting."[36]

MONTECITO RESORT LIFE

The magnificent gardens of "Casa Bienvenida" were also begun in 1928 and finished five years later. In contrast to the tasteful balance of "La Toscana" or "Il Brolino," they were more like A. E. Hanson or Florence Yoch's exuberant Hollywood gardens, full of quotable quotes in stone. One of Addison Mizner's last projects, they were a throwback to the splashier style of the teens. Like the old warhorse he was, Mizner sniffed opportunity at "Casa Bienvenida": this was a former client, Alfred Dieterich, and a welcome big spender in the late twenties days of his shrunken Florida practice.[37] In Santa Barbara, Mizner used his most opulent Palm Beach Venetian palazzo style, laced with medieval Spanish details, for the forty-room house. For the garden, he happily took advantage of the one thing Palm Beach lacked: hills. The 17 acres of formal compartments were arranged around three major vistas, of which the most impressive was a water staircase that ran downhill with much hoopla from an arched garden house toward the house in classic Italian fashion. Even though the gardens were finished in the Depression years, no expense was spared (unlike "La Toscana," where silver gazing balls were used to terminate the vistas before the statues were acquired by a subsequent owner). Life at "Casa Bienvenida" continued undiminished too. Though Alfred died, Mrs. Dieterich, the former Ethel Vreeland Post of New York, went on entertaining her guests with the unvarying rhythms of resort life: swimming at the Coral Casino in the morning, followed by lunch at the house served by a brigade of servants. Upstairs in the Florida room, in the afternoons, they played Towie, that less demanding form of bridge.[38]

"Riven Rock"

The kind of privileged eccentricity that resorters cherish found its outlets even in staid Santa Barbara. In the teens, a guest at the stately Potter Hotel might have found the revolving door fully occupied by Julius, a large and willful orangutan. Only candy would tempt him out and back to the limousine for his ride home to "Riven Rock" with Mrs. Stanley McCormick and the chauffeur. In the case of Stanley McCormick himself,

In the evening light, blue ceanothus scrambles over a sculptured hedge
beyond the lily pool at the Kirk B. Johnsons' "La Toscana."

In the rose garden, with its banquettes of Spanish tile, at "Casa del Herrero," additional sitting room is provided by the handsome art moderne chairs crafted by the owner of the garden himself, hence the name, "The House of the Blacksmith," George Steedman.

Cyrus McCormick's youngest child, it was more than eccentricity, however. Schizophrenia ran in the family, and "Riven Rock," their Santa Barbara estate, was essentially a private sanatorium for Stanley, whose mind was adjudged "collapsed" in 1906, and for his sister, Virginia, who later moved away. Part of the estate was a macaque research facility for Dr. Gilbert Hamilton, the resident family psychiatrist, who was a primate behavior specialist, hence Julius, who was purchased for a colleague of Hamilton's. Stanley, who was intelligent, well-educated, and fond of the arts, enjoyed life at "Riven Rock" during his lucid periods. There was not only a private theater showing first-run movies three times a week, but also an 87-acre landscape cared for by forty gardeners and partly designed by Lockwood de Forest.[39]

Lockwood de Forest

Lockwood de Forest let his lawn go brown in the summer—he liked the color. He also got rid of his roses—they were too ungainly most of the year for a small garden. "Without question the most avant-garde and flamboyant designer of the 20s in the South," Lockwood de Forest was about forty years ahead of his time, if one calls the sixties the moment when Californians first saw California nature and native plant succession as a suitable domestic surrounding.[40] And yet de Forest was no iconoclast; in the thirties, his many conservative Santa Barbara patrons, who would have shuddered at a Richard Neutra residence and landscape of the same period, were proud of their gardens and felt at home in them. "His schemes, though basically formal in nature, were often created solely with plant materials," says David Streatfield, and it is doubtless this formality and his bold but sophisticated planting that reassured his estate clients.[41]

De Forest came from much the same small milieu as Stanford White, the stable, genteel, well-off society of nineteenth-century New York families, professionals, and merchants, whose real-life interest was culture and the arts.[42] De Forest's family was slightly better-off and less bohemian than White's, and de Forest himself more the gentleman practitioner than the architect, who was, after all, a member of the most famous and high-powered firm of his day. But the two men shared an omniverous aesthetic sensibility, a hectic flow of ideas and energy, a bright playful confidence that the variety of solutions to any given problem was unending. De Forest, a generation younger than White, eventually found his way to abstract design in the thirties and forties, before his premature death at fifty-three in 1949. De Forest's father, also Lockwood, was a painter, collector, writer, and traveler (Egypt, Syria, Greece, and India) who started workshops in Ahmadabad to revive the art of Indian woodcarving, and in 1879 set up a partnership with Louis Comfort Tiffany to import Indian decorative art, especially carved wall panels. By 1888, de Forest, Sr., was designing the houses and spaces for

A jacaranda tree in flower sets off the white Dutch Colonial gable of "Constantia," the Arthur Meekers' escape from the Chicago winter. By the twenties, many Santa Barbara resorters were coming from the Midwest. This murkily beautiful view from the other side of the house is framed at bottom by landscape architect Lockwood de Forest's fanciful sculpting of a eugenia hedge whose outline matches the house gable.

the panels; his clients included Samuel Clemens, Cornelius Vanderbilt, and Andrew Carnegie, among others. So young Lockwood, who was born in 1896, grew up in a consciously exotic atmosphere, where space, proportion, and decoration were important matters for consideration. By 1902 the family was spending the winters in Santa Barbara; in 1912 young Lockwood was sent to the Thacher School, a boarding school in the nearby Ojai Valley. The students had their own horses and built "shacks" apart from the school buildings where they spent their weekends. Besides becoming deeply familiar with every line and hue of the California landscape, young Lockwood made a friend for life in Philadelphian Wright Ludington, a fellow student. Later, the two traveled through Italy together, and Ludington became de Forest's client, as did his father when the family moved to Santa Barbara in 1924. Wright Ludington gave his friend Lockwood what every landscape architect dreams of, a chance, as de Forest himself wrote, to "stay on the job long enough to see the planting grow as he hoped."

De Forest's formal education as a landscape architect happened in such rapid, restless stages it almost seems that he took jobs or courses only to discover he already knew most of what he was being taught. Back in Santa Barbara, he worked for six months for landscape designer Ralph Stevens before setting up his own Santa Barbara office in 1920. According to de Forest's widow, Elizabeth Kellam de Forest, Lockwood felt that Stevens understood only the typical Long Island estate garden model and used plants in conventional ways.[43]

How would de Forest's gardens differ? In 1945 he wrote, "Here in California the traditional garden design has not been a success in most cases. It has to be adapted to meet the conditions of the distant view. . . . conventional planning usually does not fit as a foreground to this distant view. If besides this . . . one adds the outdoor living room that the average person living here demands and the mechanical layout that makes for ease of maintenance, one finds that an abstract design is the best solution."[44]

William Dickinson and Arthur Meeker

Two early gardens illustrate in varying ways what he meant by "abstract design." The first, for the William R. Dickinsons, was begun in 1928 at the other exclusive area in Santa Barbara besides Montecito: Hope Ranch. North of the city and right on the coast, Hope Ranch was not developed extensively until the late twenties, because water was in short supply until irrigation was put in. Being later in date, the estate gardens tended to be more understated than those of Montecito. Since they were close to the Pacific, and the mountains were far away, ocean views predominated.[45] The Dickinsons, young, rich, Chicagoans, eschewed the popular elaborate Spanish style for their house and asked Pasadena architect Reginald Johnson for a Monterey-style house. "Monterey style"

in this case meant a large simple whitewashed brick house set irregularly around a courtyard, its spare gables a stark contrast to the vine-covered walls. De Forest's gardens and landscapes, some few of which still exist today in private hands, evoked nothing but themselves. No one went to the Dickinsons and thought of England or France or Italy or Spain—California is the place, and Californian the garden. Although it is laid out with many of the traditional divisions, including a broad lawn for the view, a rose garden, and a cutting garden, it feels untraditional, thanks to the absence of sculpture and the use of plants rather than elaborate architecture to shape the subtly modeled spaces. Boundaries are suggested, not tightly drawn, for large formal areas such as the south lawn, where the house terrace melts without a step into the grass, and a single low wall successfully implies an entire square format. The color scheme is a constant counterpoint between silver, dark green, and tawny hues, all the colors of the native California landscape.[46] One virtuoso progression that was meant to be seen in the early evening takes a visitor from the ocean-facing south lawn, with its hints of silver in the plantings of proteas that splash the long sunset shadows beneath the live oaks, through a narrow dark green path to a surprising allée of silver trees, the largest, finest grove of *Leucodendron argenteum* in the United States. At the top of the allée, a visitor turns back to a remarkable sight: above the silver-lit lines of trees are the mountains, the only place in the garden from which they can be seen. It is a sudden juxtaposition of artifice and wilderness as startling in its abstraction as Fletcher Steele's curving woodland that echoes the silhouette of Bear Mountain at "Naumkeag."

At thirty-three, and in practice for only eight years, de Forest seems to have been utterly secure in his bold plantings, shaping and simplifying the use of species that in other California gardens were often treated as background. The huge south lawn was designed to star the original live oaks, nothing more, and consequently they personify the essence of the native landscape. The exotic *Leucodendron* garden is made up of only four plants: the strange, even light of the silver trees contrasts with the wild, dark, wiry shapes of bird of paradise, *Strelitzia reginae*, planted behind them, which in turn are a contrast to the severe, tight-clipped line of hedge behind them and to the smooth grass carpet under all.

The Meeker garden, "Constantia," in Montecito, also still beautiful and private today, is very different. Here de Forest abstracted the decorative motifs of the house architecture into the garden. In 1930 Chicago architect Ambrose Cramer built a house for his parents-in-law, the meat packer Meekers from Chicago, which was directly inspired by Cecil Rhodes's house of the same name in South Africa. De Forest was faced with the problem of accommodating many functions in a comparatively small lot of 3.2 acres—ceremonial drive, entrance and service courts, service buildings, a lawn for the view, parterre and flower garden, outdoor living room—and all without destroying the large sense of scale imparted by an important Dutch Colonial house with its tall sculptured gables. Hedges, walls, and terraces divided the various spaces, and the same generous, curving gable form topped the walls and was sculpted in blackwood acacia, *A. melanoxylon,* and eugenia, *Syzygium paniculatum,* throughout the garden. The house stood at the very end of the site, overlooking the ocean view from one side. On the mountain view side, de Forest installed a long pool which reflected the peaks. The pool also meant reduced upkeep; de Forest noted in 1940 that "the water is less of a job to care for than an equal area of grass in this climate."[47] The next problem, as always in Montecito, was that of two different scales—the immensity of the mountain range which dwarfed the pool. De Forest resorted to the same device that Charles Greene used at "Green Gables"—oversized geometric forms set in the middle distance. At "Constantia" a battlemented black acacia hedge, whose huge square molars are easily a match for the peaks, stands at the end of the reflecting pool. De Forest was adept at making the kinds of choices so necessary to Californian planting plans. Here, with a South African house, why not South African plants? Particularly charming was the small sunken garden next to the house, where a collection of African and Transvaal daisies, with their enamel-like petals, bloomed throughout much of the year. Never a fool for consistancy, however, de Forest adds, "Where no native South African plants seemed to fit, material planted by the early [South African] settlers was used." A huge Brazilian jacaranda, *J. acutifolia,* stood on the ocean side, its flowers as lavender-blue as the sea, and magnolia, *M. grandiflora,* that glossy American giant, which was also a favorite of the Cape settlers, added its black-green note and deep perfume to the composition.

THREE "SPAN" GARDENS

The history of gardens is no more neatly linear than other histories, especially in a community like Santa Barbara. First, Santa Barbarans had the money, the leisure, and the confidence to carry out every change they dreamed up whenever they wanted. Second, one could say that many Santa Barbarans let themselves go more in their gardens than they generally did in person. So it's not surprising to find wide latitudes of style—as well as exaggeration, anomaly, and just plain eccentricity in a garden, as at "Lotusland" or "El Mirador." Sometimes too, in a long-lived garden the changes, like the rings of a tree, express an entire history and philosophy of design. "Val Verde" is such a garden. All three survive in one form or another today: "El Mirador" and "Val Verde" are private gardens, and "Lotusland" is open to the public on a limited basis.

Kinton Stevens, the English nurseryman who in 1885 bought the property that became "Lotusland," would probably have been delighted with operatic diva Ganna Walska's developments on the nearly 40-acre

site where he had experimented with so many exotics. The proper E. Palmer Gavits, who called the place "Cuesta Linda" in the twenties and thirties—maybe not. In 1919 they engaged architect Reginald Johnson to create a beautiful, welcoming Spanish Colonial Revival house made still more beautiful later by George Washington Smith between 1921 and 1927. The stately gardens with fountains, palms, tiles, a rill, a cascade, an olive grove, and an olive allée, were begun by Peter Riedel, the Dutch horticulturist, with Smith as a consultant.[48] Much of it remains today; Ganna Walska's new gardens extended beyond it and stretched around every side of the house.

Kinton Stevens's Victorian fancy would have been tickled by Madame Walska's forests of cactus (she was always Madame), and by the strange clearing where giant clam shells sit companionably, jaws agape, next to a zoo of spiky aloes of every kind. Madame loved stones and minerals; she was drawn to the same qualities in plants. John Tenniel, the illustrator of *Alice in Wonderland,* would have felt at home in this garden, where the grotesque statues in the outdoor theater look like the Red and White Queens, or Tweedledum and Tweedledee, and everything looks like something else. Never have so many leather-skinned, prickle-haired rare plants been so humanoid: a large group of the little-known *Beaucarnea recurvata,* a Mexican plant with a swollen baggy trunk and a small head, looks like a bunch of Southern senators about to filibuster; scores of golden barrel cactus near the house seem to have just arrived by spaceship. These wonderful and alarming effects are the result of mass planting: nothing is treated as a "specimen," so that the casualness and scale of the design make it seem spontaneous—Mother Nature's latest

In the 1920s, California gardeners first became experts at ornamenting the plain stucco walls of their Spanish Colonial Revival houses with dark shade patterns, like these cast by Euphorbia ingens *at "Lotusland," in Santa Barbara.*

creations. In addition to the encyclopedic cactus and cycad collections, among the most important and imaginatively displayed in the world, "Lotusland" also sports amazing passages of decorative glitz — handsome edgings of thick pale celadon turn out to be chunks of Coke bottle slag; the edge of the pale green aloe garden pool is heaped with pearly abalone shells.

Madame Walska was as flamboyant a performer in life as in her garden. After his marriage with Edith Rockefeller, Harold McCormick fell madly in love with and married Walska, then a beautiful Polish opera hopeful. Hopeful she remained, since nothing seemed to help her small and terrible voice. After their divorce, she moved to Santa Barbara and became an imperious local legend. She died in 1984, leaving behind her an expressive, outrageous, and original garden, which is slowly being opened to the public.[49]

In 1910, a yellow-thatched "floating teahouse" moved slowly through the lily pads of a pond high above the famous Santa Barbara ocean view. The guests sat on scarlet-cushioned benches, and while the hostess poured tea, bees hummed among the purple and white wisteria that climbed up the roof supports, springing from earth-filled boxes set around the edges of the floating platform. The peripatetic teahouse (actually controlled by a sunken cable) was the brainchild of Charles F. Eaton, who had moved to Santa Barbara in 1888 from Nice. An enthusiastic and informed amateur horticulturist, it was he who enticed Florentine naturalist Fenzi to Santa Barbara, and who made the first gardens at what he called "Riso Rivo."[50] (Serving fancy refreshments in *outre* places was a favorite Santa Barbara sport — at the Henry Bothins' "Piranhurst," the butler rushed up and down a mountain peak to a distant gazebo in a Model T, bringing lunch for ten, course by course, from the villa kitchen.)[51] But such teahouse action was minor activity in Santa Barbara's flushest years, when, as A. E. Hanson recalls, "there was always a yacht or two in harbor, and two or three parlor cars parked at the railroad station."[52] Montecito was known as "the butler belt," and one family had a housekeeper whose sole duty it was to hire and fire.[53] "Little Lolita" Mitchell, great-granddaughter of Ogden Armour of Chicago, who grew up at "Riso Rivo" after her family bought the place in 1917 and named it "El Mirador," had a gardener who followed her everywhere when she rode her pony, and picked up whatever she dropped.[54]

"El Mirador" covered about 70 acres, comparatively large for Santa Barbara. Arthur Heun, the Armour family's Chicago architect, was called in to begin with the outbuildings. Perhaps there were plans for him to build a "big house," but at the time there was already a main house on the property — Eaton's large, rambling Italianate house of an earlier day, partly frame, and partly stone construction. Very unstylish it must have looked to Lolita Armour, Ogden Armour's granddaughter, and in 1921, when there was a small fire upstairs in the old house, she had it torn down. (She did save an old wisteria vine, then reportedly the largest in the U.S. — 300 feet — and had a special pergola built for it.) That same year, she married John J. Mitchell, Jr., and they lived in a small house on the place that Heun French Provincial-ized for them. (They also had a beautiful ranch, named "Juan e Lolita" in the nearby Santa Ynez Valley.) Most of Lolita's efforts went into the gardens at "El Mirador."

By this time Elmer Awl had come to town. Awl, a five-foot-tall ex-ranch hand given to wearing white tails and a white ten-gallon hat when he got the chance, had had every reason to leave San Francisco. He had married the famous Alma de Bretteville Spreckels, sugar millionaire Adolph's widow, but decided he liked her Danish niece, Ula, better.[55] Elmer and Ula decamped for Santa Barbara, and Alma went back to calling herself Spreckels.[56] Awl took on the job of superintendent at "El Mirador," responsible for carrying out Lolita Mitchell's garden fantasies. Lolita and Elmer took dead aim at the summit of Montecito Peak, framed by two large palms planted by Eaton, and ran a long Moorish/Italian water stair from a point directly between them down to a large Japanese garden. For length and size, it beat the three other really imposing downhill water treatments in Santa Barbara — "El Fureidis," "Las Tejas," and "Cuesta Linda" ("Casa Bienvenida" was not yet built). The eleven terraces leap downhill, making a variety of water noises and wearing an assortment of palms, mostly Washingtonias, cypresses, and, in the old days, beds of tulips, violas, delphinium, roses, and lilies. From the Japanese garden at the foot a long stone pergola rises to a boulder overlook that conceals the pièce de résistance of the garden: a grotto, bristling with stalagmites and as joyfully horrific as any eighteenth-century English grotto. There is also a garden theater in a canyon that was used for entertainment. "El Mirador" was divided up in the seventies after the death of Lolita Mitchell. Appropriately enough, the long water garden she and Elmer had designed, which surely owed much to Gillespie's Persian fantasy at "El Fureidis," remained for a while in the hands of Princess Shams, eldest sister of the late deposed Shah of Iran.

Sometime in the thirties, Wright Ludington looked at the grass terraces of his villa and decided "they were simply boring." By this time, Lockwood de Forest had revamped much of the rest of the property, working first for Wright Ludington's father, C. H., who had moved permanently to "Val Verde" in 1924 from Philadelphia, buying the place from Henry Dater, J. Waldron Gillespie's cousin. De Forest's work for the Ludingtons, which stretched from 1926 until his final illness in 1946, is his own brilliant and original encapsulation of the first principles of Californian "Mediterranean gardening" worked out by Gillespie in 1906 at "El Fureidis." "Val Verde," which still exists in private hands today, also owes much to Wright Ludington himself; de Forest's old school friend had a formidable eye, and the courage always to dispense with the inessential.

This watery Eden was created by Santa Barbara landscape architect Lockwood de Forest for his friend Wright Ludington at "Val Verde." In its spare allusiveness — the columns are the pure abstraction of a pergola — de Forest's work is early modernism in a garden setting.

"Dias Felices," or "Happy Days," as the villa was first named by Dater, began as a rustic Spanish country house sitting on a terrace looking down at a classically Italianate reflecting pool. New York architect Goodhue, the architect of Gillespie's Roman villa next door, designed the Dater estate in 1915, the same year that the San Diego Exposition opened, for which he had created the dreamlike Spanish Revival buildings. The Beaux-Arts layout of "Dias Felices" had a formal rose garden, sloping terraces, and a woodland quartered with geometric paths. Just as at "El Fureidis," the reservoir on the hill above the house, an essential element in every Montecito estate before the days of public water, was treated ornamentally as a destination for a garden path. The view of the ocean toward which most of the big Montecito estates were oriented was sidelong here, angled from the principal reception rooms. "Dias Felices" was more private, showed itself off with less bravado than many houses of the same date.

De Forest, also an architect of some talent, designed a new servants' wing, garage, and service court for C. H. Ludington. He made the old reservoir, now no longer needed, into a swimming pool with a bath house that was also an art gallery, with an atrium for the display of Ludington's fine antique statues. After his father's death in the late twenties, Wright Ludington had de Forest run a long brick-paved allée down the hill from the swimming pool, opening up a view of the Pacific. Like the allée at "El Fureidis," this too was centered with a Persian-style water runnel and flanked closely by cypresses. This long walk ended some way down the

entrance drive from which one returned to the house. Although the path was indicated on the original Goodhue plan, it had never been built in Dater's day. In general, the changes that de Forest carried out for C. H. Ludington made "Val Verde" into a year-round residence, while those for his son, Wright, tied the gardens into the natural landscape.

Two characteristics mark de Forest's style. A shift in planting taste is apparent: the palms, bananas, and other lush tropicals with which Charles Gibbs Adams had heavily planted the original landscape of live oaks and sycamores gave way to de Forest's Mediterranean favorites, such as olive trees, as well as to California natives. De Forest also pruned and thinned throughout; growth was a factor of course, but in general de Forest's style, and the taste of the times, tended to be sparer, more allusive.

De Forest eliminated some of the paths in the woodland garden, and strengthened the pattern of those remaining with low concrete as edging, and masonry circles where the paths intersected. He restructured the shallow terraces that mark the descent to the reflecting pool with alternating long rows of boxwood and juniper, using his favorite contrasting hues of green and silver. Blue-gray rosemary cascades like water over the balustrade toward the water below. Near the reflecting pool, he did something few landscape architects of the teens would have done: he unbalanced a symmetrical composition. By adding another, smaller reflecting pool to one side of the old one, he pulled the viewer's eye to the right, toward what remained of the ocean view among the increasingly high trees.

But the real stroke of genius was his treatment of Ludington's "boring grass terraces." Off both living room and dining room, he raised double rows of large, plain, square columns, taller than the lofty first story of the house itself. The absence of a connecting pergola or capitals of any identifiable order conveys the sense of roofless temples, an intimation of decay, but also of happiness among the ruins. Rectangular pools of water hark back to Gillespie's similar terrace treatment at "El Fureidis." They reflect the huge honey-colored pillars, the olive and orange trees planted between them, and Ludington's exquisite statues. Of all de Forest's abstractions, this strange conceit is the most successful, the supreme paradox of a paradise both lost and regained.[57]

HEART OF THE SOUTHLAND: THE LOS ANGELES BASIN, THE HOLLYWOOD HILLS, THE SAN GABRIEL VALLEY, AND SAN DIEGO

However abstract de Forest's paradise, he and his Santa Barbaran "hill baron" clients had classical mythology and architecture as a frame of reference, more or less.[58] Even their Persian or Hispanic gardens had classical statues or architectural detailing.[59] Their Greek, Roman, or Renaissance models, first or second hand, provided the proportions as well as the ornamentation of their gardens. Either they had traveled abroad, or their libraries were full of books and periodicals that assumed such a frame of reference, or they were willing to copy their neighbors, or to go along with fashionable taste, particularly East Coast taste. Often they were concerned with getting it right, and getting it right was an important—and satisfying—part of life for these estate garden makers.

South of Santa Barbara, the point was to make an entirely new paradise, a new frame of reference, which almost necessarily implied trying any way to do it that looked even faintly promising. With a few exceptions in Pasadena, Southern California landscape architects and their clients were not attracted by the luxurious, conservative restraint that characterized gardens farther north. In fact, the strange and crowded anarchy of many estate gardens in the Los Angeles Basin mirrored the thriving popular taste for alternative philosophies and lifestyles, the more extreme the better. Neopaganism, vegetarianism, religious fundamentalism, and every other kind of *ism* "here blossomed forth in truly tropical luxuriance" as early as 1910, according to novelist Stewart Edward White.[60] Health books hyped the miraculous cures promised even to the fatally ill by the California climate (the invalid business would eventually turn into the cemetery business so adroitly dismembered by Jessica Mitford). Oil, mining, and real estate shares of the most dubious kind could be sold with ridiculous ease—unsurprisingly, since so many Californians were fresh from small-town America. Then too, the naiveté, the credulity that seems so much a part of the period and the place, perhaps only underlined the real truth: that for a while, and for some, everything was possible. Though financial success was the principal meaning of "the possible," it was not the only one.

The single promoter-developed California image that gripped Americans deepest was the view of snow-capped mountains framed by golden-fruited orange trees that appeared in thousands of descriptions and on hundred of thousands of postcards.[61] The fundamental attraction of this view is an attainable paradox which denies the idea that the pursuit of happiness must involve choices made according to reason or reality. In gardens, always a sensitive cultural geiger counter, "the pursuit of happiness" took on new and often bizarre forms deliberately far from any classical models. When Adolphus Busch of the St. Louis brewing family came to Pasadena in 1903, he made part of his estate into the 75-acre "Busch Gardens."[62] The gardens consisted of fourteen miles of paths that ran through dells and glens where "many rare trees and shrubs could easily lead one to spend a whole day." The gardens were open to the public and the most popular attractions were the many terra-cotta gnomes and fairies illustrating the brothers Grimm's and Hans Christian Andersen's fairy tales.

In 1919, Pennsylvania oil heiress Aline Barnsdall bought 36 acres on a Hollywood hill and commissioned Frank Lloyd Wright to design an "art

community." It was to have a house for her, a theater, studios, shops, cottages, and apartments. The house was built, with Aztec-inspired lintels topped with friezes of abstract hollyhocks (Barnsdall's favorite flower), and an interior garden court that served as an outdoor theater, with a fountain for a curtain. Wright, who fought with his client by telegram across half the world, nonetheless called "Hollyhock House" his California "Romanza." Architect Robert A. M. Stern quotes Wright's description of his client: "neither neo, quasi, nor pseudo . . . as near American as any Indian, as developed and traveled in appreciation of the beautiful as any European [and] as domestic as a shooting star."[63] Though the complex was never finished, Barnsdall also founded a 10-acre public park right next door, with a wading pool for children, picnic tables, and barbeques. She retained an encircling strip of land (worth $2 million in 1940, according to the WPA guidebook), where she advertised her social and political views on billboards.[64] Such universal, and often loveable, human silliness was more apparent in Hollywood than anywhere else in the United States. Some got it, some didn't. Henry James didn't get it: he loved the flowers and the climate, just like everybody else, and described the people as if they were a new species of insect. In 1904 he wrote that Southern California "has completely bowled me over—such a delicious difference from the rest of the U.S. do I find in it. (I speak of course all of nature and climate, fruits and flowers; for there is absolutely nothing else, and the sense of the shining social and human inane is utter.)"[65]

There was a serious side, of course, which rested in an acceptance of any form of behavior that might bring happiness. But by the twenties, the question was why, when land, sea, and climate conspired to make perfection available, were Americans still not happy and perfection so distant? It seemed as though, at this limitless last limit of the Pacific, that Americans were beginning to feel that nothing was worth having if you couldn't have it all. In terms of garden design, however, there were some who tried to clarify, to make choices, working with small spaces and a considered palette of plants. The result was a beautiful—though still very expensive—garden with a Mexican or Pueblo Indian cast. Such gardens lay far outside the still-vigorous estate garden tradition, with its multiple enclosures and functions and historical references from every part of the globe and every century. The gardens of the rich in Southern California ran the gamut between the two varieties.

Early Estates

The earliest estate gardens, which had been parts of the old ranchos, the huge secular land holdings that followed Spanish Mission rule, were executed in the landscape park style. In Arcadia, near Pasadena, Elia J. "Lucky" Baldwin, a miner who struck it rich, bought what remained of the great "Rancho Santa Anita" in 1875. (When the railroad rate wars of the 1880s brought thousands of new settlers from the East Coast, he made another killing, selling acre lots at the then exorbitant price of $200. Too high, said some buyers, to which supposedly Lucky answered, "Hell, we're giving the land away. We're only selling the climate.")[66] Lucky made a fabulous garden in just a few years, with canals, a gingerbread teahouse called "Queen Anne's Cottage" on the shore of one of Southern California's few freshwater lakes, and miles of winding drives, all lined with trees. To the stands of native live oaks he added specimen exotics — ginkgos, tea trees, palms, and pepper trees, *Schinus molle*, which would later become as common in Southern California as azaleas in the South.[67]

In Redlands, a city founded beside a *zanja*, or irrigation ditch, built by the Franciscan fathers of San Gabriel, the great estate was "Cañon Crest Park," home of brothers Alfred H. and Albert K. Smiley. "Cañon Crest," familiarly known as "Smiley Heights," was promoted by the Southern Pacific Railroad as one of the scenic wonders of the West Coast. Trains from the East, stopping at Redlands to allow passengers to visit, were met by tally-ho coaches drawn by four or six horses. The gardens were begun in the 1880s, when the Smileys built two homes, five miles of palm-lined drives, and two artificial lakes in a 200-acre landscape planted to resemble the tropics. They were careful not to obscure the views of the mountains and the valley floor, however. Water was a problem, but the Smileys had it piped in at great expense from springs in a neighboring valley. There were other estates built along the same line of hills, all with the same views and doubtless the same water problems. Doubtless too they also got their plants from nurseryman Franz Hosp in Riverside. Hosp, a German-American who left a thriving flower business in Cincinnati to come to Southern California, introduced such useful garden flowers as the long-blooming Cape marigold, *Dimorphotheca;* propagated invaluable roses like a climbing form of the popular 'Cecile Brunner'; and as a landscape designer set out more than 1,000 kinds of trees and shrubs for the Smileys. In California where it was worthwhile to try everything, plants mattered especially. Photographs of the garden show combinations that, to our eyes, seem oddly matched: for example, a thatched "African" hut sitting appropriately enough under palm trees is banked with colossal stands of marguerite daisies (was the idea "African daisies"?) that nearly reach the eaves. Whatever its planting style, "Smiley Heights" is pictured in Louise Shelton's first gathering of gardens in 1914, along with the gardens of Newport, Philadelphia, Old Virginia, Palm Beach, and the various exclusive North Shores (Boston, Long Island, Chicago), almost all of which fall within the boundaries of conventional good taste. Even then, it seems, California was permitted to have its own aesthetic. "Cañon Crest" eventually became a 400-acre public park.[68]

Henry and Arabella Huntington's "San Marino"

Henry Huntington's white palace, now the Huntington Art Gallery, was located on the site of an 1878 ranch house, the headquarters of "San Marino Ranch," named after a plantation in Frederick, Maryland. The new "San Marino" Huntington built was far and away the biggest and grandest estate in California south of San Simeon; today it houses what was the greatest ensemble of eighteenth-century British art outside England until Paul Mellon began buying. The nearby library contains Huntington's superb holdings of English and American history and literature.

Huntington, favorite nephew and right-hand man of Collis P. Huntington, one of the four founders of the Southern Pacific Railroad, visited J. de Barth Shorb in 1892 on his way to San Francisco on business, and had admired the views of the San Gabriel Valley and the Sierra Madre. It seems he also admired his uncle Collis's second wife for years. (The marital dance becomes confusing since Henry's first wife, Mary Alice, was actually the niece of Collis Huntington's first wife.) But at any rate, after Mary Alice divorced him for desertion, and after Collis Huntington died in 1900, Henry Huntington set about courting Collis's widow, the mysterious, imperious Arabella Worsham Huntington. (Arabella had her "mystery" well hidden; not until the nineteen-seventies was it confirmed that she had borne her Worsham son, who was adopted by Collis Huntington, out of wedlock, and had also announced the death of John Worsham, her first "husband," six years before he actually died. She had also been Collis Huntington's mistress long before his first wife's death.[69] "San Marino Ranch," which Henry Huntington bought in 1903, was intended to be the bait that would persuade the by now fifty-ish widow to marry him. Arabella, billed in the newspapers after Collis Huntington's death as "the richest woman in the world," much preferred living in Paris in her own *hôtel particulier,* improving her taste and spending millions on works of art with the help of dealer Joseph Duveen. It took Huntington until 1913 to convince her to marry him, and another six months to get her to California. By then, the great house, begun in 1907, was habitable, and the gardens were well on their way in the capable hands of Huntington's long-term head gardener, German horticulturist William Hertrich.

There was a rose garden with "a seemingly endless arbor thickly covered with climbing roses," as Mrs. Lorenzo Woodhouse wrote in her approving report of 1915; every kind of perennial; and a large, handsome Japanese garden bought lock, stock, and barrel from a Los Angeles tea garden going out of business. The Japanese atmosphere was completed by a Japanese family expressly hired for the purpose, who lived in the garden, celebrating their religious festivals and gardening in their kimonos. Water lily ponds had hot water piped in by the ingenious Hertrich to keep the giant *Victoria regia* blooming into January, and canyon gardens running high up into the foothills of the Sierra Madre. Vast quantities of native California plants were employed, loosely

Henry E. Huntington stands in front of the north facade of San Marino Ranch (1905), now the Huntington Library, Art Gallery, and Botanical Gardens. He is only slightly dwarfed by the huge standard topiary trees grown by his indefatigable superintendent, William Hertrich.

grouped in swaths and swales. As far as cacti and palms went, there was no doubt that these were serious collections, not merely gardens. Today, the Huntington Botanical Gardens' collection of desert plants is the largest and most impressive in the world. One pair of palms has a story attached. A juggernaut in politics and business, Henry Huntington was in private life a rather endearing man. Long before their marriage, in 1906, when the San Francisco earthquake and fire destroyed Arabella Huntington's old house there (where she had lived as Mrs. Collis), Henry had the singed palms uprooted and brought down to San Marino, where they were tenderly replanted and nursed back to health—and hope.

But no matter how romantic this autumn affair was, both parties were in their sixties by 1913, and certain accommodations had to be made to

age. For instance, it's rumored that the divided Italianate flight of stairs that Los Angeles architect Myron Hunt designed to connect the high south terrace with the gardens below was never built because 100 steps was just too many. Hertrich, in his memoir of the Huntingtons and the gardens, describes how the flower arrangements in the house had to be big enough for the increasingly nearsighted Arabella to see— "containers were used which would accommodate fifty to two hundred flowers," he writes.[70] Not that things ever got really slow at San Marino: Hertrich, who, according to his account, ended up delightedly supervising everything, had to accommodate an aviary in the garden for Mrs. Huntington's hundreds of birds; he was there beating off reporters when Huntington's famous purchase, Gainsborough's *Blue Boy,* arrived by private Pullman, and he dealt coolly with a shipment of 100 lively diamondback terrapin by building a special pond for them with a beach where they could lay their eggs. Hertrich made trips to San Diego to buy plants from such famous nurseries as Kate Sessions, and imported plants from points as distant as Mexico and New Jersey. He even regularly masterminded crews to move all the pictures around in the house when Joseph Duveen, now Sir Joseph and now advising both Huntingtons, arrived with railroad cars full of more treasures.

In the gardens to the north of the house stands the magnificent allée of palms and other tropicals that frames the huge mountain view. Between the trees, many moved in full grown, are the splendid Italian figures from Padua that greeted Arabella on her arrival at the ranch in 1914. Apart from this allée, and a small formal garden on the terrace level for Arabella, who liked formality, the gardens of "San Marino" are queerly put together for a house that has the style and gravity of a Newport palace. Though the rose garden and the adjoining flower garden are formal in design, they are not part of the typical Beaux-Arts estate garden's measured progression into the landscape. Perhaps this is because there was no official landscape architect. The site planning was handled by Hunt, and the gardens were laid out mostly by Hertrich following the directions of Huntington himself, a passionate and tireless experimenter more interested in "effects" than in the overall view.[71] Hertrich describes how he and Huntington would walk around the grounds with each new piece of sculpture or garden ornament, making a place for it.[72]

Contrasts abounded. Beyond the entrance gates, precious c. 1714 English wrought iron from Beddington Park, stretched a wide bright pink carpet of sand verbena, *Abronia umbellata,* a California desert flower.[73] If this odd pairing was a calculated gamble, it paid off, just as the sight of the elegant white house above the prickly desert garden succeeded, or Hunt's use of Mediterranean materials—stucco with a tile roof—worked harmoniously with a design that was clearly French-derived. With intelligence, money, and a certain kind of stubborn vision, Henry Huntington stretched the limits of the California landscape. When he married Arabella, he had never been abroad, and on their honeymoon they visited the sights, including the famous gardens of the Ile de France. Henry wrote home to his head gardener, "I tell you, Hertrich, I have seen no place as nice as the ranch."[74] For Huntington, "San Marino" was what he called "The Dream Place," which he carried out in his own style with a surreal innovativeness we now can recognize as Californian.[75]

Architect Myron Hunt's job at "San Marino" was to please Arabella Huntington. He seems to have managed with comparative ease, though it did take two visits with her in New York, sketch in hand. Myron Hunt, along with Reginald Johnson and Gordon Kaufmann, was one of the most

Frank Lloyd Wright's 1923 studio residence for Mrs. George Millard in Pasadena is framed by eucalyptus trees and mirrored in the ravine pool that forms part of the sunken garden.

successful, prolific architects in Southern California in the teens and twenties. Born in Massachusetts in 1868, he trained as an architect at MIT and studied in Europe. He practiced first in Chicago where he became one of Frank Lloyd Wright's Prairie School circle. He moved to Pasadena in 1903 for his first wife's health, and set up a partnership with Elmer Grey, another Chicago architect. Their partnership was dissolved in 1910. Hunt's main body of work ended up being handsome, regional, and even progressive, though never shocking—a perfect architecture for the new moneyed Southern Californians who wanted pleasant, modern, understated houses well suited to the climate.

Like William Delano and Thomas Hastings, he had a particular interest in landscape. "Myron loved earthwork," said Harold Coulson Chambers, his partner from 1920 on, "He was clever—extremely clever—in moving and handling earth. He liked natural swales, and his own grades looked like they simply had grown that way."[76] Hunt frequently collaborated with Paul Thiene, Florence Yoch, and the Santa Barbara firm of Cook, Hall, and Cornell, who were working on subdivision plantings as early as 1905. Hunt also contributed the foreword to Winifred Starr Dobyn's important book, *California Gardens,* published in 1931.

"San Marino" was not Hunt's first essay in grandeur. The Gurdon Wattles' garden in Hollywood, which appears in the pages of *The Ameri-*

can Architect in 1909, is a heroic ensemble of six terraces moving up and away from the house toward the mountains. Seen from the house, the complex profile of the top terrace, with triumphal arches and an elaborate balustrade, is in satisfying balance with the equally complex silhouette of the Hollywood Hills. Rampartlike white walls make the lush beds, pools, and palms within the garden seem like even more of an oasis in the chaparral-covered hillside. By contrast with the baroque weight of the terraces, the garden front of the Andalusian-inspired house couldn't be simpler—white adobelike walls and a flat tiled roof. Boldly projecting downspouts, a small reveal for a cornice, and the dark patterns of window and square-topped loggias are the only ornament.

Florence Yoch's Pasadena gardens were as far from the Wattles' handsome but heavy neoclassical garden as sedate Pasadena itself was in spirit from Hollywood. The Garden Club of America emphatically did not visit Hollywood in 1926; they paid a call on Pasadena and then motored carefully around the rest of the Los Angeles area up to Santa Barbara. Pasadena had got its respectable start thanks to the San Gabriel Orange Grove Association, a group of well-to-do Indianapolis residents who decided to emigrate to California after the exceptionally hard winter of 1873–1874. By 1875 they were thriving in vine-covered cottages, surrounded by their irrigated orchards, watching their oranges ripen—the California dream of an easy life on the land come true.[77] San Gabriel Orange Grove Association was a mouthful, so they renamed the place Pasadena, meaning "valley" in Chippewa. Visitors who came for the winter often came back the next year for life.[78] "I am fascinated and enthralled by your sun-kissed, rose-embowered semi-tropical summerland of Hellenic sky and hills of Hymettus," wrote one visitor, "In April and May the lover of nature can pass into the seventh heaven of botanical delight."[79] At the Tournament of Roses which began in 1889 as a rodeo to get rid of New Year's Eve hangovers, participants and spectators wreathed their buggies with roses to celebrate the winter blossomtime. (The Rose Bowl football game began in 1916.) Orange Grove Avenue, the main street in town, became a typical "Millionaires' Row" in the 1890s. By 1940 the WPA guidebook listed Pasadena as the richest city per capita in the United States.[80]

FLORENCE YOCH IN PASADENA
Yoch made more than 250 gardens and movie sets in her career; more than 100 were in Pasadena and nearby San Marino. Some of her gardens were as small as a third of an acre (Mrs. Irving J. Sturgis); others much larger. "Il Brolino" had been strongly Italian; many of her early Southern California gardens depended heavily on Jekyll and Lutyens, and on the idea of the English cottage garden. Her 1924 Pasadena garden for Lucile Council's parents was a close copy of Jekyll and Lutyens's town garden at 100 Cheyne Walk, and one of the Bradford Perins's garden compartments

was actually called "the cottage garden."[81] Standard grandeur with little regional flavor also had its place in her early work: one larger Pasadena garden, "Fair Oaks," begun in 1922 and completed in 1929 for the C. W. Gates, had a formal rose garden with many standard roses, and a perennial border walk with a fieldstone path. Yoch's talent was to make these English-inspired spaces smaller and more domestic; she also successfully translated planting plans from the moist English air to a much drier climate without losing any of their lushness. But as she grew older, she grew bolder. Experience taught her to chuck quotation for evocation in garden architecture, and to make original plant substitutions—instead of grass, a lawn of rosemary, alfalfa, or dichondra, *D. carolinensis*, a flat-growing plant known as lawn-leaf in the South.

Yoch's small spaces were enlivened by this superfine and regionally flavored planting sense, and by the beautifully crafted detail she and Lucile Council commissioned. Any gardener would kill to have the specially made terra-cotta tile edgings she had made for a number of her clients. But getting a Yoch garden was like getting a piano; it was no good if you couldn't play it. Yoch gave every client the chance to learn how to maintain their new gardens. In 1929, for Mrs. Preston Sturgis of Pasadena, she produced twenty-three pages of notes on care for the riot of flowers, essentially a Spanish "cottage garden." Pasadena owners often took her up on it, while most of her Hollywood clients couldn't have cared less—as George Cukor said, "Florence, you do it." Between Yoch and some of her clients one senses the same closeness of a common undertaking as between Beatrix Farrand and Mildred Bliss at "Dumbarton Oaks," and the same concern for the longevity of the garden. Like the smaller gardens of Innocenti and Webel, Yoch's successful, durable answers to the frantic experimentation of the first years of the century would form the basis of the mid-century upper-class American garden.[82]

The Bungalow Makers' Italian Garden in Pasadena
Yoch's homage to Lutyens and Jekyll was by no means the most prominent aspect of the Arts and Crafts movement in Pasadena, however. Any visitor after 1910 would have been aware of the Greene brothers' "ultimate bungalows." Charles and Henry Greene did their own site planning, just as they did their own finely crafted interiors and furniture design. Most of the gardens were really just surroundings, with outdoor living rooms sensitively placed to take advantage of existing trees or views, and places to grow flowers.[83] An exception was the large Blacker house garden built around a lake, which David Streatfield describes as "not a copy of a Japanese garden but rather one in which the arrangement of plant material and rock and the way in which one moved through the landscape evoked Japanese qualities."[84] The later one, commissioned by Cordelia Culbertson, was really an Italianate estate garden in miniature. Begun in 1911, the same year as the Fleishhacker job, it shows an even greater

At his own place in Pasadena, Myron Hunt, an architect who loved gardens, used the classic repertory—marble steps, busts and plinths, terra-cotta pots—to create an informal garden where even a rocking chair could feel at home. Landscape architect Florence Yoch worked on this garden in 1922.

The steps that begin the descent to Cordelia Culbertson's "Italian" cascade garden at "Il Paradiso" (1911) in Pasadena are canopied with white wisteria. Greene and Greene designed both house and garden, which in 1917 became the winter home of the Francis F. Prentisses of Cleveland. Charles Gibbs Adams did the plantings.

Florence Yoch and Lucille Council made three gardens in Southern California for Mrs. Reese Taylor, beginning with this one in San Marino in 1927. The entire floor of the garden is dappled with patches of woodland flowers, perhaps primroses, and ferns.

The West Coast and Hawaii

344

involvement with classical Italian garden design than the early stages of the Woodside garden.

"It is not beyond probability that where the sands of the desert now idly drift and only the call of the coyote breaks the stillness, there may rest a Villa Lante or a Fukagawa garden," wrote Charles Greene in 1905, and the Culbertson garden was his chance at a Pasadena "Villa Lante."[85] As at the Fleishhacker garden, it was the Greene brothers' happy art to make it seem that their choice of motif grew naturally out of a response to the site, and was not an arbitrary selection based on a fashionable decorative scheme. Here, the west-facing canyon on the site dictated a terraced garden, but the best view lay awkwardly north, across the main fall line of the ravine. Most Italian *catenas d'acquas* are centered on the house, but this ran downhill at a not-quite-right-angle to the U-shaped building mass, which faced the mountains. The Greenes used various angled terraces to bring a sense of inevitability to their novel solution, and splayed one wing of the house out over the view of the garden, making it perpendicular in the traditional way to the treatment of steps, landings, water channels, and lily pool below. Charles Gibbs Adams was responsible for the plantings, which by the thirties veiled the masonry with long falls of vines repeating the motif of falling water. In 1917, Miss Culbertson and her sister sold their house to Mr. and Mrs. Francis F. Prentiss, whose Cleveland garden was the work of Warren Manning. They named their new winter residence "Il Paradiso," and Mrs. Prentiss, a Standard Oil heiress, continued to commission furniture for the house and decorations for the garden from the Greenes.[86]

Mrs. Prentiss's brother, John L. Severance, and her sister, Mrs. J. B. Cox, both also had gardens in Pasadena that caught the discerning eye of Marian Cran. "Two beautiful and really mature gardens grow side by side," she writes, "There were large oaks on the lawns, deep ravines filled with azaleas, tree-ferns and running streams—drifts of forget-me-nots, red-berried cotoneasters, masses of clivias, the queer bird of paradise strelitzias and sparaxis-like bilbergias with their long pink drooping stems hung with green bells. Under the camellias grew carpets of cyclamen and violets."[87] The Severance garden, the work of Paul Thiene's Los Angeles firm, used water in every possible way, and was one of the most richly planted and beautiful gardens in Pasadena.[88] Like A. E. Hanson, Thiene was not a landscape architect but an entrepreneurial nurseryman who employed designers to carry out his projects. Lloyd Wright, Frank Lloyd Wright's son, worked with him in the teens, and those gardens tended to be abstract and informal. Later gardens of the twenties, like the Severances, were more elaborate and filled with historical detail.[89] Thiene got his start when he collaborated with the Olmsted firm on the early planning of the San Diego Exposition of 1915, setting up a nursery for the project in 1910. When the Brookline firm resigned in protest at Bertram Goodhue's relocation of the buildings in the middle of Balboa Park, instead of at the edge, Thiene stayed on as landscape advisor.[90]

For the Severances, and for many other clients, Thiene made what can be called an imposed landscape: great emphasis was placed on growing what was hard to grow, such as azaleas and camellias, rather than on what grew naturally, on making beautiful "garden pictures" regardless of what lay outside the frame, in this case, the dry, alkaline hillsides, then considered "barren." In an imposed landscape in a dry climate, water has a special resonance which it has had at least since the days of water shortages at Versailles: it was the prerogative of the rich.[91]

Archibald Young

Water was also the theme of the Archibald Young garden in Pasadena, but treated very differently. The trend toward increasing simplicity and regionalism begun by such architects as George Washington Smith and San Diegan Irving Gill was making a restrained, even minimal, garden fashionable. The Youngs' large lot was on Arroyo Seco, the dry stream that bisected the estate districts of Pasadena, and its neighbors were a number of Craftsman houses. The low white complex with its multiple tiled rooflines, and entrance gates like an Andalusian farm, was commissioned in 1929, and Smith, the architect, again called on Hanson, with whom he had worked only months before on "La Toscana" in Montecito.

It would have been almost unthinkable to have any other kind of garden than a Spanish one for this house at this stage in design history, when house and garden, among the cognoscenti at least, were conceived as a unit. Hanson's garden was the summation of provincial Spanish Revival style just as the Johnson garden in Montecito was of the Italian.[92] Water was used in threads, trickles, shallow pools, and the thinnest jets, refining to the ultimate the tradition begun in 1906 by James Waldron Gillespie. The plan was simplicity itself, just two allées crossing each other, each with a central runnel set flat in the pavement. Hanson had admired a similar treatment at Smith's own garden in Santa Barbara. The source of the water was a modest wall fountain at the house end of the cross, the three other arms terminated in small pools. A formal parterre lay off to one side, a memory, Hanson said, of the geometry of the gardens of the Generalife, seen on his 1927–1928 trip to Europe. The plantings throughout the Young garden were inspired and minimal; almost all were drought-resistant plants that grow happily somewhere around the Mediterranean.

SAN DIEGO

In San Diego, only sixteen miles north of Mexico, the influence of provincial Hispanic architectural design and naturalistic, often xerophytic, planting was still stronger. Kate Sessions, a native Californian, and an ecologist long before the term existed, lived and worked in San Diego for fifty years beginning in 1885. She was instrumental in planting the huge expanses of Balboa Park in the middle of the city (1,400 acres); she made informal, ecologically sound gardens for houses designed by such progressive architects as Irving Gill; and in her famous nursery she introduced Californians to their own flowers, coaxing them into trying such present-day standbys as the matilija poppy, *Romneya coulteri*, the golden flannelbush, *Fremontodendron mexicana*, and the San Diego county variety of the blue-flowered ceanothus that the West Coast and Texas have always called lilac, *C. cyaneus*. By the time she was in her sixties, tiny, white-haired, sunburned, lively—and dressed in an old serge skirt and men's shoes for work—she knew everything about the myth and reality of California as a place where "everything would grow." One nursery customer asked Miss Sessions (she was always Miss) what she did about rust on her hollyhocks. "I don't do anything about them," she replied tartly, "I let them alone. They do not like us and I don't like them. We have plenty of plants that do like our climate so I don't have anything to do with hollyhocks."[93]

The San Diego Exposition

At the same time that Irving Gill and Sessions were working out their regionally oriented programs, the West Coast equivalent of what Jensen was doing in the Midwest, the 1915 Panama-California Exposition in San Diego, which had an impact on estate garden style, was about to take place. Gill, who was considered too revolutionary, was ousted by Bertram Goodhue as architect for the fair. Goodhue turned to the elaborate Spanish Churrigueresque style of viceregal Mexico for the fair, a style that was grand, colorful, appropriately regional and historical, and struck just the right note of dreamy exoticism for the temporary buildings of a world's fair.[94] Gill's removal signaled the delay of modernism in California in much the same way, though far more publicly and influentially, that Charles Platt's success in gaining the McCormick commission for "Villa Turicum" in Lake Forest in 1908 stood for the defeat of the Prairie School, and the rise of the revival styles. Gill was inspired by peasant Mexican and Indian architecture as George Washington Smith was by Andalusian forms. For Gill, there were no trips to Europe to pick up ornate old doors, windows, carvings, tiles, fountains, and wrought iron as there were for Smith and his clients—Gill looked forward to cubism in a more unadorned way. His crisply cubist style, architectural historian David Gebhard argues, was close in spirit to the European avant-garde of the period, which therefore facilitated a readier acceptance on the West Coast of the International School when it arrived in the U.S. in the thirties.[95] Gill was also aware of the importance of a few plants used tellingly. He wrote about the "simple cube house, with creamy walls, sheer and plain, rising boldly into the sky, unrelieved by cornices or overhang of roof, unornamented save for the vines that soften a line or creepers that weather a pillar, or flowers that inlay color more sentiently than any tile could do."[96]

At the exposition, however, Paul Thiene, and others working on the grounds, such as John Morley who laid out the formal annual gardens, had to match Goodhue's flamboyant architecture. They did a brilliant job, using torrents of flowers, shaped trees in tubs, colored tiles, foliage more controlled and plants more harmoniously chosen than had been seen previously in California, and, of course, very un-Spanish pergolas and lawns. There were many others involved, such as Sessions herself, Frank P. Allen, Jr., the director of works until 1915, who designed the arcades and pergolas, San Diego horticulturist Fred Bodey, and Alfred D. Robinson, who dreamed up the great domed "lath house" that was such a feature of the exhibition. Now called the Botanical Building, it still exists today. The magnificent floral display *was* intended to publicize the miraculous semitropical climate, and the variety of what could be grown, as much as to be in harmony with the exposition buildings. A magazine writer described ". . . the most amazing riot of hundreds of varieties of trees and shrubs and clambering vines and small blooming plants. Over all the arcades sweeps this display of vines, with the purple bougainvillea used extensively in the plaza, and the brick red bougainvillea used dominantly along El Prado; with roses used in this patio, clematis in that, and jasmine and honeysuckle elsewhere. The effect of this floral display is of great importance. . . . It must be remembered that the majority of visitors to San Diego in 1915 will be Northerners and Easterners who have no conception of the glories of Southern California's climate and the amazing heights of beauty to which the California flora mount."[97] To satisfy the increasing American appetite for instant age, thousands of trees were moved full-grown into holes blasted in the clay hard pan that made up the slopes of Balboa Park's ravines. The red and yellow flowers of acacia, gray-foliaged plants, and an abundance of cannas, aloes, and kniphofias made for additional color in the ravines. The San Diego Exposition was an elegant lesson in creating and managing the lush look that most estate garden owners in California desired.

In San Diego, John Spreckels, eldest son of the San Francisco sugar king, Claus, had an Italianate villa with pergolas and gardens on the rooftops, and there were a few houses with names like "La Collina Ridente" in Point Loma. And of course there was Spreckels's famed beachfront Hotel del Coronado. Henry James describes the pleasures of Coronado in April, 1905: "The days have been mostly here of heavenly beauty, and the flowers, the wild flowers just now in particular, which fairly rage with radiance, over the land, are worthy of some purer planet than this. I live on oranges and olives, fresh from the tree, and I lie awake nights to listen, on purpose, to the languid list of the Pacific, which my windows overhang."[98]

Besides Spreckels, there were a few other San Franciscans who also

The planted pool that terminates the main axis of this Andalusian garden designed by A. E. Hanson for the Archibald Youngs of Pasadena (1929) is the only bravura gesture. While the rest of the garden is shaded by olives and structured with hedges of Texas privet, the sunlit pool is bright with white iris, water lilies, and petunias.

Fifty years ahead of their time, California architect Irving Gill and horticulturist Kate Sessions designed airy, modest houses and ecologically sound gardens filled with native plants, like this one at the B. F. Chase house in San Diego (1912).

saw the resort charms of Coronado. The George Newhalls, whose Lewis Hobart-designed "Newmar/La Dolphine" was one of the finest gardens on the Peninsula, commissioned a garden in Coronado by Lockwood de Forest. Kate Sessions made a garden perfectly suited to the climate and the lazy holiday air of Coronado surrounding the small adobelike bungalow designed by local architect William Templeton Johnson for a Mrs. Robert of San Francisco. Planted with native and exotic combinations that would best convey the feeling of wild California landscapes, it did so convincingly within the cultivated confines of a small home garden. "In style pure Santa Fe Mission," is how the well-known garden writer Mrs. Francis King briefly describes the house, with its rich ocher walls and dark cobalt-blue trim, which she visited in late December, 1921. She then goes on for another six pages to describe the tiny (less than a quarter of an acre) subtropical garden. It involved mostly yellow and orange flowers, much gray foliage, and cacti and aloes planted in colonies. The simple design without hedge, fence, or lawn, involved minute changes in level and sheets of low-growing plants, such as the blue-gray North African

ground morning glory, *Convolvulus sabatius, Festuca glauca,* sweet alyssum, gazania, and the native beach strawberry. "Wherever such masses of flowers occur, the foreground is apt to be cut by a yucca or an agave of different varieties," notes King, who concludes, "These masses of color are like a miniature copy of the wild-flower fields of Coronado when it was only a rabbit-and-quail park and there was plenty of rain."[99]

LOS ANGELES

At some point in 1925, during the landscape planning of E. L. Doheny, Jr.'s "Greystone" in Beverly Hills, Paul Thiene's head designer on the job, A. E. Kuehl, turned to his boss and asked him what he had in mind for the 29-acre property. "Give them everything," directed Thiene, and Kuehl designed accordingly. Around the baronial stone mansion, designed by Gordon Kaufmann, 16 acres of formal gardens were laid out, along with an Olympic-sized swimming pool, two lakes, tennis courts, a playhouse, and a picnic pavilion with a large barbeque pit. What was left of the mesquite-covered hillside was devoted to large plantings of drought-resistant material, while the sloping lawns below the house were embellished with a display of exotic trees that was practically Victorian in its variety. There was, of course, a lavish water display that included sixteen different fountains in the garden, according to Thiene's own article on water features in *Landscape Architecture.*[100] The pièce de résistance was a cascade that dropped an impressive eighty feet down a quite natural-looking man-made rock face, circulating 500 gallons per minute. The estate, one of the most expensive gardens of the decade according to historian David Streatfield, set Doheny back about $4 million. But that wouldn't have made much of a dent in the Doheny wallet. Ned Doheny was the son of Ed Doheny, the crafty oilman of Los Angeles, who engineered the Teapot Dome scandal, the great oil swindle of the twenties. Ed Doheny was the only one involved who did not go to jail, and he profited hugely from his scheme. By the time he came to trial, he was already rumored to be "richer than the richest man in America," John D. Rockefeller.[101]

However shady Ed Doheny's oil dealings were, he loved his plants and his gardens, and he loved living well. There was an elegant, understated ranch house by Los Angeles architect Wallace Neff on the 400 acres of which "Greystone" was only a small part, and then there was the estate at Chester Place, one of the first exclusive residential suburbs to be developed in Los Angeles. Doheny had made a grand estate here at the turn of the century eight years after he dug his first oil well by hand in Hancock Park, and his 200-foot-tall conservatory was known to experts worldwide for its cycad and palm collection. But there weren't enough specimens available to satisfy Doheny. Edward Howard, one of the three Howard brothers who were the most successful nurserymen in Los Angeles, was hired to spend seven years (1907–1914) in the jungles of Cuba, Guatemala, and Mexico, collecting for Doheny (who also happened to own a lot of oil and transportation in Mexico).[102] Following the still-unresolved death of his son, Ned, Doheny, Sr., broke down completely, becoming the old man in his seventies that he actually was. Like Jay Gould at Lyndhurst, Doheny was another famous capitalist villain with a soft spot for glass houses, or at least for his own. For both, the enclosed, peaceful worlds of their conservatories were more than badges of success; they were different from anything else they experienced in life. Up to the time of his death [Doheny] seldom missed a morning's visit to his conservatory," writes Victoria Padilla. "When he became too ill to walk, he insisted upon being wheeled into his greenhouse. . . ."[103]

In 1900 Los Angeles was a small city of about 100,000, with the rough edges of a former cowtown. (Most of the streets would remain unpaved until 1915, and, according to Stephen Birmingham, the few streetcars sported a sign at the back saying, "Don't Shoot Rabbits from the Rear Platform!"[104]) The surge of development that changed the small Spanish-speaking adobe town had occurred after the arrival of the railroads in 1876 and then 1886. First to arrive were the invalids; by 1880, says historian Cary McWilliams, the foothills of the San Gabriel Mountains were described as "one vast sanatorium."[105] Then came the start of the citrus industry. In 1873 Mrs. L. C. Tibbetts of Riverdale received two budded orange trees—navel oranges from Brazil that would revolutionize citrus culture in California; previously it had been limited to the rather sour and spongy varieties grown in Mexico.[106] By the end of the 1880s, raising citrus was big business. The 80s were also the time of the land boom, which collapsed in 1887, leaving acres covered with cement

In 1928, Bernard Maybeck, visionary San Francisco architect, designed the Earl C. Anthony house in Los Feliz Park, Los Angeles. Lutah Maria Riggs later designed this terrace overlooking infinity.

sidewalks, and miles planted with towns that would vanish from everything except the old maps. This initial land boom development gave the flatter areas of Los Angeles the worst possible start for estate gardens, since the rows of middle-class bungalows that would follow were enough to chase away any thought on the part of the rich of making exclusive great estate colonies. They fled to the hills, moving out farther in the classic suburban progression to Hollywood Hills, Beverly Hills, Holmby Hills, Bel-Air, with a final run up the coast to Malibu. All of these hilly communities were planned restricted residential enclaves, similar in concept to those in every other major city in the U.S. at the time.

The only proper place to live in Los Angeles that wasn't in the hills was Palos Verdes Estates, laid out by Olmsted Bros. beginning in 1924 on the big knuckle of land overlooking the ocean south of Redondo Beach. Called the "suburban City Beautiful," Palos Verdes was a juried community whose architectural restrictions were meant to protect the totally Mediterranean look of the town centers (there were intended to be six) and every villa, house, apartment, and garden.[107] The firm set up a West Coast office to deal with the project, with associate James Frederick Dawson in charge of much of the work. Perhaps it is Dawson's familiarity with the Northwest, thanks to the firm's projects there such as "The Highlands," that accounts for the presence at Palos Verdes Estates of Kirtland Cutter, the Northwest's society architect from Spokane. Cutter designed two houses for F. F. Schellenberg and James E. Buchanan, whose Olmsted Bros. gardens were illustrated in Dobyn's *California Gardens.* Frederick Law Olmsted, Jr., built himself a house on the coast designed by Myron Hunt, and made a garden behind it with a patio, lawn, and long flower borders. His next-door neighbor at "Villa Narcissa" was Frank A. Vanderlip, Jr., who had started the Palos Verdes project, originally buying 16,000 acres of the old Rancho de los Palos Verdes in 1912. In fact, Vanderlip only got as far as the guest house when the Depression intervened, but what a guest house—a sizeable stuccoed building intended to resemble an Italian farmstead. It still exists today in family hands. Original features of the garden include the courtyard garden by the front door, designed by F. L. Olmsted, Jr., its circles and squares of boxwood lit up and perfumed by callas, gardenias, and roses. To the north rises a 268-step cypress allée, with cypresses brought from Rome in 1920. Terraces and an orangerie are alive with peacocks, perhaps the descendents of Frank Vanderlip's original aviary inhabitants. Olive trees, and stone and Aleppo pines make the transition from the dark green of the cultivated gardens to the dusty gray-green of the native chaparral hillside. When the Crash hit A. E. Hanson's practice in 1929, he was hired as estate superintendent by Vanderlip, who had taken one delighted look at Harold Lloyd's garden. Hanson's job would later blossom into community planning commissions both at Palos Verdes and elsewhere in California. Vanderlip must have already appreciated great gardens when he created "Villa Narcissa"; he had grown up at "Beechwood," on the Hudson, designed for his father by Welles Bosworth in 1916.[108]

Plants and Nurseries

"Is there a modest daisy in Southern California?" asks a character in Clara Burnham's 1908 novel, *The Leaven of Love*.[109] It can't be said often enough: the chance to grow tropical plants out of doors, and the size that temperate zone plants reached growing for four seasons a year lured many people into gardening who would otherwise have had no interest. The American penchant for bigger and better led to displays of hydrangeas nine feet tall and the entire wearying range of oversized or double blossoms. Gigantism and peculiar breeding experiments had their place—Edward Howard's brother, Fred, crossed the amaryllis and the crinum, for instance, and actually got a silver medal for doing so.[110] There was an explosion of nurseries. In 1894 there were forty-five of them in Los Angeles, and by 1920 the number had increased to ninety, though Los Angeles had only half a million inhabitants. By the mid-twenties there were also twenty-one firms practicing in the Los Angeles/ Pasadena area as landscape architects. Fifteen were nurseries with design staff; the other six could be called design firms, if one includes Thiene and Hanson in that category. (The others were Yoch and Council, Edward Huntsman-Trout, Cook, Hall & Cornell, and Katherine Bashford.)[111] Good nurseries, combined with a handful of professional gardeners and estate owners, made the area a center of experiment and introduction, where Californians got a grasp of the essentials of culture in California. There were also many pitfalls. For example, any California gardener today, well aware that watering live oaks heavily will eventually kill them, would gasp at Mrs. Oakleigh Thorne's prescription: "I feel the oaks are a great responsibility," she sighed, "I water them, feed them with bonemeal, boring three or four feet; we water first and then fill up with bonemeal."[112] An entire literature arose devoted to ornamental horticulture and gardens. Charles Shinn had led off with *The Pacific Rural Handbook* in 1878, the first book specifically on California gardening. It was followed by such works as William S. Lyons's *Gardening in California* in the nineties, Belle Sumner Angier's *Gardens of California* (1906), and many others, and by a spate of periodicals, longest-lived of which was *California Garden*, a San Diego periodical with a focus on native plants that was designed especially for Southwestern Californians.[113]

In 1931 Marion Cran visited Paul Howard's Los Angeles nursery, Flowerlands, with ill-disguised unease. "Men in white overalls have 'Flowerland' in green letters on their backs," she writes. "So many seedlings in pots rather give an English eye the impression that California's amateur gardeners must be somewhat idle and extravagant, also that they must miss a good deal of the fun of their gardens. In England we enjoy growing our flowers from the seeds we sow ourselves." About trees, she goes on to say, "Americans do like to get effects in a hurry," she says, "I cannot say in how many gardens I have stood under wide spreading boughs of great trees, newly planted and held in place by wire stays.... Somehow they always make me a little uncomfortable."[114]

HOLLYWOOD

Hollywood felt no such unease, partly due no doubt to a lack of snobbery about the traditional, or proper, way to do things, partly because Hollywood's business was manufacturing illusion of just the kind that often required trees held up by wire stays. During the Depression years, only movie stars (and their studios, who often paid for their stars' lifestyles) could afford to—or wanted to—create the gardens that had once been the prerogative of American millionaires. Not that everyone was broke: nationwide, the great gardens that had been made through the twenties often grew vigorously to maturity, and were well maintained until World War II took away the labor force. But the wholehearted pleasure in formal splendor and display that flourished from the nineties up through World War I had vanished, as had the more informal and streamlined Jazz Age version of the same thing. In the thirties, it was no longer fashionable to look as rich as you were.

Except in Depression-age Hollywood. Hollywood had been named in 1887 when it was divided into streets and lots, and became a popular stagecoach excursion in the 90s.[115] A garden was actually one of the first tourist destinations. When the train came to Hollywood, its tracks stopped at the De Longpré residence, a Moorish villa on its 3 acres. French artist Paul de Longpré had purchased the land by trading three canvases with its former owner. De Longpré's specialty was floral paintings; he was also a gardener and his garden was soon a showplace, filled with beds of roses and annuals, and with pergolas, walks, and trees. In the beginning, Hollywood had blue laws, just like Pasadena, and was a temperance town. But the arrival of the movie business bent the temperance law, when a few companies began to come West in the first two decades of the new century. With Cecil B. DeMille's first Hollywood movie, a western called *Squaw Man* in 1914, the atmosphere changed. De Mille's own house and garden never achieved the heights of grandeur reached by many of his stars' estates. From 1915 till his death in 1959, he lived in a staid, substantial Italianate house in Griffith Park, a part of Hollywood described in the real estate prospectus as "a replica of Italy's finest landscape gardening linked to the city by a perfect auto road." Charlie Chaplin lived next door until 1926 when he built in Beverly Hills; DeMille then bought his old neighbor's house and had Julia Morgan design a conservatory to link the two houses. Florence Yoch made alterations to the two gardens to merge them into one which was often used for publicity stills for DeMille's films.[116]

Beverly Hills was the home of the stars. Holmby Hills and Bel-Air, which was unique in guaranteeing a view for each house built, catered to a staider crowd of rich Angelenos and Eastern and Western businessmen. In Holmby Hills, an early great garden that dated to pre-development days was that of department store owner Arthur Letts, with a deodar-lined drive, statue-decorated terraces, fountains, formal compartments, sweeping lawns, and leafy glens filled with ferns, begonias, and camellias. Miles of roadway led to a palm grove. Lett's collection of cacti and succulents was the finest in the area in 1905, and in his glasshouse were plants collected for him in the South American tropics.[117] One of the most impressive gardens in Bel-Air, which opened in 1922, was W. T. Bishop's "Il Vescovo," (1927) with a near-Palladian style villa by Gordon Kaufmann, and a severe and grand Italianate terrace garden by Florence Yoch.[118] Beverly Hills got started in 1906, when 3,000 acres were purchased by a syndicate of Los Angeles businessmen and oil millionaires that included Charles Canfield, Edward Doheny's original partner. In the panic of 1906–1907 the project lost momentum, but picked up steam again after 1911, when the Beverly Hills Hotel was built. Landscape architect Wilbur David Cook, partner with Ralph Cornell in Cook, Hall, & Cornell, laid out this most successful exercise in "The City Beautiful."[119]

Areas in Beverly Hills were zoned for use according to altitude—rich folks at the top with a view, middle-class homes laid out in the rolling land below Santa Monica Boulevard (the dividing line between better and best Beverly Hills), with provisions for service and workers on the flats. Beverly Hills was beautiful from the start: the curving streets were lined with trees, each street with a different species. A special nursery was established to grow palms, jacarandas, acacias, eucalypti, and conifers for these street plantings. The first ordinances included one that made lawns mandatory, and another that ensured that 51 percent of the surrounding landowners had to approve tree removal on any lot.

The very first to build were not movie stars, but big business, some the backers of the project like Doheny and Canfield. There were also such luminaries as E. L. Cord, maker of automobiles, and Milton Getz of Union Bank and Trust, for whom Gordon Kaufmann designed a pink Spanish-Italian-style house, while Paul Thiene designed the garden, with a long water descent to a pool. (Marion Davies and William Randolph Hearst moved in when Hearst's illness forced him to leave San Simeon in 1947; later, the house was used as a location for *The Godfather*.)

Another Beverly Hills estate that didn't belong to a movie mogul was that of Dr. Harvey S. Mudd. The garden, cited by David Streatfield as the finest garden of the twenties in Hollywood, was the work of landscape architect Edward Huntsman-Trout.[120] Huntsman-Trout was trained in the East, and like Yoch practiced exclusively on a referral basis. His

plantings were richer than Yoch's in color and texture, and his designs tended to be more formal. At the Mudd garden, which took several years to complete, he laid out a series of lawns and formal gardens on a characteristically steep Beverly Hills slope. He was proudest of his ensemble of service buildings, which disguised the dog houses and aviary, greenhouses, potting shed, and lath house as a village, faintly medieval in flavor, that climbed the hill. "I like it best when what I have done seems not to have been contrived," he said.[121]

By the late twenties, Beverly Hills' estate owners included John Barrymore, Clara Bow, Marion Davies, John Gilbert, Buster Keaton, Tom Mix, Will Rogers, Gloria Swanson, and Rudolph Valentino. Generally the architecture they wanted was lightly historical and heavily eclectic, though there was a sprinkling of modernist houses by Wright and Richard Neutra. There is a progression through the decades, from Italian-style, like DeMille's in the teens, to Spanish and Mexican in the twenties, the result of the influence of the San Diego Exposition, to modern in the thirties. In addition to the firm of Johnson & Kaufmann, four other architects who specialized in typical twenties revival styles (Mediterranean, Spanish, Tudor, Norman, and even Colonial Revival clapboard) built most of the houses, while five of the landscape architects mentioned above (Katherine Bashford mostly stuck to Pasadena) got the lion's share of the gardens. The four architects were Wallace Neff, James Dolena, Roland Coate, and Paul Williams, the only black architect of the times besides Julian Abele, Philadelphia architect Horace Trumbauer's almost invisible colleague. Williams, who was born in 1896, and had got his start as an office boy at Johnson & Kaufmann, designed 1,000 houses in his long career.

Neff, the urbane, well-educated son of the founder of Rand McNally, was Californian, born near Pasadena in 1895. His first Hollywood commission for screenwriter Frances Marion and her cowboy-turned-movie-star husband, Fred Thomson, was a Spanish-Moorish hacienda in 1923. He often designed the patio gardens for his houses, like that for razor manufacturer King C. Gillette at a ranch in Calabasas, where the intimate tiled courtyard gives way on one side to magnificent mountain views, framed and controlled by the wide arches that Neff often used.[122]

Dolena, an émigré from pre-revolutionary Russia, specialized in the neoclassical and the Colonial Revival. The Spanish-style bungalow he remodeled in 1935 for William Powell as a Georgian-Modern pavilion, was one of the last of the movie star showplaces. Benjamin Morton Purdy, a talented but little-known Los Angeles landscape architect, gave Powell a tennis court with a gallery, a sixty-foot pool, a putting green, a sunken croquet court, flower gardens, and an outdoor Georgian theater. Purdy, who has been called a "California classicist," was also capable of making a great garden out of practically nothing. In an urban hillside garden only sixty feet wide, he used the same materials as A. E. Hanson at the

Archibald Young garden in Pasadena: two lines of olive trees and ivy for groundcover. But here there was only room for six trees, so Purdy used forced perspective, planting the pair furthest from the entrance closer together to make the distance seem longer. Any garden a landscape architect took on for a movie star almost certainly had the same long list of areas devoted to sports as the Powell garden. These 10-to-30-acre ensembles were expected to provide all the amenities for modern outdoor life, in addition to flower gardens and landscaped views. Perhaps Dolena's finest effort was the simple white one-room-deep house he designed for director George Cukor in 1936. The lot was on a virtual ledge, and the house was pushed back against the hill, allowing Florence Yoch to make her finest Hollywood garden, which eased upward and downward from the house terrace in compartments of what her biographer and nephew, James Yoch, calls "Pompeian softness." James Yoch points out how similar Florence Yoch's solutions to the difficult site problems are to those of English garden designer Cecil Pinsent working in Fiesole in the first decade of the century on Villa Le Balze.[123] Notes from Yoch to Cukor on maintenance offer insights into the difficulties the designers of gardens run into with their clients and their clients' gardeners: "Please take out Cistus, Yellow Flax, and other shrubs that have been added" and more peremptorily, "Do not plant flowers along this walk any more!"[124]

Yoch's most magnificent Beverly Hills garden was created for producer Jack Warner's Southern plantation house, designed in 1935 by Roland Coate, who, like Williams, had got his start with Johnson & Kaufmann. Working with the then enormous budget of $100,000, Florence Yoch constructed a 6-acre garden whose monumental qualities (wide entrance steps, massive retaining walls, semicircular pergola of torsaded columns) match Coate's huge double portico. Yoch softened the design with her usual stray trees, an off-center fountain in a large formal pool, and little touches like a secret door, a shady path, an unexpected bench. The garden still exists in private hands today.[125]

The Warners' 18 acres were in Benedict Canyon, as were the estates of Charlie Chaplin, Harold Lloyd, and Douglas Fairbanks, Sr., and Mary Pickford. "Pickfair," sometimes described as one of the most glamorous residences of the twenties and visited by everyone from "John Barrymore to Jack Dempsey and the dukes of York," was originally a hunting lodge.[126] Wallace Neff labored to remodel it in 1925, not entirely to his satisfaction. Marion Cran didn't seem to think much of it; she briefly noted that "Mary Pickford's garden is like her ringlets were—very pretty and very well kept," and then digresses rapidly to sweet peas. She spends more time on Chaplin's estate, beginning ominously with a description of the entrance: "the curly drive was hideously suburban; cement played a loud part in the stone edging, there was the awful gazania and geranium mixture," but she was finally won over by Chaplin's hillside torrent of pink iceplant—acres of what she called "the brave simplicity of one

Comedian Harold Lloyd stands in his Beverly Hills garden designed by A. E. Hanson (1925) who employed the entire architectural arsenal of the Italian Renaissance: here, a horseshoe staircase, an ivy-wreathed catena d'acqua, *and Italian cypress.*

grand planting," beneath the dark pines.[127] Chaplin himself designed the house and grounds of what became known facetiously as "Breakaway House," since the Californian-Gothic building, as Chaplin called it, had been put together by studio carpenters, and bits soon began to fall off.[128]

By the time Marion Cran got to comedian Harold Lloyd, she was, as she admitted, "weary of sappy, rich-fed things," and she polished off the extraordinarily rich mixture ·of plants and garden architecture at "Greenacres" in one paragraph, the voice of the outraged traditional gardener crying in the wilderness. "Harold Lloyd's garden is full of features—besides flowers; a private golf course, two hard tennis courts [one of her pet hates] and a miniature English village for the young daughter. It is a medley of styles, Spanish barbecue, Italian ballroom, Japanese lily pond, English village, Indian canoes, Arizona cactus garden—one thing after another. Most exciting! Terraces, orangery—as one ecstatic female says: 'the Harold Lloyd estate in California is comparable only with the gardens of the Caliphs.' Oh, poor Harold!"[129]

English travelers had of course been dismissing America from the days of Dickens onward, and Cran had so far resisted the impulse for over 100 pages of her book. But this target was too tempting, perhaps especially because, by 1931, such an open display had become unfashionable and because shooting at movie moguls made good reading. She certainly had a target: for slightly over $2 million, Lloyd and A. E. Hanson had accumulated a shorthand version of much that earlier American estate owners had admired, particularly those of the less self-conscious 1890s, and to it they had added the sports paraphenalia of the twenties—and all in a mere 16 acres. The recital of sources is deafening: the general plan of the house was "after" Villa Gamberaia; the flight of stairs from the library to the head of the cascade was taken from the cordonata at Villa Lante, the pool in the teahouse garden was proportioned like one at Villa d'Este, and so on. Even three-year-old Gloria's miniature half-timbered village, which was built first to give her a place to play while her parents were busy with the rest of the estate, has illustrious antecedents. One naturally thinks first of Marie Antoinette's Hameau at Versailles, but a second thought might be of Arthur Curtiss James' half-scale Swiss Village for his Newport cows, which had been written up a number of times in the twenties.

But despite Cran, "Greenacres" summarized the American estate

garden and the American dream in a way perhaps only possible in movieland. The Lloyds actually enjoyed the pleasures that American estate owners always thought they would gain from their great places, but often did not. When Lloyd's movie career slacked off, life's pleasures did not dim for him: he turned to other interests—music, photography, microscopy, abstract painting. These were not the official pastimes such as shooting and yachting that Americans were supposed to take up when they became millionaires—Lloyd's pleasures are a long way from the stuffed moose on tracks behind Clarence Mackay's playhouse on Long Island! Historian Kevin Brownlow describes Lloyd as "the most unexpected combination—a thoroughly charming, democratic, artist-cumbusinessman living in a splendor that the Borgias might have envied, yet with the simplicity of a Rotarian in Grand Rapids, Michigan."[130]

HAWAII, THE FARTHEST HORIZON

For estate garden makers, Hawaii was the satisfactory stuff of legend. Nowhere else in America could one find real royalty—the Kamehameha dynasty who ruled the Hawaiian kingdom of the nineteenth century. The sons and daughters of the early American missionaries and teachers, with names like Dole and Dillingham that would become American legend themselves, soon set up their own dynasties, rooted in the fabulous fortunes they made in pineapple, sugar, railroads, real estate, and trading. In the last decades of the nineteenth century, the Hawaiian aristocracy and the Americans even did a little high-class cross-cultural trading: members of the Hawaiian royal family, like Queen Emma and King Kamehameha V, approximated British royalty as closely as possible in dress and deportment, while the Americans sprinkled their conversation, especially about gardens, with Hawaiian terminology.

Hawaii offered two great opportunities for opulent estate gardening: a climate even more deliciously tropical than Southern California, and an available labor force whose culture believed that garden-making was an artistic achievement—the Japanese. Blissfully absent from the Hawaiian garden scene were the perennial borders full of delphinium and primroses that were doggedly planted in so many inappropriate climates in the continental U.S. Instead, from "La Belle Moanalua" to "Lawai-kai," one finds the huge leaves and junglelike growth, deep perfumes, and iridescent colorings of the true tropics, as well as a Far Eastern sensitivity to plants and rocks, and a plethora of Japanese and Chinese gardens and garden architecture.

"Moanalua"

"Moanalua," on Oahu, the main island of the Hawaiian archipelago, became the property of the newly triumphant Kamehameha dynasty in 1795, but its history as a battleground dates back to the seventeenth century. Its history as an estate garden, not just a beautiful landscape of cultivated field, forest, marsh, and fishpond, can be traced to Prince Lot Kamehameha, who built a country retreat near the royal fishpond in 1853–1854. The house was used for elaborate dinner parties and the garden for hula celebrations. The last of the Kamehamehas, Princess Bernice Pauahi Bishop left the property to her trusted friend and business partner, Samuel Mills Damon, in 1884. Damon lived at "Moanalua" until his death in 1924; the family stayed in residence until the fifties. Today, the gardens are open to the public under the guidance of the Moanalua Garden Foundation.

During the forty years that Damon gardened at what he fondly called "La Belle Moanalua," he made a magnificent Victorian tropical estate. He moved King Kamehameha's cottage to a location more convenient to the railroad, and ran his own spur line close to the house. He added a ten-sided livingroom and considerably more gingerbread to the already lacy porches. He toured the gardens of England and Scotland, and came home with a Scots head gardener, Donald McIntyre, who had trained at the Royal Botanic Garden in Edinburgh. A brief look at John McLaren's work in Golden Gate Park, or at the Busch Gardens in Pasadena reveals similarities in the treatment of these landscapes, which are all richly

A monkeypod tree, the American elm of Hawaiian gardens, dominates the horizon of "Moanalua," a garden once belonging to King Kamehameha V. Scots head gardener Donald McIntyre, brought to Hawaii by subsequent owner Samuel Mills Damon in the 1880s, laid out the picturesque landscape, with its clipped shrubs and a stream banked with rockwork.

gardenesque, with their skein of paths and watercourses bending sinuously across the terrain, linking the various "garden pictures," and their collections of exotic trees grouped together or set picturesquely on the spacious lawns as single specimens. While Damon and McIntyre collected plants in Hawaii, they also imported new species that would become Hawaiian garden standbys, such as the first anthuriums from London in 1889, and orchids from Brazil, India, and the West Indies, more than 400 varieties, which were raised in glasshouses. Japanese artisans created what the Damons called a Japanese tea garden, actually

a stroll garden complete with the entire complement of a Western Japanese garden, including a teahouse, pagodas, zigzag "yatsuhashi" bridges, high-arched lacquer bridges, well-designed groups of rocks, and many Japanese species of plants. Damon also collected Hawaiian canoes, which he housed in the garden in a thatched canoe house of traditional Hawaiian design.

A force of thirty undergardeners maintained extensive kitchen gardens, which produced loquats and soursops, guavas and coffee, instead of shampooed brussels sprouts and cauliflowers. Garden buildings in-

White-trunked Indian banyans, Ficus benjamina, *cast pollarded shadows on the lawn at "La Pietra" below the classical divided Italian staircase designed by Chicago architect David Adler in 1919 for the Walter Dillinghams at Diamond Head, in Honolulu.*

cluded a marvelous structure called "Chinese Hall," for which Damon imported the roof tiles, curving eaves, and carved camphorwood wall panels from China. The windows were glazed, Western-style, and the interior was filled with splendidly carved rosewood and mahogany Western furniture. Set at the curving bank of a pond, and framed by palms, "Chinese Hall" was where Damon, who was first a minister of the Crown and then of the short-lived Hawaiian Republic, gave dinner parties and balls for up to 300. Even the Damons' renowned cuisine shared the British/Far Eastern flavor of the gardens. Their Cantonese cooks were as

adept at making scones and cakes for the high teas served at the weekly "open house" (which early tourists were welcome to attend) as they were at producing what was known in Hawaiian as "ono kaukau," their own stir-fried banquets.[1]

"La Pietra"

Walter and Mary Dillingham were also Hawaiian royalty—railroad and real estate royalty of the early twentieth century. When they made their house and gardens in 1919 they turned to Chicago architect David Adler for a purely Italian-style villa, which they named "La Pietra," after Harold Acton's great "Villa La Pietra," outside Florence. (Acton's wife was Mary Dillingham's aunt, Hortense, and the Dillinghams were married in the Tuscan garden in 1910.) Adler made a beautiful pink villa with an arcaded and paved central courtyard, and green terraces that fell away toward one of the most dazzling view in the islands, the view from Diamond Head over the harbor and city of Honolulu. The plants used were as Italian in feeling as the design. Olives and Italian cypress lined the drive, and the swimming pool was set in the middle of a pomegranate garden. Huge terra-cotta pots held citrus. But when Mediterranean species would not thrive, Mary Dillingham also used tropical plants, choosing cultivars that looked the most European, such as *Hibiscus tiliaceus,* a yellow-flowered large shrub with leaves that somewhat resemble a linden, for a classical pleached long arbor. "La Pietra" was not the Dillinghams' only estate: they also had a ranch, "Mokuleia." And, like Henry Ford with his pioneer village at "Fair Lane," Walter Dillingham also paid tribute to his humbler beginnings with a perfect replica of his missionary parents' cottage constructed at "Crowbar," a ranch holding adjacent to "Mokuleia" where he kept the polo ponies for his world-famous team.[2]

In the late twenties, Dillingham developed property he owned adjacent to "La Pietra," but had trouble enticing buyers, since "Noela Place," as he named it, was reputedly hot and dry. The first to arrive was another family member, his nephew, Harold Erdman, who commissioned a house in 1929 from Hart Wood, an associate in Bertram Goodhue's old firm (Goodhue had died in 1925). Although only an acre, the Erdmans' garden was a brilliant exercise in the use of bright color and tropical vines. In the forecourt, a copper and yellow croton brought out the warmth of the rust-colored stone walls and paving, while over the entrance tumbled a macuna vine from New Guinea, with lacquer-red flowers blooming five months of the year. Vines were the ornament of the patio behind the house, where the snow creeper, white-flowered *Porana paniculata,* which Mrs. Erdman had collected in Ceylon, hung from the upper balcony, and the white form of *Thunbergia grandiflora,* the Bengal trumpet vine (a true vine of the tropics that needs room to spread out, no wind, full sun, and rich soil) galloped over a large, sturdy arbor.[3]

"Pa'Ilima"

Orchids were the focus of the garden at "Pa'Ilima," "the place where the ilima grows." (The trouble with Hawaiian is once it is translated it is still incomprehensible.) Una Walker, wife of an important sugar planter and Hawaii's hostess-with-the-mostest, after Mary Dillingham, had what she called the Rainbow Room, where orchids were planted as a chromatic spectrum, from bluish-lavender to clear yellow. In the rock garden, she planted red orchids against the black lava rocks, and in the enormous

trees of the 7-acre garden in Nu'uanu Valley, another fashionable Honolulu neighborhood, flourished thousands of others, blazing with color. A Japanese garden dating to shortly after the turn of the century, with pagodas and bridges and lanterns, was a quiet relief after the brilliance of the flowers. Una Walker, who lived to be ninety-nine, worked in her garden every day she could till she died in 1987. The rambling white house itself, which sprouts a lanai on every side, is on the National Register of Historic Places, a perfect example of pre–air conditioning turn-of-the-century Hawaiian architecture.[4]

"Heavenly Terraces"

In 1928, the Reverend K. H. Inagaki, the Japanese pastor of the Waialua Christian Church, inexplicably left his flock and applied to Mrs. Charles Montague Cook for a job as a gardener. He explained that he wanted to make the 3-acre "yard" of the house on Makiki Heights, a newly fashionable neighborhood in Honolulu, into a "cathedral of meditation." Almost as inexplicably, Mrs. Cooke said yes, she would be happy to have him do whatever he liked—but then, Mrs. Cooke was brilliantly, charitably quixotic. The daughter of missionaries and the founder of the Honolulu Academy of Fine Arts, she in fact had just made another bold move, donating her old house site as a location for the new academy. She was starting over on Makiki Heights. During the course of the next thirteen years, the last six of which he spent in a wheelchair after a car crash, Inagaki made a sublime garden, working first for Mrs. Cooke, and then for her daughter and son-in-law, the Philip Spaldings, who developed the gardens for more than thirty years. Two of the gardeners Inagaki trained, Henry Yoshioka and Saiji Mukai, stayed at the gardens for forty-five years. The estate is now the Museum of Contemporary Art.

The house, like the Erdmans', was designed by Hart Wood in what became known as Japanese-Hawaiian style, stuccoed and tiled, with long low lines, wide verandas, spreading roofs, and sliding shoji screens that reveal small interior Far-Eastern-inspired gardens. Inagaki contrasted the sculptural rock forms, and the shrubs close-clipped in organic shapes, of the Japanese tradition with the wild jungle growth and spectacular tree forms native to Hawaii. He also contrasted closed and open spaces, formal and informal styles, and the traditional "hard" and "soft" energies of Yin and Yang. The intense spirituality of Far Eastern gardens finds its place here too: Inagaki was the sort of man who, if asked why paths curve out of sight, would answer that he didn't know, except that nature suggests there is something beyond the range of vision, an extension of the spirit that is a new vision.[5]

Stepping out on the "lanai," the sunny, breezy "heavenly terraces," of the Hawaiian name *nuumealani,* one finds a view shaped with strong horizontal lines. Nearest is a low, pierced Chinese wall, its simple profile a support for stephanotis and confederate jasmine. Beyond is another wide, flat grass terrace that drops to a slope, and above, framing the sky and the view of the distant city and harbor, is a monkeypod tree, *Samanea Saman.* To one side of the house, the terrace drops to a rectangular Chinese garden, a peaceful enclosure that is the point of entry for Inagaki's "stroll garden" in many shades of green and stone, which unrolls like a Japanese scroll painting within a framework of trees— weeping banyans, Chinese banyans, *ti (Cordyline terminalis)* and *kukui (Aleurites moluccana)* and many others from the South Pacific, South America, Zanzibar, Madagascar, New Guinea, and Australia. Even in the jungliest part of the garden, the highly successful polyglot assemblage is made harmonious by a preoccupation with line and form, a preoccupation habitual perhaps only to a culture which writes with a

brush, not a pen. Inagaki returned to Japan in 1941, and was never heard from again.[6]

"Lawai-kai"

The Reverend Daniel Dole writes to his friend, Dr. Baldwin, in January, 1871, "Queen Emma is sojourning on Kauai for a season. This is her birthday, & many natives have gone to see her, carrying some little present, as a boquet, some kind of fruit, a few eggs &c.&c. It has rained moderately all day, but the rain does not prevent the natives from riding 3 or 4 miles, to visit the Queen."[7] Queen Emma, widow of Kamehameha IV, had settled into a simple frame house on the cliff overlooking Lawai Harbor, on the northern island of Kauai. She stayed for about four

A walk through the Philip Spaldings' garden started here, on the lanai *known in Hawaiian as* nuumealani, *or "heavenly terraces." The designer of the garden was a Japanese pastor in Honolulu, who left his flock in 1928 and turned gardener. "Nuumealani" embodies a spiritual presence more successfully than most early twentieth-century Japanese gardens in America, which have pagodas and lanterns and teahouses, but do not "interpret shizen (nature)" as the Reverend Inagaki set out to do.*

months, a sort of Royal Progress visit with her retinue of servants, dancers, and musicians. Her letters to her family in Honolulu are full of requests for slips of various trees and flowers, and picks and shovels to dig a two-mile-long ditch so she could have water for her garden. Some of the trees down by the river are undoubtedly ones she planted, and the bougainvillea, both magenta and brick red, that cascades down the cliff was introduced during her stay. The red spider lily, *Crinum augustum*, is still known locally as the Queen Emma lily. In 1916 a subsequent owner lowered "Queen Emma's Cottage" carefully over the cliff where it stands today, set back from the beach, near the Allerton house, which was built in 1938. "Lawai-kai" today is open to the public; it is adjacent to the National Pacific Tropical Botanical Garden, which counts among its founders Robert Allerton and John Gregg, his companion of more than forty years, whom he adopted as his son before he died.

Robert Allerton and John Gregg had set Carl Milles's sixteen-foot-tall *Sun Singer* on its tall pedestal in the middle of a meadow in Illinois in 1932. It was the final element of a massive 1,600-acre garden of vistas and sculptures that Robert Allerton had begun in 1899, when he moved back to Illinois from Paris, the millionaire son who had decided he was not a painter. Over the next twenty-five years he discovered what he liked best was making landscapes, and "The Farms," as the 12,000-acre holding on the Sangamon River was called, jogged along a standard English country house route. Allerton was involved in the cultural life of Chicago, and at his annual party for the graduating class of architects from the University of Illinois he met young John Gregg. Gregg became Robert Allerton's other half, the architect (he held a job in David Adler's office) to the landscape architect. Gregg changed the garden as well as Allerton's life with gold buddhas, blue Chinese ceramic dogs, Balinese enclosures, and long trips to collect garden ornaments. Then home to try to duplicate the sense of lushness and tropical growth, of Far Eastern mystery and spice in the less-than-tropical Midwest. In 1932 the job was done. Robert was sixty-four; John around thirty. Interestingly in 1937, the very year they first saw "Lawai-kai," they made a final garden at "The Farms" that seems entirely unrelated in plan, scale, or feeling to all the rest. It was called "The Lost Garden," an allusion to the mythic gardens of man, beginning with Paradise. A secret garden of sensuous pleasures, it had a small lattice house with mosque-like openings and a circular staircase that led to a sunbathing roof. A copy of a Canova goddess was housed within. It seemed like a dress rehearsal for their Hawaiian adventure.

Mary Dillingham, a childhood friend of Robert Allerton's, knew his taste for the exotic—why not go visit Kauai, she said, since they had a couple of days to kill in Hawaii? So there they were in 1937 looking at a crescent beach at the mouth of the Lawai River, a blue bay, and two small bungalows below the lava cliffs hung with magenta bougainvillea. They bought it instantly—125 acres—and moved into a house of John Gregg's design. Carefully timed shiploads of garden ornaments arrived from Monticello, Illinois, including a copy of Canova's *Diana*. The two men worked side by side with their Hawaiian work force, disdaining bulldozers because, as Gregg explained, they "would have changed the contours or turned over the moss-covered rocks."

The line of the river became the spine of the garden, and Gregg and Allerton, by now masters at divining the genius of the place, made a series of garden rooms that unfolded between the river bank and the cliffs that rise behind. "Lawai-kai" was devoted to mystery and greenness. "One isn't anxious to reach an objective," said John in an interview in 1986, shortly before his death, "Here one is gradually led to see what is ahead."[8]

Water in abundance meant pools, water falls, fountains, cascades, the sound of water everywhere, and enough moisture in the air to grow plants of the rain forest (many of these, however, have to be started in the greenhouse, since the temperature of the micro-climate is about ten degrees too low for successful propagation). They took over the up-river fields of watercress and lotus root used by McBryde's tenants, cleared springs, and found burial caves, and old walls from Queen Emma's days and before. They cut back the rampant native lantana and *koa haole* (*Leucaena glauca*) to give room for more exotic plants. Their tropical collecting trips to the Fiji Islands, Ceylon, the Philippines, and Australia had a new meaning and urgency now. Plants hardy enough to grow at "The Farms" had never been as exotic as the architecture, and the truth is that much of garden life there had been devoted to discovering what would *not* grow. Here there was no need to make do with barely acceptable substitutes, no more narrow choices between wisteria and fox grape to indicate luxuriance. Now there was a huge new plant vocabulary, and gardening was planting and cutting back, not coaxing plants to reluctant life.

Cecil Beaton came to visit (for *Harper's Bazaar*) and called the place "an extraordinary masterpiece of tropical romanticism . . . a magical bamboo forest, whole walls of maidenhair fern, a phenomenal vine with brilliant turquoise flowers [the jade vine, *Strongylodon macrobotrys*, from the Philippines]." It is, he said, "a well-ordered paradise where nothing appears artificial, yet nature is so under control that not a leaf is out of place—an effect achieved by the devoted industry of the owners who emerge from the house with the first light, to put in an eight-hour day of work on their *chef d'oeuvre*."[9]

And yet, despite the magnificence of the site, and the glory of the plants, "Lawai-kai" would just be another bunch of banana leaves were it not for the fine imposition of Allerton and Gregg's plan. The spirit of classical moderation at "Lawai-kai" is expressed at the Diana Fountain, where Canova's marble huntress stands, one hand adjusting her cloak.

A trellised garden house and a tropical cliff face a copy of Canova's Diana, *far from home on the island of Kauai. Queen Emma Kamehameha was the first to garden here in 1870, but Robert Allerton and John Gregg were the ones who made it paradise.*

Gray-green with moss beneath the trees, she faces a pedimented lattice pavilion almost identical to the one in The Lost Garden. Between pavilion and statue stretch two pools, one set slightly higher than the other. Three spillways, barely a foot high, make a low counterpoint against the higher note of the jet in the upper pool. Rough, lava stone paving surrounds the pools. Wider beds planted with pothos, *Epipremnum aureum,* make the calm clearing in the forest proportionate to the size of the pavilion.

The wild aspect of "Lawai-kai" is farthest from the cultivated center. Up goes the path through a carefully planted dark jungle of house plants gone mad: sixty-foot-tall rubber plants, *Ficus elastica,* loom and unseen waters murmur nearby. Finally it is a relief to be out in the light, high on the cliff, surely not far from the original location of Queen Emma's cottage. A giddy lookout, a folly of weathered stone, surveys the flowering frangipani trees, the green marsh, and the blue Pacific. This little structure is the Phoenix Pavilion, and the ancient mythical bronze bird on its roof is a symbol of the freedom of rebirth, not just for Gregg and Allerton, who so concretely embodied that freedom in the creation of

"Lawai-kai," but for anyone who climbs up the long path.[10]

On this point of black rock overlooking the tropics, one is far from Edith Wharton at "The Mount" in Massachusetts in 1905. Yet, if estate gardens have anything to give us besides their gossip and legend, the memories of their colorful owners and gifted designers, it is the pleasure of rebirth such as that felt at "Lawai-kai," or "The Mount," or "Airdrie." At these, or at any of the other great gardens in this book, naked acts of cultural appropriation and re-use—the repetition of casinos, temples of love, water stairs, grand vistas and allées—became acts of new creation. Surviving examples have been transformed yet again by time, growth, and natural succession. No single estate can summarize the tremendous variety that fifty years of garden-making created, thanks to the push of social ambition, all the money in the world, and a cheap, abundant supply of labor—and, sometimes, a love of nature and horticulture. Today the remains of that world have been cleansed and vindicated by time: intact or ruinous, each survivor holds out an enduring promise that there is a place where, just for a moment, the ideal and the real may come close to each other, may slip into each other's places.

INTRODUCTION

1. Lewis, *Wharton*, 143.

2. "Gardenesque," a word coined by English garden designer and writer J. C. Loudon in 1832, came to mean the typical Victorian garden, which attempted to find a middle way between the old formal garden and the landscape garden. See Goode, *The Oxford Companion to Gardens*.

3. Ely, *A Woman's Hardy Garden*, 22.

4. Steele, "Background of Culture and Horticulture in the Genessee Valley," *GCA Annual Meeting Program*, 14.

5. The *H&G* spring number for 1927 contains 18 garden articles.

6. *GCA Annual Meeting Bulletin*, Seattle, 1930, 9.

7. Anna B. Warner also collaborated with her sister, Susan Warner, to write the sensational best-seller, *The Wide, Wide World*.

8. The derelict Isaac Ball house was slated for conversion as a dormitory for railroad workers.

9. Van Rensselaer's other principal work was *Henry Hobson Richardson and His Works*.

10. The term "landscape architect" was first used by English author and traveler Gilbert Meason in 1828 and subsequently by Frederick Law Olmsted and Calvert Vaux to describe their profession in writing to the NYC Board of Commissioners, resigning from the Central Park job in 1863.

11. Anderson, *Women, Design, and The Cambridge School*, 3–4.

12. Hartt, "Women and the Art of Landscape Gardening," 699.

13. Ibid., 703

14. Wilson, "The Paradox of the American Country House."

15. David Schuyler, "Jacob Weidenmann," in Tishler, *American Landscape Architecture*, 44.

16. Olmsted actively campaigned to preserve areas of natural beauty such as Yosemite Valley and Niagara Falls. Olmsted, Jr., carried on the firm's environmental concerns by helping frame the enabling legislation for the National Park Service.

17. For "Moraine Farm" see Charles E. Beveridge, "The Historical Significance of Moraine Farm."

18. Steele, "Background of Culture," GCA, 17.

19. Sargent's lasting memorial is *A Manual of Trees of North America* (1905), which described and pictured for the first time every tree that grows wild north of Mexico.

20. Sargent commissioned English plant hunter Ernest Henry Wilson's voyages to China and Japan between 1907–1919. Estate gardens would not have been the same without Wilson's flowering cherries, rhododendrons, azaleas, and *Lilium regale*.

21. According to Cleveland Amory, this popular jingle was originally delivered by a "Western man" at a Harvard alumni dinner in 1905. *Proper Bostonians*, 14.

22. Sutton, *Charles Sprague Sargent*, 105.

23. Spingarn, p. 29, quoting from Downing, *Landscape Gardening*, 2d ed. Sargent continued to amend Downing's book in subsequent editions: his changes and additional illustrations trace the gradual reemergence of formal features in the garden beginning as early as the 1850s.

24. Eastman, "Hunnewell Estate," 9.

25. Sargent, "The Columbian Exposition," 104–105.

26. Sargent, *Garden and Forest* (Mar. 15, 1893), 119–20; *Garden and Forest* (Mar. 22, 1893), 129–30. When Sargent visited the Chicago World's Fair, he brought his protegée, Beatrix Farrand.

THE NORTHEAST:
THE POWERHOUSE

THE RESORTS

1. Shelton, *Beautiful Gardens*, 70.

2. Mrs. John King Van Rensselaer, *Newport*.

3. In the 1880s, Philadelphia millionaire Fairman Rogers threw a Persian carpet on the lawn as a garden model. His gardener John Gibson needed 3,000 plants to duplicate the effect. See Phelps, *Newport in Flower*, 16.

4. James, *American Scene*, 224.

5. Mrs. J. K. Van Rensselaer and Van deWater, *Social Ladder*, 219.

6. Mrs. J. K. Van Rensselaer, *Newport*, 44.

7. Amory, *Last Resorts*, 175.

8. Ibid., 197.

9. Mrs. J. K. Van Rensselaer, *Social Ladder*, 243.

10. Amory, *Last Resorts*, 23–24.

11. The "joggle board," which provided exercise considered suitable for ladies, was a seesaw with chair backs attached. Mrs. J. K. Van Rensselaer, *Social Ladder*, 223.

12. McAllister, *Society*, 174–77.

13. Bourget, *Outre Mer*, 48.

14. Amory, *Last Resorts*, 202.

15. Mrs. J. N. Brown, "The Elms."

16. Downing and Scully, Jr., *Architectural Heritage of Newport*, 162.

17. Ernest Bowditch (1850–1918), scion of a prominent Salem family, was initially a partner of landscape gardener Robert Morris Copeland in 1871. His later Boston-based practice with Charles H. Miller involved both city planning and residential work. Bowditch often worked with the Boston architectural firm of Peabody and Stearns, as at "The Breakers." He did the original landscaping for Peabody and Stearns's original 1877 house for Pierre Lorillard; when Vanderbilt bought the house in 1886, Bowditch was called in again. After a fire, Richard Morris Hunt designed the present-day "The Breakers" for which Bowditch did the landscape, this time with his brother James. See Bowditch Papers, Essex Institute, Salem; Murphy, "Ernest W. Bowditch," 162–76; and Vanderbilt-Bowditch Correspondence, Preservation Society of Newport County.

18. On the death of Julia Berwind, in 1961, the house was purchased by the Newport Preservation Society before the gardens went downhill.

19. Mrs. J. N. Brown, "The Elms."

20. The Ecole des Beaux-Arts in Paris was the principal training ground for American neoclassical architects and landscape architects between 1880 and 1920.

21. Richard Morris Hunt was the Vanderbilt family architect; the Philadelphia Wideners had Horace Trumbauer, who designed houses for them as well as the Widener Library at Harvard, a memorial to Harry Elkins Widener, lost, along with his father, George, aboard the "Titanic." Mrs. Widener later married Alexander Hamilton Rice.

22. Maher, *Twilight*, 73.

23. Two other estates featured in this book are built on the Comstock Lode: Clarence Mackay's "Harbour Hill" on Long Island and James C. Flood's mansion in San Francisco.

24. Amory, *Last Resorts*, 253.

25. Alva Belmont was honored not for her abilities but for her patronage: she built or restored 12 houses in her lifetime, including "Marble House," Newport's showiest cottage.

26. *A Guidebook to Newport Mansions*, 79.

27. Fahnestock also had fourteen-carat gold bathroom fixtures. Amory, *Last Resorts*, 176.

28. Bourget, 50.

29. Robson, "Newport and its Gardens," 3.

30. In 1909, the Jameses tore down an 1887 McKim, Mead and White house to erect "Beacon Hill House." Landscaping was done by Olmsted Bros. Perhaps because the house was located on a rocky crag, none of the gardens was near it, but in the valley behind. The Olmsted Bros. rose garden was later replaced by a new one laid out by Manchester, Mass., rose specialist Mrs. Harriet Foote, which consisted of a 1,000-foot-long rectangle, blasted out of Rhode Island granite, filled with loam and 5,000 rose bushes, including the yellow hybrid tea rose named Harriet James for Mrs. James. John Greatorex, the Jameses' superintendent, planned the Blue Garden, a virtuoso exercise in plantsmanship. The gardens were destroyed on James's death in 1941.

31. James was the largest owner of railroad stock in the country; at his death in 1941, he was Newport's largest taxpayer.

32. Fifty-six dancers and actors, and pageant director Joseph Lindon Ward were brought from New York. See the Arthur Curtiss James scrapbook, Redwood Library, Newport.

33. Constable, "York Harbor."

34. Amory, *Last Resorts*, 287.

35. For Bowen see Bowen, *Baymeath*.

36. For "Hamilton House" see DeVito, "Hamilton House," and Emmet, "Beside a Timeless River."

37. Robin Karson, "The American Sculptor's Summer Haven," 62.

38. Painter Edward Simmons. Dryfhout, "The Gardens of Augustus Saint-Gaudens," 148.

39. Ermenc, "Economic Give-And-Take," 105–21.

40. Morgan, "Charles A. Platt's houses and gardens in Cornish, New Hampshire," 119.

41. Duncan, "Gardens of Cornish," 17.

42. Colby, "Stephen and Maxfield Parrish," 1299.

43. Platt's comfortingly classical but not overpowering houses and his clear rectangular designs for gardens pho-

tographed extremely well. His clients were both powerful and fashionable, and his work became well-known nationwide because of the play it received in shelter magazines. A monograph of his work (1913), with an admiring introduction by architectural critic Royal Cortissoz, marked the height of his renown.

44. Wilson Eyre and Bryant Fleming also regularly designed the gardens for their houses. For Platt, Ellen Shipman often made the planting plans to fit his site planning. According to Emmet ("Faulkner Farm," 177), Platt did not accept commissions for a house or a garden alone after the Anderson commission. One exception is the 1931–34 H. Wendell Endicott house at "Rockweld" in Dedham, Massachusetts, where Olmsted Associates did the site plan.

45. Platt separated garden from view at all of his houses and gardens in or near Cornish: Lazarus, Croly, Smoot, Churchill, Adams, and Slade. See Morgan, "Charles A. Platt's houses and gardens."

46. See Newton, 401.

47. Monahon, "Peterborough, Cradle of the Arts."

48. Platt worked in Peterborough at Mrs. W. H. Schofield's "Hilltop," designing an "English flower garden" (1902) and an oval Italianate garden (1914). Now the property of the Order of Discalced Carmelite Friars, "Hilltop" is being restored today.

49. Buff, "Dublin, New Hampshire," 942–50.

50. "Edgerton," the Brewsters' New Haven winter home, now a public park, has a 22-acre picturesque landscape surrounding a 1909 Jacobethan house. Architect Robert Storer Stephenson did both house and garden. National Historic Register Registration Form—Draft.

51. B. Howe, "Old Dublin Gardens."

52. Hayward, "Vermont's Historic Estate Gardens," 7.

53. Patterson, American Homes of To-day, 337.

54. The Vanderbilt houses and gardens discussed here include "The Breakers" in Newport, "Elm Court" in the Berkshires, "Florham Park" in Morristown, and "Biltmore" in Asheville. See Patterson, The Vanderbilts.

55. Both periodicals began publication in 1901. Webb purchased books by Gertrude Jekyll and William Robinson, among many others.

56. Hayward, "Vermont's Historic Estate Gardens," 7.

MASSACHUSETTS

1. Massachusetts WPA Guide, 179–83.

2. Quoted from Downing by M. G. Van Rensselaer, "A Suburban Country Place," 4.

3. One exception was the large new garden of Jack and Isabella Stewart Gardner's 40-acre "Green Hill," with its Japanese water garden and very early (1885) "Italian" garden, which incorporated classical and Renaissance fragments from her art collection.

4. For list of Faulkner Farm citations see Emmet, "Faulkner Farm," footnotes 30–40.

5. See Morgan, Platt, for "Weld," 56–58, and "Mrs. Isabel Anderson Dies."

6. Rothery, Romantic Shore, 71.

7. What started out as a live fox hunt soon gave way to "drag hunting," that practice of dragging a bag of scent, anise, or fox droppings mixed with oil and hair, for the hounds to follow.

8. See Thornton, Cultivating Gentlemen, for a discussion of Boston's 19th-century elite model farmers.

9. Endicott, Harvard Class of 1903 Fiftieth Anniversary Report, 260.

10. Richard Henry Dana, Sr., poet and essayist, father of the author of Two Years Before the Mast, owned the property until his death in 1879; the Lanes bought the land from the Danas.

11. In 1912 terraces were added to the north or landward side; after Mrs. Lane's death in 1954 the gardens were simplified.

12. The Charles Heads' "Undercliff," designed by Herbert D. Dale in 1900, was so called because the formal

garden was cut into the rocky cliff. The garden, laid out by landscape architect Martha Brooks Hutcheson, was considered her best work. In 1910 the house was sold to Dr. J. Henry Lancashire, who renamed it "Graftonwood." See "The Garden of Dr. J. Henry Lancashire, Manchester, Mass." in Wright, H&G's Book of Gardens, 61; also Patterson, American Homes of To-day, 292.

13. Alsatian George Heussler and Belgian André Parmentier of Brooklyn were the earliest professional landscape designers in America. Heussler began his American career as the gardener of Elias Hasket Derby, the Salem merchant, whose estate was famous for its greenhouses, fruit trees, and ornamental gardens.

14. Whitehill, "Glen Magna Farms."

15. For "Glen Magna" see Whitehill, "Glen Magna Farms"; Martin Filler, "Cameo Classic"; "The Endicott House and Gardens"; "History of the Endicott Garden," Yearbook of the Massachusetts Horticultural Society; and Gardner, "The Farm, The Peabody Farm, The Endicott Garden."

16. "Castle Hill" grew to 2,000 acres. One hundred and sixty-five landscaped acres and the house are open to the public today; the marshes and beaches are public parkland and conservation areas.

17. Information on "Castle Hill" from Pratt, David Adler, 16–17, 21–22.

18. Shadow Brook took its name from Hawthorne's description in The Wonder Book of a nearby rivulet, shaded "deep enough to produce a noontide twilight. Hence came the name of Shadow Brook." Its 738 acres were landscaped first by Ernest Bowditch and then by Bryant Fleming in Carnegie's day. Halfway through building the architect, H. Neill Wilson, received a telegram from Mrs. Stokes: "Please make each room one foot larger in every direction." Owens, Berkshire Cottages, 27.

19. Owens, 73.

20. Wharton, Backward Glance, 152–53.

21. Amory, Last Resorts, 11–12.

22. The incident took place in Bodian Castle in England. Wharton, Backward Glance, 249.

23. Edith Wharton, letter to Sara Foote. June 5, 1903, Wharton Archive, Beinecke Library, Yale University.

24. See Foster, "Bellefontaine at Lenox, Massachusetts," Parts 1 & 2.

25. Margaret French Cresson, GCA Bulletin, 22.

26. See Vitale, "Ferruccio Vitale."

27. Lynes, "A Gentleman's Cottage," 56.

28. Owens, 34.

29. Best known for his estate work, Barrett also laid out George Pullman's experimental city for his workers in Pullman, Illinois. Born on Staten Island in 1845, he trained for his profession by working in his brother's nursery. He ran his practice out of New Rochelle, New York. See Schermerhorn, "Nathan Franklin Barrett."

30. See Steele, "Modern Gardens for Modern Houses," "Modern Landscape Architecture," and "New Pioneering in Garden Design" for Steele's later discussions of modernism.

31. Fletcher Steele to Esther Steele, Sept. 24, 1950. Rochester Historical Society.

CONNECTICUT

1. Connecticut WPA Guide, 130.

2. Hastings graduated from the Ecole des Beaux-Arts in 1884. After working briefly for McKim, Mead & White, he and Carrère set up their own firm in 1886. Their first big job was the Ponce de Leon Hotel in Florida for Henry Flagler. During his career Hastings moved from a very correct French eighteenth-century style to a broader eclecticism, while at the same time maintaining a certain delicacy and restrained grandeur in all his work. Other Carrère and Hastings gardens mentioned in this book are "Nemours," in Delaware, and the Bingham garden theater, in Kentucky.

3. Benedict belonged to six yacht clubs, and succeeded William Vanderbilt as commodore of the prestigious Sewanhaka Corinthian in 1906.

4. For information on Benedict, see Junior League, Great Estates, 7, 1986.

5. Frishmuth's gay mouvementé work was popular for gardens. A Philadelphian born in 1880, she studied with Rodin and others in Paris, then in Berlin, and then at the Art Students' League in New York. Other garden statues by her are "Joy of the Waters," "Play Days" (also at Walhall), and "Call of the Sea" (also at "Brookgreen Gardens" and at "Villa Philbrook").

6. For "Walhall" see "Gardens on the Estate of Mrs. J. Langeloth"; "Mr. and Mrs. Frederick T. Bonham's home on Long Island Sound," 5; Greenwich in Pictures, 5; Junior League, 34–37.

7. Junior League, 89.

8. Unattributed quote, Junior League, Great Estates, 86.

9. See Jellicoe, Oxford Companion, 137.

10. For "Chelmsford," see Junior League, 103–105.

11. Connecticut WPA Guide, 332.

12. Information on New Canaan history from telephone conversation with Mrs. John King, New Canaan Historical Society Historian, Jan. 1990.

13. Important New Canaan estate gardens included those of FitzHugh Green, Mrs. William A. Carey, William Rush Taggert, Ernest Lee Conant, and that of House & Garden editor Richardson Wright. Such volumes as The Gardener's Bed-Book were based on his experiences in the garden at his eighteenth-century Comstock house.

14. Valentine, "My Grandmother's Garden," GCA, 24.

15. Ibid. For Lapham also see Bayles et al., "Story of Waveny," 21–27; and "Portrait of Lapham returns to Waveny," New Canaan Advertiser, Feb. 21, 1980.

16. Lockwood, Gardens of Colony and State, vol. I, 129–31.

17. For "Weir Farm" see "Weir Farm" National Register Inventory—Nomination Form.

18. Gilbert, born in Zanesville, Ohio, in 1859, grew up in St. Paul, Minnesota, where he set up a practice after working as Stanford White's personal assistant at McKim, Mead and White. He returned to New York when he won the competition for the U.S. Customs House in New York City. He died in England in 1934, and his son, Cass Jr., completed the U.S. Supreme Court building.

19. Both the 1730s house and Cass Gilbert's restored garden are now open to the public and administered by the Keeler Tavern Preservation Trust.

20. However, it would have been difficult to integrate a garden with the house at Branford Point; the "garden front" was the side that faced the Sound, essentially a rocky, windy ledge. Doubtless for wind protection as well as looks, the Lowell/Sargent garden, which dates from 1916, was sunken, and placed on the entrance side, on axis with the front door. See Architecture, December, 1906, and "An Italian Garden at Groton." Another Gothic fantasy now open to the public is "Gillette's Castle," on the Connecticut River in Hadlyme.

21. Plant's independent business ventures were negligible, except for the founding of the New London Ship and Engine Company. His philanthropies were local in scale; he distinguished himself with the founding grant for Connecticut College and gifts to the town of Groton.

22. At the same time he built the town house that is now Cartier's, in New York (Gibson was also the architect). The jeweler acquired his shop by a trade—Plant got a string of black-and-white pearls; Cartier got 631–651 Fifth Avenue. In 1908 he also built a hunting lodge in Lyme, and shortly afterward accumulated 2,400 surrounding acres as a game preserve.

23. For Plant see National Register of Historic Places Inventory—Nomination Form.

24. Shelton, Beautiful Gardens, 90.

25. Lowell, American Gardens; Croly, "The Architectural Work of Charles A. Platt"; Monograph of the Works of Charles A. Platt, with an introduction by Royal Cor-

tissoz; Dean, "Garden Walls"; and Shelton, *Beautiful Gardens*, 90, pl. 41.

26. Perennials did not take over entirely when bedding-out went out of style; the bushy look of the Clark garden owed much to fast-growing half-hardy and tropical annuals started in the greenhouse and set out when danger of frost was past. In old photographs, *Phlox Drummondii*, *Salvia aurea*, different lilies, and *Brugmansia × candida*, a datura bearing a white trumpet-shaped flower on a shrubby plant, have all been identified. See Huhn, "The Garden Art of Charles A. Platt," 104–107. All but the lilies would have had a greenhouse start, and even they might have been sunk in pots.

27. For the appearance of the original plantings, see photographs in the possession of the B.P.O. Elks Lodge of Rockville, the former "Maxwell Court."

28. Other houses included a town house in New York, a place in California, a weekend retreat on Long Island, and a camp in the Adirondacks.

29. The restoration of Harkness Memorial State Park, Waterford, is expected to be completed by 1992.

30. Willard Straight's Chinese garden, on Long Island, was her first Chinese garden (1915); the Rockefellers' "The Eyrie" (1926) was the best, and the best known.

31. Farrand and Rogers, who was the architect of the Harkness Tower and other Harkness commissions at Yale, would later work together on the Yale campus, creating dry moats around the buildings, which she then planted as gardens. See Richard Lyon, "The Campus Designs," in McGuire, *Beatrix Jones Farrand (1872–1959)*, 63–66.

32. Farrand's work at "Eolia" began in 1919, and though she finished in 1932, she paid an annual visit every year until her retirement.

33. A rock garden that anchors the layout to the landscape around it was the last to be attached to the sequence of gardens on the west, c. 1928–29. Farrand linked the Italian garden, boxwood garden, and rock garden together with a little rocky path that runs alongside and below the western edge of all three. Once beautifully planted with alpines, the walk constitutes another garden all by itself.

34. For Harkness see State of Connecticut, Harkness Memorial State Park Papers.

35. The garden at the Old Glebe House in Woodbury, Connecticut, is a Gertrude Jekyll design, commissioned by Annie Burr Jennings. In Greenwich, the Stanley Resors also had a Jekyll garden (1925).

36. There were many good gardens in the Jennings family: Mrs. Walter James also had a well-known garden in Cold Spring Harbor, Long Island, and Miss Annie's other sister, Mrs. Hugh D. Auchincloss, had "Hammersmith Farm" in Newport. Oliver Gould Jennings, one of the two brothers, had a formal rose garden and a rhododendron garden planted in the shade of a beech grove at "Mailands," also in Fairfield.

37. For "Sunnie-Holme," which was torn down shortly after Jennings's death, see Fairfield Historical Society, 1987 exhibition captions for "Gardens of the Golden Age," and Jennings file.

38. William Rhoads, "The Colonial Revival and the Americanization of Immigrants," in Axelrod, *Colonial Revival*, 340.

39. The Colonial Revival exaltation of white Anglo-Saxon Protestant ancestry predictably had other ugly manifestations besides xenophobia; it fed the nastiest kinds of elitism and outright anti-Semitism. William Butler, "Another City upon a Hill: Litchfield, Connecticut, and the Colonial Revival," in Axelrod, *Colonial Revival*.

40. See "Connecticut" in Lockwood, *Gardens of Colony and State*, 115–37.

41. The focus at Norfolk summer places was not cultivated display; there were many "camps." Well-known local gardens included the Carl Stoeckels' "White House," Ellen Battell Stoeckel's family homestead; the adjacent garden of

---

her cousins, the Misses Eldridge; and the places of Dr. Frederic Dennis, Sterling W. Childs, Professor M. I. Pupin, and George J. Dyer, who had a Marian Coffin garden. Saint-Gaudens designed the Joseph Battell Memorial Fountain on the landscaped town green, and Stanford White executed it.

42. James, *American Scene*, 40.

43. Ibid., 38–39.

44. Some of the non-Colonial Revival gardens were stunning, or beautiful. They included the Charles B. Curtis "Rye House" in Bantam, just outside of Litchfield, where the specialty was climbing roses, including a rose-walled tennis court, and the R. H. Liggitts' "Stonecroft," in Litchfield, where the garden laid out by the Olmsted Bros. ran down the hill to a walled octagon, and then to a river. In Sharon, the Edwin Jamesons from New York had an exquisite oval white garden laid out by Umberto Innocenti in 1933. Innocenti, who was famous for his siting abilities, settled on a fine old apple tree as the focus for the new garden. The firm then used fruit trees and small orchards, which contributed to the domestic agricultural air that characterized many of their relaxed designs for country-house gardens, which were in fact further variations on Colonial Revival schemes.

45. Packwood House also had a revival garden, created in the 1930s within the layout of a late English Renaissance garden. See Goode, 417. The Ferridays, a New York family, summered in Bethlehem from c. 1910. Arthur C. Bird of nearby Bristol Nursery, did extensive work in the garden in the twenties and thirties, following the ideas of the Ferridays, mother and daughter. (Bird also laid out the Tapping Reeve Law School garden in Litchfield, and many other estates in Litchfield, Southbury, and South Hartford.) Caroline Ferriday still owns the house. The Ferriday house and garden are destined to become the property of the Bethlehem Historical Society.

46. Alsop, "The Wasp Ascendency," 48–56.

47. For Cowles see Alsop, "The Wasp Ascendency"; Rixey, *Bamie*; and S. M. Alsop, "American Continuity."

48. Alsop, "The Wasp Ascendency," 53.

49. In Norton days, the hedges had been buckthorn. See Jones, "Memories on the Norton Place in Farmington, Connecticut," 3; for Norton also see Donahue, "Gentlemen Farmers on the Yankee Rocks."

50. The Barney House is now the Educational Conference Center of the University of Connecticut; it is open to the public for lodging.

51. The best-known and best-preserved Victorian garden in Connecticut is that of the Henry Bowen House in Woodstock, c. 1850.

52. Letters between Pope and classicist Edith Hamilton describing her informal Princeton curriculum are in the Hamilton Papers, Beinecke Library, Yale University.

53. Alfred Atmore Pope to Theodate Pope, September 5, 1898, Hill-Stead Archives, Letter #540.

54. McKim, Mead and White officially recognized her as job superintendent; their usual fee was reduced from 10% to 3.5% of the construction cost. See Hewitt, "Farmington, Connecticut," 854.

55. See New-York Historical Society, New York City, McKim, Mead and White Papers, for letters from Theodate Pope.

56. Farrand also did the landscaping for the Westover School for Girls in Middlebury, Connecticut, for which Theodate Pope was the architect (and prime mover).

57. James, *American Scene*, 39.

NEW YORK STATE

1. From *America and the Americans* (London 1855), quoted in Kouwenhoven, *The Columbia Historical Portrait*, 268.

2. Hosack purchased "Hyde Park" from a Dr. Samuel Bard. A botanist and a doctor, Hosack opened the Elgin Botanical Garden, the first of its kind in the U.S., in 1801 on the

---

site of Rockefeller Center. It folded for lack of support in 1811.

3. Parmentier's family was horticulturally distinguished. His older brother was the superintendent of the famous gardens of the duc d'Enghien in Holland. His cousin campaigned so hard to popularize the potato that it almost became a "parmentière" instead of a "pomme de terre" in France.

4. For Frederick Vanderbilt quote above see Simpson, *An American Treasure*, 79. For Frederick Vanderbilt gardens and Greenleaf see Rieley, *Vanderbilt Mansion National Historic Site Cultural Landscape Report*.

5. Amory, *Last Resorts*, 41.

6. Perkins, *Roosevelt I Knew*, 64.

7. Gould's greenhouse was cast iron. Before the Gould greenhouse was built, American builders had used wood. After, iron and later, steel, became the accepted building material for large or elaborate conservatories and greenhouses. See Britz, *The Greenhouse at Lyndhurst* and *Lyndhurst, A Property of the National Trust*.

8. In American Beaux-Arts gardens, this little temple could be called a symbol for European culture, classical learning, and the landscape tradition. Its remote classical ancestor is the Roman temple of the Sibyl at Tivoli.

9. The term "Beaux-Arts" refers to a design system and a method of architectural execution taught at the school in Paris. Estates in the Tudor, Jacobean, Queen Anne, Shingle, Neoclassic, and Art Moderne styles were carried out according to Beaux-Arts principles and methods of work. Influential American architects Richard Morris Hunt and Henry Hobson Richardson trained at the school in Paris and brought the system back at mid-century to the U.S. For more than 50 years most American architects of note either trained in Paris, in an American school modeled after the Paris school, or worked in an atelier based on Beaux-Arts principles.

The first basic principle was the importance of an overall scheme for a project, called a *parti*, a scheme to be applied down to the last detail. A second principle was the use of interpenetrating spaces to create a sense of movement, which allowed interior vistas to open up before the spectator. A third principle was using openings and changes in level to define space instead of solid walls. In gardens, the use of exterior spaces—terraces or vistas—opened naturally out of interior spaces, relating house and garden closely to each other. See Sclare, *Beaux-Arts Estates*.

10. There were few licensed women architects: Theodate Pope Riddle and Julia Morgan were among the rare exceptions.

11. Plants were furnished by the Connecticut firm of Wadley and Smythe, who worked with many great estate designers in the New York area, sometimes acting as landscape architects as well as nurserymen. They also were an informal employment agency for newly arrived English and Scottish gardeners. For Wadley and Smythe see Caldwell, Dona E., Collection, and Columbia University, Avery, Drawings Collection, Wadley and Smythe photograph album.

12. Delano and Aldrich went on to do such other important estates as Otto Kahn's "Oheka," among many others. For Rockefeller see Folsom, *Great American Mansions*, 203–206; Patterson, *American Homes*, 295–97.

13. "Greystone" is being restored and is open to the public.

14. For Untermeyer see "Greek Garden" and "A Greek Garden in America."

15. For Brewster see Howe, *American Country Houses*, 119–23; Brewster, Robert.

16. Hill, *Forty Years*, 271.

17. For "Meadowburn Farm" see Ely.

18. Some say the New York Horseshow Association list was the basis for the first Social Register.

19. Skurka, "Tuxedo Park," 72. For Tuxedo Park see also Winslow, Albert F., to Eleanor Weller, and "History of the Blair Property."

20. Mrs. Thorne was a two-garden gardener: her California garden, "Las Tejas," was if anything better than "Thornedale's." For Thorne, see "At the League Exhibit" and "Thornedale, A Cool Tapestry."

21. Allen was an early graduate of the Lowthorpe School. Other important estate works included "Wave Hill" in Riverdale, and in Mt. Kisco the garden of Miss Anne Morgan.

22. For Stillman see Reed, "A Classical Garden in Modern Times"; Dietz, "A Formal Garden."

23. Hestercombe's orangery is Lutyens's variation on an older James Wyatt orangery, which in turn was derived from Palladio. A close look at any Beaux-Arts garden will eventually turn up an Italian reference.

24. Eastman's plants came from the great Rochester nursery, Barry and Ellwanger. Fletcher Steele later simplified the plantings; now the Rochester Garden Club has restored the original Bragdon plan, and the garden is open to the public. For Eastman see Brayer, "West Garden to be Revived"; Miller, "Bringing the Country into the City."

25. After 40 years (1931–1970) as a Veterans' Hospital, "Sonnenberg Gardens" has been restored and is open to the public.

26. A quincunx is a pattern that uses five elements. As the pattern is repeated, it produces staggered rows and a diagonal, diamond-like effect.

27. The pansy garden was intended for meditation—pansies, *pensées*, represented thought in the Victorian language of flowers.

28. The cascade, ponds, and 500 feet of streambed have been restored. The rock garden plant list published in *House & Garden's Book of Gardens* (1921) contains more than 200 cultivars. For "Sonnenberg Gardens" see Townsend, Wilma T.; Doell, *Gardens of the Gilded Age*, 182–84; Hotra, "The Legacy of John Handrahan; Monroe, "Sonnenberg Gardens"; Sonnenberg Gardens, *Sonnenberg Gardens*.

29. For Kellogg, see Kellogg, Mrs. Spencer.

30. Patterson, *American Homes*, 352–53.

LONG ISLAND

1. Fitzgerald, *Great Gatsby*, 31.

2. Patterson, *American Homes*, 15.

3. Randall, *Mansions*, 15.

4. For Coe, see Thomas Hauck, "The Planting Fields," in Van Wagner, *Long Island Estate Gardens*, 15–21; Boyd, "The Residence of William R. Coe."

5. Amory, *Last Resorts*, 371.

6. Beverly Nichols, "Study in Blonde," quoted by Matz, *Otto Kahn*, 236.

7. Beatrix Farrand worked on "Oheka" from 1919–1928, softening the severe, elegant design with native plants and exotics. The long approach drive was lined with native red cedar, the water parterre enclosed by poplars, with an inner aerial hedge of clipped lindens. On a lower level south of the water parterre was the flower garden, whose plantings spilled onto the brick paths. The rose garden also used brick, and was ornamented with a *tourelle*. There was also a croquet lawn with 10-foot-high green battlemented hedges, and a Dutch garden.

8. "Talk of the Town," [Otto Kahn], *The New Yorker*, Sept. 25, 1926, 5334.

9. Matz, 143. For Kahn also see Ruhling, "Manors for the Masses"; Patterson, *American Homes*, 168–70.

10. The "Harbour Hill" event that appalled Clarence Mackay was the marriage of his daughter, Ellen, to Irving Berlin in 1923. Mackay broke off relations with Ellen.

11. For Mackay see Doell, *Gardens of the Gilded Age*, 31–34; "Clarence Mackay Rites"; Randall, 165–68; Rice, "America Masters the Lore of Gardens."

12. Sclare, *Beaux-Arts Estates*, 170.

13. Tice, *Gardening in America*, 37. Caumsett was one of the principal employers of the town, even during the Depression, since Field, on Gillies's advice, kept all the men on at a reduced schedule of three days a week.

14. For Gillies see Gillies, George; and Libby, "George H. Gillies." For Field and "Caumsett" see Sclare, 170–76. For the Hon. and Mrs. Whitelaw Reid see Shopsin, *Villard Houses*.

15. Gillies began work in 1923; Olmsted Bros. arrived in 1924. (Marian Coffin was later responsible for the design of the evergreen garden and the winter cottage plantings.) It took three years to create "Caumsett," working with 85 men and five foremen. Field would walk around the place on Saturday, and his supervision consisted of saying to Gillies, "Well, thanks very much, it's going on fine." Instant effects of age were created by the planting of enormous old trees around the house. "Mrs. Field's idea of a tree was something with its branches down to the ground," said Gillies, "so we found a couple of big ones for her at another estate out here." These made the trip by sea around Long Island, arriving on Christmas in time to be a Christmas present for Mrs. Field.

16. Six months of imposing bouquets might pass and then Field would say, "Oh, Gillies, very fine things in the front hall—what are they?" Gillies said, "I went to the house often during the day, because there were flowers to be arranged for lunch, and then often new ones for a dinner party that night." Cut flowers were not the only green things in the house—the loggia was often filled with cymbidiums as Gillies was a famous orchid grower.

17. Other New York activities included flower shows. For the New York Flower Show, Gillies traveled to Manhattan in the Fields' horse van with all the props and plants needed. In addition to attending four or five large shows annually, Gillies also mounted exhibits at the monthly meetings of the New York Horticultural Society and for a period of two years put up an exhibit weekly at the New York World's Fair of 1938–39. There were other garden associations, such as the American Horticultural Society, whose members at that time were mostly estate owners, and the New York Florists' Club, an organization of commercial growers, and even a club known as the Wall Street Farmers, a group of flowery financiers!

18. Over family objections, Hutcheson attended MIT in 1898 as a member of the first landscape gardening course and began practicing c. 1900. She made many notable estate gardens in the Northeast, especially in Connecticut, on Long Island, and on Boston's North Shore. Her book, *Spirit of the Garden*, was published in 1923.

19. New York-based Pendleton had a large Connecticut practice, and with Grace Tabor she was the author of *Suggestions for Roadside Planting* in 1933. In 1931 she is recorded as being an honorary member of the Garden Club of America.

20. Nochlin, "High Bohemia." For G. V. Whitney see also Auchincloss, *Maverick in Mauve*; Proske, *Brookgreen Gardens*.

21. For Tiffany see Martha Wren Briggs, "A Reconstruction Of The Gardens Of Louis Comfort Tiffany" in Van Wagner, 5–10; Howe, "Louis C. Tiffany"; McKean, *"Lost" Treasures*, 113–25.

22. De Forest's son, Lockwood, Jr., became one of the notable landscape architects of the 1920s and 30s in California.

23. For Stanford White biographical information and for "Box Hill" see Ferree, *American Estates*; Mooney, *Evelyn Nesbit & Stanford White*; and White, *Memoranda of the Place*.

24. Ferree, *American Estates*, 139–40.

25. For information on the firm see McKim, Mead & White, *Monograph*, and Baldwin, *Stanford White*. The most prominent, prolific firm of the Gilded Age, the three partners designed and built over 1,000 works in their 27-year-long career together (1879–1906). Within the firm, William Rutherford Mead was the engineer, Charles McKim, with his Quaker background, the advocate of moderation and classical restraint, and White, the wild man. White designed much besides architecture: according to a family story, he once designed a fishing fly for his annual salmon bout with McKim on the Restigouche River. After "thinking like a fish all day," he came up with "The Night Hawk," which is still catching fish.

26. White, *Memoranda*.

27. Auchincloss, "The Muse of Syosset."

28. Nemy, "Great Home." For Moore see also Post to Weller; "Chelsea"; "French Manoir."

29. Woolworth's "Winfield Hall" was designed and built by architect C. P. H. Gilbert for nine million dollars; the Woolworth Building (1913) by another Gilbert, Cass, at a cost of thirteen and a half million dollars. He had also given each daughter her own house on Fifth Avenue. See Maher, 337.

30. Randall, 83–84. For McCann see Nevins, "Triumph of Flora," 918–19, plates 7, 8, 9.

31. See selected client list in Flanders, *Landscape Architecture*, which includes names such as Vincent Astor, Lewis Cass Ledyard, Charles A. Stone, and Ronald Tree. It also includes a list of pastel portraits of Flanders's gardens; models, both topographic and made of porcelain; and presentation plans.

32. Smith, Charles, retired foreman of Frankenbach Nursery, interview and site visit to Kiser garden, Southampton, with MKG, Nov. 28, 1987.

33. See Flanders.

34. Symington, Mrs. J. Fife (Martha Frick) to Eleanor Weller.

35. Codman had redesigned the interiors of Edith Wharton's Newport cottage, "Land's End." The Bryce house was his first effort outside New England, and one of the first of the many Georgian houses on Long Island. *The Decoration of Houses*, which preached the unity of interior and exterior design carried out by Codman in the Bryces' house, confirmed and popularized the movement toward classical unity which Beaux Arts–trained architects in America had first set in motion only a decade before.

36. Architect Guy Lowell (1870–1927) also studied landscape architecture at the Ecole des Beaux-Arts.

37. See Valencia Libby, "Marian Cruger Coffin, The Landscape Architect and the Lady," in Nassau County, *The House and Garden*.

38. Symington to Weller. The gates she mentions are wrought-iron Thomas Hastings creations that divided the main part of the garden from the "guinea-pig" garden. An informal antechamber, this was banked with cotoneaster underplanted with bulbs that would bloom in the shade of a huge oak. The gates originally stood at the Frick carriage house entrance on 70th Street in New York City. Today, they are back at the Frick, guarding the museum courtyard garden designed by Russell Page.

39. For Hutton see Sclare, 138–43.

40. See Alsop, "Wasp Ascendency," for Pauline Sabin and her fight for prohibition repeal. Women of the Wasp ascendency, despite their confinement as wives and mothers, were concerned with many of the major socio-political issues of their time, beginning with abolition, and continuing on through suffrage, child labor laws, prohibition, and its repeal.

41. For Sabin garden see Teutonico, "Marian Cruger Coffin."

42. Amory, *Last Resorts*, 21.

43. Hewitt, "Farmington, Connecticut," 855.

44. For a portrait of Breese, see Miller, *"Tanty."*

45. Sean Scully, restoration architect of "The Orchard," interview with MKG.

46. Miller, *"Tanty,"* 84.

47. Nevins, "The Triumph of Flora," 911. For Herter see also "Daring What the Layman Dares Not."

48. Shelton, *Beautiful Gardens*, 129. For Woodhouse see also "Life in East Hampton."

49. For Sylvester see Griswold, "Water Gardens."

THE MIDDLE ATLANTIC

NEW JERSEY

1. Ferree, *American Estates*, 1.

2. Warner, "New Orleans," 187–88.

3. From "A Few Facts About Blairsden," Edith Blair Gambrill. See also Ferree, *American Estates*, 5–11.

4. Rae, *Morristown's Forgotten Past*, 86.

5. For Twombly see Burden, *The Vanderbilts in My Life*, and Fairleigh Dickinson Library, notebook and albums.

6. Shelton, *Beautiful Gardens*, 157. Shelton also mentions the Dudley Olcotts' very similar "Cherrycroft"; see Taylor, "A Formal Garden with Informal Planting."

7. See Wodell & Cottrell.

8. For Adams see "Rohallion" photograph album; Fairleigh Dickinson Library, George Moss Collection; Lowell, *American Gardens*, plate XLIV and "Rohallion" plan appendix; Shopsin, *Villard Houses*. For Barrett see Schermerhorn, "Nathan Franklin Barrett." For White, see Baldwin, *Stanford White*.

9. Weinberg, "Gardens at Moggy Hollow," *American Horticulturist*, October 1986.

10. Burt, "Princeton Grandees," 10.

11. Ibid., 13.

12. For Russell and Marquand see Greiff, "The Five Houses."

13. Lockwood, *Gardens of Colony and State*, vol. 1, 315.

14. Ibid., 310.

15. For George Gould see Geis, *Georgian Court*.

16. Information on Julian Abele from Alfred Branam.

17. For Parsons see Maher; Folsom, *Great American Mansions*, 101–106. For LeNôtre and Hardouin-Mansart see Haslehurst, *André LeNostre*.

PENNSYLVANIA
1. Maher, 75.

2. Ibid., 68.

3. Information on Philadelphia styles from Julie Leisenring (Mrs. Theodore). See also Bush-Brown, *Portraits of Philadelphia Gardens*.

4. Wallerstein, "Horace Trumbauer," 115.

5. For McIlhenney see Mellor, *Mellor, Meigs & Howe*.

6. For Pepper and Morgan see Bush-Brown.

7. For Philadelphia horticulture, see Faris, *Old Gardens*; Leighton, *American Gardens of the Nineteenth Century*; Lockwood, *Gardens of Colony and State*, vol. 1.

8. Nutting, *Pennsylvania Beautiful*, 8. For the Philadelphia Centennial Exhibition see Edward Teitelman and Betsy Fahlman, "Wilson Eyre and the Colonial Revival in Philadelphia," in Axelrod, 71–90.

9. For Sinkler see Herring, "The Highlands"; Lockwood, *Gardens of Colony and State*, vol. 1, 355–57. For Biddle see Lockwood, *Gardens of Colony and State*, vol. 1, 350–52.

10. For Clothier see Bush-Brown, 171. For Sears see Sears, Thomas.

11. Arthur Meigs, "An American Countryhouse the Property of Arthur E. Newbold," in Mellor.

12. Farrand: Clarence A. Warden, "Faraway Farm," Haverford, 1912 (includes a Chinese garden), and Frazer Harris, "Harston," Chestnut Hill, 1910, are good examples of her large and small gardens. Coffin: Randal Morgan, "Wyndmoor," Chestnut Hill (a Spanish garden, rose garden, orchid house, and English garden temple). Olmsted Bros.: See Beveridge, *The Master List . . . of the Olmsted Firm*.

13. Bush-Brown, 119.

14. Elwood, *American Landscape Architecture*, 132–34.

15. For "Boxly" see Lockwood, *Gardens of Colony and State*, 353–55; Peck, "Boxly memorandum."

16. For Lloyd see "In Memory of Mary Helen Wingate Lloyd." GCA.

17. Trollope, *Domestic Manners*, 231.

18. For Pittsburgh and the Mellons see Van Trump, *Life and Architecture in Pittsburgh*; Folsom, *Great American Mansions*, 115–19.

19. See "Renaissance Garden"; for Amateis see Proske, *Brookgreen Gardens*, 348–51.

20. Mary Beth Pastorius, telephone interview with MKG.

21. For Rea see Mrs. Frank Weller; Arnold Collection, University of Pittsburgh; Kimball, "American Country House," figs. 29–32, 135–37; *Palmer's Pictorial Pittsburgh*; Photograph file, Pennsylvania Room, Carnegie Main Library, Pittsburgh; "House of H. R. Rea."

22. For Schwab see Elwood, 78–79; Patterson, *American Homes*, 316–19, 324–27; Reif, "New Life for Garden Statues."

23. John Charles Olmsted (1852–1920) was Olmsted's nephew, adopted by him at age seven when he married his brother's widow. J. C. Olmsted carried his stepfather's park and city planning ideas forward into the twentieth century.

24. Landscape architect Rose Standish Nichols and architect William Lawrence Bottomley also worked at "Grey Towers."

25. For Pinchot see Pinchot Institute for Conservation Studies, *Final Historic Structure Report*.

DELAWARE
1. For Eleuthère du Pont see Wilkinson, *E. I. du Pont*.

2. Mrs. Alfred E. Bissell, telephone interview with MKG.

3. Thompson, *A Man and His Garden*, 86.

4. Mrs. Alfred E. Bissell, telephone interview with MKG.

5. Ruth Linton, telephone interview with MKG. See also Linton, "The Estate of Alfred I. du Pont."

6. Cantor, "Upstairs Downstairs." For H. F. du Pont see Libby, "Design of the Winterthur Gardens."

7. Libby.

8. Cantor.

9. Correll, "The Crowninshield Garden." For Crowninshield see Hagley Museum and Library, Crowninshield files and chronology.

MARYLAND
1. For Jenkins see Constable, "Windy Gates."

2. The boxwood allée came from an 18th-century Maryland house, "Nanjemoy," situated in Baltimore County in the fork of the Gunpowder River.

3. Dietz, "Stately Views."

4. Ibid.

5. In a supplement by Henry Winthrop Sargent to Downing, *Landscape Gardening*, 6th ed.

6. One original pattern remained on the top tier and Hopkins repeated it on the opposite side. For the second tier, he adapted patterns from *Formal Gardens in England and Scotland*, Inigo Triggs (New York: Scribner, 1902).

7. Historic Hampton, Inc., *Gardens and Grounds*. For Ridgely see also Bruce, "The Hampton Garden."

8. Lockwood, *Gardens of Colony and State*, 262–68.

9. For Ladew see Hardie, *Ladew*, and Olmert, "Ladew Gardens."

10. Charles Bryant to John Boogher. For Breese "The Blind" see also Shelton, *Beautiful Gardens*, 209, and plate 103.

11. See Cowgill and Rogers.

12. David Lockhart to Eleanor Weller. For Eastern Shore gardens see Talbot County, *The Art of Gardening*, and *Maryland House and Garden Pilgrimage*, 1960.

WASHINGTON, D.C.
1. Jennings, 221.

2. "The British Embassy Residence, more than any other study in this volume, is boldly rural, letting the outside in." Jennings, 219.

3. Sensibly, they avoided the summer. Like the British Embassy, Dumbarton Oaks is another private/public Washington garden. Building a museum, library, music conservatory, and scholarly center always implied some sense of public legacy. The Blisses' Washington residency began in 1933, with his retirement, and by 1940, when the garden was nearly completed they turned it over variously to Harvard and the National Park Service. Ten acres were sold to the Danish government for an embassy. The Blisses took up residence in Montecito, California, but bought a Georgetown house close to the gardens to use on their Washington visits.

4. Eleanor M. McPeck, "A Biographical Note and a Consideration of Four Major Private Gardens," in Balmori, *Beatrix Farrand's American Landscapes*, 40, 48.

5. Ibid., 61.

6. Kathy Wood, Executive Director Cleveland Park Historical Society, Washington, D.C., telephone interview with MKG.

7. Miller, *Great Houses of Washington, D.C.*, 21.

8. "Meridian House" is the headquarters of the Society of Cincinnati, a use McLaughlin had envisioned almost from the moment he built the house.

THE SOUTH

NORTHERNERS HEAD
FOR THE OLD SOUTH
1. W. R. Taylor, *Cavalier & Yankee*, 346.

2. Goode, 210.

3. Mrs. Ralph P. Hanes, interview with MKG.

4. See Howett, *Land of Our Own*, for a discussion of the philosophical and cultural meanings of the Southern landscape.

5. Cash, *Mind of the South*, 174.

6. Taylor discusses the national need to glorify the past during the economic, social, and political growing pains of the first half of the nineteenth century.

7. Henry Boykin, telephone interview with MKG.

8. Kennedy, *Architecture, Men, Women, and Money*, 291.

9. Shaffer, *Carolina Gardens*, 108.

10. Warner, *On Horseback*, 138–39.

11. See "The Gardens at Oatlands."

12. Siding with the Confederacy could not have been an easy choice for Eustis: his wife's family, the Corcorans, stayed with the Union. The Eustis family was originally from Boston: a family quarrel had sent George Peabody Eustis to New Orleans in 1822, where he married into a prominent Creole family and became chief justice of the Louisiana Supreme Court.

13. From Gertrude Jekyll's catholic color harmonies American gardeners chose the paler combinations that included silver foliage and white. Like Anna Gilman Hill, perhaps they remembered with distaste the raucous colors of their mothers' and grandmothers' bedded-out gardens. Gertrude Jekyll did not think any color was vulgar. Alfredo Siani, gardener at "Oatlands," says that study of Edith Eustis's plant lists shows that she chose the most refined forms and the softest shades of any flower, as though before the threat of bright colors and any hint of vulgarity she retreated into the secure territory of aristocratic reserve.

14. At "Enniscorthy," in Albemarle County, just east of the Blue Ridge, home of the Coles family since 1766, Mrs. Albert Morrell made "room gardens," including a rose garden, a perennial garden, and a rose arbor backed by a stand of bamboo and with yet another small garden beyond it. She also built a serpentine brick wall like that of Jefferson's design at University of Virginia. See Langhorne, *A Virginia Family*; also Elizabeth Langhorne, telephone interview with MKG.

15. Alfredo Siani, telephone interview with MKG.

16. Annie Rogers Zinn du Pont, "Description," Aug. 10, 1922.

17. Sale, *Historic Gardens*, 213.

18. For Marion du Pont Scott see Livingston, *Their Turf*.

19. The epithet "old-time" was first used widely to imply a garden design style following publication of Alice Morse Earle's *Old-Time Gardens* in 1901, one of the first revival-style garden books.

20. From Kate Mason Rowland's *The Life of George Mason, 1725–1792* (New York: G. P. Putnam's Sons, 1892), quoted in Lockwood, *Gardens of Colony and State*, vol. II, 66.

21. At "Oatlands," the Florentine tulip, *T. sylvestris*, small, fragrant, and yellow, has naturalized. The Florentine tulip was an eighteenth-century favorite, and is recommended in period florists' manuals. See Mazza, "A Gift from the Past," 4.

22. An example is the "Groombridge Garden" at "York

Notes

365

Hall," in Yorktown, Virginia, modeled after gardens at Groombridge Hall in England which are documented in Triggs's book. "York Hall" (1739) was purchased along with two adjoining houses by George Preston Blow, a descendent of the builders of Groombridge Hall. Charles Gillette designed new gardens to tie the three buildings together, for which he received the Architectural League's Honorable Mention in 1938 "for the faithful way in which the garden traditions of the South have been interpreted here and in other accomplished landscape work." See Gillette, Charles F. "Landscape Architecture at the League Exhibit in 1938," and Sale, *Historic Gardens*, 115–17.

23. Charles B. Hosmer, "The Colonial Revival in the Public Eye: Williamsburg and Early Garden Restoration," in Axelrod, 54.

24. Lockwood documents the painstaking garden excavations at Stratford Hall carried out by Morley Williams, an associate of Shurcliff's, in 1932. But although the grades, levels, wall foundations, and paths were all carefully reproduced, there was never any evidence for the very elaborate boxwood parterres that Shurcliff then proposed and Williams carried out. See *Gardens of Colony and State*, vol. II, 68–72.

25. See Charles B. Hosmer, "The Colonial Revival" in Axelrod, 54–69.

26. Ibid.

27. At the Blair House Shurcliff designed a "kitchen garden," following the discovery of the old kitchen building outline on an insurance map. The original inhabitants of Blair House would have found slim pickings in Shurcliff's "kitchen garden," which included ten clipped box bushes in a quincunx design and a lot of herbs, with not a potato or a cabbage to be seen. See Shurcliff to Perry, Shaw & Hepburn.

28. In 1886 Pinchot would join Olmsted again to advise on general layout and forestry principles at "Shelburne Farms" in Vermont.

29. For Biltmore see Newton, *Design on the Land*, 346–51; Biltmore Estate news releases. photocopies of photographs from Frederick Law Olmsted National Historic Site collections. For the Olmsted firm see Charles Beveridge, *The Frederick Law Olmsted Papers*. The partners of the firm after Frederick Law Olmsted's retirement were Frederick Law Olmsted, Jr., J. C. Olmsted, Percival Gallagher, James Dawson, Henry V. Hubbard, Edward C. Whiting, and William Marquis. Others who always worked closely with the firm were Charles S. Sargent and Arthur Shurcliff.

30. For Middleton see Lockwood, *Gardens of Colony and State*, vol. II, 243–60; Middleton Place guide booklet; and McGuire, *Gardens of America*, 23–31.

31. For "Magnolia" see Lockwood, *Gardens of Colony and State*, vol. II, 223–28; McGuire, *Gardens of America*, 60–62. To keep "Magnolia," Drayton sold his Sea Island plantation, his Charleston town house, and most of the plantation land. He floated his summer cottage down river and erected it on the foundations of the burned-out house—it forms the present-day house. In the late twenties, C. Norwood Hastie commissioned Delano & Aldrich to research and plan the reconstruction of antebellum "Magnolia." A similar pre-Revolutionary house was purchased in Charleston, and moved to "Magnolia" to cannibalize for parts. The crash of 1929 put an end to this plan, and today the bricks from the Charleston house form the paths of the garden.

32. Shaffer, *Carolina Gardens*, 65.

33. For "Mulberry" see Lockwood, *Gardens of Colony and State*, vol. II, 220–21; "Low Country Plantations"; and Shaffer, 84–87.

34. For "Orton" see Hellyer, "A Garden from a Rice Plantation"; Shaffer, 146–53; and Sprunt to Phelps. The parterre was largely the work of Dr. Frederick Hill in the 1840s.

35. Shaffer, 156.

36. Mitchell, "Pebble Hill Plantation."

37. Abbott, *Open for the Season*, 183. Local contractors often worked with Northern designers such as Warren Manning, who designed the resort "Pinehurst."

38. Cooney, *Garden Hist. Georgia*, 90–91, 405.

39. Ibid., 303–304.

40. Ibid., 18–20, 370–73. A number of Northern invaders' gardens on the barrier reef islands were Spanish. Two notable examples were Mr. and Mrs. Richard T. Cranes' on Jekyll Island, designed by the same Chicago architect, David Adler, who designed their "Castle Hill" in Danvers, Mass., and Detroiters Dr. and Mrs. H. N. Torreys' on Ossabaw Island, designed by Ellen Shipman.

41. "Joan of Arc" stands in a small park on Riverside Drive at 93rd Street, in New York City.

42. Proske, *Brookgreen Gardens*, vii.

43. For air circulation, brick garden walls in Charleston are often "pierced" with holes in a regular pattern.

44. Rose Standish Nichols: "Morningside," Mr. and Mrs. Alfred S. Bourne, Augusta; Herbert, Pray & White: Mrs. Harry Albright, Augusta; Warren Manning: "Millpond Plantation," J. H. Wade, Thomasville; Peabody, Wilson & Brown: Mr. and Mrs. Thomas Hitchcock, additions to "Mon Repos" and many other houses in Aiken. (Julian Peabody was the Hitchcocks' son-in-law.)

45. For Berckman's "Fruitlands" see Cooney, 62–63.

46. Colorado Springs was another resort that grew out of the search for health.

47. For Celestine Eustis, "Mon Repos," and general history of Aiken as a resort see Aldrich, *Tommy Hitchcock*, 17–26.

48. H. W. Smith, *Life and Sport in Aiken*, 208.

49. Aldrich, 28.

50. Once there were 20 polo fields in Aiken. Harry Worcester Smith points out that the difficulty of growing grass in South Carolina was one reason there were so many. Rotating play saved the turf. The expense and labor required to grow grass had garden implications too: shrub borders and traditional geometric parterres with brick or sand paths were easier and cheaper than a lawn.

51. Howett, "Regional Variations."

52. H. W. Smith, 191.

53. Also in Augusta was "Morningside," 16 acres laid out beginning in 1920 by Rose Standish Nichols for New Yorkers Mr. and Mrs. Alfred S. Bourne. The house terrace was furnished like a living room, and overlooked a sunken garden, planted with tulips and pansies, with a central pool flanked by tall Oriental arborvitae. There was a temple on a mount, cypress allées, and a water cascade reminiscent of that at the Villa Cigcogna in Northern Italy. See Cooney, 284–85; and "In a Georgia garden," *CLA*, Mar. 1933. Totally different was the Mr. and Mrs. Harry Chafee garden in Augusta, originally laid out in 1784 by Hannah Howard. In 1933, even after seven generations of Howards, including the Chafees, had made changes in the garden, it typified traditional Georgian taste: geometric spring-flowering parterres and no grass.

54. Cooney, 297.

55. Mrs. D. Hugh Connolly, interview with ECW.

56. Phelps, "Horticulture: an important part of Camden's heritage."

57. Hamilton Boykin, architect and a descendent, interview with MKG. For "Plane Hill" see also Boykin, *Captain Alexander Hamilton Boykin*, 29–31, 60–61, 68–69, 168–69.

58. Phelps, "Horticulture: an important part of Camden's heritage."

59. Sweet, *Camden Homes*, 61.

60. Charles Garnett, telephone interview regarding Hope du Pont Scott with MKG, June 27, 1989.

61. For a critical though sympathetic assessment of Mary Chesnut see Fox-Genovese, *Within the Plantation Household*, 334–65.

62. The Chesnuts did not occupy Kamschatka long: they moved in in 1854 and sold the house in 1858 when Chesnut was elected to the U.S. Senate. They did not have a house of their own again until 1873, when they built "Sarsfield," also in Camden.

63. Priscilla Buckley to MKG. Also see Inman, "Kamschatka."

64. Harriet Jackson Phelps, author of *Newport in Flower* and resident of Camden, in a letter of Feb. 18, 1987, states that

Reid Buckley recalls that his father worked from plans reportedly those of James Chesnut, but that these have been misplaced. It would neither have been unlikely that the Chesnuts had plans nor that they never implemented them, since they only lived in the new house for four years.

65. All information on Sarah Boylston from Evins, "Sarah Boylston and her Garden"; also see Boylston, Sarah. Richland County Historic Preservation Commission.

66. "Hampton-Preston House" became Union headquarters during the Civil War, and was later used variously as a convent, as the Governor's Mansion, and as a Presbyterian College for Women.

67. Deodar cedar, araucaria, cryptomeria, cypresses, golden arborvitae, and various yews. There was also a collection of magnolias, a ginkgo, paulownias, and all the tropicals that Victorian gardeners loved to use: bird of paradise, Sago palm, date palm, and various striped grasses.

68. Bergholz, "Southern Garden."

69. Hays, "A Colonial Garden Down South," 288.

70. *Crinum* 'Ellen Bosanquet', *Hedychium coronarium*, *Lycoris squamigera*, *L. radiata*, and *Erythronium americanum*.

FLORIDA—MAKING IT ALL UP FROM SCRATCH

1. From Thomas Higginson, *Army Life in a Black Regiment*, quoted in Lockwood, *Gardens of Colony and State*, vol. II, 306.

2. Other barrier reef resorts were Jekyll Island and Cumberland Island, southernmost of Georgia's barrier sea islands, whose first Northern invader was Andrew Carnegie. Never publicized, it was private from the 1890s until 1972 when it became a National Seashore site.

3. Another "Vizcaya" predecessor was Chicagoan Mrs. Potter Palmer's "The Oaks," in Sarasota, completed in 1911 with formal French gardens by Achille Duchêne. These gardens made a great impression on the Ringlings who built "Ca d'Zan" not far away.

4. Patterson, *American Homes*, 262.

5. Sargent came to Florida to paint John D. Rockefeller, Jr.'s portrait and stayed with James Deering's brother Charles, an old friend. Among his bold watercolors are some of "Vizcaya," which he visited and asked permission to paint.

6. Hoffman, born in 1884, graduated from Harvard and the Ecole des Beaux-Arts and started with Carrère and Hastings. In 1910 he opened his own office in New York with Harry Creighton Ingells, the best-known theatrical designer of the day. He had a long and distinguished career in domestic architecture, and was still practicing at the age of 98.

7. On their 1914 summer trip to Europe, Deering and Chalfin visited Acton, whose American wife's father, William Mitchell, the founder of the Illinois Trust and Savings Company of Chicago, must have known the Deerings. Acton's restoration at "La Pietra" was inspired and directed by Henri Duchêne, the scholar-artist who restored many classical French gardens, some of them designed by Le Nôtre. His son was Achille Duchêne. By 1914 Suarez had designed eight Florentine gardens, and he took Deering and Chalfin to visit some of them. That same summer Suarez came to the U.S. with Lady Sibyl Cutting and her daughter, Iris (the author Iris Origo). War was declared; Suarez stayed in the U.S. and got the job at "Vizcaya."

8. Chalfin also won the Lazarus Traveling Scholarship for painting and was named a Fellow of the American Academy in Rome.

9. Deering, like Anna Hyatt Huntington and so many others, was another garden maker who came south on his doctor's advice to seek a milder climate.

10. Bayley, *Vizcaya*, 93.

11. Maher, 189.

12. Curl, *Mizner's Florida*, 39.

13. For Mizner and Palm Beach see Curl, chapters 3 and 4.

14. Leonard Thomas, "Casa de Leoni" (1921); Barclay H. Warburton, "Casa Maria Marrone" (1922); Mrs. Robert Glen-

dinning; John Magee, "Lagomar"; Alfred G. Kay, "Audita."

15. See Curl, 8, and Thorndike, "Addison Mizner," 116–22.

16. Palm Beach Annual Meeting Program 1960. GCA.

17. Palm Beach Garden Slides commentary. GCA.

18. Palm Beach Annual Meeting Program 1960. GCA.

19. See Procter, *Handbook of Florida Flowers*; Walden, *Dictionary of Trees*; Workman, *Growing Native*; Palm Beach Garden Slides commentary, GCA; Palm Beach Annual Meeting Program 1960, GCA.

20. Wyeth, Princeton-educated and Beaux-Arts-trained, came to Palm Beach in 1919 and competed for the same society clients as Mizner. If Mizner's energy and bad judgment had not led him into the fatal Boca Raton adventure (see Curl, 134–204), he too might have had a fifty-year career designing houses for every street in Palm Beach. Wyeth designed houses in every style subsequent to his Spanish phase, and was also popular in Hobe Sound.

21. Curl, 165. Swiss-trained Fatio (1897–1943) came to the U.S. in 1920 and started his practice with William A. Treanor in 1921. His clients included Mortimer L. Schiff, Joseph E. Widener, and Harold S. Vanderbilt. His houses were similar to Mizner's.

22. For Urban see "Mar-a-Lago" below.

23. Thorndike, 118.

24. Curl, 83.

25. In 1938 Elizabeth Kay designed one of the seven small display gardens at the Society of the Four Arts, the elegant local civic arts center. Other contributors to the Four Arts gardens included Mrs. John S. Phipps and Mrs. Lorenzo E. Woodhouse. Remains of these gardens exist today.

26. Curl, 220.

27. See Caldwell, *Mountain Lake*, 16.

28. Bok's friend, President Calvin Coolidge, came to open the "Singing Tower" formally in 1929.

29. Olmsted Bros. moved with the increasing formality of the times: although Olmsted Senior had pioneered the picturesque landscape in America in the 1870s, by the 1910s his firm was making many more formal gardens than naturalistic ones.

30. Charles Wait got his start working for Olmsted Bros. as a draftsman and designer of architectural garden elements. He later designed the Mountain Lake clubhouse and some of the more imaginative houses at the resort.

31. All "El Caserio" and Mountain Lake Club information from Griswold interviews with Dr. and Mrs. Lyman Smith, and Griswold, "Coleridgean Fantasy."

32. Abbott, *Open for the Season*, 115.

33. It was one of only four Florida gardens listed in the 1925 GCA Visiting Gardens Directory.

34. The house behind the door is the size of a small Spanish village.

35. Previous to joining Mizner's firm, Ives trained at the New York School of the Fine Arts, worked as a draftsman for Delano & Aldrich, and worked for Maurice Fatio in Palm Beach. He later moved his practice to Hawaii.

36. Mrs. Ford Draper, telephone interview with MKG.

37. The Ringlings paid their first visit to Sarasota in 1910, when the circus took up winter quarters there. The house was built beginning in 1923 and the architect was Dwight James Baum.

38. For Ringling see Maher, 89–141.

39. "The Greatest Show on Earth," 68. Besides snakes, the grounds contain a fine 18th-century theater from Asolo and a circus museum.

40. ECW interview with Ringling Museum staff, Apr. 1983.

41. Maher, 137.

42. From Henry Ringling North and Alden Hatch, *The Circus Kings*, 201–202, quoted by Maher, 129.

43. The Ringlings wanted to be buried under "David," but ended up in New Jersey.

BACK IN THE REAL OLD SOUTH

1. Mrs. Winthrop Chanler, Amelie Rives's ex-sister-in-law, describes Rives in her memoir, *Roman Spring*, quoted by Auchincloss in *Writer's Capital*, 140–41.

2. In *The Ghost Garden* (1918) the setting is an old Southern house and garden, modeled closely after "Castle Hill." The place is possessed by the heroine's beautiful demonic ancestor, and the major scenes take place in the overgrown, terraced garden.

3. William Drake, telephone interview with MKG.

4. Troubetzkoy made a modest living as a society portrait painter.

5. Auchincloss, *Writer's Capital*, 134–35.

6. Judith Rives was also a writer, author of the memoir *Home and the World*.

7. William Rives was minister to France. The Parisian tree that bore Judith's nut was known as "The King's Tree," since it was the first and best, flowering before all the other horse chestnuts. *"Castle Hill" Grounds Tour Hand Book*.

8. Gertrude Rives Potts's account of the garden quoted by Sale in *Historic Gardens*, 216–17.

9. Jeannie Scott and Phyllis Langhorne Draper telephone interviews with MKG; Delano & Aldrich, "Mirador"; Flanders, plan of the rose garden; Patterson, "The Langhorne Home."

10. See Christian, *Homes and Gardens*, 45, and Sale, *Historic Gardens*, 173.

11. Cunningham, "Notes from Some Virginia Gardens."

12. Shelton, *Beautiful Gardens*, 220 and plates 108, 109.

13. *Homes and Gardens* followed Edith Tunis Sale's *Historic Gardens of Virginia*, 1930. Others that follow the model are *The Garden History of Georgia, 1733–1933*, and *History of Homes and Gardens of Tennessee, 1936*.

OVER THE ALLEGHENIES

1. Anne Bruce Haldeman, telephone interview with MKG.

2. For Bullitt see Bullitt, "Oxmoor"; Thomas Bullitt to Jane Terry Bullitt; and Marian Cruger Coffin, Ballard Collection.

3. MKG telephone conversation with Juan Cameron, who is married to Nora Leake, Nora Yassagi Bullitt's granddaughter. Winter, 1988.

4. See Marian Cruger Coffin, Ballard Collection.

5. "Adelicia, writing in a letter in December 1871, recorded that she had settled without recourse to the courts her difficulties with Joseph [her eldest son] . . . ." Wardin, *Belmont Mansion*, 31. All information about the Acklens and "Belmont" from this source.

6. Material for Jensen drawn from landscape historian Melanie Simo's interpretation given in the Radcliffe Seminars at Harvard University, 1985, and for "Airdrie" from on-site visits and a paper presented at the seminars.

7. Jensen's own major writing, *Siftings*, would not appear until 1956.

8. Miller, "The Prairie Spirit," 5.

9. Eaton, *Landscape Artist in America*, 15.

10. "Lanark," the neighboring Alexander house belonging to Lucy's brother, K. D. Alexander, was also landscaped by Jensen.

11. In the glass houses of Garfield Park in Chicago, Jensen had already created "natural gardens" that depicted earlier geological epochs—"When Chicago was a Jungle," etc.

12. Eaton, *Landscape Artist*, 110.

13. In Chicago's Humboldt Park Jensen made a rose garden that he later disavowed, but which at the time Wilhelm Miller praised in the first chapter of "The Prairie Spirit" as a formal garden with prairie flavor, although there are no "prairie flowers" (*Compositae*, such as daisies or rudbeckia, or other flowers with horizontal lines and upturned faces such as phlox).

14. Jensen, *The Clearing*, quoted by Eaton, *Landscape Artist*, 4.

15. The koelreuterias are not marked on Jensen's plan, nor are the plantings of *Cornus mas, Lonicera fragrantissima, Euonymus alatus*, hackberry, and various wild grape varieties. Although some of these may be adventitious, Jensen often altered a plan in execution. One note on the Airdrie plan reads, "The line of forest edge is approximate. It should follow ridge line."

16. Jensen created "prairie style" rockwork pools as far away from the prairies as Mrs. Hugh F. Van Deventer's, in Bearden, Tenn. See Brandau, *Homes and Gardens of Tennessee*, 353. "To add mystery to this hillside pool," Jensen built an overhanging ledge planted with natives, and treated the lower end of the pool as a bog garden. Above the pool was a council ring.

17. The most formal, even Italianate, garden Jensen designed was "Havenwood" for E. L. Ryerson in Lake Forest (1912), where a long allée and pool with statues purchased in Italy echoed the formality of Shaw's Italian palazzo. See Eaton, *Landscape Artist*, 97, and Colton, "The House that Was Built for a Garden."

18. Before the late twenties, Jensen's most "natural" effects were in reality quite artificial, and required much maintenance. "Airdrie" was well kept up until the thirties; then for forty years it suffered some neglect. The present restoration has revealed which plants were shaded out and which self-seeded. It wasn't till the early thirties that Jensen succeeded in using natural growth and change throughout a garden as a principal design element, as at Lincoln Memorial Gardens in Springfield, Illinois, where "Instead of the carefully laid out natural scene, only the framework is provided. Plants are to be set out in their proper environment, and natural processes allowed to take their course." Christy, "The Metamorphosis of an Artist," 66.

19. Hornbeck, "A Forest Pool," 2. Interestingly, Hornbeck apprenticed with Fletcher Steele, whose work, though different from Jensen's, bridges the traditional landscape architecture of vista and viewpoint and the modern sensibility of surrounding spaces. Steele's work, especially at "Naumkeag," and Jensen's are equally abstract, and concerned with a new kind of movement through a landscape.

20. Jensen, *The Clearing*, quoted by Eaton, *Landscape Artist*, 76.

21. W. E. Simms Planting Plan, 1916.

22. From Jens Jensen, *The Prairie Spirit*, quoted by Eaton, *Landscape Artist*, 140.

23. For Fleming see Warren, "Bryant Fleming."

24. Newton, 441.

25. Warren, "Bryant Fleming," 32.

26. Richard C. Page to ECW.

27. One of the better known Staub houses outside Texas is now the Dixon Museum, in Memphis, Tenn. Built for the Hugo Dixons in 1940, it is surrounded by 17 acres of formal forest garden designed by Hope Crutchfield, Dixon's sister, who was trained as a landscape architect but did not practice. Barnstone, *John Staub*, 318.

28. Anne Bruce Haldeman, telephone interview with MKG.

RICHMOND RISES AGAIN

1. For the development of Richmond see Dabney, *Richmond*; Brownell, *The City in Southern History*.

2. Carden G. McGehee, Jr., "The Planning, Sculpture, and Architecture of Monument Avenue, Richmond, Virginia," quoted by O'Neal, *The Work of William Lawrence Bottomley*, 22.

3. In 1911–13, Noland and Baskervill were also the architects for "Swannanoa," a large, severe, Florentine-style villa near Charlottesville with a terraced and pergola-ed rectangular Italian garden. For Henry E. Baskervill see Steele, "Henry E. Baskervill."

4. For Gillette see Lilly, "Charles Gillette"; also Gillette, Charles, work of, "New Gardens of Virginia."

5. The Weddells had good advisors: much of their furniture and art was purchased through Charles Duveen in London.

6. Lilly, "Charles Gillette," 21.

7. For Gillette's office correspondence and architectural drawings see University of Virginia.

8. Gillette lived near Windsor Farms in Rothesay Circle. The developer, Jonathan Bryan, gave Gillette the pick of the lots in exchange for his services. The house, designed by architect W. D. Blair and built in 1916, was a smallish brick and yellow stucco affair with four entrance front gables and brick-framed mullioned windows. The plantings visible in *House & Garden* December, 1921, photographs are ordinary foundation plantings that include quick-growing poplars, unlike Gillette's fine work for his clients.

9. For "Lochiel" see Lilly, "Charles Gillette," 18–25.

10. Foreword by Jaquelin T. Robertson for O'Neal, xiv.

11. Robertson, in O'Neal, xiv.

12. For Turtle Bay see Colton, "Turtle Bay Gardens."

13. Architectural historian and critic Allan Greenberg to Jaquelin T. Robertson, in O'Neal, xii.

14. Ibid., O'Neal, xiii.

15. Although Bottomley was not a horticulturist, but he had specific ideas for planting "looks" for his houses: "... each different kind of house should have its special kind of planting and landscape setting.... a stucco house ... usually looks better when seen through what we call tracery planting, perhaps with accents of evergreens. A brick or stone house, on the other hand, is apt to appear much better when there are open views of it, with the wall relieved by heavy looking vines and when there are dense masses of tree foliage behind it." Boyd, "The Country House and the Developed Landscape," 98. Bottomley's 18th-century motifs were just what Richmond's *arrivistes* wanted to cloak the recent origins of their fortunes.

16. For Lady Jean Skipwith see Lockwood, *Gardens of Colony and State*, vol. II, 102.

17. Information on designers from Mrs. Walter Robertson, telephone interview with MKG.

TWENTIETH-CENTURY GARDENS
FARTHER SOUTH

1. The New York Botanical Garden's staff have nothing to say about the virtues of this treatment. David Headley says that sodium chloride is known to be a micro-nutrient. Dora Galitzki says that in such small quantities salt will not hurt the plant. Carl Totemeier says "salt" may mean "Epsom Salts."

2. Duncan, "The Gardens of Cornish," 14.

3. Mrs. Ralph Hanes, interview with MKG. Shipman never missed a chance to use native plants. As groundcover for the Hanes' driveway turnaround circle she used two of North Carolina's signature plants: *Galax aphylla* and *Shortia galacifolia*, both rare piedmont flowers. Over them, to provide shade and humus, is a canopy of native laurel and rhododendron species.

4. Quoted in Shipman obituary, *New York Times*, Mar. 29, 1950.

5. Mrs. Ralph Hanes, June, 1988.

6. Shipman used the same cylindrical garden building in other gardens, notably "Rynwood," the Samuel Salvage garden on Long Island.

7. Shipman also designed the Hanes' garden at their summer place in Roaring Gap, N. C. Overlooking a panorama of the entire coastal plain, Shipman made a cosy nest, a small formal garden with a statue of St. Francis, a few dwarf flowering trees, and a semicircular sitting bench, sheltered by a big tree.

8. Notes from MKG interviews with Mrs. Hanes for "Carolina Grown."

9. When the garden became overgrown in the fifties, after Shipman's death, DeWitt Hanes called in Thomas Church to "give the garden some air." Church, an admirer of Shipman, did not change the character of the garden, but made those changes necessary for the continued life of any garden. He took down the bamboo arches and a pergola, and moved the garden steps back toward the house.

10. Bishir, *Early Twentieth-century Suburbs*, 67.

11. Wilson, "Reynolda House."

12. See Elwood, 147–49, for early pictures of "Reynolda," whose original plans were drawn up by Buchenland Miller and executed by Sears.

13. Mrs. C. F. Disher, telephone interview with MKG.

14. Horticultural information from T. H. McHatton's "Gardening in Georgia," in Cooney, *Garden Hist. of Georgia*, 130–38.

15. For Druid Hills and Candler see Martin, *Landmark Homes*, 170–73.

16. For Maddox see Horton, "The Summer House of a Georgian"; and Perkerson, "The Garden Theater at Woodhaven."

17. Martin, *Landmark Homes*, 155.

18. Hentz and Reid (particularly Reid) were Philip Trammell Schutze's mentors and employers. While at Georgia Tech, where he was a member of the first graduating class in the department of architecture in 1912, he worked for the firm part-time. Hentz and Reid then urged him to go to the Columbia School of Architecture. He won the American Academy's Rome Prize in 1915 and went to Europe, where he became thoroughly Italianized. After brief stints with Burrall Hoffman, Jr., and Mott Schmidt, he returned to Atlanta and the firm in 1923, and became a partner upon Reid's death in 1926.

19. All biographical information from Nancy Calhoun Motz telephone interview with MKG.

20. Reed, "America's Greatest Living Classical Architect," 10–14.

21. Cooney, 176–80.

22. Martin, *Landmark Homes*, 179.

23. The portico is after that at Duncombe House in Yorkshire, the garden staircase form comes from Bramham Park, also in Yorkshire, the statues that break the line of the eaves from Cannons, in Middlesex, the motif of the four brackets and the broken pediment suggest Badminton in Gloucestershire, etc.

24. Diego Suarez had sketched Palazzo Corsini's cascade too—it was the model for "Vizcaya's" casino mount in 1915. Perhaps Schutze took note of this, since he worked for Burrall Hoffman, Jr., in 1920. In the true classical tradition of free borrowing, Schutze simply tucked the idea away and reused it appropriately at "Swan House."

25. Cooney, 228.

26. Rousham was laid out c. 1720 by Charles Bridgeman, and in 1738 redesigned by Kent.

27. Mrs. Inman's fondness for swans occasioned the name of the house. Before the Inmans built "Swan House" they had already purchased the prize of their furniture collection: a pair of mid-eighteenth-century marble-topped consoles ornamented with swans. Georgia-born Ruby Ross Wood, one of the first well-known New York women decorators along with Elsie de Wolfe, helped with the interiors. See Lester, "The Interiors of Swan House," 31; and Mitchell, "The Swan House."

28. For "Dunaway Gardens" see "Bring the bloom back to Dunaway Gardens," n.d., and 1985 Dunaway Gardens Restoration slide show captions.

29. See Howett, "A Southern Lady's Legacy," fig. 2, 350.

30. Sarah Coleman Ferrell to Professor C. C. Cox (1901) quoted in Howett, "A Southern Lady's Legacy," 349.

31. Earl J. Draper, in "Hills and Dales," describes the pulpit outline as filled in with jack-in-the-pulpit.

32. The house had vanished, and a cotton gin house stood on the site, according to Draper, "Hills and Dales," 372.

33. The estate now comprises 1,500 acres.

34. Hamilton Boykin's "Plane Hill," in Camden, S.C., was a similar garden of the same date. Both Sarah Porter Smith's garden in Columbia, first laid out in the 1830s by John Caldwell, and the "Hampton-Preston" garden in Columbia shared many features with "The Terraces."

35. Howett, *Land of our Own*, 19.

36. Reid died at forty-one in 1926. "Hills and Dales"

was his biggest and best-known commission and he owed many later jobs to it. Among his other notable Atlanta commissions is a copy of the Somerset manorhouse, Tintinhull. A "Reid house" is still greatly prized in Atlanta today.

37. Martin, *Landmark Homes*, 162.

38. The sunken garden and five new shorter terraces rounded the corner of the house to the west, and included what was called a "Florida Garden": pink and blue hydrangeas, papaya, orange and lemon trees, and oleanders. A grotto was added to the park-and-grove part of the landscape one passes on the way up the drive. Cooney, 332.

39. Draper, "Hills and Dales," 376.

40. The photograph of "Hills and Dales" in Elwood's *American Landscape Architecture* shows this newly heightened axis, and Draper's May 1932 *House Beautiful* article illustrates the new reflecting pool below. Interestingly, Draper, whose students at the Alabama Polytechnic Institute made a complete measured plan of the garden, does not, in this article, credit Reid but refers to the garden as "a splendid example of Italian Renaissance work at the time of the Baroque period, when informalism was creeping in." Draper, "Hills and Dales," 372.

41. See Cooney, 360–63; and Lockwood, *Gardens of Colony and State*, vol. II, 321.

42. In 1916, the year "Hills and Dales" was finished, Reid bought "Mimosa Hall" (1830–1840) on 12 acres in Roswell, where he used his experiences at "Hills and Dales" to add his own new gardens. He improved the old terrace plantings without destroying their overgrown charm, and placed entrances to new formal enclosure gardens to the north without breaking up the unity of the old formal parterre. He echoed its oval beds in one of his new designs and used swept earth paths in his formal box garden.

43. Cooney, 94.

44. Lockwood. *Gardens of Colony and State*, vol. II, 329.

45. Draper, "Hills and Dales," 378.

THE DEEP SOUTH

INTRODUCTION

1. Philadelphia nurseryman Robert Buist's *American Flower-Garden Directory*, and *The Young Gardener's Assistant*, by New York seedsman T. Bridgeman, are typical works of the period. There were also regional books such as J. F. Lelievre's *Nouveau Jardinier de la Louisiane*, the first published work dealing with gardening in Louisiana.

2. About 500 garden periodicals were published in the United States during the course of the nineteenth century. Goode, 213.

3. Most information for "Petit Versailles" and "Rosedown" falls in this category.

4. For example, gloxinia, bouvardia, lantana, aphelandra, and justicia, all from South or Central America, were propagated in 1853 at "Rosedown," St. Francisville, by Martha Turnbull's gardener Charles. See Turnbull, Martha, *Rosedown Plantation. Addendum #1.* In November 1853 Turnbull's journal entry records 10 bird of paradise, Strelitzia, natives of South Africa, in bloom.

5. *Rosedown Plantation. Addendum #1.* Turnbull's note in a 1858 R. Buist's catalogue reads, "Akebia quinata (Korean introduction) is hardy." She propagated many metrosideros, a shrub with showy red or white flowers, native to New Zealand and Australia, but often lost them to frost.

6. *Rosedown Plantation. Addendum #1.* Turnbull's conservatory must have been colorful, with displays of tropical shrubs and vines such as *Hebe Andersonii*, ten feet tall with violet-tipped white flowers, and orange-yellow

Cestrum aurantiacum. She grew many plants for fragrance, such as South African honeybell, *Loasa lateritia.* The by-now-familiar star, or Confederate jasmine *(Trachelospermum jasminoides),* introduced from China, must have been new to her in 1859: she notes it as "Rhyncospermum jasminoides—very pretty white flowers, fragrant, an evergreen."

7. New Orleans and Natchez nurseries included John M. Nelson's Magnolia Nurseries and James McCabe, Gardener and Florist, in New Orlea 's, and T. Pringle and Co. in both New Orleans and Natchez.

8. For Affleck see Cotton, "Thomas Affleck."

9. In 1858 Affleck offered 50 Ghent varieties.

10. In Marion, Alabama, at "Carlisle Hall," formerly "Henworthy Hall," all the hinges and doorknobs were plated with silver. *Alabama WPA Guide,* 290. Valcour Aime, at "Petit Versailles" in Louisiana, is said to have owned a table service of solid gold, which was dumped in the river to prevent Federal confiscation during the Civil War.

ALABAMA

1. At the battles of Talledega and Horseshoe Bend.

2. The wide band of rich black loam that runs through all the cotton states is known as the Black Belt.

3. The original Confederate flag was designed and sewn by Nicola Marschall, who taught at the Judson Female Institute in Marion.

4. Taylor, *Cavalier and Yankee,* 203–205.

5. Demopolis was founded in 1817 by a band of Napoleonic exiles who called themselves the "Association of French Emigrants for the Cultivation of the Vine and Olive." Vines and olives did not thrive in Alabama, it turned out, nor did the elegant colonists, who mostly returned to France when the political climate improved for them. *Alabama WPA Guide,* 293–94.

6. List of flowers compiled by George Stritikus, Montgomery County Agent, as recalled by Mrs. Nathalie Whitfield Winn, General Whitfield's youngest daughter. See Hammond, *Ante-Bellum Mansions.*

7. For Gaines see Whitfield, *Gaineswood.*

8. For Bellingrath see *Alabama WPA Guide,* 387; Carter, *Gulf Coast Country,* 213; Folsom, *Great American Mansions,* 162–64.

9. Howard Barney, horticulturist at Bellingrath Gardens, telephone interview with MKG.

10. A hurricane later destroyed this fence.

11. Three Alabama colleges, one of them black, and two Mobile churches share the proceeds of the gardens.

12. Folsom, *Great American Mansions,* 164.

MISSISSIPPI

1. Ingraham, *The Southwest By A Yankee,* 96–97.

2. Kennedy, *Architecture, Men, Women, and Money,* 275.

3. "Linden," c. 1790; "Propinquity," c. 1790; "Hawthorne," c. 1814.

4. From "Cherokee," c. 1794–1810, to "Magnolia Hall," c. 1858, the last great Greek Revival mansion built in Natchez before the Civil War.

5. Italianate houses include "Longwood," 1858; "Edgewood," 1859; "The Towers," c. 1827, remodeled 1859–60.

6. At "Elgin Plantation," which began as a working plantation in 1800, are the remains of an enclosed, terraced formal garden far from the house. Old cedars, boxwood, and a lone camellia mark the spot. Calhoun, Dr. and Mrs. William F., hand-drawn map.

7. The best known Scots plant hunter is Robert Fortune, who introduced over 120 species from China and Japan, including forsythia and weigela. Goode, 197.

8. See Moore, "Fondly I Roam, Stories of Natchez Homes," 3; and Williams, "Memories of 'Magnolia Vale', 1985." Eighty-six-year-old (1985) Laura Metcalfe Williams, is the daughter of Mrs. R. I. Metcalfe, one of the Brown

family heirs; Mrs. Williams was partly raised at "Magnolia Vale."

9. In his book *Homestead Architecture* architect Samuel Sloan so described the house, which has also been called Moorish, Egyptian, and Byzantine. For Nutt see Hendrix, *Legend of Longwood;* Pilgrimage Garden Club, *Longwood;* and Kennedy, chapters 24–26.

10. Rushford Nutt shortened his name to Rush in honor of Benjamin Rush, and named one of his sons "Rittenhouse."

11. Kennedy, 373–75.

12. Haller Nutt owned over 800 slaves, and was known as a careful, attentive, and just master, who provided well for his slaves and doctored them himself when they fell ill. Whitwell, *Heritage,* 15.

13. Kennedy, 377, 400. Also Whitwell, 13. For the richest Natchez planters, Philadelphia was the bank, not New Orleans, providing the huge sums needed to purchase, ditch, and drain large plantations, and the amounts to tide them through the periodic declines of the cotton market. Kennedy, 367.

14. At Longwood there were governesses for the girls, tutors for the boys, and separate school buildings for each sex! Whitwell, 25.

15. The idea of an octagon as a practical residence was first published by Orson Fowler in 1853 in *A Home for All, Or the Gravel Wall and Octagon Mode of Building.*

16. This presentation of Haller Nutt and "Longwood" owes just about everything except its conclusions to Kennedy, *Architecture, Men, Women, and Money.*

17. Until the devastation of their Louisiana plantations during the Civil War forced the Nutts to move permanently to "Longwood," it was only one of three seasonal residences, the others being "Winter Quarters" and "Araby." Whitwell, 22–23.

18. Ibid., 72.

19. Pilgrimage Garden Club, *Longwood,* 10.

20. From Matilda Gresham, *Life of Walter Quintin Gresham,* quoted by Whitwell, 26.

21. Ten of the 15 acres of formal garden were planted in roses.

22. Hendrix, *Legend of Longwood,* unpaginated.

23. Whitwell, 74.

24. Thomas Jefferson, *The Works of Thomas Jefferson,* vol. x, 159, quoted by Taylor, *Cavalier and Yankee,* footnote no. 359.

LOUISIANA

1. Word, *Reflections,* 11; Frederick Law Olmsted, *Cotton Kingdom,* 113–14.

2. J. W. Dorr in the *New Orleans Crescent,* 1860, quoted by Word, *Reflections,* 9. The group of "extra heavy men" was small and close-knit: of seven planters mentioned one was Turnbull's wife's cousin and another her eldest brother. A third was Joseph Acklen, second husband of Adelicia Acklen of "Belmont."

3. Word, 20.

4. Ibid., 19.

5. As the 1850s advanced, abolitionist sentiment rose and the Turnbulls, like many other Southerners, stopped going north for pleasure, preferring Southern spas like White Sulphur Springs instead. Word, 29.

6. Fruit culture was also important. Martha Turnbull's garden diary yields the following list of fruits: seven kinds of peaches, pomegranates, blue figs, pears, apples, quinces of several varieties, nectarines, oranges, and at least four different kinds of plums besides greengages and wild plums. See Turnbull, *Rosedown Plantation, Garden Notes.*

7. In 1821, John James Audubon tutored Eliza Pirrie at "Oakley" for four months, and painted thirty-two of his bird pictures for "Birds of America." His portrait of Eliza Pirrie hangs at "Rosedown" today.

8. See Robert B. Leuchars, *A polyprosopic Forcing-house,* 43–44, fig. 7.

9. December 28, 1855: "I think hot beds are best to keep things from freezing, but never put cotton seed over them as the weight will break the glass." See Turnbull, *Rosedown Plantation, Garden Notes.*

10. William Prince and Sons, James M. Thorburn.

11. Robert Buist.

12. Sara's daughter, Nina, and her three sisters inherited the plantation, eventually leaving it debt-free to their nephews and nieces. In 1956 Catherine Fondren Underwood and her husband, Milton, purchased the plantation from the Bowman heirs, stripped the house of its later additions, and completely restored the gardens, right down to propagating old "hip" gardenias *(Gardenia Thunbergia)* and a lace-cap hydrangea cultivar *(Hydrangea macrophylla tricolor),* which were no longer available commercially.

13. Before the Civil War, a Southern lady's "I have commenced work" generally meant "I directed the work to be done," as Elizabeth Fox-Genovese points out in *Within the Plantation Household.* In Reconstruction days, it more often meant the lady worked herself, whether with assistance or not.

14. For "Afton Villa" see the National Register of Historic Places Inventory—Nomination Form.

15. Kennedy, 322.

16. Persac, who had his office in New Orleans and died in 1873, was the maker of "Norman's Chart of the Mississippi River from Natchez to New Orleans in 1858," which shows the boundaries and owners of every plantation on the lower Mississippi at that time. Persac traveled the river to make his chart, staying at plantations and presenting them with his watercolors of their places. The little figures were pasted cutouts which it is assumed Persac himself made; the watercolors were done on a drafting table with drafting tools. See Stahls, *Plantation Homes.*

17. For "Shadows-on-the-Teche" see Hall, Weeks; and Beasley, Ellen. *The Shadows-on-the-Teche Development Plan.*

18. Ripley, *Social Life in Old New Orleans.*

19. Corley, "A Girl and a Garden," 3H.

20. Aime was also a philanthropist interested in religion and education whose charitable gestures were as grand as his luxuries: for example, when Jefferson College, in Convent, went bankrupt and closed, Aime bought the place and presented it to the Marist fathers to reopen. *Louisiana WPA Guide,* 531–32.

21. Kane, *Plantation Parade,* 33.

22. Wilson, *New Orleans Architecture,* vol. 1, 100.

23. At "Longue Vue," most remarkable was the Louisiana swamp iris collection which included *Iris fulva, I. giganticaerulea,* and *I. brevicaulis,* all now in the cutting garden since the wild garden is too shady. (Shipman was not responsible for all the native plantings; Caroline Dorman, a New Orleans gardener and friend of the Sterns, helped Edith with the wildflower path in 1940.) Shipman took advantage of the mild New Orleans climate to grow tender plants, such as plumbago and ixoras, in sheltered places.

24. Edith Rosenwald grew up poor in Chicago, in suburban Metairie, before her father made all his money, and was called "Effie," for efficient, by those who knew her.

25. See Stern, "Reminiscence of Ellen Shipman."

26. The first camellias planted died almost instantly and were replaced at great expense with similar specimens.

27. For Stern see Mitchell, "Longue Vue: A Short History of the Gardens"; Stern, "Reminiscence of Ellen Shipman"; Stone, "Longue Vue"; and various Shipman garden plans from the Ellen Shipman Papers, Cornell University Libraries.

TEXAS

1. Barnstone, *John F. Staub,* 107.

2. For McFaddin-Ward see *McFaddin-Ward House,* guidebook.

3. *Texas WPA Guidebook,* 277–78.

4. For Brown see research materials prepared for exhibition labels from "Ashton Villa." For Galveston history, see Barnstone, *Galveston That Was.*

5. For Sealy see "Open Gates."

6. See "Kirby-Stewart Nuptials."

7. Coulter, "Sam Houston Park to get Staiti home."

8. In 1927 Finn copied the lake elevation of Charles Platt's "Gwinn" in Cleveland, at a bayside house in Morgan's Point, Texas, on Galveston Bay. See Barnstone, *John F. Staub,* 119.

9. For Staiti garden plan see Houston Public Library Architectural Archive, Papers of Edward Dewson, Landscape Architect and Engineer.

10. Coulter, "Sam Houston Park to get Staiti home."

11. Barnstone, *John F. Staub,* 7.

12. For Hare & Hare see Houston Public Library Architectural Archive, Hare & Hare inventory for Houston.

13. Barnstone, *John F. Staub,* 57, 133–35.

14. Ibid., note 4, 55.

15. Ibid., 160.

16. River Oaks became a success in the thirties. Between 1930–1939 John Staub built an average of two houses a year in River Oaks. The same was true for the other architect popular in the residential enclaves, Birdsall Briscoe. Briscoe, a native Texan, had begun his practice in Houston in 1910; by the time Staub came along (1921) there was enough work for both, and by the late twenties, for at least four other Houston-based architects specializing in residential work. Barnstone, *John F. Staub,* 33–34.

17. C. Matlack Price, "The New Spirit in Country House Design as Expressed by the Work of Harrie T. Lindeberg," *House Beautiful,* Feb. 1925, 128, quoted by Barnstone, *John F. Staub,* 56.

18. For "Latin-Colonial" see Barnstone, *John F. Staub,* 29–30.

19. Shipman, with Ruth London, designed the gardens of "Ravenna," the rather more academic version of "Bayou Bend" that John Staub created for the Stephen Farishes. Barnstone, *John F. Staub,* 186.

20. There are no Hogg listings in the Ellen Shipman Papers, Cornell University Libraries.

21. Warren, *Bayou Bend,* 71.

22. Ibid., 77.

23. Ibid., 79. For "Bayou Bend" gardens also see Blackburn, "The Gardens of Bayou Bend."

24. For DeGolyer see DeGolyer, Everett [garden]; AAG information sheet; Fitch, *Treasury of American Gardens.*

25. For King see *The King Ranch;* and Lea, *The King Ranch.*

26. Westkaemper, "Three Twentieth Century Gardens," 100–102.

27. For Steves see "The Builders of a Great House." Other biographical information in AAG.

28. J. Fred Buenz, telephone interview with MKG.

29. Mrs. Joan Winter, telephone interview with MKG. There are seventeen sheets of plans for Lutcher Brown in the Shipman Papers at Cornell University, all dated 1936. The design plans show variations on the axial scheme eventually carried out with the assistance of San Antonio landscape architect Day P. McNeel, and one drawing, "Preliminary Design Plan, Sketch A, March 1936," is an almost exact rendering of the garden as realized. The octagonal shape of the gazebo appears in a drawing of the garden houses dated June, 1936. The bathhouse has a columned facade just as it was eventually built, though Shipman's garden beyond and below was not executed. There are no planting plans, and no plans after 1936, which bears out Mrs. Winter's story about an early end to Shipman's involvement. However, it seems that the garden took nearly its final design form during the months that Shipman worked on it.

30. Brown, "Recollections of Mrs. Emily Brown."

31. Ibid.

32. Shipman's plans and sketches must have been of some help; see fn. 30.

33. The dairy at Robert Goodloe Harper's "Oaklands" near Baltimore was one of a series of outbuildings designed by architect Benjamin Latrobe. His design has been attributed to Stewart's *Antiquities of Athens.* The dairy is shown in three-quarter view in *An Architectural Monograph on Houses of the Southern Colonies,* one of the White Pine Series published by *Architectural Record* in 1932. "Gunston Hall's" garden porch is illustrated in another volume of the same set. Brown probably purchased the entire set when he decided to "do his own garden."

34. According to Edward M. Simmons, president of Jungle Gardens, Inc., the McIlhenny gardens at Avery Island, Louisiana, the *Camellia japonica* variety Hishi-Karaito which appeared in E. A. McIlhenny's 1941 catalogue was renamed Emily Brown by Mr. McIlhenny when it was listed in his 1949 catalogue, where it appears on page 4.

THE MIDWEST AND BEYOND

INTRODUCTION

1. Shelton, *Beautiful Gardens,* 256–57.

2. Shelton, *Beautiful Gardens,* 258.

3. Plant lists for "The New American Garden" of the 80s (primarily the work of the Washington firm of Oehme and Van Sweden) tally with Wilhelm Miller's for the Prairie Style.

4. Newton, *Design on the Land,* 353–71.

5. The Olmsted firm's design for the Court of Honor at the Chicago World's Fair promoted formal landscaping. The Fair also fostered the City Beautiful movement, which in addition to large public works such as parks and malls and drives, included by extension planned private residential developments.

6. One of the ASLA's ten founding members, Simonds (born 1857) trained as an engineer and architect. But at his first job, Graceland Cemetery in Chicago (1878), he discovered his true vocation: landscape architecture, or landscape gardening, as he called it. He worked at Graceland throughout his career, using many species of oaks indigenous to Illinois as well as graceful natives like *Nyssa sylvatica* and shrubs with spreading horizontal lines. At Frank O. Lowden's "Sinnissippi Farm," in Oregon, Illinois, on the sandstone bluffs along the river, Simonds planted white, red, and burr oaks, hickory and white pine, edged the woodland walks with shrubs, and silhouetted groups of single species against the forest. See Miller, "A New Kind of Western Home." Simonds's aim was "to teach people to take pride in their surroundings and to see nature's subtle beauty around them." Robert E. Grese, "Ossian Cole Simonds," in Tishler, 75.

7. Eaton, "Jens Jensen and the Chicago School."

8. Miller, "The Prairie Spirit," 4.

9. White, "Insurgent Architecture." In the same issue see Wilhelm Miller's "How the Middle West can come into Its Own."

10. Eaton, *Two Chicago Architects,* 188.

11. Mencken, "The Sahara of the Bozart."

12. Thomas Tallmadge, "Country House Architecture," 285.

FORMAL GARDENS IN THE MIDWEST

1. Root, "Country Place Types," 3, 11. Of six estates with plans and photographs, all but one (Walter Brewster, see below) are formal: Colonel R. R. McCormick's "Cantigny," Wheaton; Mrs. J. M. Patterson and Mrs. Charles A. Pike, Lake Forest, all three gardens by Root; and T. E. Donnelley's "Clinola," Lake Forest, with gardens variously by Howard Van Doren Shaw, H. R. White, of Pray, Hubbard, and White, and Ferruccio Vitale.

2. Meeker, *Chicago,* 95.

3. Ibid., 96. Ogden Armour pledged most of his personal fortune to bail out the company, and worked to that end until his early death in 1927 in London.

4. Arthur Heun (1866–1946) trained as an architect with his uncle, Volusin Bude, in Grand Rapids, Mich., and started his Chicago practice in 1893, specializing in domestic and club architecture. Besides "Melody Farm," he did houses for William McCormick Blair in Chicago, and in Lake Forest for the Arthur Meekers, Sr. Meeker, 88.

5. Meeker, 95. Meeker's "cypresses" would have been hardy junipers or arborvitae.

6. For "Melody Farm" see Moulton, "Mellody Farm [sic]: a Combination of Versailles and Illinois," and Wight, "Melody Farm."

7. Jensen's few private commissions at that time included Chalmers (1901) and Grommes (1903) on Lake Geneva, and the important Harry Rubens garden in Glencoe (1903), where he said he felt he achieved his mature style—a style very unlike that of "Melody Farm."

8. Notations on Jensen plans and construction photographs at Morton Arboretum indicate O. C. Simonds may have been the first landscape architect at "Melody Farm." Also, Jensen's earliest pictures date to 1909, when the house was already up; usually, Jensen's photographic series begin with the original, untouched landscape. Perhaps Arthur Heun's site plan included indications for the formal gardens, which were laid out on axis with the house. See Stephen Cristy telephone interview with MKG.

9. Meeker, 96.

10. Ibid.

11. See Morgan, *Charles Platt,* 54, 226, for network of client recommendations and relationships in the Midwest.

12. See Riley, "The Spirit of the Renaissance on the Great Lakes."

13. In 1936 Mrs. Alger gave the use of "The Moorings" to the Detroit Art Institute, and commissioned Ellen Shipman to design formal yew gardens. Grosse Pointe was Shipman City for high society gardens. In fact, garden writers Fitch and Rockwell in 1956 called her "the Midwestern landscape architect" *(Treasury),* which for a few years she was. Of the 18 gardens listed in the 1950 GCA Annual Meeting visiting list, half are by Shipman. She also laid out Lake Shore Drive in Grosse Pointe. For a notable Michigan garden by Shipman in Grand Rapids see King, *In a New Garden,* 152–56, where Shipman added gardens to the O. C. Simonds landscape.

14. See Platt plans and drawings of "Villa Turicum" at Columbia University, Avery Architectural and Fine Arts Library, Drawings and Archives Collection; also Morgan, *Charles Platt,* 113–20; and *"Villa Turicum,"* a souvenir brochure from a Lake Forest Garden Club Flower Show.

15. For other specific references see Morgan, *Charles Platt,* 120.

16. Ibid.

17. Meeker, 147.

18. Ibid.

19. Morgan points out the genius of Platt's eclecticism here: in one stroke Platt combines memories of the south front of the White House (one of his favorite buildings) and that most copied "garden gazebo" of all, the Temple of Vesta at Tivoli. Morgan, *Charles Platt,* 112.

20. Biographical sketch of Shaw from Eaton, *Two Chicago Architects.*

21. Polly Thayer Starr, "Rose Standish Nichols," in Taloumis, *Rose Standish Nichols,* 21.

22. For Nichols's gardens in Illinois see *GCA Annual Meeting Programs 1933, 1957.*

23. For Adler see Pratt, *David Adler.*

24. At the William McCormick Blairs' Colonial Revival house in Lake Forest (1926), Shipman achieved a brilliant

effect with pear trees trained like thick columns, making the fourth wall of a semi-enclosed court. See AAG lantern slide.

25. At the Joseph M. Cudahys' "Innisfail" (1930), Vitale made the original garden plan, which was abandoned for Adler's revisions for the front and back courts; only Vitale's planting plans were retained. Mrs. Cudahy was the daughter of Joy Sterling Morton, founder of the Morton Arboretum in Lisle, Illinois.

26. Pratt, 23, 60–63.

27. For Palermo see Connor, "They Made the Heights Bloom."

28. Information on Palermo gardens for E. A. Langenbach, George York/Charles Paterson, and Charles Adams gardens in the AAG.

29. For "Vouziers" see Bates, "Joseph Desloge's 'Vouziers.'"

30. University of Virginia's Papers of Charles Gillette in the Fiske Kimball Fine Arts Library reveal no Schock papers, though other Missouri gardens are on file. (Gillette's office suffered a disastrous fire.)

31. Mrs. William C. Schock, telephone conversation with MKG. For "Selma Hall" see also AAG information forms; *Selma Hall 1850–1915*; Schock to Griswold; and *St. Louis Post-Dispatch*, "'Kennett's Castle.'"

THE PRAIRIE STYLE

1. Information on "Gankler Pointe" from Henry Ford Museum, Jensen plans 1926–1932. Also Folsom, *Great American Mansions*.

2. Ford's landholdings comprised 7,000 acres. Marion Mahoney Griffin, architect wife of Walter Burley Griffin, Frank Lloyd Wright's friend and associate in the Prairie School, was the first architect of "Fair Lane" in 1913. According to a story told by the present director of "Fair Lane," Donn Werling, the Fords returned from their first trip abroad to see how the house was progressing, and Mr. Ford didn't like how the cement was being poured (too much waste). Griffin was fired, and William Van Tine of Pittsburgh completed the job. Donn Werling, telephone interview with MKG.

3. Eaton, *Landscape Artist*, 126. Also see *Conservation Planning Study—Fair Lane*; Folsom, *Great American Mansions*; *Fair Lane, the House and Gardens*; Werling, "Henry Ford, Conservationist"; and MKG telephone conversations with Werling and Gelderloos.

4. In *Landscape Artist in America*, Eaton was the first to discuss what he called the Great Meadow.

5. See Werling, and Werling telephone interview with MKG.

6. Clara Ford was president of the Women's National Farm and Garden Club for eight years in the late twenties and thirties; "Fair Lane" had a roadside produce stand.

7. In 1934 Jensen's firm landscaped the Rotunda for the Century of Progress for Ford at the Chicago World's Fair.

8. A Jensen garden with statues was the E. L. Ryersons' "Havenwood," in Lake Forest, Illinois. (Eaton, *Two Chicago Architects*, 207–209.) Architect Howard Shaw imported statues of the four seasons from Italy, which Jensen set in a formal garden that, unusually, ran axially off the entrance front. (The "garden facade" looked out over a typical Jensen meadow.) Much work remains to be done to decipher what was clearly a collaborative effort between the two men. Jensen is credited with the job in *Architectural Record* (Dec. 1917), but in the 1933 *GCA Annual Meeting Program*, Mrs. Ryerson, by then a widow, gave credit to Shaw for the architectural features, and to Rose Standish Nichols for beds, hedges, and small pools. (She herself takes credit for "change of color effect of all planting.") No mention is made of Jensen at all.

9. Harriet Foote, Manchester, Mass., rose expert, designed the garden, but again Clara Ford rearranged most of Foote's work to suit herself, according to Donn Werling.

10. Eaton, *Landscape Artist*, 126.

THE FARM, THE MANOR, THE RESORT, THE ESCAPE FROM THE CITY, THE GARDENER'S GARDEN

1. Thornton, *Cultivating Gentlemen*, introduction and ch. 1.

2. The model farm would later take a different turn, as time revealed that wasteful American farming methods had ruined the land. Pulitzer Prize-winning novelist Louis Bromfield's "Malabar Farm" in Mansfield, Ohio, had no elaborate gardens, but was devoted to soil and crop improvements and erosion control. Cason Callaway, son of the Fuller Callaways of "Hills and Dales" in La Grange, restored 2,500 run-down acres to fertile cultivation in Pine Mountain, Georgia. However, such conservation-oriented ventures were not money-makers. When Bromfield visited Callaway he said, "Cason, this is what God would do if he had the money."

3. Donald Hoffman, telephone interview with MKG. Long employed up to 350 people on the farm in the twenties. There was even a "hotel" to house about 100 single men. See Bradley, *Robert Alexander Long*, 7. "Longview" was inherited by daughter Loula Long, also a horse lover, and one of the "two all-time greats" listed in the Madison Square Garden Hall of fame for equine sports. See Bradley, 100, and Hockaday, *Kansas City Star*.

4. Washington Irving so described Missouri in 1832; from "Washington Irving to Mrs. Paris," *The Life and Letters of Washington Irving*, cited by Bradley, 199, fn. 4.

5. Bradley, 47.

6. Long's interest in public welfare and its connection with landscape was deep. See Newton, *Design on the Land*, 480–83 for Kansas City landscape architects Hare & Hare's 1922 company town for Long-Bell Lumber in Washington state.

7. Altogether different was the water lily garden on the other side of the house: fashionably "Italian" in 1912, it had a central casino with arched openings, with pergolas on either side. Large pools formed a semicircle in front of the long casino/pergola structure.

8. Later called "Lawsonia."

9. Harold Mitchell, interview with MKG.

10. Another conservatory originally stood on the south side of the garden. The east side gives onto Green Lake.

11. No landscape architect of record has yet been discovered. However, the name of "Lone Tree Farm's" longtime superintendent. W. A. Merigold, Jr., appears on several plans of 1917 (at Greenlake Conference Center). According to Mitchell, Merigold was a close associate of Mrs. Lawson in all her estate planning.

12. White, *From Camargo to Indian Hill*, 43.

13. Ibid., 22.

14. Matthews's firm, Stanley Matthews and Associates, which opened in 1920, worked principally in the public and business sectors.

15. Other Taylor gardens in the Cincinnati area included James Evans, 1919, on Grandin Road, and the brilliant formal French garden of Mrs. Norma Wendisch at "La Lanterne." Taylor's associate, Eleanor Christie, did many fine gardens, notably "Annesdale," the arboretum created by Mr. and Mrs. Stanley Rowe in Indian Hill. For other gardens see *GCA Annual Meeting Program 1954*.

16. White, *From Camargo to Indian Hill*, 50–57.

17. Photocopy of Lewis and Valentine form letter, AAG.

18. For Allerton see Shelton, *Beautiful Gardens*, 267–68, plates 126, 127; David Bowman, telephone interview with ECW; Eickman, *The Allerton Legacy*.

19. After graduating, Gregg worked for architect David Adler in Chicago until he was let go in 1929, after the Crash.

20. One more garden was made. In 1937 the distant "Lost Garden" was laid out in the woods on the other side of the river, around a small lattice house with mosquelike openings and a circular staircase that led to a sun-bathing roof. A copy of a Canova statue stood within. The house

burned in the seventies; the glade grew up.

21. See Eickman, *The Allerton Legacy*, for *The Centaur* and *The Sun Singer* gardens. In the thirties, Milles, then artist-in-residence at "Cranbrook," came to see *The Sun Singer* on its prairie, and said, "I hope that this bronze will stay there in that way till the last man has gone—when earth is dead as the moon—and still is there."

22. In 1947 Allerton and Gregg moved permanently to Hawaii to make another great garden, "Lawai-Kai," and much of "The Farm" was turned over to the University of Illinois. Allerton returned every year of his life (he lived to be ninety-one) to see the Illinois spring.

23. Miller, "Some Inspiring Examples of Roadside Planting."

24. David Bowman, telephone interview with ECW.

25. Meeker, 214–17.

26. Mrs. Brewster also wrote *The Little Garden for Little Money*.

27. For a plan see Root, "Country Place Types," 3.

28. For Brewster also see *GCA Annual Meeting 1933*.

29. Frank B. Meade and James Hamilton of Cleveland, architects, 1919.

30. The entire site was only 7 acres; the garden covered no more than a quarter of the space, and was for the most part only 25 feet wide, never exceeding 50. See Frary, "Warren Bicknell's 'Beacon Hill.'"

31. The prize was given for this garden, and for the H. G. Lapham Gardens in Brookline, Mass. "Beacon Hill" was also one of only three private gardens selected for an exhibition in London of American landscape architecture reviewed by *Landscape Architecture* in Jan. 1949.

32. Also see *GCA List of Gardens Open to Visiting Members, 1921*, 70, where it is listed as an "English" garden.

33. *Michigan WPA Guide*, 436.

34. For "Cranbrook" see Detroit Institute of Art, *Design in America*; Roger Kennedy, telephone conversation with MKG.

35. "Stan Hywet," meaning "stone quarry" in Middle English, is a salmagundi of features drawn from English Elizabethan and Jacobean country houses. The Seiberlings took their architect, Charles S. Schneider, of George B. Post & Sons, New York, on a trip to England, where they picked up ideas from Compton Wynyates, Ockwells Manor, and Haddon Hall.

36. See Blanche Linden-Ward, "Stan Hywet," in Tishler, *Landscape Architecture*, 66–70.

37. Manning, "Warren H. Manning, Landscape Designer," 149.

38. Manning's projects totalled 1,700 in 40 states at his death. Midwestern private clients included McCormicks and Mathers. Among his representative estate works were Jeptha Wade's "Millpond Plantation" in Thomasville, Ga. (1903–07), the Heffelfinger lakeside garden "Highcroft" in Lake Minnetonka, Minn. (1903), the A. A. Sprague and Stanley Field estate, Lake Forest, Ill. (1906–14), George Bullock's Centre Island garden in Oyster Bay, N.Y. (1913–26), and the John Gates Williams estate in St. Louis (1923–27). According to Newton, *Design on the Land*, 389, his best-known public works were the park and parkway system along the Susquehanna River at Harrisburg, Penn.; the Hampton Institute in Virginia; the Jamestown Exposition of 1907; municipal park systems in several states; and parts of the National Park System. He also did residential and industrial developments, including some for Frank Seiberling. For further information, see the Warren H. Manning Collection at Iowa State University, Ames.

39. Manning, "Warren H. Manning, Landscape Designer," 148.

40. See Brandau, *Homes and Gardens of Tennessee*, 346.

41. Child, "A Master Plan for Restoration and Development," 10–11. Chestnut blight and Dutch elm disease have destroyed almost all of these trees.

42. For specific gardens see Eleanor Weller-John Franklin Miller correspondence.

43. The Japanese garden, so fashionable at the time in both England and America, was a special request of Mrs.

Seiberling's. True to form, Manning proposed "the use of N. England plants to achieve effects of Japanese ideas." Seiberling-Manning correspondence, quoted by John Franklin Miller.

44. Seiberling-Manning correspondence, quoted by John Franklin Miller.

45. Lambeth, W. L., and Manning, *Thomas Jefferson as an Architect and a Designer of Landscapes*, 104.

46. The last line of Manning's obituary tribute reads, "Mr. Olmsted was a designer and a humanist, but Warren Manning was at heart a poet."

47. The Manning-Seiberling correspondence dates from 1911–1928, and consists of about 100 letters.

48. The forecourt obelisk design was taken from Gertrude Jekyll's *Garden Ornament*, which shows a 1630 design from Drummond Castle. The basecourt herb garden was based on a design from Thomas Hyll's *Gardeners Labrinthine*, 1584. See Karson, *Fletcher Steele*, 202–203.

49. Standish Backus to Fletcher Steele, 9 Nov. 1934, quoted by Karson, *Fletcher Steele*, 200.

50. Fletcher Steele to Standish Backus, 15 Nov. 1941, quoted by Karson, *Fletcher Steele*, 241.

51. Fletcher Steele, "Plant Material," *GCA Bulletin*, Sept. 1921, quoted by Karson, *Fletcher Steele*, 254–55.

52. *Michigan WPA Guide*, 231.

53. *GCA Annual Meeting Program 1950*, 12.

54. *Michigan WPA Guide*, 232–34.

55. For Newberry and McMillan, see Arbaugh, "James McMillan" and "John Stoughton Newberry."

56. Congress later voted funds to reimburse him. For the McMillan Commission's Plan of Washington see Newton, 405.

57. F. L. Olmsted, Jr., and architects David Burnham and Charles McKim went to Europe; the fourth member of the commission, sculptor Augustus Saint-Gaudens, was recovering from illness. Newton, 405.

58. Mrs. James McMillan to ECW.

59. Arbaugh, "John Stoughton Newberry," 23.

60. King, *From a New Garden*, 157–59.

61. Mrs. James McMillan to ECW.

62. Rhoda Newberry Reed, Mrs. Newberry's daughter, to Mrs. James McMillan, Aug. 27, 1987.

63. A Fleming garden also surrounded the Roy D. Chapins' large John Russell Pope Georgian house in Grosse Pointe, later the home of Henry Ford II. Where the blooming season is so short, gardens depend heavily on form and structure. In the Chapin garden, plants were treated as architecture, with clipped hedges of juniper, ilex, and holly. Fleming's taste for garden artifacts as well as this need for year-round interest led him to finish each view with an architectural feature, one a Palladian doorway from a London town house. In the Taylor garden, Fleming incorporated chunks of old sidewalk, bottom side out, into a wall, and got the mossy effect he wanted in a hurry by rubbing the rough surface with a raw potato. The moss spores caught and grew. Newton, 442.

64. B. E. Taylor, Jr., to ECW; Newton, 441–43.

65. See Crosby, *Historical Reminiscences of Lake Minnetonka*.

66. Information on "Highcroft" from Mrs. John Winsor, telephone interview with MKG; Notter, "Highcroft"; wedding announcement from *Happenings Around Lake Minnetonka: the First 100 Years 1853–1953*; and other clippings from the Warren H. Manning Collection, Iowa State University, Ames.

67. Elwood, 97–99; *GCA Annual Meeting Program 1947*, 21; Mrs. John Winsor, telephone interview with MKG.

68. For Lake Geneva history see Wolfmeyer, *Lake Geneva, Newport of the West*.

69. Shelton, *Beautiful Gardens*, 297; also see Kimball, "The American Country House."

70. Charles Yerkes, the Chicago traction magnate, was the project's patron.

71. Hutchinson, *Wychwood*, 60–61. For Hutchinson see also Fischer, "A Jaunt to Wychwood."

72. Sargent helped the Hutchinsons plan "Wychwood," gave them specimens, and introduced them to unusual plants.

73. Hutchinson, 14.

74. Ibid., 89.

75. Hutchinson, 451, quoting from an Apr., 1910 Miller article in *CLA*, one of a series entitled "Successful American Gardens."

76. Ibid., 151–54.

77. Shelton, *Beautiful Gardens*, 288.

78. For Cleveland development see *GCA Annual Meeting Program 1965*, also *Ohio WPA Guide*, and M. B. White, *The Cleveland Years 1927–1930*. Cleveland's park system began with Jeptha Wade's gift of land in 1882. In the nineties Rockefeller and others gave the land that formed the beginnings of Cleveland's "Emerald Necklace."

79. See Flanders, "The Oasis, The Garden of F. E. Drury, Esq."

80. *Ohio WPA Guide*, 223.

81. For Sherwin see *GCA Annual Meeting Program 1965*, 23.

82. A swimming pool landscaped by Bryant Fleming, with a pool house of his design, lay beyond the guest house. Warren Manning also worked at "Halfred Farms."

83. See "News of Ohio's Garden Clubs" and Rankin, "Garden of Windsor T. White." Bly Myers, White's gardener, continued on with the Rankins until the seventies. His son, born at "Halfred Farms," now manages the place.

84. For Cincinnati's horticultural history see Hedrick, *History of Horticulture*; also *GCA Annual Meeting Program 1954*.

85. Unidentified 19th-century Cincinnati account quoted in *GCA Annual Meeting Program 1954*, 11.

86. Mrs. John Campbell to ECW.

87. Douglass Wallace to MKG; "Beautiful George Godfrey Moore Home"; Mack, "Georgian mansion is Kansas Baptist Office."

88. Glover, who began practicing in Topeka in 1919, was the president of the AIA, Kansas chapter, for two years. He designed much of downtown Topeka, and many residences in luxury developments like Westboro, and, later, in Prospect Hills, Republican governor and presidential candidate Alf Landon's own real estate venture after he was defeated by Roosevelt in his second term. See "Landon Home Designed by Topeka Architect."

89. For Chatsworth see Goode, 108–109.

90. Shaw was anxious to display his learning, and promoted a Latin inscription for his main gate: *Hort. Bot. Missouriensis*. Botanist George Engelmann, his friend, persuaded him that English would be less pretentious, and the gate reads Missouri Botanical Garden.

91. Other European parks, such as the Bois de Boulogne, Versailles, or the parks of London, had begun as royal property, though public access was allowed.

92. From Asa Gray, "Engelmann," *Proceedings of the American Academy of Arts and Sciences*, vol. 19, 522, quoted by Faherty, *Henry Shaw*, 85.

93. After Shaw's death in 1889, under the first director, William Trelease, it also became a first-class botanical institution.

94. For Shaw see Faherty, *Henry Shaw*; Bry et al., *A World of Plants*; Anderson, *Henry Shaw, A Pictorial Biography*; Lemmon, "Meet Me in St. Louis"; Lacy, "Henry Shaw's Gift to St. Louis."

95. Lawrence, *Lob's Wood*, 5.

96. For all its informality, "Lob's Wood" required seven gardeners, three maids, and a cook to run properly.

97. For Krippendorf see Lawrence, *Lob's Wood*, and *Little Bulbs*.

THE PLAINS STATES AND DESERT AND MOUNTAIN

1. See "Arbor Lodge, the Morton Family Estate" and "A Notable Western Homestead."

2. See "Little Remains of Beautiful, Famous Marland Gardens Here." Marland's 1916 house is now the Ponca City Cultural Center; his second and even bigger Ponca City es-

tate is now the Marland Mansion and Gardens (1925–1928).

3. See Hare to Bernard Frazier, and "Herbert Hare's Turning Point Was A Spiral Curve."

4. See *GCA Annual Meeting Program 1956*.

THE WEST COAST AND HAWAII

THE NORTHWEST

1. Charles Prosch, *Reminiscences of Washington Territory: Scenes, Incidents, and Reflections of the Pioneer Period on Puget Sound* (1904), quoted by Morgan, *Puget's Sound*, 178.

2. Norman J. Johnston, "The Frederick Law Olmsted Plan for Tacoma," *Pacific Northwest Quarterly* (July 1975, 97–104), quoted by Morgan, *Puget's Sound*, 173.

3. Shelton, *Beautiful Gardens*, 323–25.

4. For Portland garden history see Wallace Kay Huntington, "Victorian Architecture," in Vaughan, *Space, Style and Structure*, 272–301.

5. Vaughan, 430.

6. For Kerr see Collette, "The Bishop's Close"; Wallace Kay Huntington, "Parks and Gardens of Western Oregon," in Vaughan, 417–20; *GCA Bulletin*, Sept., 1930, 86–87; Shelton, *Beautiful Gardens*, 183.

7. Shelton, *Beautiful Gardens*, 325.

8. See Wright, *H&G's Book of Gardens*, 71.

9. For Frank see "Herman Brookman House for M. Lloyd Frank," *Architect and Engineer*, Aug. 1930; Ellen Emry Heltzel, "An Era of Gracious Living," *The Oregonian*; Montague, Martha, *Fir Acres*; National Register of Historic Places Inventory—Nomination Form; Stagias, *A History of the Fir Acres Estate*; Brookman plans and drawings of "Fir Acres"; *GCA Bulletin 1930*, 89; Vaughan, 560–62.

10. Bernard Goldsmith (1869–71) and Philip Wasserman (1871–73); see also Dodds, *Oregon, A Bicentennial History*, 118–19.

11. Clark, *Washington, A Bicentennial History*, 76.

12. The second generation stayed in the Northwest: in 1906 in Coos Bay, Oregon, lumber baron Louis J. Simpson built a summer house with an indoor pool, a ballroom, and elaborate gardens that included a Japanese garden, a lily garden, and many exotics. The site is now Shore Acres State Park Botanical Garden.

13. For J. C. Olmsted see Arlyn A. Levee's "John Charles Olmsted," in Tishler, 48.

14. *GCA Bulletin 1930*, 60. The *GCA Annual Meeting Program* for 1930 lists 6 specialized nurseries in Seattle, in addition to the lily growers of Vashon Island.

15. From Matthew Josephson, *The Robber Barons: The Great American Capitalists, 1861–1901*, quoted in Morgan, *Puget's Sound*, 159.

16. Stewart, *Washington: Northwest Frontier*, vol. 3, 426–27.

17. Katie Jo Johnson, telephone interview with MKG.

18. Roberta Wightman, telephone interview with MKG. According to David Streatfield, one Olmsted garden that is a particularly "brilliant design on a steep site" is the Arthur Krauss house, now the residence of the Canadian consul, on the west shore of Lake Washington in the Madison area.

19. For similar designs that include beds of perennials in different colors see Helena Rutherfurd Ely, N. Y. State, and McAlpin, N. J.

20. *GCA Bulletin 1930*, 66.

21. Mrs. James Clapp and Mrs. William Neal Winter.

22. To judge from descriptions of gardens in the 1920s, both Seattle and Tacoma, like Boston, managed to retain a quality of life in some of their most built-up early suburbs that kept the

rich willing to maintain beautiful town gardens; the Merrill garden was perhaps the finest, but by no means the only one. See *GCA Bulletin 1930*, 23, for descriptions of Seattle neighborhoods; 58–59 for the H. F. Alexander and Robert P. Greer gardens; and 61 for the Clarence Blethen garden. In Tacoma: George Osgood, Robert Polk, Marvin McNeill, Ralph Metcalf gardens, *GCA Bulletin 1930*, 82–83. Most of these families also had summer places. The Merrills' country place was at Country Club Point.

23. In 1898 the city fathers decided Seattle had too many slopes; using the hydraulic mining techniques then employed in the gold mines of Alaska, some of the steepest hills were hosed downhill to extend the city's flatland, or dumped far out in Puget Sound. *GCA Bulletin 1930*.

24. *GCA Bulletin 1930*, 58–59.

25. Fitch, *Treasury*, 100–101.

26. See Yarwood, "History of Women in Landscape Architecture."

27. For Lord and Schryver, see Wallace Kay Huntington, "Parks and Gardens of Western Oregon," in Vaughan, 563–64.

28. For Wagner see Mrs. Joseph L. Carman III (Mrs. Wagner's granddaughter), telephone conversations and correspondence with MKG; Lockman, "Gardens: The Contours of Nature"; Verey, *American Woman's Garden*, 89–93. For H. F. Alexander, Everett Griggs, and G. Corydon Wagner, see Hunt, *History of Tacoma*, 115–17; and Stewart, *Washington: Northwest Frontier*, vol. IV, 488–91.

29. In 1900 Frederick Weyerhaeuser and ten other Midwestern lumbermen bought 900,000 acres from the Northern Pacific Railroad, which Hill controlled. This was the deal that made the Weyerhaeusers the foremost timber family in the country. Ficken, *Washington, A Centennial History*, 29. Frederick's son, John P. Weyerhaeuser, moved to Tacoma, where the family has been located ever since. He and his wife built a house on a bluff overlooking Puget Sound, where in 1922–23 Olmsted Bros. created a garden. See *GCA Bulletin 1930*, 83.

30. From *Harper's Weekly*, Jan. 12, 1894, quoted by Morgan, *Puget's Sound*, 332.

31. The "formal Roman garden" became a circular rose garden in 1945, when the subsequent owners the Lowell T. Murrays, who renamed the place "Madera," employed Seattle landscape architect John Grant to make changes in the garden. The stone pergola remained the focal point of the new rose garden. See Mrs. Joseph L. Carman III, telephone interviews with MKG.

32. Another Frederick Cole garden, "Kewn," the garden of Mrs. Gilbert Duffy, in Burien, south of Seattle on the Sound, featured virtuoso transitions from the cultivated to the wild. The Dudley Pratt statue that gave the garden its name, which signified "Quiet Place in the Woods," marked the meeting point between garden and forest. See *GCA Bulletin 1930*, 64–66; and Vaughan, 574.

33. For "Villa Carman" see Thomas Alsopp, "Parks and Gardens in the Puget Sound Area," in Vaughan, 575–76; Joseph L. Carman III, *The Garden at Villa Carman*; Mrs. Joseph L. Carman III, telephone interviews with MKG, 1987 and 1990; *Tacoma New Tribune Sunday Magazine*, Aug. 12, 1984; and *GCA Bulletin 1930*, 79, and 1977, 25.

34. Wright, *H&G's Book of Gardens*, 71.

35. See "The Gardens of Thornewood"; and *GCA Bulletin 1930*, 81–82.

36. Other articles to follow were Perkins, "Thornewood, On American Lake"; "The Residence of Mr. and Mrs. Chester Thorne at Tacoma, Washington"; and "Garden of Mr. Chester Thorne, Tacoma, Wash., Olmsted Brothers, landscape architect," in Howe, *American Country Houses of Today*.

37. Vaughan, 579.

38. For similar view designs see "Moraine Farm" in Beverly, Mass., and Charles Platt's garden in Cornish, N.H.

39. *GCA Bulletin 1930*, 82.

40. Mrs. Oakleigh Thorne would fashion a great garden in Millbrook at "Thornedale," and another equally great at "Las Tejas" in Santa Barbara.

41. Mrs. Joseph L. Carman III, to MKG.

NORTHERN CALIFORNIA

1. Maybeck, Bernard, "Program for the development of a hillside community."

2. Streatfield, "California Landscape 2," 118.

3. Ibid., 128.

4. Mullgardt, "Country House Architecture on the Pacific Coast," 423–24, 450–51.

5. Streatfield, "California Landscape 1," 40.

6. Streatfield, "Echoes of England and Italy," 378.

7. The setting for *Ramona* (1884) was partly based on Camulos Ranch, Ventura County, which was built in 1853, after American annexation. This prettified rancho with its comparatively elaborate garden is what illustrates the California rancho in Lockwood, *Gardens of Colony and State*, vol. II. See Streatfield, "California Landscape 1," 42.

8. For the Frémonts and their lifestyle see Starr, *California Dream*, 365–75.

9. See Mary Austin's *The Flock*, New York, 1906, and other volumes, cited by Starr, *California Dream*, 371, also 476 for further sources.

10. John Charles Frémont, *Memoirs of My Life*, Chicago and New York, 1887, 55, quoted by Starr, 369.

11. David Starr Jordan, *The Story of the Innumerable Company and Other Sketches*, 118, quoted by Starr, 318.

12. Warner, *Our Italy*, 18.

13. Starr, 282.

14. Private California garden theaters such as "Villa Montalvo," "Piranhurst," and "El Mirador" were used more extensively than those in other parts of the country.

15. Streatfield, "California Landscape 1," 46; also "Paradise on the Frontier."

16. Streatfield, "Echoes of England and Italy," 377.

17. *Gabriel Moulin*, 199.

18. Streatfield, "Pine & Palm," 64.

19. The $500 million Comstock Lode fortunes of the "Irish Big Four" built some legendary gardens for the second generation.

20. Streatfield, "California Landscape 2," 124.

21. Streatfield, "Pine & Palm," 64.

22. Ibid.

23. Ibid., 65.

24. Streatfield, "California Landscape 1," 46.

25. Birmingham, *California Rich*, 144.

26. Ibid.

27. *Gabriel Moulin*, 201–202.

28. Starr, 251.

29. Birmingham, *California Rich*, 185–89; and Starr, 252.

30. Starr, 253.

31. Ibid., 250.

32. Named after the 16th-century Spanish writer Garcia Ordonez de Montalvo, who first wrote about "California," as a legendary island "very near to the terrestrial Paradise."

33. Starr, 295.

34. Olmsted, R., *Here Today*, 177.

35. Birmingham, *California Rich*, 54–55.

36. Starr, 298.

37. Garnett, *Stately Homes of California*, 63–71.

38. Starr, 257–58.

39. Streatfield, "California Landscape 3," 234.

40. Simo, "The Education of a Modern Landscape Designer," 24, 30.

41. For "Newmar/La Dolphine" see Wright, *H&G's Book of Gardens*, 82; Olmsted, *Here Today*, 180; *GCA Annual Meeting Program 1935*, 63; and Simo, "Education of a Modern Landscape Designer," 19–30.

42. For "Carolands" see Olmsted, R., *Here Today*, 182–83; Eliassen, *Carolands, The Chateau Remillard*; and Darnall, "The Carolans: an Unfinished Garden."

43. Worn was the Constance Spry of the West Coast: she and her sisters were the first to use relaxed arrangements of wild flowers, and to trail a spray of brambles across a damask cloth.

44. Quoted by Littlefield, "The Classical Garden Goes West," 220. For "Filoli," see also Chatfield-Taylor, "The Flowering of Filoli"; Bailey, "California Great Estate"; Fallon, "When 'Dynasty' Came to Filoli"; *GCA Annual Meeting Program 1935*, 55; and "Lurline Roth; farewell to a great lady."

45. Starr, 410.

46. Streatfield, "Echoes of England and Italy," 379.

47. Ibid., 381.

48. Not that there was much competition: by 1929, there were fewer landscape architects and a smaller clientele than in the south. Only a mere handful of late-twenties Northern California gardens are shown in Dobyns's *California Gardens*, by comparison with those for the south. See Streatfield, "California Landscape 4," 424.

49. Makinson, *Greene & Greene, Architecture as a Fine Art*.

50. Randall Makinson, telephone interview with MKG.

51. Streatfield, "Echoes of England and Italy," 389.

52. For Fleishhacker also see Regnery, *An Enduring Heritage*, 104–107.

53. Starr, 26–27.

54. See *GCA Annual Meeting Program 1935* for Adler's other California works.

55. Cran, *Gardens in America*, 74.

56. For Pebble Beach houses and gardens by Clarence Tantau see Dobyns, pl. 70, 92, 93, 98.

57. For Phoebe Apperson Hearst's "Hacienda Del Pozo de Verona" see Ferree, *American Estates and Gardens*, 210–15.

58. Folsom, *Great American Mansions*, 123.

59. Cran, 77–78.

60. For Hearst and Julia Morgan see Ketcham, "Rediscovering San Simeon's Architect"; and Boutelle, *Julia Morgan, Architect*.

SOUTHERN CALIFORNIA

1. King, *Garden Note-Book*, 195.

2. Padilla, *Southern California Gardens*, 98.

3. Cup-of-gold was introduced into California by Hollywood nurseryman E. D. Sturtevant from seed from the Royal Botanical Gardens at Kew. See Padilla, 87.

4. Information on plant fashions from David Gebhard, Feb. 1989.

5. Woodhouse, "The Beautiful Gardens of California," 2. Much of Mrs. Woodhouse's description is lifted from Garnett, *Stately Homes of California*.

6. "Signs marked 'Private' bar the paved roads leading to the estates of such living trademarks as Stetson, Fleischmann, Armstrong, Pillsbury, and du Pont," says the *California WPA Guide*, 393. Nonetheless, a surprising number were open to the public: 40 were listed just before World War I, and over 100 by the 1920s. See also Peters, *Lockwood de Forest, Jr.*, 19.

7. Earliest Santa Barbara nurserymen were Joseph Sexton (1868), Ellwood Cooper (in the early seventies), and then Stevens in 1885, who specialized in palms. In 1892 came Florentine naturalist Dr. Emanuele Orazio Fenzi (known in California as Dr. Francesco Franceschi), who offered 2,000 different plants at "Montarioso," and set up the Southern California Acclimatizing Association, which made the first systematic study of native plants and introductions. Fenzi's 900 introductions included many plants in cultivation today. Englishman E. O. Orpet, who came to Santa Barbara in 1920 as Parks Superintendent, set up an important cactus nursery. Elizabeth de Forest, "Old Santa Barbara Gardens," 31.

8. The "Persian" gardens of Chicago playboy Ralph Isham's "Casa Blanca" were designed by Lockwood de Forest in 1916. The mosquelike, mosaic-covered indoor swimming pool exists today.

9. Underhill was the architect for C.K.G. Billings (1906), and designed the Mediterranean house and garden at F. F. Peabody's "Solana" in 1917.

10. Murphy, *On Sunset Highways,* 208.

11. For Gillespie see Garnett, 53–61; Goodhue, "'El Fureidis' at Montecito, California," and Santa Barbara Botanic Garden 1980 tour handout "Three Famous Gardens in Montecito"; Locke, "Water Gardens of California"; Oliver, *Bertram Grosvenor Goodhue,* 40–44; and Woodhouse, "The Beautiful Gardens of California," 2–5.

12. Ralph Cornell, of Cook, Hall, & Cornell, did large projects such as residential developments and public commissions. He was among the most gifted of the landscape architects in the twenties. Sensitive to the native landscape, he worked often with seedsman and wildflower expert Theodore Payne (see note 29 below), using more native plants in his work than anyone else except Kate Sessions. The UCLA campus, perhaps his masterwork, is reminiscent of the Boboli Gardens, says landscape architect Robert Fletcher, with its vegetation tunnels and focus on sculpture. Phone interview MKG. For Cornell and Payne see Mathias, *Flowering Plants,* xi–xiii.

13. Cran, 101.

14. Garnett, 74.

15. For Knapp see Garnett, 73–78; "Portfolio of Current Architecture," and Knapp, "Arcady," and *California Southland;* Waugh, "Knapp Pavilion."

16. Thorne, "When an Easterner Gardens," 178.

17. Colonel William Alston Hayne was the first to cultivate citrus in the area. Gilbar, "Las Tejas," 44.

18. A rare Santa Barbara house and garden designed by an Eastern establishment architect was the Italianate McGann villa, "Ca' di Sopra," Guy Lowell, 1916–18. See Andree, *Santa Barbara Architecture,* 190, and Hanson, *The California Gardens,* viii.

19. Gebhard, "George Washington Smith," in Andree, 92. For Thorne see also Cran, 103–106; Elizabeth de Forest, 34; Gilbar, "Las Tejas," 41–54; and Thorne, "When an Easterner Gardens," 178–80.

20. The three most important Santa Barbara landscape designers during that period were Ralph T. Stevens, Francis Underhill, and Lockwood de Forest. See Streatfield, "The Garden at Casa del Herrero."

21. Quoted by Gebhard, "George Washington Smith," in Andree, 89.

22. Another Santa Barbara architect working in the Spanish Colonial style was James Osborne Craig, who designed the El Paseo de la Guerra complex in the historical center of Santa Barbara just before the 1926 earthquake. Rich resorters (Fleischmanns, Armstrongs) contributed heavily to rebuilding after the earthquake, which in hindsight was seen as the opportunity for one of the first experiments in municipal architectural review in the country. Santa Barbara's entire downtown was rebuilt in Spanish Colonial style, and subject to strict design codes.

23. Elizabeth de Forest, 34.

24. Streatfield, "Pine and Palm," 67.

25. Streatfield, "The garden at Cass del Herrero," 287.

26. Other books on Spanish gardens they doubtless used during the twenty years of building "Casa del Herrero" included Rose Standish Nichols's *Spanish and Portuguese Gardens* (1924); C. M. Villiers-Stuart's *Spanish Gardens* and *Gardens of the Great Mughals* (1929); and Helen Morgenthau Fox's *Patio Gardens* (1929).

27. Reidel also designed the gardens of painter DeWitt Parshall's "El Cielito."

28. For Steedman see Gebhard, "Casa del Herrero"; Streatfield, "Garden at Casa del Herrero"; Verey, *American Woman's Garden,* 23–27. Also Baumgartner, "The Shade Garden: Effective Use of Drought-Tolerant Plant Material."

29. There were proportionately fewer women designers on the West Coast: Kate Sessions of San Diego was the most successful besides Yoch & Council. Others were Katherine Bashford, Pasadena, and Isabella Worn, San Francisco (see "Filoli").

30. One of Payne's largest commissions was the vanished garden of Mrs. Lorne J. Knight in Montecito where he planted wild flower meadows (see AAG lantern slide). An important public commission was the landscaping at the Los Angeles Museum of Science. Payne also sent California seeds to European institutions and seedsmen. David C. Streatfield, telephone conversation with MKG, and GCA California Garden Slides Commentary.

31. For "Il Brolino" and Yoch see James Yoch, *Landscaping the American Dream* and "Il Brolino, One of Montecito's Most Prestigious Estates."

32. Hanson, *An Arcadian Landscape,* 9.

33. Ibid., 33.

34. Ibid. The others were the George I. Cochran, Lockhart, and Archibald Young gardens.

35. Ibid., 70.

36. Ibid., 83.

37. Dieterich, son of a founder of Union Carbide, had commissioned what became known as the "million-dollar bungalow" in Millbrook, N.Y., in 1912. Curl, *Mizner's Florida,* 33.

38. Thompson, "Park Lane," 78.

39. For McCormick see *Santa Barbara Magazine,* Autumn 1975; McCormick, photograph albums, and "Riven Rock" in *Old Spanish Days,* Aug. 1933; and Peters, de Forest, Index of Folders in the Lockwood de Forest Collection, Folder 1429. "Riven Rock" took its name from a huge split boulder; the other prominent features, still surviving today, are the many boulder bridges spanning two creeks.

40. Streatfield, "California Landscape 4," 420.

41. Ibid.

42. One de Forest uncle donated a collection of American art and furniture to the Metropolitan Museum and the American Wing to house it; another was New York Botanic Garden president during the 1880s and 90s; his aunt was a photograph collector and an art historian. Peters, *Lockwood de Forest, Jr.,* 2.

43. Ibid., 7.

44. Lockwood de Forest, "Opportunity Knocks. This Time Will the Landscape Architect Miss the Bus?", 10.

45. All the Santa Barbara architects and landscape architects worked at Hope Ranch, and with each other. Besides the Dickinsons best known were the Harold Stuart Chases' "Las Terrasas," Reginald Johnson, architect, Ralph Stevens, landscape architect, the Milton Wilsons' George Washington Smith house, also with a Stevens garden, and the P. C. Bryces' G. W. Smith house with a garden by Mrs. Bryce. See Dobyns, pl. 25, 43, 51; also *GCA Annual Meeting Program 1952,* 42.

46. For de Forest silver plants must have had special meaning. Many desert and mountain plants have the glaucous bloom that indicates they are drought and wind resistant—they are the natives of the rough Californian places de Forest loved.

47. Lockwood de Forest, "In the Montecito Valley: A South African Garden in Santa Barbara, California," 55.

48. Ganna Walska took over in 1941, renamed the place after the lotus pond that became the Japanese garden and had Lockwood de Forest design the succulent garden. Later Ralph Stevens returned to work on what had been his childhood home. Succulent experts Charles Glass and Robert Foster were the last professionals to work on "Lotusland" during Walska's lifetime, designing the cycad garden, which is the most important collection of plants.

49. For "Lotusland" and Ganna Walska see Waters, "Lotusland"; the 1987 "Lotusland" visitor information; and Birmingham, *Grandes Dames.*

50. Locke, 106.

51. Morrison, "A Rich Man's Folly," 48.

52. Hanson, 29.

53. Birmingham, *California Rich,* 269.

54. Lolita Mitchell Lanning to ECW.

55. Birmingham, *California Rich,* 152.

56. Awl worked for the Mitchells until World War II when he became a lieutenant commander in the navy; on his return he became superintendent of Santa Barbara's Parks Department.

57. For Ludington and "Val Verde" see Andree, 66, 67, 270, 272; Myrick, *Montecito and Santa Barbara,* vol. 1, 179–83; Peters, *Lockwood de Forest, Landscape Architect,* 45–60; Stone, "Val Verde."

58. The great exception is Ganna Walska's "Lotusland," which actually falls outside the period covered by this book (she purchased "Cuesta Linda" in 1941) though she was working within the framework of an old Spanish Revival garden.

59. The rectangular temple at the bottom of Gillespie's Persian rill had Ionic columns. See Goodhue, "'El Fureidis' at Montecito," 103–106.

60. Stewart Edward White, *The Rules of the Game* (1910), 137, quoted in Starr, 438.

61. According to Streatfield, Charles Nordhoff was the best and best known of the promotional writers. His book, *California: For Health, Pleasure, and Residence, A Book for Travellers and Settlers* (1873), was reprinted in 1973 (Ten Speed Press).

62. See *California WPA Guide,* 248; Padilla, 106; and Twinney, "Scenes Throughout the South and Along the West Coast," 170.

63. Stern, "Designing the American Dream," 31. "Hollyhock House" later became the California Art Club.

64. *California WPA Guide,* 197–98.

65. To Mrs. William James, Apr. 5, 1905. *The Letters of Henry James,* 33.

66. *GCA Annual Meeting Program,* 13.

67. For "Lucky" Baldwin see *GCA Annual Meeting Program 1969;* and Padilla, 13. "Lucky" Baldwin's garden was the nucleus of the Los Angeles County Arboretum.

68. For Hosp and "Cañon Crest Park" see Padilla, 70–72; and Shelton, *Beautiful Gardens,* pl. 151, 152.

69. Maher, 263.

70. Hertrich, *Huntington Botanical Gardens,* 62.

71. Pasadena landscape architect Katherine Bashford worked at "San Marino" on the gardens of the historic "Old Mill," making a Spanish Colonial Revival garden patterned with paths and planted in rectangular beds. See Dobyns, pl. 185. One of Bashford's best gardens, which still exists today, is that of Mr. and Mrs. H. J. Bauer in San Marino. Primarily a spring garden, it is an informally planted border backed by a wall. The space is defined by large shrubs. See Dobyns, pl. 48.

72. Hertrich, 81.

73. Woodhouse, "Beautiful Gardens of California," 5.

74. Maher, 304.

75. For the Huntingtons and "San Marino Ranch," see Folsom, *Great American Mansions;* Hertrich; Maher, 215–309; Twinney, "Scenes Throughout the South and Along the West Coast"; and Woodhouse.

76. Maher, 297.

77. Starr, 201.

78. Padilla, 75.

79. Ibid., 72.

80. *California WPA Guide,* 247.

81. Dobyns, pl. 122.

82. For Yoch and Council's Pasadena gardens see Yoch, *Landscaping the California Dream.*

83. See Croly, "The Country House in California," for J. N. Culbertson, Freeman Ford, D. R. Gamble, and J. W. McNeill residences.

84. Streatfield, "California Landscape 3," 234. The first public Japanese ornamental garden on the West Coast was constructed for the California Mid-Winter Fair, 1894. See Streatfield, ibid., 237. Soon every estate garden had to have one.

85. Greene, "California Home Making," 26–27.

86. For Culbertson/Prentiss see Hawley, "An Italianate Garden by Greene and Greene."

87. Cran, 121.

88. Thiene also did the Pasadena garden of another

wealthy Clevelander with a beautiful garden, William Mather of "Gwinn."

89. Reginald D. Johnson, of Johnson, Kaufmann & Coates, designed the Severance house. In 1915 he also worked with Thiene on an opulent Montecito estate, the J. P. Jeffersons's "Miraflores," which was altered and freshened by Florence Yoch in 1932.

90. Streatfield, "California Landscape 3," 238.

91. The site of Versailles was flat and swampy; water had to be piped in from far away for the fountains, which sprayed on special occasions and even on a rotating schedule.

92. David Gebhard, Introduction, in Hanson, *The California Gardens*, xii.

93. MacPhail, *Kate Sessions*, 84.

94. San Diego never wanted its fair to end. After two years of display, the temporary buildings which were slated to be torn down were restored instead. They still exist today.

95. Gebhard, "The Spanish Colonial Revival in Southern California."

96. Irving Gill, "A New Architecture in a New Land."

97. Watson, "Permanent Buildings of Rare Architectural Beauty," 56.

98. To Mrs. William James, Apr. 5, 1905. *The Letters of Henry James*, 33.

99. King, *A Garden Note-Book*, 196–203.

100. Thiene, "Water Features," 43–51.

101. Folsom, *Great American Mansions*, 169–172; Birmingham, *California Rich*, 171.

102. Padilla, 103–105.

103. Ibid., 105.

104. Birmingham, *California Rich*, 107.

105. McWilliams, *Southern California Country*, 99.

106. Padilla, 61.

107. When Santa Barbara was rebuilt after the 1926 earthquake, Palos Verdes Estates surely must have served as a model.

108. For Palos Verdes Estates see Dietz, "Mediterranean Light"; Olmsted, F. L., Jr., "Palos Verdes Estates"; Smaus, "Villa Narcissa."

109. Clara Burnham, *The Leaven of Love* (1908), quoted by Padilla, 59.

110. Cran, 67, and Padilla, 84.

111. Streatfield, "California Landscape 4," 418.

112. Cran, 106.

113. Padilla, 83, 88–89, 97.

114. Cran, 87.

115. Padilla, 81.

116. For DeMille see Webb, "Cecil B. DeMille."

117. Padilla, 101.

118. A Bel-Air house that Kaufmann designed for himself had a sunny, pot-filled, Florence Yoch garden. Besides Yoch, Kaufmann's other frequent collaborator was Paul Thiene. Yoch, *Landscaping the American Dream*, 66–69.

119. Cook had worked with the Olmsted firm on the 1893 Chicago World's Fair, on the White House in 1902, and in the Chicago and Boston parks. He came west in 1905. In Hollywood, Cook designed a successful small garden for W. L. Dodge (1914–16) that was featured in an article by his partner, George D. Hall, in *The Architect and Engineer*, Apr. 1920, 87–90. The simple, rectangular spaces and minimal planting were a perfect foil for Irving Gill's crisply cubist house.

120. Streatfield, "California Landscape 4," 420.

121. Ibid., from an interview with Edward Huntsman-Trout.

122. For Wallace Neff, James E. Dolena, Roland E. Coate, and Paul Williams from Webb, "Architects to the Stars."

123. Yoch, *Landscaping the American Dream*, 88.

124. Ibid., 124.

125. Ibid., 76–78.

126. Schickel, "Mary Pickford and Douglas Fairbanks."

127. Cran, 127.

128. Berg, "Charlie Chaplin, King of the Silent Era."

129. Cran, 136.

130. Brownlow, "Harold Lloyd, A Renaissance Palace."

HAWAII

1. For "Moanalua" see Levy, "Moanalua Gardens"; Bishop Museum photographs.

2. For Dillingham see Mary Cooke to ECW; Dillingham, family photograph collection; Hibbard, *A View from Diamond Head*; Pratt, *David Adler*, 13–14.

3. For Erdman see AAG information forms; Erdman, family photograph album 1935; and *GCA Annual Meeting Programs 1935* and *1961*.

4. For Walker see AAG information forms; Warren, "Una Walker"; and *GCA Annual Meeting Programs 1935* and *1961*.

5. Murry, Engle, "A Meeting of Heaven and Earth."

6. For Spalding see AAG information forms; *GCA Annual Meeting Program 1935;* Spalding, Mrs. Samuel Cooke family photographs; and *Visitor Guide to the Spalding Gardens.*

7. Daniel Dole to Dwight Baldwin, Jan. 2, 1871, quoted by Forbes, *Queen Emma and Lawai*, 5.

8. Dworsky, "Two in the Tropics," 62.

9. Hulme, *Robert Allerton Story*, 17.

10. For Gregg Allerton and "Lawai-Kai" see Waters, "Lawai-Kai," and telephone interviews with Jennifer Eickmann, Director of Robert Allerton Park (1989), and Dr. William Theobald, Director of the National Pacifical Botanical Garden (1990).

BIBLIOGRAPHY

BOOKS

Abbott, Karl P. *Open for the Season*. Garden City: Doubleday, 1950.

Acton, Harold. *The Villas of Tuscany*. 1973. Reprint. London and New York: Thames and Hudson, 1985.

Aime, Valcour. *The Plantation Diary of the late Mr. Valcour Aime*. New Orleans: Clark and Hofeline, 1878.

Aldrich, Nelson W. *Old Money, The Mythology of America's Upper Class*. New York: Knopf, 1988.

———. *Tommy Hitchcock, An American Hero*. Gaithersburg, Va.: Fleet Street Corp. 1984.

American Country Homes of Today. New York: Architectural Book Publishing Co., 1927.

American Country Houses of Today. New York: Architectural Book Publishing Co., 1912, 1913, 1915.

American Society of Landscape Architects. *Illustrations of the Work of Members*. 4 vols. New York: House of J. Hayden Twiss, 1931–34.

Amory, Cleveland. *The Last Resorts*. New York: Harper & Bros., 1948.

———. *The Proper Bostonians*. New York: E. P. Dutton, 1947.

Anderson, Dorothy May. *Women, Design, and The Cambridge School*. West Lafayette, Ind.: PDA Publishers, 1980.

Andree, Herb, and Noel Young. *Santa Barbara Architecture*. Santa Barbara, Calif.: Capra Press, 1980.

Angier, Belle Sumner. *The Garden Book of California*. San Francisco: Paul Elder & Co., 1906.

Auchincloss, Louis. *A Writer's Capital*. Minneapolis: University of Minnesota Press, 1974.

Axelrod, Alan, ed. *The Colonial Revival in America*. New York: W. W. Norton, 1985.

Bailey, Liberty Hyde. *Cyclopedia of American Horticulture*. 4 vols. New York: Macmillan, 1900–02.

Bailey, Liberty Hyde, and Ethel Zoe Bailey. *Hortus Third*. rev. ed. The Staff of the Liberty Hyde Bailey Hortorium. New York: Macmillan, 1976.

Baker, John Cordis. *American Country Homes and Their Gardens*. Philadelphia: John C. Winston, 1906.

Baldwin, Charles C. *Stanford White*. 1931. Reprint. New York: Da Capo Press, 1971.

Balmori, Diana, Diane Kostial McGuire, and Eleanor M. McPeck. *Beatrix Farrand's American Landscapes: Her Gardens and Campuses*. Sagaponack, N. Y.: Sagapress, 1985.

Balsan, Consuelo. *The Glitter and the Gold*. New York: Harper & Bros., 1952.

Barney, Howard. *Mister Bell, A Life Story of Walter D. Bellingrath*. Theodore, Ala.: The Bellingrath Morse Foundation. 1979.

Barnstone, Howard. *The Architecture of John F. Staub, Houston and the South*. Austin: University of Texas Press, 1979.

———. *The Galveston That Was*. New York and Houston: Macmillan and The Museum of Fine Arts, 1966.

Beales, Peter. *Classic Roses*. New York: Holt Rinehart & Winston, 1985.

Bellingrath Morse Foundation. *Bellingrath Gardens and the Bellingrath Home*. Theodore, Ala.: Bellingrath Morse Foundation, 1958.

Beveridge, Charles, and Carolyn Hoffmann, comps. *The Master List of Design Projects Of The Olmsted Firm 1857–1950*. Boston: National Association for Olmsted Parks, Massachusetts Association for Olmsted Parks, 1987.

Birmingham, Stephen. *California Rich*. New York: Simon & Schuster, 1980.

———. *The Grandes Dames*. New York: Simon & Schuster, 1982.

———. *The Right People: A Portrait of the American Social Establishment*. Boston: Little, Brown, 1968.

Bishir, Catherine W., and Lawrence S. Earley, eds. *Early Twentieth-century Suburbs in North Carolina: Essays on History, Architecture and Planning*. Raleigh: North Carolina Department of Cultural Resources, 1985.

Bissell, Ervanna Bowen. *Glimpses of Santa Barbara and Montecito Gardens*. Santa Barbara, Calif.: Schauer Printing, 1926.

Blanchan, Neltje. *The American Flower Garden*. New York: Doubleday & Co., 1909.

Bourget, Paul. *Outre Mer: Impressions of America*. New York: Scribner's, 1895.

Boutelle, Sara Holmes. *Julia Morgan, Architect*. New York: Abbeville, 1988.

Bowen, Louise deKoven. *Baymeath*. Chicago: Ralph Fletcher Seymour, 1945.

Boykin, Richard Manning. *Captain Alexander Hamilton Boykin, One of South Carolina's Most Distinguished Citizens*. New York: Privately printed, 1942.

Bradley, Lenore. *Robert Alexander Long: A Lumberman of the Gilded Age*. Durham, N. C.: Forest History Society, 1989.

Brandau, Roberta Seawall. *History of Homes and Gardens of Tennessee*. Nashville: Parthenon Press for the Garden Study Club of Nashville, 1936.

Briggs, Loutrel W. *Charleston Gardens*. Columbia, S. C.: University of South Carolina Press, 1951.

Brooks, H. Allen. *The Prairie School: Frank Lloyd Wright and his Midwest Contemporaries*. New York: W. W. Norton, 1972.

Brooks, Van Wyck. *The Dream of Arcadia: American Writers and Artists in Italy, 1760–1915*. New York: Dutton, 1958.

Brown, C. Allan, and William Lake Douglas. *A Garden Heritage: The Arkansas Territorial Restoration*. Little Rock: The Arkansas Territorial Restoration Foundation, 1983.

Brown, Jane. *Gardens of a Golden Afternoon*. New York: W. W. Norton, 1982.

Brownell, Blaine A., and David R. Goldfield, eds. *The City in Southern History*. Port Washington, N. Y.: Kennikat Press, 1977.

Bry, Charlene, Marshall Crosby, and Peter Loewer. *A World of Plants: The Missouri Botanical Garden*. New York: Abrams, 1989.

Burden, Shirley. *The Vanderbilts in My Life, A Personal Memoir*. New York: Ticknor & Fields, 1981.

Burke, Doreen Bolger. *J. Alden Weir, An American Impressionist*. Wilmington: University of Delaware Press, 1983.

Bush-Brown, Louise, and James Bush-Brown. *Portraits of Philadelphia Gardens*. Philadelphia: Dorrance, 1929.

Byne, Arthur, and Mildred Stapley Byne. *Spanish Gardens and Patios*. Philadelphia: Lippincott, 1928.

Caldwell, John W. *Mountain Lake, A History*. Lake Wales, Fla.: Mountain Lake Corp., 1984.

Calvert, Frank. *Homes and Gardens of the Pacific Coast*. 1913. Reprint. Seattle: Queen Anne Historical Society, 1988.

Carter, Hodding, and Anthony Ragusin. *Gulf Coast Country*. New York: Duell, Sloan & Pearce, 1951.

Cash, W. J. *The Mind of the South*. New York: Knopf, 1941.

Cautley, Marjorie S. *Garden Design. The Principles of Abstract Design As Applied to Landscape Composition*. New York: Dodd, Mead, 1935.

Champlin, Richard L. *Trees of Newport on the Estates of the Preservation Society of Newport County*. Newport, R. I.: Preservation Society of Newport County, 1976.

Christian, Frances Archer, and Susanne Williams Massie. *Homes and Gardens in Old Virginia*. Richmond: Garrett and Massie, 1931.

Church, Thomas D. *Gardens Are for People*. New York: Reinhold Publishing Corp., 1955.

Clark, Kenneth. *Landscape into Art*. New York: Harper & Row, 1976.

Clark, Norman H. *Washington, A Bicentennial History*. New York: W. W. Norton, 1976.

Codman, Ogden, and Edith Wharton. *The Decoration of Houses*. New York: Scribner's, 1907.

Coffin, Marian Cruger. *Trees and Shrubs for Landscape Effects*. New York: Scribner's, 1940.

Cooney, Loraine, ed. *Garden History of Georgia, 1733–1933*. 1933. Reprint. Atlanta: Garden Club of Georgia, 1976.

Cran, Marion. *Gardens in America*. London: Herbert Jenkins, 1931.

Crosby, Mrs. Franklin M., ed. *Historical Reminiscences of Lake Minnetonka, 1945*. Reprint. Minneapolis, Minn.: Privately printed, 1973.

Curl, Donald W. *Mizner's Florida*. New York and Boston: Architectural History Foundation and MIT Press, 1984.

Curry, David Park. *Childe Hassam, An Island Garden Revisited*. New York: Denver Art Museum and W. W. Norton, 1990.

Dabney, Virginius. *Richmond: The Story of a City*. New York: Doubleday, 1976.

Dean, Ruth. *The Liveable House: Its Garden*. The Liveable House series. Vol. 2. New York: Moffat, Yard & Co., 1917.

Detroit Institute of Art and the Metropolitan Museum of Art, *Design in America: The Cranbrook Vision, 1925–1950*. New York: Abrams, 1983.

Dobyns, Winifred Starr. *California Gardens*. New York: Macmillan, 1931.

Dodds, Gordon B. *Oregon, A Bicentennial History*. New York: W. W. Norton, 1977.

Doell, M. Christine Klim. *Gardens of the Gilded Age: Nineteenth-century Gardens and Homegrounds of New York State*. Syracuse: Syracuse University Press, 1986.

Down Twelve Decades: A Pictorial History of Alma, Michigan. [Francis King] Alma, Mich., 1976.

Downing, Alexander Jackson. *A Treatise on the Theory and Practice of Landscape Gardening as Adapted to North America*. 1841. 6th ed. New York: A. O. Moore, 1859.

Downing, Antoinette, and Vincent Scully, Jr. *The Architectural Heritage of Newport, Rhode Island, 1640–1915*. Cambridge: Harvard University Press, 1952.

Duchêne, Achille. *Les jardins de l'avenir: hier, aujourd'hui, demain*. Paris: Vincent, Freal, 1935.

Earle, Alice Morse. *Old-Time Gardens*. New York: Macmillan, 1901.

Eaton, Leonard K. *Landscape Artist in America, The Life and Work of Jens Jensen*. Chicago: University of Chicago Press, 1964.

———. *Two Chicago Architects and their Clients*. Cambridge: MIT Press, 1969.

Eliot, Charles William. *Charles Eliot, Landscape Architect*. Boston: Houghton Mifflin, 1902.

Elliott, Brent. *Victorian Gardens*. London: B. T. Batsford, 1986.

Elwood, P. H., Jr. *American Landscape Architecture*. New York: Architectural Book Publishing, 1924.

Ely, Helena Rutherfurd. *A Woman's Hardy Garden*. New York: Macmillan, 1903.

Everett, Thomas H. *The New York Botanical Gardens Illustrated Encyclopedia of Horticulture*. 10 vols. New York: Garland Publishing, 1981.

Faherty, William Barnaby, S. J. *Henry Shaw, His Life and Legacies*. St. Louis: Missouri Botanical Garden, 1987.

Faris, John T. *Old Gardens in and about Philadelphia*. Indianapolis, Ind.: Bobbs-Merrill, 1932.

Farrand, Beatrix. *Reef Point Gardens Bulletin*. Bar Harbor, Maine: Max Farrand Memorial Fund, 1946–1959 (1963).

Favretti, Rudy, and Joy Putman Favretti. *Landscapes and Gardens for Historic Buildings*. Nashville, Tenn.: American Association for State and Local History, 1978.

Ferree, Barr. *American Estates and Gardens.* New York: Munn, 1904.

Ficken, Robert E., and Charles P. LeWarne. *Washington, A Centennial History.* Seattle: University of Washington Press, 1988.

Fitch, James M., and F. F. Rockwell. *Treasury of American Gardens.* New York: Harper & Bros., 1956.

Fitzgerald, F. Scott. *This Side of Paradise.* 1948. Reprint. New York: Scribner's, 1960.

————. *Three Novels of F. Scott Fitzgerald: The Great Gatsby, Tender is the Night, The Last Tycoon.* 1925, 1933, 1941. Reprint. New York: Scribner's, 1953.

Folsom, Merrill. *Great American Mansions and Their Stories.* New York: Hastings House, 1963.

————. *More Great American Mansions and Their Stories.* New York: Hastings House, 1967.

Ford Motor Co. Archives. *Fair Lane, The House and Gardens.* Dearborn, Mich.: Ford Motor Co. Archives, 1955.

Forum of the Civics. *A Garden Book for Houston.* Houston: Published for The Forum of the Civics by Rein, 1929.

Fox, Helen Morgenthau. *Patio Gardens.* New York: Macmillan, 1929.

Fox-Genovese, Elizabeth. *Within the Plantation Household.* Chapel Hill: University of North Carolina Press, 1988.

Fryer, Judith. *Felicitous Space, The Imaginative Structures of Edith Wharton and Willa Cather.* Chapel Hill: University of North Carolina Press, 1986.

Garnett, Porter. *Stately Homes of California.* Boston: Little, Brown, 1915.

Gebhard, David. *George Washington Smith 1876–1930.* Santa Barbara: University of California, 1964.

Geis, M. Christina, R.S.M. *Georgian Court: An Estate of the Gilded Age.* Philadelphia: The Art Alliance Press, 1982.

Goode, Patrick, and M. Lancaster, eds. *Oxford Companion to Gardens.* New York: Oxford University Press, 1986.

Goodhue, Bertram G. *The Architecture and Gardens of the San Diego Exposition.* San Francisco: Paul Elder, 1916.

Gray, David. *Thomas Hastings, Architect.* Boston: Houghton Mifflin, 1933.

Gréber, Jacques. *L'Architecture aux Etats-Unis.* 2 vols. Paris: Payot, 1920.

Greenwich in Pictures. Greenwich, Conn.: Greenwich Press, 1929.

Greiff, Constance M. *John Notman 1810–1865.* Philadelphia: The Athenaeum of Philadelphia, 1979.

Guidebook to Newport Mansions of the Preservation Society of Newport County. Newport, R. I.: Preservation Society of Newport County, n.d.

Hale, Edward Everett. *Picturesque and Architectural New England.* Vol. 2, *Picturesque Massachusetts.* Boston: D. H. Hurd, 1899.

Hammond, Ralph. *Ante-Bellum Mansions of Alabama.* New York: Bonanza Books, 1951.

Handlin, David P. *The American Home: Architecture and Society 1815–1915.* Boston: Little, Brown, 1979.

Hanford, Cornelius Holgate. *Seattle and Environs 1852–1924.* Vol. III. Chicago and Seattle: Pioneer Historical Publishing, 1924.

Hanson, A. E. *An Arcadian Landscape: The California Gardens of A. E. Hanson, 1920–1932.* Los Angeles: Hennessey and Ingalls, 1985.

Harvey, H. A., and Raymond D. McGill, comps. *The National Cyclopaedia of American Biography: revised index, permanent and current series.* New York: J. T. White & Co., 1971.

Haslehurst, F. Hamilton. *Gardens of Illusion: The Genius of Andre Le Nôtre.* Nashville: Vanderbilt University Press, 1980.

Hedrick, U. P. *A History of Horticulture in America to 1860.* 1950. Reprint, with an addendum of books published 1861–1920 by Elisabeth Woodburn. Portland, Oreg.: Timber Press, 1988.

Heiple, Robert W., and Emma B. Heiple. *A Heritage History of Beautiful Green Lake, Wisconsin.* Green Lake, Wis.: Heritage Edition, 1976.

Helfrich, G. W., and Gladys O'Neil. *Lost Bar Harbor.* Camden, Maine: Down East Books, 1982.

Hendrix, Margaret Shields. *The Legend of Longwood, A National Historic Landmark.* Natchez, Miss.: Hudson Printing Company, 1972.

Hertrich, William. *The Huntington Botanical Garden 1905–1949, Personal Recollections.* 1949. Reprint. San Marino, Calif.: Henry E. Huntington Library and Art Gallery, 1988.

Hibbard, Don, and David Franzer. *A View From Diamond Head.* Honolulu: Editions Ltd., 1986.

Hill, Anna Gilman. *Forty Years of Gardening.* New York: A. Stokes, 1938.

Historical Society of Talbot County. *The Art of Gardening: Maryland Landscapes and the American Garden Aesthetic 1730–1930.* Easton, Md.: Historical Society of Talbot County, 1985.

"History of the Endicott Garden." In *Yearbook of the Massachusetts Horticultural Society,* 1927.

Hockaday, Joan. *The Gardens of San Francisco.* Portland, Oreg.: Timber Press, 1988.

Hofstadter, Richard. *The Age of Reform, From Bryan to F.D.R.* New York: Knopf, 1955.

Howe, Samuel. *American Country Houses of Today.* New York: Architectural Book Publishing, 1915.

Howells, John Mead. *The Architectural Heritage of the Merrimack: Early Houses and Gardens.* New York: Architectural Book Publishing, c. 1941.

Hunnewell, H. H. *Life, Letters, and Diary of Horatio Hollis Hunnewell.* 3 vols. Boston: Privately Printed, 1906.

Hunt, William Lanier. *Southern Gardens, Southern Gardening.* Durham, N. C.: Duke University Press, 1982.

Hutcheson, Martha Brookes Brown. *The Spirit of the Garden.* Boston: Atlantic Monthly Press, 1923.

Hutchinson, Frances Kinsley. *Wychwood. The History of an Idea.* Chicago: The Lakeside Press, 1928.

Ingraham, Joseph Holt. *The Southwest By A Yankee.* New York, 1835.

Jackson, Helen Hunt. *Ramona.* Boston: Roberts Bros., 1884.

Jackson, J. B. *American Space, The Centennial Years: 1865–1876.* New York: W. W. Norton, 1972.

James, Henry. *The American Scene.* 1907. Reprint. Bloomington, Ind.: Indiana University Press, 1968.

————. *The Letters of Henry James,* Selected and edited by Percy Lubbock. 2 vols. New York: Scribner's, 1920.

Jefferson, Thomas. *The Writings of Thomas Jefferson.* Edited by Paul Leicester Ford. 10 vols. New York: G. B. Putnam's Sons, 1892–1899.

Jennings, J. L. Sibley, Jr., Sue A. Kohler and Jefferey R. Carson, preparers. *Massachusetts Avenue Architecture.* Vol. 2. Washington, D. C.: Commission of Fine Arts, 1975.

Jensen, Jens. *"Siftings" A Major Portion of "The Clearing" and Collected Writings.* Chicago: Ralph Fletcher Seymour, 1956.

Johnson, Thomas H., ed. *The Oxford Companion to American History.* New York: Oxford University Press, 1966.

Jones, Evan. *The Plains States.* New York: Time-Life Books, 1968.

Jones, Marshall. *This Was My Newport.* Cambridge: The Mythology Co., 1944.

Junior League of Greenwich. *The Great Estates: Greenwich, Connecticut, 1880–1930.* Canaan, N. H.: Junior League of Greenwich, Phoenix Publishing, 1986.

Kane, Harnett. *Plantation Parade.* New York: William Morrow, 1945.

Karson, Robin. *Fletcher Steele, Landscape Architect: An Account of the Gardenmaker's Life 1885–1971.* Sagaponack, N. Y.: Sagapress, 1989.

Kennedy, Roger. *Architecture, Men, Women, and Money in America 1600–1860.* New York: Random House, 1985.

Kenworthy, Richard G. *The Italian Garden Transplanted.* Troy, Ala.: Troy State University, 1988.

King, Mrs. Francis. *Chronicles of the Garden.* New York: Scribner's, 1925.

————. *In a New Garden.* New York: Knopf, 1928.

————. *Pages from a Garden Note-Book.* New York: Scribner's, 1921.

————. *The Well-Considered Garden.* New York: Scribner's, 1915.

Kolodny, Annette. *The Lay of the Land: Metaphor as Experience and History in American Life and Letters.* Chapel Hill, N. C.: University of North Carolina, 1975.

Kouwenhoven, John A. *The Columbia Historical Portrait of New York.* 1953. Revised ed. New York: Harper & Row, 1972.

Krall, Daniel. *Ellen Biddle Shipman: Dean of Women Landscape Architects.* New York: Sagapress/Abrams, forthcoming.

Lacy, Allen, ed. *The American Gardener, A Sampler.* New York: Farrar, Straus & Giroux, 1988.

Lambeth, W. A., and Warren H. Manning. *Thomas Jefferson as an Architect and a Designer of Landscapes.* Boston: Houghton Mifflin, 1913.

Langhorne, Elizabeth, K. Edward Lay, and William D. Rieley. *A Virginia Family and Its Plantation Houses.* Charlottesville: University of Virginia Press, 1987.

Lawrence, Elizabeth. *The Little Bulbs.* 1957. Reprint. Durham, N. C.: Duke University Press, 1986.

————. *Lob's Wood.* Cincinnati: Cincinnati Nature Center, 1971.

Lea, Tom. *The King Ranch.* Boston: Little, Brown, 1957.

LeBlanc, Joyce Yeldell. *The Pelican Guide to Gardens of Louisiana.* Gretna, La.: Pelican Publishing, 1974.

Leighton, Ann. *American Gardens of the Nineteenth Century: For Comfort and Affluence,* Amherst: University of Massachusetts, 1987.

Leuchars, Robert B. *A Polyprosopic Forcing-house, A Practical Treatise on the Construction, Heating, and Ventilation of Hot-Houses, etc.* Boston: John P. Jewett, 1854.

Lewis, Albert Addison. *Boxwood Gardens, Old and New.* Richmond, Va.: William Byrd Press, 1924.

Lewis, Richard Warrington Baldwin. *Edith Wharton: A Biography.* New York: Harper & Row, 1975.

Livingston, Bernard. *Their Turf: America's Horsey Set and Its Princely Dynasties.* New York: Arbor House, 1973.

Lockwood, Alice, ed. *Gardens of Colony and State.* 2 vols. New York: Scribner's, for The Garden Club of America, 1931–33.

Lockwood, Charles, and Jeff Hyland. *The Estates of Beverly Hills.* Beverly Hills: Margrant Publishing, 1984.

Logan, Harry Britton. *A Traveller's Guide to North American Gardens.* New York: Scribner's, 1974.

Long, Elias. *Ornamental Gardening for Americans.* New York: Orange Judd Co., 1885.

Longstreth, Richard. *On the Edge of the World: Four Architects in San Francisco at the Turn of the Century.* New York and Boston: Architectural History Foundation and MIT Press, 1983.

Lounsberry, Alice. *Gardens Near the Sea.* New York: Frederick A. Stokes, 1910.

Lowell, Guy, ed. *American Gardens.* Boston: Bates and Guild, 1902.

Lowenthal, David. "The Place of the Past in the American Landscape." In *Geographies of the Mind.* Edited by Martyn Bowden and David Lowenthal. New York: Oxford University Press, 1976.

McAdams, Ina May Ogletree, ed. *The Building of "Longwood."* Austin: Ina May Ogletree, 1981.

McAllister, Ward. *Society as I Have Found It.* 1890. Reprint. New York: Arno Press, 1975.

McGuire, Diane Kostial. *Gardens of America, Three Centuries of Design.* Charlottesville: Thomasson-Grant, 1989.

McGuire, Diane Kostial, and Lois Fern, eds. *Beatrix Jones Farrand (1872–1959). Fifty Years of American Landscape Architecture.* Dumbarton Oaks Colloquium on the History of Landscape Architecture VIII. Washington, D. C.: Dumbarton Oaks, Trustees for Harvard University, 1982.

McKean, Hugh F. *The "Lost" Treasures of Louis Comfort Tiffany.* New York: Doubleday, 1980.

McKim, Mead & White. *A Monograph of the Work of McKim,*

Mead & White, 1879–1915. New York: Architectural Book Publishing Co., 1915.

McLaren, John. *Gardening in California.* 1908. 2d. ed. San Francisco: A. M. Robertson, 1927.

McLaughlin, Charles Capen, ed., and Charles Beveridge, assoc. ed. *Papers of Frederick Law Olmsted.* Baltimore: Johns Hopkins University Press, 1977–.

McNamara, Katherine, ed. *Landscape Architecture: A Classified Bibliography with an Author Index.* Cambridge: Harvard University School of Landscape Architecture, 1934.

MacPhail, Elizabeth C. *Kate Sessions, Pioneer Horticulturist.* San Diego: San Diego Historical Society, 1976.

McWilliams, Carey. *Southern California Country: An Island on the Land.* 1946. Reprint. Salt Lake City: Peregrine Smith Books, 1983.

Maher, James T. *The Twilight of Splendor.* Boston: Little, Brown, 1975.

Makinson, Randell L. *Greene & Greene: Architecture as Fine Art.* Salt Lake City: Peregrine Smith Books, 1977.

Maloney, Michael, and Kenneth J. Remenschneider. *Indianapolis Landscape Architecture.* Washington, D. C.: Landscape Architecture Foundation, 1983.

Martin, Van Jones, and W. R. Mitchell, Jr. *Landmark Homes of Georgia 1733–1983.* Savannah, Ga.: Golden Coast Publishing, 1982.

Marx, Leo. *The Machine in the Garden.* 1964. Reprint. New York: Oxford University Press, 1967.

Masson, Georgina. *Dumbarton Oaks, A Guide to the Gardens.* Washington, D. C.: Dumbarton Oaks, 1968.

Mathias, Mildred E., ed. *Flowering Plants in the Landscape.* Berkeley and Los Angeles: University of California, 1982.

Matz, Mary Jane. *The Many Lives of Otto Kahn.* 1963. Reprint. New York: Pendragon Press, 1984.

Meeker, Arthur. *Chicago, with Love.* New York: Knopf, 1955.

Mellor, Meigs and Howe. *Mellor, Meigs, and Howe.* New York: Architectural Book Publishing Co., 1925.

Mencken, H. L. "The Sahara of the Bozart." In *Prejudices, Second Series.* New York: Knopf, 1920.

Miller, Frances. *"Tanty." Encounters with the Past.* [Breese] Sag Harbor, N. Y.: Sand Box Press, 1979.

———. *More About "Tanty."* Sag Harbor, N. Y.: Sand Box Press, 1979.

Miller, Hope Ridings. *Great Houses of Washington, D.C.* New York: Potter, 1969.

Miller, Wilhelm. *What England Can Teach Us About Gardening.* Garden City: Doubleday, Page, 1911.

Moffat, Frances. *Dancing on the Brink of the World: The Rise and Fall of San Francisco Society.* New York: G. P. Putnam's Sons, 1977.

Monroe, Lynn Lewis. *Sonnenberg Gardens.* Canandaigua, N. Y.: Humphrey Press for Sonnenberg Gardens, 1985.

Mooney, Michael McDonald. *Evelyn Nesbit and Stanford White, Love and Death in the Gilded Age.* New York: Morrow, 1976.

Morgan, Keith N. *Charles A. Platt.* New York and Boston: Architectural History Foundation and MIT Press, 1985.

Morgan, Murray. *Puget's Sound, A Narrative of Early Tacoma and the Southern Sound.* Seattle: University of Washington Press, 1977.

Moulin, Gabriel. *Gabriel Moulin's San Francisco Peninsula: Town and Country Homes 1910–1930.* Compiled by Donald DeNevi and Thomas Moulin. Sausalito, Calif.: Windgate Press, 1985.

Mumford, Lewis. *The Brown Decades.* New York: Dover, 1955.

Murmann, Eugene O. *California Gardens.* Los Angeles: Eugene O. Murmann, 1914.

Murphy, Thomas D. *On Sunset Highways: A Book of Motor Rambles in California.* Boston: Page, 1915.

Myrick, David F. *Montecito and Santa Barbara: From Farm to Estate.* Vol. 1. Glendale, Calif.: Trans-Anglo Books, 1988.

Newcomb, Peggy Cornett. *Popular Annuals of Eastern North America 1865–1914.* Washington, D.C.: Dumbarton Oaks, 1985.

Newcomb, Rex. *The Spanish House for America.* Philadelphia: J. B. Lippincott, 1927.

Newhall, Beaumont. *The History of Photography.* 1964. Reprint. New York: The Museum of Modern Art, 1981.

Newton, Norman. *Design on the Land, The Development of Landscape Architecture.* Cambridge, Mass.: Belknap Press, 1971.

Nichols, Rose Standish. *Italian Pleasure Gardens.* New York: Dodd, Mead, 1931.

———. *Spanish and Portuguese Gardens.* Boston: Houghton Mifflin, 1924.

Nutting, Wallace. *Connecticut Beautiful.* Framingham, Mass.: Old American Co., 1923.

———. *Pennsylvania Beautiful.* 1924. Reprint. New York: Bonanza Books, n.d.

Oakes, Donald T., ed. *A Pride of Palaces: Lenox summer Cottages, 1883–1933.* Lenox, Mass.: Lenox Library Association, 1981.

Oliver, Richard. *Bertram Grosvenor Goodhue.* New York and Boston: Architectural History Foundation and MIT Press, 1983.

Olmsted, Frederick Law. *The Cotton Kingdom.* 1861. Reprint. Indianapolis and New York: Bobbs-Merrill, 1971.

———. *A Journey in the Back Country.* 1860. Reprint. Williamstown, Mass: Corner House, 1972.

Olmsted, Roger, and T. H. Watkins. *Here Today: San Francisco's Architectural Heritage.* San Francisco: Chronicle Books, 1968.

O'Neal, William B., and Christopher Weeks. *The Work of William Lawrence Bottomley in Richmond.* Charlottesville: University Press of Virginia, 1985.

Owens, Carole. *The Berkshire Cottages: A Vanishing Era.* Englewood Cliffs, N. J.: Cottage Press, 1984.

Padilla, Victoria. *Southern California Gardens: An Illustrated History.* Berkeley and Los Angeles: University of California Press, 1961.

Palmer's Pictorial Pittsburgh. Pittsburgh, Pa.: 1905.

Parkman, Francis. *The Oregon Trail: Sketches of Prairie and Rocky Mountain Life.* Boston: Little, Brown, 1914.

Patterson, Augusta. *American Homes of To-day. Their Architectural Style, Their Environment, Their Characteristics.* New York: Macmillan, 1924.

Patterson, Jerry E. *The Vanderbilts.* New York: Abrams, 1989.

Peixotto, Ernest Clifford. *Romantic California.* New York: Scribner's, 1910.

Percy, William Alexander. *Lanterns on the Levee: Recollections of a Planter's Son.* Baton Rouge, La.: LSU Press, 1973.

Perkins, Frances. *The Roosevelt I Knew.* New York: Viking, 1946.

Phelps, Harriet Jackson. *Newport in Flower.* Newport: The Preservation Society of Newport County, 1979.

Platt, Charles A. *Italian Gardens.* New York: Harper & Brothers, 1894.

———. *A Monograph of the Work of Charles A. Platt.* Introduction by Royal Cortissoz. New York: The Architectural Book Publishing Co., 1913.

Pratt, Richard. *David Adler, The Architect and His Work.* Chicago: M. Evans & Co., 1970.

Prichard, Walter. *Walter Prichard's Outline of Louisiana Studies.* Edited and expanded by Sue Eakin. Gretna, La.: Pelican Publishing, 1972.

Prideaux, Gwynn Cochran. *Summerhouses of Virginia.* Richmond: Valentine Museum, 1976.

Procter, Lucille. *Handbook of Florida Flowers.* St. Petersburg: Great Outdoors Publishing, 1959.

Proske, Beatrice Gilman. *Brookgreen Gardens Sculpture.* Murrell's Inlet, S. C.: Brookgreen Gardens, 1968.

Rae, John W., and John W. Rae, Jr. *Morristown's Forgotten Past: The Story of a New Jersey Town.* Morristown: Privately printed: John Rae, 1979.

Randall, Monica. *The Mansions of Long Island's Gold Coast.* New York: Hastings House, 1979.

Ray, Mary Helen, and Robert P. Nicholls, eds. *The Traveler's Guide to American Gardens.* Chapel Hill, N. C.: University of North Carolina Press, 1988.

Regnery, Dorothy. *An Enduring Heritage, Historic Buildings of the San Francisco Peninsula.* Stanford: Stanford University Press, 1976.

Ripley, Eliza. *Social Life in Old New Orleans.* New York: Appleton, 1912.

Rixey, Lilian. *Bamie, Theodore Roosevelt's Remarkable Sister.* New York: David McKay, 1963.

Robertson, Ross M., and Gary M. Walton. *History of the American Economy.* New York: Harcourt Brace Jovanovich, 1979.

Root, Ralph Rodney. *Design in Landscape Gardening.* New York: Century, 1914.

———. *Landscape Garden Series,* I-X. Davenport, Iowa: The Garden Press, 1921.

Rothery, Agnes Edwards. *The Romantic Shore.* Salem, Mass.: Salem Press, 1915.

Sale, Edith Tunis, ed. *Historic Gardens of Virginia.* 1923. Reprint. Richmond: William Byrd Press, 1930.

———. *Manors of Virginia in Colonial Times.* Philadelphia: J. B. Lippincott, 1909.

Sale, Roger. *Seattle Past and Present.* Seattle: University of Washington Press, 1976.

Schmitt, Peter J. *Back to Nature: The Arcadian Myth in Urban America 1900–1930.* New York: Oxford University Press, 1976.

Sclare, Liisa, and Donald Sclare. *Beaux-Arts Estates: A Guide to the Architecture of Long Island.* New York: Viking, 1980.

Scott, Frank J. *The Art of Beautifying Suburban Home Grounds.* New York: D. Appleton & Co., 1870.

Scully, Vincent Joseph. *The Shingle Style: Architectural Theory and Design from Richardson to the Origins of Wright.* New Haven: Yale University Press, 1955.

Sedgewick, Mabel Cabot, and Robert Cameron. *The Garden Month by Month.* New York: Frederick A. Stokes, 1907.

Shaffer, E.T.H. *Carolina Gardens.* 1937. Reprint. New York: Devin-Adair, 1963.

Shelton, Louise. *Beautiful Gardens in America.* 1915. New York: Scribner's, rev ed. 1924.

———. *Continuous Bloom in America.* New York: Scribner's, 1915.

Sherman, Joe. *The House at Shelburne Farms.* Middlebury, Vt.: Paul S. Eriksson, 1986.

Shinn, Charles H. *Pacific Rural Handbook.* San Francisco: Dewey & Co., 1879.

Shopsin, Broderick. *The Villard Houses, Life Story of a Landmark.* New York: Viking, 1980.

Simpson, Jeffrey. *An American Treasure, The Hudson River Valley.* Tarrytown, N. Y.: Sleepy Hollow Press, 1986.

Sloan, Florence Adele. *Maverick in Mauve; The Diary of a Romantic Age.* With a commentary by Louis Auchincloss. New York: Doubleday, 1983.

Smith, Harry Worcester. *Life and Sport in Aiken and Those Who Made It.* New York: Derrydale Press, 1935.

Smith, Robert M., Jr., Ethel Wylly Sweet, and Henry D. Boykin. *Camden Homes and Heritage.* Camden, S. C.: Kershaw County Historical Society, 1978.

Snyder, Amy. *Grey Towers National Historic Landmark, Milford, Pennsylvania: Historic Landscape Report and Landscape Recreation Plan.* Preliminary draft. Milford, Penn.: The Pinchot Institute for Conservation Studies, USDA Forest Service, 1986.

Stahls, Paul F., Jr. *Plantation Homes of the Lafourche Country.* Gretna, La.: Pelican Publishing, 1985.

Starr, Kevin. *Americans and the California Dream 1850–1915.* New York: Oxford University Press, 1973.

Steele, Fletcher. *Design in the Little Garden.* "The Little Garden" Series, Mrs. Francis King, ed. Boston: Atlantic Monthly Press, 1924.

Stewart, Edgar I. *Washington: Northwest Frontier. Family and Personal History.* Vol. 3. New York: Lewis Historical Publishing, 1957.

Stilgoe, John. *Borderland: Origins of The American Suburb, 1820–1939.* New Haven: Yale University Press, 1988.

Stout, Henrietta Maria (Mrs. Charles H. Stout). *The Amateur's*

Book of the Dahlia. New York and Garden City: Doubleday, Page, 1922.

Stritikus, George R. *Alabama: Her People, Houses and Gardens.* Alabama: Alabama Cooperative Extension Service, 1986.

Sutton, S. B. *Charles Sprague Sargent and the Arnold Arboretum.* Cambridge: Harvard University Press, 1970.

Tabor, Grace. *Old-fashioned Gardening, A History and a Reconstruction.* New York: McBride, Nast & Co., 1913.

Taloumis, George, et al. *Rose Standish Nichols As We Knew Her: A Tribute to a Friend.* Boston: Privately printed, 1986.

Tarbell, Ida. *Florida Architecture of Addison Mizner.* New York: William Helburn, 1928.

Taylor, A. D. *The Complete Garden.* Garden City: Doubleday, 1921.

Taylor, William R. *Cavalier & Yankee.* 1957. rev. ed. Cambridge: Harvard University Press, 1979.

Thacker, Christopher. *The History of Gardens.* Berkeley and Los Angeles: University of California Press, 1979.

Thaxter, Celia. *An Island Garden.* Boston: Houghton Mifflin, 1894.

Thomas, Elizabeth Patterson. *Old Kentucky Homes and Gardens.* Louisville, Ky.: The Standard Printing Co., 1939.

Thomas, Graham Stuart. *Perennial Garden Plants or the Modern Florilegium.* London: J. M. Dent & Sons, 1976.

Thornton, Tamara Plakins. *Cultivating Gentlemen, The Meaning of Country Life Among the Boston Elite, 1785–1860.* New Haven: Yale University Press, 1990.

Tice, Patricia M. *Gardening in America, 1830–1910.* Rochester, N. Y.: The Strong Museum, 1984.

Tishler, William, ed. *American Landscape Architecture: Designers and Places.* Washington, D.C.: Preservation Press, 1989.

Triggs, Inigo. *Formal Gardens in England and Scotland.* New York: Scribner's, 1902.

Trollope, Frances. *Domestic Manners of the Americans.* 1832. Reprint. New York: Dodd Mead, 1927.

Underwood, Loring. *The Garden and Its Accessories.* Boston: Little, Brown, 1907.

Van Rensselaer, Mrs. John King. *Newport, Our Social Capital.* Philadelphia: J. B. Lippincott, 1905.

Van Rensselaer, Mrs. John King, and Frederic Van deWater. *The Social Ladder.* New York: Henry Holt & Co., 1924.

Van Rensselaer, Mrs. Schuyler [Mariana Griswold]. *Art out of Doors, Hints on Good Taste in Gardening.* New York: Scribner's, 1893.

Van Trump, James D. *Life and Architecture in Pittsburgh.* Pittsburgh: Pittsburgh History and Landmarks Foundation, 1983.

Vaughan, Thomas, and Virginia Guest Ferriday, eds. *Space, Style and Structure, Building in Northwest America.* 2 vols. Portland, Oreg.: Oregon Historical Society, 1974.

Verey, Rosemary, and Ellen Samuels. *The American Woman's Garden.* Boston: New York Graphic and Little, Brown, 1984.

Villiers-Stuart, Constance M. *Spanish Gardens: Their History, Types and Features.* New York: Scribner's, 1929.

Walden, Fred. *Dictionary of Trees: Florida and Subtropical.* St. Petersburg, Fla.: Great Outdoors Publishing, 1963.

Wallerstein, Andrew M. "Horace Trumbauer, Elkins Park, and Classicism." In *Classical America IV.* New York: Classical America, 1977.

Warner, Charles Dudley. *My Summer in the Garden.* Boston: Field, Osgood, & Company, 1870.

———. *On Horseback, A Tour in Virginia, North Carolina, and Tennessee.* Boston: Houghton Mifflin, 1889.

———. *Our Italy.* New York: Harper & Bros., 1891.

Warren, H. Langford. *Picturesque and Architectural New England.* Vol. 1, *Architectural Features.* Boston: D. H. Hurd, 1899.

Waugh, Frank A. *Formal Design in Landscape Architecture.* New York: Orange Judd, 1927.

———. *Landscape Gardening.* New York: Orange Judd, 1899.

Wharton, Edith. *A Backward Glance.* New York: D. Appleton-Century, 1934.

———. *The House of Mirth.* 1905. Reprint. Avon, Connecticut: Limited Editions Club, 1975.

———. *Italian Villas and Their Gardens.* New York: Century Co., 1904.

White, Virginia S., comp. and ed. *From Camargo to Indian Hill.* Cincinnati: The Indian Hill Historical Association, 1983.

Whitfield, Jesse G. *Gaineswood and other Memories.* Demopolis, Ala.: Privately printed, 1938.

Whitwell, William L. *The Heritage of Longwood.* Jackson, Miss.: University Press of Mississippi, 1975.

Wilder, Louise Beebe. *Adventures in My Garden and Rock Garden.* New York: Doubleday, Page, 1923.

———. *Colour in My Garden.* Garden City: Doubleday, Doran, 1918.

———. *The Fragrant Path, a book about sweet-scented flowers and leaves.* New York: Macmillan, 1932.

Wilkinson, Norman B. *E. I. du Pont, Botaniste.* Charlottesville: University Press of Virginia for Eleutherian Mills-Hagley Foundation, 1972.

Williams, Dorothy Hunt. *Historic Virginia Gardens: Preservations by the Garden Club of Virginia.* Charlottesville: University Press of Virginia, 1975.

Wilson, Samuel, Jr., and Bernard Lemann, *New Orleans Architecture.* Vol. 1, *The Lower Garden District.* Compiled and edited by Mary Louise Christovich, Roulhac Toledano, and Betsy Swanson. Gretna, La.: Friends of the Cabildo and Pelican Publishing Company, 1979.

Withey, Henry F. and Elsie Radburn. *Biographical Dictionary of American Architects, Deceased.* 1956. 2d ed. Los Angeles: Hennessey & Ingalls, 1970.

Wolfmeyer, Ann, and Mary Burns Gage. *Lake Geneva, Newport of the West.* Lake Geneva, Wis.: Lake Geneva Historical Association, 1976.

Woodward, C. Vann. *Mary Chesnut's Civil War.* New Haven: Yale University Press, 1981.

Workman, Richard W. *Growing Native: Native Plants for Landscape Use in Coastal Southern Florida.* Sanibel: The Sanibel-Captiva Conservation Foundation, 1980.

Wright, Mabel Osgood. *The Garden of a Commuter's Wife Recorded by the Gardener.* New York: Macmillan 1901.

Wright, Richardson. *The Gardener's Bed-Book.* New York: J.B. Lippincott, 1929.

———, ed. *House & Garden's Book of Gardens.* New York: Condé Nast, 1921.

Yoch, James J. *Landscaping the American Dream: The Gardens and Film Sets of Florence Yoch 1890–1972.* New York: Àbrams/Sagapress, 1989.

Ziff, Larzer. *The American 1890s.* New York: Viking Compass, 1966.

Zukowsky, John, and Robbe Pierce Stimson. *Hudson River Villas.* New York: Rizzoli, 1985.

PERIODICALS, CATALOGUES, GUIDEBOOKS, CORRESPONDENCE, EPHEMERA, UNPUBLISHED DATA, TELEPHONE INTERVIEWS, AND GCA PUBLICATIONS

For reasons of space, the following abbreviations occur:

AAG: Archive of American Gardens, Smithsonian Institution

AD: Architectural Digest	*H&G: House & Garden*
AR: Architectural Record	*LA: Landscape*
CLA: Country Life in	*Architecture*
America	MKG: Mac Griswold
GCA: Garden Club of	ECW: Eleanor Weller
America	

"Afton Villa" *National Register of Historic Places Inventory—Nomination Form.* National Park Service. Mr. and Mrs. Morrell Trimble, St. Francisville, La. 1982.

Alsop, Joseph W., and Adam Platt. "The Wasp Ascendency." [Barney] *New York Review of Books,* Nov. 9, 1989, 48–56.

Alsop, Susan Mary. "American Continuity: Remembering William Sheffield Cowles at 'Oldgate'." *AD,* Sept. 1986, 170–75.

Anderson, Edgar, and Dorothy Brockman. *"Henry Shaw: A Pictorial Biography."* Pamphlet. St. Louis: Missouri Botanical Garden, n.d.

Arbaugh, Thomas. "James McMillan." *Heritage, A Journal of Grosse Pointe Life,* Sept. 1986, 13–16.

———. "John Stoughton Newberry." *Heritage, A Journal of Grosse Pointe Life,* Aug. 1986, 21–24.

"Arbor Lodge, the Morton Family Estate." *AR,* Jan. 1906, 37–47.

Arbor Lodge State Park. Guidebook with list of trees. Nebraska City, Neb.: Arbor Lodge State Park, 1923.

"Arcady." *AR,* Jan. 1919, 66–70.

"Art out-of-doors" American Gardens 1890–1930, A Selected Bibliography. The Winterthur Museum and Gardens and The Hunt Institute for Botanical Documentation, Winterthur, 1979.

"Arthur Curtiss James dies in New York." *New York Times,* June 4, 1941.

"Ashton Villa," research materials for exhibition labels. AAG.

Aslet, Clive. "Nice Air 'N Awful Sightly Spots." [Berkshires] *Country Life,* March 12, 1987, 80–84.

"At the League Exhibit in 1938." ["Thornedale"] *LA,* July 1938, 171–72.

Auchincloss, Louis. "The Muse of Syosset." *AD,* Oct. 1986, 28.

Bailey, Janet. "California Great Estate." ["Filoli"] *Travel & Leisure,* Sept. 1988, C2–C5.

Baker, Wendy, David Bennett, and Diane Dierkes. *Landscape Architecture Analysis and Master Plan for "The Mount."* Catalogue. Lenox, Mass.: Massachusetts Council of the Arts and Humanities, Edith Wharton Restoration, Shakespeare & Co., 1982.

Bates, Ann Desloge. "Joseph Desloge's 'Vouziers' in Florissant, Missouri." Recorded by Mrs. Hal Kroeger, Jr. Feb. 9, 1987. AAG. Typescript.

Baumgartner, Sydney. "The Shade Garden: Effective Use of Drought-Tolerant Plant Material." Presented at "A California Perspective: Landscape Design Symposium," Santa Barbara, Calif., Feb. 3–4, 1989.

Bayles, Lois, Mary Louise King, and F. David Lapham. "The Story of Waveny." *New Canaan Historical Society Annual,* vol. 6, no. 3, 1969, 21–27.

Beadles, Ulysses. "Thornewood, on American Lake." Washington State Historical Society, Tacoma, Wash.

Beasley, Ellen. The Shadows-on-the-Teche Development Plan. *Shadows-on-the-Teche Archives,* New Iberia, La., 1979.

"Beautiful George Godfrey Moore Home." *Topeka Daily State Journal,* May 9, 1924.

Bell, Gracia. "Moanalua Gardens: remembrances of ali'i and a fabled estate." *Historic Hawai'i News,* Feb. 1985, 4–6.

"Bellefontaine at Lenox Massachusetts." Parts l and 2. *H&G,* Jan., Feb. 1902, 1–9; 64–71.

Berckman, Julianne Ruth. "The Development of the Mansion Grounds at Montpelier." Master's thesis, University of Connecticut, Storrs, 1983.

Berg, A. Scott. "Charlie Chaplin: King of the Silent Era at 'Breakaway House.'" *AD,* Apr. 1990, 132.

———. "Frances Marion: A Mediterranean Villa for the Oscar-Winning Writer of *The Champ,* Architecture by Wallace Neff." *AD,* Apr. 1990, 174.

Bergholz, W. R. "A Southern Garden." [Hampton-Preston House] *Farmer and Planter,* July 1861.

Beveridge, Charles E. "The Historical Significance of Moraine Farm in Beverly, Massachusetts." Mr. and Mrs. George Batchelder, "Moraine Farm," Beverly, Mass. 1984.

———. Review of American landscape architecture exhibition, London. *LA,* Jan. 1949, 83.

Biltmore Estate. Biltmore Estate news releases on rhododendrons, roses, and native azaleas and the "azalea hunters." AAG.

Binney, Marcus. "Swan House, Georgia—I." *Country Life,* May 5, 1983, 1168–71.

Bissell, Mrs. Alfred E. Tel. interview with MKG, June 1988.

Blackburn, Sadie Gwinn. "The Gardens of Bayou Bend, A Bicentennial Tour." Bayou Bend, Houston, 1975.

Bibliography

"Blairsden" photograph album. Property of Mrs. Anthony Vila, Peapack-Gladstone, N. J.

Blake, Curtis Channing. "The Architecture of Carrère and Hastings." Ph.D. diss. Columbia University, 1976.

Blanchan, Neltje. "The Formal Garden in America." *CLA*, July 1908, 271.

Bok Tower Gardens. Guidebook. Lake Wales, Fla.: American Foundation, Inc., 1981.

Bowman, David. Tel. interview with ECW, Sept. 1987. ["The Farms"]

Boyd, John Taylor, Jr. "The Country House and the Developed Landscape: William Lawrence Bottomley Expresses His Point of View about the Relation of the Country House to Its Environment in an Interview." *Arts and Decoration*, Nov. 1929, 98–100.

———. "The Residence of William R. Coe, Esq., Oyster Bay, L.I." *AR*, Mar. 21, 195–207.

Boykin, Henry. Tel. interview with MKG, Aug. 9, 1988. ["Plane Hill"]

Boylston, Sarah. Papers. Richland County Historic Preservation Commission, Columbia, S. C.

Branam, Alfred S., Jr. "For Sale: One Palace." [Stotesbury] *Philadelphia Bulletin Sunday magazine*, Feb. 11, 1968.

———. Letter to ECW, Mar. 22, 1984. List of T. Sears gardens.

"Branford House" *National Register of Historic Places Inventory—Nomination Form.* Avery Point Regional Campus, University of Connecticut, Groton.

Bratenahl, Florence. *A Cathedral Hillside and its Gardens.* Pamphlet. Washington, D. C.: All Hallows Press, 1931.

Brayer, Betsy. "West Garden of Eastman House to be Revived." *Brighton-Pittsford Post*, May 9, 1983.

Brewster, Mrs. Frederick. "Factual History of Morelands." [with plant lists] Dublin, N. H., 1953. AAG.

Brewster, Robert. Interview, tel. conversations with MKG, New York, Sept.-Oct. 1988. AAG.

"Bring the bloom back to Dunaway Gardens." Brochure. n.d.

Britz, Billie Sherrill, preparer. *The Greenhouse at Lyndhurst.* Research on Historic Properties Occasional Papers: no. l. Washington, D. C.: Preservation Press, National Trust for Historic Preservation. n.d.

"Brookside Gardens, Great Barrington, Mass." *Gardeners' Chronicle of America*, Jan. 1915, 22–23.

Brown, Catharine A. *Women and the Land, A Biographical Survey of Women who have contributed to the Development of Landscape Architecture in the United States.* Baltimore: Morgan State University, c. 1985.

Brown, Mrs. John Nicholas. " 'The Elms,' and the Newport Preservation Society." Address delivered to the Friends of the Philadelphia Art Museum, 1962. Courtesy Alfred Branam. AAG.

Brown, Mrs. Lutcher. "Recollections by Mrs. Lutcher Brown." AAG.

Brownlow, Kevin. "Harold Lloyd: A Renaissance Palace for One of the Silent Era's Great Comic Pioneers." *AD*, Apr. 1990, 160.

Bruce, Mrs. David. "The Hampton Garden." Paper read at the Annual Meeting of the GCA, 1915. AAG.

Bryant, Charles, conversation with John Boogher, Baltimore, c. 1989. [Breese, "The Blind"]

Bryant, Lynn. "Edward Huntsman-Trout, Landscape Architect." Society of Architectural Historians, Southern California Chapter, *Review* 2, Winter 1983, 1–6.

Buckley, Priscilla. Letter to MKG, July 9, 1987. AAG.

Buenz, J. Fred. Tel. interview with MKG, Sept. 1989. ["Oak Court"]

Buff, Barbara Ball. "Dublin, New Hampshire." *Antiques*, Apr. 1982, 945.

"The Builders of a Great House." [Steves] *Grinstead's Graphics*, Mar. 15, 1921, 11–26.

Bullitt, Thomas. "Oxmoor." Family history. AAG.

———. Letter to Jane Terry Bullitt. Louisville, Ky., Aug. 14., 1979. History of the house and gardens. AAG.

Burrell, Scott. "The Gardens of Virginia House." *An Occasional Bulletin.* Virginia Historical Society, June 1986.

Burt, Nathaniel. "Princeton Grandees." *Princeton History* 3, 1982, 1–27.

Buzzards Bay, Garden Club of. *"Brave Houses and Flowery Gardens" of Old New Bedford.* Ex. cat. New Bedford, Massachusetts: Garden Club of Buzzards Bay, 1976.

Cabot, Francis H. "The Rock Gardener's Louise Beebe Wilder." Revised working draft of address. Apr. 1988. AAG.

Calhoun, Dr. and Mrs. William F. Hand-drawn map of "Elgin Plantation, Natchez, Mississippi." c. 1988. AAG.

Campbell, Mrs. John. Letter to ECW, Feb. 1987. [H. F. Wood] AAG.

Cantor, Jay E. "Upstairs Downstairs: A Brandywine Perspective." Paper presented at seminar, "Country Houses and Gardens of the Brandywine Valley," Winterthur, May 4–6, 1988.

Carman, Joseph L., III. *The Garden at Villa Carman, Tacoma, Wash.* Typescript. c. 1988. AAG.

Carman, Mrs. Joseph L., III. Tel. interviews, correspondence with MKG. Tacoma, Wash., 1987–1990.

"Cass Gilbert: Architect." Ex. list, labels, and brochure. Keeler Tavern Preservation Society, Ridgefield, Conn., May 9–June 6, 1971.

"Castle Hill" Grounds Tour Hand Book. Castle Hill, n.d.

Catalog of Landscape Records in the United States Newsletter. Wave Hill, Bronx, Summer 1987–Winter, 1990.

"Cedar Crest Proposed for Nomination to National Register." *Kansas Preservation*, Nov./Dec. 1981, 3–6.

Chatfield-Taylor, Joan. "The Flowering of Filoli." *AD*, May 1989, 224–28.

"Chelsea." *Harper's Bazaar*, Sept. 1951, 2.

Child, Susan. "A Master Plan for Restoration Development of the Stan Hywet Hall Landscape Gardens." Cambridge, Mass.: Child/Hornbeck Associates, 1984.

———. "Warren Manning at Stan Hywet Hall." Presented at symposium "Masters of American Garden Design: Fletcher Steele in Context," sponsored by the American Horticultural Society, New York, Jan. 19, 1990.

Christy, Stephen F. "The Metamorphosis of an Artist: Jens Jensen." *LA*, Jan. 1976, 60–66.

———. Tel. interview with MKG, Nov. 1989.

"Clarence Mackay Rites Tomorrow at St. Patrick's." [obit.] *World-Telegram*, Nov. 14, 1938.

Clayton, Virginia Tuttle. "Reminiscence and revival: The old-fashioned garden, 1890–1910." *Antiques*, Apr. 1990, 892–905.

Close, Leslie Rose. *Portrait of an Era in Landscape Architecture, The Photographs of Mattie Edwards Hewitt.* Ex. cat. New York: Wave Hill, 1983.

Coffin, Marian Cruger. *Gardens Designed by Marian Coffin, Landscape Architect, 1865–1957: A Memorial Exhibition of Photographs of Seventeen Gardens.* Ex. cat. Hobart College, Apr. 1958.

———. 125 photographic prints from Coffin's New Haven office effects. Property of Mr. and Mrs. Richard Ballard, New Haven.

Colby, Virginia Reed. "Footprints of the Past: Ellen Biddle Shipman, Landscape Architect, 1869–1950." *Windsor Chronicle*, Jan. 23, 1987, 15.

———. "Stephen and Maxfield Parrish in New Hampshire," *Antiques*, June 1979, 1299.

Collette, Carlotta. "The Bishop's Close." *Horticulture*, Mar. 1985, 417–20.

Colton, Arthur W. "The House that Was Built for a Garden: 'Havenwood,' the Home of Edward L. Ryerson at Lake Forest, Illinois." *Garden Magazine*, Dec. 1921, 187–89.

———. "Turtle Bay Gardens, New York City." *AR*, Dec. 1920, 467–83.

Connolly, Mrs. D. Hugh. Interview with ECW, Apr. 1985. ["Morningside"] AAG.

Conrad, Glenn R. "Shadows-on-the-Teche." *Southern Accents*, Mar. 1984, 88–112.

Conservation Planning Study of Jens Jensen's Landscapes at the Henry Ford Estate, Fair Lane, Dearborn, Michigan. Henry Ford Estate, Dearborn, Mich. 1984.

Constable, Mrs. George. "Windy Gates." c. 1986. AAG.

———. "Memories of the Trip to York Harbor, Maine." 1986. AAG.

Cooke, Mary M. Letter to ECW, May 28, 1987. [Hawaii] AAG.

Corley, Dawson. "A Girl and a Garden." [Aime/"Petit Versailles"] *Baton Rouge Sunday Advocate*, Aug. 12, 1979.

"A Cornish House and Garden." [Charles Platt's garden] *AR*, Sept. 1907, 288–98.

Correll, Philip. "The Crowninshield Garden at Hagley." Paper presented at seminar, "Country Houses and Gardens of the Brandywine Valley," Winterthur, May 4–6, 1988.

Cotton, Harvey. "Thomas Affleck, Early Horticulturalist." Delivered to Natchez Historical Society, 1983. Dr. Thomas Gandy Collection, Natchez, Miss.

Coulter, Bill. "Sam Houston Park to get Staiti home." *Houston Chronicle*, Dec. 12, 1986.

Cowgill and Rogers. *"On Both Sides of the Bay." Perennials, Alpines and Rock Plants.* Catalogue, c. 1932. Cowgill Collection, Talbot County Historical Society, Easton, Md.

Croly, Herbert. "The Architectural Work of Charles A. Platt." *AR*, Mar. 1904, 144–81.

———. "The Country House in California." *AR*, Dec. 1913, 483–519.

———. "The House and Garden of Mr. Charles A. Platt." *H&G*, July 1901, 10–17.

———. "The 'Local Feeling' in the Western Country House." *AR*, Oct. 1914, 342–58.

———. "Some Recent Work of Howard Shaw." *AR*, June 1907, 421–54.

———. "A Water Front Villa: The House of Russell A. Alger, Jr." *AR*, Dec. 1914, 481–86.

Cromwell, Mabel (Mrs. Lincoln). "The Lifework of Beatrix Farrand." Program for the Garden Club of Mount Desert, with a list of Farrand's work, compiled by her c. 1950. Aug. 4, 1959. AAG.

Cunningham, Mary P. "Notes from Some Virginia Gardens." ["Chatham"] *House Beautiful*, Aug. 1930, 179–80.

Dame, Hally Brent. *History of the Maryland House and Garden Pilgrimage, 1930–1987.* c. 1987.

"Daring What the Layman Dares Not." [Herter] *Vogue*, n.d., 53–55. See undated photocopy, Herter file, East Hampton Library, East Hampton, N. Y.

Darnall, Margaretta J. "The Carolans: an Unfinished Garden." *Pacific Horticulture*, Summer 1988, 7–11.

Dean, Ruth. "Garden Walls." *CLA*, Mar. 1915, 59–61.

de Forest, Elizabeth. "Old Santa Barbara Gardens and How They Came to Be." *Pacific Horticulture*, Winter 1977–1978, 31–36.

de Forest, Lockwood. *Index of Folders in the Lockwood de Forest Collection.* Catalogue and index prepared by William F. Peters, 30 May 1981. College of Environmental Design, Documents Collection. University of California, Berkeley.

———. "In the Montecito Valley: A South African Garden in Santa Barbara, California." *LA*, Jan. 1940, 51–54.

———. "Opportunity Knocks. This Time Will the Landscape Architect Miss the Bus?" *LA*, Oct. 1945, 10.

DeGolyer, Everett [garden]. Descriptions of house and garden. Dallas Arboretum and Botanical Society Archives.

Delano & Aldrich. "Mirador, the House of Mrs. Ronald Tree, Greenwood, Va." *Southern Architect and Building News*, June 1928, 41–46.

Delano, William Adams. "Architect." *The New Yorker*, Apr. 5, 1958, 23–24.

DeVito, Susan. "Hamilton House, South Berwick, Maine." *Antiques*, Mar. 1986, 652–54.

Dietz, Paula. "A Formal Garden Laid Out in America." ["Weathersfield"] *New York Times*, Sept. 27, 1984.

———. "Mediterranean Light." *HG*, Dec. 1989.

———. "Stately Views, A Maryland Garden from the 1920's inspired by the 16th-century Villa d'Este." *New York Times Magazine*, April 15, 1984, 73–76.

Dillingham, Lowell, family photograph collection. Hawaii.

Disher, Mrs. C. F. Tel. interview with MKG, June 1989. ["Reynolda"]

Doell, M. Christine Klim, and Gerald Allan Doell. *A Report on the Site Visit to Clifton Place, Columbia, Tennessee.* Cortland, N. Y.: 1983. AAG

Donahue, Barbara. "Gentlemen Farmers on the Yankee Rocks." Barbara Donahue, Farmington, CT, 06032. 1986. Typescript.

Drake, William. Tel. interview with MKG, Nov. 3, 1988. ["Castle Hill"]

Draper, Earl J. "Hills and Dales, An Example of Early American gardens in Georgia." *House Beautiful*, May 1932, 372–78.

Draper, Mrs. Ford. Tel. interview with MKG, Oct. 24, 1988. ["The Hacienda"]

Draper, Phyllis Langhorne. Tel. interviews with MKG, June 1988. ["Mirador"]

Dryfhout, John H. "The Gardens of Augustus Saint-Gaudens." *H&G*, Dec. 1985, 144–48.

"Dunaway Gardens," slide show captions. Dunaway Gardens Restoration, Inc., Newnan, Ga., 1985.

Duncan, Frances. "The Gardens of Cornish." *Century Magazine*, May 1906, 3–19.

du Pont, Annie Rogers Zinn. Description of the creation of her garden at "Montpelier," August 10, 1922. Montpelier National Historic Site, Montpelier Station, Va.

Dworsky, Suzanne. "Two in the Tropics." [Allerton and Gregg] *Horticulture*, Mar. 1986, 54–62.

Eastman, Mary Jane. "A Garden for All Seasons: The Hunnewell Estate." *Wellesley*, May 1981, 9–11.

Eaton, Florence Taft. "The All-Season Flower Garden." [S. Untermeyer] *CLA*, August 1924, 34–38.

Eaton, Lawrence K. "Jens Jensen and the Chicago School." *Progressive Architecture*, Dec. 1960, 144–50.

"Edgerton" National Historic Register Registration Form—Draft. New Haven Colony Historical Society, Conn.

Edwards, Agnes. "Ferruccio Vitale's gardens: the interesting work in America of an Italian landscape architect." *House Beautiful*, Jan. 1916, 15–17.

Eickman, Jennifer. *The Allerton Legacy.* Guidebook. Jan. 1981.

Eliassen, John Weld, and Donald P. Ringler. *Carolands, The Chateau Remillard.* Pamphlet. Hillsborough, Calif.: John Weld Eliassen, Jr., and Donald P. Ringler, 1975.

"Ellen Biddle Shipman." [obit.] *New York Times*, Mar. 29, 1950.

Emmet, Alan. "Faulkner Farm: an Italian Garden in Massachusetts." *Journal of Garden History*, Apr.-June, 1986, 162–78.

———. "Mr. and Mrs. Harkness's Eolia: Beatrix Farrand's work with an existing plan." *Garden History*, Spring 1985, 45–59.

Endicott, H. Wendell. Harvard Fiftieth Anniversary Report, 1953. "The Endicott House and Gardens." Danvers, Mass.: Privately printed by the Endicott family, n.d. Danvers Historical Society, Danvers.

Engle, Murry. "A Meeting of Heaven and Earth." *Star-Bulletin*, Hawaii. n.d.

"Entrance Front and Garden Front, Morton F. Plant Country House," *Architecture*, Dec. 1906, Plates XC and XCI.

Erdman, Harold, family photograph album, 1935. Hawaii.

Ermenc, Christine. "Economic Give-And-Take: Farmers and Aesthetes in Cornish and Plainfield, New Hampshire, 1885–1910." *Historical New Hampshire*, Fall/Winter 1984, 105–121.

Evins, Jennie Dreher. "Sarah Boylston and her Garden." Presented at garden symposium sponsored by the South Carolina Governor's Mansion Foundation, Apr. 10–11, 1984.

Fahlman, Betsy. "The Architecture of Wilson Eyre." Master's thesis, University of Delaware, 1977.

Fahlman, Betsy, and Edward Teitelman. "Wilson Eyre: The Philadelphia Domestic Ideal." *Pennsylvania Heritage*, Summer 1982, 23–27.

Fair Lane. *Fair Lane, the House and Gardens.* Guidebook. Dearborn, Mich., 1955.

Fallon, D'Arcy. "When 'Dynasty' Came to Filoli." *Historic Preservation*, Aug. 1985, 68–72.

Farrand, Beatrix. "Laying out a Suburban Place." *CLA*, Mar. 1910, 551–52.

Fauns and Fountains: American Garden Statuary, 1890–1930. Ex. cat. Southampton, N. Y.: Parrish Art Museum, 1985.

"Ferrucio Vitale: A Minute on his Life and Service." [obit.] *LA*, July 1933, 219–20.

Filler, Martin. "Cameo Classic." [Endicott] *H&G*, Jan. 1983, 95–98.

"Fir Acres" *National Register of Historic Places Inventory—Nomination Form.* National Park Service. Lewis and Clark College, Portland, Oreg.

"Fir Acres," plans and drawings of house and gardens. Herman Brookman collection. University of Oregon, Eugene.

Fischer, John Baptiste. "A Jaunt to Wychwood, Geneva Lake, Wis." *AR*, Feb. 1915, 126–36.

Flanders, Annette Hoyt. *Landscape Architecture by Annette Hoyt Flanders, A.B., B.S., M.L.A.* New York: Privately published. Essay by Richardson Wright.

———. "The Oasis, The Garden of F. E. Drury, Esq., in the Heart of Cleveland, Ohio." *CLA*, May, 1921, 57–58.

———. Plan of the Rose Garden at "Mirador," Mar. 12, 1923. Property of Jeannie Scott, Greenwood, Va.

Fletcher, Robert. Tel. interview with MKG, Feb. 1990.

Forbes, David. *Queen Emma and Lawai.* Pamphlet. 1970. Reprint. Kauai Historical Society, 1984.

Frankenbach Nurseries, album of photographs of Southampton gardens, 1920–1940. Frankenbach Nurseries, Bridgehampton, N. Y.

Frary, I. T. "Warren Bicknell's 'Beacon Hill'." *AR*, Mar. 1923, 217.

"French Manoir." ["Chelsea"] *Town & Country*, Dec. 1946, 108–11.

Gambrill, Edith Blair. "A Few Facts About Blairsden." AAG.

Ganay, Ernest de. "Les jardins d'Achille Duchêne." *Art et Industrie*, Sept. 1935.

———. "Annual Meeting in Akron, Sept. 26–27." *Your Garden and Home*, Oct. 1939.

"Ganna Walska Lotusland." Lotusland fact sheet, 1987. AAG.

"The Gardens on the Estate of Mr. Charles M. Schwab." *CLA*, June 1920, 45–48.

"Gardens on the Estate of Mrs. J. Langeloth at Riverside, Connecticut." *CLA*, Oct. 1928, 64–69.

"Gardens and Gardening." *The Studio Garden Annual.* London and New York, 1932.

Gardens and Grounds: Hampton National Historic Site Brochure. Towson, Md.: Historic Hampton, Inc., n.d.

"The Gardens at Oatlands, Leesburg, Virginia." Brochure. National Trust for Historic Preservation, n.d.

"Gardens of Old Italian Beauty Ennoble this Romantic House: The Home of Mr. & Mrs. Earl C. Anthony, Los Feliz Park, Los Angeles." *CLA*, May 1939, 70–71.

"The Gardens of Thornewood." *Horticulture*, Mar. 1931, 94–95.

Gardner, Mrs. "The Farm, The Peabody Farm, The Endicott Garden." N.p. n.d. AAG.

Gebhard, David. Interview with MKG, Feb. 8, 1989.

———. "Casa del Herrero, the George F. Steedman house, Montecito, California." *Antiques*, Aug. 1986, 23–27.

———. "The Spanish Colonial Revival in Southern California, 1895–1930." *Journal of the Society of Architectural Historians*, May 1967, 131–47.

Gelderloos, Orin. Tel. interview with MKG, Nov. 21, 1989. ["Fair Lane"]

Gherardi, Mrs. Walter R. Letter to ECW, Apr. 10, 1984. AAG.

Gilbar, Anne. "Las Tejas." *Santa Barbara Magazine*, Feb./Mar. 1982, 40–54.

Gill, Irving. "An Architecture in a New Land." *The Craftsman*, vol. 27, no. 5. Aug. 1912.

Gillette, Charles F. "Landscape Architecture at the League Exhibit in 1938." *LA*, July 1938, 482–83.

———. "Look Here Upon This Picture, And On This: In Virginia." *LA*, Oct. 1937, 50–51.

Gillette, Charles, work of. "New Gardens of Virginia," ["Agecroft Hall," "Meadowbrook Manor," "York Hall"] *LA* Jan. 1938, 74.

Gillies, George. Interview with MKG. Huntington, N. Y., Jan. 16, 1987. AAG. Transcript.

Goodhue, Bertram G. "'El Fureidis' at Montecito, California, The Villa of James Waldron Gillespie." *H&G*, Sept. 1903, 97–100.

"A Greek Garden in America." ["Greystone"] *H&G*, April 1919, 32–33.

"Greek Gardens at Greystone." *CLA*, May 1937, 59–62.

Greene, Charles Sumner. "California Home Making." *Pasadena Daily News*, Jan. 1, 1905, 26–27.

Greene, Nathaniel Coit. "The Most Inspiring Estate in New England." [Charles S. Sargent] *New England Magazine*, Apr. 1908, 137–43.

Greenleaf, James L. "A Letter from Sicily." *LA*, July 1930, 283–86.

Greiff, Constance. "The Five Houses." *Princeton History* 3, 1982, 28–41.

Grey, Elmer. "Some Country House Architecture in the Far West." *AR*, Oct. 1922, 309–44.

Griswold, Mac. "Carolina Grown." [Ralph Hanes] *HG*, Sept. 1988, 72–75.

———. "Water Gardens." Radcliffe Seminars, 1985. AAG.

Griswold, Mac, and Eleanor Weller. "Coleridgean Fantasy." [Chapin] *Southern Accents*, Nov.-Dec. 1988, 142–49.

"Guy Lowell, F.A.I.A., 1870–1927." [obit.] *American Architect*, Feb. 20, 1927, 230.

Haglund, Karl. "H. W. S. Cleveland." *LA*, Jan. 1976.

Haldeman, Anne Bruce. Tel. interview with MKG, July 1988. AAG.

———. Completed questionnaire about her career and works in Kentucky. AAG.

Hall, George D. "The Estate of Mr. W. L. Dodge, Hollywood." *Architect and Engineer*, Apr. 1920, 87–90.

Hanes, Mrs. Ralph P. Interview with MKG. Winston-Salem, North Carolina, June 6, 1988. AAG. Notes.

Hardie, Dee. *The House and Gardens of Harvey S. Ladew.* Guidebook. Ladew Topiary Gardens: Monkton, Md.

Hare, Herbert. Letter to Bernard Frazier. ["Villa Philbrook"] Nov. 15, 1947. Philbrook Museum of Art Archives, Tulsa.

Harrigan, James M. "Francesco Franceschi and His Airy Mountain." *Pacific Horticulture*, Fall 1985, 27–31.

Hartt, Mary Bronson. "Women and the Art of Landscape Gardening." *Outlook*, Mar. 28, 1908, 695–704.

Harvard College. Harvard Class of 1903 Fiftieth Anniversary Report.

Hastings, Thomas. "Architectural Gardens." [Benedict] *Garden and Forest*, June 17, 1896, 241–43.

"Haven Wood [sic] and its Gardens." *CLA*, Jan. 1935, 44–46.

Hawley, Henry. "An Italianate Garden by Greene and Greene." [Culbertson/Prentiss] *Journal of Decorative and Propaganda Arts 1875–1945*, Summer/Fall 1986, 32–45.

Hays, Helen Ashe. "A Colonial Garden Down South." *CLA*, Jan. 1910, 288.

Hayward, Susan Cady. "Gardens of the Gilded Age: Vermont's Historic Estate Gardens are Blossoming Anew." [Webb] *Vermont Life*, Summer 1988, 3–9.

Hellyer, A. G. L., "A Garden From a Rice Plantation." *Country Life*, Jan. 4, 1973, 26–28.

"Herbert Hare's Turning Point Was A Spiral Curve." *Kansas City Star*, July 5, 1931.

Herring, Phyllis L. "The Highlands: A 20th-Century Wuthering Heights or a Potential Showplace?" *The Green Scene*, Mar. 1976.

Hewitt, Mark A. "Farmington, Connecticut: the making of a Colonial Revival country house." *Antiques*, Oct. 1988, 854.

———. "William Adams Delano and the Muttontown Enclave." *Antiques*, Aug. 1987, 316–21.

Hewitt, Susan L. "Legendary Grandeur of the Old South." *Southern Accents*, Spring 1983, 72–76.

Historic Hampton, Inc. *Gardens and Grounds: Hampton National Historic Site.* Brochure. Towson, Md.: Historic

Hampton & Preservation Maryland in cooperation with the Department of the Interior, National Park Service.

Hitchcock, Mrs. Henry. Tel. interview with MKG, Oct. 1989. [C. Gillette]

Hockaday, Laura Rollins. "Longview's Lady: Employees remember well-loved horsewoman." *Kansas City Star*, Feb. 19, 1987.

Hoffman, Donald. Tel. interview with MKG, July 1987.

Hoppin, Martha J. *The Emmets: A Family of Women Painters.* Ex. cat. The Berkshire Museum, Pittsfield, and The Danforth Museum, Framingham, Mass. 1982.

Hornbeck, Peter L. "A Forest Pool." [Simms/"Airdrie"] Childs/Hornbeck, Cambridge, Mass.

———. *Historic Landscape Preservation and Maintenance Policies and Procedures for the Richard T. Crane, Jr. Memorial Reservation.* Milton, Mass.: Trustees of Reservations, 1977.

Horton, Mrs. Thaddeus. "The Summer House of a Georgian, A country place in the South that was made attractive the first year—converting a gulch into a sunken garden." ["Woodhaven"] *CLA*, May 1908, 281–83.

Hotra, Lynda M., com "The Legacy of John Handrahan (1871–1968) in Western New York State." From *Bulletin of American Garden History.* Edited by Ellen Samuels. Winter 1987, 4.

House & Garden, Special Garden issue, 1927.

"House of H. R. Rea, Sewickley, Pa." *American Architect*, vol. CXVII, no. 2317, May 1920.

"The House of William G. Mather." *AR*, Nov. 1909, 313–20.

Howard, John Galen. "Country House Architecture on the Pacific Coast." *AR*, Oct. 1916, 322–55.

Howe, Samuel. "The Long Island Home of Mr. Louis C. Tiffany." *Town & Country*, Sept. 6, 1913, 24–26.

Howett, Catherine M. *Land of Our Own: 250 Years of Gardening Tradition in Georgia 1733–1983.* Ex. cat. Atlanta: Atlanta Historical Society, 1983.

———. "Regional Variations: Estate Traditions of Georgia and the South." Paper presented at seminar, "Country Houses and Gardens of the Brandywine Valley," Winterthur, May 4–6, 1988.

———. "A Southern Lady's Legacy: the Italian 'Terraces' of La Grange, Georgia." *Journal of Garden History*, Oct.-Dec. 1982, 343–60.

Hubbard, Theodora Kimball. "H. W. S. Cleveland." *LA*, Jan. 1930, 92–111.

Huhn, Judith A. "The Garden Art of Charles A. Platt: The Estate of Mrs. Randolph M. Clark." Master's thesis. University of Connecticut, Storrs, 1979.

Hulme, Kathryn. *The Robert Allerton Story 1873–1964.* Guidebook. Monticello, Ill.: John Gregg Allerton, 1979.

Hunt, Myron C., and Elmer Gray. "G. W. Wattles' Garden, Hollywood, California." *American Architect*, Sept. 1, 1909, 84–87.

"Il Brolino, One of Montecito's Most Prestigious Estates." *Montecito Guide*, 1983, 6–8.

"In the garden of Mr. Warren Bicknell, Cleveland." *LA*, Jan. 1924, 111.

"In a Georgia Garden." [Bourne] *CLA*, Mar. 1933.

Inman, Sue Lile. "Kamschatka, Rich in Southern History." *Southern Accents*, Nov. 1987, 119–25.

Innocenti & Webel. "Selected Projects by Innocenti & Webel." n.d. Innocenti & Webel, Greenvale, N. Y.

"An Italian Garden at Groton, Conn." ["Branford House"] *Architectural Forum*, June 1922, 221–22.

James, Arthur Curtiss, scrapbook. Redwood Library, Newport, R. I.

"James L. Greenleaf: A Minute on his Life and Service." [obit.] *LA*, Oct. 1933, 1–4.

Jensen, Jens. Letter to Mr. Stanley White, Lake Forest, Illinois, July 29, 1929. AAG. Photocopy.

Johnson, Katie Jo. Tel. interview with MKG, July 1990. [Olmsted Bros.]

Jones, Beatrix (Farrand) "The Garden as a Picture." *Scribner's Magazine*, July 1907, 2–11.

Jones, Russell Lee. "Memories of the Norton Place in Farmington, Connecticut." [Barney] Harriet Barney Lidgerwood, Farmington, Conn. n.d.

Karson, Robin. "The American Sculptor's Summer Haven." *Garden Design*, Autumn, 1985.

Kellogg, Mrs. Spencer. Letter to MKG, 1986–1988. AAG.

Kelsey, Mary Wilson. Letter to ECW, Feb. 15, 1988. AAG.

Kennedy, Roger. Telephone conversation with MKG, Dec. 1989. ["Cranbrook"]

" 'Kennett's Castle' Restored." ["Selma Hall"] *St. Louis Post-Dispatch*, July 1, 1940.

Kenworthy, Richard G. "Published records of Italianate gardens in America." *Journal of Garden History*, Jan.-Mar. 1990, 10–70.

Kern, Marjorie, and George Kern. "Gardening in dry climates." *H&G*, May 1935, 52–53.

Ketcham, Diana. "Rediscovering San Simeon's Architect." *New York Times*, Apr. 28, 1988.

Kimball, Fiske. "The American Country House." *AR*, Oct. 1919, 304–44.

Kimball, Geoffrey, comp. *The Garden Library of the New Orleans Town Gardeners.* Catalog. New Orleans, La.: Southeastern Architectural Archive, Tulane University Library, 1988.

King, Caroline. "My Moonlight Garden." *H&G*, Aug. 1915, 30–31.

King, Mrs. John. Tel. interview with MKG, Jan. 1990. [New Canaan, Conn.]

King Ranch, The. Research prepared by John A. Cypher, Jr. Kingsville, Tex., 1986. AAG.

"Kirby-Stewart Nuptials." *Southern Industrial and Lumber Review*, Dec. 20, 1906, 3–17.

Knapp, George Owen. *"Arcady," Montecito, Santa Barbara, California.* For The GCA, compliments of Mr. George Owen Knapp and Mrs. William J. Knapp, catalogued by Neville R. Stephens, landscape architect. Plant list. 1926.

———. *California Southland.* Garden Club of America Special Number, Mar. 1926.

Kocher, A. Lawrence. "The Country House. Are we developing an American Style?" *AR*, Nov. 1920, 385–402.

Krall, Daniel W. "Ellen Biddle Shipman: Dean of Women Landscape Architects." Presented at symposium "Masters of American Garden Design: Fletcher Steele in Context," sponsored by the American Horticultural Society, N. Y., Jan. 19, 1990.

Kunst, Scott G. "Landscape and Gardens." *Old-House Journal*, Apr. 1986, 128–35.

LA Partnership. *Yaddo, Saratoga Springs, New York: A Plan For Garden Restoration.* Catalogue. Saratoga Springs, N. Y.: LA Partnership, 1983.

Lacy, Allen. "Henry Shaw's Gift to St. Louis." *Horticulture*, Nov. 1984, 41–44.

Langhorne, Elizabeth. Tel. interview with MKG, Aug. 15, 1988.

Langlois, Margaret. Interview with MKG, Feb. 1990, Bethlehem, Conn. ["Ferriday"]

Lanning, Lolita Mitchell. Correspondence with ECW. 1987–1988. ["El Mirasol"] AAG.

Lees, Carlton B. "The Golden Age of Horticulture." *Historic Preservation*, Oct-Dec. 1972, 32–37.

Leisenring, Julie. Interview, tel. conversations with MKG, April-July, 1988.

Lemmon, Kenneth, "Meet Me in St. Louis." *Country Life*, May 1983, 1162–64.

Lester, Nancy K. "The Interiors of Swan House." In *Classical America IV.* New York: Classical America, 1977.

Levy, Gail K. L. Ho. "Moanalua Gardens: remembrances of ali'i and a fabled estate." *Historic Hawai'i News.* Feb. 1985.

Lewis and Valentine Collection. AAG.

Libby, Valencia. "The Design of the Winterthur Gardens." Paper presented at seminar, "Country Houses and Gardens of the Brandywine Valley," Winterthur, May 4–6, 1988.

———. "Designing Women—American Women in Landscape Architecture." Delivered at the GCA Annual Meeting, Oct. 16, 1985.

———. "George H. Gillies, Professional Gardener." *Winterthur Newsletter*, Winter, 1976, 6–7.

———. "Marian Cruger Coffin, The Landscape Architect and the Lady." *The House and Garden*, Roslyn, N.Y. 1985.

"Life in East Hampton is Lovely Like a Dream." [Woodhouse] *East Hampton Star*, Oct. 24, 1935.

Lilly, Rachel M., and Rainey, Reuben. "Charles Gillette." Barboursville, Virginia, 1986. AAG. Photocopy.

Linton, Ruth C. "Nemours, The Estate of Alfred I. du Pont." *Bulletin of American Garden History.*

———. Tel. interview with MKG, July 20, 1988. ["Nemours"]

"Little Remains of Beautiful, Famous Marland Gardens Here." *Ponca City News*, Mar. 21, 1971, 6B.

Littlefield, Doris Bayley. *Vizcaya.* Guidebook. Miami: Vizcaya, n.d.

Littlefield, Susan S. H. "The Classical Garden Goes West." *H&G*, Apr. 1984, 157–58.

Livingston, Mary. "Furnishing the Outdoor Living-Room." *H&G*, June 1915, 411–15.

Locke, Kate Greenleaf. "Water Gardens of California." *American Homes and Gardens*, Mar. 1910, 103–06.

Lockhart, David G. Letter to ECW, Apr. 9, 1984.

Lockman, Heather. "Gardens: The Contours of Nature, Landscape Pleasures in the Pacific Northwest." *AD*, May 1984, 153.

"Lockwood de Forest, January 9, 1896–March 30, 1949: A Biographical Minute." [obit.] *LA*, Oct. 1949, 35.

The Long Island Country House 1870–1930. Ex. cat. Southampton, N. Y.: Parrish Art Museum, 1988.

Lord, Priscilla Sawyer, and Virginia Clegg Gamage. *Marblehead: The Spirit of '76 Lives Here.* Philadelphia: Chilton Books, 1972.

"Low Country Plantations: Mulberry." *Colonial Homes.* Mar./Apr. 1984. 70–71.

"Lurline Roth; farewell to a great lady." [Bourn] *The Country Almanac*, Sept. 11, 1985, unpaginated.

Lyndhurst, A Property of the National Trust for Historic Preservation. Guidebook. Washington, D. C.: Preservation Press, National Trust for Historic Preservation.

Lynes, Russell. "A Gentleman's Cottage in the Berkshires." *AD*, May, 1987.

McCarthy, Mary. "The Indomitable Miss Brayton." *H&G*, Dec. 1983, 141–43.

McCormick, Stanley R., photograph albums. 2 vols. Santa Barbara Historical Society, Calif.

The McFaddin-Ward House. Guidebook. Beaumont, Tex. c. 1986.

McGuire, Diane Kostial. "Beatrix Jones Farrand (1872–1959)." Presented at symposium "Masters of American Garden Design: Fletcher Steele in Context," sponsored by the American Horticultural Society, N.Y., Jan. 19, 1990.

McIlhenny, E. A. *Camellia Catalogue 1948–1949.* Avery Island, La.

McKart, Karyn. "Two Early Nurserymen in Santa Barbara." *Pacific Horticulture*, Fall 1983, 52–56.

McKay, Alexandra. [Mrs. Benjamin Moore] Hand-drawn planting plans for "Chelsea," Muttontown, N. Y. c. 1940. AAG.

McMillan, Mrs. James. Letter to ECW, Aug. 1987. AAG.

McNabb, W. R. "Formal Gardens in the Knoxville Area 1907–1936." ["Rostrevor"] Nashville, Tenn. n.d. AAG.

Mack, George. "Designers' Showhouse opens." [Fred Anton] *Topeka Capital-Journal*, Apr. 23, 1989.

———. "Georgian mansion is Kansas Baptist Office." [George Godfrey Moore] *Topeka Capital-Journal*, Oct. 9, 1977.

Makinson, Randall. Tel. interview with MKG, Dec. 20, 1987.

Mann, Phillip. "Montecito's Microclimates." *Montecito Magazine*, Fall 1988, 47–51.

Manning, Warren H. "Warren H. Manning, Landscape Designer, A Tribute to a Pioneer in a New Profession." *AR*, Apr. 1938, 149.

[Manning] "Clients' List." Warren H. Manning Collection, Patrick Morgan Cultural Center, Center for Lowell History, University of Lowell, Mass.

———. "Photocopied Articles mentioning Warren H. Manning (1884–1984)." Warren H. Manning Collection, Dept. of Landscape Architecture, Iowa State University, Ames.

Margaret Bourke White. The Cleveland Years 1927–1930. Ex. cat. Cleveland, Ohio: New Gallery of Contemporary Art, 1976.

Maryland House and Garden Pilgrimage. *Maryland House and Garden Pilgrimage Guide 1960.* Maryland Historical Society Library, Baltimore.

" 'Maxwell Court,' A Residence and Gardens in the Italian Style at Rockville, Connecticut." *H&G,* Oct. 1903, 148–61.

Maybeck, Bernard. "Program for the development of a hillside community." *Bulletin of the Hilside Club,* 1906–07. See Jean Harris, "Bernard Ralph Maybeck," *American Institute of Architects Journal,* May 1951, 221–28.

Mazza, Karen, and Jill Winter. "A Gift from the Past." *The Oatlands Column,* Summer 1987.

"The Melancholy Estate of Edith Rockefeller McCormick." ["Villa Turicum"] Chicago Historical Society, n.d. Typescript.

"Melcombe Bingham at Glenview, Kentucky." *CLA,* Oct. 1933, 40–41.

Middleton Place guide booklet. Middleton Place Foundation, c. 1980.

Miller, John Franklin. Letters to ECW, 1987. ["Stan Hywet"] AAG.

Miller, Wilhelm. "Bringing the Country into the City." *CLA,* Sept. 1910, 524–27.

———. "The Fascinating Art of Making Vistas." [Thayer] *CLA,* Mar. 1913, 35.

———. "Lessons from a Famous Hillside Garden." [Choate] *CLA,* Aug. 1910, 433–36.

———. "A New Kind of Western Home." ["Sinnissippi Farm"] *CLA,* April 1913, 39–42.

———. "The Prairie Spirit in Landscape Gardening: What the People of Illinois Have Done and Can Do." Urbana, Ill.: University of Illinois, Coll. of Agriculture, Dept. of Horticulture, Div. of Landscape Extension, Nov. 1915.

———. "The Prairie Style of Landscape Architecture." *AR,* Oct. 1916.

———. "Some Inspiring Examples of Roadside Planting." [Allerton] *Billerica,* July 1915, 4–5.

Mitchell, Evelyn Scott. "Longue Vue: A Short History of the Gardens." Lecture. Longue Vue, New Orleans, La. 1981.

Mitchell, Harold. Interview with MKG, Apr. 1988. ["Lone Tree Farm"]

Mitchell, William Robert, Jr. "Pebble Hill Plantation: 'Slow Down, I Mean It! E. I. Poe.' " *Southern Accents,* July/Aug. 1987, 96–105.

———. "The Swan House, a Landmark of Early Twentieth-Century Life and Taste." *Southern Accents,* July/Aug. 1985, 43–52.

Monahon, Duffy. "Peterborough, Cradle of the Arts," *Monadnock Ledger,* Jan. 23, 1986.

Monroe, Lynn Lewis. "Sonnenberg Gardens, A Victorian Extravaganza." *American Horticulturist,* Aug. 1985, 19–23.

Montague, Martha, comp. *Fir Acres, the M. Lloyd Frank Estate now Palatine Hill Campus of Lewis and Clark College: Description.* Typescript. 1966. Lewis and Clark College Library, Portland, Oreg.

Moore, Edith Wyatt. "Fondly I Roam, Stories of Natchez Homes." *Natchez Times* c. 1949, with corrections and emendations by Howard B. Peabody, Jr. ["Magnolia Vale"] Collection Mr. Howard B. Peabody, Jr. Natchez, Miss.

Morgan, Keith N. "Charles A. Platt's houses and gardens in Cornish, New Hampshire." *Antiques,* July, 1982, 119.

Morris, Suzanne. "509 King William Street." [Edward Steves] *Texas Parade,* Feb. 1971, 39–41.

Morrison, Sol. "A Rich Man's Folly: The Tea House of Montecito." [Henry Bothin] *Montecito Magazine,* Spring 1984.

Motz, Nancy Calhoun. Tel. interview with MKG, Aug. 1, 1989. ["Trygvesson"]

Moulton, Robert H. "Mellody [sic] Farm: The Country Home of Mr. J. Ogden Armour." *House Beautiful,* July 1920, 32–33.

———. " Melody Farm: a Combination of Versailles and Illinois." *The Touchstone* 6, 1920.

"Mr. and Mrs. Frederick T. Bonham's home on Long Island Sound," *CLA,* Mar. 1937, 31–37.

"Mrs. Isabel Anderson Dies; Author Widow of Diplomat." *Boston Post,* Nov. 9, 1948.

"Mrs. Lorenzo E. Woodhouse Dies at 96." [obit.] *East Hampton Star,* Dec. 7, 1961.

Mullgardt, Louis Christian. "Country House Architecture on the Pacific Coast." *AR,* Oct. 1916, 323–55.

Murphy, Kevin D. "Ernest W. Bowditch and the Practice of Landscape Architecture." *Essex Institute Historical Collections,* Apr. 1989, 162–76.

———. Letter to MKG, Feb. 16, 1990. ["The Elms"]

Nassau County Museum of Art. *The House and Garden,* October 1985–January 1986. Ex. cat. Roslyn, N. Y.: Nassau County Museum of Fine Art, 1985. Essays by Pauline Metcalf and Valencia Libby.

Nemy, Enid. "Great Home has a History to Be Shared." [Benjamin Moore] *New York Times,* Oct. 13, 1983.

Nevins, Deborah. "The Triumph of Flora: Women and the American Landscape, 1890–1935." *Antiques,* Apr. 1985, 906–20.

"News of Ohio's Garden Clubs." [W. T. White] *Your Garden and Home, Ohio's Own Garden Magazine,* Oct. 1934, 44–45.

Nicholas, Nancy, comp. "Gardens Designed by Dorothy Nicholas." n.d. AAG. List of 18 gardens designed by her mother.

Nochlin, Linda. "High Bohemia, Sculptor Gertrude Vanderbilt Whitney's Long Island Studio evokes the American artistic taste of the twenties." *H&G,* Sept. 1985.

"A Notable Western Homestead." ["Arbor Lodge"] *Town & Country,* Sept. 3, 1904, 14–15.

Notter, F. H. " 'Highcroft,' Lake Minnetonka, Minn." *The Western Architect,* Feb. 1903.

O'Connor, Rory. "They Made the Heights Bloom." *Cleveland,* June 1985, 87–91.

Olmert, Michael. "Ladew Gardens: A Topiary Masterpiece in the Maryland Hunt Country." *Horticulture,* July 1984, 35–39.

Olmsted, Frederick Law, Jr. "Palos Verdes Estates." *LA,* July 1927, 255–90.

"Open Gates," description and history by an unidentified family member. AAG.

Page, Richard C. Letter to ECW, Aug. 29, 1983. ["Cheekwood"]

Paine, Nathan. Letter to Bryant Fleming, April 20, 1927.

Paine Art Center and Arboretum Archives, Oshkosh, Wisc.

Pasillé, Raymond de. "Les jardins français aux Etats-Unis, créations de MM. Duchêne et Gréber." *La Gazette illustrée des amateurs de jardins,* 1923, 16–36.

Pastorius, Mary Beth. Tel. interview with MKG, July 14, 1988.

Patterson, Augusta Owen. "The Langhorne Home in Greenwood, Virginia." *Town & Country,* June 1928, 42–50.

Payne, Rolce Redard. "Banking Land." [Charles Eliot] *H&G,* Sept. 1987.

Peck, Frederick W. G. "Boxly, The Home of Mr. and Mrs. Frederick W. G. Peck, Chestnut Hill, Philadelphia, Pennsylvania." AAG. Photocopy.

Perkerson, Medora Field. "The Garden Theater at Woodhaven near Atlanta, Georgia." *Garden Magazine,* Nov. 1924, 196.

Perkins, Mrs. John Carroll. "Thornewood, on American Lake." *House Beautiful,* Mar. 1926, 273–76.

Peters, William Fredrick. *Lockwood de Forest, Jr.* Master's thesis, University of California, Berkeley, 1980.

Phelps, Harriet Jackson [Ellis]. "Horticulture: an important part of Camden's heritage." *Chronicle-Independent,* Mar. 4, 1983.

Photographs of Thornewood, American Lake. Descriptive catalog, 44 photographs. August 3, 1987. AAG.

Pilgrimage Garden Club. *Site of National Significance: Longwood, Mississippi, Report for the Mississippi Landmarks Commission.* n.d. AAG.

Pinchot Institute for Conservation Studies. *Final Historic Structure Report, Historic Landscape Report & Management Plan on Grey Towers, Milford, Pennsylvania.* Prepared by John Milner, Associates, for the Pinchot Institute, Milford, Pa., 1980.

Pitkin & Mott. Partial list of commissions in Cleveland, Ohio, and environs. Compiled by Sally Foote, Garden Club of Cleveland. 1990. AAG.

Pittsburgh Architectural Club. *Pittsburgh Architectural Club Yearbook.* Pittsburgh, Pa., 1900, 1907, 1914.

Pond, Bremer W. "James Sturgis Pray, A Minute on his Life and Service." *LA,* Oct. 1929, 1–4.

Pool, Elizabeth. "Old Dublin Gardens." Garden Club of Dublin Program, Aug. 1984. AAG.

"Portfolio of Current Architecture: Estate of George O. Knapp, Esq." *AR,* Jan. 1919.

"Portrait of Lapham returns to Waveny," *The New Canaan Advertiser.* Feb. 21, 1980.

Post, Linda. Letter to ECW, Mar. 16, 1984. ["Chelsea"] AAG.

Pray, James Sturgis. "The Italian Garden." Parts 1–4. *American Architecture and Building News,* Feb. 10, 1900, 43–45; Feb. 17, 51–52; Mar.17, 83–85; Mar. 24, 91–92.

Price, Matlack. " 'Meridian House,' Residence of Irwin Laughlin, Esq., Washington." *Architectural Forum,* Aug. 1929, 223–28.

Prior, Edward S. "American Garden-Craft from an English Point of View." *H&G,* Nov. 1903, 201–15.

Rankin, Mrs. Alfred. "Garden of Windsor T. White." Based in part on information from Bly Myers, White's gardener. AAG.

Reed, Henry Hope. "America's Greatest Living Classical Architect: Philip Trammell Schutze of Atlanta, Georgia." *Classical America IV.* New York: Classical America, 1977.

———. "A Classical Garden in Modern Times." *Classical America.* New York: Classical America, 1973.

———. *The Elms, The Edward J. Berwind Mansion, Bellevue Avenue, Newport, Rhode Island.* Guidebook, n.d.

Reed, Rhoda Newberry. Letter to Mrs. James MacMillan, Aug. 27, 1987. AAG.

Reif, Rita. "New Life for Garden Statues." ["Immergrun"] *New York Times,* May 17, 1987.

"Renaissance Garden" in "Famous Gardens." [R. B. Mellon garden] *CLA,* Dec. 1934, 46–49.

"The Renaissance Villa of Italy Developed into a Complete Residential Type for Use in America." ["Villa Turicum"] *AR,* Mar. 1912, 201–25.

Rice, Diana. "America Masters the Lore of Gardens." *New York Times Magazine,* Aug. 9, 1925.

Rieley & Associates, Rudy J. Favretti, and Reuben M. Rainey. *Vanderbilt Mansion National Historic Site Cultural Landscape Report.* U. S. Department of the Interior, National Park Service, Contract no. CX1600–5–0037, 1988.

Riley, Phil M. "The Spirit of the Renaissance on the Great Lakes, Three Modern Mid-Western Homes, designed by Charles A. Platt." *CLA,* Sept. 1912, 28–30.

"Riven Rock, The Estate of Mr. Stanley R. McCormick." *Old Spanish Days,* Fiesta Edition, August 1933.

Robertson, Mrs. Walter. Tel. interview with MKG, July 1988. AAG.

Robson, Lloyd A. "Newport and its Gardens and Parties of the Gay Nineties." In *Mrs. Croesus Gilds the Lily,* Newport, n.d., AAG.

"Rohallion" photograph album. Property of Blake Banta, Curvon Corporation, 34 Apple St., Tinton Falls, N. J. AAG. Photocopy.

Root, Ralph Rodney. "Country Place Types of the Middle West." *AR,* Jan. 1924, 1–32.

Ruhling, Nancy. "Manors for the Masses." *Historic Preservation,* Feb. 1986, 52–54.

Ryan, Harry. Tel. interview with MKG, August 5, 1989. ["Bellingrath Gardens"]

Samuels, Ellen. "Ruth Dean: How Her Garden Grew." *East Hampton Star,* May 16, 1988.

Santa Barbara Botanic Garden. "Three Famous Gardens in Montecito." [Gillespie] Handout. July 24, 1980. AAG.

"Santa Gertrudis Ranch House, the Home of Mrs. H. M. King, near Kingsville, Texas." *AR,* July 1916, 76–83.

Sargent, Charles S. "The Columbian Exposition." *Garden and*

Forest, Dec. 1893, 104–05.

———. "Formal gardening, does it conflict with the natural style?" *Garden and Forest*. Mar. 15, 1893, 119–20.

———. "Formal gardening, where it can be used to advantage." *Garden and Forest*. Mar. 22, 1893, 129–30.

———, ed. *Garden and Forest: A Journal of Horticulture, Landscape Architecture and Forestry*. Vols. 1–9. New York: The Garden and Forest Publishing Co., 1888–1897.

Scharf, Thomas L. "Balboa Park: a San Diego Botanical Landmark." *Pacific Horticulture*, Summer 1988, 54–63.

Schermerhorn, Richard, Jr. "Nathan Franklin Barrett, Landscape Architect." *LA*, Apr. 1920, 108–13.

Schickel, Richard. "Mary Pickford and Douglas Fairbanks, Sr.: The Fabled House of Hollywood's Royal Couple." *AD*, Apr. 1990, 148.

———. "William Powell, Sophisticated Wit of My Man Godfrey and The Thin Man: Architecture by James E. Dolena." *AD*, Apr. 1990, 152.

Schock, Mrs. William C. Tel. interview, correspondence, and hand-drawn garden plan for MKG, Aug. 11, 1989. ["Selma Hall"]

———. Letter to ECW. n.d.

Scott, Jeannie. Tel. interview with MKG, Nov. 1988. ["Mirador"]

Scully, Sean. Interview with MKG. New York, July, 1986. ["The Orchard"]

Sears, Thomas. "The Work of Thomas Sears." *Architecture and Design*, Vol. 5, #21, Sept. 1941.

"Selma Hall," information form with list of notable St. Louis area gardens. AAG.

Selma Hall 1850–1915. St. Louis, Mo.: Privately printed, n.d.

Shipman, Ellen Biddle. Chronology compiled by Mrs. Front Streeter. (granddaughter.) AAG.

Shurcliff, Arthur. Letter to Perry, Shaw, and Hepburn, March 18, 1937. Colonial Williamsburg Foundation Archives.

Siani, Alfredo. Tel. interview with MKG, Aug. 22, 1988. ["Oatlands"]

Simo, Melanie. "The Education of a Modern Landscape Designer." *Pacific Horticulture*, Summer 1988, 19–30.

Skurka, Norma. "Tuxedo Park Centennial," *House Beautiful*, May, 1986, 68–77.

Smaus, Robert. "Villa Narcissa." *Los Angeles Times Magazine*, June 18, 1989, 24.

Smith, Charles. Interview and site visit to John Kiser garden, Southampton, with MKG, Nov. 28, 1987.

Smith, Dr. and Mrs. Lyman. Telephone and interviews in person with MKG, Lake Wales, Fla., Feb./Mar. 1988. ["El Caserio"]

Smith, F. A. Cushing. " 'Villa Turicum,' The Country Estate of Mrs. Rockefeller McCormick." *American Landscape Architect*, June 1930, 9.

Smith, Howard Dwight. "The Relation of the House to the Landscape." *American Architect*, Apr. 3, 1918, 397–405.

Sonnenberg Gardens. *Sonnenberg Gardens, History, Restoration, and Programs*. Pamphlet. Canandaigua, N.Y.: Sonnenberg Gardens, n.d.

Spalding, Alice Cooke. Mrs. Samuel Cooke family photograph collection. Honolulu, Hawaii.

Springarn, J. E. "Henry Winthrop Sargent and the Landscape Tradition at Wodenethe: an English Inheritance becomes an American Influence." *LA*, Oct. 1938, 24–39.

Sprunt, Kenneth M. Letter to Mrs. Henry D. Phelps, Mar. 5, 1986. ["Orton Plantation"]

Stagias, Phyllis, and Bruce Abbott. *A History of the Fir Acres Estate which became Lewis and Clark College*. Odell Manor, Lewis and Clark College. Portland, Oreg., n.d.

Steele, Fletcher. "Comfort in a Garden." *Decorators' Digest*, Feb. 1934, 11–14.

———. Letter to Esther Steele. Sept. 24, 1950. Rochester Historical Society. [Choate]

———. "Lilacs Grow Green in a Michigan Garden." [Backus] *H&G*, Sept. 1950, 11–12.

———. "Miss Mabel Choate's Place in Stockbridge, Massachusetts, has been Shaped by Two Generations of Changing

Taste." *H&G*, July 1947, 108–10.

———. "Modern Gardens for Modern Houses." *LA*, Jan. 1942, 64–65.

———. "Modern Landscape Architecture." In *Contemporary Landscape Architecture and its Sources*. Ex. cat. San Francisco: San Francisco Museum of Art, 1936.

———. "New Pioneering in Garden Design." *LA*, Apr. 1930, 159–77.

———. Review of *Jardins Français Classiques des XVII et XVIII Siècles*, by Alfred Marie. *LA*, Oct. 1949, 141–42.

Steele, Karen D. "Henry E. Baskervill: Eclectic Architect." *The Richmond Quarterly*, Summer 1984, 24–31.

Stern, Edith Rosenwald. "Reminiscence of Ellen Shipman." Longue Vue, New Orleans, La.

Stern, Robert A. M. "Designing the American Dream," *AD*, Apr. 1986, 31.

Stone, Bethia. "Val Verde." *Pacific Horticulture*, Summer 1986, 40–42.

Stone, Doris. "Longue Vue." *American Horticulture*, June 1987, 129–31.

Streatfield, David C. "Echoes of England and Italy 'On the Edge of the World': Green Gables and Charles Green." *Journal of Garden History*, Oct.-Dec. 1982, 377–98.

———. "The Evolution of the California Landscape." Parts 1–4. *LA*, "Settling Into Arcadia," Jan. 1976, 39–46; Arcadia Compromised," March 1976, 117–26; "The Great Promoters," May 1977, 229–49; "Suburbia at the Zenith," Sept. 1977, 417–24.

———. "The Garden at Casa del Herrero," *Antiques*, Aug. 1986, 287–88.

———. "Paradise on the Frontier, Victorian Gardens on the San Francisco Peninsula." *Garden History*, Spring 1984, 158–80.

———. "Where Pine and Palm Meet: The CA Garden as a Regional Expression." *Landscape Journal*, vol. 4, no. 2, 1985, 61–72.

———. Letter to ECW, June 18, 1984. List of significant California landscape architects and most important gardens. AAG.

"A Suburban Country Place." ["Holm Lea"] *Century Magazine*, May 1897, 3–17.

Swartz, Mimi. "Standing Up for King William Street." *Historic Preservation*. Oct. 1989, 22–31.

Symington, Mrs. J. Fife [Martha Frick]. Letter to ECW, c. 1987. AAG.

Talbot County Historical Society. *The Art of Gardening: Maryland Landscapes and the American Garden Aesthetic*. Ex. cat. Easton, Md.: Historical Society of Talbot County, 1985.

"Talk of the Town." ["Oheka"] *The New Yorker*, Sept. 25, 1926.

Tallmadge, Thomas E. "Country House Architecture in the Middle West." *AR*, Oct. 1922, 284–307.

Taylor, B. E., Jr. Letter to ECW, June ll, 1985. [Grosse Pointe] AAG.

Taylor, Virginia R. "A Formal Garden with Informal Planting." [Olcott] *CLA*, Mar. 1913, 42–43.

Terrell, Mrs. Arthur *Bayou Bend Gardens*. Guidebook. Houston, Tex.: Bayou Bend Gardens Foundation, n.d.

Teutonico, Jeanne Marie. "Marian Cruger Coffin: The Long Island Estates, A study of the early work of a pioneering woman in American landscape architecture." Ph.D. diss., Columbia University 1983.

Theine, Paul G. "Water Features: Notes on Experience in California Gardens." *LA*, Oct. 1927, 43–51.

Theis, Frank O'Brien, comp. *Designed Historic Landscapes in the Prairie Gateway Region*. Inventory. American Society of Landscape Architects and National Register of Historic Places, March 1987.

Theobald, Dr. William. Tel. interview with MKG, Hawaii, Sept. 1990.

Thiene, Paul G., "Water Features: Notes on Experience in California Gardens." *LA*, Oct. 1927, 43–51.

Thompson, George E., Sr. *A Man and His Garden, The story of Pierre S. du Pont's development of Longwood Gardens*.

Pamphlet. Kennett Square, Penn., 1976.

Thompson, Louis W. "Park Lane." *Santa Barbara Magazine*, May/June 1984, 34–45.

Thorne, Helen S. "When an Easterner Gardens in the Golden West." *Garden Magazine*, Apr. 1921, 178–80.

"Thornedale, A Cool Tapestry of ancient trees, brooks and ponds has been woven into a series of memorable gardens where white flowers predominate." *H&G*, Oct. 1949, 143–49.

Thorndike, Joseph J., Jr. "Addison Mizner—what he did for Palm Beach." *Smithsonian*, Winter 86, 116–22.

Townsend, Wilma T. Letter to ECW, 1986–1987.

Turnbull, Martha. *Rosedown Plantation, Garden Notes of Martha Barrow Turnbull extracted from Account Book 1836–1895*. Compiled by M. A. Lambert from Turnbull ms., St. Francisville, La., 1959, AAG. Photocopy.

———. *Rosedown Plantation. Addendum #1 Martha Turnbull: Notes Found in R. Buist's Catalogues 1857–1859*. Compiled by M. A. Lambert. Sept. 1959. AAG. Photocopy.

Turner, Suzanne. "Faithful to the Text: Magnolia Mound." *LA*, July/Aug. 1987, 72–75.

Twinney, Marc. "Scenes Throughout the South And Along the West Coast." *Gardeners' Chronicle*, June 1926, 170.

Van Rensselaer, Mariana Griswold. "A Suburban Country Place." [Charles S. Sargent] *Century*, May 1897, 3–17.

Van Valkenburgh, Michael. *Built Landscapes in the Northeast*. Brattleboro, Vt.: Brattleboro Museum and Art Center, 1984.

Van Wagner, Judy Collischan, curator. *Long Island Estate Gardens May 22–June 21, 1985*. Catalogue. Greenvale, N.Y.: Hillwood Art Gallery, Long Island University, 1985.

"Villa Turicum" The Estate of Mrs. Rockefeller McCormick, Lake Forest, Illinois, A Souvenir Brochure presented on the Occasion of the Annual Flower Show of the Lake Forest Garden Club. c. 1930. AAG. Photocopy.

Visitor Guide to Spalding Gardens. Pamphlet. Garden Club of Honolulu and Honolulu Academy of Arts, 1972.

Wallace, Douglass W. Tel. interview with MKG, Oct. 1989.; letter to MKG, Oct. 16, 1989. [Topeka, Kans.]

Wardin, Albert W., Jr. *Belmont Mansion, The Home of Joseph and Adelicia Acklen*. Guidebook. Nashville, Tenn.: Historic Belmont Association, 1981.

Warner, Charles Dudley. "New Orleans by Charles Dudley Warner." *Harper's Monthly Magazine*, Jan. 1887, 187–88.

Warren, Bonnie. "A Tribute to Classical Tradition in New Orleans." ["Longue Vue"] *Southern Accents*, Sept.-Oct. 1985.

Warren, David B. *Bayou Bend, The Interiors and the Gardens*. Guidebook. Houston, Tex.: Museum of Fine Arts, 1988.

Warren, Grace Tower. "Una Walker." *Paradise of the Pacific. Hawaii Magazine*, May 1954, 20–24.

Warren, Rhoda. "Bryant Fleming, Landscape Architect, His Years in Wyoming." *Historical Wyoming*, Oct. 1984.

Waters, W. George. "Lawai-Kai." *Pacific Horticulture*, Fall 1983, 27–33.

———. "Lotusland." *Pacific Horticulture*, Spring 1983, 20–25.

Watson, Mark S. "Permanent Buildings of Rare Architectural Beauty will Mark Coming Exposition at San Diego." *Architect and Engineer of California*, Nov. 1914, 56.

Waugh, Walter R., Jr. "Knapp Pavilion, A Brief History of 'Arcady Estate,' 1912–1945." *Montecito Magazine*, Spring/Summer 1984, 6.

Webb, Michael. "Architects to the Stars: Hollywood Legacies of Wallace Neff, James E. Dolena, Roland E. Coate and Paul Williams." *AD*, Apr. 1990, 36.

———. "Cecil B. DeMille: Hollywood Residence of a Master Showman." *AD*, Apr. 1990, 136.

Week's Hall's Notebooks. c. 1940. Shadows-on-the-Teche Archives, New Iberia, La.

Weinberg, Ruby. "The Gardens at Moggy Hollow," *American Horticulturist*, Oct. 1986, 16–20.

"Weir Farm" National Register of Historic Places Inventory—Nomination Form. Weir Farm Heritage Trust, Wilton, Conn., 1983.

Welcome to Stockbridge, Massachusetts, 1987–1988. Guidebook. Stockbridge, Mass.: Stockbridge Chamber of Commerce.

Werling, Donn. "Henry Ford, Conservationist." *Michigan Out-of-Doors*, March 1988, 18–20.

————. Tel. interview with MKG, Nov. 1989. ["Fair Lane"]

Wernick, Robert. "The Greatest Show on Earth didn't compare to home." *Smithsonian*, Sept. 1981, 68.

Westkaemper, Sarah C. *Three Twentieth Century Gardens: A Heritage of Excellence in San Antonio.* [Lutcher Brown] Master's thesis, Louisiana State University.

Wharton, Thomas K. Private Journal. May 1830–Oct. 1834. New York Public Library.

White, Charles E., Jr. "Insurgent Architecture in the Middle West: The Out-of-the-Ordinary Style that has been Developed by the Chicago School of Architects—Its Meaning and Its Destiny." *AR*, Sept. 1912.

White, Lawrence Grant. *Memoranda of the Place, and the Contents of the House, by Lawrence Grant White for his Children.* [Stanford White] Samuel White, N.Y., N.Y.

Whitehill, Walter Muir. "Glen Magna Farms, Danvers, Massachusetts." Typescript. Danvers Historical Society, Danvers, Mass., n.d.

Wight, Peter B. "Country House Architecture in the Middle West." *AR*, Oct. 1916, 291–94.

————. "Melody Farm: The Country Home of J. Ogden Armour, Esq., Lake Forest, Ill.," *AR*, Feb. 1916, 92–121.

————. "Recent Country House Work of Howard Shaw." *AR*, Dec. 1917, 499–527.

Wightman, Roberta. Tel. interview with MKG, July 1990. [The Northwest]

Wilcox, Mrs. T. B. "A Walled Garden in the Northwest." In *House and Garden's Book of Gardens.* Edited by Richardson Wright. N. Y.: Condé Nast, 1921, 71.

"William Adams Delano, Architect, Dead at 85." [obit.] *New York Herald Tribune*, Jan. 13, 1960.

Williams, Laura Metcalfe. "Memories of 'Magnolia Vale,' 1985." AAG.

Wilson, Richard Guy. "The Paradox of the American Country House." Lecture delivered at symposium, "Landscape Pleasures," Parrish Art Museum, Southampton, New York, May 1988.

Wilson, Susannah M. "Reynolda House, A lively museum of American art." *Southern Accents*, Mar./Apr. 1986, 127–34.

Winslow, Albert F. "History of the Blair Property and The Tuxedo Club." AAG.

————. Letter to Eleanor Weller, Dec. 1, 1983. [Tuxedo Park]

Winsor, Mrs. John. Tel. interview with MKG, Nov. 15, 1989. [Heffelfinger, other gardens on Lake Minnetonka]

Winter, Mrs. Joan. Tel. interview with MKG, Sept. 1989. [Lutcher Brown]

Wodell & Cotrell. History of landscape architecture firm of Wodell & Cotrell, and list of works on 35 mm slides. Compiled by Helen Page Wodell's daughter, Mrs. John Poinier. c. 1985. AAG.

Wood, Kathy. Tel. interview with MKG, Aug. 1988. [Washington, D.C.]

Woodburn, Elisabeth, *United States Landscape Collection, 1799–1938.* Sale catalog. Hopewell, N. J. , n.d.

Woodhouse, Mary Kennedy (Mrs. Lorenzo E.) "The Beautiful Gardens of California, 1915." Garden Club of East Hampton Program. East Hampton Library, N. Y.

Word, Ola Mae. *Reflections of Rosedown,* Guidebook. n.d. Rosedown Plantation, St. Francisville, La.

"W. W. Bosworth dies in France." [obit.] *New York Times,* June 5, 1956.

Yarwood, George A. "History of Women in Landscape Architecture." In *Women In Landscape Architecture.* ASLA *Bulletin* 220, American Society of Landscape Architects, July 1973.

Yoch, James. "Gardens of Florence Yoch." *Pacific Horticulture,* Summer 1989, 12–29.

SPECIAL COLLECTIONS

GARDEN CLUB OF AMERICA PUBLICATIONS

Books:

Concerning Philadelphia: Its Environs and Wilmington, Delaware. Philadelphia, 1938.

Fifty Blooming Years, 1913–1963. New York, 1963.

The Garden Club of America History, 1913–1938. Boston, 1938.

List of Gardens of the Members of the Garden Club of America open to visit by Members. Chicago: 1921; 1925.

Bulletins:

Choate, Mabel. "Correspondence." Sept. 1936.

Cresson, Margaret French. "The Chesterwood Garden." Mar. 1956.

"In Memory of Mary Helen Wingate Lloyd." Feb. 1936.

"Restoration of the Gardens at Morven, Princeton, New Jersey." Feb. 1986.

"Seattle Bound," Sept. 1930.

"Slide Programs Available." Sept. 1934.

Valentine, Caroline Lapham. "My Grandmother's Garden." Winter 1983.

Annual Meeting Programs and Reports:
(arranged chronologically)

GCA Business Meeting, Jan. 31, 1919, Colony Club, N. Y. Richmond, 1924, Detroit, 1925, California 1926. Summary by Mrs. Andrew L. Riker. Dayton, Ohio, 1928. Philadelphia, 1929. Long Island, 1931 (North Shore, N. Y.). Aiken, S. C., 1932. Evanston, Kenilworth, Winnetka, and Lake Forest, Ill. 1933. Mount Desert, Me., 1934. Piscataqua, Me., 1934. Hillsborough, Woodside-Atherton, Piedmont, Ca., 1935. Hawaii, 1935. West Point, N. Y., 1936. St. Louis, Mo., 1937. Philadelphia, May 1938. Houston, 1939. Rochester, 1941, with an article by Fletcher Steele, "Background of Culture and Horticulture in the Genesee Valley." Boston, 1946. Detroit, 1950. New Orleans, 1953. Cincinnati, 1954. Houston, 1955. Colorado Springs, 1956. Winnetka, Ill. , 1957. Piscataqua, Me., 1958. Richmond, May 1959. Palm Beach, 1960. Jupiter Island Garden Club Additional Day, Apr. 8, 1960. Hawaii, 1961. Lenox, Mass., 1962. Portland, Oreg., 1964. Cleveland, Ohio, 1965. Houston, 1967. Pasadena, Calif., 1969. Boston, 1970. Lake Placid, N. Y., 1973.

SLIDE SHOW SCRIPTS IN THE AAG

Slide shows were created according to geographical location as defined by the club zones of The Garden Club of America. All scripts are undated; all date before World War II. Regional surviving scripts or lists of slides include: California, Lake Forest Garden Club, Old Gardens of Mt. Desert, Maine, Palm Beach, Piscataqua Garden Club, and Northern and Southern Gardens, with scripts by Alice Lockwood, based on information gathered for *Gardens of Colony and State.* Scripts and lists by type of garden or garden features include Naturalistic Plantings, Rock Gardens, Uses of Water, Water in the Garden, Landscape Design, Members' Gardens (arranged in groups by details of garden architecture and planting), and Selected Members' Gardens (generally the handsomest slide views). A miscellaneous group includes Old History, Famous Southern Gardens, Old Flower Arrangements, Redwoods, Foreign Gardens, Horticulture, English Gardens, French Gardens, Japanese Gardens, and Mexican Gardens.

INSTITUTIONAL COLLECTIONS

Bishop Museum, Honolulu, Hawaii. Photographs of "Moanalua" gardens.

Dona E. Caldwell Collection, Fairfield, Conn. Correspondence, plans, and photographs: Vera Poggi Breed, Ellen Biddle Shipman, Armand R. Tibbets, and other landscape architects practicing in Connecticut.

Carnegie Main Library, Pittsburgh, Pa. Pennsylvania Room.

Columbia University, Avery Architectural and Fine Arts Library, Drawings and Archives Collection, New York, N.Y. Wadley and Smythe photograph album; Charles A. Platt Architectural Drawings; McKim, Mead & White Collection, incl. scrapbooks; Delano & Aldrich Collection; aerial photographs of Long Island estates.

Cornell University Libraries, Ithaca, N. Y., Department of Manuscripts & University Archives. Ellen Shipman Papers.

Essex Institute, Salem, Mass. Vanderbilt-Bowditch Correspondence.

Fairfield Historical Society, Fairfield, Conn. Photograph Collection, Vertical File: 375 Old Post Rd., "Sunnie-holme," Gardens of A. B. Jennings; "Gardens of the Golden Age" 1987 exhibition captions; Landscape Architecture Archive: Agnes Selkirk Clark and Herbert Kellaway Papers.

Fairleigh Dickinson University Library, Madison, N. J. Special Collections. Hamilton McKeon Twombly album of newspaper clippings; Shirley Burden photograph albums of "Florham"; George Moss Collection: Edward Dean Adams file.

Frederick Law Olmsted National Historic Site, Brookline, Mass. Frederick Law Olmsted, and Olmsted Bros. Collections.

Dr. Thomas Gandy Collection, Natchez, Miss.

Hagley Museum and Library, Wilmington, Del. Louise du Pont Crowninshield Photograph Album of her Travels; Crowninshield files; Crowninshield garden chronology.

Harvard Graduate School of Design, Cambridge, Mass. Frances Loeb Library; Clarence Fowler Collection.

Henry Ford Museum & Greenfield Village, Dearborn, Mich. The Edison Institute Archives and Library. Jens Jensen plans for Edsel Ford's "Gankler Pointe," 1926–1932; "A General Plan, The Estate of Mr. Henry Ford, Dearborn, Michigan, September 1920"; Photocopies of photographs of both estates.

Hill-Stead, Farmington, Conn. Archives.

Houston Public Library Architectural Archive, Houston Metropolitan Research Center, Houston, Tex. Papers of Edward Dewson, Landscape Architect and Engineer; Linda Anderson, comp. Hare & Hare inventory for Houston, Apr. 1980; C. C. Fleming, "Chronological Professional History."

Iowa State University. Ames, Iowa. College of Design, Department of Landscape Architecture. Warren H. Manning Collection.

New-York Historical Society. The Architectural Collections McKim, Mead & White Papers.

Richard Marchand Historic Photograph Collection, Philadelphia, Pa.

Society for the Preservation of New England Antiquities, Boston. Little & Browne Collection.

State of Connecticut Department of Environmental Protection, Hartford. Harkness Memorial State Park Papers.

University of Akron Archives. The Willard Penfield Seiberling and Seiberling Family Papers, Manning-Seiberling correspondence, 1911–1928.

University of Pittsburgh Special Collections, Pittsburgh, Pennsylvania, Hillman Library. Mary Arnold Photograph Collection.

University of Virginia, Charlottesville. Fiske Kimball Fine Arts Library. Papers of Charles Gillette.

Mrs. Frank Weller, Monkton, Md. Alfred Branam Photograph Collection.

The Henry Francis du Pont Winterthur Museum, Winterthur, Del. Archives. Marian Coffin Collection.

Works Progress Administration. Federal Writers' Projects, American Guide Series: *Alabama,* 1941; *California,* 1939; *Connecticut,* 1938; *Illinois,* 1939; *Kentucky,* 1939; *Louisiana,* 1941; *Massachusetts,* 1937; *Michigan,* 1941; *Ohio,* 1941; *Oregon,* 1940; *Texas,* 1940; *Washington,* 1941.

APPENDIX

A Catalogue of Glass Plate Photographs in the Collection of The Garden Club of America and the Archive of American Gardens/Slide Library of Notable Parks and Gardens

INTRODUCTION

Just before the First World War, and shortly after the founding of The Garden Club of America, the members commissioned a series of glass lantern slides of their gardens. The introduction of 35mm color film in the mid-1930s resulted in the demise of hand-colored lantern slides, and the Second World War brought an end to the GCA's collection. It was subsequently dispersed, largely due to a lack of proper storage facilities. In the late 1970s, Mrs. H. Jackson Phelps sought and received permission from the Executive Committee of the GCA to reassemble and expand the collection. The decision to preserve the ephemeral beauty of these gardens has given us the collection on which this book is based.

This catalogue is a description of every photograph in the archive, organized alphabetically by state, including the name of the owner and the location, with references, as well as the number of views. Where possible, we have included the name of the house, street address, architect and landscape architect, dates, the number of images, or views, of each home, and additional related information. The name of the photographer, when known, is also provided. All descriptions are based on direct study of the glass slides.

The references, or scripts, are as follows: Alice G. B. Lockwood's "Northern Gardens" and "Southern Gardens"; scripts written locally as narration for individual garden club collections; Mrs. H. Jackson Phelps's scripts, based on her own research after she reassembled the collection. In addition, I have used the following Garden Club of America publications: The Visiting Gardens List for 1921; The Visiting Gardens List for 1925; the program for the Annual Meeting of The Garden Club of America in 1933, sponsored by the Evanston, Kenilworth, Lake Forest, and Winnetka, Illinois, clubs; the September, 1934, *Bulletin*. For local information, Mrs. Henry Cadwalader, Mrs. James H. P. Garnett, and Mr. J. Peter Spang have been of help. I have been responsible for visual interpretation, based on earlier partial descriptions made by Mrs. Frank H. Weller, Jr., and Mrs. Edward A. Blackburn, Jr. A prior inventory by Mrs. Alexander H. Patterson, Jr., was of great use.

It should be noted that although there are some 3,000 glass lantern slides in the collection, there are many duplications. The use of a scene in a different slide program brought another copy of that scene into existence. At present, the listing and collating of the collection has produced the following statistics: there are 1,411 individual views of 627 gardens in 24 states. My initial compilation of the current catalogue was done in 1987–88, with additions in late 1989. New information is added as it is found and will continue to be included. This document is available through The Garden Club of America until 1992, when it will be transferred to the Office of Horticulture at the Smithsonian Institution in Washington, D.C.

On a personal note, I should like to express my great gratitude to my husband for his constant support and encouragement, as well as to our three daughters, Helen Rollins Lord, Alexandra Rollins Upton, and Elizabeth Rollins Mauran, who have unstintingly given of their knowledge of conservation, technology, and archival practice.

Helen E. Rollins (Mrs. Douglas)
January 1991

Unless otherwise stated, there is one view of each location. Please note the following abbreviations: JDS: John Duer Scott, lantern slide studio; EVA: Edward Van Altena, lantern slide studio.

ALABAMA

Theodore
Mr. and Mrs. Walter Bellingrath, "Bellingrath Gardens"; George B. Rogers, arch. and l.a., 1927; 3 views.

NORTHERN CALIFORNIA

San Francisco area
Mrs. William Alexander; Piedmont; 2 views.
Mrs. C. C. Clay; Piedmont; 2 views.
Mr. and Mrs. William Crocker, "New Place," Hillsborough; Lewis P. Hobart, arch., 1906; Bruce Porter, l.a.; 4 views.
Mrs. R. Stanley Dollar; Piedmont; 3 views.
Mrs. Eldridge Green; Piedmont.
Mrs. Duncan McDuffie; Berkeley; Willis Polk, arch.; Frederick Dawson of Olmsted Firm, l.a., c. 1925; 2 views.
Mrs. James Moffitt, "Woodland"; Piedmont; 2 views.
Mrs. Walton N. Moore; Piedmont; 2 views.
Mr. and Mrs. George Newhall, "Newmar/La Dolphine"; Hillsborough; Lewis P. Hobart, arch. and l.a., 1914; 3 views.
Mrs. Edwin L. Oliver; Piedmont.
Mrs. George Pope, "Edgecourt"; Hillsborough; see Lake Tahoe; 2 views.
Mrs. William Proctor; Piedmont; 3 views.
Mr. and Mrs. William P. Roth, "Filoli," Woodside; b. William Bowers Bourn II, Willis Polk, archs., 1915; Bruce Porter, l.a.; Isabella Worn, planting plans; now owned by National Trust for Historic Preservation; 3 views.
Mrs. Arthur G. Tasheana; Piedmont.
Mrs. Cyril B. Tobin; Hillsborough; David Adler, arch.; Isabella Worn, l.a.
Mrs. Andrew Welch; Hillsborough; formal garden designed by John McLaren; 2 views.

SOUTHERN CALIFORNIA

Pasadena
Mrs. Harry G. Bauer; Reginald D. Johnson, arch.; Katherine Bashford, l.a.; 3 views.
Mrs. James G. Boswell; Marie Clews, l.a., c. 1920; garden designed after Château La Napoule at Cannes.
Mrs. Scott Brown; 2 views.
Mrs. Ernest A. Bryant.
Mrs. James N. Clapp.
Mrs. Edward C. Harwood; Ralph Cornell, l.a.; 3 views.
Mrs. George Hume; 3 views.
Mrs. Robert Hunter.
Mrs. Frank Millard; Frank Lloyd Wright, arch. and l.a.
Mr. and Mrs. Kenyon Reynolds; 3 views.
Mrs. Harrison B. Riley; 4 views.
Mrs. Walter Seavey.
Mrs. Reese H. Taylor; Florence Yoch, l.a., 1927.
Miss Abigail van Schogell.
Mr. and Mrs. Archibald Young; Arroyo Seco; George Washington Smith, arch., 1929; A. E. Hanson, l.a.; 2 views.
Unidentified.

San Juan Capistrano
Mission of San Juan Capistrano; botanic garden.

Santa Barbara area
Blakesly Botanic Garden; 5 views.
Mrs. H. E. Bothin, "Piranhurst"; M. Garvin Hodson, l.a., 1914; Montecito.
Mrs. Sellar Bullard, "Goleta."
Miss Katherine Burke; George Washington Smith, l.a.
California Mission Garden.
Mr. and Mrs. Harold Stuart Chase, "Las Terrassas," Hope Ranch; Reginald D. Johnson, arch.; Ralph Stevens, l.a.; 3 views.
Mr. and Mrs. Hobart C. Chatfield-Taylor, "Far Afield"; Ralph Stevens, l.a.; 4 views.
Mrs. Schuyler M. Coe.
Mr. and Mrs. William R. Dickinson, Hope Ranch; Reginald D. Johnson, arch., 1928; Lockwood de Forest, l.a.; 3 views.
Mrs. W. North Duane; Montecito; 2 views.
Miss Millicent Estabrook; Lockwood de Forest, l.a., c. 1936; 2 views.
Mrs. A. Stow Fithian; owner-designed garden, with Lockwood de Forest.
Mrs. G. Hillyer Garvin; Montecito; 3 views.
Mr. and Mrs. E. Palmer Gavit, "Cuesta Linda," now "Lotusland"; 695 Asheley Road; Montecito; b. Kinton Stevens, 1882; Reginald D. Johnson, arch., 1919; George Washington Smith, arch. and l.a., 1921–27; Peter Riedel, l.a., with G. W. Smith and Mrs. Gavit; Mme. Ganna Walska, "Lotusland," 1941; d. 1984; Lockwood de Forest, l.a. for succulent garden; Ralph Stevens, l.a. until 1958; Charles Glass and Robert Foster, l.a.'s for cycad garden; 2 views.
Mrs. Frederick S. Gould; Steven Child, l.a.; Montecito; 2 views.
Mr. and Mrs. Craig Heberton, "El Hogar"; George Washington Smith, arch. and l.a., 1916.
Mrs. Bernard Hoffman, "Casa Santa Cruz"; James Osborn Craig, arch., c. 1923; Lockwood de Forest, l.a., patio, 1923; Yoch and Council, alterations, 1938; 2 views.
Mrs. Arundel Hopkins, Mission Ridge.
Mr. Kirk B. Johnson, "La Toscana"; George Washington Smith and Lutah Maria Riggs, archs., 1927; A. E. Hanson, l.a., 1928–29.
Mr. David Jones, "Pepper Hill"; Montecito; David Adler, arch.; 2 views.
Mr. and Mrs. George Owen Knapp, "Arcady"; Carleton Monroe Winslow, arch. and l.a. for terrace and upper garden, 1912; Ralph D. Cornell, l.a., 1920; Charles Gibb Adams, l.a.; Francis Underhill, l.a. for lower garden; 2 views.
Mrs. Lorne J. Knight; Montecito; Theodore Payne, l.a.; see Lake Tahoe; 3 views.
Mr. and Mrs. Arthur Meeker, "Constantia"; Montecito; Ambrose Cramer, arch., 1930; Lockwood de Forest, l.a.; 3 views.
Mr. and Mrs. John J. Mitchell (Lolita Armour), "El Mirador," formerly "Riso Rivo"; Montecito; b. Charles Eaton, c. 1888; bought by Armour family 1917; Arthur Huen, arch. for outbuildings, 1917, and remodeling small house in 1921 when large house burned; Elmer Awl, superintendent, and Mrs. Mitchell, garden designers post-1921.
Mrs. Frank H. Osgood; 3 views.
Mr. and Mrs. Reginald C. Robbins; Montecito.
Mr. and Mrs. George F. Steedman, "Casa del Herrero"; George Washington Smith, arch., 1922–30; Ralph Stevens, l.a. for estate plan; Francis Underhill and Lockwood de Forest, l.a., 1922; Peter Riedel, l.a.; later modified by owner; maintained by daughter today; 2 views.
Mr. and Mrs. Oakleigh Thorne, "Las Tejas"; b. William Alston

Hayne II, 1898; Francis W. Wilson, arch., 1917; Helen Thorne and Francis W. Wilson, l.a.; modeled after Casino Caprarola at Farnese Palace; George Washington Smith, l.a. for rose, heliotrope, and Spanish gardens, 1926 on; all clipped beds show diamond motif; 17 views.

CONNECTICUT

Fairfield
Mrs. Edgar W. Bassick; Fairfield; 8 views.
Mrs. Arthur G. Fraser.
Mrs. William E. Harmon; 3 views.
Miss Annie Burr Jennings, "Sunnie Holme," 375 Boston Post Road; Mrs. Harriet Foote and Herbert Kellaway, l.a.'s for rose garden, 1909–10; 10 views.
Mrs. Benjamin DeWill Riegel; 2 views.
Mrs. Henry B. Spelman.
Mr. and Mrs. De Ver H. Warner, "Thaddeus Burr Homestead"; Mr. and Mrs. Warner, designers of Colonial Revival garden; 2 views.

Greenwich
Mr. and Mrs. Luke Vincent Lockwood, Lockwood Road; Riverside; Alice G. B. Lockwood was author of *Gardens of Colony and State*.
Unknown, c. 1822; Clapboard Ridge.

Hartford
Mrs. Frank C. Sumner.

Litchfield, Litchfield area
Mrs. Carrington Arnold; 3 views.
Mrs. G. Herbert Bronson; 2 views.
Mrs. Frederick T. Busk, "Spruce Brook Farm"; JDS 2 views; EVA 3 views.
Mrs. B. A. Cheney; 2 views.
Mrs. Seymour Cunningham; 4 views: JDS 1; EVA 1.
Mrs. N. Curry; JDS 1 view; EVA 1 view, 1939.
Mrs. Charles B. Curtis, "Rye House"; b. 1911; Bantam; JDS 6 views.
Mrs. A. Doster; Litchfield area; 2 views.
Mrs. John Dove, "Butternut Brook Farm"; JDS 1 view.
Mrs. Finch; EVA 2 views, 1939.
Mrs. Samuel Edson Gage; West Morris; EVA 5 views, 1939.
Mrs. F. Sherman Haight; JDS 3 views.
Elbert B. Hamlin; 1924.
Mrs. Ernest Howe; 3 views.
Mrs. C. L. Hussey; 2 views.
Mrs. Ed. Jones; 2 views.
The Misses Kingsbury, "The Lindens," later "The Bull House"; William Sprats, arch., 1790; bought by Frederick J. Kingsbury, 1910; subsequent owner Ludlow Bull, 1937; 4 views.
Mrs. H. B. Lewis.
Mrs. R. H. Liggett, "Stonecroft"; Olmsted Firm, 1925–39.
Mrs. William T. Marsh.
Mrs. Harlan G. Mendenhall; JDS 3 views.
Mrs. Henry S. Munroe; 3 views.
Mrs. Reed; 3 views.
Mrs. Frank C. Sumner; 2 views.
Mrs. Robert C. Swayze; Olmsted Firm, 1924–25, 1929; EVA 3 views.
Mrs. Floyd L. Vanderpoel; 4 views.
Mrs. Gage M. Wallace; 2 views.
Miss Emily Wheeler; 3 views: JDS 1; EVA 1.
Miss May White.
Miss Alice Wolcott; 2 views.
Mrs. W. Wood; JDS 5 views.
Mrs. J. P. Woodruff; 3 views.

Middletown
Mrs. Henry Osborn Taylor.

New Canaan
Mrs. William H. Cary; 2 views.

Mrs. Henry W. Chappell; 2 views.
Mrs. Richard M. Coit; 2 views.
Mrs. Henry J. Davenport.
Mrs. P. Hanson Hiss.
Mr. and Mrs. Lewis H. Lapham, "Waveny"; William B. Tubby, arch., 1912; land bought in 1904; public park today; 4 views.
Mrs. Cyrus W. Merrell, "Lowthorpe"; 2 views.
Mrs. Raymond E. Strett.
Mrs. Samuel H. Watts; Agnes Selkirk Clark, l.a.; 5 views.

New Haven
Capt. Daniel Green, c. 1815; 2 views.

Washington
Mrs. I. N. Hebbard, "Ashland."
Arthur L. Shipman.

DELAWARE

Wilmington
Mr. and Mrs. Francis Crowninshield, "Eleutherian Mills"; Mellor, Meigs & Howe, restoration arch.; owner-designed garden; 3 views.
Mrs. Eugene du Pont, "Owl's Nest."
Mrs. Harry G. Haskell, "Hill Girt Farm," c. 1816; Noel Chamberlin, l.a., iris garden; Ellen Shipman, l.a., boxwood garden; Lewis & Valentine, nurserymen, 1920s.
Mr. and Mrs. H. Rodney Sharp, "Gilbraltar"; Marian Coffin, l.a.; Lewis & Valentine, nurserymen, 1920s; 3 views.
Mrs. Robert Wheelwright, "Goodstay."

FLORIDA

Coconut Grove
Mr. James Deering, "Vizcaya"; F. Burrell Hoffman, arch., 1912–19; Diego Suarez, l.a., 1915; Wodell & Cottrell, l.a.

Hobe Sound
Mr. and Mrs. Joseph V. Reed; 2 views.

Palm Beach
Mrs. Chester C. Bolton.
Mrs. Clifford V. Brokaw.
Mrs. Earle P. Charlton.
Mrs. Leland Cofer.
Mr. and Mrs. Hugh Dillman; 1. Addison Mizner, arch.; 2. "Sandy Loam Farm."
Mr. and Mrs. Peter Frelinghuysen; 2 views.
Mrs. Robert G. Glendenning.
Mrs. Joseph Gunster; Marion Wyeth, arch.; 2 views.
Mr. and Mrs. Alfred G. Kay, "Audita"; Addison Mizner, arch. and l.a., 1921; 7 views.
Mrs. Charles E. F. McCann (Helena Woolworth); see Long Island; 3 views.
Mr. and Mrs. George A. McKinlock; Marion Wyeth, arch.; Olmsted Firm, l.a.; 4 views.
Mrs. Paul Moore; 2 views.
Mr. and Mrs. H. C. Phipps; 2 views.
Mr. and Mrs. John S. Phipps, "Casa Bendita"; Addison Mizner, arch., 1921; see Long Island; 3 views.
Mrs. John Pillsbury; see Lake Minnetonka; 2 views.
Mrs. Rodney Proctor.
Mrs. Henry R. Rea, "Lagomar"; Addison Mizner, arch., 1924; see Pennsylvania; 2 views.
Mrs. Wiley Reynolds; Marion Wyeth, l.a.; 2 views.
Mrs. Alexander Rutherford.
Mrs. Francis A. Shaughnessy.
Mrs. Christopher D. Smither; 2 views.
Mr. and Mrs. E. T. Stotesbury, "El Mirasol"; Addison Mizner, arch., 1919; see Pennsylvania; 3 views.
Mrs. Adam G. Thompson.
Unknown (public park along Lake Worth?); 2 views.
Mrs. Woodward Vietor; Maurice Fatio, arch.; 2 views.
Mrs. Barclay H. Warburton, "Casa Maria Marrone"; Addison Mizner, arch. and l.a., 1922; 2 views.

Mrs. Frederick S. Wheeler; 2 views.
Mrs. Howard F. Whitney.
Mr. Joseph E. Widener; Maurice Fatio, arch.; 3 views.
Mrs. Lorenzo E. Woodhouse; see Long Island; 3 views.

GEORGIA

Atlanta area
Maj. and Mrs. John Dunwoody, "Mimosa Hall"; b. 1820–30; Roswell; previously owned by Neel Reid, l.a. for Callaway additions to "Hills and Dales."
Hutchinson Garden, c. 1820; Palmetto.

Augusta
Albright-Battey-Benton, "Twin Gables"; gardens, 1911; 4 views.
Judge William Barrett, Walton Way and Katherine Street.
Boardman-Clayton House, Cumming Road.
Mr. and Mrs. Alfred S. Bourne, "Morningside," 606 Milledge Road, later owned by Stevenson; Rose Standish Nichols, l.a., 1920.
Mr. and Mrs. Harry Chaffee, "Carner-Howard-Thomas-Chaffee House," 914 Milledge; Hannah Howard, design, 1784; seven generations of Howards lived there; glass slide c. 1933; 2 views.
Mr. and Mrs. Rodney Cohen; Miss Mary Lou Phinizy, c. late 1890s.
Mrs. John Speer, "Goshen Plantation"; 4 views.
Gov. Jenkins Crowell Heffernan, "Green Court," Cumming Road; Mr. and Mrs. H. P. Crowell, prior owners, 1916; 5 views.
Medical College, 1839.
Mr. William B. White, Milledge and Pickles Road; now Augusta Women's Club.

La Grange
Mr. and Mrs. Fuller E. Callaway, "Hills and Dales," 1912; formerly Mr. and Mrs. Blount Ferrell, 1841, "The Terraces"; Sarah Coleman Ferrell, design, c. 1841–1906; Neel Reid, l.a., 1914; 2 views.

Lexington
Mr. Upson Howard, "Stone Walls," 1820; 2 views.

Savannah
Mr. Robert Bolton, "White Bluff," 1799.
City of Savannah, "Bonaventure."
Mr. and Mrs. Noble Jones, "Wormsloe," 1735; Isle of Hope; 4 views.

St. Simons
Unknown. 1802.

ILLINOIS

Chicago area
Mrs. Lester Armour, North Sheridan Road, Lake Bluff; David Adler, arch. and l.a. for terrace; 3 views.
Mr. Edward H. Bennett, 89 East Deer Path, Lake Forest; 2 views.
Mr. and Mrs. Richard Bentley, 1421 North Lake Road, Lake Forest; David Adler, arch. and l.a., Ambrose C. Cramer, arch. and l.a., garage and fence.
Mr. and Mrs. William McCormick Blair, "Crab Tree Farm," Lake Bluff; Arthur Huen, arch., 1926; Ellen Shipman, l.a.; 2 views.
Mr. and Mrs. Walter Brewster, "Covin Tree," 776 North Green Bay Road, Lake Forest; Howard Van Doren Shaw, arch.; owner, l.a.; 2 views.
Mrs. Clyde M. Carr, "Wyldwoode," 55 North Mayflower Road, Lake Forest; Harrie T. Lindeberg, arch.; Warren H. Manning, l.a.; 2 views.
Mrs. Thomas Cassidy, 950 East Maplewood Road, Lake Forest.
Mr. and Mrs. William E. Clow, 900 North Green Bay Road, Lake Forest; Howard Van Doren Shaw, arch.; Rose Standish Nichols, l.a.
Mr. and Mrs. John Coleman, Jr., "Wayside," 55 North Green Bay Road, Lake Forest; Rose Standish Nichols, l.a.

The Misses Colvin, 1350 North Lake Road, Lake Forest; 3 views.

Mr. and Mrs. Joseph M. Cudahy, "Innisfail," 830 North Green Bay Road, Lake Forest; David Adler, arch. and l.a., 1930; plantings suggested by Ferruccio Vitale, l.a.; 3 views.

Mrs. Dexter Cummings, 1460 North Lake Road, Lake Forest; Harrie T. Lindberg, arch. and l.a.

Mrs. John Gary, 303 Sheriden Road, Glencoe; Frederick W. Perkins, arch., 1912; Jens Jensen, l.a.; 3 views.

Mrs. Charles C. Haffner, 880 North Green Bay Road, Lake Forest.

Mr. and Mrs. Alfred E. Hamill, "Centaurs," 1115 East Illinois Road, Lake Forest; Henry Dangler, arch., 1913; David Adler, arch. for additions and walled garden, 1927; Ferruccio Vitale, l.a., planting plan; 3 views.

Mrs. John Hamline, 395 East Woodland Road, Lake Forest.

Mrs. Edward H. Hasler, "Aldingbourne Cottage," 185 East Vine Avenue, Lake Forest; Hugh Garden, arch., 1908; Jens Jensen, l.a.; built after Aldingbourne House in Sussex, England; home of Hâsler family.

Mrs. William G. Hibbard, 840 Willow Road, Winnetka; Edward Fechheimer, arch.; Ralph Rodney Root, l.a.

Mrs. McPherson Holt, 1298 North Green Bay Road, Lake Forest.

Mrs. John Andrews King, 165 North Green Bay Road, Lake Forest; Anne Baker (associate of Annette Hoyt Flanders), l.a.; David Adler, l.a. for terrace.

Mr. and Mrs. Hugh J. McBirney, "House of the Four Winds," 81 West Laurel Avenue, Lake Forest; Howard Van Doren Shaw, arch. and l.a.; Rose Standish Nichols, l.a., planting plan; garden styled after Generalife gardens in Granada; 2 views.

Mr. and Mrs. Cyrus H. McCormick; Lake Forest; 1. "Walden"; Jarvis Hunt, 1896; remodeled by Hugh Garden, Charles Coolidge, and Russell Walcott, archs.; Warren H. Manning, l.a.; Louise Shelton, l.a., pergola; Ralph E. Griswold, l.a., new garden; Lewis & Valentine, l.a.; 6 views. 2. "Ravello," 367 Bluff's Edge Drive.

Mr. Robert McGann, 965 East Deer Path, Lake Forest; 2 views.

Mrs. Donald McLennan, 1345 North Lake Road, Lake Forest.

Miss Madeline Newall, 725 North Sheridan Road, Lake Forest.

Mrs. Augustus Peabody; unknown.

Mr. and Mrs. John T. Pirie, 930 East Rosemary Road, Lake Forest; Benjamin H. Marshall, arch.; Rose Standish Nichols, l.a.; 3 views.

Mrs. William A. P. Pullman, 700 Mayflower Road, Lake Forest; 2 views.

Mrs. Kersey Coates Reed, 1315 North Lake Road, Lake Forest; David Adler, arch., house, 1932, and "indoor winter tennis house in American Georgian style"; Ferruccio Vitale, l.a.; 2 views.

Mr. and Mrs. Edward L. Ryerson, "Havenwood"; Lake Forest; Howard Van Doren Shaw, arch., 1912; Jens Jensen, l.a.; Rose Standish Nichols, l.a.; 3 views.

Mr. and Mrs. Charles H. Schweppe, 405 North Mayflower Road, Lake Forest; Frederick W. Perkins, arch.; Pray, Hubbard and White, l.a. for terraces, forecourt, and parterre, 1914; Rose Standish Nichols, l.a., perennial and rose gardens; Fletcher Steele, l.a., hornbeam arcades from rose garden to tennis court, swimming pool, and allée, 1923; 2 views.

Mr. and Mrs. Frederick H. Scott, "Timberleigh," 175 Sheridan Road, Hubbard Woods; Otis and Clark, arch.; Jens Jensen, l.a.; Root and Hollister, l.a., small formal garden; owner-designed formal perennial garden.

Mrs. Edward Shumway, 735 East Westminster, Lake Forest; Ellen Shipman, l.a.; 2 views.

Mr. and Mrs. James Simpson, "Roscrana," 1315 North Lake Road, Glencoe; George B. Maher, arch.; remodeled by Graham, Anderson, Probst & White; Jens Jensen, l.a.; Root and Hollister, pool and perennial borders; Mrs. Charles Hubbard, tennis court, lily pool, rock and rose gardens; 5 views.

Mr. and Mrs. John Stuart, 990 Sheridan Road, Hubbard Woods; W. Corbys Zimmerman, arch., 1904; Edwin H. Clark, Inc., arch., remodeling and service buildings; Alfred Yeo-

mans, l.a.; Ray West, l.a., consultant in later years; 2 views.

Dr. and Mrs. Roy Sturtevant, 171 Laurel Avenue, Lake Forest; Ernest Walker, arch., c. 1903; 2 views.

Mrs. T. Philip Swift, 810 South Ridge Road, Lake Forest.

Mrs. Robert Thorne, Thorne Lane, Lake Forest.

Mrs. Edward K. Welles, 321 Ahwanee Road, Lake Forest; Mrs. Charles Hubbard.

Mrs. Lawrence Williams, 1050 East Illinois Road, Lake Forest; Thomas Seyster, arch.

Area Unknown
Mrs. David Minton.

LOUISIANA

Above New Orleans
Gov. Alexander Roman, "Oak Alley." 2 views.
Unknown. 2 views.

New Roads
Parlange family, "Parlange Plantation," late 18th century; 2 views.

MAINE

Kennebunkport
Miss Llewellyn Parsons; Ellen Shipman, l.a.; Olmsted Firm, l.a., 1909–29; Marvin Breckinridge Patterson, photog.; now part of the Rachel Carson National Seashore; 4 views.

Kittery Point
Mr. William Dean Howells, "Howell's Place"; b. 1902; Mr. and Mrs. John Mead Howells; Abby Howells, white garden design after 1910; Marvin Breckinridge Patterson, photog.; now Harvard University; 8 views.

Mr. and Mrs. Fergus Reid, Jr.; Gerrish Island; Marvin Breckinridge Patterson, photog.; 2 views.

Mt. Desert
Mrs. Joseph T. Bowen, "Baymeath"; Hull's Cove; Andrews, Jacques and Rantoul, arch., 1895–96; Joseph H. Curtis, l.a.

Miss Agnes Miles Carpenter, "Hauterive," c. 1899; Bar Harbor; Andrews and Rantoul, arch. 2 views.

Miss Mary Roberts Cole, "Aldersea"; Bar Harbor.

Mr. and Mrs. Ernest B. Dane, "Glengariff"; Seal Harbor; 2 views.

Mrs. John T. Dorrance, "Kenarden Lodge"; formerly John S. Kennedy; Rowe and Baker, arch., 1892; Beatrix Farrand, l.a. Bar Harbor area.

Mrs. Shepard Fabbri, "Buonriposo"; b. E. G. Fabbri, 1904; Beatrix Farrand, l.a. Bar Harbor area; 2 views.

Mr. and Mrs. Max Farrand (Beatrix Farrand), "Reef Point"; b. by Mrs. Cadwalader Jones (Farrand's mother); Bar Harbor; Rotch & Tilden, arch., 1883. Beatrix Farrand, l.a.

Mrs. Edsel Ford; Bar Harbor area; Jens Jensen, l.a.

Miss Mildred McCormick, "The Farm House"; built c. 1800; Bar Harbor; Beatrix Farrand, l.a., 1923–28.

Mrs. Gilbert Montague, "Beaulieu"; Seal Harbor.

Mr. and Mrs. William E. Patterson; Bar Harbor area; William E. Patterson, l.a.

Mr. and Mrs. John D. Rockefeller, "The Eyrie"; Seal Harbor; Beatrix Farrand, l.a., 1926–30; now owned by Mr. and Mrs. David Rockefeller.

Mr. and Mrs. Gardiner Sherman, "Keewaydin"; Mrs. Sherman later Mrs. Edward P. May; Bar Harbor; Lamb & Rich, arch., 1898; Beatrix Farrand, l.a.

Mrs. Paul Washburne; Bar Harbor area.

South Berwick
Mr. and Mrs. Harry G. Vaughan (Emily Tyson), "Hamilton House"; b. Col. Jonathan Hamilton, 1788; Herbert Browne, restoration arch.; Marvin Breckinridge Patterson, photog.; early Colonial Revival garden; now owned by the Society for the Preservation of New England Antiquities; 4 views.

York
Mr. and Mrs. John C. Breckinridge, "River House"; Guy Lowell, arch.; Marvin Breckinridge Patterson, photog.; now prop-

erty of Bowdoin College; 3 views.

Miss Elizabeth Perkins; Marvin Breckinridge Patterson, photog.; now property of Old York Historical Society; 2 views.

Mr. and Mrs. Andrew Murray Williams, "Highland Farm"; Marvin Breckinridge Patterson, photog.; 6 views.

York Harbor
Mr. and Mrs. Russell A. Alger; Ellen Shipman, l.a.; Marvin Breckinridge Patterson, photog.; see Grosse Pointe, Mich.; 3 views.

Mr. and Mrs. Fergus Reid, Sr., "Stonewall"; Marvin Breckinridge Patterson, photog.

Mr. and Mrs. Harold C. Richard; John Russell Pope, arch., 1929; Olmsted Firm, l.a.; Marvin Breckinridge Patterson, photog.

Sewalls Bathhouse; Marvin Breckinridge Patterson, photog.

MARYLAND

Baltimore
Mr. and Mrs. Miles White, 1847.

Near Easton
Unknown, "Perry Hall," 1820.

Howard County
Mr. Charles Carroll, "Doughoregan Manor," 1717; 2 views.

Towson
Ridgeley family, "Hampton," 1783, 1810; William Booth, terrace planting plans, c. 1810; 2 views.

Area Unknown
"Poplar Grove."
"Tulip Hill."

MASSACHUSETTS

Andover
Abbott Homestead, "Happy Hollow," 1685.

Brookline
Mr. Thomas Handasyd Perkins, "Shattuck Farm," 1799; 2 views.

Danvers
Mr. and Mrs. William C. Endicott, "The Farm" or "Glen Magna"; Herbert Browne, arch., remodeling c. 1892; George Huessler, l.a., 1814; Olmsted Firm, l.a., 1894; Joseph Chamberlin, designed Italian garden 1897; Herbert Browne, McIntire teahouse rose garden, 1901; 2 views.

Fall River
Mrs. James Buffington, "Borden Garden," c. 1790–1800.

Great Barrington
Mr. and Mrs. William Hall Walker, "Brookside"; b. William Stanley, 1904; Carrère and Hastings, arch.; Ferruccio Vitale, l.a., rose garden c. 1918.

Lenox
Miss H. Meyer, "Overlee Gardens."

Manchester-by-the-Sea
Mrs. Gordon Abbott, "Glass Head"; Tuck's Point; 2 views.

Mr. and Mrs. Gardiner M. Lane, "The Chimneys," 1902; 199 Summer Street; Raleigh Gildersleeve, arch.; F. L. Olmsted, Jr., l.a.

Miss Evelyn R. Sturgis, Summer Street.

Marblehead
Mr. and Mrs. Francis B. Crowninshield, "Seaside Farm"; see Wilmington, Del., and Boca Grande, Fla.

Milton
Gov. Hutchinson, 1743.

Nantucket Island
Mrs. Summers, Main Street; b. Zenas Coffin, design 1820; daughter, Mary Coffin Swift, design 1823.

New Bedford
Mr. John Arnold, "The Arnold Garden," 1821; donor of land for Arnold Arboretum, Boston. Mr. William Rotch, Jr., "Rotch-Jones-Duffie House."

Newburyport
Mr. and Mrs. Frederick S. Moseley, "Maudsley," Curzon's Mill Road; Martha Brookes Hutcheson, l.a.; see also West Newbury; 4 views.
"Osgood Brockway Garden"; John Osgood, l.a.; b. as Newburyport Academy, 1807.
"Pierce-Perry Garden," 1809.
Mr. William Wheelwright, 75 High Street.

Pride's Crossing
Mrs. H. J. Coolidge.
Mrs. William H. Moore.
Mrs. Quincy A. Shaw.

Salem
Miss Laight, c. 1810, 41 Chestnut Street.

Stockbridge
The Hon. and Mrs. Joseph H. Choate, "Naumkeag"; Miss Mabel Choate, subsequent owner; Stanford White, arch., 1885; Nathan Barrett, l.a., 1885; Fletcher Steele, l.a., 1926–58.
Mrs. C. A. deGersdorff.

Waltham
Mr. Arthur Lyman, "The Vale"; Samuel McIntire, arch., 1793; William Bell, l.a.; 2 views.

Wellesley
Mr. and Mrs. Horatio Hollis Hunnewell, "Wellesley," "Hunnewell Gardens," c. 1854; owner-designed; continues in same family.

West Newbury
Mr. and Mrs. Frederick S. Moseley, "Indian Hill"; Byfield (West Newbury); b. Mr. Benjamin Poore, the Poore Family; "Indian Hill Farm," 1688; see Newburyport; 2 views.

MICHIGAN

Unknown.

Alma
Mrs. Francis King (Louisa Yeomans), "Orchard House"; owner was l.a. and author of *The Well-Considered Garden* et al.; Nichols, Chicago, photog., 1926; 2 views.

Detroit area
Mr. and Mrs. Russell A. Alger, "The Moorings," 32 Lakeshore Drive, Grosse Pointe; Charles Platt, arch., 1908–10; Ellen Shipman, l.a.; now Grosse Pointe War Memorial; 7 views.
Mrs. C. D. Allington, 200 Provincial Road, Grosse Pointe; photos, 1926; 4 views.
Mrs. William H. Barbour, "Briar Bank," Bloomfield Hills; Fletcher Steele, c. 1924.
Mrs. Edwin H. Butler; Grosse Pointe; photos, 1926; Bryant Fleming, l.a.
Mrs. John M. Dwyer, Lakeland Court, Grosse Pointe; 2 views.
Mrs. Dexter M. Ferry, 17100 East Jefferson Avenue, Grosse Pointe; photos, 1926; 3 views.
Mrs. F. T. Murphy, 17260 East Jefferson Avenue, Grosse Pointe; 4 views.
Mr. and Mrs. John S. Newberry, 99 Lakeshore Drive, Grosse Pointe; b. 1875; A. B. Yeomans, l.a., 1908; Ellen Shipman, l.a., 1920s; 6 views.
Mrs. Stewart Pittman, 905 Three Mile Drive, Grosse Pointe.
Mrs. J. G. Rumney; 17400 East Jefferson Drive, Grosse Pointe; 2 views.
Mrs. Benjamin S. Warren; Grosse Pointe.
Mrs. Cameron B. Waterman, 330 Lincoln Road, Grosse Pointe.

MINNESOTA

Wayzata
Mrs. George C. Christian.
Mrs. Philip Little.
Mr. and Mrs. John S. Pillsbury, "Southways"; Harrie T. Lindeberg, arch.; 3 views.
Mrs. John Washburn.
Mrs. David Winton; Roy Jones, arch.; Mrs. Pearson, Excelsior, Mich., garden design.

NEVADA

Lake Tahoe
Mrs. Lorne J. Knight, "Vikingsholm"; see Montecito; 3 views.
Mrs. George Pope, see Montecito.

NEW HAMPSHIRE

Cornish
Mrs. Ellen Shipman, "Brook Place"; Ellen Shipman, l.a.

Portsmouth
"Ladd House," "Moffatt-Ladd House," Market Street; b. John Moffatt, 1770–80; now owned by Society of Colonial Dames in New Hampshire; 2 views.
Mrs. Woodbury Langdon, "Governor Langdon House," Pleasant Street, 1784; now owned by the Society for the Preservation of New England Antiquities; 2 views.
Jacob Wendell House, Pleasant Street; b. Jeremiah Hill, 1820.

NEW JERSEY

Bordentown
Joseph Bonaparte, former King of Naples, brother Napoleon, "Point Breeze," c. 1830; owner-designed.

Brunswick
Unknown, "Buccleuch," 1680; official residence of colonial governors.

Lawrenceville
Mrs. William K. Prentice, "Cherry Grove Farm," c. 1765; 1. Students Photo Service, photog. 1 view; 4 views.

Orange
Mrs. Robert Carter.
Mrs. Hendon Chubb.
Mrs. Russell Colgate.
Mrs. Harrison McFaddin.
Mrs. Ralph L. Pomeroy.
Mrs. S. H. Rollinson; 2 views.
Mrs. John E. Sloan; 2 views.
Mrs. Alfred B. Thatcher.
Mrs. John Y. G. Walker.

Princeton
Mrs. Alfred Thornton Baker, "Castle Howard Farm"; b. 1863; 2 views.
Mrs. Charles Brown.
Mrs. Malvern B. Clopton.
Mrs. C.F.W. McClure; 2 views.
Mr. and Mrs. Junius S. Morgan, "Constitution Hill"; Cope and Stewardson, arch., 1897; Students Photo Service, photog. 1 view; 3 views.
Princeton University, "Prospect"; John Notman, arch. and l.a., 1852; Beatrix Farraud, l.a. 1914–43; 2 views.
Mr. and Mrs. Moses Taylor Pyne, "Drumthwacket"; house b. 1834–35; Raleigh Gildersleeve, arch., 1893; Daniel Langton, l.a., 1905.
Mrs. Bayard Stockton, "Morven," Stockton Street; b. Richard Stockton 1720–40; house remained in family 200 years; used as Governor's Mansion by four governors, 1955–75; part of 18th-century garden said to have been modeled after Alexander Pope's at Twickenham; recent excavations indicate terraces; Mrs. Bayard Stockton laid out an "old-fashioned" garden c. 1901; 2 views.
Mrs. W. U. Vreeland; 3 views.

Red Bank
Mr. and Mrs. Andrew Varick Stout, "Brick House"; John Russell Pope, arch.; Martha Brookes Hutcheson, l.a.; 4 views.

Rumson
Mr. and Mrs. Edward Dean Adams, "Rohallion"; Stanford White, arch., 1887; Nathan Barrett, l.a.
Mrs. Howard S. Borden.
Mrs. Henry A. Caesar; Seabright; 3 views.
Mrs. J. Amory Haskell, "Oak Hill Farm"; Charles Welford Leavitt, l.a.
Mrs. Robert McCarter.
Mrs. L. R. Maehl.

Short Hills
Mrs. Moses W. Faitoute, "Twin Oaks"; 3 views.
Mrs. Bancroft Gherardi; Wodell and Coltrell, l.a., 1931; 3 views.
Mrs. Harold W. Hack; 2 views.
Mrs. Ernest L. Halbach.
Mrs. Frederic B. Ryan, "Wee Loch"; 2 views.
Mrs. Charles H. Stout.
Mrs. Tyssillio Thomas.
Mrs. W. K. Wallbridge; 2 views.
Mrs. Ruthven A. Wodell; garden designed by owner.

Summit
Mrs. Carroll P. Bassett, "Beacon Hill"; 1936.
Mrs. Clifford Brown.
Mrs. Corbin.
Miss Anne Cromwell, 1925; Mrs. James W. Cromwell, prior owner.
Mrs. Daly; 2 views.
Miss Elizabeth Gifford.
Mrs. Frederick W. Jackson.
Mrs. Livingston P. Moore; 2 views.
Mrs. Richard E. Reeves; 2 views.
Mrs. Smedberg.
Mrs. John R. Todd.
Mrs. Wallace; 1932.
Mrs. Waldron M. Ward.
Mr. Ben White.
Mrs. Richard Cade Wilson; 2 views.
Mrs. Carlton G. Winan.

Trenton
Mrs. Bruce Bedford.
Mrs. Henry C. Blackwell.
Mrs. Robert K. Bowman.
Mrs. Arthur D. Frost; 3 views.
Mrs. John M. Scudder.
Mrs. Herbert Sinclair.

NEW YORK/LONG ISLAND

Cold Spring Harbor
Mr. and Mrs. Henry W. deForest, "Nethermuir"; old garden redesigned by Olmsted Firm, 1906–27; 4 views, EVA 5 views.
Mrs. Benjamin Tappen Fairchild; 2 views, 1931 & 1936.
Dr. and Mrs. Walter B. James, "Eagle's Nest"; Umberto Innocenti (first garden), l.a.; 4 views, EVA 4 views.
Mr. and Mrs. Walter P. Jennings, "Burrwood," 1896, Shore Road; 6 views.
Mr. and Mrs. Barstow Small; EVA 3 views.

East Hampton
Mr. and Mrs. Ruger Donoho, Egypt Lane; 2 views.

Mr. and Mrs. Albert Herter, "The Creeks," Bridgehampton Road; Grosvenor Atterbury, arch., 1898; Adele Herter, garden designer; 4 views.

Mrs. William A. Lockwood, Burnett Lane.

Mrs. Scott McLanahan, Hunting Lane.

Mrs. J. H. Poor.

Mr. and Mrs. Lorenzo E. Woodhouse, Egypt's Lane; formerly the garden of Mrs. Lorenzo G. Woodhouse; today the East Hampton Nature Reserve; 2 views.

Glen Cove

Mr. and Mrs. Harold Irving Pratt, "Welwyn"; Babb, Cook and Willard, arch., 1906; Delano and Aldrich, arch; Olmsted Firm, l.a., 1906–36; James Leal Greenleaf, l.a.; Martha Brookes Hutcheson, l.a.; Lewis & Valentine, nurserymen, 1920s; 26 views.

Huntington

Mrs. Chamberlin Chanler; Lloyd Neck; Wodell & Cottrell, l.a.; 5 views.

Mrs. Winchester Noyes, "Tenacre"; EVA 4 views.

Miss Florence Sullivan, "Content"; EVA 4 views.

Mrs. Willis Delano Wood, "Fort Hill House," b. 1771; remodeled 1938; Lloyd Neck; Olmsted Bros., l.a.; Ellen Shipman, l.a. for rose garden (Olmsted Firm Master List does not include Wood); Dr. William Matheson, prior owner; 2 views.

Laurel Hollow

Mrs. Alexander A. M. White; 3 views.

Locust Valley

Mrs. John W. Davis.

Mill Neck

Mrs. Howard Slade; 4 views.

Muttontown

Mrs. Benjamin Moore, "Chelsea"; William Adams Delano, arch., c. 1920; later, Ferruccio Vitale, l.a., and Innocenti and Webel; 4 views, EVA 4 views.

Oyster Bay

Mrs. C. Comfort; 2 views.

Mrs. Nelson Doubleday; Innocenti & Webel, l.a.; EVA 4 views.

Mrs. Charles E. F. McCann (Helena Woolworth); Annette Hoyt Flanders; Innocenti and Webel, l.a.; 17 views.

Mrs. Albert Strauss; Cove Neck Road; 6 views.

Mrs. Edward M. Townsend; Townsend Place; 5 views.

Mrs. Frederick Wheeler, "Wellwood"; EVA 5 views.

Roslyn

Mrs. Harold Godwin, Bryant Avenue; 4 views, EVA 5 views.

Mrs. Henry P. Tailer, Shore Road.

Mrs. Aaron Ward (formerly Mrs. J. F. Curtis), "Willowsmere"; the owner notes in the 1921 Visiting Gardens List that "there are many vacancies due to the severe winter of 1920 and the Quarantine 37, which does not allow the importing of plants to fill them up. It should be fought by every garden lover"; 9 views.

Shelter Island

Miss Cornelia Horsford, "Sylvester Manor," settled 1652; house b. 1732; boxwood planted by original owner, Nathaniel Sylvester; Thomas Allen, l.a., 1892; for water garden; Cornelia Horsford designed a Colonial Revival garden on site of 17th-century Quaker garden; 6 views.

Southampton

Mrs. Robert C. Hill (author Anna Gilman Hill), "Grey Gardens"; see Sneden's Landing; designed by owner, possibly with assistance of landscape architect Ruth Dean; 5 views.

Syosset

Mrs. W. B. Devereaux.

Mrs. Robert Tobin, the former Mrs. James A. Burden (Adele Vanderbilt Sloane), "Woodside Acres"; William Adams Delano, arch., 1917; Olmsted Bros., l.a., 1922–24; 9 views.

Area Unknown

Mrs. Richard A. Carleton; 2 views.

Westbury

Mrs. Robert L. Bacon, "Oldacres"; Searington Road; Martha Brookes Hutcheson, l.a.; 36 views.

NEW YORK/UPSTATE

Albany area

Mrs. James F. Adams.

Mrs. Edgar H. Betts.

Unknown, "Cherry Hill."

Mrs. G. Alfred Cluett; 2 views.

Mrs. Edwin Corning.

Mrs. Erastus Corning II.

"Fort Crails."

Mrs. L. W. Gorham.

Mrs. George Ide; G. A. Glenn (photog.?).

Mrs. Rosell McKinney.

Mrs. W.L.L. Peltz; 2 views.

"The Perkins Garden."

Miss H.T.E. Pruyn.

Mrs. Robert F. Pruyn.

Mrs. Alfred Renshaw; 2 views.

Mrs. Henry K. Shaw.

Mrs. W. Leland Thompson.

Union College, "The President's Garden"; 5 views.

Unknown; 1 view.

"Van Rensselaer Manor House"; 2 views.

Mrs. Eugene Warren; Troy; 2 views.

Bedford

Mrs. Gordon Knox Bell; Katonah; Marion Coffin, l.a.; EVA 3 views.

Mrs. Whitney Blake; EVA 5 views.

Mrs. James Butler, Jr.; EVA 2 views.

Miss Elizabeth Chamberlain.

Mrs. George Chapman; EVA 3 views.

Mrs. Winthrop Cowdin; EVA 3 views.

Mrs. Charles Dickey; 3 views.

Miss Helen Clay Frick; EVA 3 views.

Mrs. O. V. Hoffman.

Mrs. Gustavus Kirby; EVA 5 views.

Miss Delia West Marble; EVA 1 view.

Mrs. L. H. May; EVA 3 views.

Mrs. Charles Mayers; Katonah; Joseph Hawkes, New York, photog.; 2 views.

Mrs. Richard W. Meade; EVA 3 views.

Mrs. James S. Metcalf.

Mr. and Mrs. George Norton Miller, "The Grove," c. 1790; previously known as "Schuyler Hall"; Rhinebeck.

Mrs. Benjamin W. Morris; EVA 5 views.

Mrs. Frank H. Potter; EVA 3 views.

Mrs. Irving Roland; EVA 4 views.

Mrs. George Schurman; EVA 3 views.

Mrs. Samuel Sloan, "Lisburne Grange"; Garrison; Fletcher Steele, l.a., 1921–37; Mrs. Sloan was chairman of Slides Committee 1919, president of GCA 1921–24; 8 views.

Mrs. Edward Tatham; EVA 3 views.

Mrs. William K. Thompson, c. 1930; Sparkhill; 2 views.

Mrs. E. Kellogg Trowbridge; Bedford Hills; EVA 5 views.

Mrs. Percy Turnure; Bedford area; 2 views.

"Van Courtland Manor House," c. 1730; Croton-on-Hudson; 2 views.

Mrs. Edmund T. Vaughan; EVA 2 views.

Mrs. William E. Verplanck, "Mount Gulian," c. 1804; Fishkill-on-Hudson; 2 views.

Mrs. A. P. Voislawsky; EVA 4 views.

Mrs. Orlando Webber; EVA 3 views, August 1937.

Mrs. Francis W. Welch; EVA 4 views.

Mr. and Mrs. Harold C. Whitman; EVA 5 views.

Mrs. Nelson B. Williams; EVA 3 views.

Canandaigua

Mrs. G. D. McKechnie; built c. 1796, Gen. Peter B. Porter.

Millbrook

Mrs. Robert L. Burton.

Mr. and Mrs. Harry H. Flagler, "Edgewood"; Marian Coffin, l.a.; 7 views.

Mr. and Mrs. Alfred B. Maclay, "Little Rest"; 8 views.

Mr. and Mrs. Charles R. Marshall.

Mrs. Victor McQuade; 2 views.

Mr. and Mrs. Oakleigh Thorne, "Thornedale"; Wodell and Cottrell and Helen Thorne, l.a., main vista garden; Nellie B. Allen, l.a., white garden; Marian Coffin, l.a., water garden; see also Santa Barbara: diamond motif is used in both locations; 10 views.

Mt. Kisco and Sneden's Landing

Mrs. Murray W. Dodge; Marian Coffin, l.a.; EVA 1 view.

Mrs. Robert C. Hill, "Neiderhurst," c. 1900; Sneden's Landing; owner-designed; Marian Coffin, l.a.; "Claude Lorrain view" garden; see also Southampton.

Mrs. Edwin O. Holter; EVA 2 views.

Mrs. Arthur H. Scribner; Mr. Greenhof and Mrs. Benjamin Morris, l.a., terrace only; Carrère and Hastings, l.a., Italian garden; EVA 3 views.

Mrs. John W. Towne, "Wingfield," c. 1920; Fletcher Steele, l.a.; EVA 6 views.

Rye

Mrs. Ethan A. Dennison; 3 views.

Mrs. Frederick A. Godley; 3 views.

Mrs. William J. Knapp; 2 views.

Unknown. "Knollwood Farms"; 1 view, May, 1926.

Mrs. Marselis Parsons.

Mrs. A. William Putnam; 2 views.

Rye Garden Club exhibit: "Monk's Garden," 1933.

Mrs. J. Rich Steers.

Mrs. Lew Wallace.

Saratoga

Mr. James Thompson, "Rose Hill," 1829; 2 views.

Schenectady

Mrs. Lawrence Achilles.

"Lansing House."

Mrs. C. Langdon Perry.

Mrs. Walter Stearn.

Tarrytown-on-Hudson

Zabriskie family, "Blithewood"; Andrew Jackson Downing, l.a.

Washington

Mrs. Herman Place, "Rose Lawn," 1830–40.

OHIO

Chillicothe

Mr. and Mrs. Thomas Worthington, "Adena"; Benjamin Latrobe, arch., 1803.

Cincinnati

Mr. and Mrs. Horace Schmidlapp; Grosvenor Atterbury, arch.; Ferruccio Vitale and Umberto Innocenti, l.a.s; all slides painted by Gladys Pratt; 9 views.

Mr. and Mrs. Charles P. Taft; Benjamin Latrobe, arch., before 1828; now Cincinnati Art Museum; 2 views.

Dayton

Mrs. E. G. Burkam.

Mrs. Nelson Emmons; 2 views.

Mr. and Mrs. George H. Mead.

Postcards of old Dayton civic plantings; 9 views.

Mrs. Adam Schantz.
Mrs. John Sutherland.

Marietta
The Mills Garden, 1814; 2 views.

OREGON

Portland
Mr. and Mrs. Peter Kerr, "Elk Rock"; John Charles Olmsted, l.a., 1905–15; now Episcopal Diocese of Oregon; 4 views.
Mr. and Mrs. Thomas Kerr, "High Hatch"; William Whidden, arch., 1900; 6 views.

PENNSYLVANIA

Kennett Square
Mr. and Mrs. Pierre S. du Pont, "Longwood Gardens," 1906; formerly Pierce Arboretum, c. 1800; owner-designed, with Lewis & Valentine, nurserymen; 3 views.

Philadelphia area
Mrs. John Hampton Barnes, "West Acres"; Devon.
Mr. Charles J. Biddle, "Andalusia," 1775; Andalusia; b. Nicholas Biddle; continues in same family; scene of organization of Garden Club of America.
Mrs. S. Lawrence Bodine, "Greenbank Farm," 1760 and 1924; Newtown Square.
Mrs. William R. Breck; Rosemont.
Mr. and Mrs. James Cheston, 4th, "Dawesfield," 1728; Ambler; 2 views.
Mr. and Mrs. Isaac Clothier, Jr., "Sunnybrook"; Radnor; Wilson Eyre and Arthur Brockie, archs. for additions, 1926; Thomas W. Sears, l.a.; 2 views.
Mrs. R. Mayer de Schauensee (Baroness); Wynnewood.
Mrs. Frederick R. Drayton, "Magnolia House"; Villanova.
Mrs. John Gibbons, "Lynfield Farm," 1700; Media; 2 views.
Mrs. Henry C. Gibson, "Fairy Hill"; Jenkintown.
Mrs. John C. Gilpin, "Sugar Loaf Orchard"; Chestnut Hill.
Mrs. Percival Glendinning, Fairmont Park; Philadelphia; now city property; 2 views.
Mrs. Robert Glendinning, "The Squirrels"; Chestnut Hill.
Unknown, "Grumblethorpe," 1744; b. John Wistar; Germantown; 2 views.
Mrs. Caspar Winter Hacker; Bryn Mawr.
Mr. and Mrs. H. Frazer Harris, "Harston," 1910; Chestnut Hill; Beatrix Farrand, l.a.; 3 views.
Mrs. Richard Haughton, "Valley Mill Farm"; Devon; 2 views.
Mrs. Benjamin R. Hoffman, "The Grange," 1684; Overbrook; 2 views.
Mr. and Mrs. Henry S. Jeanes, Jr., "The Farm House 'Laywell,'" 1843; Devon.
Mrs. John S. Jenks; Chestnut Hill.
Mrs. Stacy Lloyd, "Mill Creek House"; Ardmore.
Mrs. Randall Morgan, "Wyndmoor"; Chestnut Hill; Fletcher Steele, l.a., some areas, c. 1938, as well as orchid room in house; 2 views.
Mrs. Samuel Morris, "Edgehill"; Chestnut Hill.
Mrs. Richard T. Nalle, "Down Dale"; Chestnut Hill.
Mr. and Mrs. Eugene Newbold, "Fox Creek Farm"; Devon; Mellor, Meigs and Howe, arch. and l.a.
Mrs. John Packard III; Chestnut Hill.
Mr. and Mrs. Lewis H. Parsons, "Appleford," 1705; Villanova; 3 views.
Mrs. A. J. Drexel Paul, "Box Hill"; Radnor; 2 views.
Mrs. B. Franklin Pepper, "Ballygarth," 1919; Chestnut Hill; Willing & Sims, arch. and l.a.; 3 views.
Mrs. Charles Platt; Chestnut Hill; 2 views.
Mrs. Edgar Allen Poe, "Ropsley"; Mellor, Meigs and Howe, arch. and l.a.; b. Francis S. McIlhenny, 1917; Chestnut Hill; 3 views.
Mrs. Rudolph Rauch, "Land's End"; Villanova.
Mrs. G. Brinton Roberts, "Llanengan"; Bala Cynwyd.
Mrs. Frederic Rosengarten, "Indian Rock"; Chestnut Hill; 2 views.
Mrs. J. Clifford Rosengarten, "Woodley"; Villanova.

Mrs. Samuel P. Rotan, "Lane's End"; Chestnut Hill; garden copied from Hampton Court Palace.
Mr. and Mrs. Andrews Schofield, "Homewoods"; Chestnut Hill.
Mrs. Arthur Hoyt Scott, "Todmorden Farm," 1787; Rose Valley; garden, 1920; 3 views.
Miss Caroline Sinkler, "The Highlands"; Fort Washington (Ambler); b. Anthony Morris, 1796; George Sheaff (second owner), l.a. 1820s; Wilson Eyre, l.a., 1915; 5 views.
Mrs. J.M.R. Sinkler, "Milfern"; Paoli.
Mrs. Wharton Sinkler, "Thornbury"; Elkins Park; 2 views.
Society of Colonial Dames, "Stenton," 1718; Philadelphia; b. James Logan (William Penn's secretary); scene of beginning of Garden Club of America.
Mrs. Isaac Tatnall Starr, "Laverock Hill"; Charles Platt and Ellen Shipman, l.a.s, 1915; Chestnut Hill; 2 views.
Mrs. Frederick C. Stout; Ardmore; 2 views.
Mr. and Mrs. Frederick W. Taylor, "Boxly"; bought 1901; Chestnut Hill; Jean DuBarry, owner and garden designer, 1813; Olmsted Bros., l.a., 1901.
Mr. and Mrs. John Barnes Townsend, "Montrose," early 1900s; Radnor; Oglesby, Paul, l.a.; Lewis & Valentine, nurserymen.
Mrs. George Tyler, "Indian Council Rock"; Newtown.

Pittsburgh area
Mr. and Mrs. Henry Rea, "Farmhill," 1898; Sewickley; Hiss and Weekes, arch.

West Chester
Mrs. E. Page Allison, "Town's End Farm," 1800.
Mrs. John Groff.
Mrs. Anne Price Hemphill.
Mrs. Frank Adams Keen, "Kerwalls."

RHODE ISLAND

Bristol
"Babbitt-Morice Garden," c. 1810 and 1835; 2 views.
Mr. John De Wolf, "Linden Place," 1810; Colt family, subsequent owner; now property of the city of Bristol; 2 views.

Chepiwanoxet
Mr. and Mrs. Arthur B. Lisle, "White Swan," c. 1839; Olmsted Firm, 1926–30; Fletcher Steele, c. 1930.

Newport
Mrs. Frederick Allen, "The Mount," 1929; 2 views.
Mr. and Mrs. Hugh D. Auchincloss, Sr., "Hammersmith Farm," Harrison Avenue; Olmsted Firm, l.a., 1897; 11 views.
Miss Julie Berwind, "The Elms"; Edwin Berwind, prior owner, 1899–1936; Horace Trumbauer, arch. and site planner, 1899; Charles N. Miller, then Ernest Bowditch, l.a.; 3 views.
Mrs. Harold Brown, Bellevue Avenue; Olmsted Firm, l.a., 1894–1927; 2 views.
Mrs. John Nicholas Brown, "Harbour Court," Halidon Avenue; Ralph Adams Cram, arch.; Olmsted Firm, l.a.; Harold Hill Blossom, l.a. for enclosed garden; today New York Yacht Club; 2 views.
Mr. and Mrs. Marion Eppley, "Beacon Rock"; b. Edwin D. Morgan, Jr., 1889; McKim, Mead and White, arch.; 3 views.
Mrs. Lewis Fox Frissell, "Vedimar," Harrison Avenue; b. 1911–14; 2 views.
Mrs. Richard Gambrill, Sr., "Vernon Court," Bellevue Avenue; Carrère and Hastings, arch., 1902; Wadley and Smythe, l.a.; 2 views.
Mrs. Dudley Gilbert, "Four Acres"; 2 views.
Mrs. Edmund Grinnell, "Longacre."
Hazard family, "Vaucluse," c. 1790; Mr. Elam, Mr. Charles DeWolf, prior owners.
Col. and Mrs. L. V. Hoppin, "Auton House"; 2 views.
Miss Elise Hutton, "Shamrock Cliff"; house b. 1896; 4 views.
Mr. and Mrs. Arthur Curtiss James, "Beacon Hill House," Beacon Hill or Brenton Road (two entrances); Olmsted Firm, l.a., 1908–21; John Greatorex, estate superintendent, designed blue garden 1913; Harriet Foote, rose garden; winter visitors were directed to the winter garden; 5 views.

Mrs. Walter Belknap James, "Rockhurst," 1905; Harriet Foote designed rose garden.
Mrs. Walter James Lord; 4 views.
Mrs. Louis B. McCagg, Gibbs Avenue.
Mrs. Guthrie Nicholson, "The Glen"; John Russell Pope, arch.; 4 views.
Mrs. Samuel Nicholson, "Mariemont"; house built for Mrs. Thomas Emery, 1907; Olmsted Firm, l.a. (not listed as Emery or Nicholson in Olmsted Firm Master List); 2 views.
Dr. and Mrs. Alexander Hamilton Rice, "Miramar"; she was former Mrs. George D. Widener; Horace Trumbauer, arch., 1912; Jacques Gréber, l.a.; 4 views.
Mr. and Mrs. B. H. Ripley, "Beech Bound," b. 1895.
Mrs. Charles H. Russell, LeRoy Avenue; owner-designed garden with l.a. Louise Payson, 1930.
Mrs. Michael H. Van Buren, "Gray Craig," 1924; 2 views.
Mrs. Hubert Vos, "Zee Rust"; b. by Arthur Curtiss James; Brenton Road; 4 views.
Mr. and Mrs. Hamilton Fish Webster, "Pen Craig," Harrison Avenue; formerly Mr. and Mrs. George F. Jones, Edith Wharton's parents; 5 views.
Mr. George Peabody Wetmore, "Château sur Mer"; b. for William S. Wetmore, 1852; remodeled 1873, Richard Morris Hunt; Olmsted Firm, 1915–18; today property of the Preservation Society of Newport County; Miss Edith Wetmore; 4 views.

Portsmouth
Miss Alice Brayton, "Green Animals," c. 1860; Cory's Lane; 2 views.
Mr. and Mrs. Bradford Norman, "Brook Farm"; 2 views.

Potowomut
Mrs. William Green Roelker, "Governor Green Garden"; house built c. 1758; 2 views.

Providence
Mr. John Carter Brown, c. 1786.

Tiverton
Mrs. Edward Marvell.

SOUTH CAROLINA

Camden
Mrs. Todd.
Mrs. Ernest Woodward, "Holly Hedge," 1842; later Marion du Pont Scott, 1942; 2 views.

Charleston
Miles Brewton House, 1760; 2 views.
Mr. J. J. Pringle Smith, "Middleton Place"; house and gardens built by Middleton family beginning 1741; Ashley River; 5 views.
Smyth house, c. 1830.
Unknown.
Mr. and Mrs. Miles White, 1760; 2 views.

Sumter
Unknown, "Hill Crest," "Borough House," pre-Revolutionary; additions, 1818.

TENNESSEE

Nashville
Pres. Andrew Jackson, "The Hermitage," 1819; New England painter, Ralph Earl, possible designer of garden and driveway; 4 views.

VIRGINIA

Aldie
Mrs. A. V. Baird, "Oak Hill."
Mrs. Floyd Harris, "Stoke."

Belmont
Unknown.

Charlottesville area
Mrs. Charles E. Blue, "Ridgeway"; Charlottesville.
Mr. and Mrs. Louis Chauvenet, Jr., "Tallwood," 1804; Albemarle County; Enniscorthy family.
Mr. and Mrs. William du Pont, "Montpelier," bought 1916; built by Pres. and Mrs. James Madison, c. 1756; Charles Gillette, restoration l.a.; 3 views.
Mrs. Randolph Leitman.
Mrs. William Massie, "Rose Hill"; Greenwood; William Lawrence Bottomley, arch., 1930; Greenwood; 3 views.
Mrs. Allen Potts, Gordonsville.
Mrs. Horation Small; 3 views.
Mrs. Whitney Stone, Mrs. Samuel H. Marshall, "Morven"; Annette Hoyt Flanders, restoration l.a.; 2 views.
Prince Pierre and Princess Amelie Rives Troubetzkoy, "Castle Hill"; b. 1764, addition 1824; Charlottesville; terraces before 1765; front garden c. 1832 designed by Judith Rives; conservatories added 1840; Alden Hopkins, restoration l.a. after 1947; 3 views.
University of Virginia; Charlottesville; 3 views.

James River
Mrs. Alice Carter Bransford, "Shirley"; b. "Secretary" John Carter, 1723; 2 views.
Carter family, "Sabine Hall"; b. Robert "King" Carter for son, Col. Landon Carter; 2 views.
Mrs. Richard Crane, "Westover"; b. Col. William Byrd, 1730; 4 views.
Mr. Robert W. Daniel, "Brandon"; Brandon; b. Nathaniel Harrison, 1712; additions designed partly by Thomas Jefferson; 3 views.

Lee Family, "Stratford Hall"; b. Lee family late 1730s; Morley Williams, archeologist and l.a., 1932–33; now property of Robert E. Lee Memorial Association, Inc.; 3 views.
Mrs. Henry T. Wickham, "Hickory Hill"; b. William Fanning Wickham, 1820.

Leesburg
Mr. and Mrs. William Corcoran Eustis, "Oatlands"; b. George Carter, 1800; acquired by Stilson Hutchins of Washington, D.C., 1894, who began restoration; William Corcoran Eustis, 1903; now property of the National Trust; 2 views.

Lorton
Mr. and Mrs. Louis Hertle, "Gunston Hall"; b. George Mason, 1758; early Colonial Revival garden, c. 1912, created by the Hertles; Alden Hopkins, restoration l.a. after Hertle ownership; now operated by the National Society of Colonial Dames; 4 views.

Middleburg Area
Mrs. William Clifford.
Mrs. Fairfax Harrison; The Plains.
Mrs. Henry T. Oxnard, "Edgewood"; Upperville; 2 views.
Mr. and Mrs. Edwin G. Rust.
Unknown; 2 views.

Mount Vernon
Pres. George Washington, "Mt. Vernon," b. 1743; 4 views.

Princess Anne County
Unknown, "Buckwood."

Richmond
Unknown, "Reveille," c. 1781; one of oldest houses standing in Richmond.
Mrs. William Sale, "Tuckahoe"; b. Thomas Randolph, c. 1710.
Mr. and Mrs. George Cole Scott, "Ballyshannon," Cory Street Road.

Warrenton
Mr. and Mrs. Harry C. Groome, "Airlie."

Williamsburg Restorations
Carter-Sanders Garden; 2 views.
Coke-Garrett Garden; 2 views.
Mr. John Custis.
Governor's Palace; Perry, Shaw and Hepburn, restoration arch.; Arthur Shurcliff, restoration l.a.; 11 views.

Yorktown
"Nelson House," 1740; "York House"; b. William Nelson for son, Thomas; Charles F. Gillette, restoration l.a.

WASHINGTON STATE

Seattle
Mrs. Robert P. Buchart.
Mrs. Gilbert L. Duffy; 3 views.
Mrs. John W. Eddy.
Mr. and Mrs. Charles W. Stimson, "The Highlands," 1930; A. A. McDougall of Olmsted Firm, l.a.

Tacoma
Mr. and Mrs. Chester Thorne, "Thornewood"; Kirtland Cutter, arch., 1908; Olmsted Bros., l.a., 1908–12.

"Compton" (Pennsylvania), 133
Connecticut, 60–71; *61–65, 68, 69*
Conservation, 266, 280–81
Conservatories, 136, 139, 225, 230, 238, 268, 286, 298, 315, 348–49, 350–51; *47.*
See also Greenhouses
"Constantia" (California), 335–36; *334*
"Constitution Hill" (New Jersey), *124*
Convent (New Jersey), 121; *12*
Converse, Edmund C., 61
"Conyers Manor" (Connecticut), 61
Cook, Charles Montague, 356
Cook, Hall and Cornell, 342, 350, 351
Cook, Wilbur David, 351
Cooke, Jay, 131, 296, 302
Coolidge, Calvin, 274
Coral vine, 214
Corbett, Gail Sherman, 102
Corcoran, William, 162
Cord, E. L., 351
Cordyline terminalis, 357
Coreopsis, 219; *40*
Cornel, Dwarf *(Cornus canadensis)*, 263
Cornell, Ralph D., 327, 351
Cornell University, 201
Cornish (New Hampshire), 40–43, 212, 258; *40–43, 169*
Cornus, 106
Coronado (California), 346–48
Corydalis, 142
Cotoneaster, 345
"Cottage gardens." *See* "Old-fashioned gardens"
Cottages, 14, 28, 54, 178
Cottrell, Lois, 121
Council, Lucille, 330, 343, 350; *344*
Council rings, 200, 265, 266
"Covin Tree" (Illinois), 271–72; *270*
Cowgill, Kathleen, 151
Cowles, Anna, 70
Cowles, William Sheffield, 70
Cowslip, *287*
Cox, Mrs. J. B., 345
Cox, Kenyon, 42
Crabb, William, 242; *242*
Craig, James Osborne, 323
Craig Heberton house (California), 329
Cram, Ralph Adams, 131, 275
Cramer, Ambrose, 335
Cran, Marion, 18, 323, 324, 327, 345, 350, 352
"Cranbrook" (Michigan), 272
Crane, Richard Teller, Jr., 53, 259
Crane, Mrs. Richard Teller, Jr., 53, 259
"Creeks, The" (Long Island, New York), 114, 325; *115*
Crégier, Henri Eduard, 127
Crenier, Henri, 141
Cresson, Margaret French, 55
Crinum, 350
Crocker, C. Templeton, 318–19; *318*
Crocker, Charles, 318
Crocker, William, 319
Crocker, Mrs. William, 319
Crocus, 310
Croft, Augusta Graham, *62*
Croft, Henry W., *62*
Croly, Herbert, 42, 138
Cromwell, Oliver (New York clubman), 129
Cross, Wilbur, 67
Cross and Cross, 110, 125
"Crossways Farm" (California), 319–20
Croton, 178, 356
"Crowbar" (Hawaii), 356

Crowell, H. P., 171
Crowninshield, Francis Boardman ("Frank"), 139, 143, 186; *144*
Crowninshield, Francis Welch ("Frank"), 54
Crowninshield, Louise du Pont, 19, 139, 142–43, 186; *142, 144*
Crown-of-thorns, 179
Crowther's (English shop), 203
Cryptomeria, *31*
Crystal Springs School for Girls (California), 319
Cubism, 59, 346
"Cuesta Linda" (California), 336, 337
Cukor, George, 330, 343, 352
Culbertson, Cordelia, 343, 345; *344*
Cullinan, J. S., 237
Cunninghamia, 219
Cup-of-gold, 325
"Curchie Hill" (Oregon), 298
Curl, Donald, 184
Curlett, William, 316; *317*
Currant, Missouri, 281
Currier, Guy, 43
Curtis, Mrs. G. Warrington, 111
Cutter, Kirtland K., 307, 310, 349
Cutter and Malmgren, 307
Cutting, Bayard, 20
Cutting gardens, 18, 35, 108, 162, 235, 244; *86, 165*
Cycad, 337, 348
Cyclamen, 345
Cypress, 67, 167, 242, 255, 319, 327, 331, 337, 338, 349
  Italian, 160, 189, 356; *352*
  Monterey, *306*
"Cypress Gardens" (South Carolina), 165–67

D

Daffodil, 167, 168, 224, 235, 288
Dahlia, 67, 123, 223, 230; *124*
  Pompom, 288
Daisy, 167; *81*
  African, 336
  English *(Bellis perennis)*, 302
  Transvaal, 336
  Ursinia anthemoides, 310
Dallas (Texas), 240, 242
Dami, Luigi, 143
Damon, Samuel Mills, 353–55; *354*
Dangler, Henry, 259
Danvers (Massachusetts), 50–53; *53*
Daphne, Winter *(Daphne odora)*, 167, 303
Dater, Henry, 337–38
Datura, 178
Davies, Joseph, 154
Davies, Marion, 323, 351
Davis, Alexander Jackson, 75, 121; *74*
Davis, Bette, 43
Dawson, James Frederick, 96, 302, 349; *311*
Daylily, 38
Dean, Ruth, *115*
"Dean Hall" (South Carolina), 165, 167
Dearborn (Michigan), *264*
De Bost (merchant), 111
Dedham (Massachusetts), *51*

Deering, James, 174–76
Deer parks, 62, 89, 124, 165, 197, 233, 256, 315
de Forest, Alling, 89
de Forest, Elizabeth Kellam, 329, 335
de Forest, Lockwood, 103, 328, 329, 334–35, 337–38, 348; *309, 334, 338*
de Forest, Lockwood, Sr., 334–35
DeGolyer, Everett, 242
Delano, William, 78, 97, 106, 153, 195, 342; *78*
Delano and Aldrich, 77, 78, 97, 102, 127, 129, 138, 194
Delaware, 118, 139–43; *140–42, 144, 145*
"Delbarton" (New Jersey), 121
Delk, Edward Buehler, 290
de Longpré, Paul, 350
Delphinium, 33, 39, 44, 125, 163, 178, 208, 235, 302, 303, 305, 310, 337; *30, 37, 45*
  Shipman on, 210; *211*
DeMille, Cecil B., 233, 350–51
Demopolis (Alabama), 223–24; *222*
Dempsey, Jack, 352
Deodar, 351; *153*
Derby, Elias Hasket, *53*
Derby (New York), 89–90
De Renne, Augusta Floyd, 169
Desloges, Joseph, 261; *25, 260*
Detroit (Michigan), 170, 272, 275–76
Deutzia, 298
Devon (Pennsylvania), 132
Devore, Daniel B., 194; *193*
Devore, Mrs. Daniel B., 194; *193*
Dewing, Maria Oakley, 40
Dewing, Thomas, 40
de Wolfe, Elsie, 174
Dewson, Edward, 239, 240
Dianthus, *298*
"Dias Felices" (California), 338
Dichondra, 343
Dickens, Charles, 103
Dickinson, Emily, 43
Dickinson, William R., 335
Dieterich, Alfred, 331
Dieterich, Ethel Vreeland Post, 331
Dillingham, Mary, 355–56, 358; *355*
Dillingham, Walter, 355–56; *355*
Disney, Walt, 233
District of Columbia. *See* Washington (District of Columbia)
Dobyns, Winifred Starr, 323, 342, 349
Dodge, Marcellus Hartley, 120
Dodge, Mrs. William Hartley, 121
Doe, Mr. (gardener), 162
Dogwood, 86, 143, 148, 153, 160, 172, 194, 219, 228, 263; *20, 21, 100, 152*
  Mountain *(Cornus Nuttallii)*, 307
  Red-osier, 263
  Western, 299
Doheny, Edward L., 348–49, 351
Doheny, Edward L., Jr., 348–49
Dole, Daniel, 357
Dolena, James, 351–52
Dooley, James Henry, 207
Dooley, Sallie May, 207
Dorrance, John T., 34; *36*
Doubleday, Neltje Blanchan, 18
"Doughoregan Manor" (Maryland), 146
Dovecote, 212
Downing, Andrew Jackson, 15, 16, 23, 46, 73, 75, 121, 148, 219, 262
Dracaena, 325
Dragon tree, 325
Draper, Earl, 171, 219

Drayton, John Grimke, 158, 166, 186
Dreiser, Theodore, 282
Drew, George, 61
Drought-resistant plants, 179, 313, 327
Druid Hills (Georgia), 214–15
"Drumthwacket" (New Jersey), 123–25, 155; *125*
Drury, F. E., 282
Dryden, John F., 120
Dublin (New Hampshire), 43–44
Duchêne, Achille, 127–28, 319; *127*
Duchêne, Henri, 128
"Dumbarton Oaks" (Washington, D.C.), 34, 67, 153–54, 174; *154*
Dunaway, Hettie Jane, 217
"Dunaway Gardens" (Georgia), 217–18; *217*
Duncan, Mrs. Charles, 224
Duncan, F., *43*
Duncan, Isadora, 177
Duncan, John, 60
du Pont, Alfred I., 139–41; *141*
du Pont, Alfred Victor, 139; *141*
du Pont, Alicia Bradford, 141
du Pont, Eleuthère, 139
du Pont, Henry Algernon, 143
du Pont, Henry Francis, 19, 101, 139, 142, 286; *142*
du Pont, Jessie Ball, 141
du Pont, Pierre, 139, 269; *140*
du Pont, William, *140*
du Pont, Mrs. William, 162
Durant, William C., 276
Dusty miller, 28
Duveen, Sir Joseph, 126, 129, 340, 342
"Dynasty" (TV program), 320

E

Eagle Falls (Nevada), *291*
"Eagle Rock" (Massachusetts), 137; *51*
"Eagle's Nest" (Long Island, New York), 94
Eames, Charles, 272
Earhart, Amelia, 212
Earle, Alice Morse, 195
East End (Long Island, New York). *See* East Hampton; Southampton
Eastern Shore (Maryland), 151–52, *151*
East Hampton (Long Island, New York), 72, 79, 111–15; *92, 113, 115*
Eastman, George, 86–89, 238; *86*
Eastman, Mary Jane, *24*
Eaton, Charles F., 337
Eaton, Leonard K., 198
Ebony tree, 244
Eckbo, Garrett, 311, 319
Ecole des Beaux-Arts (Paris), 14, 76, 77, 99, 127, 208, 258, 324; *76*
"Edgewood" (Maryland), 147
"Edgewood" (New York), *83*
Edison, Thomas, 89, 274
Edisto Island (South Carolina), *159*
Edward VIII *(formerly* Prince of Wales), 99, 100, 149, 254
Effingham, Alexander, *91*
Eisele, W. G., 127
Elberon (New Jersey), 127
"El Caserio" (Florida), 185; *184*
"El Cerrito" (California), 315
Elephant's-ear, 178, 323

N

O

P

PHOTOGRAPH CREDITS

Gardens at Sylvester Manor

The authors have made every effort to reach owners of the illustrations, and wish to thank those individuals and institutions which permitted the reproduction of works in their collections. They are listed below. All other illustrations appear courtesy of The Garden Club of America, Archive of American Gardens, Collection of the Office of Horticulture, Smithsonian Institution, Washington, D.C. References are to page numbers.

American Landscape Architecture: 103; Archive of American Gardens, Katherine Lane Weems Collection: 1; Arkansas History Commission: 235; Arnold Arboretum, Photo Archives, Harvard University: 22; Ashton Villa, Galveston, Tex.: 236; Atlanta Historical Society: 216; The Ballard Collection: 110, 197; William Banks: 216; Nancy & Blake Banta: 122 (both); George & Mimi Batchelder, Beverly, Mass.: 21; Bellingrath Gardens, Courtesy Jim Ryan: 225; Mrs. Russell Bennett: 279; Biltmore Estate, Asheville, N.C.: 20; Bernice P. Bishop Museum: 354; Hedrick Blessing, photo: 259; Courtesy Alfred Branam: 76 (above); Marvin Breckenridge, Piscataqua Garden Club: 15; Robert D. Brewster: 78; Brookgreen Gardens: 169; Alice H. Callaway: 218 (above); Courtesy Castle Hill, Property of the Trustees of Reservations: 50; Patrick Chassé: 37 (below left); Cheekwood Fine Arts Center: 203, Gift of Dr. Naomi M. Kanof in Memory of her husband Max Tendler, 190; Chesterwood Museum Archives, The National Trust for Historic Preservation: 56; Donald & Janet Chubb (Douglas W. Wallace, photo): 284; Mrs. James Clement, King Ranch: 243; R.E. Clemons, photo: 240; Collection Elizabeth Whedbee Constable: 146, 147; Contemporary Museum, Honolulu: 357; Cooper Hewitt Museum Library: 52; Cornell University Libraries, Department of Manuscripts & University Archives: 63; Danvers Archive Center, Peabody Institute Library: 53; The Offices of Delano & Aldrich: 97; Lowell S. Dillingham: 355; Collection of The Driwood Moulding Co. of Florence, S.C., Merrill Folsom Collection: 164, 323; Dumbarton Oaks, Trustees for Harvard University: 153 (both); The Edison Institute, Henry Ford Museum: 264 (below); Mr. & Mrs. Long Ellis: 267; Filoli Collection: 321; The First Parish in Framingham, Framingham, Mass. (Wallace Nutting, photo): 133; Fiske Collection, 108; Frederick Law Olmsted National Historic Site, National Park Service: 95, 281 (both), 293, 303; Edith Blair Gambrill: 119; Courtesy Dr. Thomas H. Gandy, Henry Norman Collection: 227 (above), Courtesy Dr. & Mrs. Thomas H. Gandy, 227 (center and right); Garden Club of America, Rare Book Library, *La Gazette illustrée des amateurs de jardins*: 98; Garden Club of Virginia, Archive of American Gardens, Smithsonian Institution: 160, 161 (both), 191, 193, 208; M. Christina Geis: 126, Moss Archives 118; Mrs. George Gillies: 100 (both); Gottscho-Schleisner Photo Collection: 58; Grey Towers, United State Department of Agriculture, Forest Service: 138; Grosse Pointe War Memorial Assoc. (Mrs. Sidney T. Miller, photo): 257; Hagley Museum & Library: 130, 140 (both), 141; Mrs. Ralph Hanes: 211; Harris County Heritage Society Photo Collection, Litterest Dixon Collection: 239; Harvard University, Frances Loeb Library, Graduate School of Design: 55, 276, 306; Hammond Hatchett: 217; Hicks Nurseries, Inc.: 76; "The Highlands": 132; *Historic Homes & Gardens of Tennessee*, 1936, Garden Study Club of Nashville: 196; Historical Society of Talbot County, H.

Robins Hollyday Collection: 151; Walter Hunnewell: 24; Hunt Institute for Botanical Documentation, Carnegie Mellon University: 129; Huntington Library, Art Gallery & Botanical Gardens: 341; Indianapolis Museum of Art: 260; Fiammetta Innocenti, from the Collection of the North Country Garden Club: 107; International Museum of Photography at George Eastman House, painting by John C. Wenrich, 1921: 86; James D. Ireland: 257; Brereton Jones: 199; Keeler Tavern Museum, Ridgefield, Conn. (Richard Wurtz, photo): 63; Collection of Robert B. King: 94; Mrs. Hal A. Kroeger: 25, 305; Ladew Topiary Gardens (Duane Suter, photo): 150; Lake Forest Academy, Ferry Hall: 255; Lenox Library Assoc., Edith Wharton Restoration: 13; Leonards Studio, Thibodeaux, La., photo: 232; Jim Lewis, photo: 349; Library of the Boston Atheneum: 23; The Library Company of Pennsylvania: 131; Library of Congress: 58, 69, 91, 104, 155, 192, 229, LOC/Frances Benjamin Johnston: 84, copied by J. Brough Schamp: 30, 37, 49, 56, 64, 65, 92, 101 (both), 112, 115 (above left, above right, below right) 125 (above, below), 342, 344; Library of the Massachusetts Horticultural Society: 51; Library of the Pennsylvania Horticultural Society: 132; Longue Vue House & Gardens: 235; Lyndhurst, Property of National Trust for Historic Preservation: 74; Richard C. Marchand Historic Postcard Coll.: 64, 83, 280; Wayne McCall, photo: 325, 326, 336; G.C. Maugans, Plainfield, N.J.: 182; Timothy Mawson: 90; Meridian House International: 154; Mrs. William Metcalf III: 137; Middletown Place, Charleston: 165; Mission Hills Homes Company (Larry Andrew, photo): 285; Missouri Botanical Garden: 286; Monmouth College Collection: 127; Gabriel Moulin: 317, 318; Museum of the City of New York, Byron Collection: 84; Nassau County Museum Reference Library: 95; National Archives: 152; National Botanical Tropical Gardens: 359; National Museum of American Art, Smithsonian Institution, Gift of John Gellatty: 17; Naumkeag Museum & Gardens, property of the Trustees of

Reservations, Stockbridge, Mass.: 59; Mr. and Mrs. Richard Neff: 248; New-York Historical Society: 91; New York Public Library, Prints and Drawings: 166; New York State Historical Association: 77; W. Wright Olney: 12; Mr. & Mrs. John G. Ordway, Jr.: 278; Oregon Historical Society, Edna L. Holmes Collection: 300; Thomas H. Paterson: 261; Marvin Breckenridge Patterson Photo Collection: 38; Pennsylvania Historical & Museum Commission, Division of Archives & Manuscripts (Mattie E. Hewitt, photo): 130; Penrose Library, Palmer Wing of Local History: 292 (both), 293; Philbrook Museum of Art, Archives (Bob McCormack), photo: 289; *Picturesque America*, Harry Fenn: 166; Mrs. John Platt: 299; William Platt Collection (photo: DeWitt Clinton Ward): 43; Preservation Society of Newport County (Nancy Sirkis, photo): 28; Private Collection: 135, 204, 215, 246; Plan redrawn by Jamie Purinton: 211; Redwood Library & Atheneum, Newport, R.I.: 9; Jane Foster Reece: 55 (above); Richland County Historic Preservation Commission: 172; Ringling Museum of Art: 188; The Rockefeller University at Seven Springs Center, Mt. Kisco, N.Y.: 79; Mrs. Douglas Rollins: 202; Saint-Gaudens National Historic Site, National Park Service, Cornish, N.H.: 40, 42; San Antonio Conservation Society: 244; San Diego Historical Society, Ticor Collection: 348; San Mateo County Historical Museum: 321; Mrs. William O. Schock: 325; Shadows-on-the-Teche Museum, National Trust for Historic Preservation, New Iberia, La. (I.N. Martin, photo): 232; Hugh R. Sharp, Jr.: 187; Shelburne Farms (© Del Keppelman, photo): 45 (below), T. E. Marr, photo, 45 (above); Laura Maddox Smith: 215; Dr. & Mrs. Lyman Smith: 184; Society for the Preservation of New England Antiquities (Elise Vaughan): 39, 47, 48, 51; Sonnenberg Gardens, Inc., Collection of Ontario County Historical Society: 88; Stan Hywet Hall Foundation, Inc. and Mrs. John Chapman: 271; Staten Island Historical Society, Richmondtown Restoration: 91; Collection the late Chauncey Stillman: 85; George R. Stritikus, John Sartain engraving (Scott, photo): 222; Martha Frick Symington: 107; Clementine Tangeman (Jonathan Wilson, photo): 260; University Art Museum, Santa Barbara, Architectural Drawing Collection: 352; University of California, Berkeley, Bancroft Library: 338; University of California, Berkeley, College of Environmental Design, Document Collection: 320; University of Connecticut, Avery Point Campus: 65 (above, below); University of Illinois at Urbana-Champaign: 269; University of Michigan, Art & Architecture Library: 264 (above); University of Tennessee, Knoxville, Haskins Library, Special Collections Library: 205; Valentine Museum, Richmond, Va.: 159; Villa Vizcaya Museum & Gardens: 175; Virginia Historical Society: 269; Courtesy Mrs. Corydon Wagner (Charles R. Pearson, photo): 304; Wake Forest University Archives: 213; Washington State Historical Society, Tacoma: 305; Collection Eleanor Weller: 196; Western Heritage Museum, Omaha History Museum, Bostwick Fromardt, KMTV: 289 (both); The Western Reserve Historical Society, Cleveland, Ohio: 159; F. L. Peter White: 105; Robert York White Collection: 283; Jerry Wilson (hand-painted by Fred K. Martin): 344; Mrs. William Wilson (M. E. Hewitt, photo): 62; Winterthur Museum, Winterthur Archives: 142 (both); Yaddo, Gustav Lorey, photo: 87; © Paul Yeager, 1988, photo: 242.